DICTIONARY OF ACCOUNTING AND FINANCE

DICTIONARY OF ACCOUNTING AND FINANCE

qatar FINANCIAL CENTRE AUTHORITY

BLOOMSBURY

First published in 2010 by
Bloomsbury Information Ltd
36 Soho Square
London
W1D 3QY
United Kingdom

A CIP record for this book is available from the British Library.

Standard edition
ISBN-10: 1-84930-011-9
ISBN-13: 978-1-84930-011-7

Middle East edition
ISBN-10: 1-84930-012-7
ISBN-13: 978-1-84930-012-4

Mixed Sources
Product group from well-managed forests and recycled wood or fiber
FSC www.fsc.org Cert no. TT-COC-002231
© 1996 Forest Stewardship Council

Project Director: Conrad Gardner
Project Manager: Ben Hickling
Assistant Project Manager: Sarah Latham
Dictionary Editor: Susan Jellis

Cover design by Suna Cristall
Page design by Fiona Pike, Pike Design, Winchester, UK
Typeset by Marsh Typesetting, West Sussex, UK
Printed in the UK by CPI William Clowes, Beccles, NR34 7TL, UK

Contents

User Guide

The *Dictionary of Accounting and Finance* provides clear and simple definitions of more than 9,000 international finance and business terms. Updated and expanded from *QFINANCE: The Ultimate Resource*, the dictionary has been compiled by an international team of expert researchers and information specialists. It is an up-to-date, practical resource that will help the user understand both basic and complex finance terms from around the world. Easy-to-use and full of helpful information, it aims to define the world of finance.

ORDER OF TERMS

All terms are listed in strict alphabetical order, ignoring spaces and punctuation, apart from when a term is part of a phrase. For example, **asking price** is listed before **ask price**. In the case of phrases, the definition is shown at the most valid element of the phrase. For example:

bath ◇ take a bath FINANCE to experience a serious financial loss

ENTRY ANATOMY

Topic Areas

The terms have been drawn from 27 key topic areas, and each term labeled accordingly. The topic areas as they appear in the dictionary are as follows:

ACCOUNTING
BANKING
BUSINESS
CORPORATE GOVERNANCE
CURRENCY & EXCHANGE
E-COMMERCE
ECONOMICS
FINANCE
FRAUD
GENERAL MANAGEMENT
HR & PERSONNEL
INSURANCE
INTERNATIONAL TRADE
LEGAL
MARKETING
MARKETS
MERGERS & ACQUISITIONS
MORTGAGES
OPERATIONS & PRODUCTION
PENSIONS
REAL ESTATE
REGULATION & COMPLIANCE
RISK
STATISTICS
STOCKHOLDING & INVESTMENTS
TAX
TREASURY MANAGEMENT

The topic areas help to give extra context to each term, especially when the term can have more than one meaning depending on the situation in which it is used. For example:

leader 1. GENERAL MANAGEMENT, HR & PERSONNEL firm's executive who motivates others well a business executive who possesses exceptional leadership qualities as well as management skills **2.** MARKETING top performing thing the most successful product or company in a marketplace

Quick Definitions

All terms are listed with a single-sentence definition, allowing the reader to quickly grasp a concept, before reading the fuller definition available immediately following this.

Cross-References

Cross-references are used in the dictionary to link terms that are closely related, or which expand on information given in the current entry. For example:

debit side ACCOUNTING accounting column for money owed or paid out the section of a financial statement that lists payments made or owed. In ***double-entry bookkeeping***, the left hand side of each account is designated as the debit side. *See also* ***credit side***

Here, ***double-entry bookkeeping*** and ***credit side*** are shown in bold italics to show that they are also entries in the dictionary the reader may wish to refer to.

Abbreviations

Finance is full of abbreviations and acronyms, and the dictionary features many of these. Where an abbreviation is the most commonly used version of a term or phrase, the full definition is given at that entry. For example:

IBRD BANKING UN bank that helps poorest nations a United Nations organization that provides funds, policy guidance, and technical assistance to facilitate economic development in its poorer member countries. *Full form* ***International Bank for Reconstruction and Development***

and the full form points to this, as shown here:

International Bank for Reconstruction and Development BANKING *see* ***IBRD***

In cases where the full form of an abbreviation is the most commonly known form of a concept, the reader is re-directed to the expanded form when looking up the abbreviation:

UIT *abbr* STOCKHOLDING & INVESTMENTS ***unit investment trust***

which mentions:

unit investment trust STOCKHOLDING & INVESTMENTS investment company offering units in unmanaged portfolio an investment company that offers an unmanaged portfolio of securities to investors through brokers, typically in units of $1,000 each. *Abbr* ***UIT***

Variant Names

Where different words or phrases are used to refer to the same concept, these are also shown in the dictionary. The full definition is shown at the most commonly used form, with variants referring the reader to those common forms. For example:

autocorrelation STATISTICS = ***serial correlation***

directs the reader to:

serial correlation STATISTICS correlation of variable over period of time the correlation of a variable with itself over different points in time, used as an indicator of the future performance of something such as a security or economy. *Also called* ***autocorrelation***

Informal Terms

Where terms are only used informally, as slang, or are dated, this is mentioned in the entry. For example:

puff piece MARKETING press item for promotional purposes an article in a newspaper or magazine promoting a product or service (*slang*)

A

AAA[1] *abbr* ACCOUNTING ***American Accounting Association***

AAA[2] STOCKHOLDING & INVESTMENTS top investment rating the maximum safety rating given to potential investments by Standard & Poor's or Moody's, the two best known rating agencies. *Also called* ***triple A***

AAD *abbr* CURRENCY & EXCHANGE ***Arab Accounting Dinar***

AASB *abbr* ACCOUNTING ***Australian Accounting Standards Board***

AAT *abbr* ACCOUNTING ***Association of Accounting Technicians***

AB *abbr* BUSINESS ***Aktiebolag*** *or* ***Aktiebolaget***

ABA *abbr* BANKING ***American Bankers Association***

abacus FINANCE frame holding rods strung with beads for calculating a counting device used for making basic arithmetic calculations, that consists of parallel rods strung with beads. Still widely used in education worldwide and for business and accounting in China and Japan, its origins can be traced back to early civilizations. Australia's oldest accounting journal bears the same name.

abandonment option STOCKHOLDING & INVESTMENTS early investment-termination option the option of terminating an investment before the time that it is scheduled to end

abandonment value STOCKHOLDING & INVESTMENTS value of investment terminated early the value that an investment has if it is terminated at a particular time before it is scheduled to end

ABA routing number BANKING number allocated to US financial institution a unique, nine-digit bank code, which appears on the bottom of ***negotiable instruments*** such as checks, that is used to identify the US federal- or state-chartered financial institution responsible for payment. *Also called* ***routing number***

abatement FINANCE decrease in debt obligation a reduction in an amount of a liability, for example, in the amount of a person's debts, or in a company's costs of paying employee benefits

ABB *abbr* TREASURY MANAGEMENT ***activity based budgeting***

abbreviated accounts ACCOUNTING abridged UK company accounts in the United Kingdom, a shortened version of a company's ***annual accounts*** that a company classified as small- or medium-sized under the ***Companies Act*** (1989) can file with the ***Registrar of Companies***, instead of having to supply a full version

ABC *abbr* ACCOUNTING ***activity based costing***

ABI *abbr* INSURANCE ***Association of British Insurers***

Abilene paradox GENERAL MANAGEMENT theory of group decisions based on mistaken impressions a theory stating that some decisions that seem to be based on consensus are in fact based on misperception and lead to courses of action that defeat original intentions. The Abilene paradox was proposed by management professor Jerry Harvey in 1974 following a trip made by his family to the town of Abilene. One person suggested the visit and the others agreed, each believing that everyone else wanted to go. On their return, everyone admitted that they would rather have stayed at home. Harvey used this experience to illustrate the mismanagement of agreement, and of decision making in organizations when apparent consensus is actually founded on poor communication.

ability-to-pay principle TAX theory of tax liability a theory which holds that taxes should be paid only by those who can best afford them

ABM *abbr* GENERAL MANAGEMENT ***activity based management***

ABN *abbr* TAX ***Australian Business Number***

abnormal loss ACCOUNTING loss exceeding normal allowance any loss which exceeds the normal loss allowance. Abnormal losses are generally accounted for as though they were completed products.

abnormal shrinkage ACCOUNTING shrinkage contributing to abnormal loss the unexpectedly high level of reduction in inventory that has contributed to an abnormal loss

abnormal spoilage ACCOUNTING shortfall contributing to abnormal loss the unexpectedly high level of shortfall that has contributed to an abnormal loss

abnormal waste ACCOUNTING waste contributing to abnormal loss the unexpectedly high level of waste that has contributed to an abnormal loss

above par STOCKHOLDING & INVESTMENTS trading above face value used to describe a security that trades above its ***nominal value*** or ***redemption value***

above-the-line 1. ACCOUNTING indicating exceptional items in accounts used to describe entries in a company's profit and loss accounts that appear above the line separating those entries that show the origin of the funds that have contributed to the profit or loss from those that relate to its distribution. Exceptional and extraordinary items appear above the line. *See also* ***below-the-line*** *(sense 1)* **2.** ECONOMICS indicating country's revenue transactions in macroeconomics, used to describe a country's revenue transactions, as opposed to its below-the-line or capital transactions. *See also* ***below-the-line*** *(sense 2)* **3.** MARKETING relating to marketing costs for advertising used to describe marketing expenditure on advertising in media such as the press, radio, television, film, and the World Wide Web, on which a commission is usually paid to an agency. *See also* ***below-the-line*** *(sense 3)*

abridged accounts ACCOUNTING provisional UK company financial statement in the United Kingdom, financial statements produced by a company that fall outside the requirements stipulated in the ***Companies Act***. Abridged accounts are often made public through the media.

ABS *abbr* **1.** STOCKHOLDING & INVESTMENTS ***asset-backed security*** **2.** STATISTICS ***Australian Bureau of Statistics***

absolute advantage ECONOMICS favorable position of regions having low production costs an advantage enjoyed by a country or area of the world that is able to produce a product or provide a service more cheaply than any other country or area

absolute title LEGAL **1.** in UK, guaranteed right of ownership of land in the United Kingdom, an owner's guaranteed title to land, confirmed by registration with the Land Registry **2.** in UK, guaranteed right to lease in the United Kingdom, a proprietor's guaranteed valid lease on leasehold land

absorb ACCOUNTING merge production overhead costs to assign an overhead to a particular cost center in a company's production accounts so that its identity becomes lost. *See also* ***absorption costing***

absorbed account ACCOUNTING account merged with related accounts an account that has lost its separate identity by being combined with related accounts in the preparation of a financial statement

absorbed business MERGERS & ACQUISITIONS firm combined with another a company that has been merged into another company with which it is not on an equal footing

absorbed costs ACCOUNTING indirect manufacturing costs the indirect costs associated with manufacturing, for example, insurance or property taxes

absorbed overhead ACCOUNTING locally adjusted overhead an overhead attached to products or services by means of absorption rates

absorption costing ACCOUNTING method allocating overhead costs to product an accounting practice in which fixed and variable costs of production are absorbed by different cost centers. Providing all the products or services can be sold at a price that covers the allocated costs, this method ensures that both fixed and variable costs are recovered in full. However, if sales are lost because the resultant price is too high, the organization may lose revenue that would have contributed to its overhead. *See also* ***marginal costing***

absorption rate ACCOUNTING rate of merging production overhead costs the rate at which overhead costs are absorbed into each unit of production

abusive tax shelter TAX illegal tax-reduction method a tax shelter that a person claims illegally to avoid or minimize tax

ACA ACCOUNTING ICAEW Associate Chartered Accountant an Associate (member) of the Institute of Chartered Accountants in England and Wales ■ *abbr* REGULATION & COMPLIANCE ***Australian Communications Authority***

Academy of Accounting Historians ACCOUNTING US institution for accounting history a US organization founded in 1973 that promotes "research, publication, teaching, and personal interchanges in all phases of Accounting History and its interrelation with business and economic history"

ACAS *abbr* BUSINESS ***Advisory, Conciliation and Arbitration Service***

ACAUS *abbr* ACCOUNTING ***Association of Chartered Accountants in the United States***

ACCA *abbr* ACCOUNTING ***Association of Chartered Certified Accountants***

ACCC *abbr* REGULATION & COMPLIANCE ***Australian Competition and Consumer Commission***

accelerated cost recovery system ACCOUNTING use of asset depreciation to reduce US taxes in the United States, a system used for computing the depreciation of some assets acquired before 1986 in a way that reduces taxes. *Abbr* ***ACRS***

accelerated depreciation ACCOUNTING assigning higher depreciation to new assets a system used for computing the depreciation of some assets in a way that assumes that they depreciate faster in the early years of their acquisition. The cost of the asset less its residual value is multiplied by a fraction based on the number of years of its expected useful life. The fraction changes each year and charges the highest costs to the earliest years. *Also called* ***declining balance method, sum-of-the-year's-digits depreciation***

acceleration clause LEGAL clause specifying conditions for early repayment of loan a section of a contract which details how a loan may be required to be repaid early if the borrower defaults on other clauses of the contract

acceptance FINANCE signature guaranteeing payment for bill of exchange the signature on a bill of exchange, indicating that the drawee (the person to whom it is addressed) will pay the face amount of the bill on the due date

acceptance bonus FINANCE bonus paid to new employee a bonus paid to a new employee on acceptance of a job. An acceptance bonus can be a feature of a golden hello and is designed both to attract and to retain staff.

acceptance credit BANKING facility for seller to draw bill of exchange a letter of credit granted by a bank to a buyer (the "applicant") against which a seller (the "beneficiary") can draw a bill of exchange

acceptance house *UK* BANKING institution guaranteeing financial instruments an institution that accepts financial instruments and agrees to honor them should the borrower default

acceptance region STATISTICS values for which null hypothesis is acceptable the set of values in a test statistic for which the null hypothesis can be accepted

acceptance sampling OPERATIONS & PRODUCTION method of checking subset to test whole group a decision-making technique for assuring quality used in a manufacturing environment, in which acceptance or rejection of a batch of parts is decided by testing a sample of the batch. The sample is checked against established standards and, if it meets those standards, the whole batch is deemed acceptable.

accepting bank BANKING bank accepting letter of credit a bank in an exporter's own country to which an issuing bank sends a ***letter of credit*** for the exporter

accepting house BANKING firm accepting bills of exchange a company, usually an investment bank, that accepts bills of exchange at a discount, in return for immediate payment to the issuer

Accepting Houses Committee BANKING banks linked to Bank of England for lending the main London investment banks that organize the lending of money with the Bank of England and receive favorable discount rates

acceptor FINANCE addressee of signed bill of exchange a person who has accepted liability for a bill of exchange by signing its face

access BUSINESS right to sell into particular market the right to sell goods or services into a particular market without contravening related legislation

access bond MORTGAGES S. African mortgage accepting capital against other loans in South Africa, a type of mortgage that permits borrowers to take out loans against extra capital paid into the account, home-loan interest rates being lower than interest rates on other forms of credit

ACCI *abbr* BUSINESS ***Australian Chamber of Commerce and Industry***

accident insurance INSURANCE insurance against losses incurred in accidents insurance that will pay the insured person for loss or damages when an accident takes place

accommodation address BUSINESS address for receiving messages only an address used for receiving messages, which is not the address of the company's premises

accommodation bill FINANCE bill of exchange facilitating loan for another company a bill of exchange where the drawee who signs it is helping another company (the drawer) to raise a loan. The bill is given on the basis of trade debts owed to the borrower.

account 1. FINANCE arrangement for deferred payment a business arrangement involving the exchange of money or credit in which payment is deferred **2.** FINANCE record of financial dealings a record maintained by a financial institution itemizing its dealings with a particular customer **3.** ACCOUNTING record of monetary value of transactions a structured record of transactions in monetary terms, kept as part of an accounting system. This may take the form of a simple list or that of entries on a credit and debit basis, maintained either manually or as a computer record. **4.** MARKETING advertising firm's client a client of an advertising or public relations agency ◇ on account FINANCE used to describe a transaction where something is received that is to be paid for later

accountability CORPORATE GOVERNANCE responsibility for actions the allocation or acceptance of responsibility for one's own actions or those of others lower in the hierarchy

accountancy ACCOUNTING professional activities of accountants the work and profession of accountants

accountancy bodies *UK* ACCOUNTING = ***accounting bodies***

accountancy profession *UK* ACCOUNTING = ***accounting profession***

accountant ACCOUNTING somebody responsible for financial records a professional person who maintains and checks the business records of a person or organization and prepares forms and reports for financial purposes

accountant's letter ACCOUNTING independent statement about financial report a written statement by an independent accountant that precedes a financial report, describing the scope of the report and giving an opinion on its validity

accountant's opinion ACCOUNTING audit report on firm's accounts a report of the audit of a company's books, carried out by a certified public accountant

account day ACCOUNTING day of settlement of executed order the day on which an executed order is settled by the delivery of securities, payment to the seller, and payment by the buyer. This is the final day of the ***accounting period.***

account debtor ACCOUNTING body responsible for paying for something a person or organization responsible for paying for a product or service

account director MARKETING advertising firm employee in charge of client's business a senior person within an advertising agency responsible for overall policy on a client's advertising account

account executive MARKETING senior employee in charge of specific client's business an employee of an organization such as a bank, public relations firm, or advertising agency who is responsible for the business of a specific client

accounting ACCOUNTING range of activities undertaken by accountants a generic term for the activities such as bookkeeping and financial accounting conducted by accountants. Accounting involves the classification and recording of monetary transactions; the presentation and interpretation of the results of those transactions in order to assess performance over a period and the financial position at a given date; and the monetary projection of future activities arising from alternative planned courses of action. Accounting in larger businesses is typically carried out by financial accountants, who focus on formal, corporate issues such as taxation, and management accountants, who provide management reports and guidance.

Accounting and Finance Association of Australia and New Zealand ACCOUNTING organization for accountancy and financial professionals an organization for accounting and finance academics, researchers, and professionals. The Association has a variety of objectives, including the promotion of information on accounting to the public, and the provision of programs in continual professional development to both members and nonmembers. The Association's name was changed in 2002 to incorporate the Accounting Association of Australia and New Zealand and the Australian Association of University Teachers in Accounting. *Abbr* ***AFAANZ***

accounting bases ACCOUNTING fundamental accounting methods the methods used for applying fundamental accounting concepts to financial transactions and items; preparing financial accounts; determining the accounting periods in which revenue and costs should be recognized in the profit and loss account; and determining the amounts at which material items should be stated in the balance sheet

accounting bodies *US* ACCOUNTING professional organizations for accountants professional institutions and associations for accountants. These include such bodies as the Accounting Standards Board in the United Kingdom and the American Institute of Certified Public Accountants in the United States. *UK term* ***accountancy bodies***

accounting concept ACCOUNTING accepted basis for preparing accounts any of the general assumptions on which accounts are prepared. The main concepts are: that the business is a going concern; that revenue and costs are noted when they are incurred and not when cash is received or paid; that the present accounts are drawn up following the same principles as the previous accounts; and that the revenue or costs are only recorded if it is certain that they will be received or incurred.

accounting cost ACCOUNTING cost of proper financial records the cost of maintaining and checking the business records of a person or organization and of preparing forms and reports for financial purposes

accounting cycle ACCOUNTING process of regularly updating financial records the regular process of formally updating a firm's financial position by recording, analyzing, and reporting its transactions during the accounting period

accounting date ACCOUNTING end date of accounting period the date on which an accounting period ends. This can be any date, though it is usually 12 months after the preceding accounting date.

accounting department *US* ACCOUNTING company department dealing with finance the department in a company which deals with money paid, received, borrowed, or owed. *UK term* ***accounts department***

accounting equation ACCOUNTING formula relating assets, liabilities, and equity a formula in which a firm's assets must be equal to the sum of its liabilities and the owners' equity. *Also called* ***balance sheet equation***

accounting exposure ACCOUNTING risk from changing exchange rates the risk that foreign currency held by a company may lose value because of exchange rate changes when it conducts overseas business

accounting fees ACCOUNTING fees for preparing accounts fees paid to an accountant for preparing accounts. Such fees are tax-deductible.

accounting insolvency ACCOUNTING condition of liabilities exceeding assets the condition that a company is in when its liabilities to its creditors exceed its assets

accounting manager *US* ACCOUNTING manager of accounting department the manager of the accounting department in a business or institution. *UK term* ***accounts manager***

accounting manual ACCOUNTING set of instructions for keeping accounts a collection of accounting instructions governing the responsibilities of persons, and the procedures, forms, and records relating to the preparation and use of accounting data. There can be separate manuals for the constituent parts of the accounting system, for example, budget manuals or cost accounting manuals.

accounting period ACCOUNTING time between financial reports a length of time for which businesses may prepare internal accounts so as to monitor progress on a weekly, monthly, or quarterly basis. Accounts are generally prepared for external purposes on an annual basis.

accounting policies ACCOUNTING options for financial reporting the specific accounting methods selected and consistently followed by an entity as being, in the opinion of the management, appropriate to its circumstances and best suited to present fairly its results and financial position. For example, from the various possible methods of ***depreciation,*** the accounting policy may be to use ***straight line depreciation.***

accounting principles ACCOUNTING rules of financial reporting the rules that apply to accounting practices and provide guidelines for dealing appropriately with complex transactions

Accounting Principles Board ACCOUNTING former US organization with oversight of accounting in the United States, the professional organization which issued opinions that formed much of ***Generally Accepted Accounting Principles*** until 1973, when the Financial Accounting Standards Board (FASB) took over that role. *Abbr* ***APB***

accounting procedure ACCOUNTING method of keeping financial records an accounting method developed by a person or organization to deal with routine accounting tasks

accounting profession *US* ACCOUNTING set of organizations overseeing accountants collectively, the professional bodies of accountants that establish and regulate training entry standards and professional examinations, as well as ethical and technical rules and guidelines. These bodies are organized on national and international levels. *UK term* ***accountancy profession***

accounting profit ACCOUNTING difference between revenue and costs the difference between total revenue and explicit costs. Accounting profits exclude costs such as ***opportunity costs.***

accounting rate of return ACCOUNTING ratio of unadjusted profit to capital employed the ratio of profit before interest and taxation to the percentage of capital employed at the end of a period. Variations include using profit after interest and taxation, equity capital employed, and average capital for the period. *Abbr* ***ARR***

accounting ratio ACCOUNTING ratio of one accounting result to another an expression of accounting results as a ratio or percentage, for example, the ratio of ***current assets*** to ***current liabilities***

accounting records ACCOUNTING materials for preparing financial statements all documentation and books used during the preparation of financial statements. *Also called* ***books of account***

accounting reference date ACCOUNTING last day included in financial record the nominal last day of a company's ***accounting reference period,*** which ends on that date or on one no more than seven days on either side of it

accounting reference period ACCOUNTING 12 months that annual accounts cover the period covered by a company's annual accounts, which is usually one full year

accounting software ACCOUNTING programs for electronic accounts computer programs used to help maintain ***accounting records*** electronically. Such software can be used for a variety of tasks, including preparing statements and recording transactions.

accounting standard ACCOUNTING approved method of presenting financial information an authoritative statement of how specific types of transaction and other events should be reflected in financial statements. Compliance with accounting standards will usually be necessary for financial statements to give a true and fair view.

Accounting Standards Board ACCOUNTING UK standard-setting organization in the United Kingdom, a standard-setting organization established on August 1, 1990, to develop, issue, and withdraw accounting standards. Its objectives are "to establish and improve standards of financial accounting and reporting, for the benefit of users, preparers, and auditors of financial information." *Abbr* ***ASB***

accounting system ACCOUNTING everything used in producing accounting information the means, including staff and equipment, by which an organization produces its accounting information

accounting technician ACCOUNTING qualified person working in finance industry a qualified person who works in accounting and finance alongside ***certified public accountants.*** Accounting technicians have a variety of jobs, including accounts clerk, credit controller, and financial manager. Their professional body is the ***AAT.***

accounting year *UK* ACCOUNTING = ***fiscal year***

account reconciliation ACCOUNTING **1.** comparing balances of transactions a procedure for ensuring the reliability of accounting records by comparing balances of transactions **2.** comparing checkbook records with bank statement a procedure for comparing the register of a checkbook with an associated bank statement

accounts ACCOUNTING record of monetary value of transactions a structured record of transactions in monetary terms, kept as part of an accounting system. This may take the form of a simple list or that of entries on a credit and debit basis, maintained either manually or as a computer record.

accounts department *UK* ACCOUNTING = ***accounting department***

accounts manager *UK* ACCOUNTING = ***accounting manager***

accounts payable ACCOUNTING amount owed through credit the amount that a company owes for goods or services obtained on credit. *Abbr* ***AP***

accounts receivable ACCOUNTING amount owed by customers the money that is owed to a company by those who have bought its goods or services and have not yet paid for them. *Abbr* ***AR***

accounts receivable aging ACCOUNTING money owed grouped by month and customer a periodic report that classifies outstanding receivable balances according to customer and month of the original billing date

accounts receivable factoring ACCOUNTING buying of discounted invoiced debts the buying of ***accounts receivable*** at a discount with the goal of making a profit from collecting them

accounts receivable financing ACCOUNTING using money owed as collateral for loan a form of borrowing in which a company uses money that it is owed as collateral for a loan it needs for business operations

accounts receivable turnover ACCOUNTING ratio indicating length of time before customers pay a ratio that shows how long the customers of a business wait before paying what they owe. This can cause cash flow problems for small businesses.

The formula for accounts receivable turnover is straightforward. Simply divide the average amount of receivables into annual credit sales:

Sales / Receivables = Receivables turnover

If, for example, a company's sales are $4.5 million and its average receivables are $375,000, its receivables turnover is:

4,500,000 / 375,000 = 12

A high turnover figure is desirable, because it indicates that a company collects revenues effectively, and that its customers pay bills promptly. A high figure also suggests that a firm's credit and collection policies are sound. In addition, the measurement is a reasonably good indicator of cash flow, and of overall operating efficiency.

accredited investor STOCKHOLDING & INVESTMENTS investor with income of specific size an investor whose wealth or income is above a specific amount. It is illegal for an accredited investor to be a member of a private limited partnership.

accreted value STOCKHOLDING & INVESTMENTS bond's value at present interest rate the theoretical value of a bond if interest rates remained at the current level

accretion MERGERS & ACQUISITIONS firm's asset growth the growth of a company through additions or purchases of plant or value-adding services

accrual ACCOUNTING unpaid charge in accounting results a charge that has not been paid by the end of an accounting period but must be included in the accounting results for the period. If no invoice has been received for the charge, an estimate must be included in the accounting results.

accrual basis *or* **accrual concept** *or* **accrual method** ACCOUNTING recording transactions for period they refer to an accounting method that includes income and expense items as they are earned or incurred irrespective of when money is received or paid out. *See also* ***cash accounting*** *(sense 1)*

accrual bond STOCKHOLDING & INVESTMENTS = ***zero coupon bond***

accrual of discount STOCKHOLDING & INVESTMENTS annual gain for bond bought below face value the annual gain in value of a bond owing to its having been bought originally for less than its ***nominal value***

accrual of interest FINANCE addition of interest to principal the automatic addition of interest to the original amount loaned or invested. Accrual of interest costs match the cost of capital with the provision of capital.

accruals basis *or* **accruals concept** ACCOUNTING *see* ***accrual basis***

accrue 1. FINANCE increase with time to increase and be due for payment at a later date, for example, interest **2.** ACCOUNTING include item when earned or incurred to include an income or expense item in transaction records at the time it is earned or incurred

accrued dividend STOCKHOLDING & INVESTMENTS dividend earned since previous dividend payment a dividend earned since the date when the last dividend was paid

accrued expense ACCOUNTING expense incurred but not paid an expense that has been incurred within a given accounting period but not yet paid

accrued income FINANCE income due income that has been earned or accumulated over a period of time but not yet received

accrued interest STOCKHOLDING & INVESTMENTS interest accumulated since previous interest payment the amount of interest earned by a bond or similar investment since the previous interest payment

accrued liabilities FINANCE recorded but unpaid liabilities liabilities which are recorded, although payment has not yet been made. This can include liabilities such as rent and utility payments.

accruing FINANCE increasing with time added as a periodic gain, for example, as interest on an amount of money

accumulated depreciation ACCOUNTING cumulative depreciation claimed as expense the cumulative annual depreciation of an ***asset*** that has been claimed as an expense since the asset was acquired. *Also called* ***aggregate depreciation***

accumulated dividend STOCKHOLDING & INVESTMENTS dividend earned since previous dividend payment the amount of money in dividends earned by a stock or similar investment since the previous dividend payment

accumulated earnings tax TAX tax in place of dividends the tax that a company must pay because it chose not to pay dividends that would subject its owners to higher taxes

accumulated profit ACCOUNTING profit carried over into next year profit which is not paid as dividend but is taken over into the accounts of the following year

accumulated reserves FINANCE annual reserves put aside reserves which a company has put aside over a period of years

accumulating shares STOCKHOLDING & INVESTMENTS common stock issued in place of dividend common stock issued by a company equivalent to and in place of the net dividend payable to holders of common stock

accumulation unit STOCKHOLDING & INVESTMENTS unit with dividends used for more units a share in a mutual fund for which dividends accumulate and form more units, as opposed to an ***income unit,*** where the investor receives the dividends as ***income***

accuracy STATISTICS closeness of data match the degree to which data conforms to a recognized standard value

ACH *abbr* E-COMMERCE, BANKING ***automated clearing house***

acid test 1. ACCOUNTING test of organization's liquidity a test used to measure an organization's liquidity. *See also* ***acid-test ratio*** **2.** GENERAL MANAGEMENT decisive test a stringent test of the worth or reliability of something

acid-test ratio ACCOUNTING measure of organization's liquidity an accounting ratio used to measure an organization's liquidity. The most common expression of the ratio is:

(Current assets – Inventory) / Current liabilities = Acid-test ratio

If, for example, current assets total $7,700, inventory amounts to $1,200, and current liabilities total $4,500, then:

(7,700 – 1,200) / 4,500 = 1.44

A variation of this formula ignores inventories altogether, distinguishes assets as cash, receivables, and short-term investments, then divides the sum of the three by the total current liabilities, or:

(Cash + Accounts receivable + Short-term investments) / Current liabilities = Acid-test ratio

If, for example, cash totals $2,000, receivables total $3,000, short-term investments total $1,000, and liabilities total $4,800, then:

(2,000 + 3,000 + 1,000) / 4,800 = 1.25

In general, the ratio should be 1:1 or better. It means a company has a unit's worth of easily convertible assets for each unit of its current liabilities.

ACP *abbr* INTERNATIONAL TRADE ***African Caribbean and Pacific States***

acquirer 1. FINANCE buyer an organization or individual that buys a business or asset **2.** E-COMMERCE institution handling credit card transactions a financial institution, commonly a bank, that processes a merchant's credit card authorizations and payments, forwarding the data to a credit card association, which in turn communicates with the issuer. *Also called* ***clearing house*** *(sense 3)*

acquisition MERGERS & ACQUISITIONS when one organization buys another the process of one organization taking control of another, by the direct purchase of the net assets or liabilities of the other. *See also* ***merger***

acquisition accounting MERGERS & ACQUISITIONS, ACCOUNTING = ***purchase acquisition***

acquisition integration MERGERS & ACQUISITIONS merging of new company into existing company the process by which a company plans for and implements a successful integration of a newly acquired company

ACRS *abbr* ACCOUNTING ***accelerated cost recovery system***

ACT *abbr* TAX ***advance corporation tax***

action-centered leadership GENERAL MANAGEMENT model of actions of effective leaders a leadership model that focuses on what leaders actually have to do in order to be effective. The action-centered leadership model is illustrated by three overlapping circles representing the three key activities undertaken by leaders: achieving the task, building and maintaining the team, and developing the individual.

action research GENERAL MANAGEMENT study of results of researcher's own changes research that involves conducting experiments by making changes while simultaneously observing the results. The researcher takes an involved role as a participant in planning and implementing change.

active account BANKING account regularly used for transactions an account such as a bank account or investment account that is used to deposit and withdraw money frequently

active asset FINANCE asset in daily use an asset that is used in the daily operations of a business

active fund management STOCKHOLDING & INVESTMENTS proactive managing of mutual fund the managing of a mutual fund by making judgments about stock valuations instead of relying on automatic adjustments such as indexation. *See also* ***passive investment management***

active partner HR & PERSONNEL working partner in partnership firm a partner who gives a significant amount of working time to a company that is a partnership

active portfolio strategy STOCKHOLDING & INVESTMENTS proactive managing of investment portfolio the managing of an investment portfolio by making judgments about stock valuations instead of relying on automatic adjustments such as indexation

activist fiscal policy TREASURY MANAGEMENT institutional intervention to affect exchange rate the policy of a government or national bank that tries to affect the value of its country's money by such measures as changing interest rates for loans to banks and buying or selling foreign currencies

activity based budgeting TREASURY MANAGEMENT allocation of resources to individual activities the determination of which activities incur costs within an organization, establishing the relationships between them, and then deciding how much of the total budget should be allocated to each activity. *Abbr* ***ABB***

activity based costing ACCOUNTING calculating business's cost from cost of activities a method of calculating the cost of a business by focusing on the actual cost of activities, thereby producing an estimate of the cost of individual products or services.

An ABC cost-accounting system requires three preliminary steps: converting to an ***accrual method*** of accounting; defining cost centers and cost allocation; and determining process and procedure costs.

Businesses have traditionally relied on the cash basis of accounting, which recognizes income when received and expenses when paid. ABC's foundation is the accrual-basis income statement. The numbers this statement presents are assigned to the various procedures performed during a given period. Cost centers are a company's identifiable products and services, but also include specific and detailed tasks within these broader activities. Defining cost centers will of course vary by business and method of operation. What is critical to ABC is the inclusion of all activities and all resources.

Once cost centers are identified, management teams can begin studying the activities each one engages in and allocating the expenses each one incurs, including the cost of employee services.

The most appropriate method is developed from time studies and direct expense allocation. Management teams who choose this method will need to devote several months to data collection in order to generate sufficient information to establish the personnel components of each activity's total cost.

Time studies establish the average amount of time required to complete each task, plus best- and worst-case performances. Only those resources actually used are factored into the cost computation; unused resources are reported separately. These studies can also advise management teams how best to monitor and allocate expenses that might otherwise be expressed as part of general overheads, or go undetected altogether. *Abbr* ***ABC***

activity based management TREASURY MANAGEMENT management based on cost of activities a management control technique that focuses on the resource costs of organizational activities and processes, and the improvement of quality, profitability, and customer value. This technique uses ***activity based costing*** information to identify strategies for removing resource waste from operating activities. Main tools employed include: ***strategic analysis, value analysis, cost analysis, life-cycle costing,*** and ***activity based budgeting.***

activity cost pool TREASURY MANAGEMENT total cost of activity a grouping of all of the cost elements associated with an activity

activity driver analysis TREASURY MANAGEMENT assessing financial demands of activity the identification and evaluation of the activity drivers used to trace the cost of activities to cost objects. It may also involve selecting activity drivers with potential to contribute to the cost management function, with particular reference to cost reduction.

activity indicator ECONOMICS measure of economic productivity a calculation used to measure labor productivity or manufacturing output in an economy

act of God INSURANCE unforeseen event not covered by insurance an unexpected and unavoidable event or occurrence such as a storm or a flood that is not covered by an insurance policy

actual cash value INSURANCE cost of replacing something damaged beyond repair the amount of money, less ***depreciation,*** that it would cost to replace something damaged beyond repair with a comparable item

actual price MARKETS price for immediate delivery a price for a commodity that is to be delivered immediately

actuals 1. FINANCE commodities immediately available commodities that can be bought and used, as contrasted with commodities traded on a ***futures***

***contract* 2.** ACCOUNTING past earnings and expenses earnings and expenses that have occurred rather than being only projected

actual to date ACCOUNTING cumulative value already realized the cumulative value realized by something between an earlier date and the present

actual turnover FINANCE times person spends average available sum the number of times during a specific period that somebody spends the average amount of money that he or she has available to spend during that period

actuarial age INSURANCE person's statistically derived life expectancy the statistically derived life expectancy for any given person's age, used, for example, to calculate the periodic payments from an annuity

actuarial analysis INSURANCE calculation carried out by actuary a life expectancy or risk calculation carried out by an actuary

actuarial science INSURANCE statistics for calculating risk and life expectancy the branch of statistics used in calculating risk and life expectancy for the administration of pension funds and life insurance policies

actuarial tables INSURANCE lists of life expectancy by age lists showing how long people of specific ages are likely to live, used in calculating life assurance premiums

actuary INSURANCE statistician calculating life expectancy a statistician who calculates probable life spans so that the insurance premiums to be charged for various risks can be accurately determined

ACU *abbr* CURRENCY & EXCHANGE ***Asian Currency Unit***

adaptive control OPERATIONS & PRODUCTION automatic changes to industrial process a system of automatic monitoring and adjustment, usually by computer, of an industrial process. Adaptive control allows operating parameters to be changed continuously in response to a changing environment in order to achieve optimum performance.

adaptive learning GENERAL MANAGEMENT method of modifying behavior to repeat successes a style of organizational learning that focuses on prior successes and the use of these as the basis for developing future strategies and successes. Organizations use adaptive learning to make incremental improvements to existing products, services, and processes in response to the changing business environment. ***Generative learning*** is a contrasting approach to organizational learning.

adaptive measure STATISTICS choosing best statistical method a means of choosing the most appropriate method for a statistical analysis

ADB *abbr* BANKING **1.** ***African Development Bank*** **2.** ***Asian Development Bank***

ad click rate E-COMMERCE = ***click-through rate***

ADDACS *abbr* BANKING ***Automated Direct Debit Amendment and Cancellation Service***

added value 1. GENERAL MANAGEMENT = ***value added*** **2.** MARKETING addition to product that increases attractiveness an increase in the attractiveness to customers of a product or a service achieved by adding something to it

addend FINANCE number added to complete sum the initial number added to an ***augend*** in order to complete an ***addition***

addition FINANCE adding together numbers to make sum an arithmetical operation consisting of adding together two or more numbers to make a sum

additional premium INSURANCE payment for extra insurance cover a payment made to cover extra items added on to existing insurance

additional principal payment *US* ACCOUNTING making larger than necessary loan payment the payment of a lump sum to reduce the capital borrowed on a mortgage or other loan, thereby reducing the term of the loan and saving a large amount of interest expense, or the amount paid. *UK term* ***overpayment***

additional voluntary contributions PENSIONS beneficiary's extra payments into company pension extra money that an individual chooses to pay into an occupational pension plan to improve the benefits he or she will receive on retirement. *Abbr* ***AVCs***

address verification E-COMMERCE matching credit card customer's stated address to records a procedure used by the processor of a credit card to verify that a customer's ordering address matches the address in the customer's record

ADF *abbr* PENSIONS ***Approved Deposit Fund***

adhocracy GENERAL MANAGEMENT organizational system with no set rules a system of organization that emphasizes informality and flexibility and does not employ fixed rules or standard procedures for dealing with problems

adjudication of bankruptcy LEGAL legal statement of bankruptcy a legal order officially stating that somebody is bankrupt

adjustable rate mortgage MORTGAGES mortgage with fluctuating interest rate a mortgage where the interest rate changes according to the current market rates. *Abbr* ***ARM***

adjustable rate preferred stock STOCKHOLDING & INVESTMENTS preferred stocks linked to Treasury interest rate preferred stocks on which dividends are paid in line with the interest rate on Treasury bills. *Abbr* ***ARPS***

adjusted book value ACCOUNTING current value of firm's assets and liabilities the value of a company in terms of the current market values of its assets and liabilities. *Also called* ***modified book value***

adjusted futures price STOCKHOLDING & INVESTMENTS current value of futures contract the current value of a futures contract to buy a commodity at a fixed future date

adjusted gross income ACCOUNTING income after adjustments for tax purposes the amount of annual income that a person or company has after various adjustments for income or corporation tax purposes. *Abbr* ***AGI***

adjusted present value ACCOUNTING separated discounted cash flows for operations and finance where the capital structure of a company is complex, or expected to vary over time, discounted cash flows may be separated into (i) those that relate to operational items, and (ii) those associated with financing. This treatment enables assessment to be made of the separate features of each area. *Abbr* ***APV***

adjuster *US* INSURANCE assessor of insurance claims a professional person acting on behalf of an insurance company to assess the value of an insurance claim. *UK term* ***loss adjuster***

adjustment FINANCE change in financial condition a change, often a significant downward turn, in the financial condition of a business, business sector, stock market, economy, etc.

adjustment credit BANKING short-term loan from US Federal Reserve a short-term loan from the US Federal Reserve to a commercial bank and the most common borrowing method to meet reserve requirements

adjustment trigger CURRENCY & EXCHANGE factor triggering adjustment in exchange rates a factor such as a specific level of inflation that triggers an adjustment in exchange rates

adminisphere GENERAL MANAGEMENT part of firm dealing with administration the part of an organization that deals with administrative matters, often perceived negatively by employees because of the apparently unnecessary nature of decisions made by its members (*slang*)

administered price OPERATIONS & PRODUCTION retail price fixed by manufacturer the price of a good or service which is fixed by a manufacturer and which cannot be varied by a retailer

administration 1. FINANCE = ***receivership*** **2.** GENERAL MANAGEMENT management of firm's operations the management of the affairs of a business, especially the planning and control of its operations

administration costs TREASURY MANAGEMENT management costs costs of management, not including production, marketing, or distribution costs

administration school GENERAL MANAGEMENT attitude to business management a school of thought that defines management activities as a set of processes: organizing, coordinating, commanding, and controlling. *See also* ***business administration***

administrative receiver FINANCE receiver representing long-term creditor a receiver appointed by a ***debenture*** holder to liquidate the assets of a company on his or her behalf

administrator GENERAL MANAGEMENT, HR & PERSONNEL somebody appointed to return firm to solvency a licensed ***insolvency practitioner*** who is appointed by a court, the company itself, or somebody owed money to bring the company back to solvency

admissibility STATISTICS when procedure performs better than all others the property of a procedure if, and only if, there is no other of its class that performs as well or better in at least one case

ADR *abbr* STOCKHOLDING & INVESTMENTS ***American depository receipt***

ADS *abbr* STOCKHOLDING & INVESTMENTS ***American depository share***

adspend MARKETING = ***advertising expenditure***

ad valorem duty *or* **ad valorem tax** TAX sum based on something's value a tax such as Value Added Tax or duty that is calculated on the value of the products or services provided, rather than on their number or size

advance FINANCE **1.** money loaned or paid before due date money paid as a loan or as a part of a payment scheduled to be made later **2.** rise in price or rate an increase in the price, rate, or value of something **3.** pay money as loan or part payment to pay an amount of money to somebody as a loan or as a part of a payment scheduled to be made later **4.** become higher in price or rate to increase in price, rate, or value

advance corporation tax TAX former UK company tax formerly, in the United Kingdom, a tax paid by a company equal to a percentage of its dividends or other distributions of profit to its stockholders. It was abolished in 1999. *Abbr* ***ACT***

advance-decline ratio MARKETS ratio of rising stocks to falling stocks a ratio used for indicating the strength of a stock market, calculated by dividing the number of securities whose price rose by the number whose price fell. A positive result indicates a rising market and a negative result, a falling market.

advance payment FINANCE prepaid amount an amount paid before it is earned or incurred, for example, a prepayment by an importer to an exporter before goods are shipped, or a cash advance for travel expenses

advance payment bond FINANCE made under a contract or order if the supplier fails to fulfill its contractual obligations.

advance payment guarantee *or* **advance payment bond** FINANCE guarantee for recovery of advance payment a guarantee that enables a buyer to recover an advance payment made under a contract or order if the supplier fails to fulfill its contractual obligations

adverse action FINANCE refusal of credit the action of refusing somebody credit or of canceling somebody's credit

adverse balance ACCOUNTING deficit on account a deficit on an account

adverse balance of trade INTERNATIONAL TRADE level of imports higher than exports a situation where a country has more visible imports than it has exports

adverse opinion ACCOUNTING auditor's statement that accounts are misleading a statement in the auditor's report of a company's annual accounts indicating a fundamental disagreement with the company to such an extent that the auditor considers the accounts misleading

adverse selection MARKETING poor quality items sell faster the theory that poor quality goods are more likely to sell than good, because some sellers want to get rid of products, and buyers are unable to judge whether the quality or price is too low. This applies in many spheres, such as the stock market or insurance industry, as well as in the buying and selling of merchandise. Three factors come into play: (i) the variable quality of similar products on the market; (ii) the fact that buyers and sellers do not possess the same information about the product (usually the seller knows more than the buyer); (iii) sellers are more likely to want to get rid of bad quality products than good quality products.

advertisement MARKETING firm's paid announcement to sell product a public announcement by a company in a newspaper, on television or radio, or over the Internet, intended to attract buyers for a product or service

advertising MARKETING using paid announcements to try to sell products the promotion of goods, services, or ideas, through paid announcements. Advertising aims to persuade or inform the general public and can be used to induce purchase, increase brand awareness, or enhance product differentiation. An advertisement has two main components: the message, and the medium by which it is transmitted. Advertising forms just one part of an organization's total marketing strategy.

advertising agency MARKETING firm that creates paid product announcements for clients an organization that, on behalf of clients, drafts and produces advertisements, places advertisements in the media, and plans advertising campaigns. Advertising agencies may also perform other marketing functions, including market research and consulting.

advertising campaign MARKETING planned series of paid product announcements a planned program using advertising aimed at a particular target market or audience over a defined period of time for the purpose of increasing sales or raising awareness of a product or service

advertising department MARKETING part of firm that creates paid product announcements the department within an organization which is responsible for advertising its products or services. The advertising department is also the name given to the section of a publishing house that coordinates the placing of advertisements in its magazines, newspapers, or other publications. It is involved in the sale of advertising space to clients.

advertising expenditure MARKETING money spent by firm on paid product announcements the amount spent by an organization on advertising, usually per year. Advertising expenditure is analyzed by breaking it down into the main advertising channels used by companies, such as newspapers, magazines, television, radio, movie theaters, and outdoor advertising. Expenditure can show the total spending nationally, by sector, or by type and size of company, or may relate to one company's spend on advertising, including the proportion spent on specific brands. *Also called* ***adspend***

advertising manager MARKETING employee in charge of firm's paid product announcements an employee of a business who is responsible for planning and controlling its advertising activities and budgets

advertising media MARKETING TV, radio, newspapers, etc. used for product announcements the communication channels used for advertising, including television, radio, the printed press, and outdoor advertising

advertising research MARKETING gathering information about effectiveness of product announcements research carried out before or after advertising to ensure or test its effectiveness

advertorial MARKETING article influenced by advertisers a combination of an advertisement and an editorial article. The content of an advertorial is significantly influenced, and may even be entirely written, by the advertisers. Examples of advertorials include travel or leisure supplements in newspapers or magazines that are designed to attract advertisements from suppliers of relevant goods or services. A criticism of advertorials is that it is sometimes difficult to distinguish between an advertising article and ordinary journalistic articles, particularly when they appear in the same typeface as the other contents of the newspaper or magazine. To overcome this, some advertorials are headed "Advertisement."

advice of fate BANKING notification as to whether check will be honored immediate notification from a drawer's bank as to whether a check is to be honored or not

advid MARKETING promotional video a video used to promote a product or service

advising bank BANKING, INTERNATIONAL TRADE bank facilitating firm's overseas credit a bank in an exporter's own country to which an issuing bank sends a letter of credit. *Also called* ***notifying bank***

Advisory, Conciliation and Arbitration Service BUSINESS UK organization resolving workplace disputes in the United Kingdom, a public body, funded by taxpayers, that aims to prevent and resolve problems between employers and their workforces. The government established the first voluntary conciliation service in 1896, but the modern ACAS was founded in 1974 when the organization moved away from government control and became independent. It hosted talks between opposing sides in many of the high-profile labor disputes in the 1970s and 1980s, including the miners' strike in 1984. *Abbr* ***ACAS***

advisory funds STOCKHOLDING & INVESTMENTS funds invested at intermediary's discretion funds placed with a financial institution to invest on behalf of a client as the institution sees fit

advisory management STOCKHOLDING & INVESTMENTS stockbroker's provision of investment advice an advisory service offered by some stockbrokers through which clients are able to discuss a variety of investment options with their broker and receive appropriate advice. No resulting action may be taken, however, without a client's express approval.

AEO *abbr* INTERNATIONAL TRADE ***Authorized Economic Operator***

AER *abbr* FINANCE ***Annual Equivalent Rate***

AEX *abbr* MARKETS Amsterdam Stock Exchange

AFAANZ *abbr* ACCOUNTING ***Accounting and Finance Association of Australia and New Zealand***

AFBD *abbr* MARKETS ***Association of Futures Brokers and Dealers***

AfDB *abbr* BANKING ***African Development Bank***

affiliate BUSINESS **1.** firm legally linked to another a company that is controlled by another or is a member of a larger group **2.** firm owning some voting stock of another either of two companies where one owns a minority of the voting stock of the other

affiliated enterprise BUSINESS firm partly owned by another a company that is partly owned, though less than 50%, by another, and in which the stock-owning company exerts some management control or has a close trading relationship with the associate. *Also called* ***associate company***

affiliate directory E-COMMERCE list of websites with affiliate programs a directory that indexes sites belonging to *affiliate programs*. Affiliate directories offer information for companies seeking to subscribe to a program, as well as for those wanting to establish affiliate programs of their own.

affiliate marketing E-COMMERCE advertising through Internet partnerships the use of *affiliate programs* providing advertising links on websites

affiliate partner E-COMMERCE firm that advertises another firm's products on Internet a company that markets a product or service on the Internet for another company

affiliate program E-COMMERCE Internet advertising partnership between firms an advertising program in which one merchant induces others to place their banners and buttons on its website in return for a commission on purchases made by their customers.

There is no better example of the success of affiliate marketing than that of Amazon.com. The company has links on literally hundreds of thousands of external websites, linking through to its own site, from where it offers books and other products. It is a win-win situation: the external vendors can offer their visitors extra services that are easy to establish, and receive revenue from Amazon. At the same time, Amazon opens up a new channel for marketing each time a new visitor links through to its website. *Also called* ***associate program***

affinity card MARKETING credit card offering benefits a credit or debit card co-issued by a bank and another organization whose logo appears on the card. The other organization may be a charity or a commercial enterprise. If it is a charity, the issuing bank makes a donation each time the card is used. A commercial enterprise may get a portion of the revenues that the card generates and may offer benefits in the form of discounts or frequent flyer miles to the cardholder to encourage use of the card.

affirmative action HR & PERSONNEL favoring appointments from disadvantaged groups preferential treatment, usually through a quota system, to prevent, or correct, discriminatory employment practices, particularly relating to recruitment and promotion. The term is widely used in the United States, whereas in the United Kingdom, *positive discrimination* is the preferred term.

affluent society wealthy community a community in which material wealth is widely distributed

affluenza bad feelings associated with being rich feelings of unhappiness, stress, and guilt induced by the pursuit and possession of wealth (*slang*)

AFP *abbr* FINANCE ***Association for Financial Professionals***

African Caribbean and Pacific States INTERNATIONAL TRADE nations grouped for trade purposes a set of independent states that are treated in a similar way for the purposes of trade preferences. *Abbr* ***ACP***

African Development Bank BANKING bank supporting development in African countries a bank set up by African countries to provide long-term loans to help agricultural development and improvement of the infrastructure. *Abbr* ***ADB***

Afrikaanse Handelsinstituut GENERAL MANAGEMENT S. African business organization the South African national chamber of commerce for Afrikaans businesses. *Abbr* ***AHI***

AFTA *abbr* INTERNATIONAL TRADE ***ASEAN Free Trade Area***

after-acquired collateral FINANCE collateral obtained after loan agreed collateral for a loan that a borrower obtains after making the contract for the loan

after date FINANCE after date stated on bill after the date specified on a bill of exchange. Wording on a bill will state when payment has to be made, for example, "60 days after date, we promise to pay..." means 60 days after the date of the bill. *See also* ***bill of exchange***

after-hours buying MARKETS deals done after close of stock exchange buying, selling, or dealing in stock after a stock exchange has officially closed for the day, such deals being subject to normal stock exchange rules. In this way, dealers can take advantage of the fact that, because of time differences and the various stock exchanges around the world, there is almost always at least one stock exchange open throughout 24 hours.

aftermarket MARKETS trade in newly launched stock a market in new shares of stock that starts immediately after trading in the shares begins

after-sales service MARKETING help for customers after buying product customer support following the purchase of a product or service. In some cases, after-sales service can be almost as important as the initial purchase. The manufacturer, retailer, or service provider determines what is included in any warranty or guarantee package. This will include the duration of the warrant, traditionally one year from the date of purchase but increasingly two or more years, maintenance and/or replacement policy, items included/excluded, labor costs, and speed of response. In the case of a service provider, after-sales service might include additional training or help desk availability. Of equal importance is the customer's perception of the degree of willingness with which a supplier deals with a question or complaint, speed of response, and action taken.

after sight FINANCE after bill's acceptance after acceptance of a bill of exchange. Wording on a bill will state when payment has to be made, for example, "60 days after sight, we promise to pay..." means 60 days after acceptance of the bill. *See also* ***bill of exchange***

after-tax TAX after deduction of tax relating to earnings or income from which tax has already been deducted

AG FINANCE public limited company in German-speaking country used after the name of a German, Austrian, or Swiss business to identify it as a public limited company. *Full form* ***Aktiengesellschaft***

against actuals STOCKHOLDING & INVESTMENTS relating to futures trade in cash relating to a trade between owners of futures contracts that allows both to reduce their positions to cash instead of commodities

aged debt FINANCE debt that is overdue a debt that is overdue by one or more given periods, usually increments of 30 days

aged debtor FINANCE somebody with overdue debt a person or organization responsible for a debt that is overdue

agency GENERAL MANAGEMENT authority to represent somebody else a relationship between two people or organizations in which one is empowered to act on behalf of the other in dealings with a third party

agency bank BANKING bank that is foreign bank's agent a bank that does not accept deposits, but acts as an agent for another, usually foreign, bank

agency bill BANKING bill of exchange drawn on local bank a bill of exchange drawn on the local branch of a foreign bank

agency broker STOCKHOLDING & INVESTMENTS dealer trading in shares for commission a dealer who acts for a client, buying and selling stock for a commission

agency commission MARKETING money given to advertising firm for delivering business a percentage of advertising expenditure rebated to an advertising agency, media buyer, or client organization by a media owner

agency markup MARKETING additional management fee charged by advertising firm a management fee charged by an advertising agency in addition to the cost of external services that it buys on behalf of a client

agenda GENERAL MANAGEMENT list of subjects to deal with at meeting a list of topics to be discussed or business to be transacted during the course of a meeting, usually sent prior to the meeting to those invited to attend

agent GENERAL MANAGEMENT representative for somebody else a person or organization empowered to act on behalf of another when dealing with a third party

agent bank BANKING **1.** bank participating in partner bank's credit card program a bank that takes part in another bank's credit card program, acting as a depository for merchants **2.** bank acting on foreign bank's behalf a bank that acts on behalf of a foreign bank

agent's commission FINANCE money paid for agent's services money, often a percentage of sales, paid to an agent

age pension *ANZ* PENSIONS government money received by retired person a sum of money paid regularly by the government to people who have reached the age of retirement

agflation ECONOMICS rapidly rising food prices an economic situation occurring when the cost of food rises rapidly

aggregate demand ECONOMICS total money spent or invested in economy the sum of all expenditures in an economy that makes up its ***GDP,*** for example, consumers' expenditure on goods and services, investment in ***capital stock,*** and government spending

aggregate depreciation ACCOUNTING = ***accumulated depreciation***

aggregate income FINANCE total of all incomes in economy the total of all incomes in an economy without adjustments for inflation, taxation, or types of ***double counting***

aggregate output ECONOMICS all goods and services produced in economy the total value of all the goods and services produced in an economy. *Also called* ***aggregate supply***

aggregate planning OPERATIONS & PRODUCTION planning for manufacture of related products medium-range capacity planning, typically covering a period of 3 to 18 months. Aggregate planning is used in a manufacturing environment and determines not only the overall output levels planned but the appropriate resource input mix to be used for related groups of products. Generally, planners focus on overall or aggregate capacity rather than on individual products or services. Aggregate planning can be used to influence demand as well as supply, in which case variables such as price, advertising, and the product mix are taken into account.

aggregate supply ECONOMICS = ***aggregate output***

aggregator **1.** FINANCE firm selling product packages a company that combines similar products or services into larger packages, making a profit by cost savings, by reaching a larger market, or by charging more for the combined package. In the secondary mortgage market, aggregators buy individual mortgages from financial institutions and turn them into ***mortgage-backed securities,*** pooling them and selling them on at a higher price. **2.** E-COMMERCE middleman between producers and online customers an organization that acts as an intermediary between producers and customers in an Internet business web. The aggregator selects products, sets prices, and ensures fulfillment of orders.

aggressive STOCKHOLDING & INVESTMENTS describing high-risk investment strategy used to describe an investment strategy marked by willingness to accept high risk while trying to realize higher than average gains. Such a strategy involves investing in rapidly growing companies that promise capital appreciation but produce little or no income from dividends and de-emphasizes income-producing instruments such as bonds.

aggressive accounting ACCOUNTING deliberately inaccurate accounting to improve firm's position inaccurate or unlawful accounting practices used by an organization in order to make its financial position seem healthier than it is in reality (*slang*)

aggressive growth fund STOCKHOLDING & INVESTMENTS mutual fund pursuing large profits riskily a mutual fund that takes considerable risks in the hope of making large profits

AGI *abbr* ACCOUNTING ***adjusted gross income***

agile manufacturing OPERATIONS & PRODUCTION flexible method for producing goods to meet demand a manufacturing method that focuses on meeting the demands of customers by adopting flexible manufacturing practices. Agile manufacturing emerged as a reaction to ***lean production.*** It differs by focusing on meeting the demands of customers without sacrificing quality or incurring added costs. Based on the idea of the ***virtual organization,*** agile manufacturing aims to develop flexible, often short-term, relationships with suppliers, as market opportunities arise. Stock control is considered less important than satisfying the customer, and so customer satisfaction measures become more important than output measures. Agile manufacturing requires an adaptable, innovative, and empowered work force.

agility GENERAL MANAGEMENT ability to quickly respond and adapt to change the organizational capability to be flexible, responsive, adaptive, and show initiative in times of change and uncertainty. Agility has origins in manufacturing and has been cited as a source of competitive advantage by many management gurus. For others, the key to agility lies in what the organization is, as opposed to what it does. Agility grew as a reaction against the slowness of bureaucratic organizations to respond to changing market conditions. The ***virtual organization*** has been quoted as one extreme example of an agile organization.

agio **1.** FINANCE difference between two related values the difference between two values, for example, between the interest charged on loans made by a bank and the interest paid by the bank on deposits, or between the values of two currencies **2.** CURRENCY & EXCHANGE charge for exchanging currency a charge made for changing money of one currency into another, or for changing paper money into coins

AGM *UK* CORPORATE GOVERNANCE = ***annual meeting***

agreed price OPERATIONS & PRODUCTION price agreed on by buyer and seller a price for a product or service that has been accepted by both the buyer and seller

agreement among underwriters STOCKHOLDING & INVESTMENTS document forming syndicate of underwriters a document which forms a syndicate of underwriters, linking them to the issuer of a new stock issue

agreement of sale LEGAL formal contract between buyer and seller a written contract specifying the terms under which the buyer agrees to buy particular real estate and the seller agrees to sell it

agreement to sell LEGAL contract to sell at future date a contract between two parties in which one agrees to sell something to the other at a date in the future

agricultural produce ACCOUNTING slaughtered animals and harvested plants farm animals and plants once they have been slaughtered or harvested. Before this they are classified as ***biological assets.***

AHI *abbr* BUSINESS ***Afrikaanse Handelsinstituut***

AIA *abbr* ACCOUNTING ***Association of International Accountants***

AIB *abbr* BANKING ***American Institute of Banking***

AIC *abbr* STOCKHOLDING & INVESTMENTS ***Association of Investment Companies***

AICPA *abbr* ACCOUNTING ***American Institute of Certified Public Accountants***

AIFA *abbr* FINANCE ***Association of Independent Financial Advisers***

aim GENERAL MANAGEMENT goal of effort an end toward which effort is directed and on which resources are focused, usually to achieve an organization's strategy. There is considerable discussion on whether aim, goal, target, and objective are the same. In general usage, the terms are often interchangeable, so it is important that, if an organization has a particular meaning for one of these terms, it must define it in its documentation. Sometimes an aim is seen as the desired final end result, while a goal is a smaller step on the road to it.

AIM *abbr* MARKETS ***Alternative Investment Market***

air bill *US* FINANCE documents accompanying shipments by air the documentation issued by an airline for the shipment of goods by air freight. *UK term* ***air waybill***

air cover GENERAL MANAGEMENT support and protection from high-ranking employee support from a senior member of staff, usually during a time of change, upheaval, or unpopular decisions (*slang*)

airtime MARKETING amount of time that advertisement is broadcast the amount of time given to an advertisement on television, radio, or in movie theaters

air waybill *UK* FINANCE = ***air bill.*** *Abbr* ***AWB***

AITC *abbr* FINANCE ***Association of Investment Trust Companies.*** *See* ***Association of Investment Companies.***

Aktb *abbr* BUSINESS **Aktiebolag**

Aktiebolag *or* **Aktiebolaget** BUSINESS Incorporated the Swedish equivalent of Inc. *Abbr* ***Aktb***

Aktiengesellschaft FINANCE *see* ***AG***

alien corporation BUSINESS firm registered in another country a company that is based in one country, but registered in another

all equity rate FINANCE interest rate charged for high-risk project the interest rate that a lender charges because of the apparent risks of a project that are independent of the normal market risks of financing it

alligator spread MARKETS unprofitable spread in good market conditions in the US options market, a ***spread*** that remains unprofitable even with good market conditions, usually as the result of high commissions paid to brokers or agents (*slang*)

All Industrials Index MARKETS Australian index of non-mining companies a subindex of the Australian ***All Ordinaries Index*** which includes all the companies from that index that are not involved in resources or mining

All Mining Index MARKETS Australian index of mining companies a subindex of the Australian ***All Ordinaries Index*** which includes all the companies from that index that are involved in the mining industry

allocate 1. FINANCE assign item to single cost unit to assign a whole item of ***cost***, or of ***revenue***, to a single cost unit, center, account, or time period **2.** STOCKHOLDING & INVESTMENTS choose between different investments to assign assets to different investment types such as equities, bonds, or cash

allonge FINANCE attachment to bill of exchange allowing more signatures a piece of paper attached to a bill of exchange, so that more endorsements can be written on it

All Ordinaries Accumulation Index MARKETS measure of change in Australian stock prices a measure of the change in stock prices on the Australian Stock Exchange, based on the ***All Ordinaries Index***, but assuming that all dividends are reinvested

All Ordinaries Index MARKETS major index of Australian stocks the major index of Australian stocks, comprising more than 300 of the most active Australian companies listed on the Australian Stock Exchange. *Abbr* ***AO***

all-or-none underwriting MARKETS option of canceling public stock issue the option of canceling a public offering of stock if the underwriting is not fully subscribed. *Abbr* ***AON***

allotment STOCKHOLDING & INVESTMENTS UK issue of new company's stock to applicants in the United Kingdom, the act of selling shares of stock in a new company to people who have applied for them

allowable deductions TAX legitimate deductions from UK taxable income in the United Kingdom, deductions from income that are allowed by HM Revenue & Customs, reducing the total on which tax is payable

allowable expenses TAX business expenses offset against tax business expenses that can be used to reduce the amount of income on which tax is paid

allowable losses ACCOUNTING losses rightly offset against gains losses such as those on the sale of assets that can be used to reduce the amount of income on which tax is paid

allowance for bad debt ACCOUNTING accounting arrangement covering unpaid debt a provision made in a company's accounts for potentially unrecoverable debts

All Resources Index MARKETS Australian index of companies in resources industry a subindex of the Australian ***All Ordinaries Index*** which includes all the companies from that index that are involved in the resources industry

all-risks policy INSURANCE insurance policy covering all likely claims an insurance policy that covers risks of any kind, with no exclusions

alpha STOCKHOLDING & INVESTMENTS number measuring price increase a number representing an estimate of the anticipated price increase of a stock. A high alpha suggests a stock is likely to produce a good return. *See also* ***beta***

alpha rating STOCKHOLDING & INVESTMENTS expected return when market's rate is zero the return a security or a portfolio would be expected to earn if the market's rate of return were zero. Alpha expresses the difference between the return expected from a stock or mutual fund, given its beta rating, and the return actually produced. A stock or trust that returns more than its beta would predict has a positive alpha, while one that returns less than the amount predicted by beta has a negative alpha. A large positive alpha indicates a strong performance, while a large negative alpha indicates a dismal performance.

To begin with, the market itself is assigned a beta of 1.0. If a stock or trust has a beta of 1.2, this means its price is likely to rise or fall by 12% when the overall market rises or falls by 10%; a beta of 7.0 means the stock or trust price is likely to move up or down at 70% of the level of the market change.

In practice, an alpha of 0.4 means the stock or trust in question outperformed the market-based return estimate by 0.4%. An alpha of –0.6 means the return was 0.6% less than would have been predicted from the change in the market alone.

Both alpha and beta should be readily available upon request from investment firms, because the figures appear in standard performance reports. It is always best to ask for them, because calculating a stock's alpha rating requires first knowing a stock's beta rating, and beta calculations can involve mathematical complexities. *See also* ***beta rating***

alpha value STOCKHOLDING & INVESTMENTS money given to departing employee for investment in Australia and New Zealand, a sum paid to an employee when he or she leaves a company that can be transferred to a concessionally taxed investment account such as an ***Approved Deposit Fund***

alternate director CORPORATE GOVERNANCE absent director's representative at board meeting a person who is allowed to act for an absent named director of a company at a board meeting

alternative investment STOCKHOLDING & INVESTMENTS investment not in bonds or stock an investment other than in bonds or stock of a large company or one listed on a stock exchange

Alternative Investment Market MARKETS London market trading in smaller firms' stock the London market trading in stock of emerging or small companies not eligible for listing on the London Stock Exchange. It replaced the Unlisted Securities Market (USM) in 1995. *Abbr* ***AIM***

alternative minimum tax TAX US system to ensure that wealthy pay tax in the United States, a way of calculating income tax that is intended to ensure that wealthy individuals, corporations, trusts, and estates pay at least some tax regardless of deductions, but that is increasingly targeting the middle class because the threshold was never indexed for inflation. This has turned the AMT into an important political issue, with the possibility that the threshold will either be raised substantially or the AMT eliminated altogether in future. *Abbr* ***AMT***

alternative mortgage instrument MORTGAGES open-ended non-amortizing mortgage any form of mortgage other than a fixed-term amortizing loan

alternative order STOCKHOLDING & INVESTMENTS instruction for either of two specified actions an order given to a broker to do one of two things, for example, to sell a stock either when it goes up to a specified price or down to a specified price, thereby limiting gains and losses

AM *abbr* STOCKHOLDING & INVESTMENTS ***asset management***

amalgamation MERGERS & ACQUISITIONS joining of organizations for mutual benefit the process of two or more organizations joining together for mutual benefit, either through a ***merger*** or ***consolidation***

amanah FINANCE trust arrangement between parties in Islamic financing, an arrangement in which one person holds funds or property in trust for another

ambit claim *ANZ* FINANCE excessive arbitration claim anticipating compromise a claim made to an arbitration authority for higher pay or improved conditions that is deliberately exaggerated because the claimants know that they will subsequently have to compromise

American Accounting Association ACCOUNTING organization promoting accounting research a voluntary organization for those with an interest in accounting research and best practice. Its mission is "to foster worldwide excellence in the creation, dissemination, and application of accounting knowledge and skills." The association was founded in 1916. *Abbr* ***AAA***

American Bankers Association BANKING US association representing banks an association that represents banks in the United States and promotes good practice. *Abbr* ***ABA***

American depository receipt STOCKHOLDING & INVESTMENTS document indicating ownership of foreign stock a document that indicates a US investor's ownership of stock in a foreign corporation. *Abbr* ***ADR***

American depository share STOCKHOLDING & INVESTMENTS foreign stock owned by US investor a share of stock in a foreign corporation, whose ownership by a US investor is represented by an ***American depository receipt.*** *Abbr* ***ADS***

American Institute of Banking BANKING US association training bankers the part of the American Bankers Association that organizes training for people who work in the banking industry. *Abbr* ***AIB***

American Institute of Certified Public Accountants ACCOUNTING US association for certified public accountants in the United States, the national association for certified public accountants, founded in New York in 1887. *Abbr* ***AICPA***

American option *or* **American style option** STOCKHOLDING & INVESTMENTS option contract running to expiration date an option contract that can be exercised at any time up to and including the expiration date. Most exchange-traded options are of this style. *See also* ***European option***

American Stock Exchange *or* **AMEX** MARKETS New York exchange listing smaller firms a New York stock exchange listing smaller and less mature companies than those listed on the larger New York Stock Exchange.

amortization FINANCE **1.** method of recovering costs of assets a method of recovering (deducting or writing off) the capital costs of intangible assets over a fixed period of time.

For tax purposes, the distinction is not always made between amortization and depreciation, yet amortization remains a viable financial accounting concept in its own right.

It is computed using the straight-line method of depreciation: divide the initial cost of the intangible asset by the estimated useful life of that asset.

Initial cost / Useful life = Amortization per year

For example, if it costs $10,000 to acquire a patent and it has an estimated useful life of 10 years, the amortized amount per year is $1,000.

The amount of amortization accumulated since the asset was acquired appears on the organization's balance sheet as a deduction under the amortized asset.

While that formula is straightforward, amortization can also incorporate a variety of noncash charges to net earnings and/or asset values, such as depletion, write-offs, prepaid expenses, and deferred charges. Accordingly, there are many rules to regulate how these charges appear on financial statements. The rules are different in each country, and are occasionally changed, so it is necessary to stay abreast of them and rely on expert advice.

For financial reporting purposes, an intangible asset is amortized over a period of years. The amortizable life, or "useful life," of an intangible asset is the period over which it gives economic benefit.

Intangibles that can be amortized can include:

Copyrights, based on the amount paid either to purchase them or to develop them internally, plus the costs incurred in producing the work (wages or materials, for example). At present, a copyright is granted to a corporation for 75 years, and to an individual for the life of the author plus 50 years. However, the estimated useful life of a copyright is usually far less than its legal life, and it is generally amortized over a fairly short period.

Cost of a franchise, including any fees paid to the franchiser, as well legal costs or expenses incurred in the acquisition. A franchise granted for a limited period should be amortized over its life. If the franchise has an indefinite life, it should be amortized over a reasonable period not to exceed 40 years.

Covenants not to compete: an agreement by the seller of a business not to engage in a competing business in a certain area for a specific period of time. The cost of the not-to-compete covenant should be amortized over the period covered by the covenant unless its estimated economic life is expected to be less.

Easement costs that grant a right of way may be amortized if there is a limited and specified life.

Organization costs incurred when forming a corporation or a partnership, including legal fees, accounting services, incorporation fees, and other related services. Organization costs are usually amortized over 60 months.

Patents, both those developed internally and those purchased. If developed internally, a patent's "amortizable basis" includes legal fees incurred during the application process. A patent should be amortized over its legal life or its economic life, whichever is the shorter.

Trademarks, brands, and trade names, which should be written off over a period not to exceed 40 years.

Other types of property that may be amortized include certain intangible drilling costs, circulation costs, mine development costs, pollution control facilities, and reforestation expenditures.

Certain intangibles cannot be amortized, but may be depreciated using a straight-line approach if they have "determinable" useful life. Because the rules are different in each country and are subject to change, it is essential to rely on specialist advice. **2.** equal payment of principal and interest the payment of the principal and interest on a loan in equal amounts over a period of time

amortize FINANCE gradually repay debt or reduce value of assets to reduce the value of an ***asset*** gradually by systematically writing off its cost over a period of time, or to repay a ***debt*** in a series of regular installments or transfers

amortized mortgage *US* MORTGAGES mortgage with combined principal and interest payments a long-term loan, usually for the purchase of real estate, in which the borrower makes monthly payments, part of which cover the interest on the loan and part of which cover the repayment of the principal. In the early years, the greater proportion of the payment is used to cover the interest charged but, as the principal is gradually repaid, the interest portion diminishes and the repayment portion increases. *UK term* ***repayment mortgage***

amortized value FINANCE value of amortized financial instrument the value at a specific time of a financial instrument that is being amortized

amortizing swap STOCKHOLDING & INVESTMENTS interest rate swap with decreasing notional principal amount an ***interest rate swap*** in which the ***notional principal amount*** declines over the period of the contract

amount paid up MARKETS money paid for new stock an amount paid for a new issue of shares of stock, either the total payment or the first installment, if the shares are offered with installment payments

AMPS *abbr* STOCKHOLDING & INVESTMENTS ***auction market preferred stock***

AMT *abbr* TAX ***alternative minimum tax***

analysis STOCKHOLDING & INVESTMENTS evaluation of markets a systematic examination and evaluation of the financial markets and the performance of securities

analysis of variance STATISTICS isolation of one cause of statistical variation the process of separating the statistical variation caused by a particular factor from that caused by other factors

analysis of variance table STATISTICS table showing variation in statistical data a table that shows the total variation in the observations in a statistical data set

analyst STOCKHOLDING & INVESTMENTS somebody who evaluates investments a person whose job is to analyze the performance of securities and make recommendations about buying and selling

analytical review TREASURY MANAGEMENT examination of trends between financial periods the examination of ratios, trends, and changes in balances from one period to the next, to obtain a broad understanding of the financial position and results of operations and to identify any items requiring further investigation

angel investing FINANCE investing in unproven business venture willingness of an individual or network of individuals to invest in an unproven but well-researched startup business, taking an advisory role without making demands

angel investor *or* **angel** FINANCE investor in unproven business venture an individual or group of individuals willing to invest in an unproven but well-researched startup business. Angel investors are typically the first port of call for Internet startups looking for financial backing, because they are more inclined to provide early funding than ***venture capital*** firms are. After investing in a company, angel investors take an advisory role without making demands.

angel network *or* **angel investment group** FINANCE network of potential investors for entrepreneurs a network of backers, organized through a central office which keeps a database of suitable investors and puts them in touch with entrepreneurs who need financial backing

angular histogram STATISTICS circular chart showing data a histogram that represents data in a circular form. *Also called* ***pie chart***

ANN *abbr* E-COMMERCE ***artificial neural network***

announcement STOCKHOLDING & INVESTMENTS statement of company's trading prospects a statement that a company makes to provide information on its trading prospects, which will be of interest to its existing and potential investors

announcement date STOCKHOLDING & INVESTMENTS = ***declaration date***

annual accounts CORPORATE GOVERNANCE, ACCOUNTING document showing company's financial performance a profit and loss account and balance sheet, and, where a company has subsidiaries, the company's group accounts, included in the ***annual report and accounts*** for stockholders. *See also* ***annual report***

annual charge STOCKHOLDING & INVESTMENTS management fee covering administrative costs a management fee paid yearly to a stockbroker or collective fund manager by a client to cover a variety of administrative costs and ***commission***

annual depreciation ACCOUNTING reduction in book value of asset a reduction in the book value of a fixed asset at a specific rate per year, based on the estimated useful life of that asset. *See also* ***straight line depreciation***

annual depreciation provision ACCOUNTING allocation of cost of asset to specific year the allocation of the cost of an asset to a single year of the asset's expected lifetime

Annual Equivalent Rate FINANCE UK notional annual compound interest rate in the United Kingdom, a way of expressing different interest rates charged over different periods as an annual rate equivalent to a single payment of interest made on the anniversary of the loan and each subsequent year to repayment. *Abbr* ***AER***. *See also* ***compound annual return***

annual general meeting *UK* CORPORATE GOVERNANCE = ***annual meeting***

annual income FINANCE money received in one year the money received from earnings or investments during a calendar year

annualized percentage rate FINANCE monthly rate times twelve the percentage rate over a year, calculated by multiplying the monthly rate by twelve. It is not as accurate as the ***annual percentage rate,*** which includes fees and other charges. *Abbr* ***APR***

annual management charge STOCKHOLDING & INVESTMENTS charge made for managing investment account a charge made by the financial institution that is managing an investment account

annual meeting *US* CORPORATE GOVERNANCE stockholders' yearly business meeting a yearly meeting at which a company's management reports the year's results and stockholders have the opportunity to vote on company business, for example, the appointment of directors and auditors. Other business, for example, voting on dividend payments, and board- and stockholder-sponsored resolutions, may also be transacted. *Also called* ***annual stockholders' meeting***. *UK term* ***AGM***

annual percentage rate FINANCE hypothetical rate based on simple interest the interest rate that would exist if it were calculated as simple rather than compound interest.

Different investments typically offer different compounding periods, usually quarterly or monthly. The APR allows them to be compared over a common period of time: one year. This enables an investor or borrower to compare like with like, providing an excellent basis for comparing mortgage or other loan rates.

APR is calculated by applying the formula:

$$APR = [(1 + i) / m]^{m} - 1$$

In the formula, *i* is the interest rate quoted, expressed as a decimal, and *m* is the number of compounding periods per year.

The APR is usually slightly higher than the quoted rate, and should be expressed as a decimal, that is, 6% becomes 0.06. When expressed as the cost of credit, other costs should be included in addition to interest, such as loan closing costs and financial fees. *Abbr* ***APR***

annual percentage yield FINANCE effective annual return on investment the effective or true annual rate of return on an investment, taking into account the effect of ***compounding.*** For example, an annual percentage rate of 6% compounded monthly translates into an annual percentage yield of 6.17%. *Abbr* ***APY***

annual report *or* **annual report and accounts** CORPORATE GOVERNANCE, ACCOUNTING document reporting company's business performance a document prepared each year to give a true and fair view of a company's state of affairs.

Annual reports are issued to shareholders and filed at the Securities and Exchange Commission in accordance with the provisions of company legislation. Contents include a ***profit and loss account*** and ***balance sheet,*** a ***cash flow statement, auditor's report,*** directors' report, and, where a company has subsidiaries, the company's group accounts. The *financial statements* are the main purpose of the annual report, and usually include notes to the accounts. These amplify numerous points contained in the figures and are critical for anyone wishing to study the accounts in detail.

annual rest system MORTGAGES system crediting overpayments once a year a system in which extra payments or overpayments made to reduce the amount borrowed on a mortgage are credited to the account only once a year

annual return ACCOUNTING in UK, firm's report to Registrar of Companies in the United Kingdom, an official report that a registered company has to make each year to the Registrar of Companies

annual stockholders' meeting *US* CORPORATE GOVERNANCE = ***annual meeting***

annuitant PENSIONS recipient of annuity income a person who receives income from an ***annuity***

annuity PENSIONS contract for regular payments from one-off investment a contract under which a person pays a lump-sum premium to an insurance company and in return receives periodic payments, usually yearly, often beginning on retirement.

There are several types of annuities. They vary both in the ways they accumulate funds and in the ways they dispense earnings. A *fixed annuity* guarantees fixed payments to the individual receiving it for the term of the contract, usually until death; a *variable annuity* offers no guarantee but has potential for a greater return, usually based on the performance of a stock or mutual fund; a *deferred annuity* delays payments until the individual chooses to receive them; a *hybrid annuity,* also called a *combination annuity,* combines features of both the fixed and variable annuity.

annuity certain PENSIONS contract paying for set period an ***annuity*** that provides payments for a specific number of years, regardless of whether the annuitant remains alive

annuity contract INSURANCE contract providing lifelong regular payments an ***annuity*** that provides payments of a fixed sum regularly while the annuitant is alive

annuity in arrears INSURANCE annuity with delayed first payment an ***annuity*** whose first payment is due at least one payment period after the start date of the annuity's contract

anonymizer E-COMMERCE website that hides user's identity a website through which a person browsing can visit the World Wide Web without leaving any identity traces

ANSI X.12 standard E-COMMERCE accepted method of electronic business transactions an American National Standards Institute-supported protocol for the electronic interchange of business transactions. *Also called* ***X.12***

antedate *UK* GENERAL MANAGEMENT = ***predate***

anticipation note STOCKHOLDING & INVESTMENTS bond repaid with future receipts or borrowings a bond that a borrower intends to pay off with money from taxes due or money to be borrowed in a later and larger transaction

anticipatory hedging STOCKHOLDING & INVESTMENTS hedging before relevant transaction occurs hedging conducted before the transaction to which the ***hedge*** applies has taken place. *See also* ***hedge (sense 2)***

anti-dumping INTERNATIONAL TRADE preventing cheap sale of products overseas intended to prevent the sale of goods on a foreign market at a price lower than is usually charged in the home market

anti-dumping duty TAX, INTERNATIONAL TRADE import tax offsetting subsidized price of import a tax imposed by a country on imported goods, when the price of the goods includes a subsidy from the government in the country of origin. *Also called* ***countervailing duty***

anti-inflationary ECONOMICS restricting inflation restricting or trying to restrict an increase in inflation

anti-trust laws LEGAL US laws preventing monopolies in the United States, laws that prevent the formation of monopolies. Antitrust laws also attempt to curb ***trusts*** and ***cartels*** and to keep them from employing monopolistic practices to make unfair profits. They are intended to encourage competitive behavior.

ANZCERTA *abbr* INTERNATIONAL TRADE ***Australia and New Zealand Closer Economic Relations Trade Agreement***

AO *abbr* MARKETS ***All Ordinaries Index***

AON MARKETS *see* ***all-or-none underwriting***

AP *abbr* ACCOUNTING ***accounts payable***

APACS *abbr* BANKING ***Association for Payment Clearing Services***

APB *abbr* ACCOUNTING ***Accounting Principles Board***

APEC *abbr* INTERNATIONAL TRADE ***Asia-Pacific Economic Cooperation***

application server E-COMMERCE host computer network allowing dynamic information exchange an advanced type of server used to run programming languages that help websites to deliver dynamic information such as the latest news headlines, stock quotes, personalized information, or shopping carts

applied economics ECONOMICS use of economic theories for practical policies the practical application of theoretical economic principles, especially in formulating national and international economic policies

apportionment ACCOUNTING distribution of costs the sharing of costs between different internal parties, cost centers, etc.

appreciation **1.** ACCOUNTING value that asset accrues over time the value that some assets such as land and buildings accrue over time. Directors of companies are obliged to reflect this in their accounts. **2.** CURRENCY & EXCHANGE relative increase in currency value the increase in value of a currency with a ***floating exchange rate*** relative to another

appropriation ACCOUNTING sum set aside a sum of money that has been allocated for a specific purpose

appropriation account ACCOUNTING section of account showing treatment of profits the part of a ***profit and loss account*** that shows how a company's profit has been dealt with, for example, how much has been given to the stockholders as dividends and how much is being put into the reserves

approved accounts ACCOUNTING accounts agreed on by company directors accounts that have been formally accepted by a company's board of directors

Approved Deposit Fund PENSIONS fund accepting payments from superannuation fund in Australia and New Zealand, a concessionally taxed fund managed by a financial institution into which ***eligible termination payments*** can be transferred from a superannuation fund. *Abbr* ***ADF***

approved securities STOCKHOLDING & INVESTMENTS state bonds as bank reserves state bonds that can be held by banks to form part of their reserves

APR *abbr* FINANCE **1.** ***annual percentage rate*** **2.** ***annualized percentage rate***

APRA *abbr* REGULATION & COMPLIANCE ***Australian Prudential Regulation Authority***

APS *abbr* BANKING ***Asset Protection Scheme***

APV *abbr* ACCOUNTING ***adjusted present value***

APY *abbr* FINANCE ***annual percentage yield***

AR *abbr* FINANCE ***accounts receivable***

Arab Accounting Dinar CURRENCY & EXCHANGE accounting unit of Arab Monetary Fund a bookkeeping unit used between member states of the Arab Monetary Fund, equal to three IMF ***Special Drawing Rights***. *Abbr* ***AAD***

arbitrage MARKETS trade profiting from variations in market price the buying and selling of foreign currencies, products, or financial securities between two or more markets in order to make an immediate profit by exploiting the differences in market prices quoted

arbitrage fund MARKETS fund capitalizing on variations in market price a fund which tries to take advantage of price discrepancies for the same ***asset*** in different ***markets***

arbitrage pricing theory MARKETS model used for assessing return and risk a model of financial instrument and portfolio behavior that provides a benchmark of return and risk for capital budgeting and securities analysis. It can be used to create portfolios that track a market index, estimate the risk of an asset allocation strategy, or estimate the response of a portfolio to economic developments.

arbitrage syndicate MARKETS group raising capital for arbitrage deals a group of people formed to raise the capital to invest in arbitrage deals

arbitrageur MARKETS somebody buying stock for windfall profit a firm or individual who purchases stock or financial securities to make a windfall profit

arbitration GENERAL MANAGEMENT, HR & PERSONNEL process of resolving disagreement by unbiased person the settlement of a dispute by an independent third person, rather than by a court of law. Arbitration allows for claims or grievances to be settled quickly, cost-effectively, privately, and by somebody who is suitably qualified. A contract may include an arbitration clause to be invoked in the case of a dispute. *See also* ***mediation***

arbitrator GENERAL MANAGEMENT unbiased person who resolves other people's disagreements an impartial person accepted by both parties in a dispute to hear both sides and make a judgment

arbun FINANCE nonrefundable deposit allowing buyer right to cancel in Islamic financing, a nonrefundable down payment paid by a buyer to a seller upon the signing of a sale contract in which the buyer has the right to cancel the contract at any time

area sampling STATISTICS randomly selecting subregions for inspection a form of sampling in which a region is subdivided and some of the divisions are then selected at random for a complete survey

arithmetic mean STATISTICS simple average a simple average calculated by dividing the sum of two or more items by the number of items

ARM *abbr* MORTGAGES ***adjustable rate mortgage***

armchair economics ECONOMICS casual economic opinion economic forecasting or theorizing based on insufficient data or knowledge of a subject (*informal*)

arm's-length price OPERATIONS & PRODUCTION price agreed by unrelated seller and buyer a price at which an unrelated seller and buyer agree to deal on an asset or a product

ARPS *abbr* STOCKHOLDING & INVESTMENTS ***adjustable rate preferred stock***

ARR *abbr* ACCOUNTING ***accounting rate of return***

arrangement fee BANKING bank charge for arranging credit a charge made by a bank to a client for arranging credit facilities

arrears FINANCE money owed but unpaid money that is owed, but that has not been paid at the time when it was due ◇ in arrears FINANCE still owing money that should have been paid, especially in a series of payments

articles of association *UK* CORPORATE GOVERNANCE = ***bylaws***

articles of incorporation CORPORATE GOVERNANCE legal document creating US corporation in the United States, a legal document that creates a corporation and sets forth its purpose and structure according to the laws of the state in which it is established. *Also called* ***charter***

articles of partnership CORPORATE GOVERNANCE = ***partnership agreement***

artificial intelligence GENERAL MANAGEMENT computer systems thinking like humans a branch of computer science concerned with the development of computer systems capable of performing functions that normally require human intelligence, for example, reasoning, problem solving, learning from experience, and speech recognition. Artificial intelligence research combines aspects of computer science and cognitive psychology. Artificial intelligence has applications in business and management, for example, in ***expert systems.***

artificial neural network GENERAL MANAGEMENT information processing system allowing computers to learn an information processing system with interconnected components analogous to neurons, based on mathematical models that mimic some features of biological nervous systems and the ability to learn through experience. *Abbr* ***ANN***

ASB *abbr* ACCOUNTING ***Accounting Standards Board***

ascending tops MARKETS market chart pattern showing series of ascending peaks a term used to refer to an upward trend in the market as shown on a chart, in which each peak in the chart is higher than the preceding one

ASEAN Free Trade Area INTERNATIONAL TRADE conceptual agreement fostering trade around Singapore a conceptual regional free trade agreement supported by Singapore to foster trade within the region covered by the Association of Southeast Asian Nations. *Abbr* ***AFTA***

A share STOCKHOLDING & INVESTMENTS share issued to raise additional capital in the United States, a share of stock in a company issued to raise additional capital without diluting control of the company. *Also called* ***nonvoting share***. *See also* ***B share***

Asian Currency Unit ACCOUNTING unit for recording transactions in Asian Dollar market a bookkeeping unit used for recording transactions made by approved financial institutions operating in the Asian Dollar market. *Abbr* ***ACU***

Asian Development Bank BANKING bank supporting development in Asia a bank set up by various Asian countries, with other outside members, to assist countries in the region with money and technical advice. *Abbr* ***ADB***

Asian dollar BANKING, CURRENCY & EXCHANGE US dollar deposited in Asian bank a dollar deposited in a bank in Asia or the Pacific region

Asian option STOCKHOLDING & INVESTMENTS, RISK = ***average option***

Asia-Pacific Economic Cooperation INTERNATIONAL TRADE forum promoting trade in Pacific region a forum designed to promote trade and economic cooperation among countries bordering the Pacific Ocean. It was established in 1989. Members include Australia, Indonesia, Thailand, the Philippines, Singapore, Brunei, and Japan. *Abbr* ***APEC***

ASIC *abbr* REGULATION & COMPLIANCE ***Australian Securities and Investments Commission***

ask 1. *US* MARKETS security's selling price the price at which a security is offered for sale. *UK term* ***asked price*** **2.** STOCKHOLDING & INVESTMENTS value of mutual fund the net asset value of a mutual fund plus any sales charges

asked price *UK* MARKETS = ***ask*** *(sense 1)*

asking price OPERATIONS & PRODUCTION original price the price that a seller puts on something before any negotiation

ask price US MARKETS = ***ask*** *(sense 1)*

assay precious metal purity test a test used for determining the purity of a precious metal such as gold or silver

assembly OPERATIONS & PRODUCTION putting product parts together the process of joining components together to make a complete product

assembly line OPERATIONS & PRODUCTION system for putting parts together in specific order a line of production in which a number of assembly operations are performed in a set sequence. The speed of movement of an assembly line has to be matched with the skills and abilities of the workers and the complexity of the assembly process to be performed. The assembly line emerged from the ideas of ***scientific management*** and was popularized by a number of entrepreneurs, including Henry Ford in the car production industry.

assembly plant OPERATIONS & PRODUCTION factory for assembling products the factory building in which an ***assembly line*** is housed

assessed loss TAX in S. Africa tax-deductible expenses exceeding taxable income the excess of tax-deductible expenses over taxable income as confirmed by the South African Revenue Service. It may be carried forward and deducted in determining the taxpayer's taxable income in subsequent years of assessment.

assessed value FINANCE value calculated by professional adviser a value for something that is calculated officially by somebody such as an investment adviser

assessor FINANCE somebody who establishes something's worth a person who determines the value of something such as real estate for tax or insurance purposes

asset ACCOUNTING item to which value is assigned any tangible or intangible item to which a value can be assigned. Assets can be physical, such as machinery and consumer durables, or financial, such as cash and accounts receivable, or intangible, such as brand value and goodwill.

Assets are typically broken down into five different categories. ***Current assets*** include cash, cash equivalents, marketable securities, inventories, and prepaid expenses that are expected to be used within one year or a normal operating cycle. All cash items and inventories are reported at historical value. Securities are reported at market value. ***Noncurrent assets,*** or long-term investments, are resources that are expected to be held for more than one year. They are reported at the lower of cost and current market value, which means that their values will vary. ***Fixed assets*** include property, plant and facilities, and equipment used to conduct business. These items are reported at their original value, even though current values might well be much higher. ***Intangible assets*** include legal claims, patents, franchise rights, and accounts receivable. These values can be more difficult to determine. ***Accounts receivable,*** for example, reflect the amount a business expects to collect, such as, say, $9,000 of the $10,000 owed by customers. Deferred charges include prepaid costs and other expenditures that will produce future revenue or benefits.

asset allocation STOCKHOLDING & INVESTMENTS strategy maximizing return while minimizing risk an investment strategy that distributes investments in a portfolio so as to achieve the highest investment return while minimizing risk. Such a strategy usually apportions investments among cash equivalents, stock in domestic and foreign companies, fixed-income investments, and real estate.

asset-backed security STOCKHOLDING & INVESTMENTS security backed by loans a security based on the collateral of outstanding loans for which the investor receives the payments

asset backing STOCKHOLDING & INVESTMENTS assets supporting stock price support for a stock price provided by the value of the company's assets

asset base STOCKHOLDING & INVESTMENTS tangible assets of firm or person the ***tangible assets*** held by a company or individual investor at any point in time

asset-based lending FINANCE loans repaid with proceeds from acquired assets the lending of money with the expectation that the proceeds from an asset or assets will allow the borrower to repay the loan

asset class STOCKHOLDING & INVESTMENTS investment category a category into which an investment falls, for example, stocks, bonds, commodities, or real estate

asset conversion loan FINANCE loan repaid with proceeds from sale of asset a loan that the borrower will repay with money raised by selling an asset

asset cover *or* **asset coverage** FINANCE ratio showing company's solvency a ratio, derived from the net assets of a company divided by its debt, that indicates the company's solvency

asset demand ECONOMICS assets held in cash the amount of assets held as cash, which will be low when interest rates are high and high when interest rates are low

asset financing FINANCE borrowing that uses assets as collateral the borrowing of money by a company using its assets as collateral

asset for asset swap FINANCE exchange of bankrupts' debts an exchange of one bankrupt debtor's debt for that of another

asset management STOCKHOLDING & INVESTMENTS investment service combining banking and brokerage an investment service offered by some financial institutions that combines banking and brokerage services. *Abbr* ***AM*** – **asset manager**

asset play STOCKHOLDING & INVESTMENTS stock purchase assuming unknown assets the purchase of a company's stock in the belief that it has assets that are not properly documented and therefore unknown to others

asset pricing model FINANCE pricing model determining asset's future profit a pricing model that is used to determine the profit that an asset is likely to yield

Asset Protection Scheme BANKING UK insurance plan supporting banks in the United Kingdom, a government program established in 2009 that, for a fee, supports banks which have many bad loans and whose capital base is therefore compromised. It provides insurance against further losses, on the security of agreed assets, so that banks can continue to lend money. *Abbr* ***APS***

asset protection trust FINANCE trust protecting funds from creditors a trust, often established in a foreign country, used to make the trust's principal inaccessible to creditors

asset restructuring FINANCE purchase or sale of valuable assets the purchase or sale of assets worth more than 50% of a listed company's total or net assets

asset side ACCOUNTING side of balance sheet showing assets the side of a balance sheet that shows the economic resources a firm owns, for example, cash in hand or in bank deposits, products, or buildings and fixtures

assets requirements FINANCE assets needed to trade the tangible and intangible assets needed for a business to continue trading

asset stripping MERGERS & ACQUISITIONS practice of selling acquired firm's assets piecemeal the purchase of a company whose market value is below its asset value, usually so that the buyer can sell the assets for immediate gain. The buyer usually has little or no concern for the purchased company's employees or other ***stakeholders,*** so the practice is generally frowned upon. – **asset stripper**

asset substitution FINANCE purchase of risky assets undisclosed to lender the purchase of assets that involve more risk than those a lender expected the borrower to buy

asset swap 1. FINANCE exchange of assets allowing easy diversification an exchange of assets between companies so that they may dispose of parts no longer required and enter another product area **2.** STOCKHOLDING & INVESTMENTS exchange of fixed for varying payment in capital markets, the exchange of a fixed coupon payment associated with a bond for a floating rate payment, usually based on LIBOR

asset turnover ACCOUNTING measure of firm's business efficiency the ratio of a company's sales revenue to its total assets, used as a measure of the firm's business efficiency

asset valuation ACCOUNTING total value of firm's assets the aggregated value of the assets of a firm, usually the capital assets, as entered on its balance sheet

asset value MERGERS & ACQUISITIONS firm's value as combined value of assets the value of a company calculated by adding together all its assets

assign FINANCE transfer ownership of asset to transfer ownership of an ***asset*** to another person or organization

assignable cause of variation OPERATIONS & PRODUCTION apparent reason that something is different an evident reason for deviation from the norm. An assignable cause exists when variation within a process can be attributed to a particular cause that is a fundamental part of the process. Once identified, the assignable cause of the errors must be investigated and the process adjusted before other possible causes of variation are examined.

assignation *UK* LEGAL = ***assignment***

assigned risk INSURANCE poor risk that company must insure for a poor insurance risk that a company is required by law to insure itself against

assignee LEGAL somebody receiving property or rights a person to whom property or the rights to something have been transferred

assignment *US* LEGAL transfer of property or rights a legal transfer of property or the rights to something. *UK term* ***assignation***

assignor LEGAL person transferring property or rights a person who transfers property or the rights of something to somebody else

associate *ANZ* MARKETS stock exchange member without seat a member of a stock exchange who does not have a seat on it

associate company BUSINESS = ***affiliated enterprise***

associated company BUSINESS firm partly owned and controlled by another a company in which another company owns less than 50% and either has some management control over it or has a close trading relationship with it

associate director CORPORATE GOVERNANCE unelected director attending board meetings a director who attends board meetings, but has not been elected by the stockholders

associate program E-COMMERCE = ***affiliate program***

Association for Financial Professionals FINANCE US organization for professionals in finance industry in the United States, an organization for corporate financial managers that provides training and certification to members and represents their interests to government. *Abbr* ***AFP***

Association for Payment Clearing Services BANKING UK organization for payments industry the professional organization for providers of payment services to customers in the United Kingdom. *Abbr* ***APACS***

Association of Accounting Technicians ACCOUNTING UK accounting organization a professional organization founded in the United Kingdom in 1980 and offering qualifications in subjects related to accounting. It now has members and students worldwide. *Abbr* ***AAT***

Association of British Insurers INSURANCE association representing UK insurance companies an association that represents over 400 UK insurance companies to the government, the regulators, and other agencies, as well as providing a wide range of services to its members. *Abbr* ***ABI***

Association of Chartered Accountants in the United States ACCOUNTING association representing US chartered accountants a nonprofit professional and educational organization that represents over 5,000 chartered accountants based in the United States. The Association was founded in 1985. *Abbr* ***ACAUS***

Association of Chartered Certified Accountants ACCOUNTING international organization representing accountants an international accounting organization with over 300,000 members in more than 160 countries. It was formed in 1904 as the London Association of Accountants. *Abbr* ***ACCA***

Association of Futures Brokers and Dealers MARKETS organization overseeing futures and options trading a self-regulating organization that oversees the activities of dealers in the futures and options markets. *Abbr* ***AFBD***

Association of Independent Financial Advisers FINANCE UK trade association for financial advisers a UK trade association that represents the interests of independent financial advisers to the UK government and in the European Union. *Abbr* ***AIFA***

Association of International Accountants ACCOUNTING organization for accountants a professional accounting organization founded in the United Kingdom in 1928 and offering qualifications in international accounting. *Abbr* ***AIA***

Association of Investment Companies STOCKHOLDING & INVESTMENTS UK organization for investment industry the professional organization for UK investment trust companies. It was founded in 1932 and until 2006 was called the Association of Investment Trust Companies. *Abbr* ***AIC***

Association of Unit Trusts and Investment Funds STOCKHOLDING & INVESTMENTS *see* ***Investment Management Association***

assumable mortgage MORTGAGES mortgage that buyer can take over from seller a mortgage that the buyer of a property can take over from the seller

assumed bond STOCKHOLDING & INVESTMENTS bond for which new firm takes responsibility a bond for which a company other than the issuer takes over responsibility

assumption STATISTICS condition for statistical method to work accurately the conditions under which valid results can be obtained from a statistical technique

assurance *UK* INSURANCE *see* ***life insurance***

assure *UK* INSURANCE = ***insure*** *(sense 2)*

assured shorthold tenancy *UK* Real Estate tenancy for fixed short period a tenancy for a fixed period of at least six months during which the tenant cannot be evicted other than by court order. Any new tenancy without a written agreement is an assured shorthold tenancy.

assured tenancy *UK* Real Estate tenancy for indefinite period a tenancy for an indefinite period in which the tenant cannot be evicted other than by court order

assurer *or* **assuror** *UK* INSURANCE = ***insurer***

AST *abbr* MARKETS ***automated screen trading***

ASX *abbr* MARKETS ***Australian Stock Exchange***

ASX 100 MARKETS Australian index of companies a measure of the change in stock prices on the ***Australian Stock Exchange*** based on changes in the stocks of the top 100 companies. Similar indexes include the ASX 20, ASX 50, ASX 200, and ASX 300.

asymmetrical distribution STATISTICS uneven distribution of data around central point a frequency or probability distribution of statistical data that is not symmetrical about a central value in the data

asymmetric information BUSINESS information that differs between parties to transaction a situation in which consumers, suppliers, and producers do not all have the same information on which to base their decisions

asymmetric risk RISK investment risk where gains and losses differ widely the risk an investor faces when the gain realized from the move of an ***underlying asset*** in one direction is significantly different from the loss incurred from its move in the opposite direction

asymmetric taxation TAX difference in tax status between parties to transaction a difference in tax status between parties to a transaction, typically making the transaction attractive to both parties because of taxes that one or both can avoid

asynchronous transmission E-COMMERCE method of sending intermittent data the transmission of data in which the end of the transmission of one unit denotes the start of the next, rather than transmission at fixed intervals

at best MARKETS instruction to buy or sell immediately an instruction to a stockbroker to buy or sell securities immediately at the best possible current price in the market, regardless of adverse price movements. It is also applicable to the commodity or currency markets. *See also* ***at limit***

at call FINANCE repayable on demand used to describe a short-term loan that is repayable immediately upon demand

at limit MARKETS instruction to buy or sell security within limits an instruction to a stockbroker to buy or sell a security within specific limits, usually not to sell below or to buy above a set price. A time limit is stipulated by the investor, and, if there has been no transaction within that period, the instruction lapses. It is also applicable to the commodity or currency markets. *See also* ***at best***

ATM BANKING electronic machine for withdrawing money an electronic machine at which bank customers can withdraw money or access an account using an encoded plastic card. *Full form* ***automated teller machine***

ATM card *US* BANKING plastic card used in ATM a plastic card used to withdraw money or access an account at an ATM. *UK term* ***cash card***

ATO *abbr* TAX ***Australian Taxation Office***

atomize GENERAL MANAGEMENT subdivide firm to split a large organization into smaller operating units

at par MARKETS, STOCKHOLDING & INVESTMENTS describing security sold at face value used to describe a security that sells at a price equal to its face value

ATS *abbr* BANKING ***automatic transfer service***

at sight FINANCE immediately as soon as presented. A negotiable instrument which is payable at sight is called a sight draft. *See also* ***bill of exchange***

attachment LEGAL process enabling creditor to secure debtor's repayment a legal process that enables a creditor to secure dues from a debtor. A debtor's earnings and/or funds held at his or her bankers may be attached.

attachment order LEGAL court order preventing sale of debtor's property an order from a court to hold a debtor's property to prevent it from being sold until debts are paid

attention economy ECONOMICS theory that website viewing is tradable commodity a view of the economy in the late 20th century that suggests that people's attention to websites is a valuable and tradable commodity

attention management GENERAL MANAGEMENT making sure employees focus on work and goals a method of ensuring that employees are focused on their work and on organizational goals, as inattentiveness results in wasted time. An important factor in winning and sustaining attention is tapping into people's emotions.

attestation clause FINANCE clause showing that signature has been witnessed a clause showing that the signature of the person signing a legal document has been witnessed

at-the-money STOCKHOLDING & INVESTMENTS describing option where trading price matches stock price used to describe an option with a ***strike price*** roughly equivalent to the price of the underlying stock

attitude GENERAL MANAGEMENT feeling or belief about situation a mental position consisting of a feeling, emotion, or opinion evolved in response to an external situation. An attitude can be momentary or can develop into a habitual position that has a long-term influence on somebody's behavior. Attempts can be made to modify attitudes that have a negative effect in the workplace, for example, through education and training.

attitude survey MARKETING questions about people's feelings toward firm or product a piece of research carried out to assess the feelings of a target audience toward a product, brand, or organization

attributable profit ACCOUNTING profit generated by specific business activity a profit that can be shown to come from a specific area of the company's operations

attribute sampling OPERATIONS & PRODUCTION method of quality testing through random samples a random testing method for determining the quality of a finished product by inspecting a sample number of the items in each batch. The items selected are examined for a selected attribute, which is usually an abnormal or negative characteristic–for example, a sample of cars from one production run might be inspected for poor paintwork, and the number of sampled cars found with this attribute used to calculate the number of defective items in the whole batch.

auction FINANCE sale of goods by competitive bidding a sale of goods or property by competitive bidding on the spot, by mail, by telecommunications, or over the Internet

auction market preferred stock STOCKHOLDING & INVESTMENTS UK stock with dividends tracking money-market index stock in a company owned in the United Kingdom that pays dividends which track a money-market index. *Abbr* ***AMPS***

AUD *abbr* CURRENCY & EXCHANGE ***Australian dollar***

audience MARKETING everyone who reads, sees, or hears advertisement the total number of readers, viewers, or listeners who are exposed to an advertisement

audience research MARKETING research concerning target group of advertising research carried out to measure the size or composition of the target audience for a piece of advertising

audit ACCOUNTING systematic examination of firm's activities and records a systematic examination of the activities and status of an entity, based primarily on investigation and analysis of its systems, controls, and records

audit committee ACCOUNTING, GENERAL MANAGEMENT committee monitoring firm's finances a committee of a company's board of directors, from which the company's executives are excluded, that monitors the company's finances

audited accounts ACCOUNTING accounts passed by auditor a set of accounts that have been thoroughly scrutinized, checked, and approved by a team of auditors

auditing ACCOUNTING official examination of firm's accounts the work of officially examining the books and accounts of a company to see that they follow generally accepted accounting practices

audit of management GENERAL MANAGEMENT = ***operational audit***

auditor ACCOUNTING person auditing accounts a person who audits companies' accounts or procedures

Auditor-General FINANCE official responsible for legality of Australian government expenditure an officer of an Australian state or territory government who is responsible for ensuring that government expenditure is made in accordance with legislation

auditors' fees ACCOUNTING approved payment to firm's auditors fees paid to a company's auditors, which are approved by the stockholders at an annual meeting

auditors' qualification ACCOUNTING auditors' statement that firm's financial position is misrepresented a form of words in a report from the auditors of a company's accounts, stating that in their opinion the accounts are not a true reflection of the company's financial position. *Also called* ***qualification of accounts***

auditor's report ACCOUNTING auditor's confirmation of firm's financial records a certification by an auditor that a firm's financial records give a true and fair view of its profit and loss for the period

audit report ACCOUNTING official summary of audit the summary submission made by auditors of the findings of an ***audit.*** An audit report is usually of the financial records and accounts of a company. An auditor's report normally takes one of the forms approved by the accountancy professional organizations to cover all requirements imposed by law on the auditor. If reports do not support the company's records, they may be termed "qualified." A report is qualified if it contains any indication that the auditor has failed to satisfy himself or herself on any of the points that the law requires. The qualification may, for example, add a rider stating that the appointed auditor has had to rely on secondary information supplied by other auditors under circumstances in which it has been inappropriate to do otherwise. Qualifications may also refer to the inadequacy of information or explanations supplied, or to the fact that the auditor is not satisfied that proper books or other records are being kept.

audit risk ACCOUNTING, RISK danger of auditors' mistaken view the risk that auditors may give an inappropriate audit opinion on financial statements

audit trail ACCOUNTING record of steps in transaction the records of all the sequential stages of a transaction. An audit trail may trace the process of a purchase, a sale, a customer complaint, or the supply of goods. Tracing what happened at each stage through the records can be a useful method of problem solving. In financial markets, audit trails may be used to ensure fairness and accuracy on the part of the dealers.

augend FINANCE number added to complete sum the number added to an ***addend*** in order to complete an addition

Aussie Mac MORTGAGES Australian security backed by mortgages a mortgage-backed certificate issued in Australia by the National Mortgage Market Corporation. The corporation has been issuing such certificates since 1985.

austerity budget TREASURY MANAGEMENT budget to discourage consumer spending a budget imposed on a country by its government with the goal of reducing the national deficit by way of cutting consumer spending

Austrade FINANCE Australian government organization promoting trade Australian Trade Commission, a federal government body responsible for promoting Australian products abroad and attracting business to Australia. It currently has 108 offices in 63 countries.

Australia and New Zealand Closer Economic Relations Trade Agreement INTERNATIONAL TRADE intergovernmental agreement to foster trade an accord between Australia and New Zealand designed to facilitate the exchange of goods between the two countries. It was signed on January 1, 1983. *Abbr* ***ANZCERTA***

Australian Accounting Standards Board ACCOUNTING agency overseeing accounting standards the body that is responsible for setting and monitoring accounting standards in Australia. It was established under Corporations Law in 1988, replacing the Accounting Standards Review Board. *Abbr* ***AASB***

Australian Bureau of Statistics STATISTICS Australian government agency collecting data on population an Australian federal government body responsible for compiling national statistics and conducting regular censuses. It was established in 1906. *Abbr* ***ABS***

Australian Business Number TAX tax code of Australian business a numeric code that identifies an Australian business for the purpose of dealing with the Australian Tax Office and other government departments. ABNs are part of the new tax system that came into operation in Australia in 1998. *Abbr* ***ABN***

Australian Chamber of Commerce and Industry BUSINESS national organization for businesses a national council of business organizations in Australia. It represents around 350,000 businesses and its members include state chambers of commerce as well as major national employer and industry associations. *Abbr* ***ACCI***

Australian Communications Authority REGULATION & COMPLIANCE government organization overseeing communications industries the government body responsible for regulating practices in the communications industries. It was established in 1997 as a result of the merger of the Australian Telecommunications Authority and the Spectrum Management Agency. *Abbr* ***ACA***

Australian Competition and Consumer Commission REGULATION & COMPLIANCE body monitoring Australian trade practices in Australia, an independent statutory body responsible for monitoring trade practices. It was established in November 1995 as a result of the merger of the Trade Practices Commission and the Prices Surveillance Authority. *Abbr* ***ACCC***

Australian Prudential Regulation Authority REGULATION & COMPLIANCE organization overseeing solvency of financial institutions a federal government body responsible for ensuring that financial institutions are able to meet their commitments. *Abbr* ***APRA***

Australian Securities and Investments Commission REGULATION & COMPLIANCE organization overseeing financial dealings of businesses an Australian federal government body responsible for regulating Australian businesses and the provision of financial products and services to consumers. It was established in 1989, replacing the Australian Securities Commission. *Abbr* ***ASIC***

Australian Stock Exchange MARKETS principal Australian stock market the principal market for trading stock and other securities in Australia. It was formed in 1987 as a result of the amalgamation of six state stock exchanges and has offices in most state capitals. *Abbr* ***ASX***

Australian Taxation Office TAX organization overseeing federal tax system a statutory body responsible for the administration of the Australian federal government's taxation system. It is based in Canberra and is also responsible for the country's superannuation system. *Abbr* ***ATO***

AUT *abbr* STOCKHOLDING & INVESTMENTS ***authorized unit trust***

authentication E-COMMERCE procedure for verifying authenticity of online sales messages a software security verification procedure to acknowledge or validate the source, uniqueness, and integrity of an e-commerce message to make sure data is not being tampered with. The verification is typically achieved through the use of an electronic signature in the form of a key or algorithm that is shared by the trading partners.

authority GENERAL MANAGEMENT right to be in charge the right to act or command. People willingly obey a person in authority, because they believe he or she has a legitimate entitlement to exercise power.

authority chart CORPORATE GOVERNANCE diagram of organization's hierarchical relationships a diagram showing the hierarchical lines of authority and reporting within an organization. Organization charts are similar.

authority to purchase FINANCE bill bearing authorization for bank to buy it a bill drawn up and presented with shipping documentation to the purchaser's bank, allowing the bank to purchase the bill

authorization FINANCE giving approval for financial transaction the process of assessing a financial transaction, confirming that it does not raise the account's debt above its limit, and allowing the transaction to proceed. This would be undertaken, for example, by a credit card issuer. A positive authorization results in an authorization code being generated and the relevant funds being set aside. The available credit limit is reduced by the amount authorized.

authorized capital FINANCE firm's money raised from selling shares the money made by a company from the sale of authorized shares of common and preferred stock. It is measured by multiplying the number of authorized shares by their par value.

Authorized Economic Operator INTERNATIONAL TRADE internationally recognized EU trader an internationally recognized certification that an EU trader's role in the international supply chain is secure and that customs controls and procedures are compliant. *Abbr* ***AEO***

authorized share STOCKHOLDING & INVESTMENTS share issued legitimately a share that a company issued with the authority to do so

authorized share capital *UK* STOCKHOLDING & INVESTMENTS stock firm has approval to issue the type, class, number, and amount of the stocks that a company may issue, as empowered by its memorandum of association. *See also* ***nominal share capital***

authorized signatory STOCKHOLDING & INVESTMENTS issuer of documents approving financial transactions the most senior issuer of authorization certificates in an organization, recognized by a signatory authority and designated in a signatory certificate

authorized stock *US* STOCKHOLDING & INVESTMENTS stock firm has approval to issue the number of shares of stock that a corporation is allowed to issue, as stated in its articles of incorporation. *See also* ***authorized share***

authorized unit trust STOCKHOLDING & INVESTMENTS US mutual fund in the United Kingdom, a mutual fund that complies with the regulations of the Financial Services Authority. Different rules apply to different categories of mutual fund. *Abbr* ***AUT***

AUTIF STOCKHOLDING & INVESTMENTS *see* ***Investment Management Association***

autocorrelation STATISTICS = ***serial correlation***

automated clearing house BANKING, E-COMMERCE computerized network for interbank transactions ***ATM*** systems for interbank clearing and settlement of financial transactions. The network is also used for electronic fund transfers from a checking or savings account. *Abbr* ***ACH***

Automated Direct Debit Amendment and Cancellation Service BANKING UK computerized system for changing direct debits in the United Kingdom, a ***BACS*** service that allows paying banks to inform direct debit payees of a change of instruction, for example, an amendment to the customer's account details or a request to cancel the instructions. *Abbr* ***ADDACS***

automated handling OPERATIONS & PRODUCTION using computers to move goods in warehouses the use of computers to control the moving and positioning of materials in a warehouse or factory. Automated handling may involve the use of robots.

Automated Order Entry System MARKETS US system of direct access to exchange floor in the United States, a system that allows small orders to bypass the floor brokers and go straight to the specialists on the exchange floor

automated screen trading MARKETS computerized system for trading securities an electronic trading system for the sale and purchase of securities. Customers' orders are entered via a keyboard; a computer system matches and executes the deals; and prices and deals are shown on monitors, thus dispensing with the need for face-to-face contact on a trading floor. *Abbr* ***AST***

automated storage and retrieval systems OPERATIONS & PRODUCTION using computers to manage storage in warehouses the use of computerized vehicles to store, select, and move pallets around a large warehouse

automated teller machine BANKING *see* ***ATM***

automatic debit *US* BANKING bank customer's instruction for regular payments an instruction given by an account holder to a bank to make regular payments on given dates to the same payee. *Also called* ***banker's order***. *UK term* ***standing order***

automatic execution MARKETS computerized matching of buy and sell orders a trade of a security that is executed electronically by a computerized trading system that matches buy and sell orders

automatic rollover MARKETS in US, automatic repetition of fixed-term investment on the London Money Market, the automatic reinvestment of a maturing fixed term deposit for a further identical fixed term, an arrangement that can be canceled at any time

automatic transfer service BANKING automatic funds transfer protection an arrangement by which money from a depositor's savings account can be transferred automatically to his or her checking account to cover an overdraft or maintain a minimum balance. *Abbr* ***ATS***

Auto Pact INTERNATIONAL TRADE Canadian and US agreement about automobile imports an agreement between Canada and the United States, by which duties were reduced on imported cars for US automakers assembling vehicles in Canada.

Subsequent provisions of the North American Free Trade Agreement reduced its effect (*informal*).

autopoiesis E-COMMERCE process of replacing own parts a process whereby a system, organization, or organism produces and replaces its own components and distinguishes itself from its environment

availability float ACCOUNTING money representing checks written but not cashed money that is available to a company because checks that it has written have not yet been charged against its accounts

aval FINANCE guarantee of payment of bill or note in Europe, an endorsement by a third party guaranteeing the payment of a bill or promissory note

AVCs *abbr* PENSIONS ***additional voluntary contributions***

average 1. STATISTICS arithmetic mean the arithmetic mean of a sample of observations **2.** STOCKHOLDING & INVESTMENTS purchase stock regularly over period of changing prices to purchase additional shares of a stock whose price is rising or falling at intervals during the period of changing prices, in order to affect the average price paid for the stock

average accounting return ACCOUNTING percentage return of asset based on recorded value the percentage return realized on an asset, as measured by its ***book value,*** after taxes and depreciation

average adjuster INSURANCE insurer determining shared losses a person who calculates how much of an insurance is to be borne by each party

average adjustment INSURANCE insurer's determination of shared losses the calculation of the share of cost of damage to or loss of a ship

average collection period ACCOUNTING average time for cashing accounts receivable the mean time required for a firm to liquidate its accounts receivable, measured from the date each receivable is posted until the last payment is received.

Its formula is:

Accounts receivable / Average daily sales = Average collection period

For example, if accounts receivable are $280,000, and average daily sales are 7,000, then:

280,000 / 7,000 = 40

average cost of capital FINANCE average cost of getting money the average of what a company is paying for the money it borrows or raises by selling stock

average deviation STATISTICS difference between actual and average values the spread of a sample of observations, measured by calculating their mean, specifying the distance between each observation and that mean, then calculating the mean of these distances

average down STOCKHOLDING & INVESTMENTS purchase stock regularly over period of falling prices to purchase additional shares of a security whose price is falling at intervals during the price drop period, in order to lower the average price paid for the stock

average due date FINANCE date around which several payments are due the average date when several different payments fall due

average nominal maturity FINANCE average time for mutual fund to provide return the average length of time until the ***financial instruments*** of a mutual fund mature

average option *or* **average price option** STOCKHOLDING & INVESTMENTS, RISK option determined by commodity's average price an option whose value depends on the average price of a commodity during a specific period of time. *Also called* ***Asian option***

average up STOCKHOLDING & INVESTMENTS purchase stock regularly over period of rising prices to purchase additional shares of a security whose price is rising at intervals during the price rise period, in order to raise the average price paid for the stock

Average Weekly Earnings STATISTICS in Australia, official measure of wages a measure of wage levels in the Australian workforce that is calculated regularly by the Australian Bureau of Statistics. The measure is considered one of Australia's key ***economic indicators.*** *Abbr* ***AWE***

Average Weekly Ordinary Time Earnings STATISTICS in Australia, official measure of wages without overtime a measure of wage levels in the Australian workforce that excludes overtime payments, published by the Australian Bureau of Statistics

averaging STOCKHOLDING & INVESTMENTS stock trading at intervals to get average price the buying or selling of stocks at different times and at different prices to establish an average price

AWB *abbr* FINANCE ***air waybill***

AWE *abbr* STATISTICS ***Average Weekly Earnings***

"aw shucks" REGULATION & COMPLIANCE US strategy for denying responsibility for financial irregularities in the United States, a defense strategy adopted by senior executives involved in financial scandals before the ***Sarbanes-Oxley Act,*** affecting corporate governance, came into effect in 2005. Under this strategy the accused maintained that they were simply not aware of the distortion of financial reporting that took place on their watch. The new law aimed to overhaul corporate financial reporting by improving its accuracy and reliability. Accountability standards have also been considerably tightened, and chief executives are to take full responsibility for the accuracy of all financial results by signing a statement to that effect (*informal*). *See also* ***Sarbanes-Oxley Act***

ax STOCKHOLDING & INVESTMENTS expert in a particular investment a financial adviser who is the current expert on a particular security or market sector

B

B2B E-COMMERCE relating to Internet commerce between businesses used to describe an advertising or marketing program aimed at companies doing business with other companies as opposed to consumers. The term is most commonly used in reference to commerce or business that is conducted over the Internet between commercial enterprises. *Full form* ***business-to-business***

B2B advertising MARKETING advertising directed at firms advertising that is aimed at buyers for organizations rather than domestic consumers

B2B agency MARKETING advertising firm for businesses selling to other businesses an advertising agency that specializes in planning, creating, and buying advertising aimed at buyers for organizations rather than domestic consumers

B2B auction E-COMMERCE Internet site where suppliers compete for sales a Web marketplace that provides a mechanism for negotiating prices and bidding for services. Web-based B2B auctions reverse the traditional auction formula in which the goal is to help the seller get the best price. B2B Web auctions involve suppliers competing with one another by bidding down the price of their service. This inevitably benefits the buyer, as, instead of having to bid higher for a specific service or product, he or she can wait until the suppliers have bid themselves down to a reasonable price. Typically, online auctions require companies to follow a registration process in order to take part. During this process, users have to provide their credit card information and shipping preferences as well as agree to the site's code of conduct. Some sites also manage secure auctions, which restrict potential bidders to specific firms or individuals.

B2B commerce MARKETS business involving firms only, not individual customers the business conducted between companies, rather than between a company and individual consumers

B2B exchange MARKETS place for businesses to trade with each other the business-to-business marketplace that enables suppliers, buyers, and intermediaries to come together and offer products to each other according to a set of criteria

B2B marketing MARKETING = ***industrial marketing***

B2B web exchange MARKETS, E-COMMERCE marketplace adjusting prices the business-to-business marketplace that provides constant price adjustments in line with fluctuations of supply and demand

B2C MARKETS connected with Internet commerce between businesses and consumers relating to an advertising or marketing program aimed at businesses doing business directly with consumers as opposed to other businesses. The term is most commonly used in reference to commerce or business that is conducted over the Internet between a commercial enterprise and a consumer. *Full form* ***business-to-consumer***

BAA *abbr* ACCOUNTING ***British Accounting Association***

baby bonds *US* STOCKHOLDING & INVESTMENTS bonds with low values bonds in small denominations, usually less than $1,000, which small investors can afford to buy *(informal)*

backdate GENERAL MANAGEMENT **1.** put earlier date on document to put an earlier date than the current date on a document such as a check or an invoice **2.** make something apply from earlier date to make something effective from an earlier date than the current date

backdoor selling FRAUD **1.** illegal wholesaler selling directly to consumers the practice by wholesalers of selling products directly to consumers in violation of contracts with retailers **2.** selling tactic bypassing competitive bid requirement the practice by salespeople of persuading buyers who are required to obtain competitive bids to purchase goods and services without them

back duty TAX tax unpaid because information was withheld tax relating to a past period that has not been paid because of the taxpayer's failure to disclose relevant information through negligence or fraud. If back duty is found to be payable, the relevant authorities may instigate an investigation and penalties or interest may be charged on the amount.

back-end loading STOCKHOLDING & INVESTMENTS sales fee paid by investor a management charge or commission that is levied when an investor sells some types of investments such as funds and annuities. *See also* ***front-end loading***

backer FINANCE provider of financial or moral support a person or company that gives somebody financial or moral support

back interest FINANCE interest not yet paid interest that is due but has not yet been paid

backlink checking E-COMMERCE way of discovering which websites are linked a means of finding out which web pages are linked to a specific website. Backlink checking enables e-business and website managers to keep track of their own and their competitors' online popularity.

backlog OPERATIONS & PRODUCTION list of orders not yet filled the buildup of unfulfilled orders for a product or process that is behind schedule. A backlog can result from bad scheduling, production delays, an unanticipated demand for a product or process, or where the capacity of the process is not able to keep up with demand. Some large products, for example, aircraft and ships, have to be built to a backlog of orders, as it is not feasible to supply them on demand.

backlog depreciation ACCOUNTING extra depreciation on revalued asset the additional depreciation required when an asset is revalued to make up for the fact that previous depreciation had been calculated on a now out-of-date valuation

back office GENERAL MANAGEMENT staff without direct dealings with customers the administrative staff of a company who do not have face-to-face contact with the company's customers. *See also* ***front office, middle office***

back pay FINANCE overdue pay from earlier time period pay that is owed to an employee for work carried out before the current payment period and is either overdue or results from a backdated pay increase

back payment FINANCE payment due but not yet paid a payment that is due to somebody but has not yet been paid

back tax TAX tax due but not yet paid tax that is owed to a government and that is overdue

back-to-back loan FINANCE, CURRENCY & EXCHANGE arrangement for two matching loans in different currencies an arrangement in which two companies in different countries borrow offsetting amounts in each other's currency and each repays their loan at a specific future date in its domestic currency. Such a loan, often between a company and its foreign subsidiary, eliminates the risk of loss from fluctuations in exchange rates.

backup MARKETS **1.** when yields rise and prices fall a period in which the yields from bonds rise and prices fall, moving inversely to each other **2.** when market trends reverse a sudden reversal in a stock market trend, so that a ***bear market*** becomes a ***bull market*** or vice versa

backup credit BANKING secondary source of credit a ***line of credit*** to be used as a standby should the primary credit source become unavailable. *Also called* ***standby credit*** *(sense 1)*

backup facility GENERAL MANAGEMENT substitute copy to be used if original fails a secondary system, record, or contract intended to take the place of another that fails

backup withholding TAX tax payable on miscellaneous income in the United States, a withholding tax that a payer sends to the Internal Revenue Service so that somebody who has received certain types of income such as dividends or interest, or who has not provided a correct taxpayer identification number, cannot avoid all taxes on that income

backwardation MARKETS **1.** penalty paid for late delivery of stock a penalty paid by the seller when postponing delivery of stock to the buyer **2.** when cash price exceeds forward price a situation in which the ***spot price*** is higher than the ***forward price***. *See also* ***forwardation***

backward compatible E-COMMERCE usable with previous software or computers describes a computer hardware or software product that is compatible with its predecessors to the extent that it can use interfaces and data from earlier versions

backward integration OPERATIONS & PRODUCTION forming alliance with supplier to protect supply the building of relationships with suppliers in order to secure the supply of raw materials. Backward integration can involve taking control of supply companies.

backward scheduling OPERATIONS & PRODUCTION determining scheduling plan based on due date a technique for scheduling production, planning work on the basis of when the completed work is due. By using backward scheduling, managers are able to assign work to particular workstations so that the overall task is completed exactly when it is due. The technique allows potential bottlenecks and idle time for particular workstations to be identified in advance.

BACS BANKING UK electronic clearing system for straightforward payments in the United Kingdom, an electronic bulk clearing system generally used by banks and building societies for low-value and/or repetitive items such as standing orders, direct debits, and automated credits such as salary payments. It was formerly known as the Bankers Automated Clearing Service.

bad bank BANKING government bank accepting other banks' risky loans a government-owned bank created to buy and hold risky assets from other banks, in order to re-activate lending and stimulate economic activity

BADC *abbr* REGULATION & COMPLIANCE ***Business Accounting Deliberation Council***

bad check *or* **bad cheque** BANKING check returned unpaid a check that is returned uncashed for any reason to the person who wrote it

bad debt FINANCE debt that has to be written off a debt that is or is considered to be uncollectable and is, therefore, written off either as a charge to the ***profit and loss account*** or against an existing doubtful debt provision

bad debt provision ACCOUNTING estimate of uncollectable debts an accounting estimate of the amount of debts thought likely to have to be written off

bad debt reserve FINANCE firm's money set aside for uncollectable debts an amount of money that a company sets aside to cover bad debts

bad debts recovered FINANCE money written off then recovered money formerly written off as uncollectable debt that has since been recovered either wholly or in part

badwill FINANCE negative goodwill a situation in which the value of the ***separable net assets*** of a company is greater than the total value of the business *(slang)*

bai al-bithaman ajil FINANCE installment sale of goods arranged by bank in Islamic financing, a sale of goods in which a bank purchases the goods on behalf of the buyer from the seller and sells them to the buyer at a profit, allowing the buyer to make installment payments. *Also called* ***bai muajjal***

bailment FINANCE delivery of something on loan the delivery of goods from the owner to another person on the condition that they will eventually be returned

bail out FINANCE give help to firm in financial difficulty to provide sufficient financial support to a company that is having financial difficulties to ensure its survival

bailout FINANCE financial backing for firm in crisis the provision of sufficient financial support to a company that is having financial difficulties to ensure its survival

bai muajjal FINANCE = ***bai al-bithaman ajil***

bait and switch MARKETING advertising one product but selling more expensive one a marketing practice whereby customers are encouraged to enter a store by an advertisement for one product and are then persuaded to buy another more expensive product *(slang)*

balance 1. BANKING money in bank account the state of a bank account at any one time, indicating whether money is owed (a debit) or owing (a credit balance) **2.** ACCOUNTING discrepancy between debit and credit figures in double-entry bookkeeping, the amount required to make the debit and credit figures in the books equal each other **3.** ACCOUNTING difference between money paid and received the difference between the totals of the debit and credit entries in an account

balance billing FINANCE charging person for own insurance shortfall the practice of requesting payment from a receiver of a service such as medical treatment for the part of the cost not covered by the person's insurance

balance brought down ACCOUNTING figure in account to balance income and expenditure an amount entered in an account at the end of a period to balance income and expenditure

balanced budget ACCOUNTING spending plan in which income equals expenses a budget in which planned expenditure on goods and services and debt interest can be met by current income

balanced design STATISTICS experimental design with equal observations for each combination an experimental design in which the same number of observations is used for each combination of the experimental factors

balanced fund STOCKHOLDING & INVESTMENTS mutual fund with diversified investments a mutual fund that invests in a variety of types of companies and financial instruments to reduce the risk of loss through poor performance of any one type

balanced investment strategy STOCKHOLDING & INVESTMENTS spreading types of investment the practice of investing in a variety of types of companies and financial instruments to reduce the risk of loss through poor performance of any one type

balanced line OPERATIONS & PRODUCTION production system with equalized workstation times an assembly line in which the cycle time for all the workstations is equal. A balanced line is achieved by allocating the right amount of work and the correct amount of operators and machinery to produce a given flow of product over a set period, taking into account the fact that each workstation will have a different capacity and that each process involved has a different cycle time.

balanced quantity OPERATIONS & PRODUCTION materials needed by workstation to produce agreed amount an inventory measure of the quantity of materials and parts required by a workstation to achieve a planned level of output

balanced scorecard approach GENERAL MANAGEMENT emphasis on providing management with strategic information an approach to the provision of information to management in order to assist strategic policy formulation and implementation to build the long-term value of the business. It emphasizes the need to provide the user with information that addresses all relevant areas of performance in an objective and unbiased fashion. The information provided may include financial and non-financial items and cover areas such as profitability, customer satisfaction, internal efficiency, and innovation. The term originates from the best-selling business book, *The Balanced Scorecard*, written by Robert Kaplan and David Norton and published by Harvard Business School Press in 1996. Their approach applies the concept of ***shareholder value analysis***, and is based on the premise that the traditional measures used by managers to see how well their organizations are performing, such as business ratios, productivity, unit costs, growth, and profitability, are only a part of the picture. Traditional measures are seen as providing a narrowly focused snapshot of how an organization performed in the past, and give little indication of likely future performance. In contrast, the balanced scorecard offers a measurement and management system that links strategic objectives to comprehensive performance indicators.

balance off ACCOUNTING find balance by adding up totals to add up and enter the totals for both sides of an account at the end of an accounting period in order to determine the balance

balance of payments INTERNATIONAL TRADE country's trade transactions over time period a list of a country's credit and debit transactions with international financial institutions and foreign countries over a specific period. *Abbr* ***BOP***

balance of payments capital account INTERNATIONAL TRADE non-domestic items in country's balance of payments items in a country's balance of payments which refer to capital investments made in or by other countries

balance of payments current account INTERNATIONAL TRADE record of trade between countries a record of imports and exports of goods and services and the flow of money between countries arising from investments

balance of payments deficit INTERNATIONAL TRADE extent to which imports exceed exports the shortfall in income that arises when a country buys more from other countries than it sells as exports

balance of payments on capital account INTERNATIONAL TRADE record of country's non-domestic investment transactions a system of recording a country's investment transactions with the rest of the world during a given period, usually one year. Among the included transactions are the purchase of physical and financial assets, intergovernmental transfers, and the provision of economic aid to emerging nations.

balance of payments on current account INTERNATIONAL TRADE record of imports and exports a system of recording a country's imports and exports of goods and services during a given period, usually one year

balance of payments surplus INTERNATIONAL TRADE extent to which exports exceed imports the increase in income that arises when a country sells more to other countries than it buys as imports

balance of trade INTERNATIONAL TRADE gap between imports and exports the difference between a country's imports and exports of goods and services. *Abbr* ***BOT***

balance sheet ACCOUNTING statement of total assets, liabilities, and owners' equity a financial report stating the total assets, liabilities, and owners' equity of an organization at a given date, usually the last day of the accounting period. The credit side of the balance sheet states assets, while the debit side states liabilities and equity, and the two sides must be equal, or balance.

Assets include cash in hand and cash anticipated (receivables), inventories of supplies and materials, properties, facilities, equipment, and whatever else the company uses to conduct business. Assets also need to reflect depreciation in the value of equipment such as machinery that has a limited expected useful life.

Liabilities include pending payments to suppliers and creditors, outstanding current and long-term debts, taxes, interest payments, and other unpaid expenses that the company has incurred. Subtracting the value of aggregate liabilities from the value of aggregate assets reveals the value of owners' equity. Ideally, it should be positive. Owners' equity consists of capital invested by owners over the years and profits (net income) or internally generated capital, which is referred to as “retained earnings”; these are funds to be used in future operations. *Abbr* ***B/S***

balance sheet audit ACCOUNTING partial audit to check compliance with rules a limited audit of the items on a company’s balance sheet in order to confirm that it complies with the relevant standards and requirements. Such an audit involves checking the value, ownership, and existence of assets and liabilities and ensuring that they are correctly recorded.

balance sheet date ACCOUNTING annual date for balance sheet preparation the date, usually the end of a financial or accounting year, when a company’s balance sheet is drawn up

balance sheet equation ACCOUNTING = ***accounting equation***

balance sheet total ACCOUNTING total at bottom of UK firm’s balance sheet in the United Kingdom, the total of assets shown at the bottom of a balance sheet and used to classify a company according to size

balancing item *or* balancing figure ACCOUNTING number making one total equal another a number added to a series of numbers to make the total the same as another total. For example, if a debit total is higher than the credit total in the accounts, the balancing figure is the amount of extra credit required to make the two totals equal.

ball ◇ take the ball and run with it GENERAL MANAGEMENT to take an idea and implement it

balloon FINANCE **1.** = ***balloon loan*** **2.** = ***balloon payment***

balloon loan FINANCE loan with large final payment a loan repaid in regular installments with a single larger final payment including interest

balloon mortgage MORTGAGES mortgage with large final payment a mortgage for which the final payment including interest, called ***a balloon payment***, is larger than the others

balloon payment FINANCE large final payment on loan a large final payment including interest on a loan, after a number of periodic smaller payments have been made

ballpark *or* **ballpark figure** FINANCE ***rough total*** a rough, estimated figure. The term was derived from the approximate assessment of the number of spectators at a sporting event that might be made on the basis of a glance around (*slang*).

BALO FINANCE French financial publication a French government publication that includes financial statements of public companies. *Full form* ***Bulletin des Annonces Légales Obligatoires.***

BAN *abbr* STOCKHOLDING & INVESTMENTS ***bond anticipation note***

bang for the/your buck FINANCE financial benefit the leverage provided by an investment (*slang*)

bangtail MARKETING order form attached to envelope an order form for a new product that is attached by a perforated line to an envelope flap (*slang*)

bank BANKING institution holding and lending money a commercial institution that keeps money in accounts for individuals or organizations, makes loans, exchanges currencies, provides credit to businesses, and offers other financial services

bankable BANKING acceptable as security for loan acceptable by a bank as security for a loan

bankable paper BANKING document accepted by bank as security a document that a bank will accept as security for a loan

bank account BANKING facility for depositing and withdrawing money at bank an arrangement that a customer has with a bank, by which the customer can deposit and withdraw money

bank advance BANKING = ***bank loan***

bank balance BANKING money in bank account the state of a bank account at any one time, indicating whether money is owed (a debit) or owing (a credit balance)

bank base rate BANKING interest rate determining bank’s rate to customers the basic rate of interest on which the actual rate a bank charges on loans to its customers is calculated

bank bill BANKING **1.** *US* = ***banknote*** **2.** = ***banker’s bill***

bank book BANKING booklet recording deposits and withdrawals a small booklet formerly issued by banks and some other financial institutions to record deposits, withdrawals, interest paid, and the balance on savings and deposit accounts. In most cases, it has now been replaced by statements. *Also called* ***passbook***

bank card BANKING payment card issued by bank a plastic card issued by a bank and accepted by merchants in payment for transactions. The most common types are ***credit cards*** and ***debit cards***. Bank cards are governed by an internationally recognized set of rules for the authorization of their use and the clearing and settlement of transactions.

bank certificate BANKING confirmation of firm’s bank balance a document, often requested during an audit, that is signed by a bank official and confirms the balances due to or from a company on a specific date

bank charge BANKING = ***service charge***

bank confirmation BANKING verification of firm’s bank balances verification of a company’s balances requested by an auditor from a bank

bank credit BANKING maximum credit the maximum credit available to somebody from a specific bank

bank deposits BANKING money deposited in banks all money placed in banks by private or corporate customers

bank discount basis BANKING income from US Treasury bills expressed over 360 days the expression of yield that is used for US Treasury bills, based on a 360-day year

bank draft BANKING = ***banker’s draft***

bank-eligible issue BANKING US Treasury bonds available to commercial banks US Treasury obligations with a remaining maturity of ten years or less, eligible for purchase at any time by commercial banks

banker BANKING owner or senior executive of bank somebody who owns or is an executive of a bank or group of banks

banker's acceptance BANKING = ***banker's credit***

Bankers Automated Clearing Service BANKING *see* ***BACS***

banker's bill BANKING bank's order to another bank to pay money an order by one bank telling another bank, usually in another country, to pay money to somebody. *Also called* ***bank bill***

banker's check BANKING = ***banker's draft***

banker's credit BANKING financial instrument guaranteed by bank a financial instrument, typically issued by an exporter or importer for a short term, that a bank guarantees. *Also called* ***banker's acceptance***

banker's draft BANKING check drawn by bank on itself a ***bill of exchange*** payable on demand and drawn by one bank on another. Regarded as being equivalent to cash, the draft cannot be returned unpaid. *Also called* ***bank draft, banker's check.*** *Abbr* ***B/D***

bankers' hours BANKING short working day short hours of work. The term refers to the relatively short time that a bank is open to customers in some countries (*informal*).

banker's lien BANKING bank's right to hold client's property as security the right of a bank to hold some property of a customer as security against payment of a debt

banker's order BANKING = ***automatic debit***

banker's reference BANKING bank's report on customer's creditworthiness a report issued by a bank regarding a particular customer's creditworthiness

bank fee BANKING administrative charge for transaction a charge that is either paid in advance or is included in the gross capitalized cost, usually covering administrative costs such as the costs of obtaining a credit report, verifying insurance coverage, and checking documentation

Bank for International Settlements BANKING bank dealing with international finance a bank that promotes cooperation between central banks, provides facilities for international financial operations, and acts as agent or trustee in international financial settlements. The 17-member board of directors consists of the governors of the central banks of Belgium, Canada, France, Germany, Italy, Japan, the Netherlands, Sweden, Switzerland, the United Kingdom, and the United States. *Abbr* ***BIS***

bank giro BANKING = ***giro***

bank guarantee BANKING bank's undertaking to pay debt a commitment that a bank will pay a debt if the debtor defaults, for example, a bank may guarantee to pay an exporter for goods shipped if the buyer defaults

bank holding company BANKING firm owning bank or banks a company that owns one or more banks as part of its assets

bank holiday *UK* BANKING public holiday on weekday a weekday, especially a Monday, that is a public holiday when the banks are closed

bank identification number BANKING international number identifying individual bank an internationally agreed six-digit number that formerly identified a bank for credit card purposes. *Abbr* ***BIN.*** *See also* ***issuer identification number***

banking account BANKING facility for depositing and withdrawing money at bank an arrangement that a customer has with a bank, by which the customer can deposit and withdraw money

Banking Code BANKING UK banks' voluntary code of practice a voluntary code of best practice for the banking and financial services industry, which is developed and revised by the ***British Bankers' Association***

banking house BANKING financial institution providing banking services a financial organization such as a bank or ***credit union*** that is in the business of providing banking services to the public

banking insurance fund INSURANCE US fund insuring banks' deposits in the United States, a fund maintained by the Federal Deposit Insurance Corporation to provide deposit insurance for banks other than savings banks and savings and loan associations

Banking Ombudsman BANKING Australian or New Zealand official handling banking complaints an official of the Australian or New Zealand government responsible for dealing with complaints relating to banking practices

banking passport BANKING passport for holding assets abroad a second passport in another name used to hold assets confidentially and for banking transactions in another country

banking products BANKING items provided by banks for customers goods and services that banks provide for their customers, for example, statements, direct debits, and automatic debits

banking syndicate BANKING investment banks jointly offering new security a group of investment banks that jointly underwrite and distribute a new security offering

banking system BANKING network of banks providing financial services a network of commercial, savings, and specialized banks that provide financial services, including accepting deposits and providing loans and credit, money transmission, and investment facilities

bank investment contract BANKING contract between bank and investors a contract that specifies what a bank will pay its investors

bank line FINANCE = ***line of credit***

bank loan BANKING loan made to bank's customer a loan made by a bank to a customer, usually against the security of a property or asset. *Also called* ***bank advance***

bankmail BANKING agreement by bank not to finance customer's rival an agreement by a bank not to finance any rival's attempt to take over the same company that a particular customer is trying to buy (*slang*)

bank mandate BANKING written order for opening bank account a written order to a bank that asks the bank to open an account, names the person(s) allowed to sign checks on behalf of the account holder, and provides specimen signatures, etc.

banknote BANKING **1.** item of paper money a piece of paper money printed by a bank and approved as legal tender. *Also called* ***bank bill*** **2.** note from Federal Reserve Bank usable as cash in the United States, a non-interest bearing note, issued by a Federal Reserve Bank, that can be used as cash

Bank of England BANKING UK central bank the central bank of the United Kingdom, established in 1694. Originally a private bank, it became public in 1946 and increased its independence from government in 1997, when it was granted sole responsibility for setting the base rate of interest.

bank rate BANKING **1.** central bank's discount rate the discount rate offered by a country's central bank **2.** formerly, Bank of England's lending rate formerly, the rate at which the Bank of England lent to other banks. It was then also called the minimum lending rate. *See also* ***base rate***

bank reconciliation BANKING comparison of bank statement with firm's ledger the process of comparing a bank statement with a company's ledger to verify that the balances are the same

bank reserve ratio BANKING = ***required reserve ratio***

bank reserves BANKING bank's ready money the money that a bank has available to meet the demands of its depositors

bankroll FINANCE **1.** finance for project the money used for financing a project or business **2.** give money to support something to provide the financing for a project or business

bankrupt LEGAL **1.** entity legally recognized as unable to pay debts a person or corporation that has been declared by a court of law as unable to meet their financial obligations **2.** unable to pay debts legally declared unable to meet financial obligations

bankruptcy LEGAL when unable to pay debts the condition of being unable to pay debts, with liabilities greater than assets. There are two types of bankruptcy: involuntary bankruptcy, where one or more creditors bring a petition against the debtor; and voluntary bankruptcy, where the debtor files a petition claiming inability to meet his or her debts.

bankruptcy-remote RISK not likely to risk bankruptcy used to describe a strategy or business structure designed to isolate a valuable asset or entity from financial risk

bank statement BANKING statement of transactions on customer's bank account a written statement from a bank showing the balance of an account and transactions over a period of time

bank term loan BANKING bank loan lasting at least one year a loan from a bank that has a term of at least one year

bank transfer BANKING transference of money to another account an act of moving money from one bank account to another

bar *UK* CURRENCY & EXCHANGE £1,000,000 one million pounds sterling, used by traders *(slang)*

barbell STOCKHOLDING & INVESTMENTS portfolio with no medium-term bonds a portfolio that concentrates on very long-term and very short-term bonds only

bar chart GENERAL MANAGEMENT informational graph using colored bars the presentation of data in the form of a graph using blocks or bars of color or shading. A bar chart is especially useful for showing the impact of one factor against another, for example, income over time, or customer calls against sales.

barefoot pilgrim *US* STOCKHOLDING & INVESTMENTS inexperienced and unsuccessful investor an unsophisticated investor who has lost everything trading in securities *(slang)*

bargain MARKETS stock-market transaction a transaction on a stock market, especially the London Stock Exchange *(slang)*

bargaining chip FINANCE useful factor in negotiation something that can be used as a concession or inducement in negotiation

bargain tax date MARKETS date of stock-market transaction the date of a transaction on a stock market, especially the London Stock Exchange

barometer FINANCE indicator of trend an economic or financial indicator that forecasts a trend in the economy or in financial markets

barometer stock MARKETS popular security typical of market a widely held security such as a ***blue chip*** that is regarded as an indicator of the state of the market

barren money STOCKHOLDING & INVESTMENTS = ***idle capital***

barrier option STOCKHOLDING & INVESTMENTS option with trigger for trading in others an option that includes automatic trading in other options when a commodity reaches a specific price

barrier to entry MARKETS obstacle to free entry into market any impediment to the free entry of new competitors into a market

barrier to exit MARKETS obstacle to withdrawal from market any impediment to the exit of existing competitors from a market

barter FINANCE exchange of goods or services the direct exchange of goods or services between two parties without the use of money as a medium

BAS *abbr* TAX ***Business Activity Statement***

base currency CURRENCY & EXCHANGE way of expressing income from investment the currency used for measuring the return on an investment, usually the currency of the country in which the investment is made

base date MARKETS benchmark date for index calculations the reference date from which an index number such as the *retail price index* is calculated

base interest rate FINANCE US minimum expected interest rate in the United States, the minimum interest rate that investors will accept for investing in a non-Treasury security. *Also called* ***benchmark interest rate***

base pay *US* FINANCE basic salary before additional benefits a guaranteed sum of money given to an employee in payment for work, disregarding any fringe benefits, allowances, or extra rewards from an ***incentive plan***. *UK term* ***basic pay***

base period FINANCE period against which current financial period is measured a period of time against which financial or economic comparisons are made

base rate BANKING **1.** US Federal Reserve's interest rate the interest rate set by the US ***Federal Reserve*** that dictates the rate at which money is lent to other banks and which they in turn charge their customers **2.** Bank of England's interest rate the interest rate at which the Bank of England lends to other UK banks and which they in turn charge their customers

base rate tracker mortgage MORTGAGES mortgage with varying interest rate a mortgage whose interest rate varies periodically, usually annually, so as to remain a specific percentage above a standard rate

base-weighted index ECONOMICS price index comparing prices against standard time period a price index that is weighted according to prices from the base period

base year ECONOMICS benchmark year for index calculations the reference year from which an index is calculated

basic balance FINANCE relationship of current and long-term capital accounts the balance of current and long-term capital accounts in a country's balance of payments, which by implication must be financed with short-term ***capital flows*** such as short-term securities, money funds, and bank deposits

basic pay *UK* FINANCE = ***base pay***

basic rate TAX lower UK rate of income tax in the United Kingdom, the lower of the two bands of income tax, paid by the majority of people. ***Her Majesty's Revenue & Customs*** is responsible for the administration of income tax and publishes information on current tax rates and allowances on its website. *See also* ***higher rate***

basic wage FINANCE in Australia, minimum allowable pay for particular job in Australia, the minimum rate of pay set by an industrial court or tribunal for a specific occupation

basic wage rate FINANCE minimum pay in UK job in the United Kingdom, the wages paid for a specific number of hours' work per week, excluding overtime payments and any other incentives

basis FINANCE starting point for calculations a point, price, or number from which calculations are made. For example, the purchase price of a security would be used as the basis for calculating gains or losses.

basis of assessment TAX way of deciding time of tax assessment a method of deciding in which year financial transactions should be assessed for taxation

basis period TAX time when transactions are assessed for taxation the period during which financial transactions occur, used for the purpose of deciding when they should be assessed for taxation

basis point STOCKHOLDING & INVESTMENTS in bond interest rates, one hundredth of 1% one hundredth of 1%, used in relation to changes in bond interest rates. Thus a change from 7.5% to 7.4% is 10 basis points.

basis price STOCKHOLDING & INVESTMENTS **1.** price on which investment return is based the price used for calculating the gain on any investment when selling it, based on purchase price and any other costs **2.** price of bond given as yield to maturity the price of a bond shown as its annual percentage yield to maturity rather than being quoted in a currency **3.** over-the-counter securities price the price agreed between a buyer and seller on the over-the-counter market

basis risk MARKETS danger from price or interest-rate changes the risk that price variations in the cash or futures market will diminish revenue when a futures contract is liquidated, or the risk that changes in interest rates will affect the repricing of interest-bearing liabilities

basis swap MARKETS exchange of financial instruments with different interest rates the exchange of two financial instruments, each with a variable interest calculated at a different rate

basket case BUSINESS firm or person beyond recovery a company or individual considered to be in such dire circumstances as to be beyond help (*slang*)

basket of currencies CURRENCY & EXCHANGE group of currencies providing benchmark a group of currencies, each of which is weighted, calculated together as a single unit in establishing a standard of value for another unit of currency. *Also called* ***currency basket***

basket of prices FINANCE group of prices used as benchmark a group of prices used as a standard for measuring value over time

basket of securities STOCKHOLDING & INVESTMENTS set of securities traded together a group of securities that is treated as a single unit and traded together

basket of shares *US* STOCKHOLDING & INVESTMENTS set of shares of stock sold together a fixed number of shares of stock that is treated as a single unit and traded together. *UK term* ***parcel of shares***

batch E-COMMERCE credit card transactions submitted together a collection of credit card transactions including authorizations, payments, and credits saved for electronic submission to an ***acquirer*** for settlement. The merchant is encouraged to submit one large batch rather than several small ones by being charged a fee for each batch submitted.

batch production OPERATIONS & PRODUCTION producing goods in groups through individual stages a production system in which a process is broken down into distinct operations that are completed on a batch or group of products before moving to the next production stage. As batch sizes can vary from very small to extremely large quantities, batch production offers greater flexibility than other production systems.

bath ◇ take a bath FINANCE to experience a serious financial loss

Bayesian theory *or* **Bayes' theorem** STATISTICS statistical technique for predicting future based on past a statistical theory and method for drawing conclusions about the future occurrence of a given parameter of a statistical distribution by calculating from prior data on its frequency of occurrence. The theory is useful in the solution of theoretical and applied problems in science, industry, and government, for example, in econometrics and finance.

BBA *abbr* BANKING ***British Bankers' Association***

BC *abbr* TREASURY MANAGEMENT ***budgetary control***

BCA *abbr* BUSINESS ***Business Council of Australia***

BCC *abbr* BUSINESS ***British Chambers of Commerce***

BCCS *abbr* CURRENCY & EXCHANGE ***Board of Currency Commissioners***

B/D *abbr* BANKING ***banker's draft***

bean counter ACCOUNTING accountant an accountant, used to refer in a derogatory way especially to an accountant who works in a large organization (*slang*)

bear STOCKHOLDING & INVESTMENTS exploiter of unfavorable business conditions somebody who anticipates unfavorable business conditions, especially somebody who practices ***short selling***, or selling stocks or commodities expecting their prices to fall, with the intention of buying them back cheaply later. *See also* ***bull***

bear CD STOCKHOLDING & INVESTMENTS CD paying more in falling market a ***certificate of deposit*** that pays a higher interest rate when an underlying market index falls in value

bear covering MARKETS buying back stock at lower prices the point in a market at which dealers who sold stock short now buy back at lower prices to cover their positions

bearer BANKING person holding check or certificate a person who holds a check or certificate that is redeemable for payment

bearer bond STOCKHOLDING & INVESTMENTS bond owned by physical possessor of it a negotiable bond or security whose ownership is not registered by the issuer, but is presumed to lie with whoever has physical possession of the bond

bearer check *US* BANKING blank check a check with no name written on it, so that the person who holds it can cash it. *Also called* **check to bearer.** *UK term* ***cheque to bearer***

bearer instrument FINANCE financial document entitling its presenter to payment a financial instrument such as a check or bill of exchange that entitles the person who presents it to receive payment

bearer security STOCKHOLDING & INVESTMENTS security owned by physical possessor of it a stock or bond that is owned by the person who possesses it

bearish MARKETS of markets with falling prices relating to unfavorable business conditions or selling activity in anticipation of falling prices. *See also* ***bullish***

bear market MARKETS market with falling prices a market in which prices are falling and in which a dealer is more likely to sell securities than to buy them. *See also* ***bull market***

bear market rally MARKETS fast improvement in falling market a fast rise in prices, which may be temporary, after a general downward trend in a financial market

bear raid STOCKHOLDING & INVESTMENTS = ***raid***

bear spread MARKETS transactions to make profit when price falls a combination of purchases and sales of options for the same commodity or stock with the intention of making a profit when the price falls. *See also* ***bull spread***

bear tack MARKETS downward market movement a downward movement in the value of a stock, a part of the market, or the market as a whole

bear trap MARKETS reversing trends in market a situation in which a market reverses its upward trend, leading ***short investors*** to believe the trend will then continue downward and encouraging them to get into the market, at which time the market reverses again, forcing short investors to cover their positions and lose money

beauty contest *US* GENERAL MANAGEMENT situation where competing firms try to attract business a situation in which several organizations in turn compete in order to persuade another organization to use their services. *UK term* ***beauty parade***

beauty parade *UK* GENERAL MANAGEMENT = ***beauty contest***

bed ◇ get into bed with somebody GENERAL MANAGEMENT to begin a business association with a person or organization

bed and breakfast deal STOCKHOLDING & INVESTMENTS selling and buying back security overnight a transaction in which somebody sells a security at the end of one trading day and repurchases it at the beginning of the next. This is usually done to formally establish the profit or loss accrued to this security for tax or reporting purposes.

bed and spouse STOCKHOLDING & INVESTMENTS method for couples to reduce capital gains tax in the United Kingdom, a method used by married taxpayers to reduce capital gains tax. A spouse who has a capital gain and has not used all their capital gains tax allowance may sell a security, and the other spouse may buy the same security back the next day, thereby allowing the spouse who sold to offset all or part of the gain with their tax allowance, while still holding onto the stock.

before-tax profit margin TAX income before tax minus expenditure the amount by which the net income of a company before tax exceeds its expenditure

beginning inventory *US* ACCOUNTING inventory carried over to next balance sheet the closing inventory at the end of the balance sheet from one accounting period that is transferred forward and becomes the opening inventory in the one that follows. *UK term* ***opening stock***

behavioral accounting *US* ACCOUNTING accounting emphasizing psychological and social aspects an approach to the study of accounting that emphasizes the psychological and social aspects of the profession in addition to the more technical areas

behavioral science *US* HR & PERSONNEL science studying how people act academic disciplines such as sociology and psychology that relate to the study of the way in which humans conduct themselves. In the field of management, the behavioral sciences are used to study the behavior of organizations.

bells and whistles *(slang)* **1.** FINANCE features appealing to investors or producers special features attached to a derivatives instrument or securities issue that are intended to attract investors or reduce issue costs **2.** MARKETING extra unnecessary features peripheral features of a product that are unnecessary but desirable

bellwether STOCKHOLDING & INVESTMENTS security with representative price a security whose price is viewed by investors as an indicator of future developments or trends

belly ◇ go belly up FINANCE to fail financially or go bankrupt

below par STOCKHOLDING & INVESTMENTS selling at less than face value describes a stock with a market price that is lower than its par value

below-the-line **1.** ACCOUNTING showing profit distribution or sources of bottom line used to describe entries in a company's ***profit and loss account*** that show how the profit is distributed, or where the funds to finance the loss originate. *See also* ***above-the-line*** *(sense 1)* **2.** ECONOMICS showing country's capital transactions in macroeconomics, used to describe a country's capital transactions, as opposed to its ***above-the-line*** or revenue transactions. *See also* ***above-the-line*** *(sense 2)* **3.** MARKETING connected with marketing costs for everything but advertising relating to the proportion of marketing expenditure allocated to activities that are not related to advertising, such as public relations, sales promotion, printing, presentations, sponsorship, and sales force support. *See also* ***above-the-line*** *(sense 3)*

belt and braces man FINANCE lender wanting extra safeguards a very cautious lender who asks for extra collateral as well as guarantees for a loan *(slang)*

benchmark GENERAL MANAGEMENT standard used for measuring performance a point of reference or standard against which to measure performance. Originally used for a set of computer programs to measure the performance of a computer against similar models, benchmark is now used more generally to describe a measure identified in the context of a ***benchmarking*** program against which to evaluate an organization's performance in a specific area.

benchmark accounting policy ACCOUNTING one of two possible approved policies one of a choice of two possible policies within an International Accounting Standard. The other policy is marked as an "allowed alternative," although there is no indication of preference.

benchmark index MARKETS significant index an influential index for a particular market or activity

benchmarking GENERAL MANAGEMENT establishment of baselines and targets for assessing performance the establishment, through data gathering, of targets and comparators, through whose use relative levels of performance, and particularly areas of underperformance, can be identified. By the adoption of identified best practices it is hoped that performance will improve.

There are various types of benchmarking. *Internal benchmarking* is a method of comparing one operating unit or function with another within the same industry. *Functional benchmarking* compares internal functions with those of the best external practitioners of those functions, regardless of the industry they are in (also known as operational benchmarking or generic benchmarking). *Competitive benchmarking* gathers information about direct competitors, through techniques such as reverse engineering. *Strategic benchmarking* is a type of competitive benchmarking aimed at strategic action and organizational change.

benchmark interest rate FINANCE = ***base interest rate***

beneficial interest FINANCE benefiting from house as if its owner an arrangement whereby somebody is allowed to occupy or receive rent from a house without owning it

beneficial occupier REAL ESTATE occupier not owning property a person who occupies a property but does not own it fully

beneficial owner STOCKHOLDING & INVESTMENTS receiver of benefits of another's stock a person who receives all the benefits of a stock such as dividends, rights, and proceeds of any sale but is not the registered owner of the stock

beneficiary FINANCE somebody who will receive assets or proceeds a person who is designated to receive assets or proceeds from, for example, an estate or insurance policy

beneficiary bank BANKING bank dealing with gift a bank that handles a gift such as a bequest

benefit **1.** FINANCE something extra offering improvement or reward something that improves the profitability or efficiency of an organization or reduces its risk **2.** HR & PERSONNEL nonmonetary reward for employee any nonmonetary reward such as a paid vacation or employer contribution to a pension that is given to employees

benefit–cost ratio ACCOUNTING = ***cost–benefit analysis***

benefit in kind *UK* HR & PERSONNEL = ***fringe benefits***

BEP *abbr* OPERATIONS & PRODUCTION ***break-even point***

bequest FINANCE item left in will a gift that has been left to somebody in a will

Berhad BUSINESS Malay equivalent of plc a Malay term for "private." Companies can use "Sendirian Berhad" or "Sdn Bhd" in their name instead of "plc." *Abbr* ***Bhd***

Berne Union FINANCE = ***International Union of Credit and Investment Insurers***

BERR *abbr* ***Department for Business, Enterprise and Regulatory Reform***

Besloten venootschap BUSINESS limited company the Dutch term for a limited liability company. *Abbr* ***BV***

best-in-class GENERAL MANAGEMENT leading in best practice leading a market or industrial sector in efficiency. A best-in-class organization exhibits exemplary ***best practice***. Such an organization is clearly singled out from the pack and is recognized as a leader for its procedures for dealing with the acquisition and processing of materials and the delivery of end products or services to its customers. The concept of best in class is closely allied with ***total quality management***, and one tool that can help in achieving this status is ***benchmarking***.

best-of-breed MARKETING best available among computer products in marketing, sales, and competitive analysis, a computer product that is the best available software, hardware, or system in its class

best practice GENERAL MANAGEMENT most effective way of doing something the most effective and efficient method of achieving any objective or task. What constitutes best practice can be determined through a process of ***benchmarking***. An organization can move toward achieving best practice, either across the whole organization or in a specific area, through ***continuous improvement***. In production-based organizations, ***world class manufacturing*** is a related concept. More generally, a market or sector leader may be described as best-in-class.

best value GENERAL MANAGEMENT UK program encouraging local government efficiency a UK government initiative intended to ensure cost efficiency and effectiveness in the delivery of public services by local authorities. The best value initiative was announced in early 1997 to replace compulsory competitive tendering, and pilot schemes in selected local authorities began in April 1998. The Local Government Act 1999 requires councils, as part of the best value process, to review all services over a five-year period, setting standards and performance indicators for each service, comparing performance with that of other bodies, and undertaking consultation with local taxpayers and service users.

beta *or* **beta coefficient** STOCKHOLDING & INVESTMENTS number measuring changes in value a number representing an estimate of the fluctuations in value of a stock in relation to the market as a whole. A high beta indicates that a stock is likely to be more sensitive to market movements and therefore has a higher risk. *See also* ***alpha***, ***beta rating***

beta rating STOCKHOLDING & INVESTMENTS means of measuring market risk a means of measuring the volatility (or risk) of a stock or fund in comparison with the market as a whole.

The beta of a stock or fund can be of any value, positive or negative, but usually is between +0.25 and +1.75. Stocks of many utilities have a beta of less than 1. Conversely, most high-tech NASDAQ-based stocks have a beta greater than 1; they offer a higher rate of return but are also risky. Both alpha and beta ratings should be readily available upon request from investment firms, because the figures appear in standard performance reports. *See also* ***alpha rating***

b/f *abbr* ACCOUNTING ***brought forward***

BFH *abbr* TAX ***Bundesfinanzhof***

Bhd *abbr* BUSINESS ***Berhad***

bias STATISTICS distortion of statistical results inaccuracy or deviation in inferences, results, or a statistical method

bid 1. FINANCE highest realistic price the highest price a prospective buyer for a good or service is prepared to pay **2.** STOCKHOLDING & INVESTMENTS offer for most of firm's capital shares an offer to buy all or the majority of the capital shares of a company in an attempted takeover **3.** OPERATIONS & PRODUCTION statement outlining acceptable price for job a statement of what a person or company is willing to accept when selling a product or service. *Also called* ***quote***. *See also* ***tender***

bid-ask price MARKETS price charged for security in some markets, the price charged to buyers and sellers of a security, based on the ***bid-offer spread***. *See also* ***bid-offer price***

bid-ask quote MARKETS statement of amounts being offered and asked a statement of the prices that are being offered and asked for a security or option contract

bid bond FINANCE guarantee of finance for international tender offer a guarantee by a financial institution of the fulfillment of an international tender offer

bid costs MERGERS & ACQUISITIONS professional fees paid during takeover costs incurred during the takeover of a company as a result of professional advice to the purchasing company from, for example, lawyers, accountants, and bankers

bidder OPERATIONS & PRODUCTION person submitting quote a person or company that submits a quotation. *UK term* ***tenderer***

bidding war MARKETS when buyers compete for same stock or security a competition between prospective buyers for the same stock or security, during which it rises in price

bid form MARKETS form detailing offer to underwrite US municipal bonds in the United States, a form containing details of an offer to underwrite municipal bonds

bid market MARKETS market for price of stocks a market for bids (the price at which a dealer will buy stocks)

bid-offer price MARKETS price charged for security in some markets, the price charged to buyers and sellers of a security, based on the ***bid-offer spread***. *See also* ***bid-ask price***

bid-offer spread MARKETS gap between buyer's offer and seller's price the difference between the highest price that a buyer of a security is prepared to offer and the lowest price that a seller is prepared to accept

bid price MARKETS what stock exchange dealer will pay the price a stock exchange dealer will pay for a security or option contract

bid rate FINANCE, CURRENCY & EXCHANGE interest rate on Eurocurrency deposits a rate of interest paid on Eurocurrency deposits

bid-to-cover ratio MARKETS ratio of would-be and actual purchasers a number that shows how many more people wanted to buy Treasury bills than actually did buy them

bid up MARKETS **1.** make offer to raise price to bid for something merely to increase its price, not with the intention of acquiring it **2.** repeatedly increase bid price to make successive increases to the ***bid price*** for a security so that unopened orders do not remain unexecuted

Big Bang MARKETS 1980s restructuring of London Stock Exchange radical changes to practices on the London Stock Exchange implemented in October 1986. Fixed commission charges were abolished, leading to an alteration in the structure of the market, and the right of member firms to act as market makers as well as agents was also abolished *(slang)*.

big bath ACCOUNTING deliberately making bad income statement worse the practice of making a particular year's poor income statement look even worse by increasing expenses and selling assets. Subsequent years will then appear much better in comparison *(slang)*.

big beast *UK* powerful person or firm a person or a company that has a lot of financial or political power and is able to influence events *(informal)*

Big Board MARKETS New York Stock Exchange the New York Stock Exchange, where the stocks of the largest US corporations are traded. *See also* ***Little Board***

big business BUSINESS large firms with a lot of power powerful business interests or companies in general. The term is particularly used when referring to ***large-sized businesses*** or ***multinational businesses***.

Big Four 1. BANKING largest UK banks the United Kingdom's four largest commercial banks: Barclays, HSBC, Lloyds Banking Group, and NatWest (owned by Royal Bank of Scotland) **2.** ACCOUNTING largest accounting firms the four largest international auditors: PricewaterhouseCoopers, Deloitte Touche Tohmatsu, Ernst & Young, and KPMG **3.** BANKING largest Australian banks Australia's four largest banks: the Commonwealth Bank of Australia, Westpac Banking Corporation, National Australia Bank, and the Australia and New Zealand Banking Group Limited

Big GAAP ACCOUNTING in US, accounting principles for large firms in the United States, the ***Generally Accepted Accounting Principles*** that apply to large companies. It is sometimes felt that they are unnecessarily complex for smaller companies *(slang)*.

big money BUSINESS lots of money a very large amount of money

big picture GENERAL MANAGEMENT overview of situation and context a broad perspective on an issue that encompasses its surrounding context and long-term implications *(slang)*

Big Three BUSINESS largest US automobile manufacturers before 1998 before the merger of Chrysler and Mercedes in 1998, the three largest automobile manufacturers in the United States: Chrysler, Ford, and General Motors

big-ticket FINANCE expensive used to describe something that costs a lot of money *(slang)*

big uglies BUSINESS established manufacturing and industrial firms traditional manufacturing and industrial companies, thought to be unglamorous but good long-term investments *(informal)*

Bilanzrichtliniengesetz ACCOUNTING German law covering accounting the 1985 German accounting directives law. *Abbr* ***BiRiLiG***

bilateral clearing BANKING central banks' settling of accounts between countries the system of annual settlements of accounts between some countries, where accounts are settled by the central banks

bilateral credit BANKING credit to banks during clearing of checks credit allowed by banks to other banks in a clearing system to cover the period while checks are being cleared

bilateral facility BANKING arrangement for lending to single borrower a facility for making loans from one bank to one borrower, especially a corporate borrower

bilateral monopoly ECONOMICS market with one seller and one buyer a market in which there is a single seller and a single buyer

bilateral netting BANKING significant settling of contracts between banks the settling of contracts between two banks to give a new position

bilateral trade INTERNATIONAL TRADE special trade arrangement between two countries trade between two countries which give each other specific privileges such as favorable import quotas that are denied to other trading partners

bill 1. FINANCE document promising payment a written paper promising to pay money **2.** *US* FINANCE piece of paper money a piece of paper currency printed by a bank and approved as legal tender. *UK term* ***note*** **3.** LEGAL draft of new law a draft of a new law that will be discussed in a legislature **4.** OPERATIONS & PRODUCTION list of charges payable to supplier a written list of charges to be paid by a customer to a supplier **5.** OPERATIONS & PRODUCTION give bill to customer for payment to present a bill to a customer so that it can be paid

bill broker FINANCE dealer in bills of exchange an agent who buys and sells ***promissory notes*** and ***bills of exchange***

bill discount BANKING Federal Reserve's interest rate to banks the interest rate that the Federal Reserve charges banks for short-term loans. This establishes a de facto floor for the interest rate that banks charge their customers, usually a little above the ***discount rate***.

bill discounting rate FINANCE reduction in cost of US Treasury bill the amount by which the price of a Treasury bill is reduced to reflect expected changes in interest rates

billing cycle FINANCE time between requests for payment the period of time, often one month, between successive requests for payment

billion FINANCE **1.** thousand millions a sum equal to one thousand millions **2.** *UK* one million millions a sum equal to one million millions *(dated)*

billionaire FINANCE person with income over one billion a person whose net worth or income is more than one billion dollars, pounds, or other unit of currency

bill of entry INTERNATIONAL TRADE statement about imports or exports for customs a statement of the nature and value of goods to be imported or exported, prepared by the shipper and presented to a customhouse

bill of exchange FINANCE negotiable instrument a negotiable instrument, drawn by one party on another, for example, by a supplier of goods on a customer, who, by accepting (signing) the bill, acknowledges the debt, which may be payable immediately *(a sight draft)* or at some future date *(a time draft)*. The holder of the bill can thereafter use an accepted time draft to pay a bill to a third party, or can discount it to raise cash.

bill of goods FINANCE **1.** in US, batch of goods in the United States, a consignment of merchandise for transportation and delivery **2.** in US, statement about batch of goods in the United States, a statement of the nature and value of a consignment of goods to be transported and delivered

bill of lading FINANCE document acknowledging shipment of goods a document prepared by a consignor by which a carrier acknowledges the receipt of goods and which serves as a document of title to the goods consigned

bill of sale FINANCE document confirming purchase a document confirming the transfer of goods or services from a seller to a buyer

bills payable FINANCE bills that firm must pay to creditors bills, especially bills of exchange, that a company will have to pay to its creditors. *Abbr* ***B/P***

bills receivable FINANCE bills that firm's debtors will pay bills, especially bills of exchange, that are due to be paid by a company's debtors. *Abbr* ***B/R***

BIN *abbr* FINANCE ***bank identification number***

binary thinker GENERAL MANAGEMENT somebody who thinks "it's all or nothing" a person who thinks only in absolute, black-and-white terms and is incapable of appreciating the subtleties and complexities of a situation *(slang)*

binder *US* INSURANCE temporary insurance certificate a document that an insurance company issues to a customer to serve as a temporary insurance certificate until the issue of the policy itself. *UK term* ***cover note***

biological assets ACCOUNTING live animals and growing plants farm animals and plants classified as assets. International Accounting Standards require that they are recorded on balance sheets at market value. Once they have been slaughtered or harvested, the assets become *agricultural produce.*

bionomics ECONOMICS economics considered as ecosystem a theory suggesting that economics can usefully be thought of as similar to an evolving ecosystem

BiRiLiG *abbr* ACCOUNTING ***Bilanzrichtliniengesetz***

birth-death ratio STATISTICS birth count compared to death count the ratio of the number of births to the number of deaths in a population over a specific period of time

BIS *abbr* BANKING ***Bank for International Settlements***

bivariate data STATISTICS information involving two variables data in which two variables are involved in each subject

bivariate distribution STATISTICS distribution involving two variables a form of distribution in which two random variables are involved

black ◇ in the black FINANCE making a profit, or having more assets than debt

black chip *S. Africa* BUSINESS firm with black owners or stockholders a South African company that is owned or managed by black people, or is controlled by black stockholders *(slang)*

black economic empowerment ECONOMICS encouraging S. African black economic participation the promotion of black ownership and control of South Africa's economic assets

black economy ECONOMICS unofficial, untaxed economic activity economic activity that is not declared for tax purposes and is usually carried out in exchange for cash

black hole GENERAL MANAGEMENT project using resources without producing profit a project that consumes unlimited amounts of resources without yielding any profit *(slang)*

black knight MERGERS & ACQUISITIONS former friendly firm involved in takeover a former ***white knight*** that has disagreed with the board of the company to be acquired and has established its own hostile bid. *See also* ***knight***

black market MARKETS illegal market for scarce goods an illegal ***market***, usually for goods that are in short supply, but also for currency. Black market trading breaks government regulations or legislation and is particularly prevalent during times of shortage or rationing, or in industries such as pharmaceuticals or armaments that are highly regulated. *Also called* ***shadow market***

black market economy 1. ECONOMICS illegal trading a system of illegal trading in officially controlled goods **2.** CURRENCY & EXCHANGE illicit parallel currency market an illicit secondary currency market that has rates markedly different from those in the official market

Black Monday MARKETS 10.28.1927 or 10.19.1987 when financial markets dropped either of two Mondays, October 28, 1929 or October 19, 1987, that were marked by the largest stock market declines of the 20th century. Although both market crashes originated in the United States, they were immediately followed by similar market crashes around the world.

black money ECONOMICS untaxed money earned unofficially or illegally money circulating in the ***black economy*** in payment for goods and services

Black-Scholes model STOCKHOLDING & INVESTMENTS formula for determining option call price a complex mathematical formula for calculating an option's ***call price*** using the current price of the security, the ***strike price***, volatility, time until expiration, and the risk-free interest rate

Black Tuesday MARKETS 10.29.1929 when financial markets dropped Tuesday, October 29, 1929, a day on which values of stocks fell precipitously

Black Wednesday ECONOMICS 09.16.1992 when sterling crashed Wednesday, September 16, 1992, when the pound sterling left the European Exchange Rate Mechanism and was devalued against other currencies

blame culture GENERAL MANAGEMENT group's tendency to blame others for mistakes a set of attitudes, for example, within a business or organization, characterized by an unwillingness to take risks or accept responsibility for mistakes because of a fear of criticism or prosecution

blank check *or* **blank cheque** BANKING signed check with amount left blank a check with the amount of money and the name of the payee left blank, but signed by the drawer

blanket bond INSURANCE insurance against losses caused by employees an insurance policy that covers a financial institution for losses caused by the actions of its employees

blanket lien LEGAL right to somebody's property a legal right to all a person's property, including their personal effects

blended rate FINANCE intermediate interest rate an interest rate charged by a lender that is between an old rate and a new one

blind certificate E-COMMERCE computer file with user's name omitted a cookie from which the user's name is omitted so as to protect his or her privacy while making collected data available for marketing studies

blind entry **1.** ACCOUNTING uninformative bookkeeping entry a bookkeeping entry that records a debit or credit but fails to show other essential information **2.** *ANZ* FINANCE statement of cost of goods and tax a document issued by a supplier that stipulates the amount charged for goods or services as well as the amount of ***Goods and Services Tax*** payable

blind pool BUSINESS limited partnership without details of purposes a limited partnership in which the investment opportunities the general partner plans to pursue are not specified

blindside MARKETING attack somebody without warning to attack somebody in a way that he or she cannot anticipate (*slang*)

blind trust STOCKHOLDING & INVESTMENTS trust without participation of beneficiary a trust that manages somebody's business interests, with contents that are unknown to the beneficiary. People assuming public office use such trusts to avoid conflicts of interest.

block STOCKHOLDING & INVESTMENTS 10,000 or more shares of stock a very large number of shares of stock, typically 10,000 or more

block diagram STATISTICS presentation of statistical data in blocks a diagram that represents ranges of statistical data by vertical rectangular blocks

blocked account BANKING frozen bank account a bank account from which funds cannot be withdrawn for any of a number of reasons, for example, bankruptcy proceedings, liquidation of a company, or government order when freezing foreign assets

blocked currency CURRENCY & EXCHANGE currency hard to exchange a currency that people cannot easily trade for other currencies because of foreign ***exchange controls***

blocked funds CURRENCY & EXCHANGE money frozen in one place money that cannot be transferred from one place to another, usually because of foreign ***exchange controls*** imposed by the government of the country in which the funds are held

block grant FINANCE **1.** in US, federal money for local government in the United States, money that the federal government gives to a local government to spend in ways that the recipient determines **2.** in UK, government money for local authorities in the United Kingdom, money that the government gives to local authorities to fund local services

blockholder STOCKHOLDING & INVESTMENTS investor with large stake in firm an individual or institutional investor who holds a large number of shares of stock or a large dollar amount of bonds in a given company

block investment *ANZ* STOCKHOLDING & INVESTMENTS taking or having large stake in firm the purchase or holding of a large number of shares of stock or a large dollar amount of bonds in a given company

block trade STOCKHOLDING & INVESTMENTS sale of many stocks or bonds the sale of a large round number of stocks or large amount of bonds

block trading MARKETS bulk trading in securities buying and selling in very large numbers of securities

blow-off top MARKETS rapid price rise then fall a rapid increase in the price of a financial stock followed by an equally rapid drop in price (*slang*)

blowout *US* MARKETS immediate sale of complete stock issue the rapid sale of the whole of a new stock issue (*slang*)

Blue Book FINANCE UK national statistics of incomes and expenditure national statistics of personal incomes and spending patterns in the United Kingdom, published annually

blue chip STOCKHOLDING & INVESTMENTS profitable and low risk used to describe an equity or company which is of the highest quality and in which an investment would be considered as low risk with regard to both dividend payments and capital values

blue-chip stocks STOCKHOLDING & INVESTMENTS common stock in safe firm common stock in a company that is considered to be well established, highly successful, and reliable, and is traded on a stock market

blue-collar job HR & PERSONNEL job involving manual labor a position that involves mainly physical labor. With the decline in manufacturing and an increase in ***harmonization*** agreements, the term blue collar is now rarely used. Blue collar refers to the blue overalls traditionally worn in factories in contrast to the white shirt and tie supposedly worn by an office worker, known as a ***white-collar worker***.

blue-collar worker HR & PERSONNEL manual laborer a person whose job involves mainly physical labor

Blue Dogs FINANCE fiscally conservative democrats in US Congress members of a coalition of fiscally conservative Democrats in the House of Representatives of the US Congress

Blue List MARKETS information about municipal bonds in the United States, a daily list of municipal bonds and their ratings, published by Standard & Poor's

blue-sky ideas GENERAL MANAGEMENT unrealistically optimistic plans extremely ambitious, idealistic, or unrealistic proposals, apparently unconfined by conventional thinking

blue-sky laws FRAUD, REGULATION & COMPLIANCE US state laws protecting investors from fraudulent deals in the United States, state laws designed to protect investors against fraudulent traders in securities

blue-sky securities STOCKHOLDING & INVESTMENTS worthless stocks and bonds stocks and bonds that have no value, being worth the same as a piece of "blue sky" *(slang)*

blur GENERAL MANAGEMENT when big changes in firm happen quickly a period of transition for a business in which changes occur at great speed and on a large scale

BO *abbr* BANKING ***branch office***

board CORPORATE GOVERNANCE = ***board of directors***

board dismissal CORPORATE GOVERNANCE removal of firm's whole board the dismissal and removal from power of an entire board or ***board of directors***

board meeting CORPORATE GOVERNANCE directors' meeting a meeting of the board of directors of a company

Board of Currency Commissioners CURRENCY & EXCHANGE issuer of Singaporean currency the sole currency issuing authority in Singapore, established in 1967. *Abbr* ***BCCS***

Board of Customs and Excise INTERNATIONAL TRADE *see* ***Her Majesty's Revenue & Customs***

board of directors CORPORATE GOVERNANCE firm's highest management board the people selected to sit on an authoritative standing committee or governing body, taking responsibility for the management of an organization. Members of the board of directors are officially chosen by stockholders, but in practice they are usually selected on the basis of the current board's recommendations. The board usually includes major stockholders as well as directors of the company. *Also called* ***board***

Board of Inland Revenue TAX *see* ***Her Majesty's Revenue & Customs***

board of trustees STOCKHOLDING & INVESTMENTS group managing funds, assets, or property for others a committee or governing body that takes responsibility for managing–and holds in trust–funds, assets, or property belonging to others, for example, charitable or pension funds or assets

boardroom CORPORATE GOVERNANCE room for board meetings a room in which board meetings are held. A boardroom may be a room used only for board meetings or can be a multiuse room that becomes a boardroom for the duration of a board meeting.

boardroom battle CORPORATE GOVERNANCE struggle between board members a conflict or power struggle between individual board members or between groups of board members

board seat CORPORATE GOVERNANCE position on firm's board a position of membership of a board, especially a ***board of directors***

board secretary CORPORATE GOVERNANCE organization's senior administrative officer a senior employee in a public organization, with a role similar to that of a ***company secretary***

body corporate CORPORATE GOVERNANCE group acting as individual an entity such as a company or institution that is legally authorized to act as if it were one person

body of creditors BUSINESS creditors regarded as single unit the creditors of a company or individual treated as a single creditor in dealing with the debtor

body of shareholders STOCKHOLDING & INVESTMENTS shareholders regarded as single unit the shareholders of a company treated as a single shareholder in dealing with the company

bogey *US* MARKETS performance benchmark for fund managers a benchmark, often the Standard and Poor's 500 Index, against which mutual fund managers or portfolio managers measure their performance *(slang)*

boilerplate LEGAL reusable contract language standard language that can be used for the same purpose from contract to contract *(slang)*

boiler room MARKETING room for selling financial products by phone a room from which sales personnel using high-pressure sales tactics try to sell financial products or real estate of questionable value, usually by telephone and often using illegal tactics

boiler room fraud FRAUD illegal selling of worthless stock the illegal practice of calling people and pressing them to buy worthless stock in companies that do not exist or are virtually bankrupt

Bolivarism ECONOMICS socialist vision of Venezuelan president the new socialist and pan-South American vision of President Hugo Chávez of Venezuela, named for Simón Bolívar, the South American revolutionary leader who fought against Spanish colonial rule

bolsa MARKETS stock exchange a ***stock exchange*** in a Spanish-speaking country

bona fide FINANCE undertaken in good faith used to describe a sale or purchase that has been conducted in good faith, without collusion or fraud

bona vacantia FINANCE goods of intestate person with no heirs the goods of somebody who has died intestate and has no traceable living relatives. In the United Kingdom, these goods become the property of the state.

bond 1. FINANCE money given as deposit a sum of money paid as a deposit, especially on rented premises **2.** STOCKHOLDING & INVESTMENTS contract promising loan repayment with interest a certificate issued by a company or government that promises repayment of borrowed money at a set rate of interest on a particular date **3.** *S. Africa* MORTGAGES = ***mortgage bond***

bond anticipation note STOCKHOLDING & INVESTMENTS loan repaid through bonds issued later a loan that a government agency receives to provide capital that will be repaid from the proceeds of bonds that the agency will issue later. *Abbr* ***BAN***

bond covenant STOCKHOLDING & INVESTMENTS promise by lender to limit activities part of a bond contract whereby the lender promises not to do some things such as borrow beyond a specified limit

bond discount STOCKHOLDING & INVESTMENTS gap between price and higher face value the difference between the face value of a bond and the lower price at which it is issued

bonded warehouse INTERNATIONAL TRADE warehouse for dutiable or taxable goods a warehouse that holds goods awaiting duty or tax to be paid on them

bond equivalent yield STOCKHOLDING & INVESTMENTS compound interest conversion for bond comparison the interest rate on a Treasury bill, commercial paper, or discount note, usually quoted as simple interest, converted to compound interest in order to compare it with the interest on a bond. *Also called* ***equivalent bond yield****. See also* ***compound annual return***

bond fund STOCKHOLDING & INVESTMENTS mutual fund with bonds a mutual fund with an investment ***portfolio*** made up of bonds

bondholder STOCKHOLDING & INVESTMENTS entity owning bonds an individual or institution owning bonds issued by a government or company. Bondholders are entitled to payments of the interest as due and the return of the ***principal*** when the bond matures.

bond indenture STOCKHOLDING & INVESTMENTS document describing bond a document that specifies the terms and conditions of a bond

bond indexing STOCKHOLDING & INVESTMENTS matching yield from bonds and specific index the practice of investing in bonds in such a way as to match the yield of a designated index

bond issue STOCKHOLDING & INVESTMENTS sale of bonds to investors an occasion when a company or government offers ***bonds*** to investors in order to raise funding

bond market MARKETS market for government or municipal bonds a financial market in which participants trade in government or municipal bonds

bond premium STOCKHOLDING & INVESTMENTS gap between price and lower face value the difference between the face value of a bond and a higher price at which it is issued

bond quote STOCKHOLDING & INVESTMENTS up-to-date statement of bond's price a statement of the current price of a bond when traded on the open market

bond rating STOCKHOLDING & INVESTMENTS assessment of bond-issuer's reliability the rating of the reliability of a company, government, or local authority that has issued a bond. The highest rating is AAA (triple A).

bond swap STOCKHOLDING & INVESTMENTS simultaneous sale and purchase of bonds an exchange of some bonds for others, usually to gain a tax advantage or to diversify a portfolio

bond value ACCOUNTING value stated in accounts the value of an ***asset*** or ***liability*** as recorded in the accounts of a person or organization

bond-washing STOCKHOLDING & INVESTMENTS avoidance of tax on dividend income the practice of selling a bond before its dividend is due and buying it back later in order to avoid paying tax on the dividend

bond yield STOCKHOLDING & INVESTMENTS yield of bond in relation to market price the annual return on a bond (the rate of interest) expressed as a percentage of the current market price of the bond. Bonds can tie up investors' money for periods of up to 30 years, so knowing their yield is a critical investment consideration.

bonus FINANCE extra money given as reward to employee a financial incentive given to employees in addition to their ***base pay*** in the form of a one-time payment or as part of a ***bonus plan***

bonus dividend STOCKHOLDING & INVESTMENTS irregular additional dividend a one-time extra dividend in addition to the usual payment

bonus issue STOCKHOLDING & INVESTMENTS proportionate issue of new shares to stockholders the capitalization of the reserves of a company by the issue of additional shares to existing stockholders, in proportion to their holdings. Such shares are usually fully paid up with no cash called for from the stockholders.

bonus offer MARKETING sales offer of extra product for same price a sales promotion technique offering consumers an additional amount of product for the basic price

bonus plan *US* FINANCE program for rewarding employees with extra money a form of ***incentive plan*** under which a ***bonus*** is paid to employees in accordance with rules concerning eligibility, performance targets, time period, and size and form of payments. A bonus plan may apply to some or all employees and may be determined on organization, business unit, or individual performance, or on a combination of these. A bonus payment may be expressed as a percentage of salary or as a flat-rate sum. *UK term* ***bonus scheme***

bonus scheme *UK* FINANCE = ***bonus plan***

bonus shares STOCKHOLDING & INVESTMENTS **1.** increased number of shares not affecting total value shares issued to stockholders in a ***stock split***, with at least one more share for every share owned, without affecting the total value of each holding. *See also* ***stock split*** **2.** UK government reward to loyal founding stockholders in the United Kingdom, extra shares paid by the government as a reward to founding stockholders who did not sell their initial holding within a specific number of years

book STOCKHOLDING & INVESTMENTS record of trader's investments and amounts owed a statement of all the holdings of a trader and the amount he or she is due to pay or has borrowed ◇ cook the books FRAUD to use accounting methods to hide aspects of a company's financial dealings such as losses or illegal activities ◇ do the books ACCOUNTING to keep records of expenditure and income

book-building STOCKHOLDING & INVESTMENTS gathering information to determine offering price the research done among potential institutional investors to determine the optimum offering price for a new issue of stock

book cost STOCKHOLDING & INVESTMENTS total cost of stocks the price paid for a stock, including any payments to intermediaries such as brokers

book entry ACCOUNTING account entry unsupported by documentation an accounting entry indicated in a record somewhere but not represented by any document

book-entry security STOCKHOLDING & INVESTMENTS security without paper certificate a security that is recorded as a ***book entry*** but is not represented by a paper certificate

book inventory ACCOUNTING stock level recorded in accounts the number of items in stock according to accounting records. This number can be validated only by a physical count of the items.

bookkeeper ACCOUNTING maintainer of business's financial records a person who is responsible for maintaining the financial records of a business

bookkeeping ACCOUNTING recording income and expenditure the activity or profession of recording the money received and spent by an individual, business, or organization

bookkeeping barter ACCOUNTING exchange of goods treated as money transaction the direct exchange of goods between two parties without the use of money as a medium, but using monetary measures to record the transaction

book of original entry *or* **book of prime entry** ACCOUNTING chronological and classified record of transactions a chronological record of a business's transactions arranged according to type, for example, cash or sales. The books are then used to generate entries in a double-entry bookkeeping system.

books ACCOUNTING record of sales and receipts the set of records that a business keeps, showing what has been spent and earned

book sales OPERATIONS & PRODUCTION recorded sales sales as recorded in a company's sales book

books of account *UK* ACCOUNTING = ***accounting records***

book-to-bill ratio ACCOUNTING relationship between orders received and bills issued the ratio of the value of orders that a company has received to the amount for which it has billed its customers

book transfer STOCKHOLDING & INVESTMENTS recorded change in security's ownership without transfer documents a transfer of ownership of a security without physical transfer of any document that represents the instrument

book value 1. ACCOUNTING recorded value of asset the value of an asset as recorded in a company's balance sheet, usually the original cost with an allowance made for depreciation. Book value is not usually the same as ***market value*** (the amount it could be sold for). **2.** STOCKHOLDING & INVESTMENTS, ACCOUNTING firm's own valuation of its stock the value of a company's stock according to the company itself, which may differ considerably from the ***market value***. Book value is calculated by subtracting a company's liabilities and the value of its debt and ***preferred stock*** from its total assets. All of these figures appear on a company's balance sheet. For example:

	$
Total assets	1,300
Current liabilities	−400
Long-term liabilities, preference shares	−250
Book value	= 650

Book value represents a company's net worth to its stockholders. When compared with its market value, book value helps reveal how a company is regarded by the investment community. A market value that is notably higher than the book value indicates that investors have a high regard for the company. A market value that is, for example, a multiple of book value suggests that investors' regard may be unreasonably high. *Also called* ***carrying amount, carrying value***

book value per share STOCKHOLDING & INVESTMENTS, ACCOUNTING firm's own valuation of each share the value of one share of a stock according to the company itself, which may differ considerably from the market value. It is calculated by dividing the ***book value*** by the number of shares in issue.

boom FINANCE significant increase in business a period of time during which business activity increases significantly, with the result that demand for products grows, as do prices, salaries, and employment

boom and bust *or* **boom or bust** FINANCE extreme economic or market upswings and downswings a regular pattern of alternation in an economy or market between extreme growth and collapse and recession

BOP *abbr* INTERNATIONAL TRADE ***balance of payments***

border tax adjustment INTERNATIONAL TRADE taxing imported but not exported goods the application of a domestic tax on imported goods while exempting exported goods from the tax in an effort to make the exported goods' price competitive both nationally and internationally

borrow 1. FINANCE arrange to use another's assets for a time to be given money by a person or financial institution for a fixed period of time, usually paying it back in installments and with interest **2.** STOCKHOLDING & INVESTMENTS buy at delivery price and sell forward simultaneously to buy a commodity or security at the present spot price and sell forward at the same time

borrower FINANCE somebody borrowing money from lender a person who receives money from a lender with the intention of paying it back, usually with interest

borrowing FINANCE receipt of money from lender the act of borrowing money from a lender

borrowing capacity *or* **borrowing power** FINANCE amount firm can borrow in loans the amount of money available as a loan to a company at a particular time, based on the company's financial situation

borrowing costs FINANCE expense of taking out loan expenses such as interest payments incurred from taking out a loan or any other form of borrowing. In the United States, such costs are included in the total cost of the asset whereas in the United Kingdom, and in International Accounting Standards, this is optional.

borrowings FINANCE money borrowed money borrowed, usually in the form of long-term loans

boss GENERAL MANAGEMENT person managing group or process the person in charge of a job, process, department, or organization, more formally known as a manager or supervisor

Boston Box *or* **Boston matrix** BUSINESS plotting market share against growth rate a model used for analyzing a company's potential by plotting market share against growth rate. The Boston Box was conceived by the Boston Consulting Group in the 1970s to help in the process of determining which businesses a company should invest in and which it should divest itself of. A business with a high market share and high growth rate is a *star*, and one with a low market share and low growth rate is a *dog*. A high market share with low growth rate is characteristic of a ***cash cow***, which could yield significant but short-term gain, and a low market share coupled with high growth rate produces a *question mark company*, which offers a doubtful return on investment. To be useful, this model requires accurate assessment of a business's strengths and weaknesses, which may be difficult to obtain.

BOT *abbr* INTERNATIONAL TRADE ***balance of trade***

bottleneck 1. FINANCE process that holds up others an activity within an organization which has a lower capacity than preceding or subsequent activities, thereby limiting throughput. Bottlenecks are often the cause of a buildup of work in progress and of idle time. **2.** OPERATIONS & PRODUCTION somebody or something that slows down process a limiting factor on the rate of an operation. A workstation operating at its maximum capacity becomes a bottleneck if the rate of production elsewhere in the plant increases but throughput at that workstation cannot be increased to meet demand. An understanding of bottlenecks is important if the efficiency and capacity of an assembly line are to be increased. The techniques of ***fishbone charts***, *Pareto charts*, and ***flow charts*** can be used to identify where and why bottlenecks occur.

bottom fisher MARKETS financial bargain hunter an investor who searches for bargains among stocks that have recently dropped in price (*slang*)

bottom line ACCOUNTING firm's net profit or loss the net profit or loss that a company makes at the end of a specific period of time, used in the calculation of the earnings-per-share business ratio

bottom-of-the-harbor scheme *ANZ* TAX tax avoidance involving asset-stripping a tax avoidance strategy that involves stripping a company of assets and then selling the company a number of times so that it is hard to trace

bottom out MARKETS stabilize at low level to reach the lowest level in the downward trend of the market price of securities or commodities before the price begins an upward trend again

bottom-up approach 1. STOCKHOLDING & INVESTMENTS describing investment on individual potential independent of trends used to describe an approach to investing that seeks to identify individual companies that are fundamentally sound and whose stock will perform well regardless of general economic or industry-group trends **2.** GENERAL MANAGEMENT involving employee participation at all levels used to describe a consultative leadership style that promotes employee participation at all levels in decision making and problem solving. A bottom-up approach to leadership is associated with ***flat*** organizations and the empowerment of employees. It can encourage creativity and flexibility. *See also* ***top-down approach***

bottom-up budgeting TREASURY MANAGEMENT = ***participative budgeting***

bought day book ACCOUNTING record of items bought on credit a book used to record purchases for which cash is not paid immediately

bought deal STOCKHOLDING & INVESTMENTS purchase of new issue for resale to investors a method of selling stock in a new company or selling an issue of new shares in an existing company, in which an underwriter purchases all the shares at a fixed price for resale to investors

bought-in goods FINANCE goods from outside supplier components and subassemblies that are purchased from an outside supplier instead of being made within the organization

bought ledger ACCOUNTING firm's book recording expenditure a book in which all of a company's expenditure is logged

bought ledger clerk *UK* HR & PERSONNEL employee dealing with bought ledger an office employee who deals with the bought ledger or the sales ledger

bounce BANKING **1.** fail to honor check to refuse payment of a check because the account for which it is written holds insufficient money (*slang*). *Also called* ***dishonor*** **2.** be refused by bank (of a check) to be returned by a bank because there are insufficient funds in the account to meet the demand (*informal*)

bounced check BANKING check that bank fails to honor a draft on an account that a bank will not honor, usually because there are insufficient funds in the account

boundaryless organization GENERAL MANAGEMENT organizational model whose goal is flexibility a model that views organizations as having permeable boundaries. An organization has external boundaries that separate it from its suppliers and customers, and internal boundaries that provide demarcation to departments. This rigidity is removed in boundaryless organizations, where the goal is to develop greater flexibility and responsiveness to change and to facilitate the free exchange of information and ideas. The boundaryless organization behaves more like an organism encouraging better integration between departments and closer partnerships with suppliers and customers. The concept was developed at General Electric and described in the book *The Boundaryless Organization: Breaking the Chains of Organizational Structure* by Ron Ashkenas and others, which was published in 1995.

bourse MARKETS French stock exchange a European stock exchange, especially the one in Paris

boutique 1. STOCKHOLDING & INVESTMENTS small specialist firm a small firm that offers a limited number of investments or services. *See also* ***boutique investment house*** **2.** BANKING small investment bank a small investment banking firm

boutique investment house STOCKHOLDING & INVESTMENTS specialist broker a brokerage that deals in securities of only one industry. *Also called* ***niche player*** *(sense 2)*

Bowie bond STOCKHOLDING & INVESTMENTS, RISK bond backed by intellectual property an ***asset-backed security*** for which the right to royalties from intellectual property is the collateral

box ◇ think outside the box GENERAL MANAGEMENT to think imaginatively about a problem

box spread MARKETS trading in single thing an arbitrage strategy that eliminates risk by buying and selling the same thing

B/P *abbr* FINANCE ***bills payable***

BPR *abbr* GENERAL MANAGEMENT, OPERATIONS & PRODUCTION ***business process reengineering***

B/R *abbr* FINANCE ***bills receivable***

bracket creep *US* TAX incremental movement into higher tax bracket the movement of a taxpayer into increasingly higher tax brackets in a progressive tax system, usually as a result of incremental pay increases to keep pace with inflation

Brady bond STOCKHOLDING & INVESTMENTS emerging country's bond backed by Treasury bonds a bond issued by an emerging nation that has US Treasury bonds as collateral. It is named for Nicholas Brady, banking reformer and former Secretary of the Treasury.

brain drain GENERAL MANAGEMENT relocation of experts overseas for better working environment the overseas migration of specialists, usually highly qualified scientists, engineers, or technical experts, in pursuit of higher salaries, better research funding, and a perceived higher quality of working life

brainstorming GENERAL MANAGEMENT activity for generating free flow of ideas a technique for generating ideas, developing creativity, or problem solving in small groups, through the free-flowing contributions of participants. To encourage the free flow of ideas, brainstorming sessions operate according to a set of guidelines, and the production and evaluation of ideas are kept separate. Several variations of brainstorming and related techniques have emerged such as *brainwriting*, where ideas are written down by individuals, and ***buzz groups***.

brainwriting GENERAL MANAGEMENT writing down flow of ideas a variation of ***brainstorming*** in which ideas are written down by individuals

branch accounts ACCOUNTING financial records for firm's subsidiary operations the ***accounting records*** or ***financial statements*** for the component parts of a business, especially those that are located in a different region or country from the main enterprise

branch office BANKING organization in different location from headquarters a bank or other financial institution that is part of a larger group and is located in a different geographic area from the parent organization. *Abbr* ***BO***

branch tax TAX S. African tax on some foreign companies a South African tax imposed on nonresident companies that register a branch rather than a separate company

brand MARKETING name or symbol identifying product or service the distinguishing proprietary name, symbol, or ***trademark*** that differentiates a particular product or service from others of a similar nature

brand architecture MARKETING strategy for using brand on products and services the naming and structuring of ***brands*** within the product portfolio of an organization. Brand architectures may be monolithic (the corporate name is used on all products and services), endorsed (subordinate brands are linked to the corporate brand by means of either a verbal or visual endorsement), or freestanding (each product or service is individually branded for its target market). Brand architecture is influenced by the overall brand management and brand positioning strategy of the organization.

brand awareness MARKETING measure of consumers' familiarity with specific brand name the level of ***brand recognition*** that consumers have of a specific brand and its specific product category. Brand awareness examines three levels of recognition: whether the brand name is the first to come to mind when a consumer is questioned about a specific product category; whether the brand name is one of several that come to mind when a consumer is questioned about a specific product category; and whether or not a consumer has heard of a specific brand name.

brand building MARKETING efforts to gain consumer confidence in brand the establishment and improvement of a brand's identity, including giving the brand a set of values that the consumer wants, recognizes, identifies with, and trusts. Values developed in the process of brand building include psychological, physical, and functional properties that consumers desire and should always identify a property that is unique to that brand.

brand champion MARKETING employee responsible for developing and marketing brand an employee of an organization who is responsible for the development, performance, and communication of a particular brand

brand equity MARKETING brand's perceived value the estimated value that a particular brand name brings

brand extension MARKETING using known brand name to enter new market the exploitation, diversification, or stretching of a brand to revive or reinvigorate it in the marketplace. Products developed in the brand extension process may be directly recognizable derivatives or may look and feel completely different.

brand image MARKETING consumer's opinion of brand the perception that consumers have of a brand. Brand image is usually carefully developed by the brand owner through marketing campaigns or product positioning. Occasionally, the image of a brand may develop spontaneously through customer responses to a product. The image of a brand can be seriously tarnished through inappropriate advertising or association with somebody or something that has fallen from public favor.

branding MARKETING process of creating identity for brand a means of distinguishing one firm's products or services from another's and of creating and maintaining an image that encourages confidence in the quality and performance of that firm's products or services

brand leader MARKETING best-selling brand the brand that has the largest ***market share***

brand life cycle MARKETING stages from brand introduction to withdrawal from market the three phases through which brands pass as they are introduced, grow, and then decline. The three stages of the brand life cycle are the introductory period, during which the brand is developed and is introduced to the market; the growth period, when the brand faces competition from other products of a similar nature; and, finally, the maturity period, in which the brand either extends to other products or its image is constantly updated. Without careful ***brand management***, the maturity period can lead to decline and result in the brand being withdrawn. Similar stages can be observed in the ***product life cycle***.

brand loyalty MARKETING customer's inclination to stay with specific brand a long-term customer preference for a specific product or service. Brand loyalty can be produced by factors such as customer satisfaction with the performance or price of a specific product or service, or through identifying with a brand image. It can be encouraged by advertising.

brand management MARKETING responsibility for advertising, promoting, and selling product the marketing of one or more proprietary products. ***Brand managers*** have responsibility for the promotion and marketing of one or more commercial brands. This includes setting targets, advertising, and retailing, as well as coordinating all related activities to achieve those targets. In the case of multiple brand management, consideration needs be to given to questions relating to the treatment of the brands as equal or as having some differentiating value. This may affect the amount of resources committed to each brand. *See also* ***product management***

brand positioning MARKETING Identifying place in market to compete effectively the development of a brand's position in the market by heightening customer perception of the brand's superiority over other brands of a similar nature. Brand positioning relies on the identification of a real strength or value that has a clear advantage over the nearest competitor and is easily communicated to the consumer.

brand recognition MARKETING measurement of consumer's awareness of brand a measurement of the ability of consumers to recall their experience or knowledge of a particular brand. Brand recognition forms part of ***brand awareness***.

brand value MARKETING benefit to firm of brand the amount that a brand is worth in terms of income, potential income, reputation, prestige, and market value. Brands with a high value are regarded as considerable assets to a company, so that when a company is sold a brand with a high value may be worth more than any other consideration.

brand wagon MARKETING increasing use of branding the trend toward using branding in marketing concepts and techniques (*slang*)

brandwidth MARKETING measurement of awareness of product the degree to which a brand of product or service is recognized (*slang*)

breach of contract LEGAL not performing according to contract a refusal or failure to fulfill an obligation imposed by a ***contract***

breach of trust LEGAL instance of betraying people's trust a situation in which somebody does not act correctly or honestly when people expect him or her to

breadth-of-market theory MARKETS significance of relationship of rising and falling prices the theory that the health of a market is measured by the relative volume of items traded that are going up or down in price

break 1. MARKETS sharp price drop in stocks a sudden or sharp fall in prices on a financial market **2.** LEGAL fail to honor contract to fail to carry out the duties of a contract **3.** LEGAL end contract to cancel a contract

breakdown GENERAL MANAGEMENT list of individual items a detailed list or analysis of something item by item

break even ACCOUNTING make neither profit nor loss to balance income and expense, so as to show neither a net gain nor a loss

break-even MARKETING when revenue equals costs the point at which revenue from a product or project cancels out its costs

break-even analysis OPERATIONS & PRODUCTION establishing point of profit and loss balance a method for determining the point at which fixed and variable production costs are equaled by sales revenue and where neither a profit nor a loss is made. Usually illustrated graphically through the use of a ***break-even chart***, break-even analysis can be used to aid decision making, set product prices, and determine the effects of changes in production or sales volume on costs and profits.

break-even chart 1. GENERAL MANAGEMENT chart showing break-even point a management aid used in conjunction with ***break-even analysis*** to calculate the point at which fixed and variable production costs are met by incoming revenue. Lines are plotted to indicate expected sales revenue and production costs. The point at which the lines intersect marks the ***break-even point***, where no profit or loss is made. **2.** OPERATIONS & PRODUCTION chart comparing sales volumes and income a chart that indicates approximate profit or loss at different levels of sales volume within a limited range

break-even point OPERATIONS & PRODUCTION balance of profit and loss the point or level of financial activity at which expenditure equals income, or the value of an investment equals its cost, so that the result is neither a profit nor a loss. *Abbr* ***BEP***

breakout 1. MARKETS significant movement in security's price a rise in a security's price above its previous highest price, or a drop below its former lowest price, taken by technical analysts to signal a continuing move in that direction **2.** GENERAL MANAGEMENT analysis of collected data a summary or breakdown of data that has been collected

breakpoint 1. FINANCE investment size that triggers reduced charges the size of investment at which the ***front-end loading*** on larger investments in a mutual fund starts to be reduced **2.** BANKING account balance that causes interest rate change a balance reached in an account that triggers the payment of either a higher or lower interest rate

breakthrough strategy GENERAL MANAGEMENT successful new strategy a strategy that achieves significant new results in business or management

break-up value MERGERS & ACQUISITIONS value of company's assets sold individually the combined market value of a firm's assets if each were sold separately, as contrasted with selling the firm as an ongoing business. Analysts look for companies with a large break-up value relative to their market value to identify potential takeover targets.

Bretton Woods ECONOMICS agreement establishing IMF and IBRD an agreement signed at a conference at Bretton Woods, in the United States, in July 1944, that established the ***IMF*** and the ***IBRD***

bribery FRAUD offer of gift or cash to gain advantage the act of persuading somebody to exercise his or her business judgment in your favor by offering cash or a gift and thereby gaining an unfair advantage. Many organizations have ***codes of conduct*** that expressly forbid the soliciting or payment of bribes.

brick ◇ hit the bricks GENERAL MANAGEMENT to go out on strike

bricks-and-mortar E-COMMERCE relating to firms not operating online used to describe a traditional business not involved in e-commerce and incurring the cost of physical structures such as retail stores

bridge financing FINANCE borrowing in expectation of later loans short-term borrowing that the borrower expects to repay with the proceeds of later, larger loans. *See also* ***takeout financing***

bridge loan *US* FINANCE temporary loan while waiting for money a short-term loan providing funds until further money is received, for example, for buying one property while trying to sell another. *UK term* ***bridging loan***

bridging FINANCE borrowing short-term until finance is arranged the obtaining of a short-term loan to provide a continuing source of financing in anticipation of receiving an intermediate or long-term loan. Bridging is routinely employed to finance the purchase or construction of a new building or property until an old one is sold.

bridging loan *UK* FINANCE = ***bridge loan***

bring forward ACCOUNTING carry sum to next column or page to carry a sum from one column or page to the next, or from one account to the next

Brisch system OPERATIONS & PRODUCTION coding system for all firm's resources a coding system, developed principally for the engineering industry by E. G. Brisch and Partners, in which a code is assigned to every item of resources, including materials, labor, and equipment.

British Accounting Association ACCOUNTING association for accountancy education and research an organization for the promotion of accounting education and research in the United Kingdom. *Abbr* ***BAA***

British Bankers' Association BANKING nonprofit financial organization a not-for-profit trading association for the financial services and banking industries. The Association was established in 1919 and has 260 members, including 57 associate members. It addresses a variety of industry issues, including the development and revision of the voluntary ***Banking Code***, which aims to set standards of best practice. *Abbr* ***BBA***

British Chambers of Commerce BUSINESS association of accredited chambers of commerce a national network of accredited chambers of commerce. The BCC represents over 135,000 businesses in the United Kingdom. *Abbr* ***BCC***

British pound = ***pound sterling*** (*informal*)

British Private Equity and Venture Capital Association FINANCE UK organization for equity and venture firms the official organization representing UK-based private equity and venture capital firms and their advisers. *Abbr* ***BVCA***

broad tape MARKETS news service reporting financial information a news service that reports general information about securities and commodities

broken lot MARKETS = ***odd lot***

broker **1.** FINANCE, GENERAL MANAGEMENT intermediary in transaction an agent who arranges a deal, sale, or contract **2.** STOCKHOLDING & INVESTMENTS = ***stockbroker*** **3.** FINANCE, GENERAL MANAGEMENT act as intermediary in transaction to act as an agent in arranging a deal, sale, or contract

brokerage **1.** FINANCE fee for arranging deal a fee paid to somebody who acts as an agent for somebody else. For example, brokers who arrange deals for the purchase and sale of real estate, those who execute orders for securities, and those who sell insurance receive commissions. *Also called* ***broker's commission*** **2.** STOCKHOLDING & INVESTMENTS broker's business the business of being a broker, trading on a stock exchange on behalf of clients **3.** *US* STOCKHOLDING & INVESTMENTS firm trading in securities for others a company whose business is buying and selling stocks and other securities for its clients. *Also called* ***brokerage firm***, ***brokerage house***. *UK term* ***broking house***

broker-dealer STOCKHOLDING & INVESTMENTS broker who also holds stocks for resale a dealer who buys stocks and other securities and holds them for resale, and also deals on behalf of investor clients

brokered market MARKETS where brokers introduce traders a financial market in which brokers bring buyers and sellers together

brokering *US* MARKETS securities the business or job of dealing in securities. *UK term* ***broking***

broker loan rate BANKING interest charged for buying derivatives the interest rate that banks charge brokers on money that they lend for purchases ***on margin***

broker recommendation STOCKHOLDING & INVESTMENTS advice to trade or hold security a recommendation to buy, hold, or sell a stock, made by an analyst who is employed by a brokerage firm to research specific companies' strengths and weaknesses

broker's commission STOCKHOLDING & INVESTMENTS = ***brokerage*** *(sense 1)*

broking *UK* STOCKHOLDING & INVESTMENTS = ***brokering***

broking house *UK* STOCKHOLDING & INVESTMENTS firm trading in stocks and bonds for others a company whose business is buying and selling stocks and bonds for its clients. *US term* ***brokerage***

brought forward ACCOUNTING carried to next column or page indicating a sum carried from one column or page to the next, or from one account to the next. *Abbr* ***b/f.*** *See also* ***bring forward***

brownfield *US* REAL ESTATE unused urban development site an urban development site that has been previously built on but is currently unused. *UK term* ***brownfield site***

brownfield site *UK* REAL ESTATE = ***brownfield***

brown goods *UK* MARKETING audio, video, computing, and telecommunications consumer goods electronic consumer goods such as televisions, radios, and CD players, used primarily for home entertainment. *See also* ***white goods***

B/S abbr ACCOUNTING ***balance sheet***

B share STOCKHOLDING & INVESTMENTS **1.** US share with limits on voting in the United States, a share that has limited voting power. *See also* ***A share*** **2.** Australian mutual fund share with fee payable on redemption in Australia, a share in a mutual fund that has no front-end sales charge but carries a redemption fee, or ***back-end loading***, payable only if the share is redeemed. This load, called a ***contingent deferred sales charge***, declines every year until it disappears, usually after six years.

BTI abbr MARKETS ***Business Times Industrial index***

bubble MARKETS rapid rise followed by fall in asset price a rapid rise in the price of any type of asset, due mainly to people's belief that the price will continue to rise. When it rises above the real value of the asset, the price falls rapidly, analogous to a bubble bursting. *Also called* ***speculative bubble***

bubble economy ECONOMICS booming economic activity before crash an unstable boom based on speculation in any market, often followed by a financial crash

buck *US* CURRENCY & EXCHANGE *(slang)* **1.** US dollar a United States dollar **2.** one million one million of any currency unit, used by traders

bucket shop MARKETS broker engaging in delayed trades to customer's disadvantage in the United States, a firm of brokers or dealers that accepts customers' orders but does not execute the transactions until it is financially advantageous to the broker, at the customers' expense

bucket trading MARKETS broker's illegal delay of transactions for own benefit in the United States, an illegal practice in which a broker or dealer accepts customers' orders but does not execute the transactions until it is financially advantageous to the broker, at the customers' expense

budget TREASURY MANAGEMENT statement of predicted income and expenditure a quantitative statement, for a defined period of time, that may include planned revenues, expenses, assets, liabilities, and cash flows. A budget provides a focus for an organization, as it aids the coordination of activities, allocation of resources, and direction of activity, and facilitates control. Planning is achieved by means of a fixed master budget, whereas control is generally exercised through the comparison of actual costs with a flexible budget.

Budget FINANCE UK government's annual statement of financial plans in the United Kingdom, the government's annual spending plan, which is announced to the House of Commons by the Chancellor of the Exchequer. The government is legally obliged to present economic forecasts twice a year, and since the 1997 general election the main Budget has been presented in the spring while a ***pre-Budget report*** is given in the autumn. This outlines government spending plans prior to the main Budget, and also reports on progress since the last Budget.

budget account *UK* BANKING bank account for regular expenses a bank account established to control a person's regular expenditure, such as the payment of insurance premiums, mortgage, utilities, or telephone bills. The annual expenditure for each item is paid into the account in equal monthly installments, bills being paid from the budget account as they become due.

budgetary TREASURY MANAGEMENT of future financial plans relating to a detailed plan of financial operations, with estimates of both revenue and expenditure for a specific future period

budgetary control TREASURY MANAGEMENT regulation of spending regulation of spending according to a planned budget

budget committee TREASURY MANAGEMENT committee that prepares budgets the group within an organization responsible for drawing up budgets that meet departmental requirements, ensuring they comply with policy, and then submitting them to the board of directors

budget deficit ACCOUNTING amount expenditure exceeds income the extent by which expenditure exceeds revenue, especially that of a government. *Also called* ***deficit***

budget director TREASURY MANAGEMENT person responsible for budget preparation the person in an organization who is responsible for running the budget system

budgeted capacity TREASURY MANAGEMENT output level in budget an organization's available output level for a budget period according to the budget. It may be expressed in different ways, for example, in machine hours (the number of hours for which a machine is in production) or standard hours.

budgeted revenue TREASURY MANAGEMENT expected income in budget the income that an organization expects to receive in a budget period according to the budget

budgeting TREASURY MANAGEMENT preparation of budget the preparation of a budget in planning the management of income and expenditure

budget management TREASURY MANAGEMENT adjusting activities to meet budgets the comparison of actual financial results with the estimated expenditures and revenues for the given time period of a budget and the taking of corrective action as necessary

budget surplus ACCOUNTING amount income exceeds expenditure the extent by which revenue exceeds expenditure, especially that of a government. *Also called **surplus***

budget variance ACCOUNTING difference between budget estimate and reality the difference between the financial value of something estimated in the budget, such as costs or revenues, and its actual financial value

buffer inventory OPERATIONS & PRODUCTION items available to cope with changes the products or supplies of an organization maintained on hand or in transit to stabilize variations in supply, demand, production, or lead time

buffer stock OPERATIONS & PRODUCTION items available to cope with supply failure a stock of materials, or of work in progress, maintained in order to protect user departments from the effect of possible interruptions to supply

building and loan association BANKING = ***savings and loan association***

Building Societies Ombudsman REGULATION & COMPLIANCE UK official protecting customers of building societies a UK official whose duty is to investigate complaints by members of the public against building societies

building society BANKING UK financial institution supporting real estate purchases in the United Kingdom, a financial institution that offers interest-bearing savings accounts, the deposits being reinvested by the society in long-term loans, primarily mortgage loans for the purchase of real estate

bulge MARKETS sudden trend of rising prices a rapid increase in prices in the commodities market

bulk buying OPERATIONS & PRODUCTION purchase of goods cheaply in quantity the act of buying large quantities of goods at low prices

bulk handling FINANCE financing of moneys due in bulk the financing of a group of receivables together to reduce processing costs

bull STOCKHOLDING & INVESTMENTS exploiter of favorable business conditions somebody who anticipates favorable business conditions, especially somebody who buys specific stocks or commodities in anticipation that their prices will rise, often with the expectation of selling them at a large profit at a later time. *See also **bear***

bull CD STOCKHOLDING & INVESTMENTS CD paying more in rising market a ***certificate of deposit*** that pays a higher interest rate when an underlying market index rises in value. *See also **bear CD***

bulldog bond STOCKHOLDING & INVESTMENTS foreign sterling bond in UK market a bond issued in sterling in the UK market by a non-British corporation

bullet FINANCE final large loan repayment a single large repayment of the outstanding ***principal*** of a loan at maturity

bullet bond STOCKHOLDING & INVESTMENTS bond repaid with single payment a bond that can be redeemed only when it reaches its maturity date

Bulletin des Annonces Légales Obligatoires FINANCE *see **BALO***

bullet loan FINANCE loan with only interest payments until maturity a loan that involves specific payments of interest until maturity, when the ***principal*** is repaid

bullion FINANCE precious metal in bars gold, silver, or platinum produced and traded in the form of bars

bullish 1. MARKETS of markets with rising prices conducive to or characterized by buying stocks or commodities in anticipation of rising prices. *See also **bearish*** **2.** GENERAL MANAGEMENT optimistic about business anticipating favorable business conditions and optimistic about taking advantage of them

bull market MARKETS market with rising prices a market in which prices are rising and in which a dealer is more likely to be a buyer than a seller. *See also **bear market***

bull spread MARKETS transactions to make profit when price rises a combination of purchases and sales of options for the same commodity or stock, intended to produce a profit when the price rises. *See also **bear spread***

bunching MARKETS combining orders for same security from different clients a process by which brokers combine orders for the same security, so that the orders can be executed together and save clients who have placed orders for ***odd lots*** of fewer than 100 shares of stock from paying extra fees

Bund STOCKHOLDING & INVESTMENTS, RISK German government bond a bond issued by the German government with a maturity of 8.5 to 10 years

Bundesfinanzhof TAX German tax court in Germany, the supreme court for issues concerning taxation. *Abbr **BFH***

bundle FINANCE combination of products or services a package of financial products or services offered to a customer

buoyant MARKETS showing a continuous rise in prices describes a financial market or a security with continuously rising prices

buoyant market MARKETS market with rising prices a market that experiences plenty of trading activity and on which prices are rising, rather than falling

bureaucracy GENERAL MANAGEMENT rigid organizational structure an organizational structure with a rigid hierarchy of personnel, regulated by set rules and procedures. The term bureaucracy has gradually become a pejorative synonym for excessive and time-consuming paperwork and administration. Bureaucracies fell subject to ***delayering*** and ***downsizing*** from the 1980s onward, as the flatter organization became the target structure to ensure swifter market response and organizational flexibility.

burn rate FINANCE rate at which firm's capital is used the rate at which a new business spends its initial capital before it becomes profitable or needs additional funding, used by investors as a measure of a company's ability to survive, or the rate at which a mature business spends its accumulated cash and liquid securities. *Also called* ***cash burn***

bush telegraph GENERAL MANAGEMENT quick informal communication method a method of communicating information or rumors swiftly and unofficially by word of mouth or other means

business BUSINESS **1.** activity carried out for profit work such as buying, selling, or producing goods or services that a person or organization does to make a profit **2.** commercial organization a company or other organization that buys, sells, or produces goods or services to make a profit **3.** commercial transactions commercial dealings or discussions carried on between people or organizations

Business Accounting Deliberation Council REGULATION & COMPLIANCE Japanese body making accounting rules in Japan, a committee controlled by the Ministry of Finance that is responsible for drawing up regulations regarding the consolidated financial statements of listed companies. *Abbr* ***BADC***

Business Activity Statement TAX Australian document giving firm's tax details in Australia, a standard document used to report the amount of ***GST*** and other taxes paid and collected by a business. *Abbr* ***BAS***

business address BUSINESS address of firm's premises the details of number, street, and city or town where a company is located

business administration GENERAL MANAGEMENT procedures involved in operating successful business the establishment and maintenance of procedures, records, and regulations in the pursuit of a commercial activity. Business administration involves the conduct of activities leading to, and resulting from, the delivery of a product or service to the customer. Administration is often seen as paperwork and form-filling, but it reaches more widely than that to encompass the coordination of all the procedures that enable a product or service to be delivered, together with the keeping of records that can be checked to identify errors or opportunities for improvement.

business angel FINANCE investor in new company an individual who is prepared to invest money in a startup company. The amount offered by angels is typically much less than that offered by ***venture capitalists***, but angels are often willing to take greater risks.

business case GENERAL MANAGEMENT proposal showing tangible value to organization the essential value to an organization of a proposal. A business case is made through the preparation and presentation of a business plan and is used to prevent blue-sky ideas taking root without justifiable or provable value to an organization.

business center BUSINESS **1.** area where city's main businesses are the part of a city or town where the main banks, stores, and offices are located **2.** independent office providing business services an office that provides business services such as Internet access, photocopying, meeting rooms, etc., for example, to travelers in a hotel

business cluster BUSINESS cooperative of small related firms a group of small firms from similar industries that team up and act as one body. Creating a business cluster enables firms to enjoy economies of scale usually only available to bigger competitors. Marketing costs can be shared and goods can be bought more cheaply. There are also networking advantages, allowing small firms to share experiences and discuss business strategies.

business combinations MERGERS & ACQUISITIONS acquisitions or mergers in the United States, acquisitions or mergers involving two or more business enterprises

Business Council of Australia BUSINESS organization of chief executives a national association of chief executives, designed as a forum for the discussion of matters pertaining to business leadership in Australia. *Abbr* ***BCA***

business cycle ECONOMICS regular repeating pattern of economic activity a regular pattern of fluctuation in national income, moving from upturn to downturn in about five years

business day BUSINESS normal weekday a weekday when banks, businesses, and stock exchanges are open for business

business efficiency GENERAL MANAGEMENT maximizing output while minimizing input a situation in which an organization maximizes benefit and profit, while minimizing effort and expenditure. Maximization of business efficiency is a balance between two extremes. Managed correctly, it reduces costs, waste, and duplication. The greater the efficiency, the more impersonal, rational, and emotionally detached a bureaucracy becomes. The flatter organizations more prevalent today attempt to be more customer-responsive than efficient in this sense, and the notion of such an ordered and impersonal efficiency has lost favor in an era when creativity and innovation are valued as a competitive advantage.

business expenses ACCOUNTING money spent on firm's running costs money spent on running a business, not on stock or assets

business failure GENERAL MANAGEMENT bankrupt organization an organization that has gone bankrupt. A business that is at risk of failure may be saved by ***turnaround management***, which identifies and deals with the reasons for decline. *Also called* ***failure***

business gift MARKETING gift presented to customer a present, usually from a supplier to a customer, often used to maintain good relations. Business gifts may range from a pen to a gift basket and are often a form of ***merchandising***. The acceptance of a business gift is often governed by an organization's ***code of conduct*** and is often forbidden on the grounds that business gifts, particularly high value ones, may be seen as an attempt to bribe.

business hours BUSINESS period when most firms are open the time during which a business is available to be in contact with customers, usually 9:00 a.m. to 5:00 p.m.

business intelligence GENERAL MANAGEMENT collection of business data the information and information gathering techniques used by businesses

business interruption insurance INSURANCE insurance protection against interruptions to business a policy indemnifying an organization for loss of profits and continuing fixed expenses when some insurable disaster, for example, a fire, causes the organization to stop or reduce its activities. *Also called* ***consequential loss policy***

business manager GENERAL MANAGEMENT somebody responsible for firm's operations a person who is responsible for implementing the policies and procedures of a business or part of a business

business model GENERAL MANAGEMENT description of business operations a description of the way in which a specific business or type of business operates, including its structure, policies, products, services, customers, and market strategies

business name BUSINESS in UK, name that organization uses in the United Kingdom, the legal term for the name under which an organization operates

business objective GENERAL MANAGEMENT organization's goal as basis for operational policies a goal that an organization sets for itself, for example, profitability, sales growth, or return on investment. These goals are the foundation upon which the strategic and operational policies adopted by the organization are based.

business plan GENERAL MANAGEMENT outline of firm's intentions for achieving goals a document describing the current activities of a business, setting out its goals and objectives and how they are to be achieved over a set period of time. A business plan may cover the activities of an organization or a group of companies, or it may deal with a single department within the organization. In the former case, it is sometimes referred to as a corporate plan. The sections of a business plan usually include a market analysis describing the target market, customers, and competitors, an operations plan describing how products and services will be developed and produced, and a financial section providing profit, budget, and cash flow forecasts, annual accounts, and financial requirements. Businesses may use a business plan internally as a framework for implementing strategy and improving performance or externally to attract investment or raise capital for development plans. A business plan may form part of the overall corporate planning process within an organization and be used for the implementation of a company's strategy.

business process reengineering GENERAL MANAGEMENT, OPERATIONS & PRODUCTION review and change to benefit organization the initiation and control of the change of processes within an organization, in order to derive competitive advantage from improvement in the quality of products. Business process reengineering requires a review and imaginative analysis of the processes currently used by the organization. BPR, therefore, has similarities to ***benchmarking***, as this review of processes can reveal critical points where significant improvements in quality can be made. Business process reengineering was at the height of its popularity in the early to mid-1990s. It has been criticized as one of the root causes of the bouts of ***downsizing*** and ***delayering*** that have affected many parts of industry. It has also received a negative press because few BPR projects have delivered the benefits expected of them. *Abbr* ***BPR***

business property relief TAX reduction in UK inheritance tax on business property in the United Kingdom, a reduction in the amount liable to inheritance tax on some types of business property

business rate TAX UK tax on business premises in the United Kingdom, a tax on businesses calculated on the value of the property occupied. Although the rate of tax is set by central government, the tax is collected by the local authority.

business risk RISK possible risk to firm's standing the uncertainty associated with the unique circumstances of a particular company which might affect the price of that company's securities, for example, the introduction of a superior technology by a competitor

business segment ACCOUNTING distinct part of business or enterprise a distinguishable part of a business or enterprise which is subject to a different set of risks and returns from any other part. Listed companies are required to declare in their annual reports information such as sales, profits, and assets, for each segment of an enterprise.

business strategy GENERAL MANAGEMENT firm's intended means of achieving long-term goals a long-term approach to implementing a firm's business plans to achieve its business objectives

Business Times Industrial index MARKETS Asian index of stocks an index of 40 Singapore and Malaysian stocks, sponsored by the *Business Times*. *Abbr* ***BTI***

business-to-business E-COMMERCE *see* ***B2B***

business-to-consumer E-COMMERCE *see* ***B2C***

business transaction OPERATIONS & PRODUCTION instance of buying or selling an act of buying or selling goods or services in order to make a profit

business transfer relief TAX UK tax benefit in takeovers the UK tax advantage gained when selling a business for shares of stock in the company that buys it

business unit ACCOUNTING distinct part of business organization a part of an organization that operates as a distinct function, department, division, or stand-alone business. Business units are usually treated as a separate ***profit center*** within the overall business.

bust ◇ go bust FINANCE to become bankrupt (*informal*)

bust up MERGERS & ACQUISITIONS divide or subdivide firm to split up a company or a division of a company into smaller units

bust-up proxy proposal MERGERS & ACQUISITIONS approach to stockholders for leveraged buyout an overture to a company's stockholders for a ***leveraged buyout*** in which the acquirer will sell some of the company's assets in order to repay the debt used to finance the takeover

butterfly spread STOCKHOLDING & INVESTMENTS simultaneously buying and selling variety of options a complex option strategy based on simultaneously purchasing and selling calls at different exercise prices and maturity dates, the profit being the premium collected when the options are sold. Such a strategy is most profitable when the price of the underlying security is relatively stable.

buy FINANCE **1.** pay to get something to get something in exchange for money **2.** something you pay for something that you pay for relative to its being worth or not worth the amount you pay

buy and hold STOCKHOLDING & INVESTMENTS investment for long term an investment strategy based on retaining securities for a long time

buy and write STOCKHOLDING & INVESTMENTS buying stock and selling options as safeguard an investment strategy involving buying stock and selling options to eliminate the possibility of loss if the value of the stock goes down

buyback 1. MARKETS purchase by firm of its own stock an arrangement whereby a company buys its own stock on the stock market. *Also called* ***stock buyback*** **2.** STOCKHOLDING & INVESTMENTS agreed repurchase of bonds or stock the repurchase of bonds or stock, as agreed by contract. The seller is usually a ***venture capitalist*** who helped finance the forming of the company.

buydown 1. FINANCE initial payment to secure favorable interest rate an initial lump-sum payment made on a loan in order to get a more favorable ongoing rate, especially a loan secured by a mortgage **2.** MORTGAGES partial repayment of principal on mortgage the payment of principal amounts which reduces the monthly payments due on a mortgage

buyer 1. BUSINESS person buying or intending to buy somebody who is in the process of buying something or who intends to buy something **2.** OPERATIONS & PRODUCTION professional acquirer of items needed somebody whose job is to choose and buy goods, merchandise, services, or media time or space for a company, factory, store, or advertiser

buyer expectation MARKETING = ***customer expectation***

buyer's guide MARKETING information helping consumer choose from variety of products a document that offers information on a variety of related products, usually from a number of different organizations

buyer's market MARKETS when supply exceeds demand a situation in which supply exceeds demand, prices are relatively low, and buyers therefore have an advantage

buy in STOCKHOLDING & INVESTMENTS acquire controlling interest in firm to buy stock in a company so as to have a controlling interest. This is often done by or for executives from outside the company.

buying department *UK* OPERATIONS & PRODUCTION = ***purchasing department***

buying economies of scale FINANCE lower cost involved in large transactions a reduction in the cost of purchasing raw materials and components or of borrowing money due to the increased size of the purchase

buying manager OPERATIONS & PRODUCTION = ***purchasing manager***

buying power FINANCE assessment of ability to purchase products and services the assessment of a person's or organization's disposable income, regarded as determining the quantity and quality of products and services that person or organization can afford to buy

buy on close MARKETS purchase late in day a purchase of securities or insurance policies made at the end of the trading day

buy on margin STOCKHOLDING & INVESTMENTS, RISK borrow to pay for part of security purchase to purchase securities by paying cash for part of the purchase and borrowing, using the security as collateral, for the remainder

buy on opening MARKETS purchase early in day a purchase of securities or insurance policies made at the beginning of the trading day

buy or make OPERATIONS & PRODUCTION = ***purchasing versus production***

buy out MERGERS & ACQUISITIONS **1.** buy and take over business to purchase the entire stock of, or controlling financial interest in, a company **2.** buy all somebody's share to pay somebody to relinquish his or her interest in a property or other enterprise

buyout 1. MERGERS & ACQUISITIONS buying and taking over of business the purchase and ***takeover*** of an ongoing business. It is more formally known as an ***acquisition***. If a business is purchased by managers or staff, it is known as a ***management buyout***. **2.** MERGERS & ACQUISITIONS buying all of somebody's stock ownership the purchase of somebody else's entire stock ownership in a firm. It is more formally known as an ***acquisition***. **3.** PENSIONS leaver's ability to move pension assets an option to transfer benefits of a pension plan on leaving a company

buy stop order MARKETS instruction to buy stock at specific price an order to buy stock when its price reaches a specific level, above the current offering level

buy-to-let *UK* FINANCE = ***buy-to-rent***

buy-to-let mortgage *UK* MORTGAGES = ***buy-to-rent mortgage***

buy-to-rent *US* FINANCE purchase of property for rental purposes an investment in property with the intention of renting it to produce income, often to pay the original mortgage used to purchase it. *UK term* ***buy-to-let***

buy-to-rent mortgage *US* MORTGAGES mortgage to purchase property for rental a mortgage used to buy property that you intend to rent. It differs from a mortgage on property that you intend to live in, in that the mortgagee takes into consideration the income the property will produce in deciding how much to lend. *UK term* ***buy-to-let mortgage***

buzz group GENERAL MANAGEMENT small group for discussing specific issue a small discussion group formed for a specific task such as generating ideas, solving problems, or reaching a common viewpoint on a topic within a specific period of time. Large groups may be divided into buzz groups after an initial presentation in order to cover different aspects of a topic or maximize participation. Each group appoints a spokesperson to report the results of the discussion to the larger group. Buzz groups are a form of brainstorming.

BV *abbr* BUSINESS ***Besloten venootschap***

BVCA *abbr* FINANCE ***British Private Equity and Venture Capital Association***

by-bidder FINANCE somebody bidding at auction to benefit seller somebody who bids at an auction solely to raise the price for the seller

bylaws *US* CORPORATE GOVERNANCE rules for corporation's internal procedures rules governing the internal running of a corporation, such as the number of meetings, the appointment of officers, and so on. *UK term* ***articles of association***

bypass trust TAX trust saving tax by increasing beneficiaries a trust that leaves money in a will in trust to people other than the prime beneficiary in order to gain tax advantage

byproduct OPERATIONS & PRODUCTION secondary product sold for profit a secondary product, made as a result of manufacturing a main product, that can be sold for profit

C

CA *abbr* ACCOUNTING **1.** ***chartered accountant*** **2.** ***certified accountant***

C/A *abbr* FINANCE ***capital account***

c/a *abbr* BANKING ***checking account***

cable CURRENCY & EXCHANGE exchange rate between US dollar and pound a spot exchange rate between the US dollar and the pound sterling

CAC 40 MARKETS French stock market index of 40 top stocks an index of prices on the Paris Stock Exchange, based on the prices of the 40 leading stocks

CAD *abbr* OPERATIONS & PRODUCTION ***computer-aided design***

cafeteria plan *or* **cafeteria employee benefit plan** HR & PERSONNEL US employee benefit plan allowing choice of benefits in the United States, an employee benefit plan that allows employees to select a number of benefits such as contributions to a retirement plan, insurance, or cash to pay for medical expenses not covered by insurance, all or some of which may be exempt from payroll tax. *Also called* ***flexible benefit plan***

cage *US* MARKETS department of brokerage firm handling paperwork the part of a brokerage firm where the paperwork involved in the buying and selling of stocks is processed *(slang)*

calendar spread STOCKHOLDING & INVESTMENTS, RISK = ***horizontal spread***

calendar variance ACCOUNTING accounting difference from calendar months versus working days a variance that occurs if a company uses calendar months for the financial accounts but uses the number of actual working days to calculate overhead expenses in the cost accounts

calendar year January 1 to December 31 a year between the calendar dates January 1 and December 31

call STOCKHOLDING & INVESTMENTS **1.** option to buy stock an ***option*** to buy stock at an agreed price or before a particular date. Also called ***call option*** **2.** demand for agreed partial payment of share capital a request made to the holders of partly paid-up share capital for the payment of a predetermined sum due on the share capital, under the terms of the original subscription agreement. Failure on the part of the stockholder to pay a call may result in the forfeiture of the relevant holding of partly paid shares. *Also called* ***call up***

callable STOCKHOLDING & INVESTMENTS able to be repurchased before maturity used to describe a security that the issuer has the right to buy back before its maturity date. *See also* ***noncallable***

callable bond STOCKHOLDING & INVESTMENTS bond able to be bought back a bond that may be bought back by the issuer prior to its maturity date

callable capital FINANCE capital from unpaid sale of stock the part of a company's capital from the sale of stock for which the company has not yet received payment

callable preferred stock *US* STOCKHOLDING & INVESTMENTS = ***redeemable preferred stock***

call center GENERAL MANAGEMENT department or business providing information by telephone a department or business wholly focused on telephone inquiries. Call centers usually provide a centralized point of contact for an organization and support telemarketing, after-sales service, telephone helplines, or information services, either for a parent organization or on a contract basis for other businesses.

call date STOCKHOLDING & INVESTMENTS pre-maturity deadline for repurchase of bond the date before maturity on which the issuer of a ***callable bond*** has the right to buy it back

called-up share capital STOCKHOLDING & INVESTMENTS stock not paid for by stockholders the proportion of the of stock issued by a company that has not yet been paid for. *See also* ***fully paid share capital***

call in BANKING request payment of debt to ask for a debt to be paid at once

call loan BANKING bank loan repayable on demand a bank loan that must be repaid as soon as repayment is requested

call option STOCKHOLDING & INVESTMENTS = ***call*** *(sense 1)*

call payment STOCKHOLDING & INVESTMENTS sum in partial payment for stock an amount that a company demands in partial payment for stock such as a rights issue that is not paid for at one time

call price STOCKHOLDING & INVESTMENTS early redemption cost of US bond a price to be paid by an issuer for the early redemption of a US bond

call provision STOCKHOLDING & INVESTMENTS clause allowing bond to be redeemed early a clause in an ***indenture*** that lets the issuer of a bond redeem it before the date of its maturity

call purchase FINANCE purchase where either party can establish price a transaction where either the seller or purchaser can fix the price for future delivery

call risk STOCKHOLDING & INVESTMENTS, RISK risk of premature repurchase of bond the possibility that the issuer of a ***callable bond*** will buy back the bond and the bondholder will be forced to reinvest at a lower interest rate

call rule MARKETS fixing of commodity price at end of trading a commodities exchange rule whereby the price of a commodity is fixed at the end of a day's trading and remains valid until the next trading day begins

calls in arrears STOCKHOLDING & INVESTMENTS outstanding money for shares money called up for shares, but not paid at the correct time. The shares may be forfeited or a special calls in arrears account is established to debit the sums owing.

call up STOCKHOLDING & INVESTMENTS = ***call*** *(sense 2)*

CAM *abbr* OPERATIONS & PRODUCTION ***computer-aided manufacturing***

campaign MARKETING advertising and marketing plan a program of advertising and marketing activities with a specific objective

Canadian Institute of Chartered Accountants ACCOUNTING main professional body for accountants in Canada, the principal professional accountancy body that is responsible for setting accounting standards. *Abbr* ***CICA***

cancellation price STOCKHOLDING & INVESTMENTS price at which mutual fund will redeem securities the lowest value possible in any one day of a mutual fund. In the United Kingdom, it is regulated by the Financial Services Authority.

cap FINANCE upper limit an upper limit such as on a rate of interest for a loan

CAPA *abbr* ACCOUNTING ***Confederation of Asian and Pacific Accountants***

capacity OPERATIONS & PRODUCTION measure of production capability the measure of the capability of a workstation or a plant to produce output. Capacity measures can focus on a variety of factors, which typically include quantity (the number of items produced over a given period) and scope (the range of items produced by type or size).

capacity planning OPERATIONS & PRODUCTION estimation of organization's requirements to meet workload the process of measuring the amount of work that can be completed within a given time and determining the necessary physical and human resources needed to accomplish it. Capacity planning uses ***capacity utilization*** to ensure that the maximum amount of product is made and sold. The planning involves a regulation process that identifies deviations from the plan, allowing corrective action to be taken. A ***capacity requirements planning*** program can aid in the process of capacity planning.

capacity requirements planning OPERATIONS & PRODUCTION computerized system for planning resource requirements a computerized tracking process that translates production requirements into practical implications for manufacturing resources. Capacity requirements planning is part of manufacturing resource planning and is carried out after a manufacturing resource planning program has been run. This produces an *infinite capacity plan,* as it does not take account of the capacity constraints of each workstation. Where the process is extended to cover capacity requirements, a *finite capacity plan* is produced. This enables loading at each workstation to be smoothed and determines the need for additional resources.

capacity usage variance FINANCE difference in result caused by working hours the difference in gain or loss in a given period compared to budgeted expectations, caused because the hours worked were longer or shorter than planned

capacity utilization **1.** OPERATIONS & PRODUCTION measure of equipment actually used for production a measure of the plant and equipment of a company or an industry that is actually being used to produce goods or services. Capacity utilization is usually measured over a specific period of time, for example, the average for a month, or at a given point in time. It can be expressed as a ratio, where utilization = actual output divided by design capacity. This measure is used in both ***capacity planning*** and ***capacity requirements planning*** processes. **2.** ECONOMICS degree of production capability being used the output of an economy, firm, or plant divided by its output when working at full capacity

Caparo case ACCOUNTING English ruling on auditors' responsibilities in England, a court decision made by the House of Lords in 1990 that auditors owe a duty of care to present, not prospective, stockholders as a body but not as individuals

CAPEX *abbr* ACCOUNTING ***capital expenditure***

capital FINANCE investment money money that is available to be invested by a person, business, or organization in order to make a profit

capital account FINANCE firm's total capital the sum of a company's capital at a specific time. *Abbr* ***C/A***

capital adequacy ratio FINANCE percentage of bank's assets represented by capital an amount of money which a bank has to hold in the form of stockholders' equity, shown as a proportion of its risk-weighted assets, agreed internationally not to fall below 8%. *Abbr* ***CAR***. *Also called* ***capital to risk-weighted assets ratio***

capital allowance TAX tax allowance for new plant and machinery in the United Kingdom and Ireland, an allowance against income or corporation tax available to businesses or sole traders who have purchased plant and machinery for business use. The rates are set annually and vary according to the type of fixed asset purchased, for example, whether it is machinery or buildings. This system effectively removes subjectivity from the calculation of depreciation for tax purposes.

capital appreciation FINANCE increase in wealth the increase in a company's or individual's wealth at market values

capital appreciation fund STOCKHOLDING & INVESTMENTS mutual fund concentrating on capital not income a mutual fund that aims to increase the value of its holdings without regard to the provision of income to its owners

capital asset ACCOUNTING real estate owned but not traded real estate that a company owns and uses but that the company does not buy or sell as part of its regular trade

capital asset pricing model STOCKHOLDING & INVESTMENTS theory about relationship between cost and expected return a model of the market used to assess the cost of capital for a company based on the rate of return on its assets.

The capital asset pricing model holds that the expected return on a security or portfolio equals the rate on a risk-free security plus a risk premium. If this expected return does not meet or beat a theoretical required return, the investment should not be undertaken. The formula used for the model is:

Risk-free rate + (Market return – Risk-free rate) × Beta value = Expected return

The risk-free rate is the quoted rate on an asset that has virtually no risk. In practice, it is the rate quoted for 90-day US Treasury bills. The market return is the percentage return expected of the overall market, typically a published index such as Standard & Poor's. The beta value is a figure that measures the volatility of a security or portfolio of securities compared with the market as a whole. A beta of 1, for example, indicates that a security's price will move with the market. A beta greater than 1 indicates higher volatility, while a beta less than 1 indicates less volatility.

Say, for instance, that the current risk-free rate is 4%, and the S&P 500 index is expected to return 11% next year. An investment club is interested in determining next year's return for XYZ Software, a prospective investment. The club has determined that the company's beta value is 1.8. The overall stock market always has a beta of 1, so XYZ Software's beta of 1.8 signals that it is a more risky investment than the overall market represents. This added risk means that the club should expect a higher rate of return than the 11% for the S&P 500. The CAPM calculation, then, would be:

4% + (11% – 4%) × 1.8 = 16.6% expected return

What the results tell the club is that, given the risk, XYZ Software, has a required rate of return of 16.6%, or the minimum return that an investment in XYZ should generate. If the investment club does not think that XYZ will produce that kind of return, it should probably consider investing in a different company. *Abbr* ***CAPM***

capital base FINANCE funding structure as basis of firm's worth the funding structure of a company (***stockholders' equity*** plus loans and retained profits) used as a way of assessing the company's worth

capital bonus INSURANCE extra payment arising from capital gain a bonus payment by an insurance company that is produced by ***capital gain***

capital budget ACCOUNTING part of firm's budget concerned with capital expenditure a subsection of a company's master budget that deals with expected capital expenditure within a defined period. Also called ***capital expenditure budget***, ***capital investment budget***

capital budgeting TREASURY MANAGEMENT preparing budget for capital expenditure the process concerned with decision making with respect to the following issues: the choice of specific investment projects, the total amount of ***capital expenditure*** to commit, and the method of financing the investment portfolio

capital buffer FINANCE sufficient capital to counter risk the amount of capital a financial institution needs to hold above minimum requirements, calculated on an assessment of forecast risk

capital commitments ACCOUNTING authorized but unspent capital expenditure expenditure on assets which has been authorized by directors, but not yet spent at the end of a financial period

capital consumption FINANCE depreciation of fixed assets in a given period, the total depreciation of the fixed assets of a company or national economy, based on replacement costs

capital controls REGULATION & COMPLIANCE government restrictions on asset ownership regulations placed by a government on the amount of capital people may hold. Sometimes there are restrictions only on share ownership, at other times on bank accounts; also controls may apply to non-residents as well as residents.

capital cost allowance TAX Canadian tax benefit for capital depreciation in Canada, a tax advantage given for the depreciation in value of ***capital assets***

capital costs ACCOUNTING expenses on buying fixed assets expenses associated with the purchase of fixed assets such as land, buildings, and machinery

capital deepening ECONOMICS increase in country's capital-to-labor ratio the process whereby capital increases but the number of employed people falls or remains constant

capital employed FINANCE stockholders' funds plus long-term loans an amount of ***capital*** consisting of ***stockholders' equity*** plus the long-term loans taken out by a business. *See also* ***return on assets***

capital equipment ACCOUNTING equipment used for everyday operations the equipment that a factory or office uses in operating its business

capital expenditure ACCOUNTING spending on fixed assets the cost of acquiring, producing, or enhancing fixed assets such as land, buildings, and machinery. *Abbr* ***CAPEX***. *Also called* ***capital investment***

capital expenditure budget ACCOUNTING = ***capital budget***

capital expenditure proposal ACCOUNTING application for capital expenditure a formal request for authority to undertake ***capital expenditure***. This is usually supported by the case for expenditure in accordance with capital investment appraisal criteria. Levels of authority must be clearly defined and the reporting structure of actual expenditure must be to the equivalent authority level.

capital flight STOCKHOLDING & INVESTMENTS withdrawal of investments from country the transfer of large sums of money between countries to seek higher rates of return or to escape a political or economic disturbance

capital flow STOCKHOLDING & INVESTMENTS international movement of money the movement of investments from one country to another. *Also called* ***capital movement***

capital formation STOCKHOLDING & INVESTMENTS adding to capital by investment the creation of long-term assets, such as long-dated bonds or shares

capital funding planning TREASURY MANAGEMENT determining of means to finance capital expenditure the process of selecting suitable funds to finance long-term assets and ***working capital***

capital gain ACCOUNTING money made from disposing of asset the financial gain made upon the disposal of an asset. The gain is the difference between the cost of its acquisition and the net proceeds upon its sale.

capital gains distribution STOCKHOLDING & INVESTMENTS allocation of capital gains to investors a sum of money that a body such as a mutual fund pays to its owners in proportion to the owners' share of the organization's capital gains for the year

capital gains expenses ACCOUNTING cost of buying or selling assets expenses incurred in buying or selling assets, which can be deducted when calculating a capital gain or loss

capital gains reserve TAX Canadian tax benefit for customers' unpaid bills in Canada, a tax advantage given for money not yet received in payment for something that has been sold

capital gains tax TAX tax on difference between buying and selling price a tax on the difference between the gross acquisition cost and the net proceeds when an asset is sold. *Abbr* ***CGT***

capital gearing STOCKHOLDING & INVESTMENTS firm's debt per share the amount of debt of all kinds that a company has for each share of its common stock

capital goods ECONOMICS assets used for producing other goods physical assets that are used in the production of other goods

capital growth FINANCE increase in value of assets an increase in the value of assets in a fund, or of the value of stock

capital inflow FINANCE money entering country from services overseas the amount of capital that flows into an economy from services rendered abroad

capital instrument FINANCE means of raising money a security such as stocks or ***debentures*** that a business uses to raise finance

capital-intensive FINANCE requiring money rather than labor used to describe economic activities that primarily require a high proportion of ***capital*** as opposed to needing labor. *See also* ***labor-intensive***

capital investment ACCOUNTING = ***capital expenditure***

capital investment budget ACCOUNTING = ***capital budget***

capitalism ECONOMICS economic system where citizens own means of production an economic and social system in which individuals can maximize profits because they own the means of production

capitalist FINANCE investor in business a person who invests ***capital*** in trade and industry, for profit

capitalist economy ECONOMICS economy giving great commercial and financial freedom an economy in which each person has the right to invest money, to work in business, and to buy and sell products and services, without major government restrictions

capitalization **1.** FINANCE raising funds through stock split the conversion of a company's reserves into ***capital*** through a stock split **2.** STOCKHOLDING & INVESTMENTS amount invested in firm the amount of money that is invested in a company **3.** STOCKHOLDING & INVESTMENTS firm's worth the worth of the bonds and stocks issued by a company

capitalization issue *UK* STOCKHOLDING & INVESTMENTS = ***stock split***

capitalization rate FINANCE rate of raising capital through stock split the rate at which a company's ***reserves*** are converted into ***capital*** by way of a ***stock split***

capitalization ratio FINANCE proportion of firm's value in capital the proportion of a company's value represented by debt, stock, assets, and other items.

By comparing debt to total capitalization, these ratios provide a glimpse of a company's long-term stability and ability to withstand losses and business downturns.

A company's capitalization ratio can be expressed in two ways:

= Long-term debt / (Long-term debt + Owners' equity)

and

= Total debt / (Total debt + Preferred + Common equity)

For example, a company whose long-term debt totals $5,000 and whose owners hold equity worth $3,000 would have a capitalization ratio of:

5,000 / (5,000 + 3,000) = 5,000 / 8,000 = 0.625

Both expressions of the ratio are also referred to as ***component percentages***, since they compare a firm's debt with either its total capital (debt plus equity) or its equity capital. They readily indicate how reliant a firm is on debt financing. Capitalization ratios need to be evaluated over time, and compared with other data and standards. Care should be taken when comparing companies in different industries or sectors. The same figures that appear to be low in one industry can be very high in another.

capitalize **1.** FINANCE invest money in business to provide investment money for a business, in expectation of making a profit **2.** ACCOUNTING enter cost of asset in balance sheet to include money spent on the purchase of an ***asset*** as an element in a ***balance sheet***

capital lease *US* REAL ESTATE lease treated as though leased assets were purchased a lease that is treated as though the lessee had borrowed money and bought the leased assets.

If a lease agreement does not meet any of the criteria below, the lessee treats it as an ***operating lease*** for accounting purposes. If, however, the agreement meets one of the following criteria, it is treated as a capital lease: (i) The lease agreement transfers ownership of the assets to the lessee during the term of the lease. (ii) The lessee can purchase the assets leased at a bargain price (also called a bargain purchase option), such as $1, at the end of the lease term. (iii) The lease term is at least 75% of the economic life of the leased asset. (iv) The present value of the minimum lease payments is 90% or greater of the asset's value.

Capital leases are reported by the lessee as if the assets being leased were acquired and the monthly rental payments as if they were payments of principal and interest on a debt obligation. Specifically, the lessee capitalizes the lease by recognizing an asset and a liability at the lower of the present value of the minimum lease payments or the value of the assets under lease. As the monthly rental payments are made, the corresponding liability decreases. At the same time, the leased asset is depreciated in a manner that is consistent with other owned assets having the same use and economic life. *UK term* ***finance lease***

capital levy TAX tax on fixed assets a tax on fixed assets or property, rather than income. Capital levies are usually collected only once.

capital loss ACCOUNTING loss on sale of fixed asset a loss made through selling a ***capital asset*** for less than its market price

capital maintenance concept ACCOUNTING principle underpinning inflation accounting a concept used to determine the definition of profit, which provides the basis for different systems of ***inflation accounting***

capital market MARKETS market for longer-term securities a financial market dealing with securities that have a life of more than one year

capital movement STOCKHOLDING & INVESTMENTS = ***capital flow***

capital outlay ACCOUNTING = ***capital expenditure***

capital profit ACCOUNTING profit from sale of asset a profit that a company makes by selling a ***capital asset***

capital project OPERATIONS & PRODUCTION project requiring capital investment a project that involves expenditure of an organization's monetary resources for the purpose of creating capacity for production. Capital projects are usually large scale, complex, need to be completed quickly, and involve ***capital expenditure***. *See also* ***capital project management***

capital project management GENERAL MANAGEMENT control of project requiring capital expenditure control of a project that involves expenditure of an organization's monetary resources for the purpose of creating capacity for production. Capital project management often involves the organization of major construction or engineering work. Different techniques have evolved for capital project management from those used for normal ***project management***, including methods for managing the complexity of such projects and for analyzing return on investment afterward.

capital property ACCOUNTING, TAX type of asset under Canadian tax law under Canadian tax law, assets that can depreciate in value or be sold for a capital gain or loss

capital ratio ACCOUNTING firm's income as fraction of fixed assets a company's income expressed as a fraction of its ***tangible assets***. These assets include leases and company stock, as well as physical assets such as land, buildings, and machinery.

capital rationing FINANCE **1.** firm's limiting of new investment the restriction of new investment by a company because of a shortfall in its capital budget **2.** imposition of limit on capital expenditure a restriction on an organization's ability to invest capital funds, caused by an internal budget ceiling being imposed by management *(soft capital rationing)*, or by external limitations being applied to the company, as when additional borrowed funds cannot be obtained *(hard capital rationing)*

capital reconstruction MERGERS & ACQUISITIONS closing down then reconstituting firm the act of placing a company into voluntary liquidation and then selling its assets to another company with the same name and same stockholders, but with a larger capital base

capital redemption reserve ACCOUNTING in UK, firm's account underpinning trade in own stock in the United Kingdom, an account required by law to prevent a reduction in capital, where a company purchases or redeems its own stock out of ***distributable profits***

capital reduction FINANCE withdrawal of capital funds the ***retirement*** or redemption of capital funds by a company

capital reorganization STOCKHOLDING & INVESTMENTS restructuring firm's share holdings the act of changing the capital structure of a company by amalgamating or dividing existing shares to form shares of a higher or lower nominal value

capital reserves FINANCE **1.** *UK* funds unavailable for dividend payments reserves not legally available for distribution to stockholders as dividends according to the Companies Act (1985) **2.** *US* funds for future investment money that a company holds in reserve for future investment or expense

capital resource planning TREASURY MANAGEMENT assessing assets for strategic purposes the process of evaluating and selecting long-term assets to meet established strategies

capital shares STOCKHOLDING & INVESTMENTS shares with increasing value but no income shares in a mutual fund that rise in value as the capital value of the individual stocks rises, but do not receive any income

capital stock STOCKHOLDING & INVESTMENTS stock authorized by US firm's charter in the United States, the stock authorized by a company's charter, including ***common stock*** and ***preferred stock***. *See also* ***share capital***

capital structure ACCOUNTING relationship of equity capital and debt capital the relative proportions of ***equity capital*** and ***debt capital*** in a company's ***balance sheet***

capital sum INSURANCE lump sum from insurance an amount of money that an insurer pays as a ***lump sum*** on the death of an insured person or some other agreed occurrence

capital surplus STOCKHOLDING & INVESTMENTS difference between current and nominal value of stock the value of all of the stock in a company that exceeds the ***nominal value*** of the stock

capital tax TAX tax on firm's capital a tax levied on the capital owned by a company, rather than on its spending. *See also* ***capital gains tax***

capital-to-asset ratio *or* **capital/asset ratio** FINANCE = ***capital adequacy ratio***

capital to risk-weighted assets ratio FINANCE = ***capital adequacy ratio***

capital transaction FINANCE transaction bearing on non-current items a transaction affecting non-current items such as fixed assets, long-term debt, or share capital, rather than revenue transactions

capital transfer tax TAX former UK tax on asset transfers in the United Kingdom, a tax on the transfer of assets, which was replaced in 1986 by inheritance tax

capital turnover FINANCE annual sales in relation to stock value the value of annual sales as a multiple of the value of a company's stock

capital widening ECONOMICS increase in country's capital per person employed the process whereby capital is increased as a result of an increase in the number of people being employed

CAPM *abbr* **1.** OPERATIONS & PRODUCTION ***computer-aided production management*** **2.** STOCKHOLDING & INVESTMENTS ***capital asset pricing model***

capped floating rate note FINANCE floating rate note with limited interest rate a ***floating-rate note*** that has an agreed maximum rate of interest

capped rate FINANCE variable interest rate with upper limit an interest rate on a loan that may change, but cannot be greater than an amount fixed at the time when the loan is taken out by a borrower

captive finance company FINANCE provider of credit for customers of parent company an organization that provides credit and is owned or controlled by a commercial or manufacturing company, for example, a retailer that owns its store card operation or a car manufacturer that owns a company for financing the vehicles it produces

captive insurance company INSURANCE provider of insurance for customers of parent company an insurance company that has been established by a parent company to underwrite all its insurance risks and those of its subsidiaries. The benefit is that the premiums paid do not leave the organization. Many captive insurance companies are established offshore for tax purposes.

captive market MARKETS market with one supplier operating monopoly a market in which one supplier has a monopoly and the buyer has no choice over the product that he or she must purchase

capture E-COMMERCE transfer of funds in credit card transaction the submission of a credit card transaction for processing and settlement. Capture initiates the process of moving funds from the ***issuer*** to the ***acquirer***.

CAR *abbr* FINANCE ***capital adequacy ratio***

cardholder BANKING named user of credit card an individual or company that has an active credit card account with an ***issuer*** with which transactions can be initiated

card-issuing bank BANKING = ***issuer***

card-not-present merchant account E-COMMERCE account permitting online processing of credit card transactions an account that permits e-merchants to process credit card transactions without the purchaser being physically present for the transaction

cards ◇ get your cards *UK* HR & PERSONNEL = ***get your pink slip*** (*informal*)

careline MARKETING customer assistance telephone service a telephone service allowing customers to obtain information, advice, or assistance from retailers

caring economy ECONOMICS friendly relationships between firms and individuals an economy based on amicable and helpful relationships between businesses and people

carriage free *UK* OPERATIONS & PRODUCTION sent without charge to customer sent without making a charge to the customer for shipping

carriage inward OPERATIONS & PRODUCTION cost of having purchase delivered delivery expenses incurred through the purchase of goods. These may be separately itemized in financial statements.

carriage outward OPERATIONS & PRODUCTION cost of delivering purchase delivery expenses incurred through the sale of goods. These may be separately itemized in financial statements.

carriage paid *UK* OPERATIONS & PRODUCTION with shipping charge paid by seller sent by a seller who has paid for the shipping

carried interest FINANCE profit paid to private equity partners the profit that partners in a private equity enterprise receive for the services they provide

carrier OPERATIONS & PRODUCTION provider of network services to customers a telecommunications company that provides network infrastructure services and charges customers for carrying their communications over the network. Carriers do not necessarily own their own network, but may rent time on a number of networks.

carry FINANCE = ***carrying charge***

carry forward ACCOUNTING use as opening balance for next accounting period to use an account balance at the end of the current period or page as the starting point for the next period or page

carrying amount STOCKHOLDING & INVESTMENTS = ***book value*** *(sense 2)*

carrying charge FINANCE interest paid on money borrowed the interest expense on money borrowed to finance a purchase. *Also called* ***carry***

carrying cost OPERATIONS & PRODUCTION cost of temporarily holding stock any expense associated with holding stock for a given period, for example, from the time of delivery to the time of dispatch. Carrying costs will include storage and insurance.

carrying value STOCKHOLDING & INVESTMENTS = ***book value*** *(sense 2)*

carryover *or* STOCKHOLDING & INVESTMENTS amount of commodity at beginning of fiscal year the amount of a commodity that is being held at the beginning of a new fiscal year, to be added to the next year's supply. The amount of carryover may have an impact on price.

carryover day MARKETS new account's first day on London Stock Exchange the first day of trading on a new account on the London Stock Exchange

carry trade MARKETS, CURRENCY & EXCHANGE borrowings in one currency purchasing assets in another the practice of borrowing at low interest rates in one currency and using the loan to buy assets offering higher yields in another country

cartel BUSINESS association to regulate competition an alliance of business companies formed to control production, competition, and prices

cartogram STATISTICS map showing statistical data a diagrammatic map on which statistical information is represented by shading and symbols

carve-out STOCKHOLDING & INVESTMENTS = ***equity carve-out***

cash BANKING **1.** exchange check for cash to present a check and receive banknotes and coins in return **2.** banknotes and coins money in the form of banknotes and coins that are legal tender. This includes cash in hand, deposits repayable on demand with any bank or other financial institution, and deposits denominated in foreign currencies.

cash account **1.** ACCOUNTING record of money transactions a record of receipts and payments of cash, checks, or other forms of money transfer **2.** STOCKHOLDING & INVESTMENTS type of brokerage account an account with a broker that does not allow ***buying on margin***

cash accounting **1.** ACCOUNTING recording money transactions as they occur an accounting method in which receipts and expenses are recorded in the period when they actually occur. See also accrual basis **2.** TAX UK system giving automatic VAT relief on debts in the United Kingdom, a system for ***value-added tax*** that enables the taxpayer to account for tax paid and received during a given period, thus allowing automatic relief for bad debts

cash advance BANKING **1.** loan of cash against future payment a loan given in cash as early part payment of a larger sum to be received in the future **2.** loan on credit card a sum of money taken as a loan on a credit card account

cash at bank BANKING money in bank accounts the total amount of money held at the bank by a person or company

cash available to invest STOCKHOLDING & INVESTMENTS total amount available for investment with broker the amount, including cash on account and balances due soon for outstanding transactions, that a client has available for investment with a broker

cashback FINANCE **1.** giving purchaser cash refund a sales promotion technique offering customers a cash refund after they buy a product **2.** service allowing debit card payment to include cash a facility that allows consumers who pay for items by debit card in a supermarket or some other stores to add a small amount of money to the amount of their purchase and receive that amount in cash

cash balance ACCOUNTING account balance representing held cash only an account balance that represents cash alone, as distinct from an account balance that includes money owed but as yet unpaid

cash basis ACCOUNTING recording money in account only for actual transactions the bookkeeping practice of accounting for money only when it is actually received or spent

cash bonus STOCKHOLDING & INVESTMENTS extra dividend payment an unscheduled dividend that a company declares because of unexpected income

cashbook ACCOUNTING account book for cash transactions a book in which all cash payments and receipts are recorded. In a double-entry bookkeeping system, the balance at the end of a given period is included in the trial balance and then transferred to the balance sheet itself.

cash budget TREASURY MANAGEMENT estimate of cash transactions a detailed budget of estimated cash inflows and outflows incorporating both revenue and capital items. *Also called **cash flow projection***

cash burn FINANCE = ***burn rate***

cash card *UK* BANKING = ***ATM card***

cash contract OPERATIONS & PRODUCTION contract for delivery of product a contract for actual delivery of a commodity, by which the seller receives the ***spot price*** on the day of delivery

cash conversion cycle ACCOUNTING period between buying materials and selling product the time between the acquisition of a raw material and the receipt of payment for the finished product. *Also called **cash cycle***

cash cow **1.** FINANCE mature product generating cash a product characterized by a high market share but low sales growth, whose function is seen as generating cash for use elsewhere within the organization **2.** MARKETING very profitable product requiring little investment a product that sells well and makes a substantial profit without requiring much advertising or investment (*slang*) **3.** GENERAL MANAGEMENT slow-growing firm with high market share in the ***Boston Box*** model, a business with a high market share with low growth rate, which could yield significant but short-term gain. *See also **Boston Box***

cash crop ECONOMICS plants grown in quantity and sold for cash a crop such as tobacco, that is typically sold for cash rather than used by the producer

cash cycle ACCOUNTING = ***cash conversion cycle***

cash deficiency agreement FINANCE agreement to supply cash shortfall a commitment to supply whatever additional cash is needed to complete the financing of a project

cash discount FINANCE discount for paying promptly or in cash a discount offered to a customer who pays for goods or services with cash, or who pays an invoice within a particular period

cash dispenser *UK* BANKING = ***ATM***

cash dividend STOCKHOLDING & INVESTMENTS dividend in cash not shares a share of a company's current earnings or accumulated profits distributed to stockholders in cash, not in the form of ***bonus shares***

cash economy ECONOMICS sector of economy avoiding tax an unofficial or illegal part of the economy, where goods and services are paid for in cash, and therefore not declared for tax

cash equivalents STOCKHOLDING & INVESTMENTS investments convertible into cash immediately short-term investments that can be converted into cash immediately and that are subject to only a limited risk. There is usually a limit on their duration, for example, three months.

cash float FINANCE banknotes and coins for giving change banknotes and coins held by a retailer for the purpose of supplying customers with change

cash flow ACCOUNTING money from sales the movement through an organization of money that is generated by its own operations, as opposed to borrowing. It is the money that a business actually receives from sales (the cash inflow) and the money that it pays out (the cash outflow).

cash flow accounting ACCOUNTING accounting that considers only cash receipts and payments the practice of measuring the financial activities of a company in terms of cash receipts and payments, without recording ***accruals***, advance payments, debtors, creditors, and stocks

cash flow coverage ratio ACCOUNTING ratio of cash received and required the ratio of income to outstanding obligations which must be paid in cash

cash flow forecast TREASURY MANAGEMENT estimate of money coming in and going out a prediction of the amount of money that will move through an organization. This is an important tool for monitoring its solvency. *See also* ***cash budget***

cash flow life HR & PERSONNEL lifestyle dependent on income from project fees a lifestyle characterized by working for individual project fees rather than a regular salary

cash flow per common share STOCKHOLDING & INVESTMENTS cash generated for each share of common stock the amount of cash that a company derives from its activities, less any dividends paid, for each share of its common stock

cash flow projection TREASURY MANAGEMENT = ***cash budget***

cash flow risk RISK danger of receiving less cash than required the risk that a company's available cash will not be sufficient to meet its financial obligations

cash flow statement ACCOUNTING account of cash transactions a record of a company's cash inflows and cash outflows over a specific period of time, typically a year.

It reports funds on hand at the beginning of the period, funds received, funds spent, and funds remaining at the end of the period. Cash flows are divided into three categories: cash from operations; cash investment activities; and cash-financing activities. Companies with holdings in foreign currencies use a fourth classification: effects of changes in currency rates on cash.

cash fraction STOCKHOLDING & INVESTMENTS cash sum for allocation of part of share a small amount of cash paid to a stockholder to make up the full amount of part of a share which has been allocated in a ***stock split***

cash-generating unit FINANCE smallest set of assets involved in cash transactions the smallest identifiable group of assets generating cash inflows and outflows that can be measured

cash hoard FINANCE, MERGERS & ACQUISITIONS = ***cash reserves*** *(informal)*

cashier *UK* BANKING = ***teller***

cashier's check BANKING check drawn by bank on itself a bank's own check, drawn on itself and signed by the cashier or other bank official

cash in STOCKHOLDING & INVESTMENTS sell investments for cash to sell stock or other property for cash

cash in hand FINANCE, ACCOUNTING available money money that is held in coins and banknotes, not in a bank account

cashless pay HR & PERSONNEL payment directly into bank account the payment of a weekly or monthly wage through the electronic transfer of funds directly into the bank account of an employee

cashless society ECONOMICS community in which all payments are electronic a society in which all bills and debits are paid by electronic money media such as bank and credit cards, direct debits, and online payments

cash limit **1.** FINANCE fixed sum available to spend a fixed amount of money that can be spent during a specific period or on a specific project **2.** BANKING limit on single ATM withdrawal a maximum amount somebody can withdraw at one time from an ATM using an ATM card

cash loan company FINANCE S. African provider of unsecured short-term loans in South Africa, a ***microcredit*** business that provides short-term loans without collateral, usually at high interest rates

cash machine *UK* BANKING = ***ATM***

cash management OPERATIONS & PRODUCTION strategy for having cash available to produce income a strategy used by businesses to manage their cash flow in order to have more cash available for short-term investment. The strategy would include such things as accelerating cash receipts, prioritizing cash disbursements, and maintaining a cash balance to cover emergencies.

cash market MARKETS securities market based on immediate payment the market in ***gilt-edged securities*** where purchases are paid for almost as soon as they are made

cash offer FINANCE **1.** offer to buy firm for cash an offer to buy a company for cash rather than for stock **2.** offer of cash payment an offer to pay for something in cash

cash payments journal BANKING chronological record of payments from firm's bank account a chronological record of all the money paid out from a company's bank account

cashpoint *UK* BANKING = ***ATM***

cash position 1. ACCOUNTING amount of cash currently available to firm a statement of the amount of cash that a company currently has available to spend **2.** STOCKHOLDING & INVESTMENTS holdings in short-term debt the extent to which a portfolio of assets includes short-term debt securities

cash price FINANCE **1.** better deal offered to customer paying cash a lower price or better terms that apply to a sale if the customer pays cash rather than using credit **2.** = ***spot price***

cash ratio FINANCE liquid assets divided by total liabilities the ratio of a company's liquid assets such as cash and securities divided by total liabilities. *Also called* ***liquidity ratio***

cash receipts journal BANKING chronological record of deposits into firm's bank account a chronological record of all the receipts that have been paid into a company's bank account

cash reserves FINANCE, MERGERS & ACQUISITIONS available cash a large amount of cash that a company holds in order to facilitate an expected project. Cash reserves are often attractive to a company looking to make an acquisition. *Also called* ***cash hoard***

cash sale FINANCE sale paid for in cash a sale in which payment is made immediately in cash rather than put on credit

cash settlement STOCKHOLDING & INVESTMENTS **1.** early payment on options contract an immediate payment on an options contract without waiting for expiration of the normal, usually five-day, settlement period **2.** paying for securities bought the completion of a transaction by paying for securities, rather than physical delivery of them

cash surrender value INSURANCE sum received on cancellation of insurance policy the amount of money that an insurance company will pay to terminate a policy at a specific time if the policy does not continue until its normal expiration date

cash transaction FINANCE dealing involving cash payment a transaction in which the method of payment is cash, as distinct from a transaction paid for by means of a transfer of a ***financial instrument***

cash voucher FINANCE document exchangeable for cash a piece of paper that can be exchanged for cash

casino banking BANKING bank taking large investment risks a bank that is regarded as pursuing an unreasonably high-risk investment strategy

casino banking BANKING high-risk investment practices by banks the activity of pursuing a high-risk investment strategy for profit rather than providing a balanced range of banking services

casino capitalism FINANCE high-risk financial dealings a global phenomenon of increased financial risk-taking and instability, as an outcome of financial markets becoming very large and introducing many new investment products, and financial institutions being self-regulated, among other factors

casual worker HR & PERSONNEL worker who is not regular employee somebody who provides labor or services under an irregular or informal working arrangement. A casual worker is usually considered as an independent contractor rather than as an employee. Consequently, there is no obligation on the part of an employer to provide work, and there is no obligation on the part of the casual worker to accept all offers of work made by an employer.

catastrophe bond STOCKHOLDING & INVESTMENTS bond with lower value in event of disaster a bond with a very high interest rate which may be worth less or give a lower rate of interest if a disaster occurs, whether it be natural or otherwise

catastrophe future STOCKHOLDING & INVESTMENTS, RISK futures contract covering insurance losses from catastrophes a futures contract used by insurers to hedge their risk for low-probability catastrophic losses due to natural causes

catastrophe swap STOCKHOLDING & INVESTMENTS, RISK option contract covering insurance losses from catastrophes an option contract in which an investor exchanges a fixed periodic payment for part of the difference between an insurance company's premiums and its losses caused by claims due to a catastrophe

catch-up contribution PENSIONS extra payment to US pension in the United States, an additional contribution that somebody over the age of 50 is allowed to contribute to a personal retirement plan such as a ***401(k) plan*** or an ***IRA***

category killer BUSINESS large business destroying competition a major organization that puts out of business smaller or more specialized companies in a given field by offering goods or services at a lower price, or by using its brand to attract more consumer interest (*slang*)

category management MARKETING product development involving both manufacturers and retailers the process of manufacturers and retailers working together to maximize profits and enhance customer value in any given product category. Category management has developed from ***brand management*** and the techniques of efficient consumer response, and is most prevalent in the fast moving consumer goods sector. It is founded on the assumption that consumer purchase decisions are made from a variety of products within a category and not merely by brand. It has gained in prominence, as it is believed to meet customer needs better than standard brand management. *Abbr* ***CM***

cats and dogs *US* STOCKHOLDING & INVESTMENTS stocks with doubtful origins speculative stocks with dubious sales histories (*slang*)

cause and effect diagram GENERAL MANAGEMENT **1.** aid to identifying causes of variation a diagram that aids the generation and sorting of the potential causes of variation in an activity or process **2.** = ***fishbone chart***

caveat emptor BUSINESS buyer should check condition of goods purchased a Latin phrase meaning "let the buyer beware," which indicates that the buyer is responsible for checking that what he or she buys is in good condition

CBI *abbr* BUSINESS ***Confederation of British Industry***

CBO *abbr* STOCKHOLDING & INVESTMENTS, RISK ***collateralized bond obligation***

CC *abbr* BUSINESS ***close corporation*** *(sense 2)*

CCA *abbr* ACCOUNTING ***current cost accounting***

ccc *UK* FINANCE public limited company the Welsh term for a public limited company. *Full form* ***cwmni cyfyngedig cyhoeddus***

CD *abbr* BANKING ***certificate of deposit***

CDO *abbr* STOCKHOLDING & INVESTMENTS ***collateralized debt obligation***

CDS *abbr* STOCKHOLDING & INVESTMENTS ***credit default swap***

CDSC *abbr* STOCKHOLDING & INVESTMENTS ***contingent deferred sales charge***

CEIC *abbr* BUSINESS ***closed-end investment company***

ceiling FINANCE upper limit the highest point that something can reach, for example, the highest rate of a pay increase

ceiling effect STATISTICS when statistical data groups near upper limit in a statistical study, the occurrence of clusters of scores near the upper limit of the data

cellular organization GENERAL MANAGEMENT independently functioning members of single organization a form of organization consisting of a collection of self-managing firms or cells held together by mutual interest. A cellular organization is built on the principles of self-organization, member ownership, and entrepreneurship. Each cell within the organization shares common features and purposes with its sister cells but is also able to function independently.

center *US* ACCOUNTING chargeable unit of organization a department, area, or function to which costs and/or revenues are charged

central bank ECONOMICS, BANKING bank controlling country's monetary system a bank that controls the credit system and money supply of a country

central bank discount rate BANKING central bank's rate for discounting bills the rate at which a central bank discounts bills such as ***Treasury bills***

centralization FINANCE concentration of shared functions at main office the gathering together, at a corporate headquarters, of specialist functions such as finance, personnel, centralized purchasing, and information technology. Centralization is usually undertaken in order to effect economies of scale and to standardize operating procedures throughout the organization. Centralized management can become cumbersome and inefficient, and may produce communications problems. Some organizations have shifted toward ***decentralization*** to try to avoid this.

centralized purchasing OPERATIONS & PRODUCTION concentration of purchasing in single department the control by a central department of all the purchasing undertaken within an organization. In a large organization centralized purchasing is often located in the headquarters. Centralization has the advantages of reducing duplication of effort, pooling volume purchases for discounts, enabling more effective inventory control, consolidating transport loads to achieve lower costs, increasing skills development in purchasing personnel, and enhancing relationships with suppliers.

central planning ECONOMICS economy planned by government the use of an economic system in which the government plans all business activity, regulates supply, sets production targets, and itemizes work to be done

Central Provident Fund PENSIONS Singapore's retirement benefit plan in Singapore, a retirement benefit plan to which all employees and employers make compulsory contributions each month. *Abbr* ***CPF***

central purchasing OPERATIONS & PRODUCTION purchasing through firm's main office purchasing organized by a company's main office on behalf of all its departments or branches

Central Registration Depository STOCKHOLDING & INVESTMENTS *US* searchable database of investment advisers and brokers a computerized database of brokers, investment advisers, and brokerage firms that is maintained by the US Securities and Exchange Commission and is accessible to the public. *Abbr* ***CRD***

CEO *abbr* CORPORATE GOVERNANCE ***chief executive officer***

CEO churning GENERAL MANAGEMENT, HR & PERSONNEL speed at which chief executive officers lose jobs the rapid rate at which chief executive officers are often removed from their positions *(slang)*

certain annuity PENSIONS annuity payable for limited number of years an annuity that will be paid for a specific number of years only

certificate STOCKHOLDING & INVESTMENTS document of share ownership a document representing partial ownership of a company which states the number of shares that the document is worth and the names of the company and the owner of the shares

certificate authority E-COMMERCE organization verifying identities of parties in online transactions an independent organization that verifies the identity of a purchaser or merchant and issues a ***digital certificate*** attesting to this for use in e-commerce transactions

certificate of deposit BANKING document giving guaranteed interest rate for deposit a document from a bank showing that money has been deposited at a guaranteed interest rate for a specific period of time. *Abbr* ***CD***

certificate of incorporation LEGAL registration document of new company in UK in the United Kingdom, a written statement by the Registrar of Companies confirming that a new company has fulfilled the necessary legal requirements for incorporation and is now legally constituted

certificate of origin INTERNATIONAL TRADE document declaring origin of imported goods a document showing where imported goods come from or were made

certificate of tax deducted TAX *UK* statement of tax paid on interest in the United Kingdom, a document issued by a financial institution showing that tax has been deducted from interest payments on an account

certificate to commence business LEGAL authorizing document for UK public limited company in the United Kingdom, a written statement issued by the Registrar of Companies confirming that a public limited company has fulfilled the necessary legal requirements regarding its authorized minimum share capital

certified accountant ACCOUNTING UK accountant qualified by practical training in the United Kingdom, an accountant trained in industry, the public service, or in the offices of practicing accountants, who is a member of the ***Association of Chartered Certified Accountants***. Such an accountant fulfills much the same role as a ***chartered accountant*** and is qualified to audit company records. *Abbr* ***CA***

certified check BANKING check bank guarantees to pay a check that a bank guarantees is good and will be paid out of money put aside from the payer's bank account

certified public accountant ACCOUNTING US professional licensed accountant in the United States, an accountant who has passed the exam administered by the American Institute of Certified Public Accountants and has met all other educational and experience requirements to be licensed by the state in which he or she practices. Certified public accountants fulfill much the same role as ***chartered accountants*** in the United Kingdom and are qualified to audit company records. *Abbr* ***CPA***

cessation LEGAL closing down of business the discontinuation of a business for tax purposes or of its trading on the stock market

ceteris paribus STATISTICS indicator of effect of one variable on another a Latin phrase meaning "all other things being equal", used to indicate that when considering the effect of one economic variable on another, all other factors that may affect the second variable remain constant

CFD *abbr* **1.** STOCKHOLDING & INVESTMENTS ***contract for difference*** *(sense 1)* **2.** CURRENCY & EXCHANGE ***contract for difference*** *(sense 2)*

CFO *abbr* TREASURY MANAGEMENT ***chief financial officer***

CFR *abbr* OPERATIONS & PRODUCTION ***cost and freight***

CFTC *abbr* REGULATION & COMPLIANCE ***Commodity Futures Trading Commission***

CGT *abbr* TAX ***capital gains tax***

CH *abbr* REGULATION & COMPLIANCE ***Companies House***

chain of command GENERAL MANAGEMENT hierarchical structure for passing down instructions the line of authority in a hierarchical organization through which instructions pass. The chain of command usually runs from the most senior personnel, through all reporting links in an organization's or department's structure, to a targeted person or to frontline employees. ***Line management*** relies on the chain of command in order for instructions to pass throughout an organization.

chair CORPORATE GOVERNANCE *see* ***chairman***

chairman CORPORATE GOVERNANCE organization's highest executive the most senior executive in an organization, responsible for running the ***annual meeting*** and meetings of the ***board of directors***. He or she may be a figurehead, appointed for prestige or power, and may have no role in the day-to-day running of the organization. Sometimes the roles of chairman and ***chief executive officer*** are combined, and the chairman then has more control over daily operations; sometimes the chairman is a retired chief executive. In the United States, the person who performs this function is often called a *president*. Historically, the term *chairman* was more common. The terms *chairwoman* or *chairperson* are later developments, although *chair* is now the most generally acceptable. Chairman, however, remains in common use, especially in the corporate sector.

chairman's report *or* **chairman's statement** CORPORATE GOVERNANCE chair's review of year's performance and prospects a statement included in the annual report of most large companies in which the chair of the board of directors gives an often favorable overview of the company's performance and prospects

chairperson CORPORATE GOVERNANCE *see* ***chairman***

chairwoman CORPORATE GOVERNANCE woman who is organization's highest executive a woman who is the most senior executive in an organization, responsible for running the ***annual meeting***, and meetings of the ***board of directors***. *See also* ***chairman***

chamber of commerce BUSINESS association of local businesspeople an organization of local businesspeople who work together to promote trade in their area and protect common interests

Chancellor of the Exchequer FINANCE UK's chief finance minister the United Kingdom's senior finance minister, based at ***HM Treasury*** in London. The office of Chancellor dates back to the 13th century. Some of the most famous names in British politics have served in this very senior government position, including William Gladstone and Lloyd George.

change agent GENERAL MANAGEMENT administrator of major and minor changes in organization a person in an organization who is a leader in the process of change. *See also* ***change management***

change management GENERAL MANAGEMENT administration of major and minor changes in organization the coordination of a structured period of transition from situation A to situation B in order to achieve lasting change within an organization. Change management can be of varying scope, from ***continuous improvement***, which involves small ongoing changes to existing processes, to radical and substantial change involving organizational strategy. Change management can be reactive or proactive. It can be instigated in reaction to something in an organization's external environment, for example, in the realms of economics, politics, legislation, or competition, or in reaction to something within the processes, structures, people, and events of the organization's internal environment. It may also be instigated as a proactive measure, for example, in anticipation of unfavorable economic conditions in the future. Change management usually follows five steps: recognition of a trigger indicating that change is needed; clarification of the end point, or "where we want to be"; planning how to achieve the change; accomplishment of the transition; and maintenance to ensure the change is lasting. Effective change management involves alterations on a personal level, for example, a shift in attitudes or work routines, and thus personnel management skills such as motivation are vital to successful change. Other important influences on the success of change management include leadership style, communication, and a unified positive attitude to the change among the workforce. ***Business process reengineering*** is one type of change management, involving the redesign of processes within an organization to raise performance. With the accelerating pace of change in the business environment in the 1990s and 2000s, change has become accepted as a fact of business life and is the subject of books on management.

channel MARKETING way of selling products directly or through others a method of selling and distributing products to customers, directly or through intermediaries. Channels include direct sales, retail outlets, the Internet, and wholesalers.

channel communications MARKETING communications targeting customer sales organizations communications aimed at organizations that sell and distribute products to customers, for example, retailers, sales teams, or wholesalers

channel management MARKETING process of identifying, reaching, and satisfying customers the organization of the ways in which companies reach and satisfy their customers. Channel management involves more than just distribution, and has been described as management of how and where a product is used and of how the customer and the product interact. Channel management covers processes for identifying key customers, communicating with them, and continuing to create value after the first contact.

channel of distribution OPERATIONS & PRODUCTION = ***distribution channel***

channel strategy MARKETING plan for effectively getting products to customers a management technique for determining the most effective method of selling and distributing products to customers

channel stuffing FINANCE making special offers at end of fiscal year the artificial boosting of sales at the end of a fiscal year by offering distributors and dealers incentives to buy a greater quantity of goods than they actually need *(slang)*

channel support MARKETING marketing or financial support for customer sales organizations marketing or financial support aimed at improving the performance of organizations that sell and distribute products to customers, for example, retailers, sales teams, or wholesalers

chaos GENERAL MANAGEMENT situation in which change happens quickly and unexpectedly a situation of unpredictability and rapid change

chaos theory GENERAL MANAGEMENT belief in randomness of change the theory that behavior is essentially random. It emerged in the 1970s as a mathematical concept that defied the theory of cause and effect. Writers have applied the theory to management, arguing that attempts to plan and control management processes are fundamentally doomed to failure and that, instead, managers should embrace change and flexibility in order to cope with an environment that is altering at an ever-increasing rate.

CHAPS BANKING means of rapid electronic transfer of substantial funds a method for the rapid electronic transfer of funds between participating banks on behalf of large commercial customers, where transfers tend to be of significant value. *Full form* ***Clearing House Automated Payment System***

Chapter 7 LEGAL part of US Bankruptcy Act regulating liquidation process a section of the US Bankruptcy Reform Act 1978, that sets out the rules for liquidation, a choice available to individuals, partnerships, and corporations

Chapter 11 LEGAL US act protecting potential bankrupts the US Bankruptcy Reform Act (1978) that entitles enterprises experiencing financial difficulties to apply for protection from creditors and thus have an opportunity to avoid bankruptcy

Chapter 11 bankruptcy FINANCE bankruptcy protected from creditors a bankruptcy declared under the US Bankruptcy Reform Act (1978) which entitles enterprises experiencing financial difficulties to apply for protection from creditors

charge LEGAL legal interest in land as surety to creditor a legal interest in land or real estate created in favor of a creditor to ensure that the amount owing is paid off

chargeable asset TAX type of asset liable to capital gains tax an asset that will produce a ***capital gain*** when sold. Assets that are not chargeable include family homes, cars, and some types of investments such as government stocks.

chargeable gain *UK* TAX = ***taxable gain***

chargeable transfer TAX gifts liable to UK inheritance tax in the United Kingdom, gifts that are liable to ***inheritance tax***

charge account FINANCE arrangement for customer to buy on credit a facility with a retailer that enables the customer to buy goods or services on credit rather than pay in cash. The customer may be required to settle the account within a month to avoid incurring interest on the credit. *Also called* ***credit account***

charge and discharge accounting ACCOUNTING former bookkeeping system formerly, a bookkeeping system in which a person charges himself or herself with receipts and credits himself or herself with payments. This system was used extensively before the advent of double-entry bookkeeping.

charge card FINANCE card used for buying store items on account a card issued to customers by a store, bank, or other organization, used to charge purchases to an account for later payment. *See also* ***credit card***

chargee FINANCE **1.** creditor with legal interest in land a person who holds a ***charge*** over a property, and who therefore has first claim on proceeds from the sale of the property **2.** person with enforcement rights a person who has the right to force a debtor to pay

charge off ACCOUNTING unrepeated expense or bad debt an uncollectable debt or a one-time expense that appears on a company's income statement

charitable contribution ACCOUNTING firm's gift to charity a donation by a company to a charity, deductible against tax

charity accounts ACCOUNTING records of charity's financial activities the accounting records of a charitable institution, which include a statement of financial activities rather than a profit and loss account. In the United Kingdom, the accounts should conform to the requirements stipulated in the Charities Act (1993).

charter LEGAL legal document creating US corporation in the United States, a legal document that creates a corporation and sets forth its purpose and structure according to the laws of the state in which it is established. *Also called* ***articles of incorporation***

chartered accountant ACCOUNTING UK accountant qualified by professional examination in the United Kingdom, a qualified professional accountant who is a member of an Institute of Chartered Accountants. Chartered accountants are qualified to audit company accounts and some hold management positions in companies. *Abbr* ***CA***

Chartered Association of Certified Accountants ACCOUNTING formerly, UK certified accountants' association the former name of the ***Association of Chartered Certified Accountants*** in the United Kingdom

chartered bank BANKING N. American bank established by government charter in the United States and Canada, a bank that has been set up by government charter

chartered company *or* **chartered entity** BUSINESS UK organization founded by royal charter in the United Kingdom, an organization formed by the grant of a royal charter. The charter authorizes the entity to operate and states the powers specifically granted.

Chartered Institute of Management Accountants ACCOUNTING *see* ***CIMA***

Chartered Institute of Public Finance and Accountancy ACCOUNTING *see* ***CIPFA***

Chartered Institute of Taxation TAX UK organization for tax professionals in the United Kingdom, an organization for professionals in the field of taxation

charter value BANKING worth of bank's capacity to continue operating the value of a bank being able to continue to do business in the future, reflected as part of its share price

charting MARKETS stock market analysis based on charts the use of charts to analyze stock market trends and to forecast future rises or falls

chartist MARKETS stock market analyst employing charts an analyst who studies past stock market trends, the movement of stock prices, and changes in the accounting ratios of individual companies. The chartist's philosophy is that history repeats itself: using charts and graphs, he or she uses past trends and repetitive patterns to forecast the future. Although the chartist approach is considered narrower than that of a traditional analyst, it nevertheless has a good following.

chase demand plan OPERATIONS & PRODUCTION plan for matching output to customer demand a production control plan that attempts to match capacity to the varying levels of forecast demand. Chase demand plans require flexible working practices and place varying demands on equipment requirements. Pure chase demand plans are difficult to achieve and are most commonly found in operations where output cannot be stored or where the organization is seeking to eliminate stores of finished goods.

chattel mortgage MORTGAGES money borrowed using personal items as security money that is borrowed using an item of personal property, not land or buildings, as collateral

cheap money FINANCE money lent at low interest money that is lent at low interest rates, used as a government strategy to stimulate an economy either at the initial signs of, or during, a recession. *Also called* ***easy money***. *See also* ***dear money, expansionary monetary policy***

check *US* BANKING written instruction to bank to pay money an order in writing requiring the banker to pay on demand a specific sum of money to a specified person or bearer. Although a check can theoretically be written on anything (in a P. G. Woodhouse story, one was written on the side of a cow), banks issue preprinted, customized forms for completion by an account holder who inserts the date, the name of the person to be paid (the payee), the amount in both words and figures, and his or her signature. The customer is the drawer. *UK term* ***cheque***

checkbook *US* BANKING book of blank cheques a booklet with new blank checks for a bank's customer to complete. *UK term* ***cheque book***

check card *US* BANKING = ***debit card***

check digit BANKING reference number for validating transactions the last digit of a string of computerized reference numbers, used to validate a transaction

checking account *US* BANKING flexible bank account with easy withdrawal a bank account in which deposits can be withdrawn at any time by writing checks but do not usually earn interest, except in the case of some online accounts. It is the most common type of bank account. *Abbr* **c/a**. *UK term* ***current account***

check register *US* BANKING record of check transactions a control record of checks issued or received, maintained by a person or organization. *UK term* ***cheque register***

check routing symbol BANKING number on US check identifying Federal Reserve district a number shown on a US check that identifies the Federal Reserve district through which the check will be cleared

check stub *US* BANKING part of check left in checkbook a piece of paper left in a checkbook after a check has been written and taken out. *UK term* ***cheque stub***

check to bearer *US* BANKING = ***bearer check***

cheque *UK* BANKING = ***check***

cheque book *UK* BANKING = ***checkbook***

cheque card BANKING UK card guaranteeing payment of check a plastic card from a UK bank that guarantees payment of a check up to some amount, even if the user has no money in his or her account

cheque register *UK* = ***check register***

cheque stub *UK* BANKING = ***check stub***

cheque to bearer *UK* BANKING = ***bearer check***

cherry picking GENERAL MANAGEMENT selecting the best of available options the selection of what is perceived to be the best or most valuable from a series of ideas or options

Chicago Mercantile Exchange MARKETS Chicago exchange trading in futures a leading exchange for futures contracts based in Chicago. Its main product areas are interest rates, stock indexes, foreign exchange, and commodities. *Abbr* ***CME***

Chicago School ECONOMICS school of conservative economic thought a school of conservative economic thought, promoting free markets and capitalism and relying heavily on mathematical analysis. It is associated with the University of Chicago and was for many years led by Professor Milton Friedman.

chief executive officer *or* **chief executive** CORPORATE GOVERNANCE executive ultimately responsible for firm's management the person with overall responsibility for ensuring that the daily operations of an organization run efficiently and for carrying out strategic plans. The chief executive of an organization normally sits on the ***board of directors***. In a limited company, he or she is usually known as a managing director. *Abbr* ***CEO***

chief financial officer TREASURY MANAGEMENT executive responsible for firm's financial management the officer in an organization responsible for handling funds, signing checks, the keeping of financial records, and financial planning for the company. *Abbr* ***CFO***

chief information officer GENERAL MANAGEMENT executive responsible for firm's internal information systems the officer in an organization responsible for its internal information systems and sometimes for its e-business infrastructure. *Abbr* ***CIO***

chief operating officer GENERAL MANAGEMENT executive responsible for firm's day-to-day operations the officer in a corporation responsible for its day-to-day management, usually reporting to the chief executive officer. *Abbr* ***COO***

Chief Secretary to the Treasury FINANCE UK government minister controlling public expenditure in the United Kingdom, a government minister responsible to the Chancellor of the Exchequer for the control of public expenditure

Chinese wall STOCKHOLDING & INVESTMENTS obstacle to exchange of inside information the procedures enforced within a securities firm to prevent the exchange of confidential information between the firm's departments so as to avoid the illegal use of inside information

CHIPS BANKING US international wire transfer system in the United States, the computerized domestic and international wire transfer system that also serves to convert all pending payments into a single transaction. *Full form* ***Clearing House Interbank Payments System***

CHIS *abbr* FRAUD ***covert human intelligence source***

chit GENERAL MANAGEMENT **1.** official note an official note or document, usually signed by somebody in authority **2.** receipt a receipt for something or a statement of money owed

chose in action FINANCE personal right treated like property a personal right such as a patent, copyright, debt, or check that can be enforced or claimed as if it were property

chose in possession FINANCE object that can be owned a physical item such as a piece of furniture that can be owned

churn 1. STOCKHOLDING & INVESTMENTS encourage investor to change portfolio frequently to encourage an investor to change stock frequently because the broker is paid every time there is a change in the investor's portfolio (*slang*) **2.** INSURANCE encourage somebody to change insurance policy to encourage a client to change his or her insurance policy solely to earn the salesperson a commission **3.** GENERAL MANAGEMENT successive purchases of different brands of products to purchase a quick succession of products or services without displaying loyalty to any of them, often as a result of competitive marketing strategies that continually undercut rival prices, thus encouraging customers to switch brands constantly in order to take advantage of the cheapest or most attractive offers **4.** HR & PERSONNEL experience high employee turnover to suffer a high turnover rate of executives or other employees

churn rate 1. STOCKHOLDING & INVESTMENTS measure of change in investment portfolio a measure of the frequency and volume of trading of stocks and bonds in a brokerage account **2.** GENERAL MANAGEMENT rate at which customers abandon new product the rate at which new customers try a product or service and then stop using it

CICA *abbr* ACCOUNTING ***Canadian Institute of Chartered Accountants***

CIF *abbr* OPERATIONS & PRODUCTION ***cost, insurance, and freight***

CIFAS *abbr* FRAUD ***Credit Industry Fraud Avoidance System***

CIMA ACCOUNTING UK institution awarding financial degree to businesspeople a UK organization that is internationally recognized as offering a financial degree for business, focusing on strategic business management. Founded in 1919 as the Institute of Cost and Works Accountants, it has offices worldwide, supporting over 128,000 members and students in 156 countries. *Full form* ***Chartered Institute of Management Accountants***

CIO *abbr* GENERAL MANAGEMENT ***chief information officer***

CIPFA ACCOUNTING UK professional accountancy organization in the United Kingdom, one of the leading professional accountancy bodies and the only one that specializes in the public services, for example, local government, public service bodies, and national audit agencies, as well as major accounting firms. It is responsible for the education and training of professional accountants and for their regulation through the setting and monitoring of professional standards. CIPFA also provides a variety of advisory, information, and consulting services to public service organizations. It is the leading independent commentator on managing accounting for public money. *Full form* ***Chartered Institute of Public Finance and Accountancy***

circuit breaker MARKETS US provision for stopping trading a rule created by the major US stock exchanges and the ***Securities and Exchange Commission*** by which trading is halted during times of extreme price fluctuations (*slang*)

circular file GENERAL MANAGEMENT office wastebasket a wastebasket in an office (*slang*)

circular flow of income ECONOMICS model of relationship between income and spending a model of a country's economy showing the flow of resources when consumers' wages and salaries are used to buy goods and so generate income for manufacturing firms

circularization of debtors ACCOUNTING auditors' approach to debtors to identify assets the sending of letters by a company's auditors to debtors in order to verify the existence and extent of the company's assets

circular letter of credit BANKING bank's authorization of payment to every branch a letter of credit sent to all branches of the bank which issues it

circular merger MERGERS & ACQUISITIONS joining of firms sharing distribution channels a merger involving firms that have different products but similar distribution channels. *See also* ***merger***

circulating capital FINANCE = ***working capital***

circulation MARKETING number of copies of newspaper or magazine sold the number of copies sold or distributed of a single issue of a newspaper or magazine

circulation of capital FINANCE transfer of capital between investments the movement of ***capital*** from one investment to another, or between one country and another

City *or* **City of London** FINANCE area of London containing UK financial center the United Kingdom's financial center found in the historic center of London, where most banks and many large companies have their main offices. *See also* ***Wall Street***

City bonus FINANCE annual financial reward for UK employee a very large sum of money, in addition to salary, paid to an employee in London's financial industry for effective performance in increasing his or her company's profits. *See also* ***Wall Street bonus***

City Code on Takeovers and Mergers MERGERS & ACQUISITIONS UK code for fairness in takeovers in the United Kingdom, a code issued on behalf of the ***City Panel on Takeovers and Mergers*** that is designed principally to ensure fair and equal treatment of all stockholders in relation to ***takeovers***. The Code also provides an orderly framework within which takeovers are conducted. It is not concerned with the financial or commercial advantages or disadvantages of a takeover, nor with issues such as competition policy which are the responsibility of the government. The Code represents the collective opinion of those professionally involved in the field of takeovers on how fairness to stockholders can be achieved in practice.

City Panel on Takeovers and Mergers MERGERS & ACQUISITIONS independent UK group supervising takeovers in the United Kingdom, an independent nonstatutory group whose job is to supervise and regulate ***takeovers*** according to the ***City Code on Takeovers and Mergers***. *Also called* ***Takeover Panel***

City watchdog REGULATION & COMPLIANCE = ***Financial Services Authority*** (*informal*)

claim LEGAL statement of entitlement to money an official request for money, usually in the form of compensation, from a person or organization

claimant FINANCE somebody who makes benefit claim to government a person who claims a government benefit such as an unemployment or disability benefit

claim form INSURANCE form completed to make insurance claim a form that has to be filled in giving details of the reason for making an insurance claim

claims adjuster *US* INSURANCE assessor of insurance claims somebody who determines the value of a claim made under an insurance policy. *UK term* ***loss adjuster***

claims manager INSURANCE person responsible for insurance claims the person responsible for dealing with claims in an insurance company

class STOCKHOLDING & INVESTMENTS classification for common stock a type of common stock issued by a company, usually with the designations A and B, and conferring different voting rights

class action LEGAL joint civil law action a civil law action taken by a group of individuals who have a common grievance against an individual, organization, or legal entity

classical economics ECONOMICS economic theory stressing importance of free enterprise a theory focusing on the functioning of a market economy and providing a rudimentary explanation of consumer and producer behavior in particular markets. The theory postulates that, over time, the economy would tend to operate at full employment because increases in supply would create corresponding increases in demand.

classical system of corporation tax TAX system doubly taxing firm's income a system in which companies and their owners are liable for ***corporation tax*** as separate entities. A company's taxed income is therefore paid out to stockholders, who are in turn taxed again. This system operates in the United States and the Netherlands. It was replaced in the United Kingdom in 1973 by an ***imputation system***.

classified stock STOCKHOLDING & INVESTMENTS US firm's common stock divided into classes in the United States, a company's ***common stock*** divided into classes such as Class A and Class B

class interval STATISTICS division of statistical frequency distribution in a set of statistical observations, any of the intervals of the frequency distribution

class of assets ACCOUNTING categorization of assets the grouping of similar assets into categories. This is done because, under International Accounting Standards Committee rules, ***tangible assets*** and *intangible assets* cannot be revalued on an individual basis, only within a class of assets.

claw back FINANCE take back money previously allocated to recover money that has already been assigned to a specific use, especially money given in grants or tax incentives

clawback 1. FINANCE money reclaimed money taken back, especially money taken back by the government from grants or tax incentives which had previously been made **2.** MARKETS allocation of new stock to existing stockholders the allocation of new shares of stock to existing stockholders, so as to maintain the value of their holdings

clean float CURRENCY & EXCHANGE exchange rate unrestricted by government a ***floating exchange rate*** that is allowed to vary without any intervention from the country's monetary authorities

clean opinion *or* **clean report** ACCOUNTING auditor's report without reservations an auditor's report that is not qualified because of concern about the scope or treatment of some matter

clean price MARKETS bond price not including interest the price of a bond excluding accrued interest

clean surplus concept FINANCE advocating statements showing all gains and losses the idea that a company's income statement should show the totality of gains and losses, without any of them being taken directly to equity

clear OPERATIONS & PRODUCTION sell cheaply to get rid of merchandise to sell goods at a discounted price in order to dispose of inventory

clearance certificate INTERNATIONAL TRADE document giving goods customs clearance a document showing that goods have been passed by customs

clearing 1. BANKING process of passing check through banking system an act of passing of a check through the banking system, including the transfer of money from one account to another **2.** MARKETS completion of transactions and payments the process of verifying and settling orders between buyers and sellers in securities transactions

clearing bank BANKING in UK, bank employing clearing house in the United Kingdom, a bank that deals with other banks through a ***clearing house***

clearing house *or* **clearing firm** *or* **clearing corporation 1.** BANKING institution handling bank transactions an institution that settles accounts between banks, using the ***clearing system*** **2.** MARKETS institution handling securities transactions an organization that coordinates the confirmation, delivery, and settlement of securities transactions on behalf of exchanges **3.** E-COMMERCE = ***acquirer*** *(sense 2).*

Clearing House Automated Payment System BANKING *see* ***CHAPS***

Clearing House Interbank Payments System BANKING *see* ***CHIPS***

clearing system BANKING system for handling bank transactions the system of settling accounts among banks through ***clearing houses***. It allows member banks to offset claims against each other.

clear profit FINANCE profit after paying expenses the profit remaining after all expenses have been paid

clear title LEGAL = ***good title***

clerical error mistake in preparing documents a mistake made in the preparation of documents such as reports or financial accounts

clickable corporation E-COMMERCE firm operating online a company that operates on the internet. The term was popularized by a 1999 book by Jonathan Rosenoer, Douglas Armstrong, and J. Russell Gates.

click rate E-COMMERCE = ***click-through rate***

clicks-and-bricks *or* **clicks-and-mortar** E-COMMERCE organization with physical facility that also operates online combining a traditional ***bricks-and-mortar*** organization with the click technology of the Internet. Such an organization has both a virtual and a physical presence. Examples include retailers with physical stores and also websites where their goods can be bought online.

clickstream E-COMMERCE record of activity left by user surfing web the virtual trail that a user leaves behind while surfing the internet. A clickstream is a record of a user's activity on the internet, including every web page visited, how long each page is visited for, and the order in which the pages are visited. Both internet service providers and individual websites are able to track an internet user's clickstream.

click-through rate E-COMMERCE using click-throughs as measure of success of ad the percentage of viewings of an advertisement that result in a click on an on-screen device to take the user to the advertiser's website, which is a measure of the success of the advertisement. *Also called* ***ad click rate, click rate***

click wrap agreement *or* **click wrap license** E-COMMERCE contract agreed to online a contract presented entirely over the internet, the purchaser indicating assent to be bound by the terms of the contract by clicking on an "I agree" button. The term stems from "shrink wrap" agreements, licenses that become enforceable when the user removes designated packaging containing a copy of the agreement. *Also called* ***point and click agreement***

client MARKETING **1.** somebody hiring professional services a person or organization that employs the services of a professional person or organization **2.** customer a person or organization to whom goods or services are provided or sold

client base MARKETING professional's steady clients the group of regular clients of a professional person or organization

clientele effect STOCKHOLDING & INVESTMENTS influence of investors on choice of securities the preference of an investor or group of investors for buying a particular type of security

Clintonomics ECONOMICS Clinton's policy of economic intervention the policy of former President Clinton's Council of Economic Advisers to intervene in the economy to correct market failures and redistribute income

CLO *abbr* STOCKHOLDING & INVESTMENTS ***collateralized loan obligation***

CLOB INTERNATIONAL MARKETS Singaporean facility for trading in foreign stocks in Singapore, a mechanism for buying and selling foreign stocks, especially Malaysian stocks

clone fund STOCKHOLDING & INVESTMENTS mutual fund matching established fund by using derivatives a mutual fund that, by the use of derivatives, is able to duplicate the strategy and performance of a successful established mutual fund

close 1. MARKETS end of stock trading for day the end of a day's trading on a stock exchange **2.** MARKETS have a particular price at end of trading of a stock, to end the day's trading at a particular price **3.** *US* REAL ESTATE pay balance on real estate to pay off the balance owed on real estate in exchange for a deed showing ownership of the real estate. *UK term* ***complete*** ◇ close a position MARKETS to arrange affairs so that there is no longer any liability to pay, for example, by selling all securities held ◇ close the accounts FINANCE to come to the end of an accounting period and make up the profit and loss account

close company *or* **closed company** *UK* BUSINESS = ***close corporation***

close corporation *or* **closed corporation** BUSINESS **1.** *US* public corporation controlled by few shareholders a public corporation in which all of the voting stock is held by a few stockholders, for example, management or family members. Although it is a public company, stock would not normally be available for trading because of a lack of liquidity. *UK term* ***close company*** **2.** S. African business controlled by 10 or fewer in South Africa, a business registered in terms of the Close Corporations Act of 1984, consisting of not more than 10 members who share its ownership and management. *Abbr* ***CC***

closed economy ECONOMICS economic system isolated from international trade an economic system in which little or no external trade takes place

closed-end credit FINANCE credit with fixed date for full repayment a loan, plus any interest and finance charges, that is to be repaid in full by a specific future date. Loans that have real estate or motor vehicles as collateral are usually closed-end. *See also* ***open-end credit***

closed-end fund *or* **closed-end investment company** STOCKHOLDING & INVESTMENTS investment company with fixed number of shares an investment company such as an investment trust that has a fixed number of shares that can be bought and sold in the marketplace. *See also* ***open-end fund***

closed-end mortgage MORTGAGES mortgage that cannot be paid off early a mortgage with an ***indenture*** disallowing repayment before it comes to maturity. *See also* ***open-end mortgage***. *Also called* ***closed mortgage***

closed fund STOCKHOLDING & INVESTMENTS mutual fund in US closed to new investors in the United States, a mutual fund that is no longer accepting new investors, because it has become too large

closed-loop production system OPERATIONS & PRODUCTION system of recycling industrial output into new product an environmentally friendly production system in which any industrial output is capable of being recycled to create another product

closed-loop system GENERAL MANAGEMENT management control system allowing correction a management control system which includes a provision for corrective action, taken on either a feed forward or a feedback basis

closed market OPERATIONS & PRODUCTION market with supplier dealing exclusively with agent or distributor a market in which a supplier deals only with one agent or distributor and does not supply any others direct

closed mortgage MORTGAGES = ***closed-end mortgage***

closely held corporation BUSINESS US public company with few stockholders in the United States, a company whose stock is publicly traded but held by very few people

closely held shares STOCKHOLDING & INVESTMENTS publicly traded US stock with few holders in the United States, stock that is publicly traded but held by very few people

Closer Economic Relations agreement INTERNATIONAL TRADE = ***Australia and New Zealand Closer Economic Relations Trade Agreement***

closing *US* REAL ESTATE act of transferring ownership in real estate the point at which a buyer pays off the balance owed on real estate in exchange for a deed showing ownership of the real estate. *UK term* ***completion***

closing balance 1. ACCOUNTING amount carried forward to next accounting period the difference between credits and debits in a ledger at the end of one accounting period that is carried forward to the next **2.** BANKING bank balance at end of business day the amount in credit or debit in a bank account at the end of a business day

closing bell MARKETS end of period of trading the end of a trading session at a stock or commodities exchange when a bell is rung

closing costs REAL ESTATE expenses of transferring real estate ownership the charges and fees paid by buyers and sellers in a real estate or mortgage transaction at the time of closing

closing-down sale OPERATIONS & PRODUCTION sale of goods by store closing down a sale of goods that follows a store's decision to cease trading

closing entries ACCOUNTING entries at very end of accounting period in a double-entry bookkeeping system, entries made at the very end of an ***accounting period*** to balance the expense and revenue ledgers

closing out 1. MARKETS sale of commodity that ends futures contract the ending of a ***futures contract*** by the sale of the relevant commodity **2.** OPERATIONS & PRODUCTION sale of goods cheaply to offload them the act of selling goods cheaply to try to get rid of them, usually because they have not been selling well or because the seller is going out of business

closing price MARKETS last price paid during trading session the price of the last transaction for a specific security or commodity at the end of a trading session

closing quote MARKETS last price bid or offered during trading session the last bid and offer prices for a specific security or commodity recorded at the close of a trading session

closing rate CURRENCY & EXCHANGE exchange rate at end of accounting period the exchange rate of two or more currencies at the close of business at the end of an accounting period, for example, at the end of the fiscal year

closing rate method *or* CURRENCY & EXCHANGE currency conversion method in accounts a technique for translating the figures from a set of financial statements into a different currency using the ***closing rate***. This method is often used for the accounts of a foreign subsidiary of a parent company.

closing sale FINANCE sale that reduces seller's risk a sale that reduces the risk that the seller has through holding a greater number of shares or a longer term contract

closing statement REAL ESTATE statement of expenses of transferring real estate ownership a statement of all charges and fees paid by buyers and sellers in a real estate or mortgage transaction at the time of closing

closing stock ACCOUNTING inventory at end of accounting period a business's remaining stock at the end of an ***accounting period***. It includes finished products, raw materials, or work in progress and is deducted from the period's costs in the balance sheets.

cluster analysis STATISTICS statistical analysis using groupings that share characteristics a statistical method used to analyze complex data and identify groupings that share common features. Cluster analysis is a form of ***multivariate analysis*** that attempts to explain variability in a set of data. It involves finding unifying elements that enable identification of groups or clusters displaying common characteristics. It could be used, for example, to analyze results of market research and delineate groups of respondents that share specific attitudes.

clustered data STATISTICS statistical information grouped according to shared features data in which sampling units in a study are grouped into clusters sharing a common feature, or longitudinal data in which clusters are defined by repeated measures on the unit

cluster sampling STATISTICS *see* ***random sampling***

CM *abbr* GENERAL MANAGEMENT ***category management***

CMBS *abbr* STOCKHOLDING & INVESTMENTS, MORTGAGES ***commercial mortgage-backed securities***

CME *abbr* MARKETS ***Chicago Mercantile Exchange***

CML *abbr* MORTGAGES ***Council of Mortgage Lenders***

CMO *abbr* MORTGAGES ***collateralized mortgage obligation***

CN *or* **C/N** *abbr* FINANCE ***credit note***

CNCC *abbr* REGULATION & COMPLIANCE ***Compagnie Nationale des Commissaires aux Comptes***

CNS *abbr* MARKETS ***continuous net settlement***

COB *abbr* MARKETS ***Commission des Opérations de Bourse***

co-branding MARKETING, E-COMMERCE display of multiple logos to suggest joint venture the display of two or more corporate logos on a product or website in order to give the impression that the product or site is a joint enterprise

CoCo *or* **COCO** REGULATION & COMPLIANCE Canadian framework for internal regulation a system for evaluating the internal controls over financial reporting. The Criteria of Control Board (CoCo) is charged by the Board of Governors of The Canadian Institute of Chartered Accountants with issuing guidance on designing, assessing, and reporting on the control systems of organizations.

co-creditor FINANCE one of several people to whom firm owes money one of two or more people or organizations that are owed money by the same company

code of conduct GENERAL MANAGEMENT standard of ethical and social behavior and responsibility a statement and description of required behaviors, responsibilities, and actions expected of employees of an organization or of members of a professional body. A code of conduct usually focuses on ethical and socially responsible issues and applies to individuals, providing guidance on how to act in cases of doubt or confusion.

code of practice GENERAL MANAGEMENT statement of preferred organizational procedures a policy statement and description of preferred methods for organizational procedures.

Codes of practice may govern procedures for industrial relations, health and safety, and, more recently, customer service and professional development. An agreed code of practice enables activities to be carried out to a required organizational standard and provides a basis for dispute resolution.

co-director CORPORATE GOVERNANCE person involved in controlling firm one of two or more people who direct the same company

coefficient of variation STATISTICS measure of dispersion of statistical information a measure of the spread of a set of statistical data, such as a set of investment returns, calculated as the mean or standard deviation of the data multiplied by 100

co-financing FINANCE joint provision of finance the provision of money for a project jointly by two or more parties

COGS *abbr* OPERATIONS & PRODUCTION ***cost of goods sold***

cohesion fund FINANCE EU fund to equalize members' economies in the European Union, the main financial instrument for reducing economic and social disparities within by providing financial help for projects in the fields of the environment and transport infrastructure

cohort STATISTICS group of study participants with shared characteristic a group of individuals in a statistical study who have a common characteristic such as age or income

cohort study STATISTICS long-term study of people with shared characteristic a study in which a group of individuals who have a common characteristic such as age or income are observed over several years

coincident indicator ECONOMICS indicator of current economic activity a factor that provides information on economic activity taking place at the current time

COLA *abbr* FINANCE ***cost-of-living adjustment***

cold call MARKETING call strangers to sell something to make unsolicited calls to customers or consumers in an attempt to sell products or services. *Cold calling* is disliked, particularly by individual consumers, and is an inefficient way of selling, as the take-up rate is very low. *Also called* ***dial and smile***

cold start OPERATIONS & PRODUCTION new operation unsupported by previous turnover the act of beginning a new business or opening a new store with no previous turnover to base it on

Collaborative Planning, Forecasting, and Replenishment OPERATIONS & PRODUCTION *see* ***CPFR®***

collar STOCKHOLDING & INVESTMENTS, RISK preset limit a contractually imposed lower limit on a ***financial instrument***

collateral FINANCE resources providing security against loan property or goods used as security against a loan and forfeited to the lender if the borrower defaults

collateralize FINANCE provide loan with security to secure a loan by pledging assets. If the borrower defaults on loan payments, the pledged assets can be taken by the lender. – ***collateralization***

collateralized bond obligation STOCKHOLDING & INVESTMENTS, RISK investment grade pool of bonds carrying risk an ***investment gradeasset-backed security*** that consists of a portfolio of bonds, some of which may carry high risk. Pooling bonds with different degrees of risk is thought to provide enough diversification to qualify the security for an investment grade rating. *Abbr* ***CBO***

collateralized debt obligation STOCKHOLDING & INVESTMENTS investment combining bonds and loans a complex investment vehicle based on a portfolio of bonds and loans, which may include assets with an underlying risk. *Abbr* ***CDO***. *Also called* ***debt obligation***

collateralized loan obligation STOCKHOLDING & INVESTMENTS asset-backed security formed when loan is repackaged an asset-backed security that is created by repackaging loans, usually commercial loans made by a bank, at an attractive rate of interest. *Abbr* ***CLO***

collateralized mortgage obligation STOCKHOLDING & INVESTMENTS, MORTGAGES instrument with mortgages on property a financial instrument that has mortgages on property given as security in case of default. CMOs are issued against the collective value of pooled mortgages, offering interest payments based on the overall cash flow. *Abbr* ***CMO***

collateral trust certificate STOCKHOLDING & INVESTMENTS bond with stock in another firm as security a bond for which stock in another company, usually a subsidiary, is used as collateral

collecting bank BANKING bank receiving check for processing a bank into which a person has deposited a check, and which has the duty to collect the money from the account of the writer of the check

collection FINANCE collecting payments on unpaid debts the process of collecting payments on unpaid loans or bills

collection agency FINANCE business collecting outstanding payments a business that collects payments on unpaid loans or on bills

collection ratio ACCOUNTING average time for invoice to be paid the average number of days it takes a firm to convert its accounts receivable into cash.

Ideally, this period should be decreasing or constant. A low figure means the company collects its outstanding receivables quickly. Collection ratios are usually reviewed quarterly or yearly.

Calculating the collection ratio requires three figures: total accounts receivable, total credit sales for the period analyzed, and the number of days in the period (annual, 365; six months, 182; quarter, 91). The formula is:

(Accounts receivable / Total credit sales for the period) × Number of days in the period

For example: if total receivables are $4,500,000, total credit sales in a quarter are $9,000,000, and number of days is 91, then:

(4,500,000 / 9,000,000) × 91 = 45.5

Thus, it takes an average of 45.5 days to collect receivables.

Properly evaluating a collection ratio requires a standard for comparison. A traditional rule of thumb is that it should not exceed a third to a half of selling terms. For instance, if terms are 30 days, an acceptable collection ratio would be 40 to 45 days.

Companies use collection ratio information with an ***accounts receivable aging*** report. This lists aged categories of receivables, for example, 0–30 days, 30–60 days, 60–90 days, and over 90 days. The report also shows the percentage of total accounts receivable that each group represents, allowing for an analysis of delinquencies and potential bad debts. *Also called* ***days' sales outstanding***

collusive tendering FINANCE when job offerers share inside information the illegal practice among companies making offers for a job of sharing privileged information between themselves, with the objective of fixing the end result

colocation E-COMMERCE sharing of hosting center with other Internet clients the sharing of the facilities of a hosting center with other Internet clients

combination annuity INSURANCE = ***hybrid annuity***

combination bond STOCKHOLDING & INVESTMENTS bond secured by project's revenue and government credit a government bond for which the collateral is both revenue from the financed project and the government's credit

combined financial statement FINANCE summary of financial position of related firms a written record covering the assets, liabilities, net worth, and operating statement of two or more related or affiliated companies

COMEX *abbr* MARKETS ***commodity exchange***

comfort letter **1.** FINANCE parent company's support for subsidiary's loan a letter from the parent company of a subsidiary that is applying for a loan, stating the intention that the subsidiary should remain in business **2.** ACCOUNTING in US, endorsement of financial statement in the United States, a statement from an accounting firm provided to a company preparing for a public offering, which confirms that the unaudited financial information in the ***prospectus*** follows ***Generally Accepted Accounting Principles***

command economy ECONOMICS economic system controlled by government an economy in which all economic activity is regulated by the government, as formerly in China or the Soviet Union

commerce FINANCE trading on large scale the large-scale buying and selling of goods and services, usually applied to trading between different states or countries

commerce integration FINANCE marrying of old and new ways of trading the blending of Internet-based commerce capabilities with the ***legacy systems*** of a traditional business to create a seamless transparent process

commerce server E-COMMERCE **1.** computer storing e-commerce data for website a computer in a network that maintains all transactional and back-end data for an e-commerce website **2.** computer containing programs for processing online transactions a networked computer that contains the programs required to process transactions via the Internet, including dynamic inventory databases, shopping cart software, and online payment systems

commerce service provider E-COMMERCE organization providing service to firm involved in e-commerce an organization or company that provides a service to a company to facilitate some aspect of electronic commerce, for example, by functioning as an Internet ***payment gateway***. *Abbr* ***CSP***

commercial FINANCE of trading relating to the buying and selling of goods and services

commercial bank BANKING privately owned bank offering range of facilities a bank that provides financial services such as checking and savings accounts and loans to individuals and businesses. *See also* ***investment bank***

commercial bill FINANCE bill of exchange not issued by government a ***bill of exchange*** issued by a company (a ***trade bill***) or accepted by a bank (a ***banker's bill***), as opposed to a ***Treasury bill***, which is issued by a government

commercial directory BUSINESS book listing local businesses a book that lists all the businesses and businesspeople in a town

commercial hedger STOCKHOLDING & INVESTMENTS producer investing in commodities it needs a company that holds ***options*** in the commodities it uses or produces, usually in order to ensure the price stability of the commodity

commercialization FINANCE conversion of something into business the application of business principles to something in order to run it as a business

commercial law LEGAL law dealing with trade the body of law that deals with the rules and institutions of commercial transactions, including banking, commerce, contracts, copyrights, insolvency, insurance, patents, trademarks, shipping, storage, transportation, and warehousing

commercial loan FINANCE short-term renewable loan to firm a short-term renewable loan or line of credit used to finance the seasonal or cyclical working capital needs of a company

commercial mortgage-backed securities MORTGAGES stocks with cash flow from commercial mortgage stocks that are backed by the security of a mortgage on commercial rather than residential property. *Abbr* ***CMBS***

commercial paper FINANCE unsecured short-term loan note an unsecured loan note issued by a company for a short period, generally maturing within nine months

commercial property REAL ESTATE buildings and land used by business buildings and land used for the performance of business activities. Commercial property can include single offices, buildings, factories, and hotels.

commercial report FINANCE background financial report on applicant an investigative report made by an organization such as a ***credit bureau*** that specializes in obtaining information regarding a person or organization applying for something such as credit or employment

commercial substance FINANCE economic reality behind piece of business the economic reality that underlies a transaction or arrangement, regardless of its legal or technical denomination. For example, a company may sell an office block and then immediately lease it back: the commercial substance may be that it has not been sold.

commercial year FINANCE 12 months of 30 days an artificial year treated as having 12 months of 30 days each, used for calculating such things as monthly sales data and inventory levels

commission **1.** FINANCE sum paid to intermediary a payment made to an intermediary, often calculated as a percentage of the value of goods or services provided. Commission is most often paid to sales staff, brokers, or agents. **2.** *US* MARKETS broker's fee for sale a fee that a broker receives for a sale of securities. *Also called* ***placement fee***

commission agent FINANCE agent paid percentage of sales an agent whose payment is based on a specific percentage of the sales made

Commission des Opérations de Bourse MARKETS institution overseeing French stock exchanges the agency, established by the French government in 1968, that is responsible for supervising France's stock exchanges. *Abbr* ***COB***

commission house FINANCE firm charging commission on futures contracts a business that buys or sells ***futures contracts*** for clients and charges a commission for this service

Commission of the European Community = ***European Commission***

commitment STOCKHOLDING & INVESTMENTS agreement to underwrite credit an agreement by an underwriting syndicate to underwrite a ***note issuance facility*** or other credit facility

commitment document LEGAL document with contractual force confirming transaction a contract, change order, purchase order, or letter of intent pertaining to the supply of goods and services that commits an organization to legal, financial, and other obligations

commitment fee FINANCE payment to fix interest rate on forthcoming loan a fee that a lender charges to guarantee a rate of interest on a loan a borrower is soon to make. *Also called* ***establishment fee***

commitment letter FINANCE official confirmation of US loan in the United States, an official notice from a lender to a borrower that the borrower's application has been approved and confirming the terms and conditions of the loan

commitments basis FINANCE way of recording expenditure before outlay the method of recording the expenditure of a public sector organization at the time when it commits itself to it rather than when it actually pays for it

commitments for capital expenditure FINANCE amount committed to fixed assets in future the amount a company has committed to spend on fixed assets in the future. In the United Kingdom, companies are legally obliged to disclose this amount, and any additional commitments, in their ***annual report***.

committee GENERAL MANAGEMENT group of people delegated to consider particular matter a group of people appointed and authorized to study, investigate, or make recommendations on a particular matter

Committee on Accounting Procedure ACCOUNTING former US committee establishing accounting principles in the United States, a committee of the American Institute of Certified Public Accountants that was responsible between 1939 and 1959 for issuing accounting principles, some of which are still part of the ***Generally Accepted Accounting Principles***

Committee on Uniform Securities Identification Procedures REGULATION & COMPLIANCE committee that codes US securities a committee set up by the American Bankers Association to assign a code to all securities approved for trading in the United States. *Abbr* ***CUSIP***

commodities exchange MARKETS market for bulk raw materials a market in which raw materials are bought and sold in large quantities as ***actuals*** or ***futures***

commodities market MARKETS = ***commodity market***

commodity MARKETS product that can be traded an item that can be bought or sold, especially a raw material or something that has been manufactured

commodity-backed bond STOCKHOLDING & INVESTMENTS bond linked to price of commodity a bond tied to the price of an underlying commodity such as gold or silver, often used as a hedge against inflation

commodity contract MARKETS contract for transferring commodity a legal document for the delivery or receipt of a commodity

commodity exchange MARKETS exchange where commodity futures are traded an exchange where futures are traded, for example, the commodity exchange for metals. *Abbr* ***COMEX***

commodity future MARKETS fixed contract to buy or sell commodity a contract to buy or sell a commodity at a predetermined price and on a specific delivery date

Commodity Futures Trading Commission REGULATION & COMPLIANCE US agency monitoring futures trading an independent agency set up by the US government to monitor trading in ***futures contracts***. *Abbr* ***CFTC***

commodity market MARKETS market for bulk raw materials a market in which raw materials are bought and sold in large quantities as ***actuals*** or ***futures***. *Also called* ***commodities market***

commodity paper FINANCE loan secured by commodities a loan or advance for which commodities or financial documents relating to them are collateral

commodity pool FINANCE group trading in commodity options a group of people who join together to trade in ***options*** on commodities

commodity-product spread FINANCE trading in commodity and product coordinated trades in both a commodity and a product made from it

commodity trader MARKETS somebody buying and selling commodities a person whose business is buying and selling commodities

common cost **1.** ACCOUNTING cost recorded in more than one center a cost that is allocated to two or more cost centers within a company **2.** OPERATIONS & PRODUCTION cost associated with multiple items cost relating to more than one product or service and unable to be allocated to any individual one

common equity STOCKHOLDING & INVESTMENTS common stock in a company the ownership interest in a company that consists only of the common stock

common market INTERNATIONAL TRADE group of trading partners with few trade barriers an economic association, typically between nations, with the goal of removing or reducing trade barriers

common ownership BUSINESS ownership by employees collectively a situation in which a business is owned by the employees who work in it

common pricing OPERATIONS & PRODUCTION illegal price-fixing the illegal fixing of the price of a good or service by several businesses so that they all charge the same price

common seal LEGAL = ***company seal***

common-size financial statements ACCOUNTING statements with everything in percentages statements in which all the separate parts are expressed as percentages of the total. Such statements are often used for making performance comparisons between companies.

common stock *US* STOCKHOLDING & INVESTMENTS stock without first call on dividends a stock that provides voting rights but only pays a dividend after dividends for preferred stock have been paid. *UK term* ***ordinary share***

common stock ratio STOCKHOLDING & INVESTMENTS in US, proportion of capital represented by share in the United States, a measure of the interest each stockholder has in the company's capital

commorientes LEGAL people who die at same time the legal term for two or more people who die at the same time. For the purposes of inheritance law, in the event of two people dying at the same time, it is assumed that the older person died first.

communication GENERAL MANAGEMENT exchange of messages, information, ideas, etc. the exchange of messages conveying information, ideas, attitudes, emotions, opinions, or instructions between individuals or groups with the objective of creating, understanding, or coordinating activities. Communication is essential to the effective operation of an organization. It may be conducted informally through a grapevine or formally by means of letters, reports, briefings, and meetings. Communication may be verbal or nonverbal and include spoken, written, and visual elements.

communications GENERAL MANAGEMENT systems or technologies used for communicating systems or technologies such as postal, telephone, and e-mail networks, used for the communication of messages or for communicating within an organization

communications channel GENERAL MANAGEMENT methods by which people communicate a medium through which a message is passed in the process of ***communication***. Communications channels include the spoken, written, and printed word, and electronic or computer-based media such as radio and television, telephones, videoconferencing, and e-mail. The most effective channel for a specific message depends on the nature of the message and the audience to be reached, as well as the context in which the message is to be transmitted.

communications envelope E-COMMERCE = ***electronic envelope***

communication skills HR & PERSONNEL skills required for effective communication skills that enable people to communicate effectively with one another. Effective communication involves the choice of the best ***communications channel*** for a specific purpose, the technical knowledge to use the channel appropriately, the presentation of information in an appropriate manner for the target audience, and the ability to understand messages and responses received from others. The ability to establish and develop mutual understanding, trust, and cooperation is also important. More specifically, communication skills include the ability to speak in public, make presentations, write letters and reports, chair committees and meetings, and conduct negotiations.

communications management GENERAL MANAGEMENT job of ensuring effective communications the management, measurement, and control activities undertaken to ensure the effectiveness of communications

communications strategy MARKETING deciding best way to communicate with marketplace a management technique for determining the most effective method of communicating with the marketplace

communication technology GENERAL MANAGEMENT electronic systems for communicating electronic systems used for communication between individuals or groups. Communication technology facilitates communication between individuals or groups who are not physically present at the same location. Systems such as telephones, telex, fax, radio, television, and video are included, as well as more recent computer-based technologies, including ***electronic data interchange*** and e-mail.

community E-COMMERCE group of people with shared interest communicating online a group of Internet users with a shared interest or concept who interact with each other in newsgroups, mailing-list discussion groups, and other online interactive forums

community of interest GENERAL MANAGEMENT diverse group united for common cause a group of diverse people or organizations with a shared concern who have united to campaign for a common cause

community property FINANCE asset to be shared equally on divorce any asset that is acquired during marriage by either spouse and that, in some states of the United States, must be divided equally between them if they should divorce. *Also called* ***marital property***

Compagnie Nationale des Commissaires aux Comptes REGULATION & COMPLIANCE French regulatory body in France, an organization that regulates auditing by external, independent auditors. *Abbr* ***CNCC***

Companies Act REGULATION & COMPLIANCE UK legislation governing activities of firms in the United Kingdom, an Act of Parliament that regulates the working of companies. Although the first one was passed in 1844, the Acts of 1985 and 1989 consolidated previous legislation and incorporated directives from the European Union.

Companies House REGULATION & COMPLIANCE building where UK firms are registered in the United Kingdom, the office of the ***Registrar of Companies***. It has three main functions: the incorporation, re-registration, and dissolving of companies; the registration of documents that must be filed under company, insolvency, and related legislation; and the provision of company information to the public. *Abbr* ***CH***

Companies Registration Office REGULATION & COMPLIANCE office where UK firms are registered the office of the Registrar of Companies, an official UK organization at which companies' records must be deposited so that they can be inspected by the public. *Abbr* ***CRO***

companion bond STOCKHOLDING & INVESTMENTS US bond secured by mortgages in the United States, a class of a ***collateralized mortgage obligation*** that is paid off first when interest rates fall, leading to the underlying mortgages being prepaid. Conversely, the ***principal*** on these bonds will be repaid more slowly when interest rates rise and fewer mortgages are prepaid.

company BUSINESS organized group trading goods or providing services a group of people organized to buy or sell goods or to provide a service, usually for profit

company director CORPORATE GOVERNANCE somebody appointed to help run company a person appointed by the stockholders to help run a company

company law CORPORATE GOVERNANCE legislation governing firms the body of legislation that relates to the formation, status, conduct, and ***corporate governance*** of companies as legal entities

company limited by guarantee BUSINESS incorporated organization whose members have pre-agreed liability a type of organization, normally formed for nonprofit purposes, in which each member of the company agrees to be liable for a specific sum in the event of liquidation

company limited by shares BUSINESS UK organization with share holdings determining liability in the United Kingdom, a type of organization in which each member of the company is liable only for the fully paid value of the shares they own

company pension PENSIONS = ***occupational pension***

company policy CORPORATE GOVERNANCE firm's guidelines for behavior or procedure a statement of desired standards of behavior or procedure applicable across an organization. Company policy defines ways of acting for staff in areas where there appears to be latitude in deciding how best to operate. This may concern areas such as time off for special circumstances, drug or alcohol abuse, workplace bullying, personal use of Internet facilities, or business travel. Company policy may also apply to customers, for example, policy on complaints, customer retention, or disclosure of information. Sometimes a company policy may develop into a ***code of practice***.

company promoter BUSINESS somebody establishing new firm a person who organizes the setting up of a new company

company registrar CORPORATE GOVERNANCE person maintaining firm's share register the person who is responsible for maintaining the share register records of a company

company report CORPORATE GOVERNANCE statement of firm's activities and performance a document giving details of the activities and performance of a company. Companies are legally required to produce specific reports and submit them to the competent authorities in the country of their registration. These include ***annual reports*** and financial reports. Other reports may cover specific aspects of an organization's activities, for example, environmental or social impact.

company seal LEGAL firm's authenticating stamp or signature the impression of a company's official signature on paper or wax. Certain documents, such as stock certificates, have to bear this seal. *Also called* ***common seal***

company secretary CORPORATE GOVERNANCE UK firm's senior administrative officer a senior employee in an organization with director status and administrative and legal authority. The appointment of a company secretary is a legal requirement for most limited companies, except the smallest. A company secretary can also be a ***board secretary*** with appropriate qualifications. In the United Kingdom, many company secretaries are members of the Institute of Chartered Secretaries and Administrators.

comparative advantage ECONOMICS, BUSINESS benefit of higher, more efficient production an instance of higher, more efficient production in a particular area. A country that produces far more cars than another, for example, is said to have the comparative advantage in car production. It has been suggested that specialization in activities in which individuals or groups have a comparative advantage will result in gains in trade.

comparative advertising MARKETING advertising comparing firm's product with competitors' products a form of advertising that gives carefully selected details of competitor products for comparison with a company's own product, usually to the detriment of competitors. Comparative advertising is frequently used to advertise cars, where the availability of features such as a sun roof, air conditioning, advanced braking systems, fuel efficiency, safety features, and warranty terms in similarly priced cars is given.

comparative balance sheet TREASURY MANAGEMENT financial statement compared with one of different date one of two or more financial statements prepared on different dates that lend themselves to a comparative analysis of the financial condition of an organization

comparative credit analysis RISK assessment of financial risk an analysis of the risk associated with lending to different companies

compensating balance BANKING **1.** money required in bank account the amount of money a bank requires a customer to maintain in a non-interest-bearing account, in exchange for which the bank provides free services **2.** money required in bank account allowing credit the amount of money a bank requires a customer to maintain in an account in return for holding credit available, thereby increasing the true rate of interest on the loan

compensating errors ACCOUNTING mistakes after which accounts still balance two or more errors that are set against each other so that the accounts still balance

compensation FINANCE **1.** payment for work pay given to somebody in recompense for work performed **2.** money paid to unfairly dismissed employee in the United Kingdom, money paid by an employer on the order of an employment tribunal to an employee who has been unfairly dismissed

compensation fund STOCKHOLDING & INVESTMENTS fund compensating investors when stock exchange members default a fund operated by a stock exchange to compensate investors for losses incurred when members of the stock exchange default (lose more on their trading positions than they hold in capital)

compensation package HR & PERSONNEL overall employee pay and benefits offered by US employer in the United States, a bundle of rewards including pay, financial incentives, and ***fringe benefits*** offered to, or negotiated by, an employee

compensatory financing FINANCE IMF financial assistance financing from the ***International Monetary Fund*** to help a country in economic difficulty

competence GENERAL MANAGEMENT, HR & PERSONNEL ability to perform duties at level required an acquired personal skill that is demonstrated in an employee's ability to provide a consistently adequate or high level of performance in a specific job function. Competence should be distinguished from ***competency***, although in general usage the terms are used interchangeably. Early attempts to define the qualities of effective managers were based on lists of the personality traits and skills of the ideal manager. This is an input model approach, focusing on the skills that are needed to do the job. These skills are competencies and reflect potential ability to do something. With the advent of scientific management, people turned their attention more to the behavior of effective managers and to the outcomes of successful management. This approach is an output model, in which a manager's effectiveness is defined in terms of actual achievement. This achievement manifests itself in competences, which demonstrate that somebody has learned to do something well. There tends to be a focus in the United Kingdom on competence, whereas in the United States, the concept of competency is more popular. Competences are used in the workplace in a variety of ways. Training is often competence based, and the United Kingdom National Vocational Qualification system is based on competence standards. Competences are also used in reward management, for example, in competence-based pay. The assessment of competence is a necessary process for underpinning these initiatives by determining what competences an employee shows. At an organizational level, the idea of ***core competence*** is gaining in popularity.

competency GENERAL MANAGEMENT, HR & PERSONNEL innate personal ability an innate skill or ability that somebody has. *See also* **competence**

competition ECONOMICS, BUSINESS struggle between firms to win business rivalry between companies to achieve greater ***market share***. Competition between companies for customers will lead to product innovation and improvement and, ultimately, lower prices. The opposite of market competition is either a ***monopoly*** or a *controlled economy*, where production is governed by quotas. A company that is leading the market is said to have achieved ***competitive advantage***.

Competition Commission REGULATION & COMPLIANCE UK regulator of competition in the United Kingdom, an independent public body with the role of ensuring healthy competition between companies. It conducts in-depth inquiries into mergers, markets, and the regulation of the major regulated industries. It replaced the Monopolies and Mergers Commission in April 1999.

competitive advantage ECONOMICS, BUSINESS benefit of being more competitive a factor giving an advantage to a nation, company, group, or individual in competitive terms

competitive analysis BUSINESS evaluation of competitors' ability to compete analysis carried out for marketing purposes, which can include industry, customer, and ***competitor analysis***. A thorough competitive analysis done within a strategic framework can provide in-depth evaluation of the capabilities of key competitors.

competitive bid STOCKHOLDING & INVESTMENTS selling new securities at competing prices or terms a method of auctioning new securities whereby various underwriters offer the stock at competing prices or terms

competitive devaluation CURRENCY & EXCHANGE currency devaluation to increase competitiveness the devaluation of a currency to make a country's goods more competitive on the international markets

competitive equilibrium price BUSINESS price resulting in balance of buyers and sellers the price at which the number of buyers willing to buy a good equals the number of sellers prepared to sell it

competitive forces ECONOMICS, BUSINESS external factors forcing organization to become more competitive the external business and economic factors that compel an organization to improve its competitiveness

competitive intelligence BUSINESS information gathered that improves organization's competitive ability data gathered to improve an organization's competitive capacity. Competitive intelligence may include, for example, information about competitors' plans, activities, or products, and may sometimes be gained through ***industrial espionage***. Such information can have a significant impact on a company's own plans: it could limit the effectiveness of a new product launch, or identify growing threats to important accounts, for example. Unless organizations monitor competitor activity and take appropriate action, their business faces risk.

competitive local exchange carrier BUSINESS telecommunications provider competing with established provider a company that offers an alternate service to the established telephone service provider in a particular area

competitiveness index ECONOMICS, BUSINESS ranking of countries in order of competitive advantage an international ranking of states which uses economic and other information to list countries in order of their competitive performance. A competitiveness index can show which countries have overall or industry sector ***competitive advantage***.

competitive position BUSINESS situation in relation to competitors the market share, costs, prices, quality, and accumulated experience of an entity or product relative to competition

competitive pricing BUSINESS determining price by checking others setting a price by reference to the prices of comparable competitive products

competitive trader MARKETS = ***floor trader***

competitor BUSINESS person, company, or product competing with another a person, company, or product that is in commercial competition with another

competitor analysis *or* **competitor profiling** BUSINESS comparing firm's products with competitors' in developing strategy the identification and quantification of the relative strengths and weaknesses of a product or service compared with those of competitors or potential competitors that could be of significance in the development of a successful competitive strategy

complaint GENERAL MANAGEMENT customer's expression of dissatisfaction an expression of dissatisfaction with a product or service, either orally or in writing, from an internal or external customer. A customer may have a genuine cause for complaint, although some complaints may be made as a result of a misunderstanding or an unreasonable expectation of a product or service. How a complaint is handled will affect the overall level of ***customer satisfaction*** and may affect long-term customer loyalty. It is important for providers to have clear procedures for dealing rapidly with any complaints, to come to a fair conclusion, and to explain the reasons for what may be perceived by the customer as a negative response. *Also called* ***customer complaint***

complaints management GENERAL MANAGEMENT technique for handling complaints a management technique for assessing, analyzing, and responding to customer complaints

complementary goods MARKETING products depending on each other for sales goods sold separately, but dependent on each other for sales. Examples of complementary goods include toothbrushes and toothpaste or computers and computer desks.

complementor BUSINESS firm selling product that complements another firm's product a company that supplies a product that complements a product supplied by another company, for example, computers and software

complete *UK* REAL ESTATE = ***close***

completion *UK* REAL ESTATE = ***closing***

completion date BUSINESS date when something will finish the date when a financial or business transaction is due to be finalized

complex adaptive system GENERAL MANAGEMENT self-regulating system without controls a system that overrides conventional human controls because those controls will subdue inevitable change and development within that system. Complex adaptive systems are a product of the application of ***chaos theory*** and ***complexity theory*** to the world of organizations. It has been suggested that organizations that are subject to too much control are at risk of failure. Bureaucracy and the ***top-down approachtop down approach*** to management have been cited as examples of extreme control. However, if a bureaucracy is left to adapt naturally, it could become capable of self-organization and of creating new methods of operating.

complexity costs OPERATIONS & PRODUCTION business costs relating to changing economy the costs of operating a business which are difficult to quantify and relate to remaining competitive in a rapidly changing and increasingly complex economic environment. *Also called* ***costs of complexity***

complexity theory GENERAL MANAGEMENT theory that events will develop in random and complex fashion the theory that random events, if left to happen without interference, will settle into a complicated pattern rather than a simple one. Complexity theory is a development of ***chaos theory***. In a business context, it suggests that events within organizations and in the wider economic and social spheres cannot be predicted by simple models but will develop in a seemingly random and complex manner.

compliance REGULATION & COMPLIANCE fulfillment of requirements action to do what is required to meet official or agreed standards or regulations, or to do what is ordered by a court

compliance audit REGULATION & COMPLIANCE check to establish if obligations are being met an audit of specific activities in order to determine whether performance conforms with a predetermined contractual, regulatory, or statutory requirement

compliance department 1. STOCKHOLDING & INVESTMENTS, REGULATION & COMPLIANCE department in stockbroking firm enforcing stock exchange rules a department in a stockbroking firm that makes sure that the stock exchange rules are followed and that confidentiality is maintained in cases when the same firm represents rival clients **2.** REGULATION & COMPLIANCE department in firm enforcing business regulations a department that ensures that the company it is part of is adhering to any relevant laws and regulations relating to its business

compliance documentation STOCKHOLDING & INVESTMENTS, REGULATION & COMPLIANCE documents required for stock issues documents that a stock-issuing company publishes in line with regulations on stock issues

compliance officer REGULATION & COMPLIANCE officer ensuring that financial regulations are observed an employee of a financial organization who ensures that regulations governing its business are observed

component percentage FINANCE proportion of firm's value in capital the proportion of a company's value represented by debt, stock, assets, and other items. *See also* ***capitalization ratio***

composite index MARKETS index combining equities, indices, or averages an index of various equities, indices, or averages, mainly used as an indicator of the performance of the market or a specific sector of the market

compound FINANCE **1.** pay part of debt in the United Kingdom, to agree with creditors to settle a debt by paying part of what is owed **2.** calculate compound interest to calculate compound interest, based on the initial sum plus any interest that has accrued

compound annual return *or* **compounded annual return** STOCKHOLDING & INVESTMENTS return on investment including reinvestment returns the annual return on an investment after allowing for the return on reinvested intermediate ***cash flows***

compounding FINANCE **1.** calculating compound interest the calculation of ***compound interest***, based on the initial sum plus any interest that has accrued **2.** using compound interest the making of a transaction involving the payment or receipt of ***compound interest***

compound interest FINANCE interest calculated after inclusion of accrued interest interest calculated on the sum of the original borrowed amount and the accrued interest. *See also* ***simple interest***

compound option STOCKHOLDING & INVESTMENTS, RISK option with underlying asset another option an option that has a second option as the underlying asset. If the first option is exercised, the second option acts like an ordinary option.

compound rate FINANCE rate using compound interest the interest rate of a loan based on its ***principal***, the amount remaining to be paid, or any interest payments already received

comprehensive auditing ACCOUNTING = ***value for money audit***

comprehensive income FINANCE firm's income reflecting any changes in owner equity a company's total income for a given accounting period, including all gains and losses, not only those included in a normal income statement but also any that reflect a change in the value of an owner's interest in the business. In the United States, comprehensive income must be declared, whereas in the United Kingdom it appears in the statement of total recognized gains and losses.

comprehensive insurance *or* **comprehensive policy** INSURANCE insurance policy covering all likely risks an insurance policy that covers you against all risks that are deemed likely to happen

comptroller ACCOUNTING organization's senior accountant an accountant who is responsible for maintaining an organization's accounts

Comptroller of the Currency BANKING US official responsible for federal banks an official of the government responsible for the regulation of banks that are members of the Federal Reserve

compulsory acquisition STOCKHOLDING & INVESTMENTS purchasing last 10% of stocks at original price in the United Kingdom, the purchase by a bidder of the last 10% of stocks in an issue by right, at the offer price

compulsory liquidation BUSINESS enforced sale of assets to pay liabilities the closing of a business and selling its assets to pay off its liabilities, which is ordered by a court.

compulsory purchase annuity PENSIONS annuity purchased from UK personal pension plan in the United Kingdom, an annuity that must be purchased with the fund built up in a personal pension plan before age 75

compulsory winding up *UK* BUSINESS = ***compulsory liquidation***

computational error ACCOUNTING calculation mistake a mistake that was made in doing a calculation

computer-aided design *or* **computer-assisted design** OPERATIONS & PRODUCTION product design using computers the use of a computer to assist with the design of a product. Computer graphics, modeling, and simulation are used to represent a product on screen, so that designers can produce more accurate drawings than is possible on paper alone, and to perform calculations easily, thereby optimizing designs for production. *Abbr* ***CAD***

computer-aided manufacturing *or* **computer-assisted manufacturing** OPERATIONS & PRODUCTION product manufacturing controlled by computer a system in which the manufacture and assembly of a product are directed by a computer. Computer-aided manufacturing can be integrated with ***computer-aided design*** to create a CAD/CAM system. *Abbr* ***CAM***

computer-aided production management OPERATIONS & PRODUCTION use of computers to direct production management functions a system that enables all functions within an organization that are associated with production management to be directed by computer. ***MRP II*** is a well-known form of computer-aided production management. *Abbr* ***CAPM***

computer-assisted design OPERATIONS & PRODUCTION = ***computer-aided design***

computer-assisted manufacturing OPERATIONS & PRODUCTION = ***computer-aided manufacturing***

computer model STOCKHOLDING & INVESTMENTS training using Internet, intranet, or standalone computer a system for calculating investment opportunities, used by fund managers to see the right moment to buy or sell

computer telephony integration BUSINESS combining of telephone technology and computer technology the combining of computer and telephone technology to allow a computer to dial telephone numbers, route calls, and send and receive messages. One product of computer telephony integration is the process of *caller identification,* or caller ID. Caller ID identifies the telephone number a customer is calling from, searches the customer database to identify the caller, and pops up the customer account on the receiver's computer screen, using the facility known as *screen popping,* before the call is answered. *Abbr* ***CTI***

concealment of assets FRAUD hiding of assets from creditors the dishonest act of hiding assets so that creditors do not know they exist

concentration ratio MARKETS ratio indicating composition of market a ratio showing the proportion of a market that is dominated by a few large companies. This is calculated according to information about the size distribution of firms.

concentration risk RISK risk related to lack of variety in lending the risk of loss to a financial institution as a result of having too many outstanding loans concentrated in a particular instrument, with a particular type of borrower, or in a particular country

concentration services BANKING moving money into single account the placing of money from various accounts into a single account

concept board MARKETING large board for displaying advertising ideas a board used for presenting creative advertising ideas, usually a large one that members of a group can see easily

concept product MARKETING innovative product not yet on market a highly advanced and innovative product that is not yet in commercial production

concepts ACCOUNTING principles of accounting principles and abstract ideas underpinning the preparation of accounting information. *See also* ***fundamental accounting concepts***

concept search E-COMMERCE online search returning documents relating to word an online search for documents related conceptually to a word, rather than specifically containing the word itself

concept statement MARKETING summary of project's goals or nature an explanation or summary of the overall goals or nature of a project

concept testing MARKETING test of effectiveness of advertising idea research carried out to test the effectiveness of a creative advertising idea

concern BUSINESS firm and its staff a business or company and the people involved in it

concert party MERGERS & ACQUISITIONS secret plan to acquire company an arrangement by which several people or companies work together in secret, usually to acquire another company through a takeover bid

concession **1.** FINANCE price reduction for selected group a reduction in price for a specific group of people, not for everyone **2.** BUSINESS right to operate in another's premises the right of a retail outlet to operate within the premises of another establishment **3.** GENERAL MANAGEMENT agreement to ignore product's nonconformity to specification an agreement to ignore the failure of a product or service to conform to its specification, with a possible resultant deterioration in the quality of the product or service **4.** GENERAL MANAGEMENT compromise a compromise in opinion or action by a party to a dispute

concessionaire BUSINESS somebody with exclusive right to sell product a person or business that has the right to be the only seller of a product in a place

concessionally taxed TAX taxed at low rate being liable to tax at a preferential rate. Savings or benefits, for example, may be concessionally taxed.

conciliation HR & PERSONNEL dispute resolution by independent negotiator action taken by an independent negotiator to bring disputing sides together with the goal of restoring trust or goodwill and reaching an agreement or bringing about a reconciliation

concurrent engineering OPERATIONS & PRODUCTION product development by teams working in parallel a team-based cooperative approach to product design and development, in which all parties involved in ***new product development*** work in parallel. Concurrent engineering reduces or removes the time lag between the different stages of a product's development, and earlier entry into a market is therefore possible. Product quality is improved, development and product costs are minimized, and competitiveness is increased. *Also called* ***parallel engineering, simultaneous engineering***

conditional distribution STATISTICS probability distribution of specific random variable the probability distribution of a random variable while the values of one or more random variables are fixed

conditions of employment HR & PERSONNEL contract containing terms of employment terms agreed to by an employer and employee, which are legally enforceable through a ***contract of employment***. Conditions of employment include conditions that may be unique to the individual, such as notice period, remuneration, fringe benefits, and hours of work, as well as those that form organization-wide policies, such as discipline and grievance procedures and those dictated by legislation.

conditions of sale OPERATIONS & PRODUCTION agreements about how something is sold agreed ways in which a sale may take place, including information on discounts and credit terms

condominium REAL ESTATE combination of private and joint real estate ownership in the United States, a type of real estate ownership in which the owner has title to a dwelling unit, especially an apartment or town house, in a building or on land that is owned jointly with the owners of the other units

conduit IRA PENSIONS = ***rollover IRA***

Confederation of Asian and Pacific Accountants ACCOUNTING Asia-Pacific organization for accountants an umbrella organization for a number of accounting associations. *Abbr* ***CAPA***

Confederation of British Industry BUSINESS organization supporting UK businesses a corporate membership organization that aims to promote the interests of UK business. The CBI's headquarters are in London, but it has regional offices throughout the United Kingdom, a European office in Brussels, and a US base in Washington, DC. *Abbr* ***CBI***

conference GENERAL MANAGEMENT meeting for members of organizations with shared interests a type of meeting held between members of often disparate organizations to discuss matters of mutual interest. Conferences are held for a variety of reasons, including resolving problems, making decisions, developing cooperation, and publicizing ideas, products, and services. They may take place within an organization but often draw people together regionally, nationally, or internationally, and involve a large number of speakers and delegates. Many conferences are organized for commercial profit.

conference call GENERAL MANAGEMENT telephone call connecting three or more people a telephone call that connects three or more lines so that people in different locations can communicate and exchange information by voice. Conference calls reduce the cost of meetings by eliminating travel time and expenditure. Public switched telephone networks or dedicated private networks and a centrally located device called a bridge are used to connect the participants. Microphones and loudspeakers may also be used to make group-to-group communication possible. Conference calls are a type of ***teleconferencing***.

confidence indicator ECONOMICS, MARKETS number that shows how economic market will perform a number that gives an indication of how well a market or an economy will fare

confidence interval STATISTICS expected range of possible outcomes in a statistical study, the range of values of sample observations that contain the true parameter value within a given probability

confidentiality agreement GENERAL MANAGEMENT agreement to treat information as private and confidential an agreement whereby an organization that has access to information about the affairs of another organization makes an undertaking to treat the information as private and confidential. A potential buyer of a company who requires further information in the process of due diligence may be asked to sign a confidentiality agreement stating that the information will only be used for the purpose of deciding whether to go ahead with the deal and will only be disclosed to employees involved in the negotiations. Such agreements are also used where information is shared in the context of a partnership or ***benchmarking*** program.

confirmation STOCKHOLDING & INVESTMENTS, OPERATIONS & PRODUCTION document confirming transaction or agreement a written acknowledgment of a transaction or agreement, for example, from a broker confirming and detailing a securities transaction

conflict management GENERAL MANAGEMENT discovering and controlling conflict within organization the identification and control of conflict within an organization. There are three main philosophies of conflict management: all conflict is bad and potentially destructive; conflict is inevitable and managers should attempt to harness it positively; conflict is essential to the survival of an organization and should be encouraged.

conflict of interest *or* **conflict of interests** GENERAL MANAGEMENT situation in which somebody's opposing interests prejudice objectivity a situation in which a person or institution is caught between opposing concerns, loyalties, or objectives that prejudice impartiality. A conflict of interest may be between self-advantage and the benefit of an organization for which somebody works, or it could arise when somebody is connected with two or more companies that are competing. The correct course of action in such cases is for the person concerned to declare any interests, to make known the way in which those interests conflict, and to abstain from participating in the decision-making process involving those interests. A conflict of interest may also arise when an institution acts for parties on both sides of a transaction and could derive an advantage from a specific outcome.

conglomerate company BUSINESS organization owning different types of companies an organization that owns a diverse range of companies in different industries. Conglomerates are usually ***holding companies*** with subsidiaries in wide-ranging business areas, often built up through mergers and takeovers and operating on an international scale.

conglomerate diversification MERGERS & ACQUISITIONS starting different types of subsidiaries the ***diversification*** of a ***conglomerate company*** through the setting-up of ***subsidiary companies*** with activities in various areas

conglomerate merger MERGERS & ACQUISITIONS merger of companies in unrelated industries a merger of organizations that belong to different types of industry

connectivity GENERAL MANAGEMENT ability of devices or people to connect electronically the ability of electronic products to connect with others, or of individuals, companies, and countries to be connected with one another electronically

connexity GENERAL MANAGEMENT being electronically connected worldwide the condition of being closely and intricately connected by worldwide communications networks

consequential loss policy INSURANCE = ***business interruption insurance***

consideration FINANCE payment for service a sum of money paid in return for a service

consignee OPERATIONS & PRODUCTION somebody receiving goods a person who receives goods from somebody for their own use or to sell for the owner

consignment OPERATIONS & PRODUCTION goods to be sold or returned a quantity of goods given to somebody for sale, with the provision that any unsold goods will be returned

consignment stock STOCKHOLDING & INVESTMENTS stock held by dealer for somebody stock held by one party (the "dealer") but legally owned by another (the "manufacturer") on terms that give the dealer the right to sell the stock in the normal course of its business, or, at its option, to return it unsold to the legal owner

consignor OPERATIONS & PRODUCTION somebody handing goods over a person who gives goods to somebody else for sale, safekeeping, or disposal

consistency ACCOUNTING using same accounting rules every year the concept that a company should apply the same rules and standards to its accounting procedures for similar items and from one year to the next. In the United Kingdom, deviation from consistency must be noted in the company's ***annual report***.

consolidate ACCOUNTING combine accounts of holding company and its subsidiaries to combine the accounts of several subsidiary companies as well as their ***holding company*** in a single financial statement

consolidated accounts ACCOUNTING = ***consolidated financial statement***

consolidated balance sheet ACCOUNTING outline of firm's finances a balance sheet containing the most significant details of a company's finances, including those of subsidiaries

consolidated debt FINANCE debt incorporating smaller debts a single large debt into which smaller ones have been subsumed

consolidated financial statement ACCOUNTING outline of finances of parent company and subsidiaries a listing of the most significant details of the finances of a company and of all its subsidiaries. *Also called* ***consolidated accounts***

consolidated fund TAX public money for paying national debt a fund of public money, especially from taxes, used by the government to make interest payments on the national debt and other regular payments

consolidated invoice OPERATIONS & PRODUCTION combined invoice for items sent to buyer separately an invoice that covers all items shipped by one seller to one buyer during a particular period

consolidated loan FINANCE large loan for paying off smaller loans a large loan, the proceeds of which are used to eliminate smaller ones

consolidated stock STOCKHOLDING & INVESTMENTS *see* ***consols***

consolidated tape MARKETS ticker tape listing all US stock exchange activity a ticker tape that lists all transactions of the New York and other US stock exchanges

consolidated tax return TAX joint tax return for several firms a tax return that covers several companies, typically a parent company and all of its subsidiaries

consolidation 1. MERGERS & ACQUISITIONS joining several firms together the uniting of two or more businesses into one company **2.** STOCKHOLDING & INVESTMENTS creating fewer but costlier shares the combination of a specific number of lower-priced shares into one higher-priced one

consolidation accounting ACCOUNTING combining financial statements for parent firm and subsidiaries the process of adjusting and combining financial information from the individual financial statements of a parent undertaking and its subsidiary undertakings to prepare consolidated financial statements that present financial information for the group as a single economic entity

consols STOCKHOLDING & INVESTMENTS UK government bonds with no maturity date in the United Kingdom, government bonds that pay interest but do not have a maturity date. *Full form* ***consolidated stock***

consortium BUSINESS group of independent organizations allied for specific goal a group of independent organizations that join forces to achieve a particular goal, for example, to bid for a project or to conduct cooperative purchasing. A consortium goes on to complete the project if its bid is successful and is often dissolved on completion. This form of temporary alliance allows diverse skills, capabilities, and knowledge to be brought together.

consultant GENERAL MANAGEMENT specialist brought in to give advice to organization an expert in a specialized field brought in to provide independent professional advice to an organization on some aspect of its activities. A consultant may advise on the overall management of an organization or on a specific project, such as the introduction of a new computer system. Consultants are usually retained by a client for a set period of time, during which they will investigate the matter in hand and produce a report detailing their recommendations. Consultants may be established in business independently or be employed by a large consulting firm. Specific types of consultants include ***management consultants*** and ***internal consultants***.

consulting actuary PENSIONS actuary advising pension funds an independent actuary who gives mathematical and statistical advice to large pension funds

consumer ECONOMICS somebody using product or service somebody who uses a product or service. A consumer may not be the purchaser of a product or service and should be distinguished from a customer, who is the person or organization that purchased the product or service.

consumer advertising MARKETING advertising aimed at consumer market advertising aimed at individuals and the domestic and family market as opposed to industrial advertising, which is aimed at businesses

consumer behavior MARKETING consumer buying behavior the factors that affect people's decision-making on whether to buy something and what to buy. *See also* ***consumer demand***

consumer confidence ECONOMICS how people feel about economic future a measure of how people feel about the future of the economy and their own financial situation, obtained through polling

consumer council BUSINESS group representing consumers' interests a group that represents the interests of consumers

consumer credit FINANCE credit provided for purchase of goods credit given by stores, banks, and other financial institutions to consumers so that they can buy goods

Consumer Credit Act, 1974 FINANCE UK legislation regulating provision of loans in the United Kingdom, an Act of Parliament that licenses lenders and requires them to state clearly the full terms of loans that they make, including the APR

consumer demand MARKETING consumer buying behavior the patterns of ***consumer behavior*** that affect buying decisions. Consumer demand is influenced in various ways. Psychologists and marketers have identified three important factors affecting buying decisions: needs, which are things we must have, such as food; wants, which are nice to have but not essential, such as a new car; and motives, such as keeping up appearances. These factors form part of a profile which includes motivations, personality, perceptions, cognition, attitudes, and values. Other factors that influence demand include gender, age, social grouping, education, location, income, culture, and the seasons. Consumers can therefore be divided into discrete segments, each of which has a specific pattern of buying behavior. Products and services can then be targeted at specific segments of the market.

consumer durables BUSINESS purchased items intended for long-term use items that are bought and used by the public and intended to last a long time, for example, washing machines, refrigerators, or stoves

consumer-facing GENERAL MANAGEMENT **1.** engaging directly with consumers involved with or involving direct contact with consumers **2.** directly accessible by consumers able to be directly accessed by consumers, and often being the first point of contact

consumer goods marketing MARKETING promotion of products to end users the promotion of products to members of the public. Consumer goods marketing is aimed at individuals rather than organizations and promotes products directly to the end user rather than to intermediaries. Marketing strategies will be different from those used in ***industrial goods marketing***.

consumerism MARKETING influence of consumers on product manufacturing and sale the influence of the general public, as end users of products and services, on the way companies manufacture and sell their goods. Consumers exert considerable power over companies as organizations become more customer-focused. Demand is rising for products that are of high quality, ethically produced, well priced, and safe, and consumerism pressures companies to operate and produce goods and services in accordance with the public's wishes. In fact, the goals of consumerism are not at odds with those of marketing, as both have the end goal of pleasing the consumer. In practice, however, marketing does not always succeed, and there is still a need for legislation to back up the right of consumers to demand products that are of good quality and for consumer protection bodies that influence the commercial world on consumers' behalf. A particular form of consumer pressure, motivated by environmental concerns, is *green consumerism,* which campaigns for environmentally friendly goods, services, and means of production.

consumer market research MARKETING market research focusing on consumers ***market research*** that focuses on gathering and analyzing data on individual or domestic consumers, as opposed to industrial or business customers. *Also called* ***consumer research***

consumer panel MARKETING selected consumers whose purchasing habits are tracked a carefully selected group of people whose purchasing habits are regularly monitored. A consumer panel usually consists of a large cross-section of the population so as to provide meaningful data. There are two types of panel: *diary panels,* where members fill in a regular detailed diary of purchases, and, less commonly, *home audit panels,* where visits are made to the homes of members to check purchases, packaging, and used cartons. These panels run over a period of time to gain a broad overview of purchasing habits. A ***focus group*** is similar to a consumer panel, but is usually used to determine customers' views of a specific product or range of products. Members of a group meet together under the guidance of a facilitator to discuss their opinions on a face-to-face basis.

consumer price index ECONOMICS benchmark of basic retail prices an index of the prices of goods and services purchased by consumers, used to measure the cost of living or the rate of inflation in an economy. *Abbr* ***CPI***

consumer profile MARKETING detailed analysis of similar consumers for market research a detailed analysis of the purchasing habits of a group of ***consumers***, assessing influences such as age, gender, education, occupation, income, and personal and psychological characteristics. Consumer profiles are built up from extensive ***market research*** and are used for ***market segmentation*** purposes.

consumer protection MARKETING regulations protecting consumers' interests the safeguarding of consumers' interests in terms of quality, price, and safety, usually within a statutory framework. The growing purchasing power of consumers and the rise in ***consumerism*** from the late 1950s onward led to increased demands for protection against unsafe goods and services and unscrupulous trading practices.

consumer research MARKETING = ***consumer market research***

consumer services marketing MARKETING promotion and sale of services to domestic consumers the marketing of services to domestic consumers. Consumer services marketing may promote such services as banking, insurance, travel and tourism, leisure, telecommunications, and services provided by local authorities. Strategies to market these services to business constitute ***industrial services marketing***.

consumer spending MARKETING total amount of household and personal expenditure the total value of household and personal expenditure measured at macro and micro levels. At the macro level, consumer confidence can be measured by the overall levels of consumer spending; if earnings have increased at a faster rate than prices, then disposable income, or spending power, increases. At a micro level, there are market reports on the value of actual and predicted spend on a large range of consumer goods, including food, pharmaceuticals, clothing, cars, and vacations. ***Consumer demand*** is a related concept.

consumer-to-consumer commerce E-COMMERCE electronic transactions between consumers e-business transactions conducted between two individuals. The auction site eBay is a facilitator of consumer-to-consumer commerce.

consumption ECONOMICS amount of products and services used the quantity of resources used by consumers to satisfy their current needs and wants, measured by the sum of the current expenditure of the government and individual consumers

consumption tax TAX tax to encourage less use of something a tax used to encourage people to buy less of a particular good or service by increasing its price. This type of tax is often levied in times of national hardship.

contact card E-COMMERCE card that physically touches card reader a ***smart card*** in which the microprocessor chip is visible and can make physical contact with the reading device

contactless card E-COMMERCE card with chip read by radio signals a ***smart card*** in which the microprocessor chip is not visible and is accessed by the reading device by radio signals rather than by physical contact. An increasingly common use of this technology is in such applications as toll collection, where the card is accessed as the motorist displays it to the reading device in passing.

contagion ECONOMICS spreading effect of downturn across economies a situation in which a weakening economy in one country causes economies in other countries to weaken

contango MARKETS future delivery costing more than delivery now a situation where the price of commodities is higher for future delivery than it is for immediate delivery

content management E-COMMERCE dealing with words and pictures on website the means and methods of managing the textual and graphical content of a website

contestable market MARKETS economic market that any firm can participate in a market in which there are no barriers to entry, as when there is ***perfect competition***

contested takeover bid MERGERS & ACQUISITIONS takeover bid resisted by board of target firm a takeover bid where the board of the target company does not recommend it to the stockholders and tries to fight it. *Also called* ***hostile bid***

contingency LEGAL condition to be met in contract a condition in a contract which must be met before the contract becomes legally binding

contingency fund ACCOUNTING money held for unplanned expenditure money set aside from normal expenditure in case it is needed for unplanned expenses

contingency management GENERAL MANAGEMENT skill of adapting to changing situation the capacity for flexibility in varying responses and attitudes to meet the needs of different situations. Contingency management may be practiced by both individuals and organizations. Within the latter, it may be formalized through a ***contingency plan*** linked to ***risk*** or ***crisis management*** strategies, or be derived from the results of ***scenario planning***.

contingency plan GENERAL MANAGEMENT **1.** secondary plan prepared in case of situational changes a plan, drawn up in advance, to ensure a positive and rapid response to a changing situation. A contingency plan often results from ***scenario planning*** and may form part of an organization's strategy for coping with disasters. **2.** plan if situation does not progress as hoped action to be implemented only upon the occurrence of anticipated future events other than those in the accepted forward plan

contingency table STATISTICS table classifying data by variables a table in which observations on data are classified according to a number of variables

contingency tax TAX new tax to deal with particular problem a one-time tax levied by a government to deal with a particular economic problem, for example, too high a level of imports coming into the country

contingency theory GENERAL MANAGEMENT idea that management method should match situation in management, the theory that there is no single best way to organize or manage and that each firm should be organized and structured to suit the technology used and the environment around it

contingent beneficiary LEGAL person who inherits if main beneficiary is dead a person who is designated to receive assets or proceeds such as those from an insurance policy or estate, if the primary beneficiary has died

contingent deferred sales charge STOCKHOLDING & INVESTMENTS fee payable on redemption a redemption fee, or ***back-end loading***, payable on a share in a mutual fund only if the share is redeemed. It declines every year until it disappears, usually after six years. *Abbr* ***CDSC***. *See also* ***B share***

contingent liability ACCOUNTING potential liability provided for in company's accounts a liability that may or may not occur, but for which provision is made in a company's accounts, as opposed to "provisions," for which money is set aside for an anticipated expenditure

continuous budget TREASURY MANAGEMENT = ***rolling budget***

continuous compounding ACCOUNTING continuous calculation and addition of interest a system in which interest is continuously calculated and added to the initial sum plus any interest that has already accrued on a debt

continuous disclosure STOCKHOLDING & INVESTMENTS in Canada, providing full information about public firm in Canada, the practice of ensuring that complete, timely, accurate, and balanced information about a public company is made available to shareholders

continuous improvement GENERAL MANAGEMENT making frequent small changes to improve quality the seeking of small improvements in processes and products, with the objective of increasing quality and reducing waste. Continuous improvement is one of the tools that underpin the philosophies of ***total quality management*** and ***lean production***. Through constant study and revision of processes, a better product can result at reduced cost.

continuous inventory *or* **continuous stocktaking** ACCOUNTING comparing actual inventory to accounting records throughout year regular and consistent stocktaking throughout the fiscal year in order to ensure that the physical reality of the stock situation at any given time tallies with the accounting records. Any discrepancies will highlight errors or losses of stock and the accounts are adjusted to reflect this. Continuous inventory may preclude the need for an annual inventory.

continuous net settlement MARKETS automated system of tracking securities and cash balances an automated accounting system that uses a central clearing house to clear and settle securities transactions, maintaining complete records of companies' money balances. *Abbr* ***CNS***

continuous operation costing *or* **continuous process costing** OPERATIONS & PRODUCTION basing costs on process not product a costing method in which costs are first charged to the process of production, then averaged over the units produced during the relevant period. It is used where production consists of a sequence of continuous or repetitive operations.

contra account ACCOUNTING account offsetting another account an account that offsets another account, for example, when a company's supplier is not only a creditor in that company's books but also a debtor because it has purchased goods on credit

contract 1. MARKETS securities transaction an agreement to buy or sell ***securities*** or other ***financial instruments*** **2.** GENERAL MANAGEMENT legal agreement a mutually agreed, legally binding agreement between two or more parties

contract broker MARKETS broker trading for other brokers a broker who buys or sells stock on behalf of other brokers

contract costing ACCOUNTING attributing costs to individual contracts a form of ***specific order costing*** in which costs are attributed to individual contracts

contract for difference 1. STOCKHOLDING & INVESTMENTS swapping of fixed-price assets for floating-price assets an exchange of a fixed-price asset for one that has a price that varies **2.** CURRENCY & EXCHANGE currency exchange contract a ***forward exchange rate*** contract for currency. *Abbr* ***CFD***

contract hire GENERAL MANAGEMENT when firm leases resources from another firm an arrangement whereby an organization enters into a contract for the use of assets owned by another organization, as an alternative to purchasing the assets itself. Contract hire agreements usually cover a period shorter than the useful economic life of the assets concerned and often include arrangements for maintenance and replacement. Organizations frequently use contract hire arrangements for the provision of company cars or office equipment.

contracting GENERAL MANAGEMENT process of making legal supply agreement the process of making an agreement governed by a ***contract*** for the provision of goods or services to an organization

contracting out 1. PENSIONS moving employees from former UK state pension plan formerly in the United Kingdom, the withdrawal of employees by an employer or voluntarily from ***SERPS*** and their enrollment in a government-approved employer-sponsored pension plan scheme that met government standards or in a ***personal pension*** **2.** GENERAL MANAGEMENT = ***outsourcing***

contracting party LEGAL party to formal agreement a person or organization that signs a formal agreement to do or not do something

contract manufacturing OPERATIONS & PRODUCTION having another firm produce product or part the ***outsourcing*** of a requirement to manufacture a particular product or component to a third party. Contract manufacturing enables companies to reduce the level of investment in their own capabilities to manufacture, while retaining a product produced to a high quality, at a reasonable price, and delivered to a flexible schedule.

contract month MARKETS month when goods must be delivered the month in which an option expires and goods covered by it must be delivered. *Also called* ***delivery month***

contract note MARKETS full description of transaction a document with the complete description of a stock transaction

contract of employment LEGAL, HR & PERSONNEL legal agreement between employer and employee a legally enforceable agreement, either oral or written, between an employer and an employee which defines terms and ***conditions of employment*** to which both parties must adhere. Express terms of the contract are agreed between the two parties and include the organization's normal terms and conditions in addition to those that relate specifically to the individual. These terms can only be changed by employee agreement, if the contract itself allows for variation, or by terminating the contract. Terms are also implied in the contract by custom and practice or by common law. *Also called* ***employment contract***

contract purchasing OPERATIONS & PRODUCTION process of buying product through leasing a mechanism for buying leased goods. In contract purchasing, a purchaser agrees to buy goods or equipment to be paid for in a series of installments, each comprising a proportion of the capital and an interest element. After a final payment, legal ownership passes to the user.

contractual liability LEGAL legal responsibility stated in contract a legal responsibility for something as set out formally in a written agreement

contractual obligation LEGAL course of action required by contract the legal duty to take a specific course of action, as imposed by a commercial ***contract*** or a ***contract of employment***

contractual savings STOCKHOLDING & INVESTMENTS money saved regularly in long-term investments savings in the form of regular payments into long-term investments such as pension plans

contract work HR & PERSONNEL work done under contract work done according to the terms of a written agreement

contra entry ACCOUNTING account entry offsetting earlier entry an entry made in the opposite side of an account to offset an earlier entry, for example, a debit against a credit

contrarian STOCKHOLDING & INVESTMENTS investing against market trends used to describe an investor who purchases securities in opposition to the current market trend, buying when most others are selling and vice versa

contrarian research STOCKHOLDING & INVESTMENTS investigation of purchases against market trends research on market trends resulting in advice to potential buyers to purchase stocks against the current trend

contrarian stockpicking STOCKHOLDING & INVESTMENTS choosing stocks against market trends the practice of purchasing stocks against the current market trend

contributed surplus FINANCE money from sources other than earnings the part of company profits that comes from sources other than earnings, for example, from selling stock above its ***nominal value***

contribution 1. FINANCE, PENSIONS money paid into fund an amount of money placed in a fund of any kind, for example, money paid regularly into a pension **2.** FINANCE amount extra unit gains or loses the amount of money gained or lost from selling an additional unit of a product

contribution center FINANCE profitable section of business a ***profit center*** in which marginal or direct costs are equal to or less than revenue

contribution margin FINANCE profit from individual product the amount of money that an individual product or service contributes to net profit

contribution of capital FINANCE money paid as additional capital money paid to a company as additional capital

contributions holiday PENSIONS period when firm stops payments to pension plan a period during which a company stops making contributions to its pension plan because the plan is considered to be sufficiently well funded

contributory pension plan *US* PENSIONS pension provision requiring employees' contribution a pension plan into which employees must pay a portion of their salary on a regular basis. *UK term* ***contributory pension scheme***

contributory pension scheme *UK* PENSIONS = ***contributory pension plan***

control CORPORATE GOVERNANCE power to run organization the authority to direct an organization's operations and activities

control environment CORPORATE GOVERNANCE organization's management style the corporate culture of the directors and senior management of an organization

controlled company BUSINESS firm where one stockholder holds majority of voting stock a company in which a decisive proportion of the stock belongs to one owner. In the United States this is more than 25%, and in the United Kingdom, more than 50%.

controlled disbursement FINANCE payment once daily the practice of presenting checks for payment only once each day

controlled economy ECONOMICS economy with production quotas an economy in which production is governed by quotas. Controlled economies and ***monopolies*** are the opposite of market competition. *See also* ***competition***

controller ACCOUNTING organization's senior accountant an accountant who is responsible for maintaining an organization's accounts

control procedures CORPORATE GOVERNANCE rules for running organization the policies and procedures in addition to the ***control environment*** which are established to achieve an organization's specific objectives. They include procedures designed to prevent or to detect and correct errors.

control risk RISK likelihood of firm's control system allowing errors the part of an ***audit risk*** that relates to a client's internal control system

control security STOCKHOLDING & INVESTMENTS security held by somebody with management power a security held by a person who has an affiliation with the issuing company and the power to direct its management and policies, and whose resale must meet US Securities and Exchange Commission conditions

convergence 1. ECONOMICS movement toward similarity in countries' economies a situation in which the economic factors in two countries become more alike, for example, when basic interest rates or budget deficits become more similar **2.** MARKETS coming together of futures and spot prices a situation in which the price of a commodity on the futures market moves toward the ***spot price*** as settlement date approaches

conversion 1. MARKETS trading one investment product for another a trade of one convertible financial instrument for another, for example, a bond for shares of stock **2.** MARKETS trading one mutual fund's shares for another's a trade of shares of one mutual fund for shares of another in the same family **3.** PENSIONS transfer of assets to Roth IRA the process of transferring assets to a ***Roth IRA*** from another type of ***IRA***

conversion costs FINANCE expense of changing raw materials into products the cost of changing raw materials into finished or semi-finished products. Conversion costs include wages, other direct production costs, and the production overhead.

conversion discount *or* **conversion premium** STOCKHOLDING & INVESTMENTS price difference between convertible and common stock the difference between the price of convertible stock and the common stock into which it is to be converted

conversion issue STOCKHOLDING & INVESTMENTS offer of new bonds as older bonds expire the issue of new bonds, timed to coincide with the date of maturity of older bonds, with the intention of persuading investors to reinvest

conversion of funds FRAUD improper use of somebody else's money the act of using money that does not belong to you for a purpose for which it is not supposed to be used

conversion period STOCKHOLDING & INVESTMENTS period for converting loan stock into common stock a time during which convertible loan stock may be changed into common stock

conversion price 1. CURRENCY & EXCHANGE exchange rate for currency the price at which a currency is changed into a foreign currency. *Also called* ***conversion rate*** *(sense 2)* **2.** STOCKHOLDING & INVESTMENTS price offered for converting preferred stock the price at which preferred stock is converted into common stock

conversion rate 1. STOCKHOLDING & INVESTMENTS = ***conversion price*** *(sense 2)* **2.** CURRENCY & EXCHANGE = ***conversion price*** *(sense 1)* **3.** MARKETING how many people buy after consideration the percentage of inquiries by potential customers or sales calls by sales staff that results in actual sales

conversion ratio 1. STOCKHOLDING & INVESTMENTS relative value of two convertible investment products an expression of the quantity of one security that can be obtained for another, for example, shares for a ***convertible bond***.

The conversion ratio may be established when the convertible is issued. If that is the case, the ratio will appear in the indenture, the binding agreement that details the convertible's terms.

If the conversion ratio is not set, it can be calculated quickly by dividing the nominal value of the convertible security (typically $1,000) by its conversion price.

$1,000 / $40 per share = 25

In this example, the conversion ratio is 25:1, which means that every bond held with a $1,000 nominal value can be exchanged for 25 shares of common stock.

Knowing the conversion ratio enables an investor to decide whether convertibles (or a group of them) are more valuable than the shares of common stock they represent. If the stock is currently trading at 30, the conversion value is $750, or $250 less than the nominal value of the convertible. It would therefore be unwise to convert.

A convertible's indenture can sometimes contain a provision stating that the conversion ratio will change over the years. **2.** MERGERS & ACQUISITIONS number of shares traded for others during merger the number of shares of one common stock to be issued for each outstanding ordinary share of a different type when a merger takes place

conversion value STOCKHOLDING & INVESTMENTS value of investment if changed for another type the value that a security would have if converted into another type of security

convertibility CURRENCY & EXCHANGE ease of currency exchange the ability of one currency to be easily exchanged for another currency

convertible ARM MORTGAGES adjustable-rate mortgage that can be made fixed-rate an adjustable-rate mortgage that the borrower can convert into a fixed-rate mortgage under specific terms

convertible bond STOCKHOLDING & INVESTMENTS bond that can be traded for another investment a bond that the owner can convert into another asset, especially common stock

convertible currency CURRENCY & EXCHANGE easily exchanged currency a currency that can easily be exchanged for another

convertible debenture STOCKHOLDING & INVESTMENTS debenture exchangeable for stock a debenture or ***loan stock*** that can be exchanged for stock at a later date

convertible loan stock STOCKHOLDING & INVESTMENTS in UK, money loaned and redeemable as stock in the United Kingdom, money lent to a company which can be converted into shares at a later date

convertible preference shares *UK* STOCKHOLDING & INVESTMENTS = ***convertible preferred stock***

convertible preferred stock *US* STOCKHOLDING & INVESTMENTS stock that can be traded for another investment stocks that give the holder the right to exchange them at a fixed price for another security, usually common stock.

Preferred stocks and other convertible securities offer investors a hedge: fixed-interest income without sacrificing the chance to participate in a company's capital appreciation.

When a company does well, investors can convert their holdings into common stock that is more valuable. When a company is less successful, they can still receive interest and principal payments, and also recover their investment and preserve their capital if a more favorable investment appears.

Conversion ratios and prices are important facts to know about preferred stocks. This information is found on the indenture statement that accompanies all issues. Occasionally the indenture will state that the conversion ratio will change over time. For example, the conversion price might be $50 for the first five years, $55 for the next five years, and so forth. Stock splits can affect conversion considerations.

In theory, convertible preferred stocks (and convertible exchangeable preferred stocks) are usually perpetual. However, issuers tend to force conversion or induce voluntary conversion for convertible preferred stocks within ten years. Steadily increasing common stock dividends is one inducement tactic used. As a result, the conversion feature for preferred stocks often resembles that of debt securities. Call protection for the investor is usually about three years, and a 30 to 60-day call notice is typical.

About 50% of convertible equity issues also have a "soft call provision." If the common stock price reaches a specified ratio, the issuer is permitted to force conversion before the end of the normal protection period. *UK term* ***convertible preference shares***

convertibles STOCKHOLDING & INVESTMENTS securities convertible to common stock corporate bonds or shares of preferred stock that can be converted into common stock at a set price on set dates

convertible security STOCKHOLDING & INVESTMENTS investment product that can be converted to another a bond, warrant, or share of preferred stock that can be converted into another type of security, especially common stock

convertible term assurance *UK* INSURANCE = ***convertible term insurance***

convertible term insurance *US* INSURANCE extendable life insurance life insurance with an agreed termination date that the policyholder can convert to insurance until death under specific conditions

convexity ECONOMICS, FINANCE relationship of values the convex shape of a curve. The theory is that if points in a set are connected and the line between any two points is included in the set, then the set is convex. In economics, this corresponds to diminishing ***marginal utility***. In finance it can represent a convex curve in the price yield relationship of a bond or any non-linear price function, for example, that of an option.

conveyance *US* REAL ESTATE transfer of title to real estate the legal transfer of real estate from the seller to the buyer. *UK term* ***conveyancing***

conveyancing *UK* REAL ESTATE = ***conveyance***

COO *abbr* GENERAL MANAGEMENT ***chief operating officer***

cooling-off period **1.** LEGAL time allowed for reconsidering agreement a period during which somebody who is about to enter into an agreement may reflect on all aspects of the arrangement and change his or her mind if necessary **2.** HR & PERSONNEL break in negotiations allowing parties to calm down an agreed pause in a dispute, especially a labor dispute, to allow the tempers of the negotiating parties to cool before the resumption of negotiations **3.** *UK* INSURANCE period allowing cancellation of insurance a period of ten days during which somebody who has signed a life insurance policy may cancel it

cooperative BUSINESS jointly owned organization a business that is jointly owned by the people who operate it, with all profits shared equally

cooperative advertising MARKETING joint advertising by different groups with same goals a joint advertising campaign between groups with a shared objective, for example, retailer groups, or manufacturer and retailer

cooperative movement BUSINESS organized effort to share profits from joint business a movement that aims to share profits and benefits from jointly owned commercial enterprises among members. The movement was begun in Rochdale, Lancashire, England, in 1844 by 28 weavers and developed to include manufacturing and wholesale businesses as well as insurance and financial services. The Co-op in the United Kingdom and the Mondragon cooperative in Spain are two of the best-known examples.

cooperative society BUSINESS organization with customers and employees as joint partners an organization in which customers and employees are partners and share the profits

coproperty BUSINESS co-ownership of property the ownership of property by two or more people together

coproprietor BUSINESS sharer in ownership of property a person who owns a property with one other person or more

copyright LEGAL legal protection for creative material the legal protection for creative ideas, trademarks, and other brand-related material

copy testing MARKETING investigating effectiveness of advertising content research carried out to test the effectiveness of creative advertising material

copywriter MARKETING somebody who writes advertising material a person who devises the wording of an advertisement or promotional material. A copywriter may be employed by an advertising agency or, in scientific or technical areas, directly by a manufacturing or distribution company. Many copywriters also work freelance.

core business BUSINESS firm's most important activities the central, and usually the original, focus of an organization's activities which differentiates it from others and makes a vital contribution to its success. The concept of core business became prominent in the 1980s when ***diversification*** by large companies failed to generate the anticipated degree of commercial success. It was later suggested that organizations should avoid diversifying into areas beyond their field of expertise. An organization's core business should be defined by its ***core competences***.

core capability GENERAL MANAGEMENT = ***core competence***

core competence GENERAL MANAGEMENT, HR & PERSONNEL firm's important ability that makes it different a key ability or strength that an organization has acquired that differentiates it from others, gives it ***competitive advantage***, and contributes to its long-term success. Core competence is a resource-based approach to corporate strategy. The terms core competence and core capability are often used interchangeably, but some writers make distinctions between the two concepts. *Also called* ***core capability***

core values **1.** GENERAL MANAGEMENT firm's important guiding principles the guiding principles of an organization, espoused by senior management, and accepted by employees, often reflected in the ***mission statement*** of the organization. Core values often influence the culture of an organization and are usually long-standing beliefs. *Also called* ***shared values*** **2.** HR & PERSONNEL person's important guiding principles a small set of key concepts and ideals that guide somebody's life and help him or her to make important decisions

corner MARKETS control market and price to control enough of a specific good or service to be able to manipulate the price

corporate action STOCKHOLDING & INVESTMENTS firm's action that affects its shares a measure that a company takes that has an effect on the number of shares outstanding or the rights that apply to shares

corporate bond STOCKHOLDING & INVESTMENTS bond issued by firm a long-term bond with fixed interest issued by a corporation

corporate culture GENERAL MANAGEMENT shared values of organization the combined beliefs, values, ethics, procedures, and atmosphere of an organization. The culture of an organization consists of largely unspoken values, norms, and behaviors that become the natural way of doing things. An organization's culture may be more apparent to an external observer than an internal practitioner. There can be several subcultures within an organization, for example, defined by hierarchy, e.g.shop floor or executive, or by function, e.g. sales, design, or production. Changing or renewing corporate culture in order to achieve the organization's strategy is considered one of the major tasks of organization leadership, as it is recognized that such a change is hard to achieve without the will of the leader.

corporate finance FINANCE financial affairs of businesses the financial affairs of companies and institutions

corporate fraud FRAUD dishonest behavior at company level a type of fraud committed by large organizations rather than individuals, for example, auditing irregularities. Since the collapse of Enron and WorldCom in 2001 and 2002, respectively, auditing practice around the world, but especially in the United States, has come under much scrutiny. Both companies had overstated their profits, but the auditors, Arthur Andersen, had approved accounts in each case.

corporate giving GENERAL MANAGEMENT donations by firm to community monetary or in-kind donations by organizations as part of the process of community involvement

corporate governance CORPORATE GOVERNANCE system for running firm the system by which companies are directed and controlled. Boards of directors are responsible for the governance of their companies. The stockholders' role in governance is to appoint the directors and the auditors and to satisfy themselves that an appropriate governance structure is in place. The responsibilities of the board include setting the company's strategic goals, providing the leadership to put them into effect, supervising the management of the business, and reporting to the stockholders on their stewardship. The board's actions are subject to laws, regulations, and the wishes of the stockholders in the general meeting.

corporate hospitality GENERAL MANAGEMENT meals and entertainment paid for by firm entertainment provided by an organization. Corporate hospitality was originally designed to help sales people build relationships with customers, but it is now increasingly used as a staff incentive and in employee team building and training exercises.

corporate identity CORPORATE GOVERNANCE firm's distinctive features as expressed to outsiders the distinctive characteristics or personality of an organization, including corporate culture, values, and philosophy as perceived by those within the organization and presented to those outside. Corporate identity is expressed through the name, symbols, and logos used by the organization, and the design of communication materials, and is a factor influencing the ***corporate image*** of an organization. The creation of a strong corporate identity also involves consistency in the organization's actions, behavior, products, and brands, and often reflects the ***mission statement*** of an organization. A positive corporate identity can promote a sense of purpose and belonging within the organization and encourage employee commitment and involvement.

corporate image CORPORATE GOVERNANCE public's ideas about what firm is like the perceptions and impressions of an organization by the public as a result of interaction with the organization and the way the organization presents itself. Organizations have traditionally focused on the design of communication and advertising materials, using logos, symbols, text, and color to create a favorable impression on target groups, but a variety of additional activities contribute to a positive corporate image. These include public relations programs such as community involvement, sponsorship, and environmental projects, participation in quality improvement schemes, and good practice in industrial relations.

corporate planning CORPORATE GOVERNANCE process of making plans to achieve firm's objectives the process of drawing up detailed action plans to achieve an organization's goals and objectives, taking into account the resources of the organization and the environment within which it operates. Corporate planning represents a formal, structured approach to achieving objectives and to implementing the corporate strategy of an organization. It has traditionally been seen as the responsibility of senior management. The use of the term became predominant during the 1960s but has now been largely superseded by the concept of ***strategic management***.

corporate raider MERGERS & ACQUISITIONS somebody buying stake prior to hostile takeover a person or company that buys a stake in another company with a view to making a ***hostile takeover*** bid

corporate resolution CORPORATE GOVERNANCE document saying who can manage firm's money a document signed by the officers of a corporation naming those persons who can sign checks, withdraw cash, and have access to the corporation's bank account

corporate restructuring GENERAL MANAGEMENT major change in firm's activities a fundamental change in direction and strategy for an organization, which affects the way in which the organization is structured. Corporate restructuring may involve increasing or decreasing the layers of personnel between the top and the bottom of an organization, or reassigning roles and responsibilities. Invariably, corporate restructuring has come to mean reorganizing after a period of unsatisfactory performance and poor results, and is often manifested in the divestment or closure of parts of the business and the outplacement, or shedding, of personnel. In this case, corporate restructuring is used as a euphemism for delayering, rationalization, downsizing, or rightsizing.

corporate spinoff BUSINESS small firm formed from larger parent firm a small company that has been split off from a larger, parent organization

corporate strategy GENERAL MANAGEMENT firm's plans for future the direction an organization takes with the objective of achieving business success in the long term. Recent approaches have focused on the need for companies to adapt to and anticipate changes in the business environment. The formulation of corporate strategy involves establishing the purpose and scope of the organization's activities and the nature of the business it is in, taking the environment in which it operates, its position in the marketplace, and the competition it faces into consideration.

corporation *US* BUSINESS firm owned by stockholders an organization in which a number of people provide financing in return for stock. The principle of ***limited liability*** limits the maximum loss a stockholder can make if the company fails. *UK term* ***limited liability company***

corporation tax TAX tax on profits and gains a tax on profits and capital gains made by companies, calculated before dividends are paid. *Abbr* ***CT***

correction FINANCE adjustment in valuation of something a change in the valuation of something that is thought to be overvalued or undervalued which results in its being more realistically valued

correlation STATISTICS relatedness of variables the interdependence between pairs of variables in data

correlation coefficient STATISTICS measure of relatedness of variables an index of the linear relationship between two variables in data

correspondent bank BANKING bank operating as foreign bank's agent a bank that acts as an agent for a foreign bank

cost FINANCE **1.** money paid for product the amount of money that is paid to secure a good or service. Cost is the amount paid from the purchaser's standpoint, whereas the price is the amount paid from the vendor's standpoint. **2.** calculate cost of something to ascertain what must be paid to acquire a specific thing or engage in a specific activity

cost account ACCOUNTING accounting record of section of business a record of revenue and/or expenditure of a cost center or cost unit

cost accountant ACCOUNTING accountant advising on business costs an accountant who gives managers information about their business costs

cost accounting ACCOUNTING preparation of accounts detailing business costs the process of preparing special accounts of manufacturing and sales costs

cost allocation ACCOUNTING assignment of fixed expenses to cost centers the way in which overhead expenses are assigned to different cost centers

cost analysis OPERATIONS & PRODUCTION calculation of cost of new product the process of calculating in advance how much a new product will cost

cost and freight OPERATIONS & PRODUCTION including product and shipping costs, but not insurance indicates that a quoted price includes the costs of the merchandise and the transportation but not the cost of insurance. *Abbr* ***CFR***

cost audit ACCOUNTING check on cost records and accounts the verification of cost records and accounts, and a check on adherence to prescribed ***cost accounting*** procedures and their continuing relevance

cost basis ACCOUNTING price paid including purchase costs the price paid for an asset plus any expenses such as commissions associated with it at the time of purchase

cost-benefit analysis ACCOUNTING comparison of activity's costs against results a comparison between the cost of the resources used, plus any other costs imposed by an activity, for example, pollution or environmental damage, and the value of the financial and non-financial benefits derived, to establish whether there is a positive outcome. *Also called* ***benefit-cost ratio***

cost center ACCOUNTING section of business that costs firm money a department, function, section, or individual whose cost, overall or in part, is an accepted overhead of a business in return for services provided to other parts of the organization. A cost center is usually an ***indirect cost*** of an organization's products or services.

cost cutting OPERATIONS & PRODUCTION actions to reduce organization's expenses the reduction of the amount of money spent on the operations of an organization or on the provision of products and services. Cost-cutting measures such as budget reductions, salary freezes, and layoffs may be taken by an organization at a time of recession or financial difficulty or in situations where inefficiency has been identified. Alternative approaches to cost cutting include modifying organizational structures and redesigning organizational processes for greater efficiency. Excessive cost cutting may affect ***productivity*** and quality or the organization's ability to add value.

cost driver ACCOUNTING something that affects cost of activity a factor that determines the cost of an activity. Cost drivers are analyzed as part of ***activity based costing*** and can be used in ***continuous improvement*** programs. They are usually assessed together as multiple drivers rather than singly. There are two main types of cost driver: the first is a ***resource driver***, which refers to the contribution of the quantity of resources used to the cost of an activity; the second is an ***activity driver***, which refers to the costs incurred by the activities required to complete a specific task or project.

cost-effective OPERATIONS & PRODUCTION giving best results for least expense offering the maximum benefit for a given level of expenditure. When limited resources are available to meet specific objectives, the cost-effective solution is the best that can be achieved for that level of expenditure and the one that provides good value for money. The term is also used to refer to a level of expenditure that is perceived to be commercially viable.

cost-effectiveness analysis TREASURY MANAGEMENT measurement of how much positive results cost a method for measuring the benefits and effectiveness of a particular item of expenditure. Cost-effectiveness analysis requires an examination of expenditure to determine whether the money spent could have been used more effectively or whether the resulting benefits could have been attained through less financial outlay.

cost factor ACCOUNTING activity or item incurring business cost an activity or item of material, equipment, or personnel that incurs a cost

cost function ECONOMICS ratio of total cost to quantity produced a mathematical function relating a firm's or an industry's total cost to its output and factor costs

cost inflation ECONOMICS = ***cost-push inflation***

costing OPERATIONS & PRODUCTION calculating total expenses related to product the determination of the total cost of a product, from the purchase of ***raw materials*** to delivery to the consumer. There are a large number of costing techniques, including ***life-cycle costing***, ***activity based costing***, and ***operating costing***.

cost, insurance, and freight OPERATIONS & PRODUCTION including product, shipping, and insurance costs indicates that a quoted price includes the costs of the merchandise, transportation, and insurance. *Abbr* ***CIF***

cost of appraisal OPERATIONS & PRODUCTION money spent to check quality of products the costs incurred in order to ensure that outputs produced meet required quality standards

cost of capital TREASURY MANAGEMENT interest paid on operating capital interest paid on the capital used in operating a business

cost of conformance OPERATIONS & PRODUCTION money spent on quality requirements the costs of achieving specific quality standards for a product or service. *See also* ***cost of appraisal, cost of prevention***

cost of entry OPERATIONS & PRODUCTION expense of bringing out new product the costs of introducing a new product to the market. Cost of entry calculations include the cost of all research, development, production, testing, marketing, advertising, and distribution of the new product.

cost of external failure OPERATIONS & PRODUCTION cost of correcting quality of products after sale the costs arising from inadequate quality which are identified after the transfer of ownership from supplier to purchaser. *See also* ***cost of internal failure***

cost of goods sold OPERATIONS & PRODUCTION **1.** money spent on products to sell for a retailer, the cost of buying and acquiring the goods it sells to its customers **2.** money spent on supplying services for a service firm, the cost of the employee services supplied **3.** money spent manufacturing products to sell for a manufacturer, the cost of buying the raw materials and manufacturing finished products. *Abbr* ***COGS***

cost of internal failure TREASURY MANAGEMENT cost of correcting quality of products before sale the costs arising from inadequate quality which are identified before the transfer of ownership from supplier to purchaser. *See also* ***cost of external failure***

cost of living FINANCE money spent on housing, food, and basics the average amount spent by somebody on accommodations, food, and other basic necessities. In the United States, a broad definition might sometimes include education and healthcare. Salaries are usually increased annually to cover rises in the cost of living.

cost-of-living adjustment *US* FINANCE, HR & PERSONNEL = ***cost-of-living increase***

cost-of-living allowance *UK* FINANCE, HR & PERSONNEL = ***cost-of-living increase***

cost-of-living increase FINANCE, HR & PERSONNEL extra pay to cover price rises a small increase in salaries made to account for rises in the ***cost of living***

cost-of-living index FINANCE, HR & PERSONNEL information on changes in prices over time an index that shows changes in the cost of living by comparing current prices for a variety of goods with the prices paid for them in previous years

cost of nonconformance OPERATIONS & PRODUCTION money lost by not meeting quality requirements the cost of failure to deliver the required standard of quality for a product or service. *See also* ***cost of external failure, cost of internal failure***

cost of prevention OPERATIONS & PRODUCTION money spent to avoid producing low-quality products the costs incurred prior to or during production in order to prevent substandard or defective products or services from being produced

cost of sales OPERATIONS & PRODUCTION = ***cost of goods sold*** *(sense 3)*

cost per click-through E-COMMERCE system paying online advertiser for each ad click a pricing model for online advertising, where the seller gets paid whenever a visitor clicks on an ad

cost-plus pricing OPERATIONS & PRODUCTION deciding price by adding amount to product's cost a standard ***markup*** added to the cost of a product or service to establish a selling price. Many companies simply add a percentage of production costs to arrive at a selling price. The degree of markup depends on the level of anticipated sales. It may incorporate a desired return on investment. Low volume luxury goods may have a high markup; high volume goods may have a relatively lower markup.

cost price OPERATIONS & PRODUCTION selling price yielding no profit to seller a selling price that is the same as the price paid by the seller, which results in no profit being made

cost-push inflation ECONOMICS price increases caused by rise in production costs inflation in which price rises result from increased production costs or similar factors rather than from customer demand

cost reduction OPERATIONS & PRODUCTION cutting costs to increase profits the process of identifying and eliminating unnecessary costs to improve the profitability of a business

costs ACCOUNTING amounts of money paid out for something amounts of money that are paid out for something, especially on a regular basis

cost savings OPERATIONS & PRODUCTION benefits from reducing costs the benefits to an organization derived from reducing expenditures

costs of complexity OPERATIONS & PRODUCTION = ***complexity costs***

cottage industry BUSINESS commercial activity performed by individuals or small businesses an industry made up of small businesses, often run from the home of the proprietor

Council of Mortgage Lenders MORTGAGES UK association for mortgage industry in the United Kingdom, the trade association for the mortgage industry, whose members account for about 98% of UK residential mortgage lending. *Abbr* ***CML***

council tax TAX local tax paid in UK in the United Kingdom, a tax paid by individuals or companies to a local authority. Introduced in April 1993, the rate of council tax depends on the estimated value of the residential or commercial property occupied.

counterbid FINANCE **1.** higher bid competing with another bid a higher bid made in reply to a previous bid by another bidder **2.** make counterbid to make a higher bid in reply to a previous bid

counter-claim LEGAL **1.** claim for damages responding to another a claim for damages made in reply to a previous claim **2.** make counter-claim to put in a counter-claim for something

countercyclical ECONOMICS falling when other factor rises tending to increase as another factor decreases and decreasing as it increases. *See also* ***procyclical***

countercyclical stock STOCKHOLDING & INVESTMENTS stock price moving against economic trend a stock that tends to rise as the economy weakens and fall as it strengthens

counterfeit FRAUD **1.** illegally produce imitation goods or money to produce forged or imitation goods or money intended to deceive or defraud. Counterfeited goods of inferior quality are often sold at substantially lower prices than genuine products and may bear the ***brand*** or ***trade name*** of the company. Counterfeiting violates ***trademark*** and ***intellectual property*** rights and may damage the reputation of producers of authentic goods. National and international legislation provides some recourse to companies against counterfeiters, but strategies such as consumer warnings and labeling methods are also used to minimize the impact of counterfeiting. Efforts to eliminate counterfeiting are coordinated by the International Anti-Counterfeiting Coalition. **2.** *also* counterfeited relating to illegally produced imitations used to describe goods or money illegally produced but appearing authentic

counterfoil BANKING small paper record of transaction a slip of paper kept after writing a check, an invoice, or a receipt, as a record of the deal that has taken place

countermand GENERAL MANAGEMENT cancel order given earlier to say that an order must not be carried out

counter-offer BUSINESS higher or lower offer responding to another a higher or lower offer made in reply to another offer

counterparty LEGAL other person in legal agreement a person or organization with whom the person or organization in question is entering into a contract

counterparty risk RISK risk associated with other party to contract the possibility that the person or persons with whom a contract exists will fail to fulfill the terms of their side of the contract

counterpurchase INTERNATIONAL TRADE import bartered for exporter's commitment to further trade a reciprocal trading practice involving a traditional export transaction plus the commitment of the exporter to buy additional goods or services from that country. *See also* ***countertrade***

countersign FINANCE sign document after other signatory to sign a document that has already been signed by somebody else

countertrade INTERNATIONAL TRADE system of trade between two parties a variety of reciprocal trading practices. This umbrella term encompasses practices ranging from the direct exchange of goods for goods where no cash changes hands (***barter***) to more complex variations: *counterpurchase*, which involves a traditional export transaction plus the commitment of the exporter to buy additional goods or services from that country; and ***buyback***, in which the supplier of a plant or equipment is paid from the future proceeds resulting from the use of the plant. Countertrade conditions vary widely from country to country and can be costly and administratively cumbersome.

countervailing duty TAX, INTERNATIONAL TRADE = ***anti-dumping duty***

country risk INTERNATIONAL TRADE risk of doing business in particular country the risk associated with undertaking transactions with, or holding assets in, a particular country. Sources of risk might be political, economic, or regulatory instability affecting overseas taxation, repatriation of profits, nationalization, currency stability, etc.

coupon STOCKHOLDING & INVESTMENTS **1.** paper requesting bond payment a piece of paper attached to a government bond certificate which a bondholder presents to request payment **2.** interest rate of bond the rate of interest paid on a bond issued at a fixed rate. *Also called* ***coupon rate*** **3.** interest payment on bond an interest payment made to a bondholder, originally on presentation of a dated coupon to the company or an agent of the issuer ◊ clip coupons FINANCE to collect periodic interest on a bond

coupon rate STOCKHOLDING & INVESTMENTS = ***coupon*** *(sense 2)*

coupon security STOCKHOLDING & INVESTMENTS government security carrying coupon and paying interest a government security that carries a coupon and pays interest, as opposed to a ***zero-coupon security***, that pays no interest but is sold at a discount from its face value. *See also* ***zero-coupon security***

covariance STATISTICS measure of two variables' tendency to change together the value that is predicted from the product of the deviations of two variables from each of their means

covariate STATISTICS less important variable affecting important variable a variable that is not crucial in an investigation but may affect the crucial variables from which a model is being built

covenant FINANCE legal financial agreement a financial agreement conditional on future events, for example, changes in the capital structure and rating of a firm, or fundamental changes in business strategy such as to divest of a major asset or to acquire another company. Covenants are frequently included in bond offerings or bank loan/syndication terms. In the United Kingdom, when payments are made by an individual under covenant to a charity, the charity can reclaim the tax paid by the donor.

cover *UK* INSURANCE = ***coverage*** *(sense 2)*

coverage **1.** MARKETING how many customers reached the percentage of a target audience reached by different media **2.** *US* INSURANCE level of insurance protection the amount or type of protection guaranteed by an insurance policy. *UK term* ***cover***

covered bond STOCKHOLDING & INVESTMENTS bond with loan as security a bond that has mortgage or other loans given as security in case of default

covered option STOCKHOLDING & INVESTMENTS option backed by actual stock an ***option*** whose owner holds the stock for the option. A covered option can be either a ***call option*** or a ***put option***.

covered warrant STOCKHOLDING & INVESTMENTS futures contract a type of ***futures contract*** issued by a financial institution allowing the holder to buy or sell a quantity of its ***financial instruments***

cover note *UK* INSURANCE = ***binder***

covert human intelligence source FRAUD somebody providing information about illegal activity in the United Kingdom, a person who supplies information about somebody being investigated, for example, for fraud, without the knowledge of the person being investigated. *Abbr* ***CHIS***

CP *abbr* FINANCE ***commercial paper***

CPA *abbr* ACCOUNTING ***certified public accountant***

CPF *abbr* PENSIONS ***Central Provident Fund***

CPF® OPERATIONS & PRODUCTION business practice encouraging collaboration between buyers and sellers a business practice that uses information sharing among buyers and sellers throughout the supply chain to make products available to customers when they need them, while reducing suppliers' costs such as inventory and transportation. *Full form* ***Collaborative Planning, Forecasting, and Replenishment***

CPI *abbr* ECONOMICS ***consumer price index***

CPI inflation ECONOMICS inflation rate of economy using consumer price index the rate of ***inflation*** in an economy calculated using data from a ***consumer price index***

CPIX *ANZ* ECONOMICS consumer price index the ***consumer price index*** excluding interest costs, on the basis that these are a direct outcome of monetary policy

crack E-COMMERCE disable copy protection on software, CD, or DVD to defeat the copy protection that is intended to prevent somebody from illegally copying and distributing a software product, music CD, or DVD

crash **1.** MARKETS very large drop in stock price a precipitous drop in value, especially of the stocks traded in a market **2.** ECONOMICS large and sudden economic decline a sudden and catastrophic downturn in an economy. While there were several in the 20th century, the crash in the United States in 1929 is one of the most famous. However, the events of 2008 have had even more severe global consequences.

crawling peg CURRENCY & EXCHANGE incremental control on exchange rates a method of controlling exchange rates, allowing them to move up or down slowly

CRD *abbr* STOCKHOLDING & INVESTMENTS ***Central Registration Depository***

creative accounting FRAUD accounting methods used to conceal firm's true state the use of accounting methods to hide aspects of a company's financial dealings in order to make the company appear more or less successful than it is in reality (*slang*). *See also* ***corporate fraud***

creative destruction MERGERS & ACQUISITIONS process of new firms and products replacing old a way of describing the endless cycle of innovation, which results in established goods, services, or organizations being replaced by new models. The term was first mentioned by Joseph Schumpeter in *Capitalism, Socialism and Democracy* (1942), but used heavily during the dot-com boom of the late 1990s and early 2000s.

creative thinking *or* **creativity** GENERAL MANAGEMENT coming up with original interesting ideas the generation of new ideas by approaching problems or existing practices in innovative or imaginative ways. Psychologists have disagreed on the nature of creative thinking. Until about 1980, research concentrated on identifying the personality traits of creative people, but more recently psychologists have focused on the mental processes involved. Creative thinking involves reexamining assumptions and reinterpreting facts, ideas, and past experience. A growing interest in creative thinking as a source of ***competitive advantage*** has developed in recent years, and creative thinking is considered important, not just for the development of new products and services, but also for its role in organizational decision making and problem solving. Many organizations actively seek a corporate culture that encourages creative thinking. There are a number of techniques used to foster creative thinking, including brainstorming. Creative thinking is linked to innovation, the process of taking a new idea and turning it into a market offering.

credit FINANCE **1.** positive amount of assets after liabilities are deducted the amount of money left over when a person or organization has more ***assets*** than ***liabilities***, and those liabilities are subtracted from the total of the assets **2.** lender's belief that borrower will repay loan the trust that a lender has in a borrower's ability to repay a loan, or a loan itself **3.** arrangement to pay later for product bought now a financial arrangement between the vendor and the purchaser of a good or service by which the purchaser may buy what he or she requires, but pay for it at a later date ◇ post a credit ACCOUNTING in bookkeeping, to enter a credit item in a ledger

credit account FINANCE = ***charge account***

credit availability FINANCE ease of borrowing the ease with which money can be borrowed at a given time

credit balance FINANCE sum owed on credit account the amount of money that a customer owes on a ***charge account***

credit bureau FINANCE US firm evaluating people's ability to repay loans a company that assesses the creditworthiness of people for businesses or banks. *See also* ***mercantile agency***

credit capacity FINANCE total amount somebody can borrow and repay the amount of money that a person or organization can borrow and be expected to repay

credit card BANKING card from bank used to pay for things a card issued by a bank or financial institution and accepted by a merchant in payment for a transaction for which the cardholder must subsequently reimburse the issuer. *See also* ***charge card***

credit ceiling FINANCE = ***credit limit***

credit column ACCOUNTING accounting column recording money received the right-hand column in accounts showing money received

credit committee RISK group assessing creditworthiness a committee that evaluates a potential borrower's credit status and ability to repay loans

credit company FINANCE firm that lends money a company that extends credit to people. It may be an independent company or a subsidiary of a parent company such as an automobile manufacturer whose products are being bought.

credit control RISK monitoring of customers' credit management a system of checks designed to ensure that customers pay on time and do not owe more than their credit limit

credit controller FINANCE employee who manages payment of overdue invoices a member of staff whose job is to expedite the payment of overdue invoices

credit cooperative FINANCE group borrowing together an organization of people who join together to gain advantage in borrowing

credit creation FINANCE ability of banks to lend more money the collective ability of finance companies, banks, and other lenders of money to make money available to borrowers. While a central bank can create money, it cannot create credit.

credit crunch FINANCE inability or reluctance of banks to lend money the collective inability or unwillingness of finance companies, banks, and other lenders to make money available to borrowers (*informal*). *Also called* ***credit squeeze, liquidity squeeze***

credit default swap STOCKHOLDING & INVESTMENTS, RISK assumption of credit risk in return for payments a ***derivative instrument*** similar in structure to an insurance policy, in which the buyer of the instrument agrees to make payments to the seller in return for a guarantee that the seller will assume the credit risk of a third party. *Abbr* ***CDS***

credit deposit E-COMMERCE credit card transaction amount put in seller's bank the value of the credit card purchases deposited in a merchant's bank account after the acquirer's fees are deducted

credit derivative STOCKHOLDING & INVESTMENTS, RISK contract transferring lender's risk a ***financial instrument*** or ***derivative*** by which the lender's risk is devolved to a third party and separately traded

credit entity FINANCE person borrowing or lending a borrower from a finance company, bank, or other lender of money, or the lender of the funds

credit entry ACCOUNTING entry for income or value an item in a financial statement recording money received or the value of an asset

credit exposure RISK lender's risk that borrower will not repay the risk to a lender that a borrower will default and not fulfill their contractual payment

credit facility BANKING arrangement to supply credit an arrangement with a bank or supplier that enables a person or organization to be given credit or borrow money when it is needed, for example, a ***letter of credit***, ***revolving credit*** or a ***term loan***. *Also called* ***lending facility***

credit freeze FINANCE period when government limits banks' lending a period during which lending by banks is restricted by government

credit granter FINANCE lender a person or organization that lends money

credit history FINANCE record of somebody's repayment of loans a potential borrower's record of debt repayment. Individuals or organizations with a poor credit history may find it difficult to find lenders who are willing to give them a loan.

Credit Industry Fraud Avoidance System FRAUD UK fraud prevention service in the United Kingdom, a nonprofit membership organization established for the purpose of preventing financial crime. *Abbr* ***CIFAS***

crediting rate STOCKHOLDING & INVESTMENTS interest rate on insurance policy the interest rate paid on an insurance policy which is an investment

credit limit FINANCE total amount somebody is allowed to borrow the highest amount that a lender will allow somebody to borrow, for example, on a credit card. *Also called* ***credit ceiling***

credit line FINANCE = ***line of credit***

credit-linked note RISK fixed-income security with embedded credit default swap a fixed-income security with an embedded ***credit default swap*** which is sold to investors willing to take the risk of default in return for a high yield on their investment

credit market MARKETS market trading in debt securities the market in which debt securities such as loans, corporate bonds, commercial paper, and ***credit default swaps*** are bought and sold

credit note FINANCE = *abbr* ***c/n.*** = ***credit slip***

creditor FINANCE somebody you owe money for goods or services a person or an entity to whom money is owed as a consequence of the receipt of goods or services in advance of payment

creditor days FINANCE number of days firm takes to pay creditors the number of days on average that a company requires to pay its creditors.

To determine creditor days, divide the cumulative amount of unpaid suppliers' bills (also called trade creditors) by sales, then multiply by 365. If suppliers' bills total $800,000 and sales are $9,000,000, the calculation is:

(800,000 / 9,000,000) × 365 = 32.44 days

The company takes 32.44 days on average to pay its bills.

Creditor days is an indication of a company's creditworthiness in the eyes of its suppliers and creditors, since it shows how long they are willing to wait for payment. Within reason, the higher the number the better, because all companies want to conserve cash. At the same time, a company that is especially slow to pay its bills (100 or more days, for example) may be a company having trouble generating cash, or one trying to finance its operations with its suppliers' funds. *See also* ***debtor days***

creditor nation INTERNATIONAL TRADE country with balance of payments surplus a country where payments received exceed those made over the same period

creditors' committee FINANCE lenders' group seeking money from bankrupt borrower a group that directs the efforts of creditors to receive partial repayment from a bankrupt person or organization. *Also called* ***creditors' steering committee***

creditors' meeting FINANCE meeting of bankrupt's creditors a meeting of those to whom a bankrupt person or organization owes money

creditors' settlement FINANCE agreement for partial repayment by bankrupt borrower an agreement on partial repayment to those to whom a bankrupt person or organization owes money

creditors' steering committee FINANCE = ***creditors' committee***

credit rating *or* **credit ranking** FINANCE **1.** evaluation of creditworthiness an assessment of a person's or an organization's ability to pay back money that they owe according to the terms on which it was borrowed, based on a broad assessment of financial health including previous loans and other outstanding financial obligations **2.** process of evaluating creditworthiness the process of assessing a person's or an organization's ability to pay back money that they owe according to the terms on which it was borrowed

credit rating agency *US* FINANCE firm evaluating creditworthiness a company that assesses a person's or an organization's ability to pay back money that they owe according to the terms on which it was borrowed, on behalf of businesses or banks. *UK term* ***credit-reference agency***

credit rationing FINANCE, RISK process of making it harder to borrow money the process of making credit less easily available or subject to high interest rates

credit receipt *US* FINANCE = ***credit slip***

credit-reference agency *UK* FINANCE = ***credit rating agency***

credit references FINANCE list of previous lenders when opening credit account details of individuals, companies, or banks who have given credit to a person or company in the past, supplied as references when somebody is opening a credit account with a new supplier

credit report FINANCE information concerning person's or organization's creditworthiness information about the ability of a person or organization to pay back money that they owe, used by financial institutions in determining decisions relevant to granting credit

credit risk RISK possibility that debtor will default the possibility that a person or an organization will not be able to pay back money that they owe according to the terms on which it was borrowed

credit sale FINANCE sale for which buyer can pay later a sales transaction by which the buyer is allowed to take immediate possession of the purchased goods and pay for them at a later date

credit scoring FINANCE calculation during credit rating a calculation done in the process of assessing a person's or an organization's ability to pay back money that they owe according to the terms on which it was borrowed

credit side ACCOUNTING part of financial statement with assets the section of a financial statement that lists assets. In ***double-entry bookkeeping***, the right-hand side of each account is designated as the credit side. *See also* ***debit side***

credit slip *US* FINANCE statement that store owes customer money a receipt saying that a store owes a customer an amount of money for returned goods and entitling the person to goods of that value. *UK term* ***credit note***

credit spread RISK difference between debt yield of firm and benchmark the difference between the yield on the debt of a particular company and the yield on a risk-free asset such as a US ***Treasury bond*** having the same maturity

credit spread option STOCKHOLDING & INVESTMENTS, RISK option contract based on firm's credit spread an option contract on the ***credit spread*** of the debt of a particular company whose payoff is based on changes in the credit spread

credit spread swap STOCKHOLDING & INVESTMENTS, RISK exchange of fixed for credit-spread payment a ***swap*** in which one party makes a fixed payment to the other on the swap's settlement date and the second party pays the first an amount based on the actual credit spread

credit squeeze FINANCE = ***credit crunch***

credit standing FINANCE somebody's reputation for repaying debt the reputation that somebody has with regard to meeting financial obligations

credit system FINANCE means of making loans a set of rules and organizations involved in making loans on a commercial basis

credit union BANKING financial institution providing banking services to members a cooperative financial organization that provides banking services, including loans, to its members at relatively low rates of interest

creditworthiness FINANCE reliability in repaying debt the extent to which a person or organization is financially reliable enough to borrow money or be given credit

creditworthy FINANCE reliable in repaying debt regarded as being reliable in terms of ability to pay back money owed according to the terms on which it was borrowed

creeping takeover MERGERS & ACQUISITIONS takeover through gradual acquisition a takeover of a company achieved by the gradual acquisition of small amounts of stock over an extended period of time (*slang*)

creeping tender offer MERGERS & ACQUISITIONS gradual acquisition of firm's stock an acquisition of many shares in a company by gradual purchase, especially to avoid US restrictions on tender offers

CREST MARKETS UK electronic transaction system in the United Kingdom, the paperless system used for settling stock transactions electronically

crisis management GENERAL MANAGEMENT firm's methods of dealing with unexpected negative situation actions taken by an organization in response to unexpected events or situations with potentially negative effects that threaten resources and people or the success and continued operation of the organization. Crisis management includes the development of plans to reduce the risk of a crisis occurring and to deal with any crises that do arise, and the implementation of these plans so as to minimize the impact of crises and assist the organization to recover from them. Crisis situations may occur as a result of external factors such as the development of a new product by a competitor or changes in legislation, or internal factors such as a product failure or faulty ***decision making***, and often involve the need to make quick decisions on the basis of uncertain or incomplete information. *See also* ***risk management, disaster management***

Criteria of Control Board REGULATION & COMPLIANCE Canadian financial regulator a group that issues guidance on designing, assessing, and reporting on the control systems of organizations, under the aegis of the the Canadian Institute of Chartered Accountants. *Abbr* ***CoCo***

criticality OPERATIONS & PRODUCTION evaluation of ways something can fail a ranking of the severity of the various ways in which a system, device, or process can fail, their frequency of occurrence, and the consequences of their failure

critical mass GENERAL MANAGEMENT when firm or project becomes clearly worth continuing the point at which an organization or project has gained sufficient momentum or ***market share*** to be either self-sustaining or worth the input of extra investment or resources

critical-path method *or* **critical-path analysis** GENERAL MANAGEMENT, OPERATIONS & PRODUCTION way of determining activities necessary for success a planning technique used especially in project management to identify the activities within a project that are critical for its success. In critical-path method, individual activities within a project and their duration are recorded in a diagram or flow chart. A critical path is plotted through the diagram, showing the sequence in which activities must be completed in order to complete the project in the shortest amount of time, incurring the least cost.

critical region STATISTICS set of test results causing rejection of hypothesis the range of values of a test statistic that lead a researcher to reject the null hypothesis

critical restructuring GENERAL MANAGEMENT very large changes in firm's organization major economic or social changes that fundamentally reshape traditional patterns of organization

critical success factor GENERAL MANAGEMENT aspect essential to firm's success any of the aspects of a business that are identified as vital for successful targets to be reached and maintained. Critical success factors are usually identified in such areas as production processes, employee and organization skills, functions, techniques, and technologies. The identification and strengthening of such factors may be similar to identifying ***core competences***, and is considered an essential element in achieving and maintaining ***competitive advantage***.

critical value STATISTICS standard against which hypothesis is rejected the value with which a researcher compares a statistic from sample data in order to determine whether or not the null hypothesis should be rejected

CRM *abbr* MARKETING ***customer relationship management***

CRO *abbr* REGULATION & COMPLIANCE ***Companies Registration Office***

crony capitalism ECONOMICS system in which well-connected people control wealth a form of capitalism in which business contracts are awarded to the family and friends of the government in power rather than by open-market tender

cross MARKETS transaction with shared broker a transaction in securities in which one broker acts for both parties

crossborder services ACCOUNTING accounting services for client in another country accounting services provided by an accounting firm in one country on behalf of a client based in another country

crossborder trade INTERNATIONAL TRADE trade between neighboring countries the buying and selling of goods and services between two countries that have a common frontier

cross currency swap CURRENCY & EXCHANGE = ***currency swap*** *(sense 1)*

cross-docking OPERATIONS & PRODUCTION immediately matching items between incoming and outgoing shipments a procedure used in ***logistics*** to reduce handling and warehousing costs by immediately matching items from incoming shipments on the loading dock with outgoing shipment requirements and transferring them to the outgoing vehicles

crossed cheque *UK* BANKING check that can only be deposited a check with two lines across it showing that it can only be deposited at a bank and not exchanged for cash

crossed market MARKETS where price to buy exceeds price to sell a situation in which a bid to buy a stock or option is higher than the offer to sell

cross-functional OPERATIONS & PRODUCTION working as team with different functions toward goal used to describe a group of employees who have different functions within an organization and who work together as a team to achieve an objective

cross-hedging MARKETS hedging with related futures contract a form of hedging using an option on a different but related commodity, especially a currency

cross holdings STOCKHOLDING & INVESTMENTS, MERGERS & ACQUISITIONS reciprocal stockholdings designed to combat takeovers a situation in which two companies own stock in each other in order to stop either from being taken over

cross listing OPERATIONS & PRODUCTION trying to sell same thing in multiple places the practice of offering the same item for sale in more than one place

cross rate CURRENCY & EXCHANGE exchange rate of two currencies against third currency the rate of exchange between two currencies expressed in terms of the rate of exchange between them and a third currency, for example, sterling and the peso in relation to the dollar. *Also called* ***exchange cross rate***

cross-sectional study STATISTICS survey collecting various information at once a statistical study in which a variety of information is collected at the same time, for example, in a single telephone call

cross-sell OPERATIONS & PRODUCTION sell range of complementary products at same time to sell customers a range of products or services offered by an organization at the same time, for example, offering insurance services while selling somebody a mortgage

crowding out *or* **crowding out effect** MARKETS effect of major borrowing by government on credit markets the effect on credit markets produced by extremely large borrowing by a national government, causing an increase in interest rates and a reduction in some areas of investment

Crown Agent INTERNATIONAL TRADE UK government representative on international board a person appointed by the UK government to sit on a board that provides financial, commercial, and other services to some foreign governments and international organizations

crown jewels FINANCE company's most valuable properties an organization's most valuable ***assets***, often the motivation behind ***takeover bids***

cryptography E-COMMERCE method of restricting who can access website a powerful means of restricting access to part or all of a website, whereby only a user with an assigned "key" can request and read the information

CSP *abbr* E-COMMERCE ***commerce service provider***

CT *abbr* TAX ***corporation tax***

CTI *abbr* BUSINESS ***computer telephony integration***

culture shock GENERAL MANAGEMENT confusion on exposure to unfamiliar situation the effects on an employee or organization when faced with new, unfamiliar, or rapidly changing circumstances. Symptoms of culture shock include uncertainty, stress, confusion, disorientation, or simply not knowing how to act in the circumstances. Culture shock can occur in a number of scenarios, for example, when expatriates come across new cultures and customs in a foreign country; when new staff are thrown into the deep end of a busy department; when two organizations merge with poor strategic, operational, or cultural synergy; or when public sector organizations adopt private sector practices. The degree of shock can be reduced through careful analysis, planning, training, and consequent preparedness.

cum FINANCE with the Latin word for "with." Its opposite is "ex-."

cum-all STOCKHOLDING & INVESTMENTS including all normal benefits of stock ownership including all of the entitlements that are attached to owning a share of stock. *See also* ***ex-all***

cum coupon STOCKHOLDING & INVESTMENTS with coupon attached or before payment of interest with a coupon attached or before interest due on a security is paid

cum dividend *or* **cum div** STOCKHOLDING & INVESTMENTS including unpaid dividend including the next dividend still to be paid

cum rights STOCKHOLDING & INVESTMENTS including rights an indication that the buyer of the stock is entitled to participate in a forthcoming ***rights issue***

cumulative increasing over time added to regularly and becoming increasingly larger over a period of time

cumulative interest FINANCE total interest the total interest added to capital originally invested

cumulative method GENERAL MANAGEMENT system of adding things together a system in which items are added together, used, for example, in some forms of electing officers to a number of posts

cumulative preference share *UK* STOCKHOLDING & INVESTMENTS = ***cumulative preferred stock***

cumulative preferred stock *US* STOCKHOLDING & INVESTMENTS preferred stock whose dividends accumulate if not paid a type of ***preferred stock*** that will have the dividend paid at a later date even if the company is not able to pay a dividend in the current year. *UK term* ***cumulative preference share***

cumulative voting CORPORATE GOVERNANCE system of election of directors a voting system that allows a stockholder one vote per share of stock owned multiplied by the number of directors to be elected. Stockholders may distribute these votes among the candidates in any way they choose.

currency CURRENCY & EXCHANGE money of particular country the system of money in general circulation in a particular country

currency backing CURRENCY & EXCHANGE gold or securities supporting currency gold, other valuable metal, or government securities, that support the strength of a country's currency

currency band CURRENCY & EXCHANGE allowable range of variation in exchange rate exchange rate levels between which a ***currency*** is allowed to move without full revaluation or devaluation

currency basket CURRENCY & EXCHANGE = ***basket of currencies***

currency clause CURRENCY & EXCHANGE clause fixing exchange rate for contract a clause in a contract that avoids problems of payment caused by exchange rate changes by fixing in advance the exchange rate for the various transactions covered by the contract

currency future STOCKHOLDING & INVESTMENTS option on currency a contract for buying or selling currency at a particular exchange rate within a set period

currency hedging STOCKHOLDING & INVESTMENTS, RISK reducing risk by diversifying currency holdings a method of reducing ***exchange rate risk*** by diversifying currency holdings and adjusting them according to changes in exchange rates

currency mismatching CURRENCY & EXCHANGE depositing low-interest loan in country with high-interest the practice of borrowing money in the currency of a country where interest rates are low and depositing it in the currency of a country with higher interest rates. The potential profit from the interest rate margin may be offset by changes in the exchange rates, which increase the value of the loan in the company's balance sheet.

currency note CURRENCY & EXCHANGE paper money a piece of paper money, representing a promise to pay the bearer a specific sum on demand

currency reserves CURRENCY & EXCHANGE government's reserves of foreign currency foreign money held by a government to support its own currency and to pay its debts

currency risk CURRENCY & EXCHANGE, RISK likelihood of adverse exchange rate the possibility of a loss due to future changes in exchange rates

currency swap CURRENCY & EXCHANGE **1.** agreement to use one currency for another an arrangement between two parties to exchange an amount of one currency for another currency, later returning the original amounts. This is useful, for instance, where both parties hold a currency other than the one they need at a specific time. *Also called* ***cross currency swap*** **2.** selling and buying same amount of foreign currency the selling or buying of a particular amount of a foreign currency for immediate delivery, accompanied by selling or buying the same amount of the same currency on the ***futures market***

currency unit CURRENCY & EXCHANGE coin or bill in specific monetary system each of the notes and coins that are the medium of exchange in a country

current account BANKING **1.** record of transactions between two parties a record of transactions between two parties, for example, between a bank and its customer, or a branch and head office, or two trading nations. *Abbr* ***c/a*** **2.** *UK* = ***checking account***

current account equilibrium INTERNATIONAL TRADE balance of country's imports and exports a country's economic circumstances when its expenditure equals its income from trade and ***invisible earnings***

current account mortgage MORTGAGES long-term real estate loan a long-term loan, usually for the purchase of real estate, in which the borrower pays interest on the sum loaned in monthly installments and repays the principal in one lump sum at the end of the term. When calculating the interest payments, the lender takes into account the balance in the borrower's checking and/or savings accounts. It is the borrower's responsibility to make provisions to accumulate the required capital during the period of the mortgage, usually by contributing to tax efficient investment plans or by relying on an anticipated inheritance. *See also* ***mortgage***

current assets FINANCE cash, or asset to be converted to cash cash or other assets, such as stock and long-term investments, held for conversion into cash in the normal course of trading

current assets financing FINANCE using current assets to back loan the use of current assets such as cash, debtors, and stock as collateral for a loan

current cash balance STOCKHOLDING & INVESTMENTS money that broker's client has available to invest the amount, which excludes balances due soon for outstanding transactions, that a client has available for investment with a broker

current cost accounting ACCOUNTING accounting based on current replacement cost of assets a method of accounting that notes the cost of replacing assets at current prices, rather than valuing assets at their original cost. *Abbr* ***CCA***. *See also* ***historical cost accounting***

current earnings FINANCE firm's most recent annual earnings the annual earnings most recently reported by a company, which exclude interest and tax

current liabilities FINANCE debt to be repaid within one year liabilities which fall due for payment within one year. They include that part of any long-term loan due for repayment within one year.

current principal factor FINANCE part of original loan left to be paid the portion of the initial amount of a loan that remains to be paid

current ratio FINANCE ratio of current assets to current liabilities a ratio of ***current assets*** to ***current liabilities***, used to measure a company's liquidity and its ability to meet its short-term debt obligations.

The current ratio formula is a simple one:

Current assets / Current liabilities = Current ratio

Current assets are the ones that a company can turn into cash within 12 months during the ordinary course of business. Current liabilities are bills due to be paid within the coming 12 months.

For example, if a company's current assets are $300,000 and its current liabilities are $200,000, its current ratio would be:

300,000 / 200,000 = 1.5

As a rule of thumb, the 1.5 figure means that a company should be able to get hold of $1.50 for every $1.00 it owes.

The higher the ratio, the more liquid the company. Prospective lenders expect a positive current ratio, often of at least 1.5. However, too high a ratio is cause for alarm too, because it indicates declining receivables and/or inventory, which may mean declining liquidity. *Also called* ***working capital ratio***

current stock value STOCKHOLDING & INVESTMENTS value of all stock held the value of all stock in an investor's set of holdings, including stock in transactions that have not yet been settled

current value FINANCE current assets minus current liabilities a ratio indicating the amount by which ***current assets*** exceed ***current liabilities***

current yield STOCKHOLDING & INVESTMENTS interest on bond divided by market price the interest being paid on a bond divided by its current market price, expressed as a percentage. *Also called* ***income yield***

curriculum vitae *UK* HR & PERSONNEL = ***résumé***

cushion FINANCE firm's surplus money money left after a company has serviced its debts and therefore available to meet unexpected demands

cushion bond STOCKHOLDING & INVESTMENTS high-interest bond a bond that pays a high rate of interest and so depreciates less when interest rates rise but is at risk of being *called* if interest rates fall

CUSIP *abbr* REGULATION & COMPLIANCE ***Committee on Uniform Securities Identification Procedures***

custodial account BANKING bank account for child in the United States, a bank account opened, normally by a parent or guardian, in the name of a minor who is too young to control it

custodian BANKING manager of trust funds a legal guardian, whether a person or an institution, whose principal function is to maintain and grow the assets contained in a trust

customer MARKETING somebody who buys product or service a purchaser of a product or service. A customer is a person or organization that purchases or obtains goods or services from other organizations such as manufacturers, retailers, wholesalers, or service providers. A customer is not necessarily the same person as the ***consumer***, as a product or service can be paid for by one party, the customer, and used by another, the consumer.

customer capital FINANCE value of firm's customer relationships the value of an organization's relationships with its customers, which involves factors such as market share, customer retention rates, and profitability of customers

customer care MARKETING = ***customer relations***

customer-centric model GENERAL MANAGEMENT emphasis on customers a business model organized around the needs of the customer

customer complaint GENERAL MANAGEMENT *see* ***complaint***

customer demand MARKETING amount of product customers will and can buy the quantity of a product or service that customers are willing and able to purchase at a given price during a given period of time

customer equity FINANCE value of firm's customer relationships the total asset value of the relationships that an organization has with its customers. The term was coined by Robert C. Blattberg and John Deighton in their article "Manage Marketing by the Customer Equity Test," *Harvard Business Review*, Jul/Aug, vol. 74 no. 4, pp. 136–144. Customer equity is based on ***customer lifetime value***, and an understanding of customer equity can be used to optimize the balance of investment in the acquisition and retention of customers. It is also known as ***customer capital*** and forms one component of the ***intellectual capital*** of an organization.

customer expectation MARKETING what potential buyer thinks or feels about product the needs, wants, and preconceived ideas of a customer about a product or service. Customer expectation will be influenced by his or her perception of the product or service and can be created by previous experience, advertising, hearsay, awareness of competitors, and brand image. The level of customer service is also a factor, and a customer might expect to encounter efficiency, helpfulness, reliability, confidence in the staff, and a personal interest in his or her patronage. If customer expectations are met, then customer satisfaction results. *Also called* ***buyer expectation***

customer flow MARKETING how many customers pass through store, airport, etc. the number and pattern of customers coming into a store or passing through a train or bus station, airport, or other large service, retail, or leisure area. Customer flow can be monitored by observation, time lapse or normal closed circuit television, or, less satisfactorily, by analysis of purchase data. This provides useful information about the number of customers, flow patterns, bottlenecks, areas not visited, and other aspects of consumer behavior.

customer focus GENERAL MANAGEMENT firm's attention to what customers want or need an organizational orientation toward satisfying the needs of potential and actual ***customers***. Customer focus is considered to be one of the keys to business success. Achieving customer focus involves ensuring that the whole organization, and not just frontline service staff, puts its customers first. All activities, from the planning of a new product to its production, marketing, and after-sales care, should be built around the customer. Every department and every employee should share the same customer-focused vision. This can be aided by practicing good ***customer relationship management*** and maintaining a ***customer relations*** program.

customer knowledge management GENERAL MANAGEMENT use of information from customers to improve firm the acquisition and use of customer-related knowledge to create value for both the organization and the purchasers of its products and services. Customer knowledge management is a form of ***knowledge management*** which focuses on the human aspects of customer knowledge acquired through direct interaction with the customer as well as quantitative transactional data. Some writers restrict the concept to the use of knowledge residing in, or acquired from, customers as opposed to information *about* customers collected by ***customer relationship management*** systems. Interactive technologies, conversations with customers, and user groups may be used to create knowledge-sharing and partnership between the organization and its customers.

customer lifetime value FINANCE expected profit from customer over time the ***net present value*** of the profit an organization expects to realize from a customer for the duration of their relationship. Customer lifetime value focuses on customers as assets rather than sources of revenue; the volume of purchases made, customer retention rates, and profit margins are factors taken into account in calculations. Strategies for increasing customer lifetime value aim to improve customer retention and lengthen the life of the relationship with the customer. It is a key factor in the customer equity of an organization.

customer profitability FINANCE amount of firm's profits due to customers the degree to which a ***customer*** or segment of customers contributes toward an organization's profits. Customer profitability has been shown to be produced primarily by a small proportion of customers, perhaps 10% to 20%, who generate up to 80% of a company's profits. Up to 40% of customers may generate only moderate profits, and the other 40% may be loss making. Such data enables companies to focus efforts on the most profitable segments.

customer recovery MARKETING attempts to win back firm's customers activities intended to win back customers who no longer buy from an organization

customer relations MARKETING how firm deals with buyers of its products the approach of an organization to winning and retaining customers. The most critical activity of any organization wishing to stay in business is its approach to dealing with its customers. Putting customers at the center of all activities is seen by many as an integral part of quality, pricing, and product differentiation. On one level, customer relations means keeping customers fully informed, turning complaints into opportunities, and genuinely listening to customers. On another level, being a customer-focused organization means ensuring that all activities relating to trading–for example, planning, design, production, marketing, and after-sales of a product or service–are built around the customer, and that every department and individual employee understands and shares the same vision. Only then can a company deliver continuous ***customer satisfaction*** and experience good customer relations. *Also called* ***customer care***

customer relationship management MARKETING development of connections with buyers of firm's products the cultivation of meaningful relationships with actual or potential purchasers of goods or services. Customer relationship management aims to increase an organization's sales by promoting customer satisfaction, and can be achieved using tools such as relationship marketing.

CRM is particularly important in the sphere of e-commerce, as there is no personal interaction between the vendor and the customer. A website therefore has to work hard to develop the relationship with customers and demonstrate that their business is valued. A CRM system generally includes some or all of the following components: customer information systems, ***personalization*** systems, ***content management*** systems, ***call center*** automation, ***data warehousing***, ***data mining***, sales force automation, and campaign management systems. All these elements combine to provide the essentials of CRM: understanding customer needs; anticipating their information requirements; answering their questions promptly and comprehensively; delivering exactly what they order; making deliveries on time; and suggesting new products that they will be genuinely interested in. *Abbr* ***CRM***

customer retention MARKETING maintaining connections with buyers of firm's products the maintenance of the patronage of people who have purchased a company's goods or services once and the gaining of repeat purchases. Customer retention occurs when a customer is loyal to a company, a brand, or a specific product or service, expressing long-term commitment and refusing to purchase from competitors. A company can adopt a number of strategies to retain its customers. Of critical importance to such strategies are the wider concepts of customer service, customer relations, and relationship marketing. Companies can build loyalty and retention through the use of a number of techniques, including ***database marketing***, the issue of loyalty cards redeemable against a variety of goods or services, preferential discounts, free gifts, special promotions, newsletters or magazines, members' clubs, or customized products in limited editions. It has been argued that customer retention is linked to employee loyalty, since loyal employees build up long-term relationships with customers.

customer satisfaction MARKETING how happy buyers are with firm's products the degree to which ***customer expectations*** of a product or service are met or exceeded. Corporate and individual customers may have widely differing reasons for purchasing a product or service and therefore any measurement of satisfaction will need to be able to take into account such differences. The quality of after-sales service can also be a crucial factor in influencing any purchasing decision. More and more companies are striving, not just for customer satisfaction, but for customer delight, that extra bit of added value that may lead to increased customer loyalty. Any extra added value, however, will need to be carefully costed.

customer service MARKETING how firm helps buyers of its products the way in which an organization deals with its ***customers***. Customer service is most evident in sales and ***after-sales service***, but should infuse all the processes in the ***value chain***. Good customer service is the result of adopting ***customer focus***. Poor customer service can be a product of poor ***customer relations***.

customization GENERAL MANAGEMENT changing products for individual customers the process of modifying products or services to meet the requirements of individual customers

customs barrier INTERNATIONAL TRADE measure designed to restrict trade a provision intended to make trade more difficult, for example, a high level of duty

customs broker INTERNATIONAL TRADE shipper's agent clearing goods through customs a person or company that takes goods through customs for a shipping company

customs clearance INTERNATIONAL TRADE **1.** passage granted to imports or exports by customs the act of passing goods through customs so that they can enter or leave the country **2.** document proving payment of customs duty a document given by customs to a shipper to show that customs duty has been paid and the goods can be shipped

customs declaration INTERNATIONAL TRADE form stating dutiable imports a statement showing goods being imported on which duty will have to be paid

customs duty INTERNATIONAL TRADE tax on imports and exports tax paid on goods brought into or taken out of a country

customs entry point INTERNATIONAL TRADE border point for declaring goods to customs a place at a border between two countries where goods are declared to customs

customs formalities INTERNATIONAL TRADE procedures followed by customs officials a declaration of goods by the shipper and examination of them by the customs authorities

customs seal INTERNATIONAL TRADE seal showing contents not examined by customs officials a seal attached by a customs officer to a box, to show that the contents have not passed through customs

customs tariff INTERNATIONAL TRADE list of import taxes a list of taxes to be paid on imported goods

customs union INTERNATIONAL TRADE agreement allowing goods to cross borders without duties an agreement between several countries that goods can travel between them without ***duty*** being paid, while goods from other countries are subject to duties

cutthroat BUSINESS extremely competitive aggressively ruthless, especially in dealing with competitors

cutting-edge GENERAL MANAGEMENT technologically advanced at the forefront of new technologies or markets

CV *abbr UK* HR & PERSONNEL curriculum vitae = ***résumé***

cwmni cyfyngedig cyhoeddus *UK see* **ccc**

cybermarketing E-COMMERCE advertising via the Internet the use of Internet-based promotions of any kind. This may involve targeted e-mail, bulletin boards, websites, or sites from which the customer can download files.

cybersales E-COMMERCE electronic sales sales made electronically through computers and information systems

cyberspace E-COMMERCE Internet as imagined world of electronic data the online world and its communication networks

cyberterrorism E-COMMERCE terrorist methods to disrupt information systems the use of techniques that disrupt or damage computer-based information systems to cause fear, injury, or economic loss

cyberwar E-COMMERCE using Internet to damage other's computer networks the use of information systems such as the Internet to exploit or damage an adversary's computer-based network processes

cycle time OPERATIONS & PRODUCTION **1.** time taken to get product to market the total time taken from the start of the production of a product or service to its completion. Cycle time includes processing time, move time, wait time, and inspection time, only the first of which creates value. **2.** = ***lead time*** *(sense 3)*

cyclical factors BUSINESS effects of trade cycle on businesses the way in which a ***trade cycle*** affects businesses

cyclical stock STOCKHOLDING & INVESTMENTS stock affected by business cycles a stock whose value rises and falls in line with economic cycles

cyclical unemployment ECONOMICS recurring temporary lack of employment unemployment, usually temporary, caused by a lack of ***aggregate demand***, for example, during a downswing in the business cycle

cyclic variation STATISTICS regular recurrence of change the repeatable systematic variation of a variable over time

D

D/A *abbr* BANKING ***deposit account*** *(sense 1)*

daily price limit MARKETS daily allowable change in option price the amount by which the price of an ***option*** is allowed to rise or fall during a single trading day

daily trading limit MARKETS permitted daily futures or options price range the highest and lowest prices that are allowed for a futures or options contract during a single trading day

Daimyo bond CURRENCY & EXCHANGE Japanese bond for European investors a Japanese ***bearer bond*** that can be cleared through European clearing houses

daisy chaining MARKETS illegal practice to inflate price of security an illegal financial practice whereby traders create artificial transactions in order to make a particular security appear more active than it is in reality (*slang*)

daman FINANCE contract whereby one person underwrites obligation of another in Islamic financing, a contract of guarantee in which the guarantor agrees to be responsible for a debt or obligation of another. *Also called* ***dhaman***

D&B *abbr* BUSINESS ***Dun and Bradstreet***

data STATISTICS information from statistical survey the measurements made and observations collected during a statistical investigation

database GENERAL MANAGEMENT organized collection of information a structured collection of related information held in any form, especially on a computer. The creation of a database assists organizations in keeping records and facilitates the retrieval of specific facts or different categories of information as and when required. Databases of various kinds may form part of an organization's ***MIS***.

database management system STATISTICS computer program for managing information a dedicated computer program designed to manipulate a collection of information

database marketing MARKETING collecting information about customers to target advertising the collection and analysis of information about customers and their buying habits, lifestyles, and other such data. Database marketing is used to build profiles of individual customers, who are then targeted with customized mailings, special offers, and other incentives to encourage spending.

data capture MARKETING collecting customer information through response forms the acquisition of information through advertisement coupons, inquiry forms, or other means that require a customer response

data cleansing MARKETING making sure information is accurate the process of ensuring that data is up to date and free of duplication or error

data dredging STATISTICS using information from outside study to draw conclusions the process of making comparisons with, and drawing conclusions from, data which was not part of the original basis of a study

data fusion E-COMMERCE merging information from different sources into consistent system the integration of data and knowledge collected from disparate sources by different methods into a consistent, accurate, and useful whole

data mining **1.** E-COMMERCE using software to find patterns in online databases the process of using sophisticated software to identify commercially useful statistical patterns or relationships in online databases **2.** MARKETING pulling information from firm's databases for management decisions the extraction of information from a ***data warehouse*** to assist managerial decision making. The information obtained in this way helps organizations gain a better understanding of their customers and can be used to improve customer support and marketing activities.

data protection MARKETING methods of keeping personal information in databases safe the safeguards that govern the storage and use of personal data held on computer systems and in paper-based filing systems. The growing use of computers to store information about individuals has led to the enactment of legislation in many countries designed to protect the privacy of individuals and prevent the disclosure of information to unauthorized persons.

data reduction STATISTICS summarizing large data sets the process of summarizing large data sets into histograms or frequency distributions so that calculations such as means can be made

data screening STATISTICS checking data for significant anomalies the process of assessing a set of observations to detect significant deviations such as ***outliers***

data set STATISTICS collection of statistical information all of the measurements or observations collected in a statistical investigation

data smoothing algorithm STATISTICS method for removing meaningless data a procedure for removing meaningless data from a sequence of observations so that a pattern can be detected

Datastream MARKETS online financial data system a data system available online that gives financial information, for example, about securities, prices, and stock exchange transactions

data transfer E-COMMERCE how much information is downloaded from website the amount of data downloaded from a website. This information can be useful, particularly for measuring the number of visitors to a website.

data warehouse GENERAL MANAGEMENT information database used for business analysis a collection of subject-orientated data collected over a period of time and stored on a computer to provide information in support of managerial decision making. A data warehouse contains a large volume of information selected from different sources, including operational systems and organizational databases, and brought together in a standard format to facilitate retrieval and analysis. ***Data mining*** techniques are used to access the information in a data warehouse.

dated date STOCKHOLDING & INVESTMENTS start date for calculation of interest the date on which interest begins to accrue on a fixed-income security, which is also the date the security is issued

date of maturity STOCKHOLDING & INVESTMENTS = ***maturity date***

dawn raid STOCKHOLDING & INVESTMENTS large morning purchase of firm's stock a sudden, planned purchase of a large amount of a company's stock at the beginning of a day's trading. Up to 15% of a company's stock can be bought in this way, and the purchaser must wait for seven days before buying more. A dawn raid may sometimes be the first step toward a ***takeover***.

DAX MARKETS main German stock exchange the principal German stock exchange, based in Frankfurt. *Full form* ***Deutscher Aktienindex***

day book ACCOUNTING book for recording daily sales and purchases a book in which an account of sales and purchases made each day can be recorded

dayn FINANCE debt obligation in Islamic financing, a debt incurred as the result of any contract or financial transaction

Day of the Jackal Fraud FRAUD UK identity fraud using dead child's birth certificate in the United Kingdom, a form of identity fraud in which a person obtains the birth certificate of a dead child and uses it to acquire a false identity and passport

day order CURRENCY & EXCHANGE in dollar trading, order with one day's validity an order that is valid only during one trading day

days' sales outstanding ACCOUNTING = ***collection ratio***

day trader MARKETS trader operating by the day a trader who turns holdings into cash at the end of each day

day trading MARKETS operating by the day the practice of turning holdings into cash at the end of each day

DC *abbr* BANKING ***documentary credit***

D/C *abbr* BANKING ***documentary credit***

DCF *abbr* FINANCE ***discounted cash flow***

DCM *abbr* MARKETS ***Development Capital Market***

DD *abbr* **1.** BANKING ***direct debit*** **2.** ACCOUNTING ***due diligence*** *(sense 1)*

dead account BANKING inactive account an account that is no longer used

dead cat bounce MARKETS brief rise in stock price after large drop a short-term increase in the value of a stock following a precipitous drop in value *(slang)*

deadweight loss ECONOMICS inefficiency caused by imbalance economic inefficiency caused by a fall in quantities of a product produced, for example, when a monopoly producer keeps production low to maintain high prices, or by a tax

deal 1. BUSINESS business transaction a business arrangement or agreement between two or more people, usually to their mutual benefit **2.** BUSINESS trade in something as business to buy and sell something as a business **3.** MARKETING bargain something offered for sale on favorable terms ◇ cut somebody a deal BUSINESS to agree on terms for a business arrangement with somebody

dealer 1. BUSINESS person who buys and sells something a person engaged in the purchase and sale of goods or services **2.** MARKETS person trading for self, not clients a person or firm that buys or sells on their own account, not as a broker on behalf of clients

dealership MARKETING business selling products for specific manufacturer a retail outlet distributing, selling, and servicing products such as cars on behalf of a manufacturer

deal flow STOCKHOLDING & INVESTMENTS presentation of new investments the rate at which new offers of investments are being presented to underwriters

dealing room MARKETS area in stock exchange used for trading securities a room at a stock exchange where the buying and selling of stocks takes place

dealings BUSINESS business between people or organizations business activities conducted between people or organizations

dear money FINANCE money lent at high interest to restrict spending money that is lent at a high interest rate and will therefore restrict a borrower's expenditure. *See also* ***cheap money***

death benefit INSURANCE payment made when insured person dies insurance benefit paid to the family of somebody who dies in an accident at work

death by committee GENERAL MANAGEMENT termination of proposal by committee inertia the prevention of serious consideration of a proposal by assigning a committee to look at it

death duty *UK* TAX = ***estate tax***

death tax *US* TAX *(informal)* = ***estate tax***

debenture BUSINESS acceptance by firm of debt obligation the written acknowledgment of a debt by a company, usually given under its seal and containing provisions as to payment of interest and principal. A debenture may be secured on some or all of the assets of the company or its subsidiaries.

debenture bond FINANCE **1.** documentation of unsecured bond a certificate showing that a ***debenture*** has been issued, and giving its terms and conditions **2.** US loan without security in the United States, a long-term unsecured loan, a common type taken out by companies

debenture capital FINANCE loan that company secures with assets money borrowed by a company, using its fixed assets as security

debenture holder FINANCE somebody holding a bond a person who holds a bond or certificate of debt for money lent

debenture stock FINANCE stock paying fixed interest on fixed schedule a form of debt instrument in which a company guarantees payments on a fixed schedule or at a fixed rate of interest

debit ACCOUNTING charge against account in bookkeeping a bookkeeping entry that shows an increase in assets or expenses, or a decrease in liabilities, revenue, or capital. It is entered in the left-hand side of an account in ***double-entry bookkeeping***.

debit balance ACCOUNTING balance showing more money owed than received the difference between debits and credits in an account where the value of ***debits*** is greater

debit card BANKING bank card that functions like check a card issued by a bank or financial institution and accepted by a merchant in payment for a transaction. Unlike the procedure with a ***credit card***, purchases are deducted from the cardholder's account at the time when the transaction takes place. *Also called* ***check card***

debit column ACCOUNTING left side of double-entry bookkeeping system the left-hand side of an account, showing increases in a company's assets or decreases in its liabilities

debit entry ACCOUNTING entry for expenditure an item in a financial statement recording money spent

debit note FINANCE document showing that customer owes money a document that shows how much money a person or company owes. *Abbr* ***D/N***

debits and credits ACCOUNTING record of firm's financial transactions figures entered in a company's accounts to record increases and decreases in ***assets***, expenses, liabilities, revenues, or capital

debit side ACCOUNTING accounting column for money owed or paid out the section of a financial statement that lists payments made or owed. In ***double-entry bookkeeping***, the left hand side of each account is designated as the debit side. *See also* ***credit side***

debt FINANCE **1.** money owed an amount of money owed to a person or organization **2.** money borrowed money borrowed by a person or organization to finance personal or business activities

debt bomb ECONOMICS economic volatility caused by default of major institution instability in an economy as a result of a major financial institution defaulting on its obligations

debt capital FINANCE money raised as loan capital that is raised that carries an obligation to pay back the principal together with interest

debt collection agency FINANCE business specializing in getting debts repaid a business that secures the repayment of debts for third parties on a commission or fee basis

debt-convertible bond STOCKHOLDING & INVESTMENTS bond convertible from variable to fixed interest a floating-rate bond that can be converted to a fixed rate of interest. *See also* ***droplock bond***

debt counseling *or* FINANCE guidance for people in financial difficulty a service offering advice and support to individuals who are financially stretched

debt/equity ratio MARKETS relationship between firm's debts and value the ratio of what a company owes to the value of all of its outstanding shares of stock

debt factoring FINANCE purchase of firm's accounts receivable at discount the business of buying debts at a discount. A factor collects a company's debts when due, and pays the creditor in advance part of the sum to be collected, thus "buying" the debt.

debt finance *UK* FINANCE = ***debt financing***

debt financing *US* FINANCE raising of capital by long-term borrowing the activity of raising capital from long-term borrowing such as the sale of bonds or notes. *UK term* ***debt finance***

debt forgiveness FINANCE lender's canceling of debt the writing off of all or part of a nation's debt by a lender

debt instrument FINANCE written agreement between borrower and lender any document used or issued for raising money, for example, a bill of exchange, bond, or promissory note

debt market FINANCE market trading in debts a market in which corporate or municipal, government, or public debts are bought and sold

debtnocrat BANKING person in position to make very large loans a senior bank official who specializes in lending extremely large sums, for example, to emerging nations (*slang*)

debt obligation STOCKHOLDING & INVESTMENTS = ***collateralized debt obligation***

debtor FINANCE person owing money a person or organization owing money to another. *Also called* ***obligor***

debtor days FINANCE average time it takes to collect payment the number of days on average that it takes a company to receive payment for what it sells.

To determine debtor days, divide the cumulative amount of accounts receivable by sales, then multiply by 365. If accounts receivable total $600,000 and sales are $9,000,000, the calculation is:

$(600{,}000 / 9{,}000{,}000) \times 365 = 24.33$ days

The company takes 24.33 days on average to collect its debts.

Debtor days is an indication of a company's efficiency in collecting monies owed. Obviously, the lower the number the better. An especially high number is a telltale sign of inefficiency or worse. *See also* ***creditor days***

debtor nation INTERNATIONAL TRADE country owing more money than it is owed a country whose foreign debts are larger than money owed to it by other countries

debtors' control FINANCE systems for prompt repayment strategies used to ensure that borrowers pay back loans on time

debt ratio FINANCE relationship between firm's debts and assets the debts of a company shown as a percentage of its ***equity*** plus loan capital

debt rescheduling FINANCE negotiation of new terms for debt repayment the renegotiation of debt payments. Debt rescheduling is necessary when a company can no longer meet its debt payments. It can involve deferring debt payments, deferring payment of interest, or negotiating a new loan. It is usually undertaken as part of ***turnaround management*** to avoid ***business failure***. Debt rescheduling is also undertaken in less developed countries that encounter national debt difficulties. Such arrangements are usually overseen by the ***International Monetary Fund***.

debt security STOCKHOLDING & INVESTMENTS security issued as evidence of debt to purchaser a security issued by a company or government which represents money borrowed from the security's purchaser and which must be repaid at a specified maturity date, usually at a specified interest rate

debt service FINANCE combined interest and principal due on money borrowed the payments due under a loan agreement, i.e. interest payable and payments of principal

debt/service ratio ECONOMICS measurement of debt against gross income the ratio of a country's or company's borrowing to its equity or ***venture capital***

debt swap FINANCE exchange of country's debt for local currency a method of reducing exposure to long-term debt of nations with undeveloped economies by purchasing the debt at a discount and exchanging it with the central bank for local currency

decentralization GENERAL MANAGEMENT giving decision-making power to larger group the dispersal of decision-making control. Decentralization involves moving power, authority, and decision-making control within an organization from a central headquarters or from high managerial levels to subsidiaries, branches, divisions, or departments. As an organizational concept, decentralization implies delegation of both power and responsibility by top management in order to promote flexibility through faster decision making and improved response times. Decentralization is, therefore, strongly related to the concept of empowerment, though the latter is perhaps more focused on direct working front-line staff.

decile STATISTICS value representing one-tenth of frequency distribution one of the nine values that divide the total number of items in a ***frequency distribution*** into ten groups, each containing an equal number of items

decision analysis GENERAL MANAGEMENT = ***decision theory***

decision maker GENERAL MANAGEMENT somebody authorized to make important decisions for firm somebody with the responsibility and authority to make decisions within an organization, especially those that determine future direction and strategy. ***Decision theory*** is used to assist decision makers in the process of ***decision making***.

decision making GENERAL MANAGEMENT process of determining what to do the process of choosing between alternate courses of action. Decision making may take place at an individual or organizational level. The process may involve establishing objectives, gathering relevant information, identifying alternatives, setting criteria for the decision, and selecting the best option. The nature of the decision-making process within an organization is influenced by its culture and structure, and a number of theoretical models have been developed. ***Decision theory*** can be used to assist in the process of decision making. Specific techniques used in decision making include heuristics and decision trees. Computer systems designed to assist managerial decision making are known as decision support systems.

decision-making unit MARKETING group of employees responsible for purchase decisions a group of people within an organization who directly or indirectly influence the purchase of a product or service

decision support system GENERAL MANAGEMENT computer system containing information used for management decisions a computer system designed to collect, store, process, and provide access to information to support managerial decision making. Decision support systems were developed in the 1970s to facilitate unstructured and one-off decision making, as the standard reporting capabilities of ***MIS***s were perceived to be more suitable for routine day-to-day decisions. Data on an organization's external operating environment, as well as internal operational information, is included and an interactive interface allows managers to retrieve and manipulate data. Modeling techniques are used to examine the results of alternative courses of action.

decision theory GENERAL MANAGEMENT analysis of how people determine course of action a body of knowledge that attempts to describe, analyze, and model the process of ***decision making*** and the factors influencing it. Decision theory encompasses both formal mathematical and statistical approaches to solving decision problems, using quantitative techniques such as probability and ***game theory***, and more informal behavioral approaches. It is used to inform and assist decision making in organizations. *Also called* ***decision analysis***

decision tree GENERAL MANAGEMENT chart helping people determine course of action a diagram designed to help decision makers by representing available options and possible outcomes as branches of a tree. Decision trees provide an overview of multiple-stage ***decision making*** by showing successive decision points arising from previous choices. Values representing the relative probability of individual outcomes may be assigned to each branch of the tree in order to compare strategies and select the most favorable.

declaration date STOCKHOLDING & INVESTMENTS day when firm sets next dividend in the United States, the date when the directors of a company meet to announce the proposed dividend per share that they recommend be paid

declaration of dividend STOCKHOLDING & INVESTMENTS firm's official announcement of next dividend a formal announcement by a company's directors of the proposed dividend per share that they recommend be paid. It is subsequently put to a stockholders' vote at the company's annual meeting.

declaration of income TAX = ***income tax return***

declaration of solvency BUSINESS official notice of UK firm's creditworthiness in the United Kingdom, a document, filed with the ***Registrar of Companies***, that lists the assets and liabilities of a company seeking voluntary liquidation to show that the company is capable of repaying its debts within 12 months

declared value TAX figure on customs form the value of goods as entered on a customs declaration

declining balance method ACCOUNTING = ***accelerated depreciation***

deconstruction GENERAL MANAGEMENT breaking up old-fashioned business systems the breaking up of traditional business structures to meet the requirements of the modern economy

decreasing term life insurance *or* **decreasing term life assurance** INSURANCE life insurance with death benefit decreasing over time life insurance that is in effect for a specified period of time and provides a death benefit that decreases incrementally during the period the policy is in effect

de-diversify BUSINESS sell off firm's marginal interests to sell off parts of a company or group that are not considered directly relevant to its main area of interest

deductible *US* INSURANCE portion of insurance claim paid by policyholder the part of a commercial insurance claim that has to be met by the policyholder rather than the insurance company. A deductible of $1,000 means that the company pays all but $1,000 of the claim for loss or damage. *UK term* ***excess***

deduction FINANCE deducting from total, or amount deducted a subtraction of money from a total, or an amount of money subtracted from a total

deduction at source TAX taking taxes directly from salary in the United Kingdom, the collection of taxes from an organization or individual paying an income, rather than from the recipient of the income, for example, from an employer paying wages, a bank paying interest, or a company paying dividends

deed LEGAL legal evidence of real estate sale a legal document, most commonly one that details the transfer or sale of real estate

deed of arrangement LEGAL agreement to terms of repayment by insolvent debtor in the United Kingdom, a legal document that sets out the agreement between an insolvent person and his or her ***creditors***

deed of assignment LEGAL document transferring real estate to creditor in the United Kingdom, a legal document detailing the transfer of real estate from a ***debtor*** to a ***creditor***

deed of covenant LEGAL legal promise to make payments in the United Kingdom, a legal document in which a person or organization promises to pay a third party a sum of money on an annual basis, with tax advantages. A deed of covenant was often used for making regular payments to a charity before the introduction of ***Gift Aid***.

deed of partnership LEGAL legal agreement for partnership in the United Kingdom, a legal document formalizing the agreement and financial arrangements between the parties that make up a partnership

deed of transfer STOCKHOLDING & INVESTMENTS documentation of transfer of stock ownership in the United Kingdom, a legal document that attests to the transfer of stock ownership

deed of variation LEGAL procedure for changing deceased person's will in the United Kingdom, an arrangement that allows the will of a deceased person to be amended, provided specific conditions are met and the amendment is signed by all the original beneficiaries

deep-discount bond STOCKHOLDING & INVESTMENTS bond selling at far less than value a bond offered at a large discount on the face value of the debt so that a significant proportion of the return to the investor comes by way of a capital gain on redemption, rather than through interest payments

deep-discounted rights issue STOCKHOLDING & INVESTMENTS new shares priced below market value a rights issue where the new shares are priced at a very low price compared to their current market value to ensure that stockholders take up the rights

deep-in-the-money call option STOCKHOLDING & INVESTMENTS profitable contract to buy securities a ***call option*** that has an exercise price below the market price of the underlying asset and has therefore become very profitable. *See also* ***deep-out-of-the-money call option***

deep-in-the-money put option STOCKHOLDING & INVESTMENTS profitable contract to sell securities a ***put option*** that has an exercise price above the market price of an underlying asset and has therefore become very profitable. *See also* ***deep-out-of-the-money put option***

deep market MARKETS market in which volume will not affect price a commodity, currency, or stock market in which the volume of trade is such that a considerable number of transactions will not influence the market price

deep-out-of-the-money call option STOCKHOLDING & INVESTMENTS unprofitable contract to buy securities a ***call option*** that has an exercise price above the market price of the underlying asset and has little intrinsic value. *See also* ***deep-in-the-money call option***

deep-out-of-the-money put option STOCKHOLDING & INVESTMENTS unprofitable contract to sell securities a ***put option*** that has an exercise price below the market price of an underlying asset and has little intrinsic value. *See also* ***deep-in-the-money put option***

deep pocket BUSINESS firm giving financial assistance to another a company that provides much-needed funds for another company (*slang*)

de facto standard GENERAL MANAGEMENT successful product's recognized standing in market a standard set in a given market by a highly successful product or service

defalcation FINANCE misuse of money entrusted to somebody's care the improper and illegal use of funds by a person who does not own them, but who has been charged with their care

default 1. STOCKHOLDING & INVESTMENTS be unable to cover loss on trades as a member of an exchange, to lose more on a trading position than is held in capital **2.** LEGAL not do what you have contracted to do to fail to comply with the terms of a contract, especially to fail to pay back a debt

defaulter FINANCE person failing to make scheduled payments a person who defaults, for example, somebody who fails to make scheduled payments on a loan

default notice LEGAL = ***notice of default***

default risk STOCKHOLDING & INVESTMENTS, RISK risk of non-payment the possibility that the issuer of a bond will be unable to make payments of principal and interest when they are due

defeasance LEGAL clause specifying how contract might be broken a clause in a collateral deed that says a contract or bond will be revoked if something happens or if some act is performed

defended takeover bid MERGERS & ACQUISITIONS offer to buy firm that opposes being sold a bid for a company takeover in which the directors of the target company oppose the action of the bidder

defensive security STOCKHOLDING & INVESTMENTS security providing earnings despite falling market a security that has very little risk and provides a return even when the stock market is weak

defensive stock STOCKHOLDING & INVESTMENTS stock not affected by external factors stock that prospers predictably regardless of external circumstances such as an economic slowdown, for example, the stock of a company that markets a product everyone must have

deferment FINANCE putting off of something a postponement of something, for example, taxes or interest on a loan, until a later date

deferred annuity STOCKHOLDING & INVESTMENTS investment offering return 12+ months after last premium an investment that does not pay out until at least one year after the final premium has been paid

deferred common stock *US* STOCKHOLDING & INVESTMENTS stock paying dividends only after others are paid a type of stock usually held by founding members of a company, often with a higher dividend that is only paid after other shareholders have received their dividends and, in some cases, only when a specific level of profit has been achieved. This type of stock is rarely issued in the United States. *Also called* ***deferred share***. *UK term* ***deferred ordinary share***

deferred consideration BUSINESS purchase in which final payment has conditions attached installment payments for the acquisition of new subsidiaries, usually made in the form of cash and stock, where the balance due after the initial deposit depends on the performance of the business acquired

deferred coupon STOCKHOLDING & INVESTMENTS bond that delays interest payments a ***coupon*** that pays no interest at first, but pays relatively high interest after a specific date

deferred credit *or* **deferred income** ACCOUNTING money received but not yet recorded as income revenue received but not yet reported as income in the profit and loss account, for example, payment for goods to be delivered or services provided at a later date, or government grants received for the purchase of assets. The deferred credit is treated as a credit balance on the balance sheet while waiting to be treated as income. *See also* ***accrual basis***

deferred creditor FINANCE creditor paid after all others a person who is owed money by a bankrupt person or organization but who is paid only after all other creditors

deferred interest bond STOCKHOLDING & INVESTMENTS bond that delays interest payments a bond that pays no interest at first, but pays relatively high interest after a specific date

deferred month STOCKHOLDING & INVESTMENTS distant month for option a month relatively late in the term of an ***option***

deferred ordinary share *UK* STOCKHOLDING & INVESTMENTS **1.** stock paying no dividend in early years a type of stock that pays no dividend for a specific number of years after its issue date but then is treated the same as the company's common stock **2.** = ***deferred common stock***

deferred payment **1.** FINANCE money to be repaid later money owed that will be repaid at a later date **2.** OPERATIONS & PRODUCTION payment in installments payment for goods by installments over a period of time

deferred revenue ACCOUNTING income carried into next accounting period revenue carried forward to future accounting periods

deferred share STOCKHOLDING & INVESTMENTS = ***deferred common stock***

deferred tax TAX tax payable later a tax that may become payable at some later date

deficiency FINANCE amount of shortfall the amount by which something such as a sum of money is less than it should be

deficit ACCOUNTING = ***budget deficit***

deficit financing FINANCE covering shortfall the borrowing of money because expenditure will exceed receipts

deficit spending FINANCE spending financed by borrowing government spending financed through borrowing rather than through taxation or other current revenue

defined contribution pension plan PENSIONS employer's retirement plan with specific investments in the United States, a retirement plan arranged by an employer in which the money contributed by both the employer and employee is invested, so that the retirement benefit is not fixed but is dependent on how well the investments do

deflation ECONOMICS long-term decline in prices a reduction in the general level of prices sustained over several months, usually accompanied by declining employment and output

deflationary ECONOMICS causing drop in prices causing a decline in the prices of goods and services

deflationary fiscal policy ECONOMICS government policy of raising taxes and reducing spending a government policy that raises taxes and reduces public expenditure in order to reduce the level of ***aggregate demand*** in the economy

deflationary gap ECONOMICS failure in exploiting economic potential a gap between ***GDP*** and the potential output of the economy

deflator ECONOMICS inflation-related reduction in national income the amount by which a country's ***GDP*** is reduced to take into account ***inflation***

degearing BUSINESS reduction in firm's long-term debt a reduction in a company's loan capital in relation to the value of its common stock plus reserves. *See also* ***leverage***

degressive tax TAX tax decreasing as taxable amount increases a tax for which the amount to be paid decreases as the amount that is liable for taxation increases. *See also* ***progressive tax***

delayed settlement processing E-COMMERCE storing credit card transactions online until shipment a procedure for storing authorized transaction settlements online until after the merchant has shipped the goods to the purchaser

delayering GENERAL MANAGEMENT removing layers of firm's management the removal of supposedly unproductive layers of middle management to make organizations more efficient and customer-responsive. The term came into vogue during the 1980s.

del credere FINANCE extra charge to protect against nonpayment an amount added to a charge to cover the possibility of its not being paid

del credere agent FINANCE sales agent who guarantees purchaser's payment an agent who agrees to sell goods on commission and pay the principal even if the buyer defaults on payment. To cover the risk of default, the commission is marginally higher than that of a general agent.

delegatee GENERAL MANAGEMENT person being allocated task a person who is given the responsibility and authority to undertake a specific activity

delegation GENERAL MANAGEMENT putting somebody else in charge of activity the process of entrusting somebody else with the appropriate responsibility and authority for the accomplishment of a specific activity. Delegation involves briefing somebody else to perform a task for which the delegator holds individual responsibility, but which need not be executed by him or her. There are various degrees of delegation: for example, a manager may delegate responsibility, but not necessarily full authority, and continue to supervise the activity. Delegation should be a positive activity, for example, as an aid to employee development, rather than a negative one, for example, passing on an unpopular task. It should be accompanied by support and encouragement from the delegator to the delegatee. An extension of delegation is empowerment, in which complete authority for a task is passed to somebody else, who takes full responsibility for its objectives, execution, and results.

delegator GENERAL MANAGEMENT person allocating task a person who gives somebody else the responsibility and authority to undertake a specific activity

deleverage FINANCE pay off debt to reduce the size of a company's debt, possibly by selling off some assets

delinquent BUSINESS late in repaying money owed used to describe a person or organization that is late in paying an account, or a debt that remains unpaid

delisting REGULATION & COMPLIANCE removal of firm from stock exchange the action of removing a company from being traded on a recognized stock exchange – ***delist***

delivered price OPERATIONS & PRODUCTION price that includes shipping and handling a price that includes any expenses incurred during packing and transportation of the item to its final destination

delivery 1. FINANCE handing over of bill of exchange for payment the transfer of a bill of exchange or other negotiable instrument to the bank that is due to make payment **2.** OPERATIONS & PRODUCTION act of delivering commodity to buyer the transportation of a commodity by a seller to a purchaser as set out in a futures contract

delivery date MARKETS date for delivery of commodity the date on which a commodity bought or sold in a futures contract must be delivered

delivery month MARKETS = ***contract month***

delivery notice MARKETS notification of details of handover a written notice to the buyer of a commodity on a ***futures contract*** of its delivery and terms of settlement

Delphi technique GENERAL MANAGEMENT forecasting method avoiding group pressure a qualitative forecasting method in which a panel of experts respond individually to a questionnaire or series of questionnaires, before reaching a consensus. The Delphi technique requires individual submission of, and response to, the questionnaire on the topic under investigation, in order to avoid the effect of a dominant personality influencing a group discussion. A summary of the written replies is then distributed so that responses can be revised in the light of the views expressed. This cycle is repeated until the coordinator of the group is satisfied that the best possible consensus has been reached. The Delphi technique was developed at the Rand Corporation during the late 1940s and 1950s and owes its name to the Greek oracle at Delphi, which was believed to make predictions about the future.

delta STOCKHOLDING & INVESTMENTS option price change compared with associated asset the amount of change in the price of an option as compared to a corresponding change in the price of its underlying asset

demand 1. FINANCE request for payment an act of asking somebody for payment of money owed **2.** MARKETING measure of consumers' willingness to buy the need that consumers have for a product or their eagerness and ability to buy it

demand bill FINANCE bill of exchange payable on demand a ***bill of exchange*** that must be paid when payment is asked for

demand deposit BANKING account balance available for writing checks money in a deposit account that the holder can withdraw at any time by writing a check

demand forecasting FINANCE estimation of consumer demand for product or service the activity of estimating the quantity of a product or service that consumers will purchase. Demand forecasting involves techniques including both informal methods such as educated guesses and quantitative methods such as the use of historical sales data or current data from test markets. Demand forecasting may be used in making pricing decisions, in assessing future capacity requirements, or in making decisions on whether to enter a new market.

demand management OPERATIONS & PRODUCTION predicting and meeting customer demand the ***supply chain*** activity of ***forecasting***, effectively planning for, and meeting ***customer demand*** for a product

demand note FINANCE promissory note that is payable on demand a promissory note that has no specific date for payment but instead must be paid when it is presented

demand price FINANCE price buyer is willing to pay the price that purchasers are willing to offer to pay for a given quantity of goods

demand-pull inflation ECONOMICS inflation caused by increased demand inflation caused by rising demand that cannot be met

demand risk RISK risk of customer demand not matching firm's forecast the risk for a company that demand for a product will either exceed their expectations and ability to meet the demand or fall short of their expectations and leave them with product they cannot sell

demassifying GENERAL MANAGEMENT tailoring mass medium to customers' needs the process of changing a mass medium to a medium that is customized to meet the requirements of individual consumers

demerge MERGERS & ACQUISITIONS separate parts of firm to split up an organization into a number of separate parts

demerger MERGERS & ACQUISITIONS separation of company into independent parts the separation of a company into several distinct entities, especially used of companies that have grown by acquisition

demographics STATISTICS characteristics and statistics of human population the characteristics of the size and structure of a human population, including features such as its distribution and age range

demography STATISTICS study of human population statistics the study of the size and structural characteristics of human populations

demonetize CURRENCY & EXCHANGE discontinue coin or note to withdraw a coin or note from a country's currency

demurrage BUSINESS payment made to compensate for late shipment compensation paid to a customer when shipment of a good is delayed at a port or by customs

demutualization *or* BANKING conversion of mutual society to public corporation the process by which a mutual society becomes a publicly owned corporation

Denial of Service Attack E-COMMERCE attempt to prevent Internet use an attempt to limit or prevent a user or users from accessing the Internet, a network, or using their e-mail, for example, by flooding it with more requests than it can handle

denomination CURRENCY & EXCHANGE value on coin, banknote, or stamp a unit of money imprinted on a coin, banknote, or stamp

department GENERAL MANAGEMENT section of firm responsible for particular function a section of an organization, usually centered on a specialized function, under the responsibility of a head of department or team leader

departmental budget ACCOUNTING budget for department a budget of income and/or expenditure applicable to a specific department. *See also* ***functional budget***

departmentalization GENERAL MANAGEMENT dividing firm into sections the division of an organization into sections. Departmentalization is usually based on operating function, and organizations will commonly have departments for, for example, finance, personnel, or marketing. Such organizational structure is typical of a ***bureaucracy***. It may be used in ***centralization***, when a particular activity is undertaken by one department in one location on behalf of the whole organization, but may equally be a feature of a *decentralized* organization, in which departments are used as individual operating units responsible for their own management.

Department for Business, Enterprise and Regulatory Reform British government department a British government department dealing with areas such as enterprise, business law, markets, energy policy, and business regulation. It was created in 2007 to bring together the functions of the ***Department of Trade and Industry*** and regulatory functions formerly performed within the Cabinet Office. *Abbr* ***BERR***

Department of Trade and Industry former British government department the former British government department that dealt with areas such as commerce, international trade, and the stock exchange. Its functions are now taken over by the ***Department for Business, Enterprise and Regulatory Reform***. *Abbr* ***DTI***

dependency ratio ECONOMICS proportion of society economically dependent on work force a measure of the proportion of a population that is too young or too old to work and is therefore economically dependent on that part of the population that is productively working. *Also called* ***support ratio***

dependent variable STATISTICS variable that changes in response to another a variable or factor whose value changes as a result of a change in another (the ***independent variable***)

deposit **1.** BANKING money added to bank account money placed in a bank for safekeeping or to earn interest **2.** BUSINESS partial payment to reserve something part of the price of an item given by a customer in advance so that the item will not be sold to somebody else before the full price is paid **3.** OPERATIONS & PRODUCTION add money to bank account to pay money into a bank account

deposit account BANKING **1.** interest-paying account requiring prior notice for withdrawal a bank account that pays interest on deposited funds but on which prior notice must be given in order to withdraw money. *Abbr* ***D/A*** **2.** interest-paying UK building society account in the United Kingdom, a building society account that is held by somebody who is not a member of the society. Deposit accounts are generally paid a lower rate of interest, but in the event of the society going into liquidation deposit account holders are given preference. *See also* ***share account***

depositary BUSINESS somebody who entrusts valuable items to institution a person or organization that has placed money or documents for safekeeping with a ***depository***

depositor BANKING somebody who deposits money in financial institution a person or business that places money in a bank, savings and loan, or other type of financial institution

depository BANKING institution responsible for keeping valuable items safe a bank or organization with whom money or documents can be placed for safekeeping

Depository Trust and Clearing Corporation BUSINESS US company for handling securities transactions in the United States, a holding company with several subsidiaries, which is set up to efficiently handle clearance, settlement, and depository services for the securities industry. *Abbr* ***DTCC***

deposit protection INSURANCE insurance against loss of deposits insurance that depositors have against loss by a financial institution. In the United States, the Federal Deposit Insurance Corporation (FDIC) provides this.

deposit slip *or* **deposit receipt** *US* BANKING receipt for deposits made in bank account the slip of paper that accompanies money or checks being paid into a bank account. *UK term* ***paying-in slip***

deposit-taking institution BANKING banking institution serving general public an institution that is licensed to receive money on deposit from private individuals and to pay interest on it, for example, a bank or savings and loan

depreciable cost ACCOUNTING expense spread over several accounting periods an expense that may be set against the profits of more than one accounting period

depreciate 1. FINANCE lose value over time to lose value, or decrease the value of something, usually over a period of time **2.** ACCOUNTING make allowance for asset's progressive loss of value to make an allowance in business accounts for the loss of value of an asset over time

depreciation 1. ACCOUNTING loss of value an allocation of the ***cost*** of an ***asset*** over a period of time for accounting and tax purposes. Depreciation is charged against earnings, on the basis that the use of capital assets is a legitimate cost of doing business. Depreciation is also a non-cash expense that is added into net income to determine cash flow in a given accounting period.

To qualify for depreciation, assets must be items used in the business that wear out, become obsolete, or lose value over time from natural causes or circumstances, and they must have a useful life beyond a single tax year. Examples include vehicles, machines, equipment, furnishings, and buildings, plus major additions or improvements to such assets. Some intangible assets also can be included under certain conditions. Land, personal assets, stock, leased or rented property, and a company's employees cannot be depreciated.

Straight line depreciation is the most straightforward method. It assumes that the net cost of an asset should be written off in equal amounts over its life. The formula used is:

(Original cost – Scrap value) / Useful life in years

For example, if a vehicle cost $30,000 and can be expected to serve the business for seven years, its original cost would be divided by its useful life:

(30,000 – 2,000) / 7 = 4,000 per year

The $4,000 becomes a depreciation expense that is reported on the company's year-end income statement under "operation expenses."

In theory, an asset should be depreciated over the actual number of years that it will be used, according to its actual drop in value each year. At the end of each year, all the depreciation claimed to date is subtracted from its cost in order to arrive at its ***book value***, which would equal its market value. At the end of its useful business life, any portion not depreciated would represent the salvage value for which it could be sold or scrapped.

For tax purposes, some accountants prefer to use the ***declining balance method*** to record larger amounts of depreciation in the asset's early years in order to reduce tax bills as soon as possible. In contrast to the straight-line method, this assumes that the asset depreciates more in its earlier years of use.

The table below compares the depreciation amounts that would be available, under these two methods, for a $1,000 asset that is expected to be used for five years and then sold for $100 as scrap.

Straight-line method of depreciation

Year	Annual depreciation	Year-end book value
1	$900 x 20% = $180	$1,000 - $180 = $820
2	$900 x 20% = $180	$820 - $180 = $640
3	$900 x 20% = $180	$640 - $180 = $460
4	$900 x 20% = $180	$460 - $180 = $280
5	$900 x 20% = $180	$280 - $180 = $100

Declining-balance method of depreciation

Year	Annual depreciation	Year-end book value
1	$1,000 x 40% = $400	$1,000 - $400 = $600
2	$600 x 40% = $240	$600 - $240 = $360
3	$360 x 40% = $144	$360 - $144 = $216
4	$216 x 40% = $86.40	$216 - $86.40 = $129.60
5	$129.60 x 40% = $51.84	$129.60 - $51.84 = $77.76

The depreciation method to be used for a particular asset is fixed at the time that the asset is first placed in service. Whatever rules or tables are in effect for that year must be followed as long as the asset is owned.

Depreciation laws and regulations change frequently over the years as a result of government policy changes, so a company owning property over a long period may have to use several different depreciation methods. **2.** CURRENCY & EXCHANGE decrease in value of currency a reduction of a currency's value in relation to the value of other currencies

depreciation rate ACCOUNTING annual rate at which asset loses value the rate at which the value of an asset decreases each year in business accounts

depressed market MARKETS market where supply outweighs demand a market in which there are more goods available than there are customers who are willing to buy them, leading to lower prices. A stock market that is depressed, with falling prices, is called a ***bear market***.

depression ECONOMICS long-term decline in economic activity a prolonged slump or downturn in the business cycle, marked by a high level of unemployment

deprival value FINANCE = ***value to the business***

deregulation REGULATION & COMPLIANCE lessening of government controls a reduction in government controls over a specific business activity with the intention of stimulating competition

deregulatory model REGULATION & COMPLIANCE belief in less government regulation the theory that less government regulation in the economy will result in more competition and a more efficient marketplace

derivative STOCKHOLDING & INVESTMENTS security with price link to underlying asset a ***security*** such as an ***option***, the price of which has a strong correlation with an underlying commodity, currency, or ***financial instrument***

derivative instruments *or* **derivatives** STOCKHOLDING & INVESTMENTS securities based on other securities or market conditions forms of traded securities, such as option contracts, which are derived from ordinary bonds and shares, exchange rates, or stock market indices.

Derivative Trading Facility MARKETS Australian computer system for trading options a computer system and associated network operated by the Australian Stock Exchange to facilitate the purchase and sale of exchange-traded options. *Abbr* ***DTF***

descending tops MARKETS chart pattern with each successive peak lower a term used to refer to a chart pattern that shows falling market, in which each high is lower than the previous one

designated account BANKING account requiring second person for extra identification an account opened and held in one person's name, but that also includes another person's name for extra identification purposes

design for manufacturability *or* **design for assembly** *or* **design for production** OPERATIONS & PRODUCTION designing products for ease of manufacture the process of designing products to optimize the manufacturing process while assuring the product's highest quality, performance, and reliability for the price

design for supply OPERATIONS & PRODUCTION designing desirable products that keep costs low the process of designing products that will meet ***customer demand*** without sacrificing quality or customer service, while minimizing costs throughout the ***supply chain***

design protection MARKETING = ***copyright***

de-skilling HR & PERSONNEL replacing need for particular job skills with technology the removal of the need for skill or judgment in the performance of a task, often because of new technologies. While it can be argued that de-skilling has adversely affected some manual workers in traditional manufacturing industries, the technologies used in modern production systems require a wider range and higher level of skill among the workforce as a whole.

desk research MARKETING investigation conducted from office research carried out in an office, using documents, telephone interviews, or the Internet

Deutscher Aktienindex MARKETS *see* ***DAX***

devaluation ECONOMICS reduction of official currency exchange rate a reduction in the official fixed rate at which one currency exchanges for another under a fixed-rate regime, usually to correct a balance of payments deficit

developing country ECONOMICS poor nation with little industrial development a country, often a producer of primary goods such as cotton or rubber, that cannot generate investment income to stimulate growth and that possesses a national income that is vulnerable to change in commodity prices

development area *or* **development zone** BUSINESS area receiving government aid to attract commercial development a geographic area that has been given special help from a government to encourage businesses and factories to be set up there

development capital FINANCE money for expansion financing acquired or provided for the expansion of an established business

Development Capital Market MARKETS closed sector of Johannesburg exchange for developing companies a sector on the South African stock exchange for listing smaller developing companies which was closed to new listings in 2004 due to low liquidity. *Abbr* ***DCM***

development cycle MARKETING *see* ***new product development***

dhaman FINANCE = ***daman***

Diagonal Street *S. Africa* FINANCE financial district of Johannesburg the financial center of Johannesburg or, by extension, South Africa (*informal*)

dial and smile *US* MARKETING call strangers to sell something to call potential customers of a product or service to try to make a sale (*slang*)

DIAMONDs STOCKHOLDING & INVESTMENTS shares in selected firms on American Stock Exchange shares in a fund, traded on the American Stock Exchange, that is made up of the 30 companies represented in the ***Dow Jones Industrial Average***

dicing and slicing MARKETING analyzing information in different ways the analysis of raw data to extract information under different categories (*slang*)

dictum meum pactum MARKETS my word is my bond Latin for the phrase "My word is my bond," the motto of the London Stock Exchange

differential costing FINANCE way to determine costs based on production levels a costing method that shows the difference in costs that results from different levels of activity such as making one thousand or ten thousand extra units of a product

differential pricing MARKETING selling product at different prices in different places a method of pricing that offers the same product at different prices, for example, in different markets, countries, or retail outlets

differential tariff TAX charge that varies by class or source a tax on goods or services which varies according to their class or source

differentiation MARKETING = ***product differentiation***

digital cash E-COMMERCE form of electronic cash carrying no user information an anonymous form of ***digital money*** which can be linked directly to a bank account or exchanged for physical money. As with physical cash, there is no way to obtain information about the buyer from it, and it can be transferred by the seller to pay for subsequent purchases. *Also called* ***e-cash, electronic cash***

digital certificate E-COMMERCE electronic document that shows buyer is authentic an electronic document issued by a recognized authority which validates a purchaser. It is used much as a driver's license or passport is used for identification purposes in a traditional business transaction.

digital coins E-COMMERCE form of electronic cash for small payments a form of electronic payment authorized for instant transactions which facilitates the purchase of items priced in small denominations of ***digital cash***. Digital coins are transferred from customer to merchant for a transaction such as the purchase of a newspaper using a ***smart card*** for payment.

digital coupon E-COMMERCE online form used for obtaining lower product price a voucher or similar form that exists electronically, for example, on a website, and can be used to reduce the price of goods or services

digital divide E-COMMERCE inequality of access to information technology the difference in opportunities available to people who have access to modern information technology and those who do not. Factors such as urban living, education level, economic class, and industrialization affect the digital divide.

digital economy ECONOMICS economic system based on online business transactions an economy in which the main productive functions are in electronic commerce, for example, trade on the Internet

digital goods E-COMMERCE products sold and delivered electronically merchandise that is sold and delivered electronically, for example, over the Internet

digital hygienist GENERAL MANAGEMENT employee who inspects other employees' Internet usage somebody within a company who is responsible for checking employees' e-mails and surfing habits for non-work-related activity *(slang)*

digital money E-COMMERCE electronic cash related to real-world currency a series of numbers with an intrinsic value in some physical currency. Online digital money requires electronic interaction with a bank to conduct a transaction; offline digital money does not. Anonymous digital money is synonymous with ***digital cash***. Identified digital money carries with it information revealing the identities of those involved in the transaction. *Also called* ***e-money, electronic money***

digital strategy GENERAL MANAGEMENT plan based on information technology a business strategy that is based on the use of information technology

digital wallet E-COMMERCE shopper's software used for making online payments software stored on the hard drive of an online shopper's computer allowing the user to pay for purchases electronically. The wallet can hold in encrypted form such items as credit card information, digital cash or coins, a digital certificate to identify the user, and standardized shipping information. *Also called* ***electronic wallet***

digitizable E-COMMERCE able to be converted to electronic form capable of being converted to digital form for distribution via the Internet or other networks

dilution levy FINANCE charge to compensate for effect of investors' transactions an extra charge levied by fund managers on investors buying or selling units in a fund, designed to offset any potential effect on the value of the fund of such purchases or sales

dilution of equity *US* STOCKHOLDING & INVESTMENTS sale of additional stock resulting in reduced value a situation in which a company makes more shares of common stock available without an increase in its assets, with the end result that each share is worth less than before. *UK term* ***dilution of shareholding***

dilution of shareholding *UK* STOCKHOLDING & INVESTMENTS = ***dilution of equity***

dip MARKETS small temporary fall in securities prices a slight temporary fall in the price of securities after a long-term gain

direct action marketing MARKETING = ***direct response marketing***

direct channel MARKETING way of selling and delivering directly to buyers a method of selling and distributing products direct to customers. Direct channels include direct selling, mail order, and the Internet.

direct cost OPERATIONS & PRODUCTION cost relating to production a variable cost directly attributable to production. Items that are classed as direct costs include materials used, labor deployed, and marketing budget. Amounts spent will vary with output. *See also* ***indirect cost***

direct debit BANKING arrangement for charging customer's account automatically a system by which a customer allows a company to make charges to his or her bank account automatically and where the amount charged can be increased or decreased with the agreement of the customer. *Abbr* ***DD***. *See also* ***automatic debit***

directive LEGAL **1.** official order an official or government instruction that something should happen **2.** new law in EU in the EU, a decision made centrally that is applied through the domestic law of member states

direct labor HR & PERSONNEL employees who actually make products or perform services personnel directly involved in the manufacturing of products or the provision of services. Direct labor includes ***blue-collar workers***.

direct labor cost percentage rate FINANCE product overhead attributed to labor costs an ***overhead absorption rate***, based on labor costs, which can readily be allocated to individual units of production

direct labor hour rate FINANCE product overhead attributed to labor hours an ***overhead absorption rate***, based on labor hours, which can readily be allocated to individual units of production

direct mail MARKETING sending advertising directly to potential customers the sending by mail, fax, or e-mail of advertising communications addressed to specific prospective customers. Direct mail is one tool that can be used as part of a marketing strategy. The use of direct mail is often administered by third-party companies that own databases containing not only names and addresses, but also social, economic, and lifestyle information. It is sometimes seen as an invasion of personal privacy, and there is some public resentment of this form of advertising. This is particularly true of e-mailed direct mail, known as spam. By enabling advertisers to target a specific type of potential customer, however, direct mail can be more cost-efficient than other advertising media. It is frequently used as part of a relationship marketing strategy.

direct mail preference service MARKETING arrangement for removing name from firm's mailing list an arrangement that allows individuals and organizations to refuse direct mail by having participating organizations remove them from their mailing lists

direct marketing MARKETING = ***direct response marketing***

director HR & PERSONNEL **1.** person elected by stockholders to help run company a person appointed by the stockholders to be one of the people with the responsibility of running the company. A director is usually in charge of one or other of its main functions, for example, sales or human resources, and is usually a member of the board of directors. **2.** person in charge of something the person who is in charge of a project, an official institute, or other organization

directorate CORPORATE GOVERNANCE group directing firm's course the governing or controlling body of an organization responsible for the organization's corporate strategy and accountable to its stakeholders for business results. A directorate may also be known as a ***board of directors*** or council, or, at an inner level, the executive or management committee.

director's dealing STOCKHOLDING & INVESTMENTS stock transactions by firm's director the purchase or sale of a company's stock by one of its directors

director's fees FINANCE money paid to company director money paid to a director of a company for attendance at board meetings

directors' report CORPORATE GOVERNANCE board of directors' annual report the annual report prepared by the board of directors and distributed to the company's stockholders

direct response marketing *or* **direct response advertising** MARKETING methods for trying to sell directly to consumers the use of direct forms of advertising to elicit inquiries or sales from potential customers directly to producers or service providers. Direct response marketing aims to bypass intermediaries such as wholesalers or retailers. Forms of communication used include direct mail, home shopping channels, and television and press advertisements. *Also called* ***direct action marketing, direct marketing***

direct selling MARKETING selling products to consumers without intermediate steps the selling of products or services directly to customers without the use of intermediaries such as wholesalers, retailers, or brokers. Direct selling offers many advantages to the customer, including lower prices and shopping from home. Potential disadvantages include lack of after-sales service, an inability to inspect products prior to purchase, lack of specialist advice, and difficulties in returning or exchanging goods. Methods of direct selling include mail order catalogs and door-to-door and telephone sales. Direct selling has increased with the growth of the Internet, which enables producers to make direct contact with potential customers.

direct share ownership *UK* STOCKHOLDING & INVESTMENTS = ***direct stock ownership***

direct stock ownership *US* STOCKHOLDING & INVESTMENTS ownership of stock by private individuals the ownership of stock by private individuals, buying or selling through brokers, and not via holdings in mutual funds. *UK term* ***direct share ownership***

direct tax TAX tax paid directly by producer or provider a tax on income or capital that is paid directly rather than added to the price of goods or services

dirty float CURRENCY & EXCHANGE exchange rate influenced by central bank's actions abroad a floating exchange rate that cannot float freely because a country's central bank intervenes on foreign exchange markets to alter its level

dirty price FINANCE cost of debt plus unpaid interest the price of a debt instrument that includes the amount of accrued interest that has not yet been paid

disaggregation MERGERS & ACQUISITIONS breaking up group of allied firms the breaking apart of an alliance of companies to review their strengths and contributions as a basis for rebuilding an effective business web

disaster management GENERAL MANAGEMENT firm's response to major unexpected negative events the actions taken by an organization in response to unexpected events that are adversely affecting people or resources and threatening the continued operation of the organization. Disaster management includes the development of *disaster recovery plans*, for minimizing the risk of disasters and for handling them when they do occur, and the implementation of such plans. Disaster management usually refers to the management of natural catastrophes such as fire, flooding, or earthquakes. Related techniques include ***crisis management***, ***contingency management***, and ***risk management***.

disaster recovery plan GENERAL MANAGEMENT plan for firm's response to disaster a plan for minimizing the risk of disasters and for handling them when they do occur. It usually refers to natural catastrophes such as fire, flooding, or earthquakes. *See also* ***disaster management***

disbursement FINANCE paying out of money the payment of money, for example, as an expense or to get rid of a debt

disbursing agent FINANCE = ***paying agent***

discharged bankrupt LEGAL person released from bankruptcy a person who has been released from being bankrupt because his or her debts have been paid

discipline HR & PERSONNEL rules of expected behavior or performance standards of required behavior or performance. Good practice requires an organization to establish a disciplinary procedure in order to ensure just decisions. A disciplinary procedure should consist of a formal system of documented warnings and hearings, with rights of representation and appeal at each stage.

disclaimer LEGAL statement denying legal responsibility for something a statement expressing a refusal to accept legal responsibility for something such as the outcome of an event or the validity of a claim

disclosure REGULATION & COMPLIANCE legal obligation to reveal pertinent facts the act of declaring facts that were previously unknown, such as share ownership which might affect business decisions, especially to comply with legal requirements

disclosure of information LEGAL giving potentially confidential information to outsiders the release of information to a third party or parties which may be considered confidential. The disclosure of information in the public interest may be prohibited, permitted, or required, by legislation in a variety of contexts. For example: ***data protection*** legislation restricts the disclosure of personal data held by organizations; ***company law*** requires the publication of certain financial and company data; and ***whistleblowing*** legislation entitles employees to divulge information relating to unethical or illegal conduct in the workplace. ***Restrictive covenants*** and ***confidentiality agreements*** also regulate the information that may be disclosed to third parties.

disclosure of shareholding STOCKHOLDING & INVESTMENTS public disclosure of holdings in firm a public announcement of a shareholding in a company, required by the regulatory authorities and stock exchanges if a shareholding exceeds a given percentage

discount 1. FINANCE price reduction to encourage buying a reduction in the price of goods or services in relation to the standard price. A discount is a selling technique that is used, for example, to encourage customers to buy in large quantities or to make payments in cash. It can also be used to improve sales of a slow-moving line. The greater the purchasing power of the buyer, the greater the discounts that can be negotiated. Some companies inflate original list prices to give the impression that discounts offer value for money; conversely too many genuine discounts may harm profitability. **2.** STOCKHOLDING & INVESTMENTS reduced share price offered by investment trust the difference between the share price of an investment trust and its ***net asset value***

discount allowed BUSINESS amount of seller's price reduction the amount by which the seller agrees to reduce his or her price to the customer

discount broker STOCKHOLDING & INVESTMENTS broker with lower fees offering fewer services a broker who charges relatively low fees because he or she provides restricted services

discount brokerage *US* FINANCE finance firm offering fewer, cheaper services a brokerage that offers fewer services for a reduced commission than a standard brokerage

discounted bond STOCKHOLDING & INVESTMENTS low-yield bond priced below face value a bond that is sold for less than its face value because its yield is not as high as that of other bonds

discounted cash flow FINANCE forecast return on investment subject to cost-of-funds adjustment a calculation of the forecast return on capital investment by discounting future cash flows from an investment, usually at a rate equivalent to the company's minimum required rate of return. *Abbr* ***DCF***

discounted dividend model STOCKHOLDING & INVESTMENTS calculation of stock's value by discounting future dividends a method of calculating a stock's value by reducing future dividends to the present value. *Also called* ***dividend discount model***

discounted value STOCKHOLDING & INVESTMENTS = ***present value***

discount house FINANCE firm trading in discounted bills of exchange in the United Kingdom, a financial company that specializes in buying and selling ***bills of exchange*** at a reduced price

discount loan FINANCE loan issued with interest payments deducted a loan that amounts to less than its face value because payment of interest has been subtracted

discount market MARKETS market for borrowing and lending money a market for borrowing and lending money, through certificates of deposit, Treasury bills, etc.

discount rate 1. BANKING interest rate banks pay for loans the rate charged by a central bank on any loans it makes to other banks **2.** E-COMMERCE fee seller pays for credit card transaction settlement a percentage fee that an e-commerce merchant pays to an account provider or independent sales organization for settling an electronic transaction

discount received BUSINESS amount of customer's price reduction the amount by which the purchaser receives a reduction in price from the seller

discount security FINANCE low-priced security not paying interest a security that is sold for less than its face value in lieu of bearing interest

discount window BANKING Federal Reserve loans to member banks in the United States, the system by which the Federal Reserve grants loans to a member bank by giving advances on the security of Treasury bills that the bank is holding

discrete variable STATISTICS statistical variable with whole-number value in a statistical study, a variable such as the number of deaths in a population which has only a whole-number value

discretionary account STOCKHOLDING & INVESTMENTS account allowing broker to make trading decisions a securities account in which the broker has the authority to make decisions about buying and selling without the customer's prior permission. *Also called* ***managed account***

discretionary client STOCKHOLDING & INVESTMENTS client who lets broker manage funds without consultation a client whose funds are managed at the discretion of a broker without the broker needing to refer to the client for prior permission

discretionary funds STOCKHOLDING & INVESTMENTS funds broker can manage without consulting client funds managed at the discretion of a broker without the broker needing to refer to the owner for prior permission

discretionary management STOCKHOLDING & INVESTMENTS investment agreement allowing broker to make decisions an arrangement between a stockbroker and his or her client whereby the stockbroker makes all investment decisions. It is the opposite of an ***advisory management*** arrangement.

discretionary order STOCKHOLDING & INVESTMENTS transaction handled by broker alone a security transaction in which a broker controls details such as the time of execution

discretionary spend *UK* FINANCE = ***discretionary spending***

discretionary spending *US* FINANCE money for things you want but don't need the amount of money available after direct taxation to an individual or family to spend on items other than necessities such as food, clothing, and homes. *UK term* ***discretionary spend***

discretionary trust FINANCE trust arrangement giving trustee full decision-making power a trust where the trustees decide how to invest the income and when and how much income should be paid to the beneficiaries

discriminant analysis STATISTICS statistical method of identifying variables that differentiate groups a statistical technique designed to predict the groups or categories into which individual cases will fall on the basis of a number of independent variables. Discriminant analysis attempts to identify which variables or combinations of variables accurately discriminate between groups or categories by means of a scatter diagram or classification table called a "confusion matrix." Discriminant analysis has applications in finance, for example, credit risk analysis, or in the prediction of company failure, and in the field of marketing, for market segmentation purposes.

discriminating monopoly ECONOMICS sole producer tailoring prices to markets a company able to charge different prices for its output in different markets because as the only producer it has power to influence prices for its goods

discrimination HR & PERSONNEL unfairly treating people differently because of prejudice unfavorable treatment in employment based on prejudice. Major forms of outlawed discrimination include those based on sex, race, disability, and, in some countries, age.

diseconomies of scale OPERATIONS & PRODUCTION increased unit cost with increased production a situation in which increased production increases, rather than decreases, unit costs

disequilibrium FINANCE imbalance in economy, as between supply and demand an imbalance in the economy when supply does not equal demand, or when a country's balance of payments is in deficit

disequilibrium price ECONOMICS product price causing supply and demand imbalance the price of a good set at a level at which demand and supply are not in balance

dishonor BANKING not pay check because funds are inadequate to refuse payment of a check because the account for which it is written does not contain enough money. *Also called* ***bounce*** *(sense 1)*

disinflation ECONOMICS removal of inflation through monetary policies the elimination or reduction of inflation or inflationary pressures in an economy by fiscal or monetary policies

disintermediation 1. FINANCE direct trading in money market the process of savers and borrowers making transactions directly in the money market rather than by making deposits and taking loans from banks **2.** E-COMMERCE removing middlemen to sell directly to customer the elimination of intermediaries, for example, the wholesalers found in traditional retail channels, in favor of direct selling to the consumer. *See also* ***reintermediation***

disinvest 1. FINANCE reduce investment by non-replacement of capital assets to reduce investment by not replacing capital assets when they wear out **2.** STOCKHOLDING & INVESTMENTS reduce investment by selling stock to reduce investment overall or in a specific area by selling stock

disinvestment FINANCE **1.** reduction in investment through non-replacement of capital assets a process of reducing investment by not replacing capital assets when they wear out **2.** reduction in investment by selling stock a process of reducing investment overall or in a specific area by selling stock

dismissal HR & PERSONNEL firing employee the termination of somebody's employment by his or her employer

DISPENSATION TAX UK employer's tax allowance for business expenses in the United Kingdom, an arrangement between an employer and ***Her Majesty's Revenue & Customs*** in which business expenses paid to an employee are not declared for tax

dispersion STATISTICS degree of deviation from mean the amount by which a set of observations deviates from its mean

disposable income *or* **disposable personal income** TAX income after tax and other deductions income that is left for spending after taxes and other deductions have been made from the income of a person or organization. *See also* ***net pay***

dispute HR & PERSONNEL disagreement between parties a disagreement. An ***industrial dispute*** is a disagreement between an employer and an employees' representative, usually a labor union, over pay and conditions and can result in industrial action. A ***commercial dispute*** is a disagreement between two businesses, usually over a contract. There are three main types of dispute resolution: litigation, arbitration, and alternative dispute resolution.

disqualification LEGAL court decision disallowing person from becoming company director a court order that prevents somebody from being a director of a company. A variety of offenses, even those termed as "administrative," can result in some people being disqualified for up to five years.

distrain BUSINESS take control of assets to pay debt to seize ***assets*** belonging to a person or organization in order to pay off a debt

distressed property FINANCE property subject to repossession property originally purchased with the aid of a loan on which payments have stopped and the borrower has defaulted

distress merchandise OPERATIONS & PRODUCTION goods sold cheaply to pay company's debts goods that are sold at sharply reduced prices in order to settle a company's debts

distress sale OPERATIONS & PRODUCTION sale of goods cheaply to pay company's debts a sale of goods at sharply reduced prices in order to settle a company's debts

distributable profit STOCKHOLDING & INVESTMENTS profit usable as dividends profit that can be distributed to stockholders as dividends if the directors decide to do so

distributed profit STOCKHOLDING & INVESTMENTS profit passed on as dividends profit passed to stockholders in the form of dividends

distribution OPERATIONS & PRODUCTION supplying of manufactured goods to retailers the act of sending goods from the manufacturer to the wholesaler and then to retailers

distribution center OPERATIONS & PRODUCTION place for holding products to be sent out a warehouse or storage facility where the emphasis is on processing and moving goods on to wholesalers, retailers, or consumers rather than on storage

distribution channel OPERATIONS & PRODUCTION means of moving products from suppliers to customers the route by which a product or service is moved from a producer or supplier to customers. A distribution channel usually consists of a chain of intermediaries, including wholesalers, retailers, and distributors, which is designed to transport goods from the point of production to the point of consumption in the most efficient way. *Also called* ***channel of distribution***

distribution list E-COMMERCE named group of e-mail addresses a list of e-mail addresses given one collective name. Internet users can send a message to all the addresses on the list simultaneously by referring to the list name.

distribution management OPERATIONS & PRODUCTION handling movement of goods from production to sale the management of the efficient transfer of goods from the place of manufacture to the point of sale or consumption. Distribution management encompasses such activities as warehousing, materials handling, packaging, stock control, order processing, and transportation.

distribution of income **1.** STOCKHOLDING & INVESTMENTS payment of dividends to stockholders the payment of accumulated dividends to stockholders on record, usually on an annual basis **2.** ECONOMICS wealth range in society the way income is spread across society as a whole, as a measure of the equality or inequality of wealth

distribution resource planning OPERATIONS & PRODUCTION computerized system managing needs for finished products a computerized system that integrates distribution with manufacturing by identifying requirements for finished goods and producing schedules for ***inventory*** and its movement within the distribution process. Distribution resource planning systems receive data on sales forecasts, customer order and delivery requirements, available inventory, ***logistics***, and manufacturing and purchasing ***lead times***. This data is analyzed to produce a time-phased schedule of resource requirements that is matched against existing supply sources and production schedules to identify the actions that must be taken to synchronize supply and demand. The effective integration of material requirements planning and distribution resource planning systems leads to the more effective and timely delivery of finished goods to the customer, and to reduced inventory levels and lower material costs. *Abbr* ***DRP***

distributions STOCKHOLDING & INVESTMENTS income from investment any income arising from a bond fund or an equity

distributive network E-COMMERCE interconnected system for moving products a system or infrastructure that enables products and services to move around. Offline distributive networks include roads, telephone companies, electrical power grids, and the mail service. In the new economy, distributive networks include online banks and Web-enabled mobile telephones.

distributor MARKETING intermediary between manufacturer and seller an organization that distributes products to retailers on behalf of a manufacturer

distributor support MARKETING aid from manufacturer to firm that distributes products marketing or financial support by manufacturers aimed at improving the performance of organizations that distribute their products

District Bank BANKING member bank of Federal Reserve in the United States, one of the 12 banks that make up the ***Federal Reserve***. Each District Bank is responsible for all banking activity in its assigned region.

divergence MARKETS contradictory indications of trends a situation in which two or more indicators such as a stock price and an index move in opposite directions, showing a shift in a trend

diversification GENERAL MANAGEMENT, MERGERS & ACQUISITIONS developing new areas for growth or risk reduction a strategy to increase the variety of business, service, or product types within an organization. Diversification can be a growth strategy, taking advantage of market opportunities, or it may be aimed at reducing risk by spreading interests over different areas. It can be achieved through ***acquisition*** or through internal research and development, and it can involve managing two, a few, or many different areas of interest. Diversification can also be a corporate strategy of investment in acquisitions within a broad portfolio range by a large ***holding company***. One distinct type is ***horizontal diversification***, which involves expansion into a similar product area, for example, a domestic furniture manufacturer producing office furniture. Another is ***vertical diversification***, in which a company moves into a different level of the ***supply chain***, for example, a manufacturing company becoming a retailer.

diversified investment company FINANCE varied mutual fund a mutual fund with a range of types of investments

divestiture FINANCE firm's sale of asset the sale by a company of an asset, for example, to get money to pay off a debt

divestment **1.** MERGERS & ACQUISITIONS selling or closing part of firm the sale or closure of one or several businesses, or parts of a business. Divestment often takes place as part of a rationalization effort to cut costs or to enable an organization to concentrate on core business or competences, and may take the form of a ***management buyout***. **2.** STOCKHOLDING & INVESTMENTS giving up ownership in firm the proportional or complete reduction in an ownership stake in an organization

dividend STOCKHOLDING & INVESTMENTS profits paid to stockholders part of a company's net profits paid out to qualified stockholders at a fixed amount per share

dividend check *US* STOCKHOLDING & INVESTMENTS check in payment of dividend a check issued to qualified stockholders that makes payment of a dividend. *UK term* ***dividend warrant***

dividend clawback STOCKHOLDING & INVESTMENTS arrangement for reinvestment of dividends an agreement that dividends will be reinvested as part of the financing of a project

dividend cover STOCKHOLDING & INVESTMENTS ability of net profit to pay firm's dividend the number of times a company's dividends to ordinary stockholders could be paid out of its net after-tax profits. This measures the likelihood of dividend payments being sustained, and is a useful indication of sustained profitability.

If the figure is 3, a firm's profits are three times the level of the dividend paid to stockholders.

Dividend cover is calculated by dividing earnings per share by the dividend per share:

Earnings per share / Dividend per share = Dividend cover

If a company has earnings per share of $8, and it pays out a dividend of 2.1, dividend cover is

8 / 2.1 = 3.80

An alternative formula divides a company's net profit by the total amount allocated for dividends. So a company that earns $10 million in net profit and allocates $1 million for dividends has a dividend cover of 10, while a company that earns $25 million and pays out $10 million in dividends has a dividend cover of 2.5:

10,000,000 / 1,000,000 = 10

and

25,000,000 / 10,000,000 = 2.5

A dividend cover ratio of 2 or higher is usually adequate, and indicates that the dividend is affordable. A dividend cover ratio below 1.5 is risky, and a ratio below 1 indicates a company is paying the current year's dividend with retained earnings from a previous year's, a practice that cannot continue indefinitely. On the other hand, a high dividend cover figure may disappoint an investor looking for income, since the figure suggests directors could have declared a larger dividend. *See also* ***payout ratio***

dividend discount model STOCKHOLDING & INVESTMENTS = ***discounted dividend model***

dividend forecast STOCKHOLDING & INVESTMENTS predicted amount of next dividend a prediction of the amount that an expected dividend will pay per share

dividend limitation STOCKHOLDING & INVESTMENTS restriction on dividend payments for bond a provision in a bond limiting the dividends that may be paid

dividend mandate STOCKHOLDING & INVESTMENTS permission to directly deposit dividends in bank account an authorization by a stockholder to the company in which he or she has a holding to pay dividends directly into his or her bank account

dividend payout STOCKHOLDING & INVESTMENTS money paid as dividends to stockholders money distributed by a company in the form of dividends to qualified stockholders

dividend payout ratio STOCKHOLDING & INVESTMENTS = ***payout ratio***

dividend per share STOCKHOLDING & INVESTMENTS amount of dividend per share of stock held an amount of money paid by a company as dividend for each share of stock held

dividend reinvestment plan STOCKHOLDING & INVESTMENTS arrangement for reinvesting dividends in firm's stock a plan that provides for the reinvestment of dividends in the stock of the company paying the dividends. *Abbr* ***DRIP***

dividend rights STOCKHOLDING & INVESTMENTS rights to receive dividends the entitlement of a stockholder to receive a share of the company's profits

dividends-received deduction STOCKHOLDING & INVESTMENTS, TAX tax break on dividends from subsidiary company a tax advantage on dividends that a company receives from a company it owns

dividend warrant *UK* STOCKHOLDING & INVESTMENTS = ***dividend check***

dividend yield STOCKHOLDING & INVESTMENTS relative size of dividend dividends paid out expressed as a percentage of a stock's price

D/N *abbr* FINANCE ***debit note***

documentary credit *or* **documentary letter of credit** BANKING provision for payment in international transactions an arrangement, used in the finance of international transactions, whereby a bank undertakes to make a payment to a third party on behalf of a customer. *Abbr* ***D/C***

dog GENERAL MANAGEMENT firm with low market share and growth in the ***Boston Box*** model, a business with a low market share and low growth rate. *See also* ***Boston Box***

dog-eat-dog MARKETING extremely competitive ruthlessly willing to harm competitors, especially in the marketplace (*slang*)

dogs of the Dow MARKETS stocks with smallest yield according to Dow Jones in the United States, the stocks in the ***Dow Jones*** Industrial Average that pay the smallest dividends as a percentage of their prices (*informal*)

dollar CURRENCY & EXCHANGE currency unit in US and some other countries a unit of currency used in the United States and other countries such as Australia, Bahamas, Barbados, Bermuda, Brunei, Canada, Fiji, Hong Kong, Jamaica, New Zealand, Singapore, and Zimbabwe

dollar area CURRENCY & EXCHANGE region using US dollar for trading an area of the world where the US dollar is the main trading currency

dollar cost averaging *US* FINANCE regular repeating of investment the regular periodic purchase of the same amount in dollars of the same security regardless of its price. *UK term* ***pound cost averaging***

dollar gap CURRENCY & EXCHANGE shortage of US dollars a situation in which the supply of US dollars is not enough to satisfy the demand for them from overseas buyers

dollar roll MARKETS arrangement to sell then repurchase stock in the United States, an agreement to sell a stock and buy it back later for a specified price

dollars-and-cents *US* FINANCE influenced by money used to describe a situation in which cost and return are considered the determining factors

dollar stocks STOCKHOLDING & INVESTMENTS stocks in US companies stocks issued by companies incorporated in the United States

domestecutive BUSINESS woman working from home a woman who works or runs a business from her home

domestic consumer ECONOMICS user of product for personal purposes a ***consumer*** who uses a product for personal, domestic, or household purposes

domestic currency CURRENCY & EXCHANGE money legally accepted in home country the legal ***currency*** of the jurisdiction that issued it

domestic economy ECONOMICS economy of home country the production, consumption, and distribution of wealth within a specific country

domestic market MARKETS market in home country the market for goods and services in the country where a company is based

domestic production OPERATIONS & PRODUCTION production of goods for home country use the production of goods and services for internal consumption in the producer country rather than for export

domestic tax TAX tax on residents and businesses in home country tax levied on companies doing business and individuals living in a specific country

domestic trade BUSINESS trade inside firm's home country trade by a company within the country in which it is based. *Also called* ***home trade***

domicile LEGAL country of somebody's residence or firm's registration the country in which somebody has his or her permanent residence or where a company's office is registered

domicilium citandi et executandi *S. Africa* FINANCE address for delivering legal documents the address where a summons or other official notice should be served if necessary, which must be supplied by somebody applying for credit or entering into a contract

dominant influence TREASURY MANAGEMENT undisputed influence over financial policy influence that can be exercised to achieve the operating and financial policies designed by the holder of the influence, notwithstanding the rights or influence of any other party

donor FINANCE giver of gift a person who gives a gift, especially money

dormant account BANKING inactive bank account a bank account that is no longer used by the account holder

dormant company ACCOUNTING firm not doing business for a while a company that has not made any transactions during a specific ***accounting period***

dot.com E-COMMERCE firm selling on Internet an e-commerce enterprise, marketing its products only through the Internet

double bottom MARKETS bullish chart pattern with "W" shape a chart pattern in which the price of a security drops, recovers moderately, drops again, then recovers a second time and continues its upward trend, regarded as an indicator of a bullish market

double counting ACCOUNTING using same cost or benefit twice in calculation the counting of a cost or benefit element twice when carrying out analysis. This can happen when the total sales in a market is calculated as the sum of all sales made by companies, without deducting the purchases companies make from other firms in the market.

double digit growth ECONOMICS rapid growth of firm or economy an increase of between 10% and 99% in the productivity or size of a company, business activity, or economy within a specific period of time

double digit inflation ECONOMICS rapid growth of inflation rate a rate of inflation between 10% and 99%, usually calculated on an annual basis

double dipping FRAUD fraudulently receiving two incomes from government in the United States, the illegal practice of receiving income from a government pension as well as social security payments, or of holding a government job while receiving a government pension

double dip recession ECONOMICS brief recovery preceding further recession a pattern in an economic cycle that shows two periods of recession separated by a brief period of growth. *Also called* ***W-shaped recession***

double-entry bookkeeping ACCOUNTING type of bookkeeping system used by most businesses the most commonly used system of bookkeeping, based on the principle that every financial transaction involves the simultaneous receiving and giving of value, and is therefore recorded twice

double indemnity INSURANCE commitment to pay double insurance for accidental death a provision in an insurance policy that guarantees payment of double its face value on the accidental death of the holder

double taxation TAX having to pay tax twice on same income the taxing of something twice, usually the combination of corporation tax and tax on the dividends that stockholders earn

double taxation relief TAX tax break between countries on taxes already paid a reduction of tax payable in one country by the amount of tax on income, profits, or capital gains already paid in another country

double top MARKETS bearish chart pattern with "M" shape a chart pattern in which the price of a security rises, drops moderately, rises again, then drops a second time and continues its downward trend, regarded as an indicator of a bearish market

Dow Jones FINANCE provider of business and financial news Dow Jones and Company, Inc., a US corporation that provides business and financial news worldwide and compiles the ***Dow Jones Averages***

Dow Jones Averages MARKETS stock price listing of selected US traded stocks an index of the prices of selected stocks on the New York Stock Exchange compiled by Dow Jones & Company, Inc

Dow Jones Industrial Average *or* **Dow Jones Index** MARKETS index of stocks in major industrial firms an index of 30 predominately industrial stocks actively traded on the New York Stock Exchange, used as an indicator of the performance of stocks in the United States

downgrade MARKETS **1.** reduce projection for stock price to change the forecast for a stock price to a lower one **2.** reduce bond rating to change the credit rating for a ***bond*** to a lower one

down payment FINANCE partial payment at time of purchase a part of the full price of something paid at the time it is bought, with the remaining part to be paid later

downshifting GENERAL MANAGEMENT reducing work and income for simpler, better life the concept of giving up all or part of your work commitment and income in exchange for improved quality of life Downshifting is integral to the idea of ***portfolio working***, in which individuals opt out of a formal employee relationship to sell their services at a pace and at a price to suit themselves

downside factor *or* **downside potential** STOCKHOLDING & INVESTMENTS possibility of loss in value the possibility of incurring a loss when an investment declines in value

downside risk STOCKHOLDING & INVESTMENTS risk of loss in value the risk that an investment will decline in value. *See also* ***upside potential***

downsizing **1.** BUSINESS expense cuts to make organization more efficient organizational restructuring involving outsourcing activities, replacing permanent staff with contract employees, and reducing the number of levels within the organizational hierarchy, with the intention of making the organization more flexible, efficient, and responsive to its environment **2.** HR & PERSONNEL reducing number of firm's employees the reduction of the size of a business, especially by laying staff off. Downsizing may be part of a rationalization process, or corporate restructuring, with the removal of hierarchies or the closure of departments or functions either after a period of unsatisfactory results or as a consequence of strategic review. The terms "upsizing" and "resizing" are applied when an organization increases the number of staff employed.

downstream OPERATIONS & PRODUCTION at later stage at a point later in the production process

downstream progress GENERAL MANAGEMENT easy advancement toward goals movement by a company toward achieving its objectives which is easy because it involves riding a wave or trend and benefiting from favorable conditions. *See also* ***upstream progress***

downswing MARKETS decline in stock prices a downward movement in stock prices following a period of steady or rising prices

downtick MARKETS trade at price lower than in previous trade a transaction in which the price of a particular security is lower than the price in the transaction immediately preceding it

downtime OPERATIONS & PRODUCTION period when machinery is not working a period of time during which a machine is not available for use because of maintenance or breakdown

downturn FINANCE, MARKETS downward trend a downward trend in sales, profits, a stock market, or an economy

Dow Theory MARKETS idea that movements in selected stocks predict prices the theory that stock market prices can be forecast on the basis of the movements of selected industrial and transportation stocks

draft BANKING document ordering payment a written order to pay a particular sum from one account to another, or to a person. *See also* ***sight draft, time draft***

drawback TAX tax rebate on imports that produce exports a rebate on customs duty for imported goods that are used in producing exports

drawdown FINANCE decision to use money made available earlier the act of obtaining money that has previously been made available under a credit agreement

drawee BANKING payer of bill of exchange or check the individual or institution to whom a bill of exchange or check is addressed, who will pay the sum indicated

drawer BANKING person who writes check or bill the person who writes a check or a bill asking an individual or institution to pay money to the payee indicated

drawing account BANKING account for tracking money withdrawn an account that permits the tracking of withdrawals, used, for example, by a ***sole proprietor*** or ***partner***

drawing rights FINANCE member country's right to borrow from IMF fund a right of a member country of the ***International Monetary Fund*** to borrow money from the fund in a foreign currency. *See also* ***Special Drawing Right***

drilling down MARKETING investigating more detailed subject information a technique for managing data by arranging it in hierarchies that provide increasing levels of detail

DRIP *abbr* STOCKHOLDING & INVESTMENTS ***dividend reinvestment plan***

drip feed **1.** FINANCE gradual provision of capital a method of providing capital to a small startup company in which investors contribute capital as needed over a period of time **2.** STOCKHOLDING & INVESTMENTS regular increase in investment a method of investing in securities in which investors invest a specific amount of money on a regular basis

drip method MARKETING calling potential customers repeatedly until they buy a marketing method that involves calling potential customers at regular intervals until they agree to make a purchase (*slang*)

drive time MARKETING time when people drive to or from work the time of the day when most people are likely to be in their cars, usually early in the morning or late in the afternoon, considered to be the optimum time to broadcast a radio commercial (*slang*)

drop a bundle MARKETS spend or lose large sum of money to spend or lose a lot of money, especially on the stock market (*slang*)

drop lock FINANCE change from floating to fixed interest rate the automatic conversion of a debt instrument with a floating rate to one with a fixed rate when interest rates fall to an agreed percentage

droplock bond STOCKHOLDING & INVESTMENTS bond becoming fixed rate if interest rate falls a floating-rate bond that will convert to a fixed rate of interest if interest rates fall to a specific level. *See also* ***debt-convertible bond***

DRP *abbr* OPERATIONS & PRODUCTION ***distribution resource planning***

dry goods textiles and housewares textiles, clothing, and general housewares

DTCC *abbr* BUSINESS ***Depository Trust and Clearing Corporation***

DTF *abbr* MARKETS ***Derivative Trading Facility***

DTI *abbr* ***Department of Trade and Industry***

dual currency bond CURRENCY & EXCHANGE bond issued and paying interest in different currencies a bond that pays interest in a currency other than the one used to buy it

dual economy ECONOMICS different growth rates for manufacturing and services an economy in which the manufacturing and service sectors are growing at different rates

dual listing MARKETS listing of stock on two exchanges the listing of a stock on two or more stock exchanges, often including a regional exchange in addition to a nationwide exchange

dual pricing MARKETS selling product at different prices in different markets the practice of setting different prices for the same product in the different markets in which it is sold

dual trading FINANCE working as agent for buyer and seller the practice of acting as agent for both a broker's firm and its customers

duck ◇ get your ducks in a row *or* line up your ducks GENERAL MANAGEMENT **1.** to get everything properly organized **2.** to get all concerned parties to agree to a plan of action

dud check BANKING check not honored because of insufficient funds a check that cannot be cashed because the person writing it does not have enough money in the account to pay it

due bill STOCKHOLDING & INVESTMENTS notice of transfer from seller to buyer a notification that a security has been transferred from the seller to the buyer, giving details of the amounts such as cost, dividends, or interest owed either the seller or buyer

due date FINANCE deadline for payment of debt the date on which a debt is required to be paid

due diligence 1. ACCOUNTING detailed check of firm's accounts before sale the examination of a company's accounts prior to a potential ***takeover*** by another organization. This assessment is often undertaken by an independent third party. *Abbr* ***DD*** **2.** GENERAL MANAGEMENT investigation of firm before purchase or investment the collection, verification, analysis, and assessment of information about the operations and management of a company undertaken by a potential purchaser or investor. Due diligence aims to confirm that the purchaser or investor has an accurate picture of the target company and to identify risks and benefits associated with the prospective deal. Due diligence usually starts after the signing of a letter of intent by both parties and information disclosed during the process is normally protected by the signing of a ***confidentiality agreement***. Due diligence often leads on to negotiations on the detailed terms of the agreement. The process may cover the financial, legal, commercial, technical, cultural, and environmental aspects of the organization's operations as well as its ***assets*** and ***liabilities***, and may be conducted with the assistance of professional advisers.

due-on-sale clause MORTGAGES obligation to pay off mortgage upon property sale a provision requiring a homeowner to pay off a mortgage upon sale of the property

dumping INTERNATIONAL TRADE selling commodity abroad at greatly reduced price the selling of a commodity on a foreign market at a price below its ***marginal cost***, either to dispose of a temporary surplus or to achieve a monopoly by eliminating competition – ***dump***

Dun and Bradstreet BUSINESS organization that collects and provides credit information an international organization that sources credit information from companies and their creditors which it then makes available to subscribers. *Abbr* ***D&B***

duopoly ECONOMICS market with only two sellers of product a market in which only two sellers of a good exist. If one decides to alter the price, the other will respond and influence the market's response to the first decision.

durable power of attorney LEGAL power to act for another a ***power of attorney*** that allows one person to act on behalf of another if that person should become unable to act on their own behalf, for example, because of mental incompetence

duration STOCKHOLDING & INVESTMENTS time to receive current value of payments the time in years that it will take to receive the present value of all the payments from a fixed-income investment, calculated using the effect that a 1% change in the interest rate will have on the investment. This calculation is mainly used to measure the sensitivity of changes in bond prices to changes in interest rates.

Dutch auction FINANCE auction in which price bidding goes down an auction in which the lot for sale is offered at an initial price that, if there are no bidders, is then reduced until there is a bid

duty TAX tax on goods, especially imports and exports a tax that must be paid on goods, especially on imported and exported goods

duty-free TAX exempt from customs duty sold without the requirement for any customs duties to be paid

dynamic pricing FINANCE pricing from demand pricing that changes in line with patterns of demand

dynamic programming GENERAL MANAGEMENT mathematical approach to solving production and inventory problems a mathematical technique used to solve complex problems in the fields of production planning and inventory control. Dynamic programming divides the problem into steps or decision stages that can be addressed sequentially, usually by working backward from the last stage. Applications of the technique include maintenance and replacement of equipment, resource allocation, and process design and control.

E

EAA *abbr* ACCOUNTING ***European Accounting Association***

EAI *abbr* OPERATIONS & PRODUCTION ***enterprise application integration***

e-alliance E-COMMERCE union of organizations for Internet commerce a partnership forged between organizations in order to achieve business objectives for enterprises conducted over the web. There has been a surge in such alliances since the Internet took off in the mid-1990s, and studies show that the most successful have been those involving traditional offline businesses and online entities, known as the clicks-and-mortar strategy, for example, that between Amazon.com and Toys 'R' Us. Toys 'R' Us had the physical infrastructure and brand, while Amazon.com had the online infrastructure and experience of making e-commerce work.

E&O *abbr* ACCOUNTING ***errors and omissions***

early adopter GENERAL MANAGEMENT one of first users of new technology an individual or organization that is among the first to make use of a new technique, strategy, technology, etc.

early withdrawal BANKING taking money out of time deposit account early the removal of money from a deposit account before the due date. Early withdrawal often incurs a penalty that the account holder must pay.

earned income FINANCE money earned for work performed money generated by a person's or organization's labor, for example, wages, salaries, fees, royalties, and business profits. *See also* ***unearned income***

Earned Income Credit TAX US tax credit for low paid in the United States, a federal income tax credit for low-income individuals and families with income generated from employment. *Abbr* ***EIC***

earning potential **1.** BUSINESS amount person can earn the amount of money somebody should be able to earn in his or her professional capacity **2.** STOCKHOLDING & INVESTMENTS potential dividend earnings the amount of dividend that a share potentially can produce

earnings **1.** ACCOUNTING money available to business after expenses income or profit from a business, quoted gross or net of tax, which may be retained and distributed in part to the stockholders **2.** FINANCE money obtained through work a sum of money gained from paid employment, usually quoted before tax, including any extra rewards such as ***fringe benefits***, allowances, or incentives

earnings before interest and taxes ACCOUNTING *see* ***EBIT***

earnings before interest, tax, depreciation, and amortization *or* ACCOUNTING *see* ***EBITDA***

earnings cap PENSIONS in UK, maximum earnings for pension purposes in the United Kingdom, the top limit of earnings that can be used in calculating a retirement pension paid from an ***occupational pension*** plan

earnings credit BANKING in US, amount offsetting bank charges in the United States, an allowance that reduces bank charges on checking accounts

earnings drift FINANCE pay increases outstripping official rates a situation in which an increase in pay is greater than that of officially negotiated rates

earnings growth STOCKHOLDING & INVESTMENTS increase in profit per share of stock an increase in the profit a company earns as expressed on a per-share basis

earnings momentum STOCKHOLDING & INVESTMENTS change in profit per share of stock an increase or decrease in a company's earnings per share as compared to the same period of time in the previous year, used by investors as a measure of how its stock will perform

earnings performance STOCKHOLDING & INVESTMENTS dividend-yielding pattern of stock a measure of how well a specific stock does in providing dividends

earnings per share STOCKHOLDING & INVESTMENTS profit allotted to each share of common stock a financial ratio that measures the portion of a company's profit allocated to each outstanding share of common stock. It is the most basic measure of the value of a share, and also is the basis for calculating several other important investment ratios.

EPS is calculated by subtracting the total value of any preferred stock from net income (earnings) for the period in question, then dividing the resulting figure by the number of shares outstanding during that period.

(Net income – Dividends on any preferred stock) / Average number of shares outstanding

Companies usually use a weighted average number of shares outstanding over the reporting period, but shares outstanding can either be "primary" or "fully diluted." Primary EPS is calculated using the number of shares that are currently held by investors in the market and able to be traded. Diluted EPS is the result of a complex calculation that determines how many shares would be outstanding if all exercisable warrants and options were converted into shares at the end of a quarter.

Suppose, for example, that a company has granted a large number of share options to employees. If these options are capable of being exercised in the near future, that could significantly alter the number of shares in issue and thus the EPS, even though the net income is the same. Often in such cases, the company might quote the EPS on the existing shares and the fully diluted version. *Abbr* ***EPS***

earnings-related contributions FINANCE payments into social security fund based on earnings contributions to social security that rise as the person's earnings rise, especially ***National Insurance*** contributions in the United Kingdom

earnings-related pension PENSIONS in UK, pension linked to salary in the United Kingdom, a pension that is linked to the size of the beneficiary's salary

earnings report *US* STOCKHOLDING & INVESTMENTS published financial report of US firm a company's financial statements, which must be published according to US law. *UK term* ***published accounts***

earnings retained ACCOUNTING = ***retained profits***

earnings season STOCKHOLDING & INVESTMENTS time when firms announce earnings the time of year when major companies declare their results for the previous period

earnings surprise STOCKHOLDING & INVESTMENTS gap between actual and expected earnings a considerable difference in size between a company's actual and anticipated earnings

earnings yield FINANCE earnings as percentage of stock price money earned by a company during a year, expressed as a percentage of the price of one of its shares

EASDAQ MARKETS European stock exchange for technology and growth companies a stock exchange for technology and growth companies based in Europe and modeled on the ***NASDAQ*** in the United States. *Full form* ***European Association of Securities Dealers Automated Quotations***

eased *UK* MARKETS describes stock market that is slightly down used in stock market reports to describe a market that has experienced a slight fall in prices

easy market MARKETS stock market with few buyers a market in which fewer people are buying, with the effect that prices are lower than hoped

easy money FINANCE = ***cheap money***

easy money policy FINANCE government policy to encourage borrowing a government policy that aims to expand the economy by making money more easily accessible to the public. This is done by strategies such as lowering interest rates and offering easy access to credit.

easy terms *UK* FINANCE = ***installment plan***

EBIT ACCOUNTING income minus costs revenue minus the cost of goods sold and normal operating expenses. *Full form* ***earnings before interest and taxes***

EBITDA ACCOUNTING use of earnings to measure firm's performance the earnings generated by a business's fundamental operating performance, frequently used in accounting ratios for comparison with other companies. Interest on borrowings, tax payable on those profits, depreciation, and amortization are excluded on the basis that they can distort the underlying performance.

It is calculated as follows:

Revenue – Expenses (excluding tax and interest, depreciation, etc.) = EBITDA

It is important to note that EBITDA ignores many factors that impact on true cash flow, such as working capital, debt payments, and other fixed expenses. Even so, it may be useful for evaluating firms in the same industry with widely different capital structures, tax rates, and depreciation policies. *Full form* ***earnings before interest, tax, depreciation, and amortization***

EBQ OPERATIONS & PRODUCTION size cheapest and easiest to produce the optimum batch size for the manufacture of an item or component, at the lowest cost. The batch size is a tradeoff between unit costs that increase with batch size and those that decrease. The point of lowest combined or total cost indicates the most economic batch size for production. *Full form* ***economic batch quantity***. *Also called* ***economic lot quantity***. *See also* ***economic order quantity***

EBRD BANKING European bank helping to develop market economies a bank, established in 1991, to develop programs to tackle a variety of issues. These included the creation and strengthening of infrastructure; industry privatization; the reform of the financial sector, including the development of capital markets and the privatization of commercial banks; the development of productive competitive private sectors of small and medium-sized enterprises in industry, agriculture, and services; the restructuring of industrial sectors to put them on a competitive basis; and the encouragement of foreign investment and cleaning up the environment. The EBRD had 41 original members: the European Commission, the European Investment Bank, all the then EU countries, and all the countries of Eastern Europe except Albania, which finally became a member in October 1991, followed by all the republics of the former USSR in March 1992. *Full form* ***European Bank for Reconstruction and Development***

e-business E-COMMERCE **1.** carrying out of business over Internet the conduct of business on the Internet, including the electronic purchasing and selling of goods and services, servicing customers, and communications with business partners. *Also called* ***electronic business*** **2.** firm operating over Internet a company that conducts the main part of its business on the Internet

EC *abbr* INTERNATIONAL TRADE ***European Community***

e-cash E-COMMERCE = ***digital cash***

ECB BANKING bank responsible for EU monetary policy the financial institution that replaced the European Monetary Institute in 1998 and that is responsible for carrying out EU monetary policy and administering the euro. *Full form* ***European Central Bank***

ECBC *abbr* FINANCE ***European Covered Bond Council***

ECGD *abbr* INTERNATIONAL TRADE ***Export Credit Guarantee Department***

ECML *abbr* E-COMMERCE ***electronic commerce modeling language***

ECN *abbr* MARKETS ***Electronic Communications Network***

ECOA *abbr* FINANCE US law ensuring equal treatment for borrowers ***Equal Credit Opportunity Act***

e-collaboration E-COMMERCE cooperation using Internet collaboration among people or organizations made possible by means of electronic technologies such as the Internet, videoconferencing, and wireless devices

e-commerce E-COMMERCE business conducted electronically, especially via Internet the exchange of goods, information products, or services via an electronic medium such as the Internet. Originally limited to buying and selling, it has evolved to include such functions as customer service, marketing, and advertising. *Also called* ***electronic commerce, web commerce***

e-commerce processes E-COMMERCE stages of trading over Internet the flow of information through planning, design, manufacture, sales, order processing, distribution, and quality in an e-business

e-company E-COMMERCE e-commerce business a company engaged in e-commerce or that conducts the main part of its business on the Internet

econometric model ECONOMICS set of mathematical equations representing economic relationships a way of representing the relationship between economic variables as an equation or set of equations with statistically precise parameters linking the variables

econometrics ECONOMICS study of mathematical equations for representing economic relationships the branch of economics concerned with using mathematical models to describe relationships in an economy, for example, between wage rates and levels of employment

economic assumption ECONOMICS belief on which economic model is based an assumption built into an economic model, for example, that output will grow at 2.5% in the next tax year

economic batch quantity OPERATIONS & PRODUCTION *see* ***EBQ***

economic benefit FINANCE benefit measurable in money a benefit to a person, business, or society that can be measured in financial terms

economic cycle ECONOMICS recurrent expansion and slowdown of trade a repeated sequence of business activity expanding, then slowing down, and then expanding again

economic development ECONOMICS rise in country's living standards improvements in the living standards and wealth of the citizens of a country

Economic Development Board BUSINESS organization promoting foreign investment in Singapore's economy an organization established in 1961 that works to promote investment in Singapore by providing various services and assistance programs to foreign and local companies. *Abbr* ***EDB***

economic efficiency BUSINESS *see* ***efficiency***

economic forecaster ECONOMICS person predicting future economic performance a person whose job is to predict how a country's economy will perform in the future

economic goods ECONOMICS products or services sold in market services or physical objects that can command a price in the market

economic growth ECONOMICS increase in country's economic activity and income an increase in the national income of a country created by the long-term productive potential of its economy

economic indicator ECONOMICS statistical measurement of country's economy a statistic that may be important for a country's long-term economic health, for example, rising prices or falling exports

economic life ECONOMICS country's manufacturing and trade conditions the conditions of trade and manufacture in a country that contribute to its prosperity or poverty

economic lot quantity OPERATIONS & PRODUCTION *see* ***EBQ***

economic miracle ECONOMICS dramatic rebuilding of economies after World War II the rapid growth after 1945 in countries such as Germany and Japan, where in ten years economies shattered by World War II were regenerated

economic model ECONOMICS computerized forecast of economic trends a computerized plan of a country's economic system, used for forecasting economic trends

economic order quantity OPERATIONS & PRODUCTION amount for best inventory control the most economic inventory replenishment order size, which minimizes the sum of inventory ordering costs and holding costs. *Abbr* ***EOQ***

economic paradigm ECONOMICS fundamental economic belief a basic unchanging economic principle, one that governs the way economists view the world

economic planning ECONOMICS government's plans for future of economy plans made by a government for the financial state of a country over different future time periods

Economic Planning and Advisory Council REGULATION & COMPLIANCE advisory group for Australia's economic policies a committee of businesspeople and politicians appointed to advise the Australian government on economic issues

economic pressure ECONOMICS country's negative economic conditions a condition in a country's economy in which economic indicators are unfavorable

economic profit ACCOUNTING total revenue less total cost the difference between the total revenue and total cost associated with a specific business

economic relations INTERNATIONAL TRADE trade and finance interactions between countries the arrangements for cooperation in international trade, finance, and investment existing between individual countries and sets of countries

economics ECONOMICS study of society's wealth the study of the consumption, distribution, and production of wealth in societies

economic sanctions INTERNATIONAL TRADE trade restrictions to bring about political changes restrictions on trade with a country in order to influence its political situation or to make its government change its policy

economic surplus ECONOMICS positive balance of costs against output the positive difference between an economy's output and the costs incurred in factors such as wages, raw materials, and depreciation

economic theory of the firm ECONOMICS idea that firm's responsibility is to serve stockholders the theory that the only duty that a company has to those external to it is financial. The economic theory of the firm holds that stockholders should be the prime beneficiaries of an organization's activities. The theory is associated with ***top-down leadership*** and ***cost cutting*** through rationalization and ***downsizing***. With immediate stock price dominating management activities, the economic theory of the firm has been criticized as being too short-term, as opposed to the longer-term thinking behind ***stakeholder theory***.

economic value added FINANCE evaluating performance by comparing earnings to capital investment a way of judging financial performance by measuring the amount by which the earnings of a project, an operation, or a corporation exceed or fall short of the total amount of capital that was originally invested by its owners.

EVA is conceptually simple: from net operating profit, subtract an appropriate charge for the opportunity cost of all capital invested in an enterprise (the amount that could have been invested elsewhere). It is calculated using this formula:

Net operating profit less applicable taxes – Cost of capital = EVA

If a company is considering building a new plant, and its total weighted cost over ten years is $80 million, while the expected annual incremental return on the new operation is $10 million, or $100 million over ten years, then the plant's EVA would be positive, in this case $20 million:

$100 million – $80 million = $20 million

An alternative but more complex formula for EVA is:

(% Return on invested capital – % Cost of capital) × Original capital invested = EVA

EVA is frequently linked with shareholder value analysis, and an objective of EVA is to determine which business units best utilize their assets to generate returns and maximize shareholder value; it can be used to assess a company, a business unit, a single plant, office, or even an assembly line. This same technique is equally helpful in evaluating new business opportunities. *Abbr* ***EVA***

economic welfare ECONOMICS society's well-being in economic terms the level of prosperity in an economy, as measured by employment and wage levels

economies of scale ECONOMICS savings achieved by mass production the cost advantages of a company producing a product in larger quantities so that each unit costs less to make. *See also* ***diseconomies of scale***

economies of scope ECONOMICS savings achieved when multiple products share same technology the cost advantages of a company producing a number of products or engaging in a number of profitable activities that use the same technology

economist ECONOMICS somebody who studies society's wealth a person who studies the consumption, distribution, and production of wealth in societies

economy ECONOMICS production, consumption, and distribution of society's wealth the distribution of wealth in a society and the means by which that wealth is produced and consumed

economy drive BUSINESS effort to save money or materials a concerted effort to save money or materials, as by reducing expenditures or avoiding waste

economy efficiency principle ECONOMICS theory about relationships in efficient economy the principle that if an economy is efficient, no one can be made better off without somebody else being made worse off

ecopreneur BUSINESS environmentalist entrepreneur an entrepreneur who is concerned with environmental issues

ECP *abbr* MARKETS ***Eurocommercial paper***

EDB *abbr* BUSINESS ***Economic Development Board***

EDC *abbr* E-COMMERCE ***electronic data capture***

EDI *abbr* E-COMMERCE ***electronic data interchange***

EDI envelope E-COMMERCE = ***electronic envelope***

EEA *abbr* INTERNATIONAL TRADE ***European Economic Area***

EEC *abbr* INTERNATIONAL TRADE ***European Economic Community***

e-economy ECONOMICS economy based largely on online business transactions an economy that is characterized by extensive use of the Internet and information technology

effect STATISTICS result of change of statistical variable the change in a response that is created by a change in one or more of the explanatory ***variables*** in a statistical study

effective annual interest rate FINANCE average annual interest rate on deposit the average interest rate paid on a deposit for a period of a year. It is the total interest received over 12 months expressed as a percentage of the principal at the beginning of the period.

effective capacity OPERATIONS & PRODUCTION output under normal operating conditions the volume that a workstation or process can produce in a given period under normal operating conditions. Effective capacity can be influenced by the age and condition of the machine, the skills, training, and flexibility of the workforce, and the availability of ***raw materials***.

effective date FINANCE, OPERATIONS & PRODUCTION actual starting date the date when an action such as the issuing of new stock is effective

effective demand FINANCE demand for product by those able to buy demand for a product made by people and organizations with sufficient wealth to pay for it

effective exchange rate CURRENCY & EXCHANGE exchange rate of one currency against others a rate of exchange for a currency calculated against a group of currencies whose values have been weighted

effectiveness BUSINESS *see* ***efficiency***

effective price STOCKHOLDING & INVESTMENTS stock price adjusted for rights issue the price of a stock adjusted to take into account the effects of existing stockholders being offered a rights issue. *See also* ***rights issue***

effective rate FINANCE true interest rate including all factors the real interest rate to be paid on a loan or deposit, which includes compounding and other factors

effective sample size STATISTICS size of sample with extraneous factors removed the remaining size of a sample after irrelevant or excluded factors have been removed

effective spread STOCKHOLDING & INVESTMENTS difference between new issue price and underwriter's price the difference between the price of a newly issued stock and what the underwriter pays, adjusted for the effect of the announcement of the offering

effective strike price STOCKHOLDING & INVESTMENTS actual price paid when option is exercised the price of an option at a specific time, adjusted for fluctuation since the initial offering

effective tax rate TAX actual tax rate paid by taxpayer after adjustments the average tax rate applicable to a given transaction, whether it is income from work undertaken, the sale of an asset, or a gift, taking into account personal allowances and scales of tax. It is the amount of money generated by the transaction divided by the additional tax payable because of it.

effective yield *UK* STOCKHOLDING & INVESTMENTS = yield to maturity

efficiency BUSINESS meeting goals economically the achievement of goals in an economic way. Efficiency involves seeking a good balance between economy in terms of resources such as time, money, space, or materials, and the achievement of an organization's goals and objectives. A distinction is often made between technical and economic efficiency. *Technical efficiency* means producing maximum output with minimum input, while *economic efficiency* means the production and distribution of goods at the lowest possible cost. In management, a further distinction is often made between efficiency and *effectiveness*, with the latter denoting performance in terms of achieving objectives.

efficiency ratio FINANCE measure of relationship between income and overhead expenses a way of measuring the proportion of operating revenues or fee income spent on overhead expenses.

Often identified with banking and financial sectors, the efficiency ratio indicates a management's ability to keep overhead costs low. In banking, an acceptable efficiency ratio was once in the low 60s. Now the goal is 50, while better-performing banks boast ratios in the mid-40s. Low ratings usually indicate a higher return on equity and earnings.

This measurement is also used by mature industries, such as steel manufacture, chemicals, or car production, that must focus on tight cost controls to boost profitability because growth prospects are modest.

The efficiency ratio is defined as operating overhead expenses divided by turnover. If operating expenses are $100,000, and turnover is $230,000, then

100,000 / 230,000 = 0.43 efficiency ratio

However, not everyone calculates the ratio in the same way. Some institutions include all non-interest expenses, while others exclude certain charges and intangible asset amortization.

A different method measures efficiency simply by tracking three other measures: accounts payable to sales, days' sales outstanding, and stock turnover. This indicates how fast a company is able to move its merchandise. A general guide is that if the first two of these measures are low and the third is high, efficiency is probably high; the reverse is likewise true.

To find the stock turnover ratio, divide total sales by total stock. If net sales are $300,000, and stock is $140,000, then

300,000 / 140,000 = 2.14 stock turnover ratio

To find the accounts payable to sales ratio, divide a company's accounts payable by its annual net sales. A high ratio suggests that a company is using its suppliers' funds as a source of cheap financing because it is not operating efficiently enough to generate its own funds. If accounts payable are $50,000, and total sales are $300,000, then

50,000 / 300,000 = 0.14 = 14% accounts payable to sales ratio

efficiency variance FINANCE disparity between actual and standard cost of production the difference between the standard cost of making a product and actual costs of production. A separate variance can be calculated for materials, labor, and overhead.

efficient capital market MARKETS stock market in which prices quickly reflect information a market in which stock prices reflect all the information available to the market about future economic trends and company profitability

efficient markets hypothesis ECONOMICS theory on limitations of financial information the hypothesis that exploiting stock market information cannot bring an investor unexpected returns because stock prices already reflect all the information available to the market about future economic trends and company profitability. *Abbr* ***EMH***

EFT *abbr* E-COMMERCE ***electronic funds transfer***

EFTA *abbr* INTERNATIONAL TRADE ***European Free Trade Association***

EFTPOS *abbr* E-COMMERCE ***electronic funds transfer at point of sale***

EGM *abbr* CORPORATE GOVERNANCE ***extraordinary general meeting***

EIB BANKING organization that finances EU development a financial institution whose main task is to further regional development within the EU by financing capital projects, modernizing or converting undertakings, and developing new activities. *Full form* ***European Investment Bank***

EIC *abbr* TAX ***Earned Income Credit***

EIS *abbr* GENERAL MANAGEMENT **1.** ***environmental impact statement*** **2.** ***electronic information system***. *See also* ***MIS***

either-way market CURRENCY & EXCHANGE currency market buying and selling at same price a currency market with identical prices for buying and selling, especially for the euro

elastic ECONOMICS sensitive to price changes responsive to changes in the price of a product

elasticity ECONOMICS relationship between supply, demand, and price a measurement of the relationship between supply, demand, and price

In practical terms, elasticity indicates the degree to which consumers respond to changes in price. It is obviously important for companies to consider such relationships when contemplating changes in supply, demand, and price.

Demand elasticity measures how much the quantity demanded by a customer changes when the price of a product or service is increased or lowered. This measurement helps companies to find out whether the quantity demanded will remain constant despite price changes. Supply elasticity measures the impact on supply when a price is changed. The reverse can also be calculated, that is, how much the market clearing price for a good or service changes in response to changes in the supply or demand function. This is called the price elasticity, or demand or supply elasticity, respectively.

The general formula for elasticity is:

Elasticity = % change in x / % change in y

In theory, x and y can be any variable. However, the most common application measures price and demand. If the price of a product is increased from \$20 to \$25, or 25%, and demand in turn falls from 6,000 to 3,000, elasticity would be calculated as:

−50% / 25% = −2

A value greater than 1 means that demand is strongly sensitive to price, while a value of less than 1 means that demand is not price-sensitive.

elected officers HR & PERSONNEL officials chosen in election officials such as directors or union representatives who are chosen by a vote of the members or stockholders of an organization and who hold a ***decision making*** position on a committee or board

electronic banking BANKING remote bank transactions by computer the use of computers to carry out banking transactions such as withdrawals through ATMs or transfer of funds at point of sale

electronic business E-COMMERCE = ***e-business***

electronic cash E-COMMERCE = ***digital cash***

electronic check *US* E-COMMERCE means of paying electronically a payment system in which fund transfers are made electronically from the buyer's checking account to the seller's bank account. *UK term* ***electronic cheque***

electronic cheque *UK* E-COMMERCE = ***electronic check***

electronic commerce E-COMMERCE = ***e-commerce***

electronic commerce modeling language *or* E-COMMERCE standardized format for electronic purchases a standardization of field names to streamline the process by which e-merchants electronically collect information from consumers about order shipping, billing, and payment. *Abbr* ***ECML***

Electronic Communications Network MARKETS system for direct securities trading a computerized securities trading system that allows investors who have accounts with brokers with access to the system to trade directly and anonymously. *Abbr* ***ECN***

electronic data capture E-COMMERCE use of computers for card transactions the use of a point-of-sale terminal or other data-processing equipment to validate and submit credit or debit card transactions. *Abbr* ***EDC***

electronic data interchange E-COMMERCE standardized way of transmitting business documents a standard for exchanging business documents such as invoices and purchase orders in a standard form between computers through the use of electronic networks such as the Internet. *Abbr* ***EDI***

electronic envelope E-COMMERCE opening and closing data in electronic transmission the header and trailer information that precedes and follows the data in an electronic transmission to provide routing information and security. *Also called* ***communications envelope, EDI envelope, envelope***

electronic funds transfer E-COMMERCE payment system using electronic medium a payment system that processes financial transactions between two or more parties or institutions. *Abbr* ***EFT***

electronic funds transfer at point of sale E-COMMERCE payment by card swipe, immediately transferring funds the payment for goods or services by a bank customer using a card that is swiped through an electronic reader on the register, thereby transferring the cash from the customer's account to the retailer's or service provider's account. *See also* ***debit card***

electronic information system GENERAL MANAGEMENT information collection system supporting decision making a management information system designed specifically to collect and store information from both internal and external sources for use by senior managers in making strategic decisions. *Abbr* ***EIS***. *See also* ***MIS***

electronic money E-COMMERCE = ***digital money***

electronic payment system E-COMMERCE method for payments over Internet a means of making payments over an electronic network such as the Internet

electronic point of sale E-COMMERCE automated checkout system a computerized checkout system in stores that records sales by scanning bar codes, automatically updates the retailer's inventory lists, and provides a printout of the customer's purchases. *Abbr* ***epos***

electronic procurement E-COMMERCE = ***e-procurement***

electronic retailer E-COMMERCE = ***e-retailer***

electronic shopping E-COMMERCE making purchases over Internet the process of selecting, ordering, and paying for goods or services over an electronic network such as the Internet. *Also called* ***online shopping***

electronic software distribution E-COMMERCE making computer programs available over Internet a form of electronic shopping in which computer programs can be purchased and downloaded directly from the Internet

electronic store E-COMMERCE website for selling goods a website that is specifically designed to provide product information and handle transactions, including accepting payments

electronic trading STOCKHOLDING & INVESTMENTS securities trading using computers the buying and selling of investment instruments using computer systems

electronic wallet E-COMMERCE = ***digital wallet***

elephant FINANCE financial institution whose high-volume trading increases prices a very large financial institution such as a bank that makes trades in high volumes, thereby increasing prices *(slang)*

eligible liabilities BANKING liabilities considered when calculating bank's reserves liabilities that must be taken into account in the calculation of a bank's reserves

eligible paper FINANCE **1.** US financial instruments accepted for rediscounting in the United States, first class paper, such as a bill of exchange or a check, acceptable for rediscounting by the Federal Reserve System ▶ **2.** UK financial instruments accepted as loan security in the United Kingdom, bills of exchange or securities accepted by the Bank of England as security for loans to discount houses. *See also* ***lender of last resort***

eligible reserves BANKING total amount of money held by US bank the sum of the cash held by a US bank plus the money it holds at its local Federal Reserve Bank

eligible termination payment TAX in UK, termination pay eligible for concessional tax in the United Kingdom, a sum paid to an employee when he or she leaves a company, that can be transferred to a concessionally taxed investment account, such as an ***Approved Deposit Fund***. *Abbr* ***ETP***

e-mail blast MARKETING e-mail appeal to large group a single instance of sending out an e-mail to a large group to reach potential customers

e-marketplace E-COMMERCE place on Internet for trading an Internet-based environment that brings together business-to-business buyers and sellers so that they can trade more efficiently online.

The key benefits for users of an e-marketplace are reduced purchasing costs, greater flexibility, saved time, better information, and better collaboration. However, the drawbacks include costs in changing procurement processes, cost of applications, set-up, and integration with internal systems, and transaction/subscription fees.

There are three distinct types of e-marketplace: independent, in which public environments seek simply to attract buyers and sellers to trade together; consortium-based, in which sites are established on an industry-wide basis, typically when a number of key buyers in a particular industry get together; and private, in which e-marketplaces are established by a particular organization to manage its purchasing alone.

embargo INTERNATIONAL TRADE government order stopping trade with foreign country a government order that stops a type of trade, such as exports to, or imports from, a specific country

embezzlement FRAUD illegal use of money for personal benefit the illegal use of somebody else's money for personal benefit by the person to whom it has been entrusted

emergency credit FINANCE special credit given by US Federal Reserve in the United States, credit given by the ***Federal Reserve*** to an organization that has no other means of borrowing capital

emerging country *or* **emerging nation** ECONOMICS country experiencing development and economic growth a country in the early stages of becoming industrialized and undergoing economic growth and foreign investment

emerging economy ECONOMICS *see* ***emerging market*** *(sense 1)*

emerging market 1. ECONOMICS country experiencing development and economic growth a country that is becoming industrialized and undergoing economic growth. *Also called* ***emerging economy*** **2.** MARKETS financial market in emerging nation a financial market in a newly industrialized country, often with a high growth rate but with some risks

EMH *abbr* ECONOMICS ***efficient markets hypothesis***

emoluments FINANCE payments from employment wages, salaries, fees, or any other monetary benefit derived from employment

e-money E-COMMERCE = ***digital money***

emotional capital GENERAL MANAGEMENT interaction of employees the intangible organizational asset created by employees' cumulative emotional experiences that give them the ability to successfully communicate and form interpersonal relationships. Emotional capital is increasingly being seen as an important factor in company performance. Low emotional capital can result in conflict between staff, poor teamwork, and poor ***customer relations***. By contrast, high emotional capital is evidence of emotional intelligence and an ability to think and feel in a positive way, which results in good interpersonal communication and self-motivation. A related concept is ***intellectual capital***.

employability HR & PERSONNEL possession of useful skills the potential for obtaining and keeping fulfilling work through the development of skills that are transferable from one employer to another. Employability is affected by market demand for a particular set of skills and by personal circumstances. Employees may take responsibility for developing their own employability through learning and training, or, as part of the ***psychological contract***, employers may assist their employees in enhancing their employability. An important factor in employability is the concept of learning throughout life.

employee HR & PERSONNEL person contracted to work for another somebody hired by an employer under a ***contract of employment*** to perform work on a regular basis at the employer's behest. An employee works either at the employer's premises or at a place otherwise agreed, is paid regularly, and enjoys ***fringe benefits*** and employment protection.

employee ownership STOCKHOLDING & INVESTMENTS when shares are in employees' hands the possession of shares in a company, in whole or in part, by the workers. There are various forms of employee ownership that give employees a greater or lesser stake in the business. These include: ***employee stock ownership plans***, employee ***buyout***s, ***cooperatives***, and employee trusts. Ownership does not necessarily lead to greater ***employee participation*** in decision making, although the evidence suggests that where employees are involved in this, the company is more successful.

employee participation HR & PERSONNEL inclusion of employees in decision making the involvement of employees in decision making. Employee participation can take either a representational or direct form. Representation takes place through bodies such as consultative committees. Direct participation can be achieved through communication methods such as letters, employee attitude surveys, and team briefing, or through initiatives such as self-managed teams and suggestion programs.

Employee Retirement Income Security Act LEGAL US law setting benefit plan standards in the United States, a federal law that sets the minimum requirements for retirement and health benefit plans in the private sector. *Abbr **ERISA***

employee share ownership plan *UK* STOCKHOLDING & INVESTMENTS = ***employee stock ownership plan***

employee share scheme STOCKHOLDING & INVESTMENTS making stock available to employees in the United Kingdom, a plan to give, or encourage employees to buy, a stake in the company that employs them by awarding free or discounted stock. Such plans may be available to some or all employees, and plans approved by HM Revenue & Customs enjoy tax advantages. Types of plan include ***employee share ownership plans***, ***stock options***, ***Save as You Earn***, and employee share ownership trusts. Among the potential benefits are improved employee commitment and productivity, but the success of a plan may depend on linking it to employee performance and the performance of the price of stock.

employee stock fund STOCKHOLDING & INVESTMENTS US firm's fund for buying stock for employees in the United States, a fund from which money is taken to buy shares of a company's stock for its employees

employee stock ownership plan *US* STOCKHOLDING & INVESTMENTS system of allocating stock to employees a plan sponsored by a company by which a trust holds stock in the company on behalf of ***employees*** and distributes that stock to employees. In the United States, stock can only be sold when an employee leaves the organization, and is thus thought of as a form of pension provision. In the United Kingdom, stock can be disposed of at any time. There are two types of employee stock ownership plans in the United Kingdom: the case-law employee stock ownership plan, which can benefit all or some employees but may not qualify for tax benefits; and the employee stock ownership trust. *UK term **employee share ownership plan**. Abbr **ESOP***

employee stock purchase plan STOCKHOLDING & INVESTMENTS making stock available to employees in the United States, a plan to encourage employees to buy a stake in the company that employs them by awarding free or discounted stock. Such plans may be available to some or all employees, and plans approved by the Internal Revenue Service enjoy tax advantages. Among the potential benefits are improved employee commitment and productivity, but the success of a plan may depend on linking it to employee performance and the performance of the price of stock. *Abbr **ESPP***

employer HR & PERSONNEL person or organization with employees a person or organization that pays people to perform specific activities. An employer usually contracts an ***employee*** to fill a permanent or temporary position to perform work on a regularly paid basis within the relevant legal framework of the country of residence.

employers' association BUSINESS organization assisting employers a body that regulates relations between employers and employees, represents members' views on public policy issues affecting their business to national and international policymakers, and supplies support and advice. An employers' association represents companies within one or many sectors at regional, national, or international level and is usually a nonprofit, nonparty political organization, funded by subscriptions paid by its members.

employer's contribution PENSIONS employer's payments into employee's pension money paid regularly by an employer toward an employee's retirement pension

employers' liability insurance INSURANCE insurance covering employee accidents insurance to cover accidents that may happen to employees at work, and for which the company may be responsible

employment contract HR & PERSONNEL = ***contract of employment***

employment equity *S. Africa* HR & PERSONNEL offering opportunities to qualified people from disadvantaged groups the policy of giving preference in employment opportunities to qualified people from sectors of society that were previously discriminated against, for example, black people, women, and physically challenged people

employment law LEGAL, HR & PERSONNEL rules regulating employers and employees the collection of statutes, common law rules, and decisions in court or employment tribunal cases that govern the rights and duties of employers and employees. The ***contract of employment*** forms the cornerstone of employment law, which also embraces ***discrimination*** and ***severance*** rights, collective bargaining, health and safety, union membership, and industrial action.

employment pass HR & PERSONNEL in S. Africa, work permit for professionals in South Africa, a visa issued to a foreign national who is a professional with a qualifying salary level

empowerment GENERAL MANAGEMENT, HR & PERSONNEL conferring authority on employees the redistribution of power and decision-making responsibilities, usually to employees, where such authority was previously a management prerogative. Empowerment is based on the recognition that employee abilities are frequently underused, and that, given the chance, most employees can contribute more. Empowered workplaces are characterized by managers who focus on energizing, supporting, and coaching their staff in a blame-free environment of trust.

EMS CURRENCY & EXCHANGE first stage in European monetary union the first stage of economic and monetary union of the EU, which came into force in March 1979, giving stable, but adjustable, exchange rates. *Full form **European Monetary System***

EMU ECONOMICS movement toward common European currency a program for the integration of European economies and the introduction of a common currency. The timetable for European monetary union was outlined in the Maastricht Treaty in 1991. The criteria were that national debt must not exceed 60% of GDP; budget deficit should be 3% or less of GDP; inflation should be no more than 1.5% above the average rate of the three best performing economies of the EU in the previous 12 months; and applicants must have been members of the ***ERM*** for two years without having realigned or devalued their currency. The ERM was abandoned with the introduction of the ***euro*** in 12 countries in 2002. *Full form* ***European Monetary Union***

encash *UK* CURRENCY & EXCHANGE = ***cash*** *(sense 1)*

encryption E-COMMERCE putting information in code for transmission over Internet a means of encoding information, especially financial data, so that it can be transmitted over the Internet without being read by unauthorized parties.

Within an Internet security system, a secure server uses encryption when transferring or receiving data from the Web. Credit card information, for example, that could be targeted by a hacker, is encrypted by the server, turning it into special code that will then be decrypted only when it is safely within the server environment. Once the information has been acted on, it is either deleted or stored in encrypted form.

encryption key E-COMMERCE system for encoding and decoding information a sequence of characters known to both or all parties to a communication, used to initiate the ***encryption*** process

encumbrance MORTGAGES debt using real estate as collateral a liability such as a mortgage or charge that is attached to a property or piece of land

end consumer MARKETING somebody using product or service a person who uses a product or service. An end consumer may not be the purchaser of a product or service and should be distinguished from a customer.

endogenous variable STATISTICS dependent variable in an econometric study, the dependent variable, such as the stock price of a company, that is acted on by an independent variable, such as the company's earnings growth rate

endorse BANKING sign reverse side of check to sign a bill or check on the back to show that its ownership is being passed to another person or company

endorsement MARKETING explicit approval of product the public approval of a product by a person or organization. The endorsement can be used to promote the product to other organizations that may be more cautious in their approach to adopting new products.

endowment FINANCE donation of money for specified purpose a gift of money, especially to a nonprofit organization, to be used for a specific purpose

endowment assurance *UK* INSURANCE = ***endowment insurance***

endowment fund FINANCE fund for nonprofit organization a mutual fund established to provide income for a nonprofit institution

endowment insurance *US* INSURANCE insurance paying on policy's maturity or death an insurance policy that pays a set amount to the policyholder when the policy matures, or to a beneficiary if the policyholder dies before it matures. Part of the premium paid is for the life coverage element, while the remainder is invested in real estate and stocks (either a "with-profits" or "without-profits" policy) or, in the case of a share-linked policy, is used to purchase shares in a life fund. The sum the policyholder receives at the end of the term depends on the size of the premiums and the performance of the investments. *See also* ***term insurance***. *UK term* ***endowment assurance***

endowment mortgage MORTGAGES loan with both interest and endowment policy payments a long-term loan, usually for the purchase of real estate, in which the borrower makes two monthly payments, one to the lender to cover the interest on the loan, and the other as a premium paid into an endowment insurance policy. At the end of the loan's term, the proceeds from the endowment policy are used to repay the principal. *See also* ***mortgage***

endowment policy INSURANCE *see* ***endowment insurance***

endpoint STATISTICS when final event in study happens a point at which a definable event in a study takes place

energy audit GENERAL MANAGEMENT investigation of sourcing and employment of energy a review, inspection, and evaluation of sources and uses of energy within an organization to ensure efficiency and lack of waste

energy conservation GENERAL MANAGEMENT prevention of overuse of fuel the minimization of fuel consumption. Energy conservation, through the monitoring and control of the amounts of electricity, gas, and other fuels used in the workplace, can help reduce costs and damage to the environment. An energy management plan provides a systematic method of assessing, evaluating, and improving an organization's energy usage. This forms part of an organization's approach to environmental management.

engagement letter BUSINESS letter formalizing business relationship between professional and client a letter, usually required by professional standards, sent by a professional such as an accountant to a client, setting out the work the accountant is to do and further administrative matters such as any limit on the accountant's liability

entail LEGAL restriction on somebody inheriting real estate a legal condition that passes ownership of a property to specific persons only

enterprise 1. GENERAL MANAGEMENT bold undertaking a venture characterized by innovation, creativity, dynamism, and risk. An enterprise can consist of one project, or may refer to an entire organization. It usually requires several of the following attributes: flexibility, initiative, problem-solving ability, independence, and imagination. Enterprises flourish in the environment of delayered, nonhierarchical organizations but can be stifled by bureaucracy. **2.** BUSINESS firm a commercial business or company

enterprise application integration OPERATIONS & PRODUCTION sharing of information and proceedings using software the unrestricted sharing of data and business processes via integrated and compatible software programs. As businesses expand and recognize the need for their information and applications to be shared between systems, they are investing in enterprise application integration in order to streamline processes and keep all the parts of their organizations, for example, human resources and inventory control, connected. *Abbr* ***EAI***

enterprise culture GENERAL MANAGEMENT attitudes and behavior fostering bold undertakings an organizational or social environment that encourages and makes possible initiative and innovation. An organization with an enterprise culture is usually more competitive and more profitable than a bureaucracy. Such an organization is believed to be more rewarding and stimulating to work in. A society with an enterprise culture facilitates individuality and requires people to take responsibility for their own welfare. Conservative governments in the United Kingdom during the 1980s and 1990s promoted an enterprise culture by introducing market principles into all areas of economic and social life. These included policies of deregulation of financial services, privatization of utilities and national monopolies, and commercialization of the public sector. The enterprise culture is now supported by both main political parties.

enterprise investment scheme TAX tax incentives for investors in unquoted UK firms in the United Kingdom, a plan to promote investment in unquoted companies by which qualifying gains are exempt from capital gains tax

enterprise portal E-COMMERCE website collating useful information a website that assembles a wide range of content and services for employees of a particular organization, with the goal of bringing together all the key information they need to do a better job. The key difference between an enterprise portal and an intranet is that an enterprise portal contains not just internal content, but also external content that may be useful, such as specialized news feeds, or access to industry research reports. Ensuring that content is relevant, current, and frequently refreshed is essential for such sites to succeed, and enterprise portals are thus expensive to maintain.

Enterprise Risk Management RISK procedure for reducing risk to organization the process of planning and establishing control systems in order to minimize the risks that an organization faces, including financial, strategic, operational, and hazard risks. *Abbr* ***ERM***

enterprise zone FINANCE, BUSINESS district where government gives incentives for economic development an area in which the government offers financial incentives such as tax relief to encourage new business activities. *Abbr* ***EZ***

entertainment expenses HR & PERSONNEL reclaimable money spent on customers or suppliers costs, reimbursable by an employer, that are incurred by an employee in hosting social events for clients or suppliers in order to obtain or maintain their patronage or goodwill

entitlement GENERAL MANAGEMENT assumption of deserving reward the expectation that an organization or individual will make large profits regardless of their contribution to the economy or company

entitlement offer FINANCE nontransferable offer an offer that cannot be transferred to anyone else

entrepot port OPERATIONS & PRODUCTION international port dealing in re-exports a town with a large international commercial port dealing in re-exports

entrepreneur BUSINESS somebody who starts and operates new business somebody who sets up a business or enterprise. An entrepreneur typically demonstrates effective application of a number of enterprising attributes, such as creativity, initiative, risk taking, problem-solving ability, and autonomy, and will often risk his or her own capital to establish a business.

entropy STATISTICS measure of system's information transfer rate a measure of the rate of transfer of the information that a system such as a computer program or factory machine receives or outputs

entry ACCOUNTING item written in accounts ledger an item of written information put in an accounts ledger

entry barrier MARKETING hindrance to entering market a perceived or real obstacle preventing a competitor from entering a market

envelope E-COMMERCE = ***electronic envelope***

environmental accounting ACCOUNTING including costs to environment in decision making the practice of including the indirect costs and benefits of a product or activity, for example, its environmental effects on health and the economy, along with its direct costs when making business decisions. *Also called* ***full cost accounting, green accounting***

environmental audit GENERAL MANAGEMENT assessment of success of environmental policies the regular systematic gathering of information to monitor the effectiveness of environmental policies. An environmental audit is concerned with checking conformity with legislative requirements and environmental standards, as well as with company policy. The audit may also cover potential improvements in environmental performance and systems.

environmental impact assessment GENERAL MANAGEMENT study of effect on environment of proposed project a study, undertaken during the planning phase before an investment is made or an operation started, to consider any potential environmental effects

environmental impact statement GENERAL MANAGEMENT findings of environmental impact assessment a report on the results of a particular environmental impact assessment. *Abbr* ***EIS***

environmental management GENERAL MANAGEMENT control of organization's impact on environment a systematic approach to minimizing the damage created by an organization to the environment in which it operates. Environmental management has become an issue in organizations because consumers now expect them to be environmentally aware, if not environmentally friendly. Senior managers and directors are increasingly being held liable for their organizations' environmental performance, and the onus is on them to adopt a ***corporate strategy***

that balances economic growth with environmental protection. Environmental management involves reducing pollution, waste, and the consumption of natural resources by implementing an environmental action plan. This plan brings together the key elements of environmental management, including an organization's ***environmental policy*** statement, an ***environmental audit***, environmental management system, and external standards.

environmental policy GENERAL MANAGEMENT intentions regarding minimizing harm to environment a statement of organizational intentions regarding the safeguarding of the environment

EOQ *abbr* FINANCE, OPERATIONS & PRODUCTION ***economic order quantity***

epos *or* **EPOS** *or* **EPoS** *abbr* E-COMMERCE ***electronic point of sale***

e-procurement E-COMMERCE purchasing of products over Internet the business-to-business sale and purchase of goods and services over an electronic network such as the Internet. *Also called* ***electronic procurement***

EPS *abbr* STOCKHOLDING & INVESTMENTS ***earnings per share***

Equal Credit Opportunity Act FINANCE US law ensuring equal treatment for borrowers in the United States, a federal law that gives all consumers an equal opportunity to obtain credit by requiring creditors to follow specific rules regarding the information they can obtain from applicants. *Abbr* ***ECOA***

equal opportunities HR & PERSONNEL provision of same chances to all the granting of equal rights, privileges, and status regardless of gender, age, race, religion, disability, or sexual orientation. Equality in employment is regulated by law in most Western countries. An organizational equal opportunities policy works to go farther than the regulatory framework demands. Such a policy should focus on preventing discriminatory or harassing behavior in the workplace and achieving equal access to training, job, and promotion opportunities. ***Affirmative action***, referred to as positive discrimination in the United Kingdom, is a controversial approach to encouraging the advancement of minorities. ***Diversity management*** builds on and goes beyond equal opportunities by looking at the rights of individuals rather than groups.

equal pay HR & PERSONNEL paying men and women at same rate the principle and practice of paying men and women in the same organization at the same rate for like work, or work that is rated as of equal value. Work is assessed either through an organization's job evaluation plan or by the judgment of an independent expert appointed by an industrial committee. Although many countries have legislation on equal pay, a gap still exists between men's pay and women's pay and is attributed to sexual discrimination in job evaluation and payment systems.

equal treatment HR & PERSONNEL avoidance of discrimination at work a principle of the European Union that requires member states to ensure that there is no ***discrimination*** with regard to employment, vocational training, and working conditions. The principle of equal treatment is applied through Europe-wide directives and national legislation of the member states.

equilibrium ECONOMICS balance in economy the state of balance in the economy where supply equals demand or a country's balance of payments is neither in deficit nor in excess

equilibrium price ECONOMICS product price causing balanced supply and demand the price at which the supply of and the demand for a good are equal. Suppliers increase prices when demand is high and reduce prices when demand is low.

equilibrium quantity ECONOMICS amount regulating supply and demand the quantity that needs to be bought for supply to match demand at a specific price. Suppliers increase quantity when demand, and therefore the price, is high and reduce quantity when demand or price is low.

equilibrium rate of interest ECONOMICS when expected and actual interest rates match the rate at which the expected interest rate in a market equals the actual rate prevailing

equipment trust certificate STOCKHOLDING & INVESTMENTS US bond issued to pay for equipment in the United States, a bond sold for a 20% down payment and collateralized by the equipment purchased with its proceeds

equities STOCKHOLDING & INVESTMENTS stock in corporation a stockholder's holdings in a corporation

equity 1. FINANCE value of asset minus outstanding loans the value of an asset minus any loans outstanding on it **2.** FINANCE value of company owned by stockholders the value of a company that is the property of its stockholders, calculated as the value of the company's assets minus the value of its liabilities, not including the ordinary share capital **3.** STOCKHOLDING & INVESTMENTS ownership of company's stock ownership in a company in the form of stock **4.** STOCKHOLDING & INVESTMENTS stockholder's right to share in company's profit the right of a stockholder to receive dividends from the profit of a company in which the shares of stock are owned

equity accounting ACCOUNTING listing subsidiary's profits on parent company's books a method of accounting that puts part of the profits of a subsidiary into the parent company's books

equity capital STOCKHOLDING & INVESTMENTS stock owned by stockholders the part of the nominal value of the stock owned by the stockholders of a company. *See also* ***share capital***

equity carve-out STOCKHOLDING & INVESTMENTS sale of shares of stock to fund spin-off a situation in which an established company sells off shares of stock to investors in order to create an independent company from a subsidiary part of the business. *Also called* ***carve-out***

equity claim FINANCE claim on residual earnings a claim on earnings that remain after debts are satisfied

equity contribution agreement FINANCE agreement to contribute equity an agreement to buy a proportion of the ***capital stock*** of a company in order to provide funds for a project

equity derivative STOCKHOLDING & INVESTMENTS derivative instrument based on stock a ***derivative instrument*** whose ***underlying asset*** is a stock. The most common equity derivative is an ***option***.

equity dilution STOCKHOLDING & INVESTMENTS decrease in percentage of ownership in firm the reduction in the percentage of a company represented by each share for an existing stockholder who has not increased his or her holding in the issue of new common stock

equity dividend cover *UK* ACCOUNTING calculation of firm's ability to pay dividend an accounting ratio, calculated by dividing the distributable profits during a given period by the actual dividend paid in that period, that indicates the likelihood of the dividend being maintained in future years.

equity finance *UK* FINANCE = ***equity financing***

equity financing *US* FINANCE money contributed for share in business the money introduced into a business by its owners. If it is a for-profit company, then the equity is introduced in exchange for shares and investors can expect a share of any profit. In the case of limited companies, it takes the form of dividends. *UK term* ***equity finance***

equity floor MARKETS payment agreement based on market drop an agreement for one party to pay another whenever some indicator of a stock market's value falls below a specific limit

equity fund STOCKHOLDING & INVESTMENTS mutual fund that is invested in equities a mutual fund that is invested mainly in stocks, not in government securities or other funds

equity gearing FINANCE relationship of borrowings to equity the ratio between a company's borrowings and its ***equity***

equity kicker MARKETS investment incentive promising share of future revenue an incentive given to people to lend a company money, in the form of a warrant to share in future earnings

equity multiplier FINANCE US firm's worth as multiple of stock price in the United States, a measure of a company's worth, expressed as a multiple of each dollar of its stock's price

equity risk premium STOCKHOLDING & INVESTMENTS extra return expected on equities compared to bonds an extra return on equities over the return on bonds, because of the risk involved in investing in equities

equity swap STOCKHOLDING & INVESTMENTS, RISK agreement between parties to exchange cash flows an agreement in which one party agrees to exchange its cash flow, which is linked to a benchmark such as the ***London Interbank Offered Rate*** or the rate of return on an ***index***, for another party's fixed or floating rate of interest

equity sweetener FINANCE incentive for people to lend firm money an incentive to encourage people to lend a company money. The sweetener takes the form of a warrant that gives the lender the right to buy stock at a later date and at a specific price.

equivalent annual cash flow FINANCE return on annuity compared to other investment the value of an annuity required to provide an investor with the same return as some other form of investment

equivalent bond yield STOCKHOLDING & INVESTMENTS = ***bond equivalent yield***

equivalent taxable yield TAX return on taxable investment compared to other investment the value of a taxable investment required to provide an investor with the same return as some other form of investment

ERDF *abbr* FINANCE ***European Regional Development Fund***

e-retailer E-COMMERCE retail business operating over Internet a business that uses an electronic network such as the Internet to sell its goods or services. *Also called* ***electronic retailer, e-tailer***

ergonomics GENERAL MANAGEMENT, HR & PERSONNEL study of efficient working environments the study of workplace design and the physical and psychological impact it has on workers. Ergonomics is about the fit between people, their work activities, equipment, work systems, and environment to ensure that workplaces are safe, comfortable, efficient, and that productivity is not compromised. Ergonomics may examine the design and layout of buildings, machines, and equipment, as well as aspects such as lighting, temperature, ventilation, noise, color, and texture. Ergonomic principles also apply to working methods such as systems and procedures, and the allocation and scheduling of work.

ERISA *abbr* LEGAL ***Employee Retirement Income Security Act***

ERM CURRENCY & EXCHANGE former system for stabilizing European Community exchange rates a system to maintain exchange rate stability used in the past by member states of the European Community. *Full form* ***Exchange Rate Mechanism*** ■ *abbr* RISK ***Enterprise Risk Management***

ERR *abbr* STOCKHOLDING & INVESTMENTS ***expected rate of return***

error account BANKING account for recording transactions made in error an account for the temporary placement of funds involved in a financial transaction known to have been executed in error

error rate ACCOUNTING proportion of errors made the number of mistakes per thousand entries or per page

errors and omissions ACCOUNTING bookkeeping mistakes mistakes arising from incorrect record keeping or accounting. *Abbr* ***E&O***

ESC *abbr* GENERAL MANAGEMENT, HR & PERSONNEL ***European Social Charter***

escalator clause LEGAL contract clause permitting price increases a clause in a contract that allows for regular price increases for a product or service to cover projected cost increases

escape clause LEGAL clause specifying conditions under which contract is void a clause in a contract that allows one of the parties to avoid carrying out the terms of the contract under specific conditions

escheat LEGAL government claim on property in absence of heirs the reversion of real or personal property to the government upon the death of a person who has no legal heirs

escrow LEGAL safe keeping by third party of valuable item an agreement between two parties that holds that something such as a good, document, or amount of money should be held for safe keeping by a third party until specific conditions are fulfilled

escrow account BANKING account holding money until contract conditions are met an account where money is held until specific conditions, such as a contract being signed, or a consignment of goods being safely delivered, are met

e-shock E-COMMERCE unstoppable advance of e-commerce the forward momentum of electronic commerce, considered as powerful and irresistible

ESOP *abbr* STOCKHOLDING & INVESTMENTS ***employee stock ownership plan***

ESPP *abbr* STOCKHOLDING & INVESTMENTS ***employee stock purchase plan***

essential industry ECONOMICS industry necessary to nation's economy an industry regarded as crucial to a country's economy and often supported financially by a government by way of tariff protection and tax breaks

establishment fee FINANCE = ***commitment fee***

estate FINANCE deceased person's assets the net assets of somebody who has died

estate duty TAX former tax paid on estate before distribution in the United Kingdom until 1975, a tax paid on the property left by a dead person before it is passed to the heirs. *See also* ***inheritance tax***

estate tax TAX tax paid on estate before distribution to heirs in the United States, a tax paid on the property left by a dead person before it is passed to the heirs

estimate FINANCE **1.** approximation of something's value an approximate calculation of an uncertain value. An estimate may be a reasonable guess based on knowledge and experience or it may be calculated using more sophisticated techniques designed to forecast projected costs, profits, losses, or value. **2.** approximation of cost of work a written statement of an approximate price for work to be undertaken by a business

estimation STATISTICS predicted numerical value the provision of a numerical value for a parameter of a population that has been sampled

estimator FINANCE person who calculates expected job costs a person whose job is to calculate the likely cost for carrying out work

estoppel LEGAL ruling denying somebody right to give evidence a rule of evidence whereby somebody is prevented from denying or asserting a fact in legal proceedings

e-tailer E-COMMERCE = ***e-retailer***

e-tailing E-COMMERCE operating retail business over Internet the practice of doing business over an electronic network such as the Internet

ETF *abbr* MARKETS ***exchange-traded fund***

ethical fund FINANCE fund providing money to firms having moral practices a fund that invests in companies that operate by moral standards approved of by their investors, such as not manufacturing or selling weapons, not trading with countries with poor human rights records, or using only environmentally acceptable sources of raw materials

ethical index STOCKHOLDING & INVESTMENTS list of stock in conscientious firms a published index of stock in companies that operate by moral standards approved of by their investors

ethical investment STOCKHOLDING & INVESTMENTS investing only in socially responsible firms investment only in companies whose policies meet the ethical criteria of the investor. *Also called* ***socially conscious investing***

Ethical Investment Research Service STOCKHOLDING & INVESTMENTS organization determining which firms have moral practices an organization that does research into companies and recommends those that follow specific ethical standards

ETP *abbr* TAX ***eligible termination payment***

EU *abbr* ECONOMICS ***European Union***. *See also* ***single market***

Euribor *abbr* MARKETS ***Euro Interbank Offered Rate***

euro *or* **Euro** CURRENCY & EXCHANGE currency of nations belonging to EU the currency of 12 member nations of the European Union. The euro was introduced in 1999, when the first 11 countries to adopt it joined together in an Economic and Monetary Union and tied their currencies' exchange rate to the euro. Notes and coins were brought into general circulation in January 2002, although banks and other financial institutions had before that time carried out transactions in euro. The official plural of euro is "euro," although "euros" is widely used.

euro account BANKING account operated in euro a checking account or savings account in euro

Eurobank BANKING US bank dealing in Eurocurrency a bank that handles transactions in ***Eurocurrency***

Eurobond STOCKHOLDING & INVESTMENTS bond issued and traded in different currencies a bond issued in the currency of one country and sold to investors from another country. *Also called* ***global bond***

Eurocheque BANKING check good in any European bank a check that can be cashed at any bank in the world displaying the European Union crest. The Eurocheque system is based in Brussels.

Euroclear MARKETS European payment system for securities a user-owned system for routing and settling securities transactions throughout Europe

Eurocommercial paper MARKETS form of short-term loan short-term loans without collateral obtained by companies in foreign countries. *Abbr* ***ECP***

Eurocredit BANKING, CURRENCY & EXCHANGE credit in currency of another country a loan made in a currency other than that of the lending institution

Eurocurrency BANKING, CURRENCY & EXCHANGE deposits in currency of another country money deposited in one country but denominated in the currency of another country, for example, dollars deposited in a British bank

Eurodeposit BANKING, CURRENCY & EXCHANGE deposit in Eurocurrency a short-term deposit of ***Eurocurrency***. Eurodeposits have a variable interest rate based on the Euro Interbank Offered Rate.

Eurodollar BANKING, CURRENCY & EXCHANGE US dollar deposited in foreign bank a dollar deposited in a European bank or other bank outside the United States

Euroequity MARKETS European stock not traded domestically a stock in an international company that is traded outside its country of origin

Euroequity issue MARKETS security for foreign country a capital issue in a currency and a country other than that of the issuer

Euro Interbank Offered Rate MARKETS lending rate for euro the ***Interbank Offered Rate*** for loans in euro. *Abbr* ***Euribor***

euroland ECONOMICS = ***eurozone***

euro LIBOR MARKETS LIBOR denominated in euros the ***London Interbank Offered Rate*** denominated in euro rather than US dollars

Euro-note CURRENCY & EXCHANGE security in Eurocurrency market a form of ***Eurocommercial paper*** in the Eurocurrency market

Euro-option MARKETS option to buy European bonds an option to buy European bonds at a later date

European Accounting Association ACCOUNTING European organization for accounting academics an organization for accounting academics. Founded in 1977 and based in Brussels, the EAA aims to be a forum for European research in accounting. It holds an annual congress and since 1992 has published a journal, *European Accounting Review*. *Abbr* ***EAA***

European Association of Securities Dealers Automated Quotations MARKETS *see* ***EASDAQ***

European Bank for Reconstruction and Development BANKING *see* ***EBRD***

European Central Bank BANKING *see* ***ECB***

European Commission EU executive body the main executive body of the European Union, made up of members nominated by each member state. *Also called* ***Commission of the European Community***

European Community INTERNATIONAL TRADE former organization of European nations the name of the immediate precursor of the ***EU***. *Abbr* ***EC***

European Covered Bond Council FINANCE representative organization for various financial institutions the official organization bringing together bond issuers, analysts, investment bankers, rating agencies, and a wide range of interested market participants. *Abbr* ***ECBC***

European Economic Area INTERNATIONAL TRADE EU and EFTA member countries an area comprising the countries of the European Union and the members of EFTA, formed by an agreement on trade between the two organizations. *Abbr* ***EEA***

European Economic Community INTERNATIONAL TRADE former organization of European nations the name of the precursor of the ***European Community*** before it became the ***EU***. *Abbr* ***EEC***

European Free Trade Association INTERNATIONAL TRADE free-trade group linked with EU a group of countries (Iceland, Liechtenstein, Norway, and Switzerland) formed to encourage free trade between its members, and linked with the European Union in the European Economic Area. *Abbr* ***EFTA***

European Investment Bank BANKING *see* ***EIB***

European Monetary System CURRENCY & EXCHANGE *see* ***EMS***

European Monetary Union CURRENCY & EXCHANGE movement toward common European currency *see* ***EMU***

European option STOCKHOLDING & INVESTMENTS option exercisable only on expiration date an option that the buyer can exercise only on the day that it expires. *See also* ***American option***

European Private Equity and Venture Capital Association FINANCE group providing information for investors an organization that provides information and networking opportunities for investors, entrepreneurs and policymakers in the ***equity financing*** industry. *Abbr* ***EVCA***

European Regional Development Fund FINANCE fund supporting less developed European areas a fund set up to provide grants to less industrially developed parts of Europe. *Abbr* ***ERDF***

European Social Charter ECONOMICS charter containing rights of EU members a charter adopted by the European Council of the EU in 1989. The 12 rights it contains are: freedom of movement, employment, and remuneration; social protection; improvement of living and working conditions; freedom of association and collective bargaining; worker information; consultation and participation; vocational training; equal treatment of men and women; health and safety protection in the workplace; pension rights; integration of those with disabilities; and protection of young people. *Abbr* ***ESC***

European Union ECONOMICS organization of European nations a social, economic, and political organization involving 27 European countries. It came into effect in 1993 as a result of the signing of the Maastricht Treaty by 15 countries; other countries joined later. Precursors were the European Community (EC), and the European Economic Community (EEC). *Abbr* ***EU***

Euroyen CURRENCY & EXCHANGE yen deposited in bank abroad a Japanese yen deposited in a bank outside Japan

Euroyen bond STOCKHOLDING & INVESTMENTS Eurobond in yen a Eurobond denominated in yen but issued outside of Japan by a non-Japanese company

eurozone ECONOMICS countries using euro the area of Europe comprising those countries that have adopted the euro as a common currency. *Also called* ***euroland***

EVA *abbr* FINANCE ***economic value added***

EVCA *abbr* FINANCE ***European Private Equity and Venture Capital Association***

event marketing MARKETING promotion of social functions the promotion and marketing of a specific event such as a conference, seminar, exhibition, or trade fair. Event marketing may encompass ***corporate hospitality*** activities, business or charity functions, or sporting occasions. The planning, marketing, and managing of the function on the day are sometimes entirely ***outsourced*** to companies specializing in event management.

event risk STOCKHOLDING & INVESTMENTS chance of loss on bond the possibility that a bond rating will drop because of an unexpected event such as a takeover or restructuring

evergreen loan FINANCE loan supplying flow of capital a series of loans providing a continuing stream of capital for a project

exact interest ACCOUNTING annual interest calculated over 365 days annual interest calculated on the basis of a full 365 days, as opposed to ordinary interest that is calculated on 360 days

ex-all STOCKHOLDING & INVESTMENTS without rights to anything pending having no right with respect to stocks in any pending transaction such as a split or the issuance of dividends. *Abbr* ***xa***. *See also* ***cum-all***

excellence GENERAL MANAGEMENT, OPERATIONS & PRODUCTION attainment of highest standards a state of organizational performance achieved through the successful integration of a variety of operational and strategic elements which enables an organization to become one of the best in its field. Excellence is initially evident when an organization rises above its competitors, and it is usually measured by the ability to sustain a leading or significant market share. The strategic and operational elements contributing to excellence include the organization's approach to ***total quality management***, core competency, ***benchmarking***, ***customer service***, the ***balanced scorecard approach***, and ***leadership***. Taken all together, these components should produce an organizational approach to the generation, development, and delivery of products and services which is better, cheaper, and smarter than that of the competition. Attempts at becoming an excellent organization have spawned terms such as ***best practice*** and ***world class manufacturing*** and are usually associated with a holistic approach to ***competitive advantage***.

exceptional items ACCOUNTING **1.** ordinary business costs of unusual size or nature costs that arise from normal business dealings, but that must be recorded because of their unusual size or nature **2.** unusual items included in pre-tax balance sheet items in a balance sheet that do not appear there each year and that are included in the accounts before the pre-tax profit is calculated, as opposed to ***extraordinary items*** that are calculated after the pre-tax profit

exception reporting GENERAL MANAGEMENT providing only significant information the passing on of information only when it breaches or transcends agreed norms. Exception reporting is intended to reduce information overload by minimizing the circulation of repetitive or old information. Under this system, only information that is new and out of the ordinary will be transmitted.

excess 1. FINANCE assets less liabilities in a financial institution, the amount by which assets exceed liabilities **2.** *UK* INSURANCE = ***deductible***

excess capacity OPERATIONS & PRODUCTION underutilized manufacturing capability spare manufacturing capability that is not being used

excess liquidity BANKING cash in bank exceeding required amount cash held by a bank above what is required by the regulatory authorities

excess profit FINANCE unusually high profit a level of profit that is higher than a level regarded as usual

excess profits tax TAX tax levied in unusual situation a tax levied by a government on a company that makes extraordinarily large profits in times of unusual circumstances, for example, during a war. An excess profits tax was imposed in both the United States and the United Kingdom during World War II.

excess reserves BANKING reserves in financial institution exceeding required amount reserves held by a financial institution that are higher than those required by the regulatory authorities. As such reserves may indicate that demand for loans is low, banks often sell their excess reserves to other institutions.

excess return FINANCE profit from investment the amount received from an investment in excess of the basic interest rate or the cost of capital by which an activity is financed

exchange 1. MARKETS place for buying and selling a ***market*** where goods, services, or financial instruments are bought and sold **2.** STOCKHOLDING & INVESTMENTS converting one form of security to another the conversion of one type of security for another, for example, the exchange of a bond for stock **3.** E-COMMERCE environment for conducting business the main type of business-to-business marketplace. The ***B2B exchange*** enables suppliers, buyers, and intermediaries to come together and offer products to each other according to a set of criteria. ***B2B Web exchanges*** provide constant price adjustments in line with fluctuations of supply and demand. In E2E or "exchange-to-exchange" e-commerce, buyers and sellers conduct transactions not only within exchanges but also between them. **4.** FINANCE barter to trade goods and services for other goods and services **5.** CURRENCY & EXCHANGE trade one country's currency for another to trade the currency of one country or economic zone for that of another

exchange controls CURRENCY & EXCHANGE regulations governing foreign exchange dealings the regulations by which a country's banking system controls its residents' or resident companies' dealings in foreign currencies and gold

exchange cross rate CURRENCY & EXCHANGE = ***cross rate***

exchange dealer CURRENCY & EXCHANGE foreign currency trader a person who buys and sells foreign currency

exchange equalization account CURRENCY & EXCHANGE bank account for regulating value of British pound the Bank of England account that sells and buys sterling for gold and foreign currencies to smooth out fluctuations in the exchange rate of the British pound

exchange offer STOCKHOLDING & INVESTMENTS offer of one security for another an offer to trade one security for another, usually to stockholders of a company in financial trouble and at less favorable terms

exchange option STOCKHOLDING & INVESTMENTS option allowing holder to exchange assets an option that allows the holder to trade one asset for another.

The option may be either a ***European option***, which can be exercised only on the expiration date, or an ***American option***, which can be exercised at any time up to and including the expiration date. *Also called **Margrabe option***

exchange premium CURRENCY & EXCHANGE surcharge for buying foreign currency an extra cost above the usual rate for buying a foreign currency

exchange rate CURRENCY & EXCHANGE rate for converting one currency to another the rate at which one country's currency can be exchanged for that of another country

Exchange Rate Mechanism CURRENCY & EXCHANGE *see **ERM***

exchange rate movements CURRENCY & EXCHANGE changes in value between currencies the fluctuations in value between currencies that can result in losses to businesses that import and export goods and to investors

exchange rate parity CURRENCY & EXCHANGE relative value of currencies the relationship between the value of one currency and another

exchange rate risk CURRENCY & EXCHANGE, RISK chance of incurring loss on converting currencies the risk of suffering loss on converting another currency to the currency of a company's own country.

Exchange rate risks can be arranged into three primary categories. (i) Economic exposure: operating costs will rise due to changes in rates and make a product uncompetitive in the world market. Little can be done to reduce this routine business risk that every enterprise must endure. (ii) Translation exposure: the impact of currency exchange rates will reduce a company's earnings and weaken its balance sheet. To reduce translation exposure, experienced corporate fund managers use a variety of techniques known as ***currency hedging***. (iii) Transaction exposure: there will be an unfavorable move in a specific currency between the time when a contract is agreed and the time it is completed, or between the time when a lending or borrowing is initiated and the time the funds are repaid. Transaction exposure can be eased by ***factoring*** (transferring title to foreign accounts receivable to a third-party factoring house).

Although there is no definitive way of forecasting exchange rates, largely because the world's economies and financial markets are evolving so rapidly, the relationships between exchange rates, interest rates, and inflation rates can serve as leading indicators of changes in risk. These relationships are as follows. Purchasing Power Parity theory (PPP): while it can be expressed differently, the most common expression links the changes in exchange rates to those in relative price indices in two countries:

Rate of change of exchange rate = Difference in inflation rates

International Fisher Effect (IFE): this holds that an interest-rate differential will exist only if the exchange rate is expected to change in such a way that the advantage of the higher interest rate is offset by the loss on the foreign exchange transactions. Practically speaking, the IFE implies that while an investor in a low-interest country can convert funds into the currency of a high-interest country and earn a higher rate, the gain (the interest rate differential) will be offset by the expected loss due to foreign exchange rate changes. The relationship is stated as:

Expected rate of change of the exchange rate = Interest-rate differential

Unbiased Forward Rate Theory: this holds that the forward exchange rate is the best unbiased estimate of the expected future spot exchange rate.

Expected exchange rate = Forward exchange rate

exchange rate spread CURRENCY & EXCHANGE difference in buying and selling price of currencies the difference between the price at which a broker or other intermediary buys and sells foreign currency

exchange-traded MARKETS traded on exchange bought and sold on an exchange, as opposed to over-the-counter

exchange-traded fund MARKETS fund traded like stocks a group of stocks that can be traded on a stock exchange like a single stock and is linked to a specific market index. *Abbr **ETF***

Exchequer BANKING UK government's bank account in the United Kingdom, the government's account at the Bank of England into which all revenues from taxes and other sources are paid

Exchequer stocks STOCKHOLDING & INVESTMENTS UK government stocks UK government stocks used to finance government expenditure. They are regarded as a very safe investment.

excise duty TAX tax on specific goods a tax on goods such as alcohol or tobacco produced and sold within a specific country

excise license TAX license permitting sale of specific products a license issued against payment to allow somebody to trade in products such as wine that are subject to excise duty

excise tax TAX tax on specific goods a tax levied for a particular purpose

exclusion clause LEGAL clause listing items not covered by agreement a clause in an insurance policy or warranty that states which items or events are not included in the cover provided

exclusive agency *US* BUSINESS exclusive agreement to operate an agreement to be the only person to represent a company or to sell a product in a particular area. *UK term **sole agency***

exclusive agreement MARKETING sole right to sell product an agreement by which a person or company is made sole agent for selling a product in a market

exclusive economic zone ECONOMICS area in country with special economic conditions a zone in a country in which specific economic conditions apply. The Special Economic Zone in China, where trade is conducted free of state control, is an example.

ex coupon STOCKHOLDING & INVESTMENTS without interest coupons without the interest coupons or after interest has been paid

ex dividend STOCKHOLDING & INVESTMENTS giving buyer no dividend right used to describe bonds or stocks that, when they are sold, do not provide the buyer with the right to a forthcoming dividend

execution 1. STOCKHOLDING & INVESTMENTS completion of securities trade the process of completing an order to buy or sell securities **2.** LEGAL carrying out contract the process of carrying out the terms of a legal order or contract

execution only MARKETS handling security transaction without giving advice used to describe a stock market transaction undertaken by an intermediary who acts on behalf of a client without providing advice. *See also **active fund management, discretionary management***

executive CORPORATE GOVERNANCE **1.** person in senior management an employee in a position of senior responsibility in an organization. An executive is involved in planning, strategy, policy making, and ***line management***. **2.** any person with responsible job a person with a significant role in an organization or project, for example, a ***manager, consultant, executive officer***, or *agent*

executive chairman CORPORATE GOVERNANCE organization's highest executive the most senior executive in an organization when the roles of chair and chief executive are combined, and the executive chairman has some control over daily operations. *See also **chairman***

executive director CORPORATE GOVERNANCE director in senior management position a senior employee of an organization, usually with responsibility for a specific function and usually, but not always, a member of the ***board of directors***

executive officer CORPORATE GOVERNANCE = ***executive*** *(sense 2)*

executive pension plan PENSIONS UK pension plan for firm's top executives in the United Kingdom, a pension plan for senior executives of a company. The company's contributions are a tax-deductible expense but are subject to a cap. The plan does not prevent the executive from being a member of the company's group pension plan although the executive's total contributions must not exceed a specific percentage of his or her salary.

executive share option scheme *UK* STOCKHOLDING & INVESTMENTS = ***executive stock option plan***

executive stock option plan *US* STOCKHOLDING & INVESTMENTS stock purchase arrangement for top employees an arrangement whereby some directors and employees are given the opportunity to purchase stock in the company at a fixed price at a future date. In some jurisdictions, such arrangements can be tax efficient if specific local tax authority conditions are met. *UK term **executive share option scheme***

executive summary GENERAL MANAGEMENT statement outlining main points of business plan a concise summary at the beginning of a business plan of the objectives, products and/or services, marketing plans, operations, etc. of the proposed business, designed to attract investors

executor LEGAL person responsible for distribution of deceased person's assets a person appointed under a will to ensure the deceased's estate is distributed according to the terms of the will

exempt gift TAX in US, untaxed gift in the United States, a gift that is not subject to ***gift tax***

exempt investment fund TAX UK investment for people having certain tax advantages in the United Kingdom, a collective investment, usually a mutual fund, for investors, such as charities or contributors to pension plans, who have tax privileges

exemption TAX allowance per person subtracted from taxable income an amount per family member that somebody can subtract when reporting income to be taxed

exempt purchaser STOCKHOLDING & INVESTMENTS institutional investor exempt from securities commission filing requirements an institutional investor who may buy newly issued securities without filing a prospectus with a securities commission

exempt security STOCKHOLDING & INVESTMENTS security exempt from legal requirement a security that is not subject to a provision of law such as margin or registration requirements

exempt supply TAX in UK, item exempt from VAT in the United Kingdom, an item or service on which ***VAT*** is not levied, for example, the purchase of, or rent on, real estate and financial services

exercise STOCKHOLDING & INVESTMENTS to use the right to act to put into effect a right to carry out a transaction with previously agreed terms, especially in trading ***options***

exercise date STOCKHOLDING & INVESTMENTS date when option may be taken the date on which the holder of an option can put its terms into effect

exercise notice STOCKHOLDING & INVESTMENTS option holder's notice of wish to exercise option an option holder's notification to the option writer of his or her desire to exercise the option

exercise of warrants STOCKHOLDING & INVESTMENTS using warrant to buy stock the process of activating the right given by a warrant to purchase stock at a specific date

exercise price STOCKHOLDING & INVESTMENTS **1.** price at which option is taken the price at which an option will be put into effect **2.** = ***strike price***

exercise value STOCKHOLDING & INVESTMENTS profit from cashing in option the amount of profit that can be realized by cashing in an ***option***

ex-gratia payment HR & PERSONNEL exceptional extra payment a one-time extra payment in addition to normal pay, made out of gratitude or courtesy, or in recognition of a special contribution

exhibition MARKETING large event for displaying goods an event organized to bring together buyers and sellers at a single venue

Eximbank BANKING US bank lending money to foreign importers a bank founded in 1934 that provides loans direct to foreign importers of US goods and services. *Full form **Export-Import Bank***

existential culture GENERAL MANAGEMENT attitudes and behavior fostering individuals a form of corporate culture in which the organization exists to serve the individual, rather than individuals being servants of the organization. Existential culture was identified by Charles Handy. It typically consists of a group of professionals who work together, but have no leader.

exit STOCKHOLDING & INVESTMENTS termination of investment the way in which an investor can realize the gains or losses of an investment, for example, by selling the company they have invested in

exit charge *or* **exit fee** STOCKHOLDING & INVESTMENTS fee charged to sell out of investment a charge sometimes made by a trust when selling shares in a mutual fund

exit fee STOCKHOLDING & INVESTMENTS = ***exit charge***

exit P/E ratio FINANCE final price/earnings ratio the ***price/earnings ratio*** when a company changes hands, as by a takeover or sale

exit price MARKETS price at which investment is sold the price at which an investor sells an investment or at which a firm sells all its merchandise and leaves a market

exit strategy BUSINESS planned disposal of business a plan for disposing of a business and realizing the value of the investment made in it. The development of an exit strategy involves establishing the value of the business, identifying and selecting exit options, identifying and removing obstacles, and preparing and implementing a plan. Exit options include the sale of the business, ***merger***, flotation or public listing, ***management buyout***, ***franchising***, family succession, ceasing to trade, or ***liquidation***.

ex-legal STOCKHOLDING & INVESTMENTS US bond not displaying legal opinion in the United States, a municipal bond that is issued without the legal opinion of a law firm printed on it

ex officio CORPORATE GOVERNANCE by virtue of one's office because of an office held. An officeholder such as a treasurer may attend a committee meeting "ex officio" because of the office held in the wider organization, even if they are not otherwise a member of that committee.

exogenous variable STATISTICS variable from outside study in an econometric study, any variable that has an impact on it from outside

exotic option STOCKHOLDING & INVESTMENTS. RISK complicated option traded in over-the-counter market a complex option contract whose underlying asset or terms of payoff differ from those of either a standard ***American option*** or ***European option***. Exotic options are usually traded in the ***over-the-counter market***.

expansionary monetary policy FINANCE lending at low interest to stimulate economy a government strategy of lending money at low interest rates to stimulate an economy that is entering or experiencing a recession

expected rate of return *or* **expected return** STOCKHOLDING & INVESTMENTS probable return on investment the projected percentage return on an investment, based on the weighted probability of all possible rates of return.

It is calculated by the following formula:

$$ERR = \sum_{i=1}^{-} (P(i) \times r_i)$$

where P(*i*) is the probability of outcome *i* and r_i is the return for outcome *i*.

The following example illustrates the principle that the formula expresses:

The current price of ABC, Inc. stock is trading at $10. At the end of the year, ABC shares are projected to be traded:

- 25% higher if economic growth exceeds expectations-a probability of 30%;
- 12% higher if economic growth equals expectations-a probability of 50%;
- 5% lower if economic growth falls short of expectations-a probability of 20%.

To find the expected rate of return, simply multiply the percentages by their respective probabilities and add the results:

$$(30\% \times 25\%) + (50\% \times 12\%) + (25\% \times -5\%) = 7.5 + 6 + -1.25 = 12.25\%\ ERR$$

A second example:

- if economic growth remains robust (a 20% probability), investments will return 25%;
- if economic growth ebbs, but still performs adequately (a 40% probability), investments will return 15%;
- if economic growth slows significantly (a 30% probability), investments will return 5%;
- if the economy declines outright (a 10% probability), investments will return 0%.

Therefore:

$$(20\% \times 25\%) + (40\% \times 15\%) + (30\% \times 5\%) + (10\% \times 0\%) = 5\% + 6\% + 1.5\% + 0\% = 12.5\%\ ERR$$

Abbr ***ERR***. *See also* **capital asset pricing model**

expected value FINANCE future value based on probability of an occurrence the future value of a course of action, weighted according to the probability that the course of action will actually occur. If the possible course of action produces income of $10,000 and has a 10% chance of occurring, its expected value is 10% of $10,000 or $1,000.

expenditure FINANCE amount spent an amount of money spent on a particular thing, or the total amount spent

expenditure switching ECONOMICS switching government spending from one area to another government action to divert domestic spending from one sector to another, for example, from imports to home-produced goods

expense ACCOUNTING **1.** cost required a cost incurred in buying goods or services **2.** money spent a charge against a company's profit

expense account HR & PERSONNEL **1.** money allowed for business travel and entertainment money that businesspeople are allowed by their companies to spend on traveling and entertaining clients in connection with business **2.** facility to draw or reclaim money for expenses an amount of money that an employee or group of employees can draw on to reclaim personal ***expenses*** incurred in carrying out activities for an organization

expense ratio STOCKHOLDING & INVESTMENTS percentage of management costs passed on the percentage of the assets held in a mutual fund that includes management fees and other costs of operating the fund and that are passed on to stockholders

expenses HR & PERSONNEL money spent by employee as part of work personal costs that are reimbursed by the employer to any employee carrying out activities for an organization

experience curve GENERAL MANAGEMENT = ***learning curve***

experiential learning HR & PERSONNEL learning through experience and analysis a model that views learning as a cyclical process in four stages: concrete experience, reflective observation, abstract conceptualization, and active experimentation. Experiential learning relates to participants' activities and reactions to a training event, in contrast to passive learning. Proposed by David A. Kolb in 1971, the model was later expanded by other practitioners including Peter Honey and Alan Mumford.

experimental design STATISTICS how experiment is set up the planning of the procedures to be used in an experimental study

expert system GENERAL MANAGEMENT computer program providing expert knowledge and procedures a computer program that emulates the reasoning and decision making of a human expert in a particular field. The main components of an expert system are the knowledge base, which consists of facts and rules about appropriate courses of action based on the knowledge and experience of human experts; the inference engine, which simulates the inductive reasoning of a human expert; and the user interface, which enables users to interact with the system. Expert systems may be used by nonexperts to solve well-defined problems when human expertise is unavailable or expensive, or by experts seeking to find solutions to complex questions. They are used for a wide variety of tasks, including medical diagnostics and financial decision making, and are an application of ***artificial intelligence***.

expiration cycle MARKETS system showing stock option's expiration date in options trading, a way of designating the month on which a stock option expires. An option is assigned to one of three cycles, January (with expiration dates in January, April, July, and October), February (with expiration dates in February, May, August, and November), and March (with expiration dates in March, June, September, and December).

expiration date *US* STOCKHOLDING & INVESTMENTS last day on which to exercise an option the last day on which somebody who holds an option to buy or sell an asset can exercise that option. *UK term* ***expiry date***

expiry date *UK* STOCKHOLDING & INVESTMENTS = ***expiration date***

explicit cost FINANCE cost of using resources not owned by producer the cost of resources that are bought from outside the company producing the good or service. *See also* ***implicit cost***

exploding bonus FINANCE potential recruits' bonus that diminishes with time a bonus offered to recent graduates that encourages them to sign for a job as quickly as possible as it reduces in value with every day of delay (*slang*)

exponential smoothing STATISTICS statistical method of identifying long-term trends a statistical technique used in quantitative ***forecasting***, particularly in the areas of inventory control and ***sales forecasting***, that adjusts data to give a clearer view of trends in the long term. In exponential smoothing, values are calculated using a formula that takes all previous values into account but assigns greatest weight to the most recent data.

exponential trend STATISTICS trend in statistics over time a statistical trend that is revealed as observations are collected at uniformly spaced intervals over a period of time

export INTERNATIONAL TRADE **1.** sending goods abroad for sale the practice or business of sending goods from one country to another to be sold. *See also* ***exports*** **2.** send goods abroad for sale to send goods from one country to another to be sold

export agent INTERNATIONAL TRADE facilitator of trade abroad an intermediary who acts on behalf of a company to open up or develop a market in a foreign country. Export agents are often paid a commission on all sales and may have exclusive rights in a particular geographic area. A good agent will know or get to know local market conditions and will have other valuable information that can be used to mutual benefit.

exportation INTERNATIONAL TRADE act of sending goods abroad for sale the act of sending goods to foreign countries for sale

Export Credit Guarantee Department INTERNATIONAL TRADE UK government department helping exporters with finances a UK government department that provides financial and insurance assistance for exporters. The Export Credit Guarantee Department works to benefit organizations exporting UK goods and services and sets up insurance for UK companies investing overseas. *Abbr* ***ECGD***

exporter INTERNATIONAL TRADE firm sending goods abroad for sale a company that sends goods from one country to another to be sold

Export-Import Bank BANKING, INTERNATIONAL TRADE *see* ***Eximbank***

exporting INTERNATIONAL TRADE selling products abroad the process of selling goods to other countries. Exporting provides access to nondomestic markets and can be coordinated by an export manager. As with all business activities, careful market research needs to be undertaken. This can be conducted by the company itself or through an experienced export agent. Many companies produce goods almost entirely for export. Services also can be exported, but require different delivery mechanisms through subsidiary offices, or local ***franchise*** or ***licensing agreements***.

export-led growth ECONOMICS increase in economy based on exports growth in which a country's main source of income is from its export trade

export license LEGAL government permit allowing exportation of something a government permit allowing goods to be sent to another country for sale

exports INTERNATIONAL TRADE goods sent abroad for sale goods sent to another country to be sold. *See also* ***export***

ex-rights STOCKHOLDING & INVESTMENTS sold without rights for sale without rights such as voting or conversion rights. The term can be applied to transactions such as the purchase of new shares.

ex-rights date MARKETS date of first ex-rights trade the date when a stock first trades ex-rights, with the rights remaining with the seller rather than transferring to the buyer

extendable bond STOCKHOLDING & INVESTMENTS bond whose maturity can be postponed a bond whose maturity can be delayed by either the issuer or the holder

extendable note STOCKHOLDING & INVESTMENTS note whose maturity can be postponed a note whose maturity can be delayed by either the issuer or the holder

extended credit FINANCE **1.** credit with long repayment terms credit that allows the borrower a long time before payment is required **2.** long repayment term offered by US Federal Reserve in the United States, an extra long period of credit offered to commercial banks by the Federal Reserve

extended fund facility ECONOMICS time allowance for repaying IMF a credit facility operated by the ***International Monetary Fund*** that allows a country up to eight years to repay money it has borrowed from the fund

Extensible Business Reporting Language FINANCE *see* ***XBRL***

extension GENERAL MANAGEMENT extra time granted for something an additional period of time allowed for something, for example, the repayment of a debt or the filing of a tax return

external account BANKING account of overseas resident in UK bank an account held at a United Kingdom-based bank by a customer who is an overseas resident

external audit ACCOUNTING periodic independent audit of firm's accounts a periodic examination of the books of account and records of an entity conducted by an independent third party (an auditor) to ensure that they have been properly maintained; are accurate and comply with established concepts, principles, and accounting standards; and give a true and fair view of the financial state of the entity. *See also* ***internal audit***

external communication GENERAL MANAGEMENT informal exchange of information the exchange of information and messages between an organization and other organizations, groups, or individuals outside its formal structure. The goals of external communication are to facilitate cooperation with groups such as suppliers, investors, and stockholders, and to present a favorable image of an organization and its products or services to potential and actual customers and to society at large. A variety of channels may be used for external communication, including face-to-face meetings, print or broadcast media, and electronic communication technologies such as the Internet. External communication includes the fields of PR, media relations, advertising, and marketing management.

external debt ECONOMICS country's debts to nonresidents the part of a country's debt that is owed to creditors who are not residents of the country

external finance FINANCE investors' money money that a company obtains from investors, for example, by loans or by issuing stock

external funds FINANCE third-party money money that a business obtains from a third party rather than from its own resources

external growth BUSINESS growth as result of joining with another firm business growth as a result of a merger, a takeover, or through a partnership with another organization

external market INTERNATIONAL TRADE international market for securities issued outside single country a securities market in which securities issued outside the jurisdiction of any one country are offered simultaneously to investors in a number of countries

external trade INTERNATIONAL TRADE trade with other countries commercial activity carried out with foreign countries. *See also* ***internal trade, crossborder trade***

extraordinary general meeting CORPORATE GOVERNANCE general meeting other than regular annual meeting any general meeting of an organization other than the ***AGM annual meeting***. Directors can usually call an extraordinary general meeting at their discretion, as can company members who either hold not less than 10% of the paid-up voting shares, or who represent not less than 10% of the voting rights. Directors are obliged to call an EGM if there is a substantial loss of capital. Fourteen days' written notice must be given, or 21 days' written notice if a special resolution is to be proposed. Only special business can be transacted at the meeting, the general nature of which must be specified in the convening notice. *Abbr* ***EGM***

extraordinary item ACCOUNTING exceptional inclusion in firm's accounts an item, such as an acquisition or a sale of assets,that is included in a company's accounts but is not likely to occur again. These items are not taken into account when a company's ***operating profit*** is calculated.

extraordinary resolution CORPORATE GOVERNANCE vote held on exceptional issue in the United Kingdom, an exceptional issue that is put to the vote at a company's general meeting, for example, a change to the company's articles of association, requiring 14 days' notice

extrapolate STATISTICS estimate value beyond set of known values to estimate from a set of values that lies beyond the range of the data collected

extreme value STATISTICS smallest or largest values in statistical study either of the smallest or largest variate values in a sample of observations from a statistical study

EZ *abbr* FINANCE, BUSINESS ***enterprise zone***

F

face value **1.** FINANCE amount on banknote the amount printed on a banknote, showing its value **2.** STOCKHOLDING & INVESTMENTS value displayed the value shown on a ***financial instrument*** such as bonds or stocks, often different than the actual value

facilitation HR & PERSONNEL making it easier for others to do something the process of helping groups, or individuals, to learn, find a solution, or reach a consensus, without imposing or dictating an outcome.

Facilitation works to empower individuals or groups to learn for themselves or find their own answers to problems without control or manipulation. Facilitators need good communication skills, including listening, questioning, and reflecting. Facilitation is used in a variety of contexts including training, conflict resolution, and negotiation.

facility FINANCE total credit offered the total amount of credit that a lender will allow a borrower under a specific agreement

facility fee FINANCE charge for arranging credit a charge made by a lender to a borrower for arranging credit facilities

facility takeover *UK* FRAUD type of identity theft a type of fraud in which a person impersonates another person and falsely claims a change of address in order to gain access to and control that person's financial accounts

factor 1. FINANCE collector of corporate debt a business that purchases or lends money on ***accounts receivable*** based on an evaluation of the ***creditworthiness*** of prospective customers of the business, for a small percentage of the debt amount **2.** STATISTICS statistical variable in a statistical study, a variable such as one affecting the price of an asset which can be isolated and modeled separately

factor analysis STATISTICS study of relationships between variables the examination of the relationships existing between the variables observed in a statistical study

factor four OPERATIONS & PRODUCTION quadrupling productivity to reduce waste a concept of environmentally friendly production based on increasing the productivity of resources by a factor of four to reduce waste

factoring FINANCE **1.** transferring of foreign debts the practice of transferring title to foreign ***accounts receivable*** to a third-party ***factor*** that assumes responsibility for collections, administrative services, and any other services requested. Major exporters use factoring as a way of reducing exchange rate risk. The fee for this service is a percentage of the value of the receivables, anywhere from 5% to 10% or higher, depending on the currencies involved. Companies often include this percentage in selling prices to recoup the cost. **2.** selling firm's debts at discount the sale of ***accounts receivable*** to a third party (the ***factor***) at a discount, in return for cash. A factoring service may be "with recourse," in which case the supplier takes the risk of the debt not being paid, or "without recourse," when the factor takes the risk. *See also* ***invoice discounting*** **3.** buying of debts the practice of buying up a business's ***accounts receivable***, providing it with ***working capital***

factoring charges FINANCE cost of selling debts to third party the cost of selling ***accounts receivable*** to an agent for a commission

factor market ECONOMICS place where capital or labor is traded a market in which ***factors of production*** are bought and sold, for example, the capital market or the labor market

factors of production OPERATIONS & PRODUCTION land, labor, and capital the three things needed to produce a product: land, labor, and capital

factory OPERATIONS & PRODUCTION place for manufacturing goods a building or set of buildings housing workers and equipment for the sole purpose of manufacturing goods, often on a large scale

factory gate price OPERATIONS & PRODUCTION manufacturing cost of goods the actual cost of manufacturing goods before any additional charges are added to give a profit. The factory gate price includes direct costs such as labor, raw materials, and energy, and indirect costs such as interest on loans, plant maintenance, or rent.

failure GENERAL MANAGEMENT = ***business failure***

Failure Mode and Effects Analysis RISK way of identifying and dealing with potential failures a method for identifying and ranking the seriousness of ways in which a product, process, or service could fail, and finding ways in which to minimize the risk of those potential failures. *Abbr* ***FMEA***

fair dealing MARKETS legal trading in stock the buying and selling of stock in a legal and open manner

fair market value *or* **fair value** FINANCE asset's or liability's worth in arm's length transaction the amount for which an asset or liability could be exchanged in an arm's length transaction between informed and willing parties, other than in a forced or liquidation sale.

fair price OPERATIONS & PRODUCTION good price for both buyer and seller a price that is favorable for both buyer and seller

fair trade INTERNATIONAL TRADE agreement waiving duties on some imports an international business system by which countries agree not to charge import duties on some items imported from their trading partners

fair value accounting *UK* ACCOUNTING = ***historical cost accounting***

fair wear and tear OPERATIONS & PRODUCTION, INSURANCE damage caused by normal use the acceptable and expected level of damage caused by normal use

fallen angel STOCKHOLDING & INVESTMENTS highly rated security whose value has dropped a stock that was once very desirable but has now dropped in value (*slang*)

falling knife STOCKHOLDING & INVESTMENTS stock whose price has taken steep drop a stock whose price has fallen at a rapid rate over a short time period

false accounting ACCOUNTING, FRAUD criminal accounting practices the criminal offense of changing, destroying, or hiding accounting records for a dishonest purpose

false market MARKETS, FRAUD market influenced by illegal manipulation of stock prices a market in stocks caused by persons or companies conspiring to buy or sell and so influence the stock price to their advantage

falsification FRAUD making false accounting entries the activity of making false entries in financial accounts

family business BUSINESS business owned and run by family a ***small or medium-sized business*** that is controlled and operated by members of a family. It may be organized as a sole proprietorship, partnership, corporation, or limited liability company

family of funds STOCKHOLDING & INVESTMENTS related group of mutual funds a selection of mutual funds with different objectives that is offered by one investment company, allowing investors to easily transfer money from one fund to another with little cost. *Also called* ***fund family***

Fannie Mae MORTGAGES US institution financing housing the largest source of financing for housing in the United States, which funds mortgages by issuing debt securities in US and international securities markets. Fannie Mae was created in 1938 as a federal agency and chartered in 1968 by the US Congress as a stockholder-owned private company. On September 7, 2008, after Fannie Mae reported billions of dollars in losses from subprime loans, its government regulatory agency, the Federal Housing Finance Agency put Fannie Mae under its conservatorship. In addition, the US Treasury agreed to provide up to $100 billion of capital as needed to ensure Fannie Mae's continued operation. *Full form* ***Federal National Mortgage Association***. *See also* ***Freddie Mac***

FAQ E-COMMERCE commonest questions about something FAQ pages are often included on websites to provide first-time visitors with answers to the most likely questions they may have. FAQ pages are also used in newsgroups and software applications. *Full form* ***frequently asked question***

far month MARKETS most distant month in futures trading the latest month for which there is a futures contract for a particular commodity. *See also* ***nearby month***

FAS ACCOUNTING US accounting standards in the United States, the standards of financial reporting and accounting established by the FASB. *Full form* ***Financial Accounting Standards***

FASB ACCOUNTING US accounting organization in the United States, an institution responsible for establishing the standards of financial reporting and accounting for companies in the private sector. The ***Securities and Exchange Commission*** performs a comparable role for public companies. *Full form* ***Financial Accounting Standards Board***

FASTER MARKETS New Zealand Stock Exchange's computerized trading system a computer-based clearing, settlement, registration, and information system operated by the New Zealand Stock Exchange. *Full form* ***Fully Automated Screen Trading and Electronic Registration***

fast track GENERAL MANAGEMENT route providing rapid results a rapid route to success or advancement. The fast track involves competition and a race to get ahead, and is associated with high ambition and great activity. An employee can be on a fast track, for example, to promotion, but an activity also can be said to take the fast track, for example, to rapid product development.

fat cat BUSINESS highly paid chief executive a derogatory term used to describe a chief executive of a large company or organization who secures extremely large pay, pension, and termination packages, and may receive large bonuses

FCA ACCOUNTING ICAEW Fellow Chartered Accountant a Fellow (long-term member) of the Institute of Chartered Accountants in England and Wales

FCCA ACCOUNTING ACCA Fellow, Chartered Certified Accountant a Fellow (long-term member) of the Association of Chartered Certified Accountants

FCM *abbr* STOCKHOLDING & INVESTMENTS ***futures commission merchant***

FCMA ACCOUNTING CIMA Fellow Chartered Management Accountant a Fellow (long-term member) of the Chartered Institute of Management Accountants

FDI *abbr* STOCKHOLDING & INVESTMENTS ***foreign direct investment***

FDIC *abbr* INSURANCE ***Federal Deposit Insurance Corporation***

feasibility study GENERAL MANAGEMENT assessment of ease of doing something an investigation into a proposed plan or project to determine whether and how it can be successfully and profitably carried out. Frequently used in ***project management***, a feasibility study may examine alternative methods of reaching objectives or be used to define or redefine the proposed project. The information gathered must be sufficient to make a decision on whether to go ahead with the project, or to enable an investor to decide whether to commit finances to it. This will usually require analysis of technical, financial, and market issues, including an estimate of resources required in terms of materials, time, personnel, and finance, and the expected return on investment.

Fed BANKING = ***Federal Reserve***

Federal Deposit Insurance Corporation INSURANCE US agency insuring deposits in commercial banks the US federal agency that manages insurance funds that insure deposits in commercial banks and in savings and loans associations. *Abbr* ***FDIC***

Federal Funds FINANCE US reserves deposits held in reserve at the Federal Reserve by the US banks. The *Federal Funds rate*, the rate that the Federal Reserve charges banks for borrowing reserves, is the key US monetary policy rate.

Federal Home Loan Mortgage Corporation MORTGAGES, RISK *see* ***Freddie Mac***

federal income tax TAX deductions from employees' pay funding US government in the United States, money deducted from employees' salaries in order to fund Federal services and projects

Federal Insurance Contributions Act HR & PERSONNEL *see* ***FICA***

Federal National Mortgage Association MORTGAGES, RISK *see* ***Fannie Mae***

Federal Open Market Committee ECONOMICS committee that oversees US monetary policy the 12-member committee of the ***Federal Reserve Board*** that meets eight times a year to determine US monetary policy by setting interest rates or by buying and selling government securities. *Abbr* ***FOMC***

federal organization GENERAL MANAGEMENT combining of subsidiaries for benefits of scale a form of organization structure in which subsidiaries federate to gain benefits of scale. In a federal organization, the leader provides coordination and vision, and initiatives are generated from the component subsidiary organizations. Federal organization is one of the many ways in which organizations restructure in order to deal with the dilemmas of power and control. Federal organization offers an enabling framework for autonomy to release corporate energy for people to do things in their own way, provided that it is in the common interest, and for people to be well informed so as to be able to interpret that common interest. Royal Dutch Shell, Unilever, and ABB are exemplars of federalism.

Federal Reserve BANKING system of federal government control of US banks the central banking system of the United States, founded in 1913 by an Act of Congress. The board of governors, made up of seven members, is based in Washington, DC, and 12 Reserve Banks are located in major cities across the United States. It regulates money supply, prints money, fixes the discount rate, and issues bonds for government debt. *Also called* ***Federal Reserve System, Fed***

Federal Reserve bank BANKING major US bank any of the 12 banks that are members of the US ***Federal Reserve***

Federal Reserve Board BANKING supervisory board of the US Federal Reserve the seven-member Board of Governors, appointed by the President of the United States and confirmed by the Senate, that supervises the ***Federal Reserve*** and formulates monetary policy. Appointees to the Board of Governors serve for 14 years. *Abbr* ***FRB***

Federal Reserve note CURRENCY & EXCHANGE US paper money a piece of paper money issued by the Federal Reserve Bank and approved as the legal tender of the United States

Federal Reserve System BANKING = ***Federal Reserve***

Federation of Small Businesses BUSINESS organization representing UK small businesses in the United Kingdom, a not-for-profit membership organization representing the interests of small businesses. The FSB was established in 1974 and has over 174,000 members. *Abbr* ***FSB***

Fed funds rate BANKING interest rate on interbank loans in Federal Reserve the rate charged by US banks for lending money deposited with the ***Federal Reserve*** to other banks

Fed pass BANKING US Federal Reserve's easing of credit the addition of reserves to the ***Federal Reserve*** in order to increase availability of credit

Fedwire BANKING US electronic transfer system the US ***Federal Reserve***'s electronic system for transferring funds

fee FINANCE payment to professional for services money paid for work carried out by a professional person such as an accountant

feedback GENERAL MANAGEMENT information about performance to facilitate improvement the communication of responses and reactions to proposals and changes, or of the findings of appraisals of performance, with the goal of enabling improvements to be made. Feedback can be either positive or negative.

feedback control GENERAL MANAGEMENT identification and regulation of outputs the measurement of differences between planned outputs and actual outputs achieved, and the modification of subsequent action and/or plans to achieve future required results

feeding frenzy MARKETS frantic buying in a financial market, a period of extremely active buying (*slang*)

fee work FINANCE work done for organization by non-employees work on a project carried out by independent workers or contractors, rather than employees of an organization

fempreneur BUSINESS independent businesswoman = ***lipstick entrepreneur***

femterprise BUSINESS firm with woman owner a business that has been started or is owned by a woman

FHLMC MORTGAGES *see* ***Freddie Mac***

fiat money FINANCE government-recognized money coins or banknotes that have little intrinsic value in the material of which they are made but that are recognized by a government or other issuing authority, such as the European Central Bank, as having value

FICA HR & PERSONNEL in US money deducted for Social Security and Medicare in the United States, a federal law that requires employers to deduct a percentage of their employees' income for payment into the trust fund that provides Social Security and Medicare benefits. Employers and employees are each responsible for half the payment, while self-employed individuals are responsible for the entire payment but are allowed a tax deduction for half. *Full form* ***Federal Insurance Contributions Act***

FICO score FINANCE US system for assessing credit rating a score used by lenders in the United States to assess a person's ability to pay back a loan, based on the person's payment history, current debt, types of credit used, length of credit history, and new credit. Scores range from 300 to 850. The system was devised by the Fair Isaac Corporation (FICO).

fictitious assets ACCOUNTING book assets with no resale value assets such as pre-payments that do not have a resale value but are entered as assets on a company's ***balance sheet***

FID *abbr* TAX ***Financial Institutions Duty***

fiduciary LEGAL **1.** person acting for another a person who controls property or acts on behalf of or for the benefit of another person **2.** on behalf of another controlled or managed for another person

fiduciary deposit BANKING bank-managed deposit a bank deposit that is managed for the depositor by the bank

field research MARKETING direct contact with customers to gain information the collection of data directly from contact with customers and potential customers through surveys, interviews, and other forms of ***market research***

field trial MARKETING test of product in actual use a limited pilot test of a product under real conditions. A field trial is undertaken to test the physical or engineering properties of a product in order to identify and iron out any technical shortcomings prior to marketing. Customers may be involved in some trials, for example, in testing a new laundry detergent. Field trials should not be confused with test marketing, which is used to determine the likely market for, and likely consumer response to, a new product or service.

field work MARKETING work in real environment practical work, study, or research carried out in the real world away from the desk. In a marketing context, field work forms primary ***market research*** and involves obtaining customers' views and opinions on a face-to-face basis or through mail questionnaires or telephone surveys.

FIFO OPERATIONS & PRODUCTION inventory control system a method of inventory management in which the stock of a given product first placed in store is used before more recently produced or acquired goods or materials. *Full form* ***first in first out***

FIF Tax *abbr* TAX ***Foreign Investment Funds Tax***

figures ACCOUNTING financial results a company's financial results calculated for a particular period of time

filing date *UK* TAX = ***filing deadline***

filing deadline *US* TAX due date for income tax returns the date by which income tax returns must be filed with the relevant taxation authority. *UK term* ***filing date***

fill STOCKHOLDING & INVESTMENTS buy or sell an investment upon client's order to carry out a client's instructions to buy or sell a security or commodity

filter GENERAL MANAGEMENT extracting useful information from large amounts of data a process for analyzing large amounts of incoming information to identify any material that might be of interest to an organization

FIMBRA *abbr* REGULATION & COMPLIANCE ***Financial Intermediaries, Managers and Brokers Regulatory Association***

final average monthly salary PENSIONS earnings on which most US pensions are based the earnings on which most defined benefit pensions are based. *UK term* ***pensionable earnings***

final closing date MERGERS & ACQUISITIONS final day for acceptance of takeover the last date for the acceptance of a ***takeover bid***, when the bidder has to announce how many stockholders have accepted the offer

final demand FINANCE last reminder before legal action of debt a last reminder from a supplier to a customer to pay an outstanding debt. Suppliers often begin legal proceedings if a final demand is ignored.

final discharge FINANCE last debt payment the final payment on the amount outstanding on a debt

final dividend STOCKHOLDING & INVESTMENTS year-end dividend payment the ***dividend*** paid at the end of a year's trading. The final dividend must be approved by a company's stockholders.

final salary pension PENSIONS in UK, benefit on retirement based on earnings in the United Kingdom, a retirement benefit regularly paid to employees or their survivors by an employer, based on salary at or near retirement. Employers set up pension plans by depositing an amount of money in the employee's name into a pension fund, which may be contributed to by the employer or both the employer and the employee. The fund is invested and benefits are paid to the employee from the fund upon retirement. Either the employer or employee may assume the risk of investment failure depending upon the type of pension.

final sale *US* FINANCE sale of nonreturnable items a sale that does not allow the purchaser to return the goods. *UK term* ***firm sale***

finance FINANCE **1.** *UK* = ***financing*** **2.** supply money for business or project to provide an amount of money for a particular purpose. *See also* ***fund***

Finance Act TAX legislation granting British government power of taxation an annual Act of the British Parliament that gives the government the power to obtain money from taxes as proposed in the ***Budget***

Finance and Leasing Association FINANCE financing and leasing firms' UK organization in the United Kingdom, an organization representing firms engaged in business financing and the leasing of equipment and cars

finance bill TAX public-spending bill a proposal for legislation giving a government the power to obtain money from taxes

finance company FINANCE business lending money for purchases a business that lends money to people or companies against ***collateral***, especially to make purchases of some kind. *UK term* ***finance house***

finance house *UK* FINANCE = ***finance company***

finance lease *UK* FINANCE = ***capital lease***

finance market MARKETS = ***money market***

finances FINANCE money available for spending the financial status of a person or organization

financial FINANCE of finance relating to the management of money

financial accountant TREASURY MANAGEMENT UK accountant acting as adviser or financial director a qualified accountant, a member of the Institute of Financial Accountants, who advises on accounting matters or who works as the financial director of a company

financial accounting **1.** TREASURY MANAGEMENT financial reports for investors and external parties the form of accounting in which financial reports are produced to provide investors or others outside a company with information on a company's financial status. *See also* ***management accounting*** **2.** ACCOUNTING process of producing financial statements the process of classifying and recording a company's transactions and presenting them in the form of profit and loss accounts, balance sheets, and cash flow statements, for a given ***accounting period***

Financial Accounting Standards ACCOUNTING *see* ***FAS***

Financial Accounting Standards Board ACCOUNTING *see* ***FASB***

financial adviser FINANCE investment adviser somebody whose job is to give advice about investments

financial aid FINANCE money provided to help somebody or something monetary assistance given to an individual, organization, or nation. International financial aid, from one country to another, is often used to fund educational, health-related, or other humanitarian activities.

financial analyst STOCKHOLDING & INVESTMENTS = ***investment analyst***

financial capital FINANCE funds for buying physical assets funds that can be used for the purchase of assets such as buildings and equipment. *See also* ***real capital***

financial control TREASURY MANAGEMENT management of firm's finances the policies and procedures established by an organization for managing, documenting, and reporting its financial transactions

financial correspondent FINANCE reporter who covers money matters a reporter who writes articles on money matters or reports on them on television or radio

financial distress FINANCE situation close to bankruptcy the condition of being in severe difficulties over money, especially being close to ***bankruptcy***

financial economies of scale FINANCE benefits gained by increasing scale of activity financial advantages gained by being able to do things on a large scale

financial engineering STOCKHOLDING & INVESTMENTS converting or creating financial instruments the conversion of one form of financial instrument into another, such as the swap of a fixed-rate instrument for a floating-rate one, or the creation of a new type of financial instrument – **financial engineer**

financial futures *or* **financial futures contract** MARKETS contract to purchase financial instrument for future delivery a contract for the purchase of a specific ***basket of securities***, such as interest rates, exchange rates, share prices, or indices, for delivery at a date in the future. *Also called* ***financials***

financial futures market MARKETS market in financial instruments for future delivery the market in ***basket of securities***, such as interest rates, exchange rates, share prices, or indices, for delivery at a date in the future

financial incentive scheme FINANCE in UK, money rewarding improved performance in the United Kingdom, a program offering employees a cash bonus, share options or other monetary reward for improved commitment and performance and as a means of motivation. *See also* ***non-financial incentive scheme***

financial institution FINANCE organization investing large sums of money an organization, such as a bank, savings and loan, pension fund, or insurance company, that invests large amounts of money in securities

Financial Institutions Duty TAX Australian tax on money deposited in financial institutions a tax on monies paid into financial institutions imposed by all state governments in Australia except for Queensland. Financial institutions usually pass the tax on to customers. *Abbr* ***FID***

financial instrument STOCKHOLDING & INVESTMENTS contract that is evidence of financial transaction any contract that gives rise to both a financial asset of one entity and a financial liability or equity instrument of another entity. Financial instruments include both primary financial instruments such as bonds, currency, and stocks, and derivative financial instruments, whose value derives from the underlying assets.

Financial Intermediaries, Managers and Brokers Regulatory Association REGULATION & COMPLIANCE former UK financial regulator a former UK financial regulatory authority, now incorporated into the ***Financial Services Authority***. *Abbr* ***FIMBRA***

financial intermediary FINANCE financial institution handling deposits and/or loans an institution that accepts deposits or loans from individuals and lends money to clients. Banks, ***savings and loan associations***, and finance companies are all financial intermediaries.

financial leverage FINANCE relationship between firm's borrowings and stockholders' funds the relationship between a company's borrowings (which includes both prior charge capital and long-term debt) and its stockholders' funds (common share capital plus reserves). Calculations can be made in a number of ways, and may be based on capital values or on earnings/interest relationships. Overdrafts and interest paid thereon may also be included:

Profit before interest and tax / Profit before tax

shows the effect of interest on the operating profit.

Profit before interest and tax / Interest expense

shows the number of times that profit will cover interest expense.

Total long-term debt / (Shareholders' funds + long-term debt)

shows the proportion of long-term financing which is being supplied by debt.

Total long-term debt / Total assets

a measure of the capacity to redeem debt obligations by the sale of assets.

(Operating cash flows – Taxation paid – Returns on investment and servicing of finance) / Repayments of debt due within one year

measures ability to redeem debt.

A company with a high proportion of prior charge capital to shareholders' funds is highly leveraged, and is lowly or lightly leveraged if the reverse situation applies.

financial market MARKETS market for buying and selling financial instruments a market in which financial instruments are traded. The financial markets are stock exchanges, commodity exchanges, bond markets, and the foreign exchange market.

financial obligation FINANCE something you must pay a sum of money that you are committed to pay, especially a debt. *See also* ***collateralized debt obligation***

financial obligations FINANCE things you must spend money on things that you must use your money to pay for, such as rent, household expenses, dependent family members, etc.

Financial Ombudsman REGULATION & COMPLIANCE UK organization handling complaints against financial institutions in the United Kingdom, an organization responsible for investigating and resolving complaints involving money from members of the public against a company, institution, or other organization. The Ombudsman is not a governmental body, but it does operate under an Act of Parliament in the form of the Financial Services and Markets Act 2000.

financial performance FINANCE firm's ability to generate revenue a measure of a company's ability to generate income over a given period of time

financial planner FINANCE somebody giving advice about money a professional investment adviser who analyzes a person's financial situation and goals and prepares a plan to meet those goals. *See also* ***independent financial adviser***

financial planning FINANCE money management for future the activity of producing strategies for the acquisition of funds to finance activities and meet established goals

Financial Planning Association of Australia FINANCE Australian organization for financial planners a national organization representing companies and individuals working in the Australian financial planning industry. Established in 1992, the Association is responsible for monitoring standards among its members. *Abbr* ***FPA***

financial position FINANCE value of firm's assets and liabilities the amount of money that a person or organization has in terms of assets and liabilities

financial pyramid STOCKHOLDING & INVESTMENTS, RISK investment pattern tapering from safe to risky an investment strategy, typically having four levels of risk. The first and largest percentage of assets are in safe, liquid investments; the second, in investments that provide income and long-term growth; the third, in riskier investments with a chance of greater return; and the fourth and smallest percentage, in the riskiest investments with the chance of greatest return.

financial report ACCOUNTING document detailing firm's financial position a document that gives the financial position of a company or other organization

Financial Reporting Council REGULATION & COMPLIANCE UK regulator for corporate reporting in the United Kingdom, an independent regulator responsible for setting standards for corporate reporting and actuarial practice, as well as monitoring and enforcing accounting and auditing standards. They also oversee the regulatory activities of the professional accounting bodies and operate independent disciplinary arrangements for public interest cases involving accountants and actuaries. *Abbr* ***FRC***

Financial Reporting Review Panel ACCOUNTING UK group for examining questionable accounting practices in the United Kingdom, a review panel established to examine contentious departures from accounting standards by large companies. It is a subsidiary body of the ***Financial Reporting Council***.

Financial Reporting Standards Board ACCOUNTING New Zealand accounting organization in New Zealand, an organization that is responsible for setting and monitoring accounting standards. *Abbr* ***FRSB***

financial resources FINANCE money available for spending the money that is available for a person or organization to spend

financial review FINANCE examination of organization's finances an examination of the state of an organization's finances

financial risk FINANCE, RISK investors' chance of loss the possibility of financial loss in an investment or speculation

financials MARKETS = ***financial futures***

Financial Services Act REGULATION & COMPLIANCE UK legislation regulating providers of financial services in the United Kingdom, an Act of Parliament that regulates the offering of financial services to the general public and to private investors

Financial Services Authority REGULATION & COMPLIANCE UK organization overseeing financial system in the United Kingdom, an independent non-governmental organization formed in 1997 following reforms in the regulation of financial services. Banking and investment services supervision was merged into the remit of the previous regulator, the ***Securities and Investments Board***, which then changed its name to become the Financial Services Authority. The FSA's four statutory objectives were specified by the Financial Services and Markets Act 2000: maintaining market confidence; increasing public knowledge of the finance system; ensuring appropriate protection for consumers; and reducing financial crime. *Abbr* ***FSA***. *Also called* ***City watchdog***

Financial Services Compensation scheme FINANCE fund compensating customers of insolvent UK financial firm in the United Kingdom, an independent organization set up by law to pay compensation to customers who have made claims against an authorized financial services firm in the event that the firm is unable, or likely to be unable, to pay the claims

financial services industry FINANCE financial institutions dealing in money management the business activity of the financial institutions that offer money management services such as banking, investment, brokerage, and insurance

financial statements ACCOUNTING documents reporting company's financial performance summaries of accounts to provide information for interested parties. The most important financial statements are the balance sheet, income statement, statement of cash flows, and the shareholders' equity statement. *See also* ***annual report***

financial supermarket FINANCE firm providing many different financial services a company that offers a variety of financial services. For example, a bank may offer loans, mortgages, retirement plans, and insurance alongside its existing range of normal banking services.

Financial Times FINANCE British financial newspaper a respected British financial daily newspaper, printed in 23 cities across the world and available in 140 countries, as well as online. *Abbr* ***FT***

Financial Times Index *or* **Financial Times Ordinary Index** MARKETS UK market index of thirty blue chip companies an index based on the market prices of thirty ***blue chip*** companies. This index is the oldest of the Financial Times indices, and is now considered too narrow to have much relevance.

financial year *UK* **1.** ACCOUNTING = ***fiscal year*** **2.** TAX for UK corporations, April 1 to March 31 in the United Kingdom, for corporation tax purposes, the period from 1 April of a given year to 31 March of the following year

financier FINANCE somebody who provides financing a person who specializes in the provision of financing to other people or organizations

financing *US* FINANCE money required to pay for something the money needed by an individual or company to pay for something, for example, a project or inventory. *UK term* ***finance***

financing gap 1. FINANCE difference between money available and money needed a shortfall between the funds available and the funds needed for a project. For example, a company planning expansion is able to finance some of this activity from internally generated cash and some from existing finance agreements but any shortfall requires the raising of new funds. **2.** ECONOMICS funding shortfall from canceling poorer countries' debts a gap in funding for institutions such as the ***International Monetary Fund*** caused by canceling the debts of poorer countries such as those in West Africa

financing vehicle FINANCE product providing funds for activity a method or product used to provide the funds for an activity

finder's fee FINANCE fee for finding new client a fee paid to somebody who finds a client for another person or company, for example, somebody who introduces a new client to a brokerage firm

fine-tuning ECONOMICS making small changes to improve economic position the process of making small adjustments in areas such as interest rates, tax bands, or the money supply, to improve a nation's economy

finish MARKETS end of stock trading for day the end of a day's trading on a stock exchange

finished goods OPERATIONS & PRODUCTION items ready for sale completed goods that are available for distribution or sale to customers

finite capacity plan OPERATIONS & PRODUCTION plan for resource requirements a plan produced where ***capacity requirements planning*** covers capacity requirements, enabling ***loading*** at each workstation to be smoothed and determining the need for additional resources. *See also* ***capacity requirements planning***

finite population STATISTICS fixed-size group a statistical population that has a limited size

FIRB *abbr* REGULATION & COMPLIANCE ***Foreign Investment Review Board***

fire sale 1. FINANCE sale of anything at a large discount a sale of anything at a very low price, usually because the seller is facing ***bankruptcy*** **2.** OPERATIONS & PRODUCTION sale of fire-damaged goods a sale of goods that have been damaged during a fire

firm BUSINESS **1.** company a business or company. This wide sense is the one in which the word is used in this dictionary. **2.** partnership a business run by ***partners***

firm order MARKETS order to broker to sell or buy an order to a broker to sell or buy a security on a specific date or at a specific price

firm quote MARKETS bid to trade with time limit a bid to buy or offer to sell a security that a ***market maker*** is obligated to meet within a specified period of time

firm sale *UK* FINANCE = ***final sale***

first call MARKETS firm processing earnings forecasts a company that gathers and reports brokerage analysts' earnings forecasts for use by brokers and investors in making investment recommendations and decisions

first in first out OPERATIONS & PRODUCTION *see* ***FIFO***

first mover MARKETING innovating firm the company that first introduces a new type of product or service to a market. Those organizations that follow a first mover to market are known as *followers* or *laggards*– terms that also describe companies that are not the recognized leaders in a sector.

first mover advantage GENERAL MANAGEMENT advantage of being first with new product the benefit produced by being the first to enter a market with a new product or service. First mover advantages include becoming a market leader in a new area; establishing a new leading ***brand***; being able to charge a premium until competitor products appear; enhanced reputation, design, and copyright protection; and possibly setting an industry standard to which other competitors may have to aspire. Disadvantages include cheaper, and possibly better, *follower* products; the possibility of having to reduce prices or continuously having to add value to stay ahead; first mover development costs; a possible shift in consumer tastes away from the product; obsolescence; and a follower product being accepted as the industry standard.

first quarter ACCOUNTING first part of fiscal year the period of three months from January to the end of March, or the period of three months at the start of any fiscal year. *Abbr* ***Q1***

first-round financing FINANCE initial funding the first infusion of capital into a project

fiscal TAX relating to finance, especially to tax relating to financial matters, especially in respect of governmental collection, use, and regulation of money through taxation

fiscal agent BANKING agent in finance matters a bank or trust that takes over the fiscal responsibilities of another party

fiscal balance ECONOMICS balance of income and expenditure the extent to which government receipts differ from government outlay. If outlays exceed receipts then the fiscal balance is negative or in deficit; if receipts exceed outlays then the balance is positive or in surplus.

fiscal drag *UK* TAX increase in tax paid as inflation rises the effect that inflation has on taxation in that, as earnings rise, the amount of tax collected increases without a rise in tax rates

fiscal measures TAX tax changes introduced for economic reasons tax changes made by a government to improve the working of the economy

fiscal policy ECONOMICS, TAX government's methods for managing economy the central government's policy on lowering or raising taxation or increasing or decreasing public expenditure in order to stimulate or depress ***aggregate demand***

fiscal year *US* ACCOUNTING, TAX firm's 12-month accounting period a twelve-month period used by a company for accounting and tax purposes. A fiscal year is not necessarily the same as a calendar year.
UK term ***financial year****. Abbr* ***FY***

fishbone chart GENERAL MANAGEMENT diagram for investigation of causes of problems a diagram that is used to identify and categorize the possible causes of problems. Within such a chart, which resembles the shape of the skeleton of a fish, the topic or problem to be discussed is placed in a box at the right-hand side that corresponds to the fish's head, and the major items to be investigated are shown as branches at an angle to the horizontal spine. Questions are asked to identify possible causes of problems in each area and the results are added to the diagram as additional layers of branches. This ensures that all aspects of the problem are considered systematically. The fishbone chart is also known as a ***cause and effect diagram***. It is frequently used in brainstorming and problem solving.

fixation MARKETS setting of commodity's price on options market the act by a government of stating the price of a commodity on an options market

fixed annuity INSURANCE *see* ***annuity***

fixed asset ACCOUNTING asset that firm keeps long-term a long-term business asset such as a machine or building that will not usually be traded

fixed assets register ACCOUNTING register of tangible assets a record of individual tangible fixed assets belonging to a company or organization

fixed-asset turnover ratio ACCOUNTING measure of how firm uses its assets a measure of the use a business makes of its capital assets. It is calculated by dividing sales by net fixed assets.

fixed capital FINANCE durable assets such as buildings and machinery assets in the form of buildings and machinery, that are long-lasting and can be used repeatedly for production

fixed charge FINANCE creditor's right to specific asset the right of a creditor to a claim on a specific asset, as opposed to a ***floating charge*** that applies to all a company's assets. *Also called* ***specific charge***

fixed cost ACCOUNTING cost that remains fixed when sales fluctuate a cost that does not change according to sales volumes, for example, overhead such as rent or production costs

fixed deduction TAX agreed UK tax deduction for general expenses in the United Kingdom, a deduction agreed by HM Revenue & Customs and a group of employees which covers general expenditure on clothes or tools used in the course of employment

fixed deposit BANKING deposit paying fixed interest over set period a deposit that pays a fixed rate of interest over a defined period

fixed exchange rate CURRENCY & EXCHANGE set rate of exchange between currencies a rate of exchange of one currency against another that cannot fluctuate, and can only be changed by devaluation or revaluation

fixed exchange rate system CURRENCY & EXCHANGE currency exchange system with unchanging rates a system of currency exchange in which there is no change of rate

fixed expenses FINANCE unvarying overhead costs costs that do not vary with different levels of production, for example, rent, staff salaries, and insurance

fixed income FINANCE income that remains unchanged each year income that does not change from year to year, for example, from an annuity

fixed interest FINANCE **1.** with unvarying interest rate used to describe a loan or financial product that has an interest rate that does not go up or down **2.** interest rate that stays the same interest that is paid at a rate that does not vary over a period of time

fixed-interest loan FINANCE loan with unchanging interest rate a loan whose rate of interest stays the same over the whole period of the loan

fixed-interest security STOCKHOLDING & INVESTMENTS investment paying constant interest an investment such as a government bond that produces an amount of interest that does not change with changes in short-term interest rates. *Also called* ***fixed-rate security***

fixed interval re-order system OPERATIONS & PRODUCTION = ***periodic inventory review system***

fixed-price agreement OPERATIONS & PRODUCTION contract setting prices for period of time an agreement whereby a company provides a service or a product at a price that stays the same for the whole period of the agreement

fixed rate FINANCE unchanging interest rate an interest rate for loans that does not change with fluctuating conditions in the market and stays the same for the whole period of the loan

fixed-rate loan FINANCE loan with unchanging interest rate a loan with an interest rate that is set at the beginning of the term and remains the same throughout

fixed-rate mortgage MORTGAGES mortgage with unchanging interest rate a mortgage for which the interest rate on the loan it secures is set at the beginning of the term and remains the same throughout

fixed-rate security STOCKHOLDING & INVESTMENTS = ***fixed-interest security***

fixed scale of charges FINANCE range of standard charges a set of charges that does not vary according to individual circumstances but is applied consistently in all cases of the same kind

fixed yield FINANCE constant percentage return on investment a percentage return on an investment which does not change over a period of time

fixtures and fittings REAL ESTATE items sold along with property the objects in a property that are sold with the property, both those which cannot be removed and those which can. Fixtures and fittings are a category of ***fixed assets***.

flag MARKETS chart pattern that confirms price trend a pattern on a chart showing a period during which securities prices consolidate a previous advance or fall

flat 1. MARKETS steady market price due to low demand used to describe market prices that do not fall or rise, because of low demand **2.** GENERAL MANAGEMENT without hierarchy used to describe a management structure that is not strongly hierarchical

flat rate FINANCE unvarying standard rate a price, payment or interest rate that remains the same regardless of other factors which may change

flat tax TAX tax unrelated to income a tax levied at one unchanging rate regardless of the level of somebody's income. *See also* ***progressive tax***

flat yield STOCKHOLDING & INVESTMENTS interest rate as percentage of fixed-interest security price an interest rate that is a percentage of the price paid for a ***fixed-interest security***

flat yield curve FINANCE graph using unified interest rate for bonds a visual representation of relative interest rates that shows the same interest rates for long-term bonds as for short-term bonds. As investors are assumed to prefer shorter maturities to longer ones, other factors being equal, a flat yield curve is normally assumed to imply that investors can expect lower short-term rates in future.

flexed budget FINANCE budget responsive to changes in trade a budget that changes in response to changes in sales turnover and output

flexible benefit plan HR & PERSONNEL = ***cafeteria plan***

flexible exchange rate system CURRENCY & EXCHANGE currency exchange system with fluctuating rates a system of currency exchange in which rates change from time to time

flexible manufacturing system OPERATIONS & PRODUCTION **1.** various stages of production under central computer control an integrated system of computer-controlled machine tools and transport and handling systems under the control of a larger computer. Flexibility is achieved by having an overall method of control that coordinates the functions of both the machine tools and the handling systems. **2.** computer-controlled system producing variety of parts an integrated, computer-controlled production system that is capable of producing any of a variety of parts, and of switching quickly and economically between them ▶ *Abbr* ***FMS***

flexible spending account HR & PERSONNEL US employee benefit based on voluntary salary deductions in the United States, an employee benefit plan, a type of ***cafeteria plan***, funded by voluntary salary reduction, that the employee may use for specific expenses that are exempt from payroll taxes. *Also called* ***salary reduction plan***

flight of capital FINANCE removal of investment money because of economic uncertainty the rapid movement of investment money out of one country because of lack of confidence in that country's economic future

flight to quality STOCKHOLDING & INVESTMENTS movement of investors to low-risk securities a tendency of investors to buy safe well-established securities when the economic outlook is uncertain

flip 1. BUSINESS new company run for short-term success a startup company that works to build market share quickly and generate short-term personal wealth for its founders through flotation or sell-off **2.** REAL ESTATE develop property for quick profit to buy a property, fix it up, and then resell it in a short period in order to make a profit

float 1. FINANCE delay between presentation of check and actual payment the period between the presentation of a check as payment and the actual payment to the payee or the financial advantage provided by this period to the drawer of a check **2.** FINANCE cash held for small transactions a small cash balance maintained to facilitate low-value cash transactions. Records of these transactions should be maintained as evidence of expenditure, and periodically a float or petty cash balance will be replenished to a predetermined level. **3.** STOCKHOLDING & INVESTMENTS sell stocks or bonds to sell stocks or bonds. *See also* ***new issue***

floater FINANCE variable-rate loan a loan with an interest rate that varies over time

floating asset FINANCE short-term asset replaced by another an asset that it is assumed will be consumed during the company's normal trading cycle and then replaced by the same type of asset

floating capital FINANCE amount of company's money invested in current assets the portion of a company's money that is invested in current assets, as distinct from that invested in ***fixed assets*** or ***capital assets***

floating charge FINANCE charge linked to company's assets overall a charge linked to any of the company's assets in a category, but not to a specific item

floating debenture FINANCE debenture running for lifetime of firm a ***debenture*** secured on all of a company's assets which runs until the company is closed down

floating debt FINANCE loan frequently renewed a borrowing for less than one year that is repeatedly renewed

floating exchange rate CURRENCY & EXCHANGE currency exchange rate that is allowed to vary an exchange rate for a specific currency that can vary according to market demand, and is not fixed by a government

floating rate FINANCE interest rate fluctuating as market fluctuates an interest rate that is not fixed and which changes according to fluctuations in the market

floating-rate note FINANCE, CURRENCY & EXCHANGE Eurocurrency loan with variable interest rate a Eurocurrency loan that is not given at a fixed rate of interest. *Abbr* ***FRN***

floor **1.** FINANCE lower limit a lower limit on an interest rate, price, or the value of an asset **2.** MARKETS = ***trading floor***

floor broker MARKETS = ***pit broker***

floor effect STATISTICS when statistical data groups approach lower limit in a statistical study, the occurrence of clusters of scores near the lower limit of the data

floor limit BANKING limit on credit card sale without bank authorization the highest sale through a credit card that a retailer can accept without having to obtain authorization from the issuing bank

floor price MARKETS lowest possible price the lowest possible price that something can be sold for

floor trader MARKETS exchange member trading for own account a member of an exchange who buys and sells securities mainly for their own account on the ***trading floor*** of an exchange. *Also called* ***competitive trader***

flotation MARKETS funds raised by sale of stock the financing of a company by selling stock in it or a new debt issue, or the offering of stock and bonds for sale on the stock exchange. *See also* ***initial public offering***

flow chart *or* **flow diagram** GENERAL MANAGEMENT diagrammatic representation of stages a graphic representation of the stages in a process or system, or of the steps required to solve a problem. A flow chart is commonly used to represent the sequence of functions in a computer program or to model the movement of materials, money, or people in a complex process. Two primary symbols used in flow charts are the ***process box***, indicating a process or action taking place, and the ***decision lozenge***, indicating the need for a decision.

flow line production *or* **flow production** OPERATIONS & PRODUCTION processing in stages in single direction a production method in which successive operations are carried out on a product in such a way that it moves through the factory in a single direction. Flow line production is most widely used in mass production on production lines. More recently, it has been linked with batch production. Under flow line production, inventory is often kept to the minimum necessary to ensure continued activity. Stoppages and interruptions to the flow indicate a fault, and corrective action can be taken. Assembly line production is an extreme version of flow line production.

flow on BUSINESS pay raise awarded to match another a pay increase awarded to one group of employees as a result of a pay raise awarded to another group working in the same field

flow theory GENERAL MANAGEMENT idea about people's reaction to change a theory of the way in which people become engaged with, or disengaged from, change. Flow theory suggests that people harmonize in change situations, and open, honest, trusting relationships emerge. The theory recognizes the unpredictability and rigidity of human nature when faced with change. *See also* ***change management***

flow trader MARKETS person trading for client a trader in an organization such as an investment bank who buys and sells products for the bank's clients rather than trading aggressively on behalf of the bank itself. *See also* ***proprietary trading***

fluff it and fly it MARKETING make product look good, then sell it to enhance a product's appearance and then put it on the market *(slang)*

FMA *abbr* STOCKHOLDING & INVESTMENTS ***Fund Managers' Association***

FMEA *abbr* RISK ***Failure Mode and Effects Analysis***

FMS *abbr* OPERATIONS & PRODUCTION ***flexible manufacturing system***

FNMA MORTGAGES *see* ***Fannie Mae***

FOB *or* **f.o.b.** *abbr* FINANCE ***free on board*** *(sense 1)*

focus group MARKETING group giving reactions and opinions a carefully selected representative variety of consumers or employees used for the purposes of providing feedback on preferences and responses to a selected range of issues. A focus group usually operates with a facilitator to guide discussion.

folio ACCOUNTING numbered page in account book a page with a number, especially two facing pages in an account book which have the same number

followback survey STATISTICS follow-up check on statistical population a further survey of a statistical population carried out a period of years after an original survey

follower MARKETING firm moving into area created by another a company that follows the first company to introduce a new type of product or service to a market. *See also* ***first mover***

FOMC *abbr* ECONOMICS ***Federal Open Market Committee***

footfall MARKETING how many people walk past store a measure of the number of people who walk past a store

Footsie MARKETS *see* ***FTSE 100 Share Index***

Forbes 500 FINANCE list of largest US public companies a list of the 500 largest public companies in the United States, ranked according to various criteria by *Forbes* magazine

forced sale BUSINESS sale enforced by court order a sale that takes place as the result of a court order or because it represents the only reasonable way for a company or individual to avoid a financial crisis

force field analysis GENERAL MANAGEMENT means of making change more acceptable a technique for promoting change by identifying positive and negative factors and by working to lessen the negative forces while developing the positive ones

force majeure LEGAL incident that contractual parties cannot predict or control something that happens that is out of the control of the parties who have signed a contract, for example, a strike, war, or storm

forecast STATISTICS estimation of value of variable a prediction of the value of a variable in a statistical study

forecast dividend STOCKHOLDING & INVESTMENTS expected year-end dividend a dividend that a company expects to pay at the end of the current trading year. *Also called* ***prospective dividend***

forecasting GENERAL MANAGEMENT estimation or prediction of future the prediction of outcomes, trends, or expected future behavior of a business, industry sector, or the economy through the use of statistics. Forecasting is an ***operational research*** technique used as a basis for management planning and decision making. Common types of forecasting include trend analysis, ***regression analysis***, ***Delphi technique***, ***time series*** analysis, ***correlation***, and ***exponential smoothing***.

foreclose *US* FINANCE acquire mortgaged property when owner defaults to acquire a property because the owner cannot or will not repay money that he or she has borrowed to buy the property. *UK term* ***repossess***

foreclosure *US* FINANCE act of recovering security on unpaid loan the acquisition of property when an owner cannot or will not repay the loan that was taken out to buy the property. *UK term* ***repossession***

foreign bill FINANCE bill of exchange payable only overseas a bill of exchange that is not payable in the country where it is issued

foreign currency CURRENCY & EXCHANGE other country's money the currency or interest-bearing bonds of a foreign country

foreign currency account BANKING, CURRENCY & EXCHANGE bank account operated in foreign currency a bank account in the currency of another country, for example, a dollar account in a bank in the United Kingdom

foreign currency reserves CURRENCY & EXCHANGE foreign money held by government foreign money held by a government to support its own currency and pay its debts. *Also called* ***foreign exchange reserves, international reserves***

foreign debt CURRENCY & EXCHANGE debt owed to other country hard-currency debt owed to a foreign country in payment for goods and services

foreign direct investment STOCKHOLDING & INVESTMENTS investment in firm by foreign company or government investment in a company outside the country of the investor, who sets up subsidiaries or acquires usually about 10% of the stock with voting rights, thus gaining influence in the foreign company's management. *Abbr* ***FDI***

foreign dividend STOCKHOLDING & INVESTMENTS in UK, dividend paid from overseas in the United Kingdom, a dividend paid from another country, possibly subject to special rules under UK tax codes

foreign draft CURRENCY & EXCHANGE check drawn and payable in different countries a check that is drawn in one country and payable in another

foreign equity market MARKETS market equities of overseas companies the market in one country for equities of companies in other countries

foreign exchange CURRENCY & EXCHANGE **1.** foreign currencies currencies and financial instruments used to buy goods abroad or as investments. *Also called* ***forex*** **2.** dealings in foreign currencies dealings in the currencies of other countries, on foreign-exchange markets

foreign exchange broker *or* **foreign exchange dealer** CURRENCY & EXCHANGE trader in foreign currencies a person whose business is to buy and sell foreign currencies

foreign exchange dealing CURRENCY & EXCHANGE trade in foreign currencies the business of buying and selling currencies of other countries

foreign exchange market CURRENCY & EXCHANGE **1.** market for trading foreign currencies a market where people buy and sell foreign currencies **2.** dealings in foreign currencies dealings in the currencies of other countries

foreign exchange option CURRENCY & EXCHANGE contract guaranteeing minimum rate in currency exchange a contract that, for a fee, guarantees a worst-case exchange rate for the future purchase of one currency for another. Unlike a ***forward transaction***, the option does not obligate the buyer to deliver a currency on the settlement date unless the buyer chooses to. These options protect against unfavorable currency movements while preserving the ability to participate in favorable movements.

foreign exchange reserves CURRENCY & EXCHANGE = ***foreign currency reserves***

foreign exchange transfer CURRENCY & EXCHANGE sending of money abroad the process of sending money from one country to another

foreign income dividend STOCKHOLDING & INVESTMENTS dividend from earnings abroad a dividend paid from earnings in countries other than the one in which the investment was made

Foreign Investment Funds Tax TAX Australian tax on offshore investments a tax imposed by the Australian government on ***unrealized capital gains*** made by Australian residents from offshore investments. It was introduced in 1992 to prevent overseas earnings from being taxed at low rates and never brought to Australia. *Abbr* ***FIF Tax***

Foreign Investment Review Board REGULATION & COMPLIANCE Australian institution regulating foreign investment in Australia, a non-statutory body that regulates and advises the federal government on foreign investment. It was established in 1976. *Abbr* ***FIRB***

foreign investments STOCKHOLDING & INVESTMENTS money invested abroad money invested in countries other than your own

foreign money order CURRENCY & EXCHANGE money order for somebody abroad a money order in a foreign currency that is payable to somebody living in a foreign country

foreign reserve CURRENCY & EXCHANGE centrally held foreign currency the currency of other countries held by an organization, especially a country's central bank

foreign subsidiary company BUSINESS *see* ***subsidiary company***

foreign tax credit TAX tax benefit for taxes paid abroad a tax advantage for taxes that are paid to or in another country

forensic accounting **1.** ACCOUNTING, FRAUD accounting that assists in identifying financial fraud an accounting practice that specializes in investigating and presenting expert court testimony concerning crimes involving financial matters **2.** ACCOUNTING reference to accounts to check legality of activities the use of accounting records and documents in order to determine the legality or otherwise of past activities

forex *or* **Forex** CURRENCY & EXCHANGE = ***foreign exchange***

forfaiting INTERNATIONAL TRADE purchase of exporter's goods by third party the purchase of an exporter's goods by a third party at a discount. This party then collects payment from the importer with the shipped goods serving as collateral.

forfeit clause LEGAL contractual clause stating forfeit if contract not fulfilled a clause in a contract which states that goods or a deposit will be taken if the contract is not fulfilled by one of the signers

forfeiture LEGAL punitive loss of property or right loss of property or the right to something, usually because of an unlawful act

form 3 STOCKHOLDING & INVESTMENTS US form for reporting first securities transactions in the United States, a form that must be filed with the Securities and Exchange Commission within 10 days of the first securities transaction by officers, directors, or 10% shareholders in a company reporting their holdings in the company

form 4 STOCKHOLDING & INVESTMENTS US form for reporting changes in securities holdings in the United States, a form that must be filed with the Securities and Exchange Commission reporting any changes in the securities holdings of officers, directors, or 10% shareholders in a company

formal documents MERGERS & ACQUISITIONS documents detailing takeover bid documents that provide the full details of a takeover bid

form letter GENERAL MANAGEMENT identical letter sent to different people a letter that can be sent without any change to several correspondents

form T STOCKHOLDING & INVESTMENTS US form for reporting transactions after market close in the United States, a required form used by brokers to report to the National Association of Securities Dealers all securities transactions that have taken place after the markets have closed

Fortune 500 FINANCE list of largest US industrial companies a list of the 500 largest industrial companies in the United States, compiled annually by *Fortune* magazine

Forum of Private Business BUSINESS UK small-business support group in the United Kingdom, a business support and lobby group representing more than 25,000 small businesses. *Abbr* ***FPB***

forwardation MARKETS when cash price is lower than forward price a situation in which the spot price of a futures product is lower than the ***forward price***

forward contract MARKETS contract for future delivery a private contract for delivery of a commodity at a later date

forward cover FINANCE cash purchase of commodity fulfilling futures contract the purchase for cash of the quantity of a commodity needed to fulfill a futures contract

forward delivery MARKETS, OPERATIONS & PRODUCTION delivery at agreed future date a delivery at some date in the future that has been agreed to by the buyer and seller

forwarder OPERATIONS & PRODUCTION agent who handles shipping and customs for clients a person or company that arranges shipping and customs documents for several shipments from different companies, putting them together to form one large shipment

forward exchange rate CURRENCY & EXCHANGE rate for future foreign currency purchase a rate for purchase of foreign currency at a fixed price for delivery at a later date. *Also called* ***forward rate*** *(sense 2)*

forwarding agent BUSINESS somebody preparing shipping and customs documents a person or company that arranges shipping and customs documents for clients

forward integration OPERATIONS & PRODUCTION way to ensure products will be distributed a means of guaranteeing ***distribution channels*** for products and services by building relationships with, or taking control of, ***distributors***. Forward integration can free the supplier from the threat or influence of major buyers and can also provide a barrier to market entry by potential rivals. ***Backward integration*** can provide similar guarantees on the supply side.

forward interest rate FINANCE interest rate set for future loan an interest rate specified for a loan to be made at a future date

forward-looking study STATISTICS ongoing statistical survey a survey of a statistical population carried out for a period such as a year after an original survey

forward margin MARKETS difference between current and future price the difference between the current price (***spot price***) and the future price (***forward price***)

forward market MARKETS market for purchases delivered at future date a market for the buying of foreign currency, stocks, or commodities for delivery at a later date at a prearranged price

forward price MARKETS contracted price for future delivery the price set in an ***option*** contract for a security or commodity to be delivered at a future date

forward pricing STOCKHOLDING & INVESTMENTS setting of investment price using future valuation the establishment of the price of a share in a mutual fund based on the next asset valuation

forward rate **1.** FINANCE rate for loan the rate at which there is no economic arbitrage between receiving an interest rate today and receiving an interest rate starting at some point in the future **2.** CURRENCY & EXCHANGE = ***forward exchange rate***

forward rate agreement STOCKHOLDING & INVESTMENTS, RISK contract trading fixed interest for variable interest a contract traded in the ***over-the-counter market*** in which parties agree to exchange a fixed interest rate or currency exchange rate for a variable rate on an agreed amount of money for an obligation beginning at a future time

forward sales MARKETS sale for future delivery sales of stock, commodities, or foreign exchange for delivery at a later date

forward scheduling OPERATIONS & PRODUCTION way of establishing when each stage must start a method for determining the start times for the various operations involved in a particular ***job***. Forward scheduling is most often used when the operations department sets the delivery date for a job, rather than the sales or marketing departments. Jobs are scheduled for the various operations as the workstations are expected to become available. The customer can then be informed of the projected delivery date. *See also* ***backward scheduling***

forward trading MARKETS buying or selling for future delivery the activity of buying or selling stock, commodities, or foreign exchange for delivery at a later date

forward transaction MARKETS agreement to buy and sell currency in future an agreement to buy one currency and sell another on a date some time beyond two business days. This allows an exchange rate on a given day to be specified for a future payment or receipt, thereby eliminating exchange rate risk.

founders' shares *UK* STOCKHOLDING & INVESTMENTS stock issued to firm's founders stock held by founding members of a company, often with a higher dividend that is only paid after other stockholders have received their dividends and, in some cases, only when a specific level of profit has been achieved. *See also* ***deferred common stock***

401(k) plan PENSIONS type of US retirement plan in the United States, a personal retirement plan arranged by an employer for an employee, invested in bonds, mutual funds, or stock. The employee contributes a proportion of salary, on which tax can be deferred; the employer can also make contributions.

fourteen hundred MARKETS warning of stranger in London Stock Exchange formerly, an exclamation used as a warning when a stranger walked onto the ***trading floor*** of the London Stock Exchange

fourth level of service GENERAL MANAGEMENT high level of increased value a very high rating in a system of measuring the value added to a product or service

fourth market MARKETS direct trading, without brokers trading conducted directly without brokers, usually by large institutions

fourth quarter ACCOUNTING last period of fiscal year the period of three months from October to the end of the year, or the period of three months at the end of a fiscal year. *Abbr* ***Q4***

FPA *abbr* FINANCE ***Financial Planning Association of Australia***

FPB *abbr* BUSINESS ***Forum of Private Business***

fractional certificate STOCKHOLDING & INVESTMENTS certificate relating to part of share a certificate for less than a full share (***fractional share***)

fractional currency CURRENCY & EXCHANGE paper money in very small denominations the paper money that is in denominations smaller than one unit of a standard national currency

fractional share STOCKHOLDING & INVESTMENTS less than full share of stock one part of a full share of stock, usually created as the result of a dividend reinvestment plan or a ***stock split***

franchise MARKETING authorization to provide another's products an agreement enabling a third party to sell or provide products or services owned by a manufacturer or supplier. A franchise is granted by the manufacturer, or *franchisor*, to a *franchisee*, who then retails the product. The franchise is regulated by a *franchise contract*, or *franchise agreement*, that specifies the terms and conditions of the franchise. These may include an obligation for the franchisor to provide national advertising or training for sales staff in return for the meeting of agreed sales targets by the franchisee. The franchisee usually retains a percentage of sales income. In other cases, a franchise may involve the ***licensing*** of a franchisee to manufacture a product to the franchisor's specification, and the sale of this product to retailers. Franchises can also be organized by issue of a ***master franchise***.

franchise agreement *or* **franchise contract** MARKETING *see* ***franchise***

franchise chain MARKETING group of stores with same franchise a number of retail outlets operating the same ***franchise***. A franchise chain may vary in size from a few to many thousands of outlets and in coverage from a small local area to worldwide.

franchisee MARKETING holder of franchise a third party with a contract to sell or provide products or services owned by a manufacturer or supplier. The franchisee usually retains a percentage of sales income. *See also* ***franchise***

franchisor MARKETING granter of franchise a manufacturer or supplier who has made an agreement enabling a third party to sell or provide products or services that it owns. *See also* ***franchise***

franco FINANCE free available at no cost

franked payment STOCKHOLDING & INVESTMENTS **1.** dividends with tax credits dividends carrying tax credits paid by a company to stockholders **2.** dividend free of UK corporation tax in the United Kingdom, a dividend received by a company from another UK company, exempt from corporation tax

fraud FRAUD dishonest methods used for personal benefit the use of dishonesty, deception, or false representation in order to gain a material advantage or to injure the interests of others. Types of fraud include false accounting, theft, third party or investment fraud, employee collusion, and computer fraud. *See also* ***corporate fraud***

fraud ring FRAUD group organized to defraud others an organized group of people or companies who defraud others, for example, by stealing identities to gain access to financial information, by forging mortgage documents, or by filing false insurance claims

fraudulent misrepresentation LEGAL making false statements to deceive the action of making a false statement with the intention of deceiving a customer

FRB *abbr* BANKING ***Federal Reserve Board***

FRC *abbr* REGULATION & COMPLIANCE ***Financial Reporting Council***

Freddie Mac MORTGAGES, RISK US institution financing housing a stockholder-owned private company chartered in 1970 by the US Congress to fund home mortgages by issuing debt securities in US and international securities markets. On September 7, 2008, after Freddie Mac reported more than $2 billion in losses from subprime loans, its government regulatory agency, the Federal Housing Finance Agency, put Freddie Mac under its conservatorship. *Full form* ***Federal Home Loan Mortgage Corporation****. Abbr* ***FHLMC****. See also* ***Fannie Mae***

freebie MARKETING something given away free a product or service that is given away, often as a business promotion

free coinage CURRENCY & EXCHANGE minting from donated metals a government's minting of coins from precious metals provided by citizens

free competition BUSINESS unregulated competition for business between companies a situation in which companies are allowed to compete with each other to win business without government intervention or restrictions

free currency CURRENCY & EXCHANGE currency that can be traded without restriction a currency that is allowed by the government to be bought and sold without restriction

free enterprise ECONOMICS freedom to trade without government control the trade carried on in a free-market economy, where resources are allocated on the basis of supply and demand

free gold FINANCE government gold not part of national reserve gold held by a government but not pledged as a reserve for the government's currency

freeholder REAL ESTATE person who owns property a person who owns a property legally and unconditionally, with rights to grant leases

freehold property REAL ESTATE property held free and clear property that the owner holds legally and unconditionally, with rights to grant leases

free issue STOCKHOLDING & INVESTMENTS = ***bonus issue***

freelance GENERAL MANAGEMENT, HR & PERSONNEL self-employed working on the basis of being self-employed, and possibly working for several employers at the same time, perhaps on a temporary basis. Freelance workers have been described as ideally suited to ***portfolio working***.

freelancer HR & PERSONNEL self-employed person somebody who works on a ***freelance*** basis, offering skills and expertise to different employers anywhere in the world. A freelancer works independently and may follow a pattern of ***portfolio working***.

free market ECONOMICS system of trade without government controls a market in which supply and demand are unregulated, except by the country's competition policy, and rights in physical and intellectual property are upheld

free market economy ECONOMICS economic system operating without government controls an economic system in which the government does not intervene or unduly regulate business activity

free on board OPERATIONS & PRODUCTION **1.** including all costs till goods are on carrier including in the price all the seller's costs until the goods are on the ship for transportation **2.** including all costs to point of delivery including in the price all the seller's costs until the goods are delivered to a place ▶ *Abbr* ***f.o.b.***

free period BANKING permitted delay between credit card purchase and payment the period allowed to credit card holders before payment for credit card purchases is requested

free port INTERNATIONAL TRADE port without customs duties a port where no customs duties are charged

free reserves BANKING bank reserves without restrictions the part of a bank's reserves that are above the statutory level and so can be used for various purposes as the bank wishes

free-standing additional voluntary contributions plan PENSIONS additional personal pension a separate pension plan taken out by somebody in addition to an ***occupational pension***

free trade INTERNATIONAL TRADE unrestricted trade between nations a system in which trading of goods between one country and another takes place without any restrictions or customs barriers

free trade area *or* **free trade zone** INTERNATIONAL TRADE group of countries trading without restrictions a group of countries engaged in trading between themselves without restrictions or customs barriers

free trader INTERNATIONAL TRADE person favoring free trade a person who is in favor of free trade

freeze-out STOCKHOLDING & INVESTMENTS compulsory purchase of minor stockholdings in acquired company the exclusion of minority stockholders in a company that has been taken over. A freeze-out provision may exist in a ***takeover*** agreement, which permits the acquiring organization to buy the noncontrolling shares held by small stockholders. A fair price is usually set, and the freeze-out may take place at a specific time, perhaps two to five years after the takeover. A freeze-out can still take place, even if provision for it is not made in a corporate charter, by applying pressure to minority stockholders to sell their shares to the acquiring company.

freight OPERATIONS & PRODUCTION goods being transported goods loaded for onward transport, most often by sea or by air

freight forwarder OPERATIONS & PRODUCTION firm consolidating shipments of freight an organization that collects shipments from a number of businesses and consolidates them into larger shipments for economies of scale. A freight forwarder often also deals with route selection, price negotiation, and documentation of distribution, and can act as a distribution agent for a business. By consolidating loads, a freight forwarder can negotiate cheaper rates of transportation than the individual businesses and can prebook space to ensure a more rapid delivery schedule.

frequency analysis MARKETING way of comparing chances of reaching target audience a technique for comparing the number of opportunities to reach the same target audience in different media

frequency distribution STATISTICS classifying statistical data and recording frequencies in a statistical study, the process of dividing a sample of observations into classes and listing the number of observations in each class

frequency polygon STATISTICS representation of frequency a diagrammatic representation showing the values in a ***frequency distribution***

frequently asked question E-COMMERCE *see* ***FAQ***

frictional unemployment ECONOMICS temporarily between jobs a situation in which people are temporarily out of the labor market. They could be seeking a new job, incurring search delays as they apply, attending interviews, and relocating.

friction-free market MARKETS market in which competing products are very similar a market in which there is little differentiation between competing products, so that the customer has exceptional choice

friendly society BANKING in UK, association whose dues help members in need in the United Kingdom, a group of people forming an association to pay regular subscriptions to a fund that is used to help members of the group when they are in financial difficulties

fringe benefits HR & PERSONNEL supplements to main pay from employer rewards given or offered to employees in addition to their wages or salaries and included in their employment contract. Fringe benefits range from share options, company cars, expense accounts, cheap loans, medical insurance, and other types of ***incentive schemeincentive plan*** to discounts on company products, subsidized meals, and membership of social and health clubs. Many of these benefits are liable for tax. In the United States, a ***cafeteria plan*** permits employees to select from a variety of such benefits, although usually some are deemed to be core and not exchangeable for others. Minor benefits, sometimes appropriated rather than given, are known as ***perks***.

FRN *abbr* FINANCE, CURRENCY & EXCHANGE ***floating-rate note***

front company BUSINESS, FRAUD firm hiding illegal activities of controlling firm a company established as a legitimate business to conceal the illegal activities of the business controlling it

front end GENERAL MANAGEMENT section of firm dealing directly with customers the part of an organization that deals with customers on a face-to-face basis

front-end loading FINANCE early deduction of charges and commission the practice of taking the commission and administrative expenses from the early payments made to an investment or insurance plan. *See also* ***back-end loading***

front office GENERAL MANAGEMENT staff that interacts with customers and clients the members of staff in a financial institution or brokerage who deal directly with customers and clients. *See also* ***back office, middle office***

frozen account BANKING bank account made inoperable by court order a bank account whose funds cannot be used or withdrawn because of a court order

frozen credits BANKING credits that are not movable credits in an account which cannot be moved, usually owing to a legal dispute

FRSB *abbr* ACCOUNTING ***Financial Reporting Standards Board***

FSA *abbr* REGULATION & COMPLIANCE ***Financial Services Authority***

FSB *abbr* BUSINESS ***Federation of Small Businesses***

FT *abbr* FINANCE ***Financial Times***

FTASI *abbr* MARKETS ***FTSE Actuaries Share Indices***

FTSE MARKETS Financial Times-Stock Exchange an abbreviation of "Financial Times-Stock Exchange," used in the name of various indices of the London Stock Exchange published in the Financial Times

FTSE 30 Share Index *or* **FTSE 30** MARKETS index of influential UK companies an index showing the stock prices of 30 influential companies on the London Stock Exchange. Although in existence since 1935, the FTSE 30 Share Index is now one of the less popular indices.

FTSE 100 Share Index *or* **FTSE 100** MARKETS index of most-highly capitalized UK public companies an index, established in 1984, that is based on the stock prices of the 100 most highly capitalized public companies in the United Kingdom

FTSE 250 Index *or* **FTSE 250** MARKETS index of medium-capitalized UK companies an index of medium-capitalized companies not included in the ***FTSE 100 Share Index***. It represents over 17% of UK market capitalization.

FTSE Actuaries Share Indices MARKETS several indices based on London stock prices several indices based on prices on the London Stock Exchange, which are calculated by and published in the Financial Times in conjunction with the Actuaries Investment Research Committee. *Abbr* ***FTASI***

FTSE All-Share Index MARKETS average of UK stock prices an average of the stock prices of all the companies listed on the London Stock Exchange. As this encompasses over 1,000 companies, this index is often used as a reliable barometer of the performance of different companies. This index aggregates the FTSE 100, FTSE 250, and FTSE Small Cap Indices.

FTSE Small Cap Index MARKETS index of UK companies with smallest capitalization an index that indicates the performance of companies with the smallest market capitalization, representing roughly 2% of market capitalization in the United Kingdom

FTSE TMT Index MARKETS index of UK companies in technology, media, and telecommunications an index which indicates the performance of companies in the United Kingdom in three key business areas: technology, media, and telecommunications. *Abbr* ***FTSE TMT***

fulfillment MARKETING dealing with approaches from customers the process of responding to customer inquiries, orders, or sales promotion offers

fulfillment house MARKETING firm handling approaches from customers for others an organization that specializes in responding to inquiries, orders, or sales promotion offers on behalf of a client

full bank BANKING bank offering full domestic and international services a local or foreign bank permitted to engage in the full range of domestic and international services

full cost accounting ACCOUNTING = ***environmental accounting***

full coupon bond STOCKHOLDING & INVESTMENTS bond with competitive interest rate a bond whose interest rate is competitive in the current market

full cover *UK* INSURANCE = ***full coverage***

full coverage *US* INSURANCE insurance for most risks insurance that provides coverage against a wide range of risks. *UK term* ***full cover***

full employment HR & PERSONNEL situation in which all capable workers have jobs a situation in which all the people who are fit to work have jobs

full faith and credit FINANCE US government debt repayment guarantee an unconditional guarantee by the US government to repay the principal and interest on all its debt

full price OPERATIONS & PRODUCTION standard price with no discounts the regular price for a product, with no special discounts applied

full rate OPERATIONS & PRODUCTION standard charge with no discounts the standard charge for a service, with no special discounts applied

full-service banking BANKING provision of banking and financial services a type of banking that offers a whole range of services including mortgages, loans, and pension plans

full-service broker FINANCE broker managing portfolios and giving financial advice a broker who manages portfolios for clients, and gives advice on stocks and financial questions in general

full time HR & PERSONNEL standard working hours the standard hours of attendance expected in an organization. *See also* ***part time***

Fully Automated Screen Trading and Electronic Registration MARKETS *see* ***FASTER***

fully connected world GENERAL MANAGEMENT population in touch by networks a world in which most people and organizations are linked by networks such as the Internet

fully diluted earnings per (common) share STOCKHOLDING & INVESTMENTS earnings including commitments to issue more stocks the amount earned per share taking into account commitments to issue more shares, for example, as a result of convertibles, stock options, or warrants

fully diluted earnings per share STOCKHOLDING & INVESTMENTS earnings per share taken over all ordinary shares the amount earned per share calculated over the whole number of shares on the assumption that convertible shares and options have been converted to ordinary shares

fully diluted shares STOCKHOLDING & INVESTMENTS total shares, including convertible shares and stock options total number of shares that would be outstanding assuming that convertible shares have been converted to ordinary shares and that stock options have been exercised

fully distributed issue STOCKHOLDING & INVESTMENTS issue fully sold out to investors an issue of stocks sold entirely to investors rather than being held by dealers

full year ACCOUNTING 12 months a 12-month period, especially with reference to financial information such as earnings, sales, profits, and outlook for the future

full-year forecast ACCOUNTING prediction of future 12 months' earnings or losses a prediction of the expected earnings or losses of a business for the future over a 12-month period

full-year results ACCOUNTING past 12 months of financial data the financial information of a business, especially its profits or losses, calculated for the preceding 12-month period

fully paid share capital *or* **fully paid-up capital** STOCKHOLDING & INVESTMENTS total paid by investors for capital holdings the amount of the share capital when all calls have been paid on all issued shares. *See also* ***called-up share capital, paid-up capital***

functional budget TREASURY MANAGEMENT budget for activity or department a budget of income and/or expenditure applicable to a specific function. A function may refer to a process or a department. Functional budgets frequently include the following: production cost budget (based on a forecast of production and plant utilization); marketing cost budget; sales budget; personnel budget; purchasing budget; and research and development budget. *See also* ***departmental budget***

functional relationship STATISTICS relationship between statistical variables the relationship between variables in a statistical study in which there is no bias or any other distorting factor

fund FINANCE **1.** money earmarked for something an amount of money set aside for a particular purpose **2.** money invested money invested in an investment trust as part of a mutual fund, or given to a financial adviser to invest on behalf of a client. *See also* ***funds*** **3.** supply money for purpose to provide an amount of money for a particular purpose. *See also* ***finance***

fundamental accounting concepts ACCOUNTING basic assumptions for accounts broad basic assumptions that underlie the periodic financial accounts of business enterprises. *See also* **concepts**

fundamental analysis STOCKHOLDING & INVESTMENTS assessment of influences affecting firm's performance an assessment of how the external and internal influences on a company's activities should affect investment decisions. *See also* ***technical analysis***

fundamentals BUSINESS, MARKETS most basic business components the basic components such as assets, profitability, and dividends of a company or a stock market

funded FINANCE **1.** backed by long-term loans supported by money in the form of long-term loans **2.** based on a fund a future financial commitment,such as the payment of a pension, that is supported by an existing fund of money

funded debt FINANCE long- or medium-term debt long-term debt or debt that has a maturity date in excess of one year. Funded debt is usually issued in the public markets or in the form of a private placement to qualified institutional investors.

fund family STOCKHOLDING & INVESTMENTS = ***family of funds***

funding FINANCE **1.** finance for business or project the financial support that is available for a business or project **2.** changing short-term debt into long-term loan the conversion of a short-term debt into a loan that has a maturity date in excess of one year

funding risk RISK likelihood of difficulty in raising funds the risk that it might be difficult to realize assets or otherwise raise funds to meet commitments associated with ***financial instruments***. *See also* ***liquidity risk***

fund management STOCKHOLDING & INVESTMENTS business of investing clients' money the business of dealing with the investment of sums of money on behalf of clients

fund manager STOCKHOLDING & INVESTMENTS manager of investments somebody who manages the investments of a mutual fund or other financial institution. *Also called* ***investment manager***

Fund Managers' Association STOCKHOLDING & INVESTMENTS UK organization for fund managers an association representing the interests of UK-based institutional fund managers. It now forms part of the ***Investment Management Association***. *Abbr* ***FMA***

fund of funds STOCKHOLDING & INVESTMENTS mutual fund investing in several underlying mutual funds a registered mutual fund that invests in a variety of underlying mutual funds. Subscribers own units in the fund of funds, not in the underlying mutual funds.

funds FINANCE money available to spend money that is available to a person, business, or organization for spending. *See also* ***insufficient funds***

fungibility BUSINESS, FINANCE interchangeability of product the ability to be easily substituted for or combined with another similar product

fungible **1.** FINANCE substitutable indistinguishable for business purposes from other items of the same type. Such products may be easily combined in making up shipments. **2.** STOCKHOLDING & INVESTMENTS interchangeable used to describe an asset, especially a security, that can be exchanged for a similar asset

funny money **1.** CURRENCY & EXCHANGE forged currency money that is counterfeit or forged **2.** FRAUD questionable money money obtained from a legally or morally suspect source

future STOCKHOLDING & INVESTMENTS contract for future delivery a contract to deliver a commodity at a future date at a fixed price. *Also called* ***futures contract***

future delivery OPERATIONS & PRODUCTION delivery at prearranged future date a delivery at some date in the future that has been arranged by the buyer and seller

future option STOCKHOLDING & INVESTMENTS contract for future trade at set price a contract in which somebody agrees to buy or sell an option for purchasing or selling a commodity, currency, or security at a prearranged price for delivery in the future. *Also called* ***futures option***

futures STOCKHOLDING & INVESTMENTS items traded now for later delivery stock, currency, or commodities that are bought or sold now for delivery at a later date

futures commission merchant STOCKHOLDING & INVESTMENTS broker for futures somebody who acts as a broker for ***futures contracts***. *Abbr* ***FCM***

futures contract STOCKHOLDING & INVESTMENTS *see* ***future***

futures exchange CURRENCY & EXCHANGE exchange for futures an exchange on which ***futures contracts*** are traded

futures market MARKETS market for trade in items with fluctuating prices a market for buying and selling securities, commodities, or currencies that tend to fluctuate in price over a period of time. The market's goal is to reduce the risk of uncertainty about prices in the period ahead.

futures option STOCKHOLDING & INVESTMENTS *see* ***future option***

futures research GENERAL MANAGEMENT consideration of what could happen in future the identification of possible future ***scenarios*** with the goal of anticipating and perhaps influencing what the future holds. Futures research is important to the process of ***issues management***. It usually identifies several possible scenarios for any set of circumstances, and enables an informed decision to be made.

future value FINANCE projected value of sum of money the value that a sum of money will have in the future, taking into account the effects of inflation, interest rates, or currency values.

Future value calculations require three figures: the sum in question, the percentage by which it will increase or decrease, and the period of time. In this example, these figures are $1,000, 11%, and two years.

At an interest rate of 11%, the sum of $1,000 will grow to $1,232 in two years:

$1,000 × 1.11 = $1,110 (first year) × 1.11 = $1,232 (second year, rounded to whole dollars)

Note that the interest earned in the first year generates additional interest in the second year, a practice known as compounding. When large sums are in question, the effect of compounding can be significant.

At an inflation rate of 11%, by comparison, the sum of $1,000 will shrink to $812 in two years:

$1,000 × 1.11 = $901 (first year) × 1.11 = $812 (second year, rounded to whole dollars)

In order to avoid errors, it is important to express the percentage as 1.11 and multiply and divide by that figure, instead of using 11%; and to calculate each year, quarter, or month separately. *See also* ***present value***

futuristic planning GENERAL MANAGEMENT planning for potentially radically different future planning for a period that extends beyond the planning horizon in the form of future expected conditions that may exist in respect of the entity, products/services, and environment, but that cannot usefully be expressed in quantified terms. An example would be working out the actions needed in a future with no automobiles.

futurize GENERAL MANAGEMENT keep technologically up to date to ensure that an organization is taking full advantage of the latest technologies

fuzzy accounting ACCOUNTING, FRAUD accounting practices that mislead investors company accounting practices designed to inflate earnings or earnings estimates in order to attract investors

fuzzy search E-COMMERCE computer search giving near and exact matches a computer search that returns not only exact matches to the search request, but also close matches that include possibilities and allow for such things as spelling errors

FY *abbr* ACCOUNTING ***fiscal year***

G

G7 FINANCE group of seven major industrial nations the major industrial nations established in 1985 to discuss the world economy, consisting of Canada, France, Germany, Italy, Japan, the United Kingdom, and the United States. *Full form* ***Group of Seven***

G8 FINANCE G7 countries plus Russia the group of eight major industrial nations consisting of the ***G7*** plus Russia. *Full form* ***Group of Eight***

G10 FINANCE nations contributing to General Arrangements to Borrow fund the group of ten countries who contribute to the General Arrangements to Borrow fund: Belgium, Canada, France, Germany, Italy, Japan, the Netherlands, Sweden, the United States, and the United Kingdom. Switzerland joined in 1984. *Full form* ***Group of Ten***. *Also called* ***Paris Club***

G20 ECONOMICS group of industrial and emerging countries a forum for discussion between 20 industrialized and emerging-market countries on issues related to global economic stability. *Full form* ***Group of Twenty***

GAAP *abbr* ACCOUNTING ***Generally Accepted Accounting Principles***

GAB FINANCE international fund providing large loans to countries a fund financed by the ***G10*** that is used when the IMF's own resources are insufficient, for example, when there is a need for large loans to one or more industrialized countries. *Full form* ***General Arrangements to Borrow***

gain FINANCE increase in amount or value an increase in the amount or level of something, for example, in a company's profit or in the value of stocks on a stock exchange

gain sharing FINANCE sharing profits from efficiency improvements with employees a group-based ***bonus plan*** to share profits from improvements in production efficiency between employees and the company

galloping inflation ECONOMICS very rapid inflation inflation that increases rapidly by large amounts

game theory GENERAL MANAGEMENT technique for investigating consequences of strategies and conflicts a mathematical technique used in ***operational research*** to analyze and predict the outcomes of games of strategy and conflicts of interest. Game theory is used to represent conflicts and problems involved in formulating marketing and organizational strategy, with the goal of identifying and implementing optimal strategies. It involves assessing likely strategies to be adopted by players in a given situation under a particular set of rules.

gamma STOCKHOLDING & INVESTMENTS rate of change in option price the rate of change in the ***delta*** of an option for a unit change in the price of the underlying asset. It is a measure of ***convexity***.

gap analysis **1.** FINANCE analyzing shortfall between current results and ultimate goals a method of improving a company's financial performance by analyzing the reasons for the gap between current results and long-term objectives **2.** MARKETING investigation of gaps in market or availability a marketing technique used to identify gaps in market or product coverage. In gap analysis, consumer information or requirements are tabulated and matched to product categories in order to identify product or service opportunities or gaps in product planning.

gap financing FINANCE short-term loan arrangement the process of arranging an extra loan such as a ***bridge loan*** in order to make a purchase not fully covered by an existing loan

garage **1.** MARKETS part of New York Stock Exchange the annex to the main floor of the New York Stock Exchange **2.** *UK* TAX move assets or liabilities for tax advantage to transfer assets or liabilities from one financial center to another to take advantage of a tax benefit

garbatrage *US* STOCKHOLDING & INVESTMENTS stocks benefiting from unrelated takeover stocks that rise because of a ***takeover*** but that are not connected to the target company (*slang*)

garden leave GENERAL MANAGEMENT full pay without working in a ***contract of employment***, a clause that allows the employer to keep an employee on full pay, but not require him or her to work, during the employee's contractual ***notice period***. Garden leave thereby prevents the employee from working for another employer until the notice period has expired, by which time any confidential information the employee holds is likely to have become commercially out of date.

garnishee FINANCE person ordered to redirect debt payment to another a person who owes money to a creditor and is ordered by a court to pay that money to a creditor of the original creditor, and not to the actual creditor

garnishee order LEGAL order requiring debt payment to third party a court order, making somebody pay money not directly to a creditor, but to a third party. For example, a court may order an employer to take money from an employee's pay and pay it to somebody to whom the employee owes money. *Also called **garnishment** (sense 2)*

garnishment 1. FINANCE withholding of income to repay debt a procedure by which wages or salary are withheld from an employee in order to pay off the employee's debt **2.** LEGAL = ***garnishee order***

GAS *abbr* ACCOUNTING ***Government Accountancy Service***

gatekeeper GENERAL MANAGEMENT controller of dissemination of information somebody within an organization who controls the flow of information and therefore influences policy

gateway E-COMMERCE where computer networks meet and exchange data a point where two or more computer networks meet and can exchange data

GATT INTERNATIONAL TRADE international treaty promoting multilateral trade a treaty signed in Geneva in 1947 that aimed to foster multilateral trade and settle trading disputes between adherent countries. Initially signed by 23 nations, it started to reduce trade tariffs and, as it was accepted by more and more countries, tackled other barriers to trade. It was replaced on January 1, 1995, by the World Trade Organization. *Full form **General Agreement on Tariffs and Trade***

gazump *UK* REAL ESTATE accept higher offer, negating earlier verbal agreement to agree verbally to sell to one buyer, but before the agreement becomes legally binding, to accept a higher offer from another buyer. Gazumping is usually associated with the real estate market, although it can occur in any market where the prices are rising rapidly.

gazunder *UK* REAL ESTATE undercut price verbally agreed earlier to agree verbally to buy at one price, but before the agreement becomes legally binding, to offer a lower price. Gazundering is usually associated with the real estate market, although it can occur in any market where the prices are falling rapidly.

GBE *abbr* GENERAL MANAGEMENT ***Government Business Enterprise***

GB pound CURRENCY & EXCHANGE = ***pound sterling***

GDP ECONOMICS all goods and services produced by economy the total flow of goods and services produced by an economy over a quarter or a year, measured by the aggregate value of goods and services at market prices. *Full form **gross domestic product***

GDP per capita ECONOMICS total economic output divided by population ***GDP*** divided by the country's population so as to achieve a figure per person in the population

GEAR ECONOMICS redistributive economic program in S. Africa the macroeconomic reform program of the South African government, intended to foster economic growth, create employment, and redistribute income and opportunities in favor of the poor. *Full form **Growth, Employment, and Redistribution***

geared investment trust *UK* STOCKHOLDING & INVESTMENTS = ***leveraged investment company***

gearing FINANCE, RISK = ***leverage***

gearing ratios FINANCE = ***leverage ratios***

geisha bond STOCKHOLDING & INVESTMENTS = ***shogun bond***

general account MARKETS account with investment broker who lends money the US Federal Reserve Board's term for a ***margin account*** set up for a brokerage customer

General Agreement on Tariffs and Trade INTERNATIONAL TRADE *see **GATT***

General Arrangements to Borrow FINANCE *see **GAB***

general audit ACCOUNTING comprehensive examination of firm's accounts an examination of all books and accounts belonging to a company

general average INSURANCE sharing of insured loss by all policyholders a process by which the cost of lost goods is shared by all parties to an insurance policy, as in cases when some goods have been lost in an attempt to save the rest of the cargo

General Commissioners TAX in UK, officials appointed to hear tax appeals in the United Kingdom, an independent group of people from a variety of backgrounds appointed by the Lord Chancellor to hear appeals from taxpayers against Her Majesty's Revenue & Customs. In Scotland, Commissioners are appointed by Scottish ministers.

general expenses ACCOUNTING routine costs of running business minor expenses of various kinds incurred in the running of a business

general fund FINANCE mutual fund with wide-ranging investments a mutual fund that has investments in a variety of stocks

general insurance INSURANCE insurance against losses excluding life insurance insurance relating to various potential losses such as theft or damage, but excluding life insurance

general ledger ACCOUNTING book listing firm's financial transactions a book that lists all of the financial transactions of a company

general lien LEGAL **1.** right to hold property until debt paid a right to hold the goods or property of a debtor until a debt has been paid **2.** right to hold debtor's personal property only a right to hold the personal possessions of a debtor until a debt is paid, but not his or her house or land. *See also **banker's lien***

Generally Accepted Accounting Principles ACCOUNTING guidelines relating to fair accounting practices a summary of best practice in respect to the form and content of financial statements and auditors' reports, and of accounting policies and disclosures adopted for the preparation of financial information. GAAP has statutory or regulatory authority in the United States and Canada and some other countries, but not in the United Kingdom. *Abbr* ***GAAP***

general manager GENERAL MANAGEMENT manager involved in all aspects of organization a ***manager*** whose work encompasses all areas of an organization. A general manager is traditionally a nonspecialist, has a working knowledge of all aspects of an organization's activities, and oversees all operating functions. In large companies and the public sector, specialist managers with expert knowledge may control departments, while a general manager provides unifying ***leadership*** from the top.

general meeting CORPORATE GOVERNANCE meeting of company's stockholders a meeting of all the stockholders of a company or of all the members of an organization

General National Mortgage Association MORTGAGES *see* ***Ginnie Mae***

general obligation bond STOCKHOLDING & INVESTMENTS municipal bond financing public undertakings a municipal or state bond that is repaid out of general funds. *Abbr* ***GO bond***

general partner BUSINESS partner in firm who has no limited liability a partner in a business whose responsibility for its debts is not limited and whose personal assets may be at risk if the company's assets are not sufficient to discharge its debts

general partnership BUSINESS business where all partners share profits and liabilities a business in which each partner has a share in the administration, profits, and losses of the operation

general undertaking REGULATION & COMPLIANCE directors' undertaking to obey Stock Exchange regulations an agreement, signed by all the directors of a company applying for Stock Exchange listing, that promises that they will work within the regulations of the Stock Exchange

generative learning GENERAL MANAGEMENT learning that fosters experimentation and open-mindedness a style of organizational learning that encourages experimentation, risk taking, openness, and system-wide thinking. Organizations have successfully used this style of learning to transform themselves in the face of technological, social, and market change. ***Adaptive learning*** is a contrasting approach.

generic strategy MARKETING marketing strategy any of three strategies for marketing products or services: cost leadership, differentiation, and focus. The first implies supplying products in a more cost-effective way than competitors; the second refers to adding value to products or services; and the third focuses on a specific product market segment with the goal of establishing a monopoly.

gensaki STOCKHOLDING & INVESTMENTS bond sale incorporating repurchase agreement the Japanese term for a bond sale incorporating a repurchase agreement at a later date

gentleman's agreement GENERAL MANAGEMENT reliable unwritten agreement a verbal agreement between two people who trust each other to keep the agreement without a formal contract

Gesellschaft mit beschränkter Haftung BUSINESS *see* ***GmbH***

gharar FINANCE uncertainty prohibited in Islamic business dealings in Islamic financing, excessive uncertainty in a business transaction of any type. It is one of three prohibitions in Islamic law, the others being ***maysir*** and ***riba***.

ghosting MARKETS, FRAUD illegal price fixing of stock an illegal practice in which two or more market makers, who are required by law to compete, join to influence the price of a stock

Giffen good ECONOMICS = ***inferior good***

Gift Aid TAX in UK, tax advantage on gifts to charity in the United Kingdom, a system through which a charity receiving a gift of money from a taxpayer can also directly receive the tax that had been paid on the sum at the standard rate

gift inter vivos TAX gift between living persons a gift that is made to another living person. *Abbr* ***GIV***

gift-leaseback TAX leasing back of gifted property the practice of giving somebody a property and then leasing it back, usually for tax advantage or charitable purposes

gift tax TAX in US, tax paid by giver on gift in the United States, a tax on money or property given to another living person, which is to be paid by the giver. Exemptions exist for gifts below a specific value, gifts between spouses, etc.

gift with reservation FINANCE gift that benefits donor in some way in the United Kingdom, a gift with some benefit retained for the donor, for example, the legal transfer of a dwelling when the donor continues in residence

gilt STOCKHOLDING & INVESTMENTS *see* ***gilt-edged security***

gilt-edged STOCKHOLDING & INVESTMENTS issued by blue-chip company used to describe a security issued by a blue-chip company, which is therefore considered very secure (*informal*)

gilt-edged security STOCKHOLDING & INVESTMENTS UK government security paying regular fixed interest in the United Kingdom, a security issued by the government that pays a fixed rate of interest on a regular basis for a specific period of time until the redemption date, when the principal is returned. Their names, for example, Exchequer 10½% 2005 (abbreviated to Ex 10½% '05) or Treasury 11¾% 2003–07 (abbreviated to Tr 11¾% '03–'07) indicate the rate and redemption date. Thought to have originated in the 17th century to help fund the war with France, today they form a large part of the ***national debt***. *Also called* ***gilt***. *See also* ***index-linked gilt, short-dated gilts***

gilt repos MARKETS UK market in trading gilts in the United Kingdom, the market in prearranged sales and repurchase of gilt-edged securities, launched in 1996 by the Bank of England to make gilts more attractive to overseas investors

gilt strip STOCKHOLDING & INVESTMENTS UK bond yielding single cash payment at maturity in the United Kingdom, a ***zero coupon bond*** created by splitting the interest payments from a gilt-edged security so that it produces a single cash payment at maturity

gilt unit trust STOCKHOLDING & INVESTMENTS UK mutual fund investing in gilts in the United Kingdom, a mutual fund where the underlying investments are ***gilt-edged securities***

Ginnie Mae MORTGAGES US securities agency in the United States, a government agency that issues mortgage-backed bonds. *Full form* ***General National Mortgage Association***

giro 1. BANKING UK bank transfer in the United Kingdom, a system of transferring money from one bank account to another. *Also called* **bank giro 2.** FINANCE UK state benefit in the United Kingdom, a benefit paid by the state (*slang*)

GIV *abbr* TAX ***gift inter vivos***

give up MARKETS three-way trade a transaction involving three brokers in which broker A, who is busy, asks broker B to execute a trade for a client with broker C. The trade is recorded as broker A's transaction, so broker A receives a commission, and broker B, who actually executed the trade, gives up the transaction.

glamour stock STOCKHOLDING & INVESTMENTS fashionable investment a currently fashionable and popular security (*slang*)

Glass–Steagall Act REGULATION & COMPLIANCE US law separating banking and brokerage industries in the United States, a law enacted in 1933 that enforces the separation of the banking and brokerage industries. Some provisions have since been repealed, most notably: (1) allowing the Federal Reserve to regulate interest rates in savings accounts, and (2) prohibiting a bank holding company from owning other financial companies.

global bank BANKING bank with worldwide business a bank that is active in the international markets and has a presence in several continents

global bond STOCKHOLDING & INVESTMENTS = ***Eurobond***

global bond issue STOCKHOLDING & INVESTMENTS bond issue allowing transfer of titles between markets an issue of a bond that incorporates a settlement mechanism allowing for the transfer of titles between markets

global brand MARKETING brand name known everywhere the brand name of a product that has worldwide recognition. A global brand has the advantage of economies of scale in terms of production, recognition, and packaging. *Also called* ***global product***

global coordinator STOCKHOLDING & INVESTMENTS overall manager of global stock issue the lead manager of a global offering who is responsible for overseeing the entire issue and is usually supported by regional and national coordinators

global custody FINANCE bundle of financial services for institutional investors a financial service, usually available to institutional investors only, that includes the safekeeping of securities certificates issued in markets across the world, the collection of dividends, dealing with tax, valuation of investments, foreign exchange, and the settlement of transactions

global depositary receipt STOCKHOLDING & INVESTMENTS certificate for shares of stock traded abroad a certificate held by a bank in one country representing shares of stock that are traded on an exchange in a foreign country but can be purchased through various banks worldwide

global economy ECONOMICS, INTERNATIONAL TRADE international trade relations the economic relations between countries in a world where markets in individual countries have now spread beyond national boundaries and are more integrated with those of other countries. *Also called* ***world economy***

global hedge STOCKHOLDING & INVESTMENTS = ***macrohedge***

globalization GENERAL MANAGEMENT expanding operations worldwide the creation of international strategies by organizations for overseas expansion and operation on a worldwide level. The process of globalization has been precipitated by a number of factors, including rapid technology developments that make global communications possible, political developments such as the fall of communism, and transportation developments that make traveling faster and more frequent. These produce greater development opportunities for companies with the opening up of additional markets, allow greater customer harmonization as a result of the increase in shared cultural values, and provide a superior competitive position with lower operating costs in other countries and access to new raw materials, resources, and investment opportunities.

global marketing MARKETING marketing to sell products worldwide a marketing strategy used mainly by multinational companies to sell goods or services internationally. Global marketing requires that there be harmonization between the marketing policies for different countries and that the marketing mix for the different countries can be adapted to the local market conditions. Global marketing is sometimes used to refer to overseas expansion efforts through ***licensing***, ***franchises***, and ***joint ventures***.

global marketplace ECONOMICS, INTERNATIONAL TRADE market encompassing whole world a worldwide trading system that has grown up since the 1970s, in which goods can be produced wherever the production costs are cheapest wherever they are ultimately sold

global offering STOCKHOLDING & INVESTMENTS worldwide offering of securities the offering of securities in several markets simultaneously, for example, in Europe, the Far East, and North America

global pricing contract OPERATIONS & PRODUCTION contract for single worldwide price a contract between a customer and a supplier whereby the supplier agrees to charge the customer the same price for the delivery of parts or services anywhere in the world. As

globalization increases, more customers are likely to press their suppliers for global pricing contracts. Through such contracts suppliers can benefit by gaining access to new markets and growing their business, achieving economies of scale, developing strong relationships with customers, and thereby gaining a ***competitive advantage*** that is difficult for competitors to break. There are risks involved, too, for example, being in the middle of a conflict between a customer's head office and its local business units, or being tied to one customer when there are more attractive customers to serve.

global product MARKETING *see* ***global brand***

glocalization GENERAL MANAGEMENT expanding and adapting operations worldwide the process of tailoring products or services to different local markets around the world. Glocalization is a combination of globalization and localization. Improved communications and advances in technology have made worldwide markets accessible to even small companies but, rather than being homogenous, the global market is in fact made up of many different localities. Success in a globalized environment is more likely if products are not globalized or mass marketed, but glocalized and customized for individual local communities that have different needs and different cultural approaches.

glue GENERAL MANAGEMENT unifying factor a common factor such as information that unifies organizations, supply chains, and other commercial groups (*informal*)

GM *abbr* FINANCE ***gross margin***

GmbH BUSINESS corporation the German term for a corporation. *Full form* ***Gesellschaft mit beschränkter Haftung***

GNMA MORTGAGES *see* ***Ginnie Mae***

gnomes of Zurich BANKING Swiss bankers bankers and currency dealers based in Switzerland, who have a reputation for secrecy. The term is often used to refer in a derogatory way to unknown currency speculators who cause upheavals in the currency markets (*informal*).

GNP ECONOMICS country's total economic output plus foreign investment income the ***GDP*** plus domestic residents' income from investment abroad less income earned in the domestic market accruing to noncitizens abroad. *Full form* ***gross national product***

GNP per capita ECONOMICS GNP divided by population the ***GNP*** divided by the country's population so as to achieve a figure per person in the population

goal GENERAL MANAGEMENT target of effort an end toward which effort is directed and on which resources are focused, usually to achieve an organization's strategy. There is considerable discussion on whether objective, goal, target, and aim are the same. In general usage, the terms are often interchangeable, so it is important that, if an organization has a particular meaning for one of these terms, it must define it in its documentation. Sometimes an objective is seen as the desired final end result, while a goal is a smaller step on the road to it.

GO bond STOCKHOLDING & INVESTMENTS = ***general obligation bond***

go-go fund STOCKHOLDING & INVESTMENTS, RISK high-risk mutual fund a mutual fund that trades heavily and predominantly in high-return, high-risk investments

going concern BUSINESS company currently trading a company that is actively trading and making a profit

going short FINANCE selling asset for repurchase at lower price borrowing and then selling an asset one does not own with the intention of acquiring it at a later date at a lower price for delivery to the purchaser. *See also* ***bear***

gold bond STOCKHOLDING & INVESTMENTS bond with gold as collateral a bond for which gold is collateral, often issued by mining companies

gold bug STOCKHOLDING & INVESTMENTS investor who believes gold prices will rise a person who believes that gold is the best investment

gold bullion FINANCE gold bars gold in the form of bars

gold card BANKING credit card for wealthy customer a gold-colored credit card, generally issued to customers with above average incomes, that may include additional benefits such as an overdraft at an advantageous interest rate. It may require an annual fee.

gold certificate LEGAL document stating ownership of gold a document that shows ownership of gold that the owner may not be storing

golden handcuffs FINANCE financial incentive to remain in organization a financial incentive paid to encourage employees to remain in an organization and dissuade them from leaving for a rival business or to start their own company (*informal*)

golden handshake *or* **golden goodbye** FINANCE generous payment for departing senior executive a sum of money given to a senior executive on his or her involuntary departure from an employing organization as a form of severance pay. A golden handshake can be offered when an executive is required to leave before the expiration of his or her contract, for example, because of a ***merger*** or corporate restructuring. It is intended as compensation for loss of office. It can be a very large sum of money, but often it is not related to the perceived performance of the executive concerned (*informal*)

golden hello FINANCE **1.** generous financial arrangement for new employee a welcome package for a new employee which may include a bonus and stock options. A golden hello is designed as an incentive to attract employees. Some of the contents of the welcome package may be contingent on the performance of the employee. **2.** support for employer hiring new employee a payment from a government to an employer who takes on new staff when jobs are hard to find in a recession

golden parachute *or* **golden umbrella** FINANCE generous financial package on dismissal from employment a clause inserted in the contract of employment of a senior employee that details a financial package payable if the employee is dismissed.

A golden parachute provides an executive with a measure of financial security and may be payable if the employee leaves the organization following a ***takeover*** or ***merger***, or is dismissed as a result of poor performance.

golden share STOCKHOLDING & INVESTMENTS government's controlling interest in newly privatized company a controlling interest retained by a government in a company that has been privatized after having been in public ownership

gold fix *or* **gold fixing** FINANCE twice-daily setting of gold price a system by which the world price for gold is set twice a day in US dollars on the London Gold Exchange and in Paris and Zurich

gold point CURRENCY & EXCHANGE price variation in gold-backed currency an amount by which a currency that is linked to gold can vary in price

gold reserve CURRENCY & EXCHANGE central bank's gold holdings gold coins or bullion held by a central bank to support a paper currency and provide security for borrowing

gold standard CURRENCY & EXCHANGE system valuing currency against gold a system in which a currency unit is defined in terms of its value in gold

good faith deposit FINANCE sum given to confirm deal a deposit made by a buyer to a seller to show a firm intention to complete the transaction

good for the day MARKETS describing instructions valid only on specific day used to describe instructions to a broker that are valid only for the specific day indicated

good for this week *or* **good for this month** *UK* MARKETS = ***good this week, good this month***

goods OPERATIONS & PRODUCTION things that are bought and sold items, materials, and products that can be transported and are for sale

goods and chattels FINANCE movable personal property movable personal possessions, as opposed to land and buildings

Goods and Services Tax TAX **1.** Australian tax on goods and services in Australia, a government-imposed consumption tax, currently of 10%, added to the retail cost of goods and services **2.** former Canadian tax on goods and services a former Canadian tax on goods and services. It was a value-added tax and was replaced by the ***harmonized sales tax***. *Abbr* ***GST***

goods received note OPERATIONS & PRODUCTION receipt for goods a record of goods issued at the point of receipt

good this week *or* **good this month** *US* STOCKHOLDING & INVESTMENTS describes instructions valid only during particular week/month used to describe instructions to a broker that are valid only for the duration of the week/month given. *Abbr* ***GTM***. *UK terms* ***good for this week, good for this month***

good 'til cancel MARKETS describing order effective up to 60 days used to describe an order to buy or sell a security that is effective until an investor cancels it, up to a maximum of 60 days. *Abbr* ***GTC***

good title LEGAL unquestionable property ownership ownership of a property that cannot be legally challenged successfully. *Also called* ***clear title***

goodwill ACCOUNTING business assets such as reputation and expertise an ***intangible asset*** of a company which includes factors such as reputation, contacts, and expertise, for which a buyer of the company may have to pay a premium.

Goodwill becomes an intangible asset when a company has been acquired by another. It then appears on a balance sheet in the amount by which the price paid by the acquiring company exceeds the net tangible assets of the acquired company. In other words

Purchase price – Net assets = Goodwill

If an airline is bought for $12 billion and its net assets are valued at $9 billion, $3 billion of the purchase would be allocated to goodwill on the balance sheet.

go private STOCKHOLDING & INVESTMENTS change to private status without stock market listing to revert from being a public limited company quoted on a stock exchange to a private company without a stock market listing

go public STOCKHOLDING & INVESTMENTS become public corporation to place stock of a private company for sale on a stock exchange in order to raise funds

gourde CURRENCY & EXCHANGE Haitian currency unit a unit of currency used in Haiti

governance CORPORATE GOVERNANCE management of firm the process of managing a company, especially with respect to the soundness or otherwise of its management

Government Accountancy Service ACCOUNTING body monitoring accounting practice in UK Civil Service in the United Kingdom, a part of ***HM Treasury*** whose remit is to ensure that best accounting practice is observed and conducted across the whole of the Civil Service. *Abbr* ***GAS***

government bond STOCKHOLDING & INVESTMENTS investment product issued by government a bond or other security issued by a government on a regular basis as a method of borrowing money for government expenditure

government borrowing FINANCE money government borrows to fund public spending the total amount of money that a country's central government has borrowed to fund its spending on public services and benefits. *See also* ***national debt***

Government Business Enterprise GENERAL MANAGEMENT partly nationalized Australian business an Australian business that is fully or partly owned by the state. *Abbr* ***GBE***

Government National Mortgage Association MORTGAGES *see* ***Ginnie Mae***

government securities/stock STOCKHOLDING & INVESTMENTS securities or stock issued by government securities or stock such as US Treasury bonds or UK gilt-edged securities that are issued by a government

GPM *abbr* MORTGAGES ***graduated payments mortgage***

graduated payments mortgage MORTGAGES US mortgage with initial low payments in the United States, a mortgage with a fixed interest rate but with low payments that gradually increase over the first few years. *Abbr* ***GPM***

graduated pension scheme PENSIONS former UK government pension linking benefits to individual salaries in the United Kingdom, a government pension arrangement where the benefit was calculated as a percentage of a person's salary. Former contributors still receive payments but there are no new contributors.

graduated tax TAX = ***progressive tax***

grand total FINANCE sum of all subtotals the final total, which is a result of adding several subtotals

granny bond *UK* STOCKHOLDING & INVESTMENTS savings type for older people a long-term savings opportunity for older people, with a tax advantage or a return linked to the rate of inflation (*informal*). *See also* ***index-linked savings certificate***

grant 1. FINANCE money given to fund something money given by a government or other organization to help pay for something such as education or research **2.** LEGAL transfer something legally to somebody else to transfer money, property, or rights to somebody in a legal transaction

grant of probate LEGAL in UK, document certifying validity of will in the United Kingdom, a document that states the validity of a will and upholds the appointment of the executor(s)

grantor STOCKHOLDING & INVESTMENTS seller of option a person who sells an ***option*** to another person

grapevine GENERAL MANAGEMENT unofficial means of communication an informal communication network within an organization that conveys information through unofficial channels independent of management control. Information travels much more quickly through the grapevine than through formal channels and may become distorted. A grapevine may reinterpret official corporate messages or spread gossip and rumor in the absence of effective organization channels. It can, however, also complement official communication, provide feedback, and strengthen social relationships within the organization.

graph STATISTICS representation of relationship between variables a diagram depicting the relationship between dependent and independent variables through the use of lines, curves, or figures on horizontal and vertical axes. Time is the most common independent variable, showing how the dependent variable has altered over a defined period.

graveyard market MARKETS **1.** market for infrequently traded stocks a market for stock that is infrequently traded either through lack of interest or because of little or no value **2.** market where sellers face large losses a ***bear market*** where investors who dispose of their holdings are faced with large losses, as potential investors prefer to stay liquid until the market shows signs of improving

gravy train BUSINESS business activity yielding large profits easily any type of business activity in which a person or organization makes a large profit without much effort

gray knight *US* MERGERS & ACQUISITIONS unreliable friendly firm involved in takeover a ***white knight*** that does not have the confidence of the company to be acquired in a ***takeover***. *UK term* ***grey knight***. *See also* ***knight***

gray market *US* **1.** MARKETS unofficial market for stock before official trading an unofficial market run by dealers, in which new issues of stock are bought and sold before they officially become available for trading on a stock exchange, even before the stock allocations become known **2.** MARKETS market for imported goods a ***market*** in which goods are sold that have been manufactured abroad and imported. A gray market product is one that has been imported legally, in contrast to one on the ***black market***, which is illegal. Such markets arise when there is a supply shortage, usually for exclusive goods, and the goods are offered for sale at lower prices than the equivalent goods manufactured in the home country. **3.** MARKETING older people's shopping preferences the market segment occupied by older members of a population ▶ *UK term* ***grey market***

gray marketing *US* MARKETING targeting older people marketing aimed at older age groups such as the middle-aged and elderly. *UK term* ***grey marketing***

gray wave *US* BUSINESS describing companies with good prospects for distant future used to describe a company that is thought likely to have good prospects in the distant future. It gets its name from the fact that investors are likely to have gray hair before they see their expectations fulfilled (*slang*). *UK term* ***grey wave***

Great Depression ECONOMICS 1930s global economic crisis the world economic crisis that began after the US stock market collapsed in 1929 and continued through the 1930s, resulting in mass unemployment and poverty, especially in North America

greater fool theory STOCKHOLDING & INVESTMENTS strategy assuming overpriced stock will attract buyer the investing strategy that assumes it is wise to buy a stock that is not worth its current price. The assumption is that somebody will buy it from you later for an even greater price.

green accounting ACCOUNTING = ***environmental accounting***

greenback CURRENCY & EXCHANGE US paper money a piece of US paper money of any denomination

green card HR & PERSONNEL work permit for noncitizens in US an identity card and work permit issued by the US government to a person living and working in the United States who is not a US citizen. It is officially known as a "United States Permanent Resident Card."

green chips BUSINESS promising small companies small companies considered to have potential for growth

green currency CURRENCY & EXCHANGE former EU currency for agricultural prices in the European Union, currency formerly used for calculating agricultural payments. Each country had an exchange rate fixed by the Commission, so before the introduction of the euro there were currencies such as "green francs" and "green marks."

green dollar *US* FINANCE spending and investment based on environmental awareness money spent on environmentally sound products and services and investing in companies with environmentally sound policies and practices. *UK term* ***green pound***

green investing STOCKHOLDING & INVESTMENTS investment in green technologies investing in companies developing environmentally sound technologies and products to counter the economic effects of climate change

greenmail MARKETS stock purchase threatening takeover to prompt profitable resale the purchase of enough of a company's stock to threaten it with ***takeover***, so that the company is forced to buy back the stock at a higher price to avoid the takeover (*slang*)

Green Paper UK government report on proposed law in the United Kingdom, a report from the government on proposals for a new law to be discussed in Parliament. *See also* ***White Paper***

green pound **1.** *UK* FINANCE = ***green dollar*** **2.** CURRENCY & EXCHANGE monetary unit used for converting EU agricultural prices in the European Union, a currency unit formerly used for converting agricultural prices into pounds sterling

green shoe *or* **greenshoe option** STOCKHOLDING & INVESTMENTS option in stock issue covering potential shortfall an option offered by a company raising the capital for the issue of further shares of stock to cover a shortfall in the event of overallocation. It gets its name from the Green Shoe Manufacturing Company, which was the first to include the feature in a public offering (*slang*).

green taxes TAX taxes that discourage environmental damage taxes levied to discourage behavior that will be harmful to the environment

Gresham's Law ECONOMICS theory that cheaper money replaces more valuable money the principle that "bad money will drive out good." If two forms of money with the same denomination exist in the same market, the form with the higher metal value will be driven out of circulation because people hoard it and use the lower-rated form to spend.

grey knight *UK* MERGERS & ACQUISITIONS = ***gray knight***

grey market *UK* MARKETS = ***gray market***

grey marketing *UK* MARKETING = ***gray marketing***

grey wave *UK* BUSINESS = ***gray wave***

gross ACCOUNTING without deductions before taxes and other deductions have been taken into account

gross borrowings ACCOUNTING total of firm's loans and overdrafts the total of all money borrowed by a company including items such as overdrafts and long-term loans but without deducting cash in bank accounts and on deposit

gross domestic product ECONOMICS *see* ***GDP***

gross earnings FINANCE total pay before deductions a person's salary or wage before subtracting payroll deductions such as taxes and retirement savings

gross income FINANCE total income before deductions a person's salary or wage plus any other money received from other sources, before subtracting payroll deductions, such as taxes and retirement savings, and any other taxes

gross income yield ACCOUNTING yield before tax the yield of an investment before tax is deducted

gross interest ACCOUNTING interest earned before tax is deducted the interest earned on a deposit or security before the deduction of tax. *See also* ***net interest***

gross lease FINANCE lease that exempts lessee from some payments a lease that does not require the lessee to pay for things the owner usually pays for. *See also* ***net lease***

gross margin **1.** FINANCE difference between borrower's interest payments and lender's costs the difference between the interest rate paid by a borrower and the cost of the funds to the lender **2.** ACCOUNTING percentage difference between income and costs the difference between revenue and cost of revenue expressed as a percentage **3.** OPERATIONS & PRODUCTION difference between unit's manufacturing cost and sale price the difference between the manufacturing cost of a unit of output and the price at which it is sold ▶ *Abbr* ***GM***

gross national product ECONOMICS *see* ***GNP***

gross negligence GENERAL MANAGEMENT failure to act responsibly a breach of a duty to act with expected care in conducting activities. *See also* ***negligence***

gross profit ACCOUNTING difference between total sales revenue and production costs the difference between an organization's sales revenue and the cost of goods sold. Unlike ***net profit***, gross profit does not include distribution, administration, or finance costs. *Also called* ***trading profit***

gross profit margin ACCOUNTING *see* ***profit margin***

gross receipts ACCOUNTING total revenue the total revenue received by a business, before tax and other deductions have been taken into account. *See also* ***net receipts***

gross redemption yield *UK* STOCKHOLDING & INVESTMENTS = ***yield to maturity***

gross sales ACCOUNTING sales before discounts the total of all sales before discounts

gross spread MARKETS difference between public's and underwriter's price for security the difference between the price of a security offered to the public and the price the underwriter pays

gross turnover ACCOUNTING total turnover all of a business's income less statutory allowances, and other taxes on this income

gross yield STOCKHOLDING & INVESTMENTS income derived from securities before tax the income return derived from securities before the deduction of tax

gross yield to redemption *UK* STOCKHOLDING & INVESTMENTS = ***gross redemption yield***

ground rent REAL ESTATE **1.** rent paid to owner of land under building a rent paid by the main tenant to the owner of the ground on which a building sits **2.** rent paid on vacant land in the United States, a rent paid on land by a tenant to the owner of the land

group BUSINESS firm with subsidiaries a commercial organization consisting of a parent company and subsidiaries under common ownership

group balance sheet ACCOUNTING = ***consolidated balance sheet***

group investment STOCKHOLDING & INVESTMENTS shared investment an investment made by more than one person

group life assurance *UK* INSURANCE = ***group life insurance***

group life insurance *US* INSURANCE life insurance policy covering several individuals a life insurance policy that covers a number of people such as members of an association or club, or employees at a company. *UK term* ***group life assurance***

Group of Eight FINANCE *see* ***G8***

Group of Seven FINANCE *see* ***G7***

Group of Ten FINANCE *see* ***G10***

Group of Twenty FINANCE *see* ***G20***

groupthink GENERAL MANAGEMENT desire for agreement that compromises judgment a phenomenon that occurs during ***decision making*** or ***problem solving*** when a team's desire to reach an agreement overrides its ability to appraise the problem properly. It is similar to the ***Abilene paradox*** in that it is based on people's desire to conform and please others.

growth 1. FINANCE firm's economic increase an increase in productivity, sales, or earnings that an organization experiences **2.** OPERATIONS & PRODUCTION increase in demand for product the second stage in a product life cycle, following the launch, when demand for the product increases rapidly

growth and income fund STOCKHOLDING & INVESTMENTS mutual fund seeking capital increase with large dividends a mutual fund that tries to maximize growth of capital while paying significant dividends

growth capital FINANCE funding that firm uses to expand funding that allows a company to accelerate its growth. For new startup companies, growth capital is the second stage of funding after ***seed capital***.

growth company BUSINESS firm increasing in size or output a company whose contribution to the economy is growing because it is increasing its workforce or earning increased foreign exchange for its exported goods

growth curve STATISTICS line on graph showing increase over time a line plotted on a graph that shows a statistical increase over a period of time

Growth, Employment, and Redistribution INTERNATIONAL TRADE *see* ***GEAR***

growth equity STOCKHOLDING & INVESTMENTS promising investment product an equity that is thought to have good prospects of growth, usually with a high price/earnings ratio. *Also called* ***growth stock***

growth fund STOCKHOLDING & INVESTMENTS mutual fund focusing on capital increase a mutual fund that tries to maximize growth of capital without regard to dividends

growth index BUSINESS numerical scale representing firm's economic increase an index showing the growth in a company's revenues, earnings, dividends, or other figures

growth industry FINANCE area of business expanding quickly an industry that is developing and expanding at a faster rate than other industries

growth prospects FINANCE potential for economic increase the likelihood that something such as a specific stock or a country's economy will considerably improve its performance

growth rate ECONOMICS how much and how fast economy is growing the rate of an economy's growth as measured by its technical progress, the growth of its labor force, and the increase in its ***capital stock***

growth stock STOCKHOLDING & INVESTMENTS = ***growth equity***

GST *abbr* TAX ***Goods and Services Tax***

GTC *abbr* MARKETS ***good 'til cancel***

GTM *abbr* MARKETS ***good this month***

GTW *abbr* MARKETS ***good this week***

guarantee FINANCE promise to cover another person's contractual duties a promise made by a third party, or guarantor, that he or she will be liable if one of the parties to a contract fails to fulfill their contractual obligations. A guarantee may be acceptable to a bank as security for borrowing, provided the guarantor has sufficient financial means to cover his or her potential liability.

guaranteed bond STOCKHOLDING & INVESTMENTS bond with guaranteed principal and interest a bond on which the principal and interest are guaranteed by an institution other than the one that issues it, or a stock in which the dividends are similarly guaranteed. *Also called* ***guaranteed stock***

guaranteed fund STOCKHOLDING & INVESTMENTS investment whose losses third party promises to cover a fixed term investment where a third party promises to repay the investor's principal in full should the investment fall below the initial sum invested

guaranteed income bond INSURANCE UK life insurance bond providing fixed income a bond issued by a UK life insurance company designed to provide an investor with a fixed rate of income for a specific period of time. Only those policies with an independent third party guarantee can receive this denomination.

guaranteed investment certificate *UK* INSURANCE = ***guaranteed investment contract***

guaranteed investment contract *US* INSURANCE investment guaranteeing interest but not principal an investment instrument issued by an insurance company that guarantees interest but not principal. *UK term* ***guaranteed investment certificate***

guaranteed renewable policy INSURANCE policy valid as long as payments continue an insurance policy that remains in effect as long as the premiums are paid

guaranteed stock STOCKHOLDING & INVESTMENTS = ***guaranteed bond***

guarantor BUSINESS somebody promising to repay borrower's loan if necessary a person or organization that guarantees repayment of a loan if the borrower defaults or is unable to pay

guarantor of last resort FINANCE person or entity guaranteeing bad debt repayment a person, organization, or government that guarantees repayment of a debt that cannot otherwise be repaid

guardian LEGAL court-appointed person managing affairs of another a person appointed by law to act on behalf of somebody, especially a child, who cannot act on his or her own behalf

guardian ad litem LEGAL somebody representing child in court case a person who acts on behalf of a minor who is a defendant in a court case

gun jumping FINANCE profitable trading based on inside information trading that takes place on the basis of privileged information *(slang)*

gunslinger STOCKHOLDING & INVESTMENTS investment manager investing in high-risk stocks a portfolio manager who invests in high-risk stocks hoping that they will yield high returns *(slang)*

GW *abbr* E-COMMERCE ***payment gateway***

H

haggle FINANCE discuss to agree on price of item to reach a price with a buyer or seller by the gradual raising of offers and lowering of the price asked until a mutually accepted figure is obtained

haircut 1. FINANCE difference between loan amount and value of collateral the difference between the market value of a security and the amount lent to the owner using the security as collateral **2.** STOCKHOLDING & INVESTMENTS estimate of investment loss an estimate of possible loss in investments

half-life MORTGAGES years it takes to repay half of mortgage the number of years needed to repay half the principal borrowed on a mortgage

half-normal plot STATISTICS plot of statistical data to identify anomalies a way of plotting statistical data which is used to check for the presence of values in the data that fall outside the expected range

half-stock STOCKHOLDING & INVESTMENTS $50 stock a stock that has a nominal value of fifty US dollars

half-year ACCOUNTING half of accounting period six months for which accounts are presented

hammer MARKETS take firm off London Stock Exchange to remove a business from trading on the London Stock Exchange because it has failed ◇ hammering the market MARKETS the practice of ***short selling*** by speculators who think prices are about to drop so they can buy back before delivery and make a profit

handle 1. BUSINESS to deal in particular product, service, or market to buy, sell, or trade in a particular product, service, or market **2.** STOCKHOLDING & INVESTMENTS whole-number price of share of stock or currency the price of a stock or foreign currency, quoted as a whole number

handling charge OPERATIONS & PRODUCTION money charged for preparing goods for dispatch money to be paid for packing, invoicing, or dealing with goods which are being shipped

hand off *US, Canada* GENERAL MANAGEMENT transfer responsibility for project to give responsibility for a project to another person or organization

hand signals MARKETS signs made with hands in stock exchange the signs used by ***traders*** on the ***trading floors*** at exchanges for futures and options to overcome the problem of noise

hands-off GENERAL MANAGEMENT without constant supervision characterized by an absence of close and constant management attention

hands-on GENERAL MANAGEMENT closely involved characterized by first-hand personal involvement in the management of an activity

hang out loan FINANCE outstanding amount on loan the amount of a loan that is still outstanding after the termination of the loan

Hang Seng index MARKETS Hong Kong Stock Exchange indicator an index of the prices of selected stocks on the Hong Kong Stock Exchange

hara-kiri swap FINANCE exchange of interest rates with no profit margin an interest rate swap made without a profit margin

hard capital rationing FINANCE *see* ***capital rationing*** *(sense 2)*

hard cash CURRENCY & EXCHANGE money in bills money in the form of bills and coins, as opposed to checks or credit cards

hard commodities MARKETS nonperishable raw materials metals such as copper, zinc, mercury, tin, aluminum, and lead, and other solid raw materials. *See also* ***commodity, soft commodities***

hard currency CURRENCY & EXCHANGE money traded in foreign exchange market a currency that is traded in a foreign exchange market and for which demand is persistently high relative to its supply. *See also* ***soft currency***

hardening FINANCE **1.** stabilizing after changes becoming stable after a period of fluctuation **2.** describing prices that are slowly rising used to describe prices that are slowly moving upward

hard landing ECONOMICS sudden economic recession after growth period the rapid decline of an economy into recession and business stagnation after a sustained period of growth

harmonization 1. FINANCE equality of financial and social regulation the convergence of financial and social regulation in the countries of the European Union **2.** GENERAL MANAGEMENT equalizing pay and conditions the resolution of inequalities in the pay and conditions of employment between different categories of employees **3.** GENERAL MANAGEMENT equalizing benefits of related companies the alignment of the systems of pay and benefits of two companies that become one by merger, acquisition, or takeover **4.** GENERAL MANAGEMENT equalizing treatment of full- and part-time employees the process of removing differences between groups of employees, such as full- and part-time staff, with regard to terms and conditions of employment such as rates of pay, pension rights, and vacation entitlement

harmonized sales tax TAX Canadian tax on goods and services a Canadian tax on goods and services. It is a value-added tax that replaced the Goods and Services Tax. *Abbr* ***HST***

harvesting strategy MARKETING slowing marketing activity before sale of product ends a reduction in or cessation of marketing for a product prior to it being withdrawn from sale, resulting in an increase in profits on the back of previous marketing and advertising campaigns

head and shoulders MARKETS graph showing three rallies in firm's stock price a pattern in a graph plotting a company's stock price which resembles the silhouette of a person's head and shoulders (three rises and falls, with the most pronounced rise and fall in the middle). Analysts see this pattern as an indication of an impending larger fall in price.

headcount reduction HR & PERSONNEL reducing number of employees a reduction in the number of people employed by a company in circumstances such as a drop in the amount of sales

headline rate of inflation ECONOMICS inflation measure including wide range of costs a measure of inflation that attempts to take account of most costs and services. In the United States, the headline rate is based on the Consumer Price Index. In the United Kingdom, it is based on the Retail Price Index, which takes account of homeowners' mortgage costs.

head of household TAX US tax status for somebody with dependents in the United States, a federal tax filing status that qualifies a person to pay less income tax if they are unmarried or considered unmarried on the last day of the year, have paid more than half of the cost of keeping a home for the year, and have had a dependent child or other qualified dependent such as a parent living with them for more than half the year

headquarters *or* **head office** BUSINESS firm's main office the main office of an organization where most of the administrative work is done and where the board of directors meets

heads of agreement GENERAL MANAGEMENT key items agreed on the most important subjects or items dealt with in a commercial agreement

head tax TAX tax on each adult a tax paid by all adult inhabitants of a country, regardless of their income

health saving account FINANCE US savings plan for medical expenses in the United States, a savings plan with tax benefits that is designed to help individuals accumulate money for qualified medical expenses. *Abbr* ***HSA***

health warning STOCKHOLDING & INVESTMENTS message on UK advertisements about risks of investing in the United Kingdom, a legally required warning message printed on advertisements for investments, stating that the value of investments can fall as well as rise *(slang)*

heavy 1. MARKETS experiencing more activity than usual used to describe a market in which trading is more active than usual **2.** STOCKHOLDING & INVESTMENTS investing too much in one type of stock having too many investments in related industries or stock **3.** STOCKHOLDING & INVESTMENTS high-priced used to describe a stock that has such a high price that small investors are reluctant to buy it. In this case the company may decide to split the stock so as to make it more attractive.

heavy industry OPERATIONS & PRODUCTION manufacturing sector making large products a manufacturing industry that requires a lot of resources, uses heavy raw materials such as coal, and makes large products such as ships or engines

hedge STOCKHOLDING & INVESTMENTS **1.** method of protecting against possible loss a protection against a possible loss on an investment which involves taking an action that is the opposite of an action taken earlier **2.** take action to reduce risk of investment loss to take measures to offset risk of loss on an investment, especially by investing in counterbalancing securities as a guard against price fluctuations

hedge fund STOCKHOLDING & INVESTMENTS, RISK risky type of investment fund an investment fund that takes considerable risks, including investment in unconventional instruments, in the hope of generating great profits. There are many types of hedge funds, using very different strategies. Some are highly geared and some use arbitrage, futures, and options to achieve their objectives.

hedging STOCKHOLDING & INVESTMENTS, RISK strategy for protecting against possible financial losses financial transactions intended to protect against possible losses from existing financial activities or investments, for example, buying investments at a fixed price for delivery later or investing in counterbalancing securities ◇ hedging against inflation STOCKHOLDING & INVESTMENTS investing in order to avoid the impact of inflation, thus protecting the purchasing power of capital. Historically, equities have generally outperformed returns from savings accounts in the long term and beaten the ***retail price index***. They are thus considered as one of the best hedges against inflation, although no stock market investment is without risk.

held order STOCKHOLDING & INVESTMENTS large order that seller waits to process an order that a dealer does not process immediately, often because of its large size

hereditament LEGAL property that can be inherited any property, including personal, land, and buildings, that somebody can inherit

Her Majesty's Revenue & Customs TAX, INTERNATIONAL TRADE UK government department that collects tax in the United Kingdom, the government department responsible for the administration and collection of all forms of tax, including VAT, income tax, and excise duties. HMRC combines the duties of two formerly separate departments, the Inland Revenue and HM Customs and Excise. *Abbr* ***HMRC***

Herstatt Risk CURRENCY & EXCHANGE, RISK risk of delivery failure in foreign currency transaction the risk in foreign currency exchange transactions that one party to the exchange will fail to make payment after having received payment from the other party

heuristics GENERAL MANAGEMENT exploration of possible solutions in problem solving a method for problem solving or decision making that arrives at solutions through exploratory means such as experimentation, trial and error, or evaluation

hidden asset ACCOUNTING firm's property recorded at lower than actual value an asset that is shown in a company's accounts as being worth much less than its true market value

hidden economy ECONOMICS = ***black economy***

hidden reserves ACCOUNTING firm's unrecorded reserves funds that are set aside but not declared in the company's balance sheet

hidden tax TAX tax that not everyone is aware of a tax that is not immediately apparent. For example, while a consumer may be aware of a tax on retail purchases, a tax imposed at the wholesale level, which consequently increases the cost of items to the retailer, will not be apparent.

high concept GENERAL MANAGEMENT succinct idea a compelling idea that is expressed clearly and concisely

high-end GENERAL MANAGEMENT of most expensive, advanced, or powerful kind relating to the most expensive, most advanced, or most powerful in a variety of products such as computers

higher rate TAX upper UK income tax rate in the United Kingdom, the higher of the two bands of income tax. ***Her Majesty's Revenue & Customs*** is responsible for the administration of income tax and publishes information on current tax rates and allowances on its website. *See also* ***basic rate***

high finance FINANCE dealing with very large amounts of money the lending, investing, and borrowing of very large sums of money organized by financiers

high-flier *or* **high-flyer** STOCKHOLDING & INVESTMENTS stock that increases quickly in price a heavily traded stock that increases in value considerably over a short period

high gearing FINANCE when firm borrows a lot of money a situation in which a company has a high level of borrowing compared to its stock price

high-income STOCKHOLDING & INVESTMENTS describing fund yielding high returns used to describe a fund that yields a high rate of return

highly geared company *or* **highly-geared company** = ***highly leveraged company***

highly leveraged company *US* BUSINESS firm with relatively large debts a company that has a large amount of debt in proportion to its equity. *UK term* ***highly geared company***

high net worth individual FINANCE somebody with at least $4 million a person whose net assets, excluding the value of a home, are worth more than $4 million, by some classifications. It is estimated that some 10 million worldwide fall into this category. *Abbr* ***HNWI***

high-powered GENERAL MANAGEMENT able and dynamic having, showing, or requiring great dynamism and ability

high-premium convertible debenture STOCKHOLDING & INVESTMENTS bond unlikely to be converted a convertible bond with an exercise price that makes it unlikely to be converted in the foreseeable future. It therefore has a low option premium.

high-pressure MARKETING forceful and persistent used to describe a selling technique in which the sales representative attempts to persuade a buyer forcefully and persistently

high-risk company BUSINESS, RISK firm running high business risks a company that is exposed to high levels of business risk

High Street bank BANKING major UK bank with local offices a UK bank that provides ***retail banking*** services and has many local offices for customers to visit, as distinguished from an ***investment bank*** or a bank that provides services only on the Internet

high-tech crime FRAUD crime committed using computer technologies illegal activities using the Internet or other computer technologies. *Also called* ***hi-tech crime***

high yield STOCKHOLDING & INVESTMENTS, RISK higher than usual yield a higher rate of return than is usual for a particular type of investment or company

high-yield bond STOCKHOLDING & INVESTMENTS, RISK = ***junk bond***

high yielder STOCKHOLDING & INVESTMENTS, RISK high-performing but risky investment product a security that has a higher than average rate of return and is consequently often a higher risk investment

hire 1. HR & PERSONNEL give job to somebody to employ somebody new to work for you or your organization **2.** *UK* FINANCE = ***rent***

hire purchase *UK* FINANCE = ***installment plan***

historical cost *or* **historic cost** ACCOUNTING original cost of item bought in past the record of the value of a firm's asset reflecting its original price when it was purchased

historical cost accounting ACCOUNTING record keeping based on original cost of items the preparation of accounts on the basis of historical cost, with assets valued at their original cost of purchase. *UK term* ***fair value accounting***. *See also* ***current cost accounting***

historical cost depreciation ACCOUNTING discounting asset's value based on original cost the accounting practice of depreciating a firm's asset based on its original cost

historical figures ACCOUNTING figures or values correct at the time figures or values that were correct at the time of purchase or payment, as distinct from a current value

historical summary ACCOUNTING UK report of firm's results in past in the United Kingdom, an optional synopsis of a company's results over a period of time, often five or ten years, featured in the annual accounts

historical trading range MARKETS = ***trading range***

historic pricing STOCKHOLDING & INVESTMENTS basing mutual fund prices on most recent holdings the establishment of the price of a share in a mutual fund on the basis of the most recent values of its holdings

hi-tech crime FRAUD = ***high-tech crime***

HMCE INTERNATIONAL TRADE *see* ***Her Majesty's Revenue & Customs***

HM Customs and Excise INTERNATIONAL TRADE *see* ***Her Majesty's Revenue & Customs***

HMRC *abbr* TAX, INTERNATIONAL TRADE ***Her Majesty's Revenue & Customs***

HM Revenue & Customs TAX, INTERNATIONAL TRADE = ***Her Majesty's Revenue & Customs***

HM Treasury FINANCE UK government department that manages public funds the UK government department responsible for managing the country's public revenues. While the incumbent prime minister holds the title of First Lord of the Treasury, the department is run on a day-to-day basis by the ***Chancellor of the Exchequer***.

HNWI *abbr* FINANCE ***high net worth individual***

hockey stick BUSINESS performance curve that falls then rises sharply a performance curve, typical of businesses in their early stages, that descends then rises sharply in a straight line, creating a shape similar to that of a hockey stick

hold STOCKHOLDING & INVESTMENTS own security for long time to own a security over a long period of time

holdback E-COMMERCE reserve funds covering possible disputed charges funds from a merchant's credit card transactions held in reserve for a predetermined time by the merchant account provider to cover possible disputed charges. *Also called* ***reserve account***

holder FINANCE owner of financial obligation the person who is in possession of a ***bill of exchange*** or ***promissory note***

holder of record STOCKHOLDING & INVESTMENTS official owner of stock the person who is registered as the owner of stock in a company

holding *or* **holdings** STOCKHOLDING & INVESTMENTS investment owned by somebody an investment, or set of investments, that a person owns at a specific time

holding company BUSINESS parent firm that owns other firms a parent organization that owns the majority of share capital in other companies in order to gain control of them. A holding company may have no other business than the holding of stock in other companies.

holding period STOCKHOLDING & INVESTMENTS period between purchase and sale of asset the length of time an asset was held from the time of purchase to the time of sale, used for determining whether a capital gain or loss is taxed as short-term (less than one year) or long-term (one year or more)

home banking BANKING using computer at home for banking services a system of banking using a personal computer at home to carry out various financial transactions such as paying invoices or checking transactions in a bank account

home loan MORTGAGES money used for house purchase a loan of money to enable the purchase of a house

homeowner's insurance policy *US* INSURANCE insurance for house and contents an insurance policy that protects homeowners against loss of or damage to a home or its contents and provides coverage for personal liability if somebody is injured while on the premises. *UK terms* ***home policy, household policy***

home policy *UK* INSURANCE = ***homeowner's insurance policy***

home run FINANCE investment with rapid returns an investment that produces a high rate of return in a short time

home trade *UK* BUSINESS = ***domestic trade***

homogenization INTERNATIONAL TRADE imposition of uniformity on separate markets and cultures the removal of characteristic differences between separate markets and cultures. Globalization is frequently blamed for homogenization.

honorarium FINANCE modest payment for simple duties a payment made to somebody for performing a specific service, often a token amount

horizontal diversification BUSINESS developing new but related areas expansion into a related but different product area, for example, a domestic furniture manufacturer producing office furniture. *See also* ***diversification***

horizontal equity ECONOMICS belief in similar taxation for similar incomes the theory that individuals in similar financial situations should be taxed at the same rate

horizontal integration BUSINESS merging of similar functions or organizations the merging of functions or organizations that operate on a similar level. Horizontal integration involves the amalgamation of companies producing the same types of goods or operating at the same stage of the supply chain. It may also describe the merging of departments within an organization that perform similar tasks. *See also* ***vertical integration***

horizontal merger MERGERS & ACQUISITIONS combining of firms in same industry the amalgamation of two or more organizations from the same industry under single ownership, through the direct *acquisition* by one organization of the net assets or liabilities of the other. *See also* ***merger***

horizontal spread STOCKHOLDING & INVESTMENTS, RISK simultaneous buying and selling of two options a purchase of one ***option*** accompanied by the sale of another with the same ***exercise price*** but a different date of maturity. *Also called* ***calendar spread***

horse-trading GENERAL MANAGEMENT shrewd bargaining bargaining in which the goods are not directly comparable and the valuations are frequently subjective

hostile bid MERGERS & ACQUISITIONS = ***contested takeover bid***

hostile takeover MERGERS & ACQUISITIONS unwelcome acquisition of firm the acquisition by a company of a controlling interest in the voting share capital of another company whose directors or stockholders are opposed to the action. *See also* ***takeover***

hot card BANKING stolen credit card a credit card that has been stolen and might be used fraudulently

hot issue STOCKHOLDING & INVESTMENTS new investment product expected to perform well a new security that is expected to trade at a significant premium to its issue price. *See also* ***hot stock***

hot money 1. FRAUD stolen money money that has been obtained by dishonest means. *See also* ***money laundering*** **2.** STOCKHOLDING & INVESTMENTS funds transferred for short-term gain money that is moved on short notice from one financial center to another to secure the best possible return

hot stock MARKETS stock whose price rises rapidly a stock, usually a new issue, that rises quickly on the stock market. *See also* ***hot issue***

house FINANCE finance firm a business organization, especially a financial institution that handles the purchase and sale of securities to investors

house call STOCKHOLDING & INVESTMENTS warning by brokerage firm of low margin account notice from a brokerage firm that the amount of money in a client's margin account is less than the required amount

household policy *UK* INSURANCE = ***homeowner's insurance policy***

house journal GENERAL MANAGEMENT periodic bulletin giving internal information an informal publication issued periodically by an organization or agency to aid the internal communication process

house poor FINANCE with all money invested in house a situation in which the cost of owning a home is too high in proportion to the homeowner's income

HSA *abbr* FINANCE ***health saving account***

HST *abbr* TAX ***harmonized sales tax***

human asset accounting HR & PERSONNEL = ***human capital accounting***

human capital HR & PERSONNEL staff the ***employees*** of an organization. The term builds on the concept of capital as an asset of an organization, implying recognition of the importance and monetary worth of the skills and experience of its employees. It is measured through ***human capital accounting***.

human capital accounting HR & PERSONNEL attempted valuation of employee knowledge and skills an attempt to place a financial figure on the knowledge and skills of an organization's ***employees*** or ***human capital***. *Also called* ***human asset accounting, human resource accounting*** *(sense 1)*

human resource accounting HR & PERSONNEL **1.** = ***human capital accounting*** **2.** record keeping of value of firm's employees the identification, recording, and reporting of the investment in, and return from the employment of, the personnel of an organization

human resource forecasting GENERAL MANAGEMENT estimates of future employment needs and supply the prediction of future levels of demand for, and supply of, workers and skills at organizational, regional, or national level. A variety of techniques are used in manpower forecasting, including the statistical analysis of current trends and the use of mathematical models. At national level, these include the analysis of census statistics; at organizational level, projections of future requirements may be made from sales and production figures. Human resource forecasting forms part of the human resource planning process. *Also called* ***manpower forecasting***

human resource management HR & PERSONNEL management of employees as individuals a model of ***personnel management*** that focuses on the individual rather than taking a collective approach. It is characterized by an emphasis on strategic integration, employee commitment, workforce flexibility, and quality of goods and services.

human resource planning GENERAL MANAGEMENT efforts to balance employment needs with supply the development of strategies to match the supply of workers to the availability of jobs at organizational, regional, or national level. Human resource planning involves reviewing current personnel resources, forecasting future requirements and availability, and taking steps to ensure that the supply of people and skills meets demand. At a national level, this may be conducted by government or industry bodies, and at an organizational level, by human resource managers. *Also called* ***manpower planning***

hurdle rate 1. BANKING rate above which loan is profitable for bank a minimum rate of return needed by a bank to fund a loan, representing the rate below which a loan is not profitable for the bank **2.** STOCKHOLDING & INVESTMENTS minimum return before fees due the minimum rate of return required on a fund before the fund manager can begin taking fees **3.** *UK* STOCKHOLDING & INVESTMENTS growth rate needed to repay stock's redemption price the rate of growth in a portfolio required to repay the final fixed redemption price of zero dividend preference shares

hurricane bond STOCKHOLDING & INVESTMENTS, RISK catastrophe bond for hurricane insurance risk a type of ***catastrophe bond*** that transfers some of the insurance risk from insurers to investors in the event of a hurricane

hybrid STOCKHOLDING & INVESTMENTS combination of investment types a combination of financial instruments, for example, a bond with warrants attached, or a variety of cash and derivative instruments designed to mirror the performance of a financial market

hybrid annuity INSURANCE part fixed part variable annuity a type of ***annuity*** that combines features of both a fixed annuity (guaranteeing fixed payments to the individual receiving it for the term of the contract, usually until death) and a variable annuity (offering no guarantee but having potential for a greater return, usually based on the performance of a stock or mutual fund). *Also called* ***combination annuity***

hybrid financial instrument STOCKHOLDING & INVESTMENTS investment type with features of other types a ***financial instrument*** such as a convertible bond that has characteristics of multiple types of instruments, often convertible from one to another

hyperinflation ECONOMICS extremely high rate of inflation a very rapid growth in the rate of inflation so that money loses value and physical goods replace currency as a medium of exchange. This happened, for example, in Latin America in the early 1990s and in Zimbabwe in the 2000s.

hyperpartnering E-COMMERCE temporary commercial partnerships using Internet technology a form of commerce in which companies use Internet technology to form partnerships and execute transactions at high speed and low cost in order to take advantage of business opportunities as soon as they appear

hypothecate FINANCE **1.** use real estate to back loan to use the mortgage on real estate as collateral for a loan **2.** use money for defined purpose to designate money, especially public funds, to be used for a specific purpose only

hypothecation FINANCE **1.** using assets as loan collateral without transferring ownership an arrangement in which assets such as securities are used as collateral for a loan but without transferring legal ownership to the lender **2.** designating money for specific purpose the process of earmarking money derived from specific sources for related expenditure, for example, using taxes collected on gasoline sales solely on public transportation

hypothesis testing STATISTICS checking sample data against knowledge of sample the process of testing sample data from a statistical study to determine whether it is consistent with what is known about the sample population

hysteresis ECONOMICS dependency of equilibrium on change the way in which equilibrium is dependent on the changes that take place as an economy experiences change

I

IAS *abbr* TAX, STOCKHOLDING & INVESTMENTS ***installment activity statement***

IASB *abbr* ACCOUNTING ***International Accounting Standards Board***

IASC *abbr* ACCOUNTING ***International Accounting Standards Committee***

IB *abbr* BANKING ***investment bank***

IBOR *or* **IBR** *abbr* MARKETS ***Interbank Offered Rate***

IBR MARKETS *see* ***Interbank Offered Rate***

IBRC INSURANCE former association of UK insurance brokers in the United Kingdom, a statutory body established under the Insurance Brokers Registration Act of 1977 which was deregulated following the establishment of the Financial Services Authority and the General Insurance Services Council. Its complaints and administration functions passed to the Institute of Insurance Brokers. *Full form* ***Insurance Brokers Registration Council***

IBRD BANKING UN bank that helps poorest nations a United Nations organization that provides funds, policy guidance, and technical assistance to facilitate economic development in its poorer member countries. *Full form* ***International Bank for Reconstruction and Development***

ICA *abbr* INSURANCE ***Insurance Council of Australia***

ICAEW *abbr* ACCOUNTING ***Institute of Chartered Accountants in England and Wales***

ICAI *abbr* ACCOUNTING ***Institute of Chartered Accountants in Ireland***

ICANZ *abbr* ACCOUNTING ***Institute of Chartered Accountants of New Zealand***

ICAS *abbr* ACCOUNTING ***Institute of Chartered Accountants of Scotland***

ICC BUSINESS association to support private business an organization that represents business interests to governments, working to improve trading conditions and foster private enterprise. *Full form* ***International Chamber of Commerce***

ICSA *abbr UK* FINANCE ***Institute of Chartered Secretaries and Administrators***

ICSID *abbr* BANKING ***International Centre for Settlement of Investment Disputes***

IDA *abbr* FINANCE ***International Development Association***

identity theft FRAUD use of another's identity for criminal purpose the use of another person's personal and financial information, such as credit card numbers, Social Security numbers, or passport information, without their knowledge, to commit a crime

idle capital *or* **idle cash** FINANCE firm's unused money and property the money and assets of a business that are not being invested productively. *Also called* ***barren money, sideline cash***

IDR *abbr* STOCKHOLDING & INVESTMENTS ***International Depository Receipt***

IFA *abbr* **1.** FINANCE ***independent financial adviser*** **2.** ACCOUNTING ***Institute of Financial Accountants***

IFAD *abbr* FINANCE ***International Fund for Agricultural Development***

IFC *abbr* FINANCE ***International Finance Corporation***

IFRS *abbr* ACCOUNTING ***International Financial Reporting Standards***

IHT *abbr* TAX *US* ***inheritance tax***

IIB *abbr* INSURANCE ***Institute of Insurance Brokers***

IIN *abbr* BANKING ***issuer identification number***

ijara *or* **ijarah** FINANCE agreement by bank to purchase then lease item in Islamic financing, a leasing arrangement in which a bank or financier purchases an item for a customer, then leases it to the customer at a profit

ijara wa-iqtina FINANCE agreement by customer to buy item after leasing it in Islamic financing, a leasing arrangement with a bank similar to ijara in which the customer agrees to purchase the item at a prearranged price at the end of the lease term

ILG *abbr* STOCKHOLDING & INVESTMENTS ***index-linked gilt***

illegal parking STOCKHOLDING & INVESTMENTS, FRAUD concealing true ownership an illegal stock market practice of using another company's name when purchasing securities (*slang*)

illiquid FINANCE **1.** lacking easy access to cash used to describe a person or business that lacks cash or assets such as securities that can readily be converted into cash **2.** not easily convertible to cash used to describe an asset that cannot be easily converted into cash

illiquid market STOCKHOLDING & INVESTMENTS securities market with low trading volume a securities market in which very little trading is taking place

IMA *abbr* STOCKHOLDING & INVESTMENTS **1.** ***investment management agreement*** **2.** ***Investment Management Association***

imaginization GENERAL MANAGEMENT business approach encouraging creativity and innovation an approach to creativity concerned with improving our ability to see and understand situations in new ways, with finding new ways of organizing, with creating shared understanding and personal empowerment, and with developing a capability for continuing self-organization

IMF FINANCE international lending organization an international organization based in Washington, DC, that was established by industrialized nations to monitor economic and financial developments, lend to countries with balance of payments difficulties, and provide expert policy advice and technical assistance. *Full form* ***International Monetary Fund***

immediate annuity PENSIONS single-premium annuity with immediate payments a type of ***annuity*** that is purchased with a single premium and whose payments begin immediately

immediate holding company BUSINESS subsidiary UK firm with its own subsidiaries in the United Kingdom, a company with one or more subsidiaries that is itself a subsidiary of another company (the holding company)

immovable property REAL ESTATE land and buildings land and permanent structures such as buildings

impact day MARKETS first day of trading the day when the terms of a new issue of stock are announced

impaired capital FINANCE firm's total capital lower than stock value a company's capital that is worth less than the nominal value of its stock

impaired credit FINANCE when somebody's credit rating is reduced a situation in which a person becomes less creditworthy than before

impairment of capital FINANCE how much firm's stock value exceeds total capital the extent to which the value of a company is less than the nominal value of its stock

imperfect competition MARKETS = ***monopolistic competition***

impersonation of the deceased fraud FRAUD fraud using deceased person's identity in the United Kingdom, a situation in which a person uses the identity of somebody who has recently died to commit a crime such as accessing financial information or obtaining a passport. *Abbr* ***IOD fraud***

implicit cost FINANCE cost of using resources owned by producer the cost of using resources that are owned by a company that is producing a good or service. *See also* ***explicit cost***

import INTERNATIONAL TRADE product or service introduced from abroad a product or service brought into another country from its country of origin either for sale or for use in manufacturing

import duty INTERNATIONAL TRADE, TAX tax on imported products a tax on goods imported into a country. Although it may simply be a measure for raising revenue, it can also be used to protect domestic manufacturers from overseas competition.

importer INTERNATIONAL TRADE firm bringing goods into country for sale a company that brings goods from one country to another to be sold

import license INTERNATIONAL TRADE government-issued document allowing importation of goods a document issued by a government which allows goods that are to be sold to be brought into the country from another country

import penetration INTERNATIONAL TRADE proportion of foreign goods in domestic market the degree to which one country's imports dominate the ***market share*** of those from other industrialized countries

import quota INTERNATIONAL TRADE set amount of product allowed into country a fixed quantity of a particular type of goods, which the government allows to be brought into the country from another country

import restriction INTERNATIONAL TRADE government action limiting goods brought into country an action by a government to reduce the level of imported goods, for example, by setting quotas and imposing duties

import surcharge INTERNATIONAL TRADE, TAX extra tax on imported goods to discourage imports an extra duty levied on imported goods in an attempt to limit imports in general and to encourage local manufacture

imprest account ACCOUNTING type of petty cash record in the United Kingdom, a record of the transactions of a type of petty cash system. An employee is given an advance of money, an imprest, for incidental expenses and, when most of it has been spent, he or she presents receipts for the expenses to the accounts department and is then reimbursed with cash to the total value of the receipts.

imprest system ACCOUNTING petty cash system involving written receipts in the United Kingdom, a system of controlling a petty cash fund, in which cash is paid out against a written receipt, and the receipt is used to get more cash to bring the fund up to the original level

improvement curve GENERAL MANAGEMENT = ***learning curve***

imputation system TAX dividend tax credit for tax paid by firm a system in which recipients of dividends gain tax advantage for taxes paid by the company that paid the dividends

imputed interest FINANCE, TAX taxable interest considered paid but not paid interest that is considered to be paid and may be taxed, even though it has not yet been paid

IMRO *abbr* REGULATION & COMPLIANCE ***Investment Management Regulatory Organisation***

inactive account BANKING bank account that is not in use a bank account that is not used over a particular period of time

inactive market MARKETS market with little trading taking place a stock or commodities market in which there is little interest shown by potential investors, resulting in few trades

'inan BUSINESS business partnership where partners contribute money and work in Islamic financing, a type of partnership in which the partners contribute both capital and work to a business

Inc. *abbr* BUSINESS ***incorporated***

incentive plan *US* FINANCE program rewarding improved performance a program set up to give benefits to employees to reward them for improved commitment and performance and as a means of motivation. An incentive plan is designed to supplement ***base pay*** and ***fringe benefits***. A *financial incentive plan* may offer stock options or a cash bonus, whereas a nonfinancial *incentive plan* offers benefits such as additional paid vacations. Awards from incentive plans may be made on an individual or team basis. *UK term* ***incentive scheme***

incentive scheme *UK* FINANCE = ***incentive plan***

incentive stock option STOCKHOLDING & INVESTMENTS US plan allowing employees to buy stock in the United States, an employee stock option plan that gives each qualifying employee the right to purchase a specific number of the corporation's shares at a set price during a specific time period. Tax is only payable when the stocks are sold.

incestuous share dealing STOCKHOLDING & INVESTMENTS stock trading among firms in same group stock trading by companies within a group in the stock of the other companies within that group. The legality of such transactions depends on the objective of the deals.

inchoate instrument FINANCE incomplete monetary contract a ***negotiable instrument*** that is incomplete because, for example, the date or amount is missing. The person to whom it is delivered has the authority to complete it in any way he or she considers fit.

incidence of tax TAX indicating who must pay tax used to indicate where the final burden of a tax lies. For example, although a retailer pays any sales tax to the tax collecting authority, the tax itself is ultimately paid by the customer.

incidental expenses FINANCE small amounts spent on unplanned items small amounts of money spent at various times in addition to the usual larger budgeted amounts

income 1. FINANCE money received money received by a company or individual **2.** FINANCE money created money generated by a business **3.** STOCKHOLDING & INVESTMENTS interest or dividends received from investments money received from savings or investments, for example, interest on a bank account or dividends from stock

income bond STOCKHOLDING & INVESTMENTS bond repaid from profits a bond that a company repays only from its profits

income distribution 1. FINANCE, HR & PERSONNEL levels of earnings across group or area the distribution of income across a specific group such as a company or specific area such as a region or country, showing the various wage levels and the percentage of individuals earning at each level **2.** *UK* STOCKHOLDING & INVESTMENTS = ***income dividend***

income dividend *US* STOCKHOLDING & INVESTMENTS money paid to investors from group investment earnings payment to investors of the income generated by a collective investment, less management charges, tax, and expenses. It is distributed in proportion to the number of shares held by each investor. *UK term* ***income distribution***

income elasticity of demand FINANCE demand changing with income a proportional change in demand in response to a change in income

income fund STOCKHOLDING & INVESTMENTS fund focused on high income a fund that attempts to provide high income rather than capital growth

income gearing FINANCE ratio of firm's loan interest payments to profits the ratio of the interest a company pays on its borrowing shown as a percentage of its pre-tax profits

income redistribution ECONOMICS government policy to balance income levels through taxation a government policy to redirect income to a targeted sector of a country's population, for example, by lowering the rate of tax paid by low-income earners

income shares *UK* STOCKHOLDING & INVESTMENTS = ***income stock***

income smoothing ACCOUNTING accounting method to make income appear steady a form of ***creative accounting*** that involves the manipulation of a company's financial statements to show steady annual profits rather than large fluctuations

incomes policy ECONOMICS UK government policy to limit wage and price increases in the United Kingdom, any government policy that seeks to restrain increases in wages or prices by regulating the permitted level of increase

income statement ACCOUNTING = ***profit and loss account***

income stock *US* **1.** STOCKHOLDING & INVESTMENTS stock expected to pay high dividends common stock sought because of its relatively high yield as opposed to its potential to produce capital growth **2.** MARKETS split fund shares receiving income, not capital appreciation certain funds, for example, investment trusts, that issue split level funds where holders of the income element receive all the income (less expenses, charges, and tax), while holders of the capital element receive only the capital gains (less expenses, charges, and tax) ▶ *UK term* ***income shares***

income stream FINANCE money received from product or activity the income received by a company from a particular product or activity

income support FINANCE UK government subsidy for people with low incomes in the United Kingdom, a government benefit paid to low-income earners who are working less than 16 hours per week, and may be disabled or have family care responsibilities. *Abbr* ***IS***

income tax TAX tax on money received a tax levied directly on the income of a person or a company and paid to a local, state, or federal government. *Abbr* ***IT***

income tax allowance TAX untaxed part of person's income in the United Kingdom, a proportion of somebody's income that is not subject to tax. Allowances are announced each year by the ***Chancellor of the Exchequer*** in the ***Budget***. *See also* ***income tax***

income tax return TAX report of earnings for tax purposes a standard format used for reporting income and computing the tax due on it. *Also called* ***declaration of income***

income unit STOCKHOLDING & INVESTMENTS in UK, share in mutual fund in the United Kingdom, a share in a mutual fund that makes regular dividend payments to its stockholders

income yield STOCKHOLDING & INVESTMENTS = ***current yield***

inconvertible CURRENCY & EXCHANGE describing currency not easily converted used to describe a currency that cannot be easily converted into other currencies

incorporated BUSINESS set up as corporation in the United States, legally established as a corporation. *Abbr* ***inc.***

incorporation LEGAL process of forming corporation the legal process of creating a corporation or company. Incorporated entities have a legal status distinct from that of their owners, and limited liability.

incorporeal chattels LEGAL intellectual properties intangible properties such as patents or copyrights

incremental scale *UK* HR & PERSONNEL system of salaries increasing by regular yearly amounts a scale that includes standard increases, especially a salary scale that increases by regular annual amounts

indebted FINANCE owing money to somebody else used to describe a person, company, or country that owes money to another person, a financial institution, or another country

indemnity FINANCE agreement to pay compensation an agreement by one party to make good the losses suffered by another. *See also* ***indemnity insurance, letter of indemnity***

indemnity insurance INSURANCE insurance paid to reimburse damages or losses an insurance contract in which the insurer agrees to cover the cost of losses suffered by the insured party. Most insurance contracts take this form except personal accident and life insurance policies, where fixed sums are paid as compensation, rather than reimbursement, for a loss that cannot be quantified in monetary terms.

indenture STOCKHOLDING & INVESTMENTS agreement about bond a formal document showing the terms of agreement on a ***bond issue***

independent authenticator BUSINESS firm that guarantees other firms are genuine a company that has the authority, either from the government or a controlling body, to issue certificates of authentication when they are sure that a company is who it claims to be

independent company BUSINESS firm not owned by another firm a company that is not owned or controlled by any another company

independent financial adviser FINANCE somebody giving unbiased advice about money a person who gives impartial advice to clients on financial matters and who is not employed by any financial institution, although commission for the sale of products may be received. *Abbr* ***IFA***. *See also* ***financial planner***

independent variable STATISTICS factor whose change in value affects other factors a factor whose value, when it changes, influences one or more other variables

index 1. FINANCE amount representing value of group an amount calculated to represent the relative value of a group of things **2.** MARKETS number indicating value of stocks in market a standard that represents the value of stocks in a market, for example, the Hang Seng, Dow Jones Index, or Nikkei average

index arbitrage MARKETS simultaneously trading stocks and stock index futures the buying or selling of a basket of stocks against an index option or future

indexation FINANCE connecting rate to standard price index the linking of a rate to a standard index of prices, interest rates, stock prices, or similar items

indexed portfolio STOCKHOLDING & INVESTMENTS stock in all firms in stock exchange index a portfolio of stock in all the companies that form the basis of a specific stock exchange index

index fund STOCKHOLDING & INVESTMENTS mutual fund linked to stock exchange index a mutual fund composed of companies listed in an important stock market index in order to match the market's overall performance. *Also called* ***index tracker, tracker fund***. *See also* ***managed fund***

index futures STOCKHOLDING & INVESTMENTS futures contract on stock exchange index a ***futures contract*** trading in one of the major stock market indices such as the ***Standard & Poor's 500 Index***. *See also* ***Dow Jones Averages***

index-linked FINANCE changing in relation to numerical scale varying in value in relation to an index, especially the ***consumer price index***, or the ***retail price index*** for index-linked securities in the United Kingdom

index-linked bond STOCKHOLDING & INVESTMENTS investment product with index tied to index a security where the income is linked to an index such as a financial index. *See also* ***index-linked gilt, index-linked savings certificate***

index-linked gilt STOCKHOLDING & INVESTMENTS UK bond with payments linked to retail prices in the United Kingdom, an inflation-proof government bond, first introduced for institutional investors in 1981 and then made available to the general public in 1982. It is inflation-proof in two ways: the dividend is raised every six months in line with the ***retail price index*** and the original capital is repaid in real terms at redemption, when the indexing of the repayment is undertaken. The nominal value of the stock, however, does not increase with inflation. Like other gilts, ILGs are traded on the market. Price changes are principally dependent on investors' changing perceptions of inflation and real yields. *Abbr* ***ILG***

index-linked savings certificate STOCKHOLDING & INVESTMENTS UK savings type with payments linked to inflation rate a certificate issued by the UK National Savings & Investments organization, with a return linked to the ***retail price index***. *See also* ***granny bond***

index-linked security *UK* STOCKHOLDING & INVESTMENTS = ***inflation-proof security***

index number ECONOMICS number indicating relative economic change a weighted average of a number of observations of an economic attribute, for example, retail prices expressed as a percentage of a similar weighted average calculated at an earlier period

index of leading economic indicators ECONOMICS predictor of future economic performance a statistical measure that uses a set of economic variables to predict the future performance of an economy

index option STOCKHOLDING & INVESTMENTS option to purchase shares in market index an option to purchase shares in a stock market index. This allows an investor to trade within a particular sector and eliminates some of the risk of investing in individual stocks.

index tracker STOCKHOLDING & INVESTMENTS = ***index fund***

index tracking MARKETS managing stocks to match stock exchange performance an investment technique whereby a portfolio is maintained in such a way as to match the growth in a stock market index

indicated dividend STOCKHOLDING & INVESTMENTS predicted annual dividends if current rate stays same the forecast total of all dividends in a year if the amount of each dividend remains as it is

indicated yield STOCKHOLDING & INVESTMENTS predicted annual income the forecast yield at the current dividend rate

indication price *UK* MARKETS approximate price of investment product an approximation of the price of a security as opposed to its firm price

indicative price MARKETS investment product price as shown on trading screen the price shown on a screen-based system for trading securities such as the UK Stock Exchange Automated Quotations system. The price is not firm, as the size of the bargain will determine the final price at which market makers will actually deal.

indicator STATISTICS something that shows situation's trend over time a variable that, followed over time, gives an indication of a trend with regard to a particular situation

indifference curve ECONOMICS curve on graph representing customers' product satisfaction a line on a graph showing how consumers view different combinations of products. The line joins various points, each point representing a combination of two products, and each combination giving the customer equal satisfaction.

indirect channel MARKETING selling and distribution via intermediary the selling and distribution of products to customers through intermediaries such as wholesalers, distributors, agents, dealers, or retailers

indirect cost ACCOUNTING unchanging expense not directly related to production a fixed or overhead cost that cannot be attributed directly to the production of a particular item and is incurred even when there is no output. Indirect costs may include the ***cost center*** functions of finance and accounting, information technology, administration, and personnel. *See also* ***direct cost***

indirect labor costs OPERATIONS & PRODUCTION pay for staff not directly involved in production the cost of paying employees such as cleaners or cafeteria staff who are not directly involved in making a product. Such costs cannot be allocated to a ***cost center***.

indirect tax TAX tax not paid directly to government a tax such as sales tax that is not paid directly to the government that levies it but is collected and paid by a third party

indirect taxation TAX process of collecting taxes paid through third party the process of levying taxes that are not paid directly to a government, but are paid through a third party. A sales tax, for example, is paid by the purchaser of a product to the seller, who then pays the tax to the government.

individual retirement account PENSIONS *see* ***IRA***

Individual Savings Account STOCKHOLDING & INVESTMENTS *see* ***ISA***

Individual Voluntary Arrangement LEGAL UK payment agreement between debtors and lenders in the United Kingdom, a legally binding arrangement between debtors and creditors by which debtors offer the creditors the best deal they can afford by realizing their assets, thus avoiding the expense of bankruptcy proceedings

induction *UK* HR & PERSONNEL = ***orientation***

industrial action *UK* GENERAL MANAGEMENT = ***job action***

industrial dispute *UK* GENERAL MANAGEMENT = ***labor dispute***

industrial espionage GENERAL MANAGEMENT underhand methods of obtaining rival's commercial secrets the practice of spying on a business competitor in order to obtain its trade or commercial secrets. Information sought through industrial espionage will often refer to new products, designs, formulas, manufacturing processes, marketing surveys, research, or future plans. The goal of industrial espionage is either to injure the business prospects or market share of the target company, or to use the secrets discovered for another organization's commercial benefit.

industrial goods OPERATIONS & PRODUCTION goods produced for industry goods used in industrial processes, including processed or raw materials, machinery, components, and equipment

industrial goods marketing MARKETING marketing of goods to organizations marketing directed at organizations, businesses, and other institutions, rather than at the individual end user of a product. It may require different marketing strategies from those used in ***consumer goods marketing*** to be effective.

industrial marketing MARKETING marketing of goods or services to organizations the marketing of goods or services to companies, as opposed to individual consumers. Industrial marketing involves a number of key differences from selling to consumers. These include a smaller customer base with higher value or larger unit purchases, more technically complex or specially tailored products, professionally qualified purchasers, closer buyer--seller relationships, and possible group-purchasing decision making. *Also called* ***B2B marketing***

industrial market research MARKETING research into marketing of products to organizations research into the marketing of services and goods to industry, businesses, and other institutions. Industrial market research is used as an aid to ***decision making*** and concerns the manufacture, selling, and distribution of products with the goal of reducing costs and increasing profits. It considers factors such as the available labor force, location of the firm, export market potential, and use of resources.

industrial production ECONOMICS total output of factories and mines the output of a country's productive industries. Until the 1960s, this commonly related to iron and steel or coal, but since then lighter engineering in automobile or robotics manufacture has taken over.

industrial revenue bond STOCKHOLDING & INVESTMENTS bond to pay for building a bond that a private company uses to finance construction

industrial services marketing MARKETING marketing of services to organizations the marketing of services such as maintenance contracts, insurance, training, transportation, office cleaning, and advertising to industry, businesses, and other institutions. Many services offered to industry are also offered to the consumer, but promoting them to consumers requires strategies derived from ***consumer services marketing***.

industrial tribunal HR & PERSONNEL UK court deciding employment disagreements in the United Kingdom, a court that can hear and decide disputes involving employment. These include disputes relating to discrimination, unfair dismissal, breach of contract, and pay.

industry BUSINESS **1.** all components of manufacturing process all factories, companies, or processes involved in the manufacturing of products **2.** companies providing similar products or services a group of companies making the same type of product or offering the same type of service

ineligible bills FINANCE bills unacceptable for discounting those ***bills of exchange*** that cannot be ***discounted*** by a central bank

inertia selling MARKETING selling by sending unsolicited goods in the United Kingdom, a method of selling, regarded by some as unethical, that involves the sending of unsolicited goods on a sale or return policy. Inertia selling relies on the passive reaction of a potential purchaser to choose to pay for the goods received rather than undertake the effort to send them back. The receiver of the goods is not bound by law to pay for them but must keep them in good condition until they are collected or returned.

infant industry BUSINESS new area of business an industry in the early stages of development

inference STATISTICS conclusion about statistical population based on observation a conclusion drawn by a researcher about a statistical population after observing individuals in the population

inferior good ECONOMICS item demanded less as income rises a good that a consumer buys in decreasing quantities as his or her income rises. *Also called* ***Giffen good***

infinite capacity plan OPERATIONS & PRODUCTION plan for resource requirements disregarding workstation limitations a plan produced where ***capacity requirements planning*** does not take account of the capacity constraints of each workstation. *See also* ***capacity requirements planning***

inflation ECONOMICS increase in prices over time a sustained increase in a country's general level of prices which devalues its currency, often caused by excess demand in the economy

inflation accounting ACCOUNTING record-keeping method including effects of inflation the adjustment of a company's accounts to reflect the effect of inflation and provide a more realistic view of the company's position

inflationary ECONOMICS tending to cause increase in prices characterized by excess demand or high costs creating an excessive increase in the country's money supply

inflationary gap ECONOMICS situation where demand is greater than production capacity a gap that exists when an economy's resources are utilized and ***aggregate demand*** is more than the full-employment level of output. Prices will rise to remove the excess demand.

inflationary spiral ECONOMICS cycle of rising prices and wages a situation in which, repeatedly, in inflationary conditions, excess demand causes producers to raise prices and employees to demand wage rises to sustain their living standards. *Also called* ***wage-price spiral***

Inflation linked bond STOCKHOLDING & INVESTMENTS, RISK government bond with inflation protection a bond issued by a government that is indexed to protect against inflation

inflation-proof ECONOMICS indexed to inflation so as to preserve value used to describe a pension, wage, or investment that is indexed to inflation so that its value is preserved in times of inflation

inflation-proof security *US* STOCKHOLDING & INVESTMENTS security growing with inflation a security that is indexed to inflation or a cost-of-living index. *UK term* ***index-linked security***

inflation rate ECONOMICS rate at which prices increase over time the rate at which general price levels increase over a period of time

inflation target ECONOMICS central bank's goal for increase in prices a range or figure for the rate of increase in prices that the central bank of a country aims to reach at a specific date in the future

inflation tax TAX **1.** government gain from inflation the decrease in buying power imposed by inflation on holders of currency and fixed-return assets, to the government's gain as it inflates the money supply **2.** tax on firms that give large pay raises an income policy that taxes companies that grant pay raises above a specific level

infomediary E-COMMERCE website providing industry information for companies a website that provides and aggregates relevant customer or industry information for other companies

infomercial MARKETING commercial including helpful information a television or cinema commercial that includes helpful information about a product as well as advertising content

info rate MARKETS provisional rate a money market rate quoted by dealers for information only

informal economy ECONOMICS untaxed, unofficial economic activity the economy that runs in parallel to the formal economy but outside the reach of the tax system, most transactions being paid for in cash or goods

information management GENERAL MANAGEMENT acquisition and organization of information the acquisition, recording, organizing, storage, dissemination, and retrieval of information. Good information management has been described as getting the right information to the right person in the right format at the right time.

information space E-COMMERCE Web as information source the abstract concept of all the knowledge, expertise, and information accessible on the Web

infrastructure GENERAL MANAGEMENT basic support system the basic parts of a system that function together to support something, for example, the network and systems that support computing or the public services and facilities that support business activity

ingot CURRENCY & EXCHANGE gold or silver bar a bar of gold or silver

inheritance FINANCE property received from somebody who has died property that is received from somebody through a will or by legal succession

inheritance tax TAX **1.** US tax paid on inherited property in some states of the United States, tax paid on property received by inheritance or legal succession, calculated according to the value of the property received **2.** UK tax paid on estate before distribution to heirs in the United Kingdom, tax payable on wealth or property worth above a specific amount and inherited after somebody's death. The threshold in 2009–10 was £325,000, and the estate is liable for 40% tax on the excess amount. *Abbr* ***IHT***

initial capital FINANCE money used for starting firm the money that is used to start a business. Sources of initial capital might include personal funds, bank loans, grants, or credit from suppliers.

initial margin STOCKHOLDING & INVESTMENTS required deposit on open positions the deposit required of members of the ***London Clearing House*** on all open positions, long or short, to cover short-term price movements. It is returned to members when the position is closed. *See also* ***variation margin***

initial offer STOCKHOLDING & INVESTMENTS in UK, first offer on another firm's stock in the United Kingdom, the first offer that a company makes to buy the stock of another company

initial public offering STOCKHOLDING & INVESTMENTS first time firm's stock are sold the first instance of making particular stock available for sale to the public. *Abbr* ***IPO***. *See also* ***flotation***

initial sales OPERATIONS & PRODUCTION product sales when product is new to market the sales of a new product or service immediately after its introduction to the market

initial yield STOCKHOLDING & INVESTMENTS expected yield of new investment fund the yield that an investment fund is estimated to provide at its launch

injunction LEGAL court ruling preventing specific action a court order preventing a person or organization from doing something

inland bill CURRENCY & EXCHANGE in UK, bill belonging to one country in the United Kingdom, a bill of exchange that is payable and drawn in the same country

inland freight charge OPERATIONS & PRODUCTION fee for transporting products within country a charge for transporting goods from one part of a country to another part of the same country

Inland Revenue TAX, INTERNATIONAL TRADE *see* ***Her Majesty's Revenue & Customs***

Inland Revenue Department TAX New Zealand government agency responsible for taxes the New Zealand government body responsible for the administration of the national taxation system. *Abbr* ***IRD***

innovation GENERAL MANAGEMENT creation of new product or service the creation, development, and implementation of a new product, process, or service with the goal of improving efficiency, effectiveness, or ***competitive advantage***. Innovation may apply to products, services, manufacturing processes, managerial processes, or the design of an organization. It is most often viewed at a product or process level, where product innovation satisfies a customer's needs, and process innovation improves efficiency and effectiveness. Innovation is linked with creativity, and involves taking new ideas and turning them into reality through invention, research, and new product development.

inputs OPERATIONS & PRODUCTION things needed for producing products and services resources such as materials, staff, equipment, and funds that are required to produce a product or service

input tax TAX *see* ***VAT***

input tax credit TAX refund of Canadian Goods and Services Tax in Canada, an amount paid as ***Goods and Services Tax*** on supplies purchased for business purposes, which can be offset against Goods and Services Tax collected

inside director CORPORATE GOVERNANCE full-time director of firm a director who works full-time in a corporation. *See also* ***outside director***

inside information *or* **insider information** STOCKHOLDING & INVESTMENTS secret knowledge about firm information that is of advantage to investors but is only available to people who have personal contact with a company

inside quote MARKETS range of buyers' and sellers' prices a range of prices for a security, from the highest offer to buy to the lowest offer to sell

insider BUSINESS somebody with secret information about firm somebody who has access to information that is privileged and unavailable to most members of the public

insider dealing *or* **insider trading** MARKETS, FRAUD trading stock using secret information profitable, usually illegal, trading in securities carried out using information not available to the public

insolvency FINANCE lacking money to pay debt the inability to pay debts when they become due. Insolvency will apply even if total assets exceed total liabilities, if those assets cannot be readily converted into cash to meet debts as they mature. Even then, insolvency may not necessarily mean ***business failure***. ***Bankruptcy*** may be avoided through ***debt rescheduling*** or ***turnaround management***.

insolvency practitioner FINANCE UK insolvency specialist in the United Kingdom, a licensed professional who advises on or acts in all formal insolvency procedures

insolvent FINANCE unable to pay debts used to describe a person or business that is unable to pay debts, because the debts are more than the amount of assets that can be readily turned into cash

insourcing GENERAL MANAGEMENT use of internal staff, not external contractor or consultant the use of in-house personnel or an internal department to meet an organization's need for specific services. Insourcing is seen as a reaction to the growing popularity of ***outsourcing***, a practice that has not always met expectations.

inspector of taxes TAX UK government tax official in the United Kingdom, an official who reports to HM Revenue & Customs and is responsible for issuing tax returns and assessments, determining tax liabilities, and conducting appeals on tax matters

installment FINANCE one of several payments for initial public offering one of two or more payments made for the purchase of an initial public offering

installment activity statement TAX STOCKHOLDING & INVESTMENTS Australian form for reporting payments on investment income a standard form used in Australia to report ***pay-as-you-go*** installment payments on investment income. *Abbr* ***IAS***

installment loan *US* FINANCE fixed-interest loan with regular payments a loan that is repaid with fixed regular installments, and with a rate of interest fixed for the duration of the loan. *UK term* ***instalment credit***

installment plan *US* FINANCE method of paying for purchase with regular payments a method of buying something by paying for it in regular equal amounts over a period of time. *UK terms* ***hire purchase, easy terms***

instalment credit *UK* FINANCE = ***installment loan***

instant access account BANKING UK savings account with easily accessible funds in the United Kingdom, a savings account that pays interest, but from which the account holder can withdraw money immediately whenever he or she needs it

Institute of Chartered Accountants in England and Wales ACCOUNTING UK accounting organization the largest professional accounting body in Europe, providing certification by examinations, ensuring high standards of education and training, and supervising professional conduct. *Abbr* ***ICAEW***

Institute of Chartered Accountants in Ireland ACCOUNTING Ireland-wide accounting organization the oldest and largest professional body for accountants in Ireland, the ICAI was founded in 1888. Its many objectives include promoting best practice in chartered accountancy and maintaining high standards of professionalism among its members. It publishes a journal, *Accountancy Ireland,* and has offices in Dublin and Belfast. *Abbr* ***ICAI***

Institute of Chartered Accountants of New Zealand ACCOUNTING New Zealand accounting organization the only professional accounting body in New Zealand, representing over 26,000 members in that country and abroad. ICANZ has overseas branch offices in Fiji, London, Melbourne, and Sydney. *Abbr* ***ICANZ***

Institute of Chartered Accountants of Scotland ACCOUNTING Scottish accounting organization the world's oldest professional body for accountants, based in Edinburgh. *Abbr* ***ICAS***

Institute of Chartered Secretaries and Administrators *UK* FINANCE association of administrators and administrative assistants an organization that works to promote the efficient administration of commerce, industry, and public affairs. Founded in 1891 and granted a royal charter in 1902, it represents the interests of its members to government, publishes journals and other materials, promotes the standing of its members, and provides educational support and qualifying programs. *Abbr* ***ICSA***

Institute of Directors CORPORATE GOVERNANCE UK organization for directors of firms in the United Kingdom, an individual membership association whose stated objective is to "serve, support, represent, and set standards for directors." Founded in 1903 by Royal Charter, the IoD it is an independent, nonpolitical body. It is based in London, but also has offices in Belfast, Birmingham, Bristol, Edinburgh, Manchester, and Nottingham. *Abbr* ***IoD***

Institute of Financial Accountants ACCOUNTING UK organization for accountants a UK professional organization, established in 1916, that works to set technical and ethical standards in financial accounting. *Abbr* ***IFA***

Institute of Financial Services BANKING UK organization for financial education in the United Kingdom, the trading name of the Chartered Institute of Bankers, especially when involved with education

Institute of Insurance Brokers INSURANCE UK association of insurance brokers in the United Kingdom, the professional body for insurance brokers and the caretaker for the deregulated Insurance Brokers Registration Council's complaints program. *Abbr* ***IIB***

institutional buyout MERGERS & ACQUISITIONS purchase of firm by financial institution the ***takeover*** of a company by a financial institution that backs a group of managers who will run it

institutional investor STOCKHOLDING & INVESTMENTS organization that invests an institution such as an insurance company, bank, or labor union that makes investments

institutional survey STATISTICS statistical analysis of firms a statistical investigation in which an institution such as a company is the unit of analysis

instrument 1. FINANCE way of achieving something a means to an end, for example, a government's expenditure and taxation in its quest for reducing unemployment **2.** STOCKHOLDING & INVESTMENTS investment product a generic term for either securities or derivatives. Instruments can be negotiable or nonnegotiable. *See also* ***financial instrument, negotiable instrument*** **3.** LEGAL legal document an official or legal document

insufficient funds FINANCE too little money in bank account for check a lack of enough money in a bank account to pay a check drawn on that account

insurable interest INSURANCE personal interest in insured property a relationship between a person insuring something and the thing insured that would cause the person financial loss if the thing insured were damaged or destroyed

insurable risk INSURANCE quantifiable risk a risk that can be accurately assessed on the basis of past experience and for which insurance policy may be acquired. *See also* ***risk***

insurance 1. INSURANCE contract to pay for others' losses a legally binding arrangement in which individuals or companies pay another company to guarantee them compensation if they suffer loss resulting from risks such as fire, theft, or accidental damage **2.** MARKETS any method of reducing investment risk in financial markets, hedging or any other strategy that reduces risk while permitting participation in potential gains

Insurance and Superannuation Commission INSURANCE Australian government insurance agency an Australian federal government body responsible for regulating the superannuation and insurance industries. *Abbr* ***ISC***

insurance broker INSURANCE somebody who sells insurance a person or company that acts as an intermediary between companies providing insurance and individuals or companies that need insurance

Insurance Brokers Registration Council INSURANCE *see* ***IBRC***

insurance company INSURANCE firm that pays for damage or injury a company whose business is guaranteeing people compensation if they suffer financial loss as a result of events such as death, fire, and accidental damage

Insurance Council of Australia INSURANCE Australian organization supporting insurance firms an independent body representing the interests of businesses involved in the insurance industry. It was established in 1975 and currently represents around 110 companies. *Abbr* ***ICA***

insurance coverage *or* INSURANCE guaranteed compensation for specified risks the type and amount of compensation against specific risks that is guaranteed by an ***insurance policy***

insurance intermediary INSURANCE somebody that gives insurance advice and arranges policies a person or company that provides advice on insurance and can arrange policies. *See also* ***IIB, IBRC***

insurance policy INSURANCE contract specifying terms of insurance a document that sets out the terms and conditions for providing compensation against specific risks

insurance premium INSURANCE regular payment to insurance firm a regular payment made by a person or a company to a company for a specific ***insurance policy***

insurance premium tax TAX UK tax on general insurance in the United Kingdom, a tax on household, motor vehicle, travel, and other general insurance

insurance reserves *US* INSURANCE insurance firm's funds in reserve the assets that an insurance company maintains to meet future claims or losses. *UK term* ***technical reserves***

insure INSURANCE **1.** agree to compensate in declared circumstances to make a contract to pay compensation if a particular loss or event occurs **2.** *US* insure somebody's life to insure somebody's life, so that the insurance company will pay compensation when that person dies. *UK term* ***assure***

insured INSURANCE protected by insurance covered by a contract of insurance for specific risks such as loss, damage, illness, or death

insured account INSURANCE US bank account protected by insurance in the United States, an account with a bank or savings institution that belongs to a federal or private insurance organization

insured bond STOCKHOLDING & INVESTMENTS bond protected by insurance a bond whose principle and interest payments are insured against default

insurer INSURANCE insurance provider a company that provides insurance for a variety of risks

intangible asset FINANCE non-material resource an asset such as intellectual property or ***goodwill***. *Also called* ***invisible asset***. *See also* ***tangible asset***

intangibles FINANCE non-material costs and benefits to business the benefits to a business such as customer goodwill and employee loyalty, and costs such as training time and lost production, that cannot easily be quantified

integrated implementation model GENERAL MANAGEMENT product development with simultaneous stages a model of ***new product development*** that strives to achieve both flexibility and acceleration of development. All activities such as design, production planning, and test marketing are performed in parallel rather than going through a sequential linear progression. *See also* ***new product development***

integration BUSINESS joining business under central authority the act of bringing several businesses together under a central control

intellectual assets FINANCE knowledge, experience, and skills of workers the knowledge, experience, and skills of its staff that an organization can make use of

intellectual capital FINANCE firm's combined intangible assets the combined intangible assets owned or controlled by a company or organization that provide ***competitive advantage***. Intellectual capital assets can include the knowledge and expertise of employees, brands, customer information and relationships, contracts, ***intellectual property*** such as patents and copyright, and organizational technologies, processes, and methods. Intellectual capital can be implicit and intangible, stored in people's heads, or explicit and documented in written or electronic format.

intellectual property FINANCE ownership of items such as copyrights and patents the ownership of rights to ideas, designs, and inventions, including ***copyrights***, ***patents***, and ***trademarks***. Intellectual property is protected by law in most countries, and the World Intellectual Property Organization is responsible for harmonizing the law across different countries and promoting the protection of intellectual property rights.

intellectual property crime FRAUD crime involving counterfeiting and copyright piracy illegal activities involving the manufacture and distribution of counterfeit and copyrighted products

intellectual property rights LEGAL rights to ownership of intellectual property the legal rights a person or company has to the ownership of their ideas, designs, and inventions, including ***copyrights***, ***patents***, and ***trademarks***. *Abbr* ***IPRs***

interactive planning GENERAL MANAGEMENT process allowing participation in futures design and achievement a process that promotes participation in both the design of a desirable future and the developments that enable this future to be achieved rather than waiting for it to happen. Interactive planning is associated with Russell Ackoff, and was outlined in *Creating the Corporate Future* (1981).

interbank loan BANKING loan made to another bank a loan that one bank makes to another bank

interbank market MARKETS, BANKING lending of money amongst banks a market in which banks lend money to or borrow money from each other for short periods

Interbank Offered Rate *or* **Interbank Rate** MARKETS interest rate that banks charge each other the rate of interest at which banks lend to each other on the ***interbank market***. *Abbr* ***IBOR***

interchange E-COMMERCE, BANKING transaction between issuing and acquiring banks a transaction between an ***acquirer*** and an ***issuer***

interchangeable bond STOCKHOLDING & INVESTMENTS bond whose form can be changed a bond whose owner can change it at will between registered and coupon form, sometimes for a fee

interchange fee E-COMMERCE BANKING charge on interchange, paid by acquiring bank the charge on a transaction between the acquiring bank and the issuing bank, paid by the acquirer to the issuer

intercommodity spread STOCKHOLDING & INVESTMENTS options for purchase and sale of related goods a combination of purchase and sale of options for related commodities with the same delivery date

intercompany pricing OPERATIONS & PRODUCTION setting prices for product sales between firms the setting of prices by companies within a group to sell products or services to each other, rather than to external customers

inter-dealer broker STOCKHOLDING & INVESTMENTS intermediary between dealers a broker who arranges transactions between dealers in government securities

interest FINANCE borrowing charge or payment the rate that a lender charges for a loan or ***credit facility***, or a payment made by a financial institution for the use of money deposited in an account

interest arbitrage *UK* FINANCE switching funds between countries for higher interest rates transactions in two or more financial centers in order to make an immediate profit by exploiting differences in interest rates. *See also* ***arbitrage***

interest assumption FINANCE predicted amount of interest the expected rate of return on a portfolio of investments

interest-bearing FINANCE paying or requiring interest used to describe a deposit, account, shares, etc., that pay interest, or a loan that requires interest

interest-bearing account *or* **interest-bearing deposit** BANKING money in bank account that earns interest a deposit of money, or a bank account, that receives interest

interest charge BANKING fee paid for borrowing money an amount of money paid by a borrower as interest on a loan

interest cover FINANCE amount of money available for payment of interest the amount of earnings available to make interest payments after all operating and nonoperating income and expenses, except interest and income taxes, have been accounted for.

Interest cover is regarded as a measure of a company's creditworthiness because it shows how much income there is to cover interest payments on outstanding debt.

It is expressed as a ratio, comparing the funds available to pay interest (earnings before interest and taxes, or EBIT) with the interest expense. The basic formula is

EBIT / Interest expense = Interest coverage ratio

If interest expense for a year is $9 million, and the company's EBIT is $45 million, the interest coverage would be

45 million / 9 million = 5:1

The higher the number, the stronger a company is likely to be. A ratio of less than 1 indicates that a company is having problems generating enough cash flow to pay its interest expenses, and that either a modest decline in operating profits or a sudden rise in borrowing costs could eliminate profitability entirely. Ideally, interest coverage should at least exceed 1.5; in some sectors, 2.0 or higher is desirable.

Variations of this basic formula also exist. For example, there is:

(Operating cash flow + Interest + Taxes) / Interest = Cash flow interest coverage ratio

This ratio indicates the firm's ability to use its cash flow to satisfy its fixed financing obligations. Finally, there is the fixed-charge coverage ratio, that compares EBIT with fixed charges:

(EBIT + Lease expenses) / (Interest + Lease expenses) = Fixed-charge coverage ratio

"Fixed charges" can be interpreted in many ways, however. It could mean, for example, the funds that a company is obliged to set aside to retire debt, or dividends on preferred stock.

interested party BUSINESS somebody with financial relationship to firm a person or company that has a financial interest in a company

interest-elastic investment STOCKHOLDING & INVESTMENTS investment with variable rate of return an investment with a rate of return that varies with the rise and fall of interest rates

interest expense FINANCE cost of borrowing money the cost of the interest payments on borrowed money

interest-free credit FINANCE loan for which no fee is charged credit or a loan on which no interest is paid by the borrower

interest group GENERAL MANAGEMENT group promoting members' interests a group that is concerned with promoting the economic interests of its members, for example, a business association, professional association, or labor union

interest-inelastic investment STOCKHOLDING & INVESTMENTS investment with fixed rate of return an investment with a rate of return that does not vary with the rise and fall of interest rates

interest in possession trust FINANCE UK trust whose income can be distributed immediately in the United Kingdom, a trust that gives one or more beneficiaries an immediate right to receive any income generated by the trust's assets. It can be used for real estate, enabling the beneficiary either to enjoy the rent generated by the property or to reside there, or as a life policy, a common arrangement for inheritance tax planning.

interest-only mortgage MORTGAGES loan on which interest is paid before principal a long-term loan, usually for the purchase of real estate, in which the borrower only pays interest to the lender during the term of the mortgage, with the principal being repaid at the end of the term. It is thus the borrower's responsibility to make provisions to accumulate the required capital during the period of the mortgage. *See also* ***mortgage***

interest payment FINANCE borrowing or lending charge an amount of money paid by a financial institution for the use of money deposited in an account, or money paid by a borrower as interest on a loan

interest rate FINANCE percentage of money charged for borrowing the amount of interest charged for borrowing a sum of money over a specific period of time

interest rate cap MORTGAGES highest allowed interest rate an upper limit on a rate of interest, for example, in an adjustable-rate mortgage

interest rate effect ECONOMICS interest rate change leading to increased investment the increase in investment that takes place when companies take advantage of lower interest rates to invest more

interest rate exposure *UK* FINANCE possible loss related to changes in interest rates the risk of a loss associated with movements in the level of interest rates. *See also* ***bond***

interest rate floor MORTGAGES lowest allowed interest rate a lower limit on a rate of interest, for example, in an adjustable-rate mortgage

interest rate future MARKETS futures contract for interest a ***futures contract*** with an underlying asset that bears interest. *See also* ***future***

interest rate guarantee FINANCE **1.** limit on fluctuation a limit that is set to prevent interest rates moving outside a specific range **2.** legal protection from interest-rate changes a tailored indemnity protecting the purchaser against future changes in interest rates

interest rate option STOCKHOLDING & INVESTMENTS contract for interest a contract conferring the right but not an obligation to pay or receive a specific interest rate under stated terms. *See also* ***option***

interest rate risk FINANCE risk of investment loss due to rising interest the risk that the value of a fixed-income investment will decrease if interest rates rise

interest rate swap FINANCE trade of loans with different interest rates an exchange of two debt instruments with different rates of interest, made to tailor cash flows to the participants' different requirements. Most commonly a longer-term fixed rate is swapped for a shorter-term floating one.

interest-sensitive FINANCE affected by changes in interest rates used to describe assets, generally purchased with credit, that are in demand when interest rates fall but considered less attractive when interest rates rise

interest yield FINANCE set rate of return paid on investment a rate of gain generated by an investment that pays a fixed rate of return, usually a percentage of the amount invested

interfirm cooperation GENERAL MANAGEMENT agreement between firms to collaborate commercially a formal or informal agreement between organizations to collaborate in achieving common or new goals more efficiently or effectively. Interfirm cooperation may take the form of a ***joint venture***.

interim certificate LEGAL document showing partial stock ownership a ***certificate of deposit*** certifying partial ownership of stock that is not totally paid for at one time

interim dividend STOCKHOLDING & INVESTMENTS dividend for part of tax year a dividend whose value is determined on the basis of a period of time of less than a full ***fiscal year***

interim financial statement FINANCE financial statement for part of tax year only a financial statement that covers a period other than a full ***fiscal year***. Although UK companies are not legally obliged to publish interim financial statements, those listed on the London Stock Exchange are obliged to publish a half-yearly report of their activities and a profit and loss account that may either be sent to stockholders or published in a national newspaper. In the United States, the practice is to issue quarterly financial statements. *Also called* ***interim statement***

interim financing FINANCE providing of temporary finance financing by means of bridge loans, between the purchase of one asset and the sale of another

interim payment STOCKHOLDING & INVESTMENTS partial payment of dividend early in year a distribution to stockholders of part of a dividend in the first part of a financial year

interim statement FINANCE = ***interim financial statement***

intermarket spread MARKETS trading in similar options in different markets a combination of purchase and sale of options for the same commodity with the same delivery date on different markets

intermediary FINANCE agent for financial transactions a person or organization that arranges financing, insurance, or investments for others

intermediate goods OPERATIONS & PRODUCTION items for producing other items goods bought for use in the production of other products

intermediation FINANCE acting as agent in financial transaction the process of arranging financing through an intermediary. Financial institutions act as intermediaries when they lend depositors' money to borrowers.

internal audit RISK audit by firm's own employees an audit of a company undertaken by its employees, usually to check on its internal controls. *See also* ***external audit***

internal benchmarking GENERAL MANAGEMENT *see* ***benchmarking***

internal consultant GENERAL MANAGEMENT expert within company advising colleagues an employee who uses knowledge and expertise to offer advice or business solutions to another department or business unit within an organization

internal consulting GENERAL MANAGEMENT advising colleagues elsewhere in firm the activity of offering advice or business solutions to another department or business unit within an organization. *See also* ***internal consultant***

internal control GENERAL MANAGEMENT management system for controlling firm's activities a system set up by the management of a company to monitor and control the company's activities

internal cost analysis ACCOUNTING investigation into organization's activities to establish profitable areas an examination of an organization's value-creating activities to determine sources of profitability and to identify the relative costs of different processes. Internal cost analysis is a tool for analyzing the ***value chain***. Principal steps include identifying those processes that create value for the organization, calculating the cost of each value-creating process against the overall cost of the product or service, identifying the cost components for each process, establishing the links between the processes, and working out the opportunities for achieving relative cost advantage.

internal differentiation analysis GENERAL MANAGEMENT assessment of what makes product or service distinctive an examination of processes in the ***value chain*** to determine which of them create differentiation of the product or service in the customer's eyes, and thus enhance its value. Internal differentiation analysis enables an organization to focus on improving the identified processes to maximize ***competitive advantage***. Steps involve identification of value-creating activities, evaluation of strategies that can enhance value for the customer, and assessment of which differentiation strategies are the most sustainable.

internal growth BUSINESS growth by developing existing business organic growth created within a business, for example, by inventing new products and so increasing its market share, producing products that are more reliable, offering a more efficient service than its competitors, or being more aggressive in its marketing. *See also* ***external growth***

internal marketing MARKETING implementation of marketing principles within organization the application of the principles of marketing within an organization. Internal marketing involves the creation of an internal market by dividing departments into business units, with control over their own operations and expenditure, with attendant impacts on corporate culture, politics, and power. Internal marketing also involves treating employees as internal customers with the goal of increasing employees' motivation and focus on customers.

internal rate of return FINANCE interest rate indicating worthwhile profit in a discounted cash flow calculation, the rate of interest that reduces future income streams to the cost of the investment; practically speaking, the rate that indicates whether or not an investment is worth pursuing.

Let's assume that a project under consideration costs $7,500 and is expected to return $2,000 per year for five years, or $10,000. The IRR calculated for the project would be about 10%. If the cost of borrowing money for the project, or the return on investing the funds elsewhere, is less than 10%, the project is probably worthwhile. If the alternative use of the money will return 10% or more, the project should be rejected, since from a financial perspective it will break even at best.

Typically, managements require an IRR equal to or higher than the cost of capital, depending on relative risk and other factors.

The best way to compute an IRR is by using a spreadsheet (such as Excel) or financial calculator.

If using Excel, for example, select the IRR function. This requires the annual cash flows to be set out in columns and the first part of the IRR formula requires the cell reference range of these cash flows to be entered. Then a guess of the IRR is required. The default is 10%, written 0.1.

If a project has the following expected cash flows, then guessing IRR at 30% returns an accurate IRR of 27%, indicating that if the next best way of investing the money gives a return of -20%, the project should go ahead.

Now	–2,500
Year 1	1,200
Year 2	1,300
Year 3	1,500

IRR can be misleading, especially as significant costs will occur late in the project. The rule of thumb "the higher the IRR the better" does not always apply. For the most thorough analysis of a project's investment potential, some experts urge using both IRR and net present value calculations, and comparing their results. *Abbr* ***IRR***

Internal Revenue Code TAX US federal tax laws the complex series of federal tax laws in the United States

Internal Revenue Service TAX *see* ***IRS***

internal trade BUSINESS trade within one country commercial activity that is carried out within a specific country. *Also called* ***home trade***. *See also* ***external trade***

internal versus external sourcing OPERATIONS & PRODUCTION = ***purchasing versus production***

International Accounting Standards Board ACCOUNTING organization that sets accounting standards an independent and privately funded standard-setting organization for the accounting profession, based in London. The Board, whose members come from nine countries and a variety of backgrounds, is committed to developing a single set of high quality, understandable, and enforceable global standards that require transparent and comparable information in general purpose financial statements. It also works with national accounting standard setters to achieve convergence in accounting standards around the world. *Abbr* ***IASB***

International Accounting Standards Committee ACCOUNTING former organization promoting international agreement on accounting standards formerly, an organization based in London that worked toward achieving global agreement on accounting standards, replaced by the ***International Accounting Standards Board***. *Abbr* ***IASC***

International Bank for Reconstruction and Development BANKING *see* ***IBRD***

International Centre for Settlement of Investment Disputes BANKING part of World Bank Group one of the five institutions that comprise the World Bank Group, based in Washington, DC. It was established in 1966 to undertake the role previously undertaken in a personal capacity by the president of the World Bank in assisting in mediation or conciliation of investment disputes between governments and private foreign investors. The overriding consideration in its establishment was that a specialist institution could help to promote increased flows of international investment. Although ICSID has close links to the World Bank, it is an autonomous organization. *Abbr* ***ICSID***

International Chamber of Commerce BUSINESS *see* ***ICC***

International Depository Receipt STOCKHOLDING & INVESTMENTS outside US, document indicating ownership of stock the equivalent of an ***American depository receipt*** in the rest of the world, an IDR is a negotiable certificate issued by a bank that indicates ownership of stock. *Abbr* ***IDR***

International Development Association FINANCE agency helping poorest nations an agency administered by the International Bank for Reconstruction and Development to provide assistance on concessionary terms to the poorest countries. Its resources consist of subscriptions and general replenishments from its more industrialized and developed members, special contributions, and transfers from the net earnings of the International Bank for Reconstruction and Development. *Abbr* ***IDA***

International Finance Corporation FINANCE UN agency encouraging private investment in developing nations a United Nations organization promoting private sector investment in developing countries to reduce poverty and improve the quality of people's lives. It finances private sector projects that are profit-oriented and environmentally and socially sound, and helps to foster development. The International Finance Corporation has a staff of 2,000 professionals around the world who seek profitable and creative solutions to complex business issues. *Abbr* ***IFC***

International Financial Reporting Standards ACCOUNTING standards for preparing financial statements a set of rules and guidelines established by the ***International Accounting Standards Board*** for standardizing the preparation of financial statements so that investors, organizations, and governments have a basis for comparison. *Abbr* ***IFRS***

international fund FINANCE mutual fund with domestic and foreign investments a mutual fund that invests in securities both inside and outside a country

International Fund for Agricultural Development FINANCE UN agency in poor countries a specialized United Nations agency with a mandate to combat hunger and rural poverty in countries with developing economies. Established as an international financial institution in 1977 following the 1974 World Food Conference, it has financed projects in over 100 countries and independent territories, to which it has committed US$7.7 billion in grants and loans. It has three sources of finance: contributions from members, loan payments, and investment income. *Abbr* ***IFAD***

International Monetary Fund FINANCE *see* ***IMF***

international money market MARKETS, CURRENCY & EXCHANGE exchange of foreign currencies a market in which currencies can be borrowed and lent and converted into other currencies

International Organization of Securities Commissions REGULATION & COMPLIANCE institution overseeing international securities transactions an organization of securities commissions from around the world, based in Madrid. Its objectives are to promote high standards of regulation, exchange information, and establish standards for, and effective surveillance of, international securities transactions. *Abbr* ***IOSCO***

international reserves CURRENCY & EXCHANGE = ***foreign currency reserves***

International Securities Market Association MARKETS association concerned with international securities market the self-regulatory organization and trade association for the international securities market. Its primary role is to oversee the fast-changing marketplace through the issuing of rules and recommendations relating to trading and settlement practices. Established in 1969, the organization has over 600 members from 51 countries. *Abbr* ***ISMA***

International Swaps and Derivatives Association STOCKHOLDING & INVESTMENTS organization for derivative traders a professional association for international traders in derivatives, founded in 1985. *Abbr* ***ISDA***

international trade INTERNATIONAL TRADE buying and selling activity between countries the sale and purchase of goods and services that takes place between trading partners in different countries

International Union of Credit and Investment Insurers INSURANCE association concerned with exports and foreign investments an organization that works for international acceptance of sound principles of export credit and foreign investment insurance. Founded in 1934, the London-based Union has 51 members in 42 countries that play a role of central importance in world trade, both as regards exports and foreign direct investments. *Also called* ***Berne Union***

Internet merchant E-COMMERCE businessperson selling over Internet a businessperson who sells a product or service over the Internet

Internet payment system E-COMMERCE fund transfer system using Internet any mechanism for fund transfer from customer to merchant or business to business via the Internet. There are many payment options available, including credit card payment, credit transfer, electronic checks, direct debit, smart cards, prepaid plans, loyalty plan points-based approaches, person-to-person payments, and cellphone plans.

Getting the online payment system right is critical to the success of e-commerce. Currently, the most common form of online consumer payment is by credit card (90% in the United States; 70% in Europe). The most common business-to-business payments, however, are still offline, probably because such transactions often involve large sums of money.

Good online payment systems share key characteristics: ease of use; robustness and reliability; proper authentication (to combat fraud); efficient integration with the vendor's own internal systems; and security and assurance procedures that check that the seller gets the money and the buyer gets the goods.

Internet security E-COMMERCE protection of computer files from unauthorized access the means used to protect websites and other electronic files from attack by hackers and viruses. The Internet is, by definition, a network; networks are open, and are thus open to attack. A poor Internet security policy can result in a substantial loss of productivity and a drop in consumer confidence.

interpolation STATISTICS way of calculating approximate value a method of estimating an unknown value such as a return on an investment using values that are known

interquartile range STATISTICS difference between first and third quartiles the difference between the first and third quartiles of a statistical sample, used to measure the spread of variables in the data

interstate commerce BUSINESS trade between US states in the United States, commerce that involves more than one state and is therefore subject to regulation by Congress. *See also* ***intrastate commerce***

intervention ECONOMICS government action to influence market forces government action to manipulate market forces for political or economic purposes

intervention mechanism CURRENCY & EXCHANGE central banks' means of maintaining fixed exchange rates a method such as buying or selling of foreign currency used by central banks in maintaining equivalence between exchange rates

inter vivos trust FINANCE trust set up between living people a legal arrangement for managing somebody's money or property, set up by one living person for another living person

in the money STOCKHOLDING & INVESTMENTS having intrinsic value used to describe an option that, if it expired at the current market price, would have significant ***intrinsic value***. *See also* ***out of the money***

intraday MARKETS during one trading day within a single day of trading

intrapreneur GENERAL MANAGEMENT worker deploying entrepreneurial skills within firm an employee who uses the approach of an entrepreneur within an organizational setting. An intrapreneur must have freedom of action to explore and implement ideas, although the outcome of such work will be owned by the organization rather than the intrapreneur, and it is the organization that will take the associated risk. Managers of organizations in which intrapreneurs are allowed to operate subscribe to the view that innovation can be achieved by encouraging creative and exploratory activity in semiautonomous units.

intrastate commerce BUSINESS trade within US state in the United States, commerce that occurs within a single state. *See also* ***interstate commerce***

intrinsic value STOCKHOLDING & INVESTMENTS gap between share price and option price with reference to an option or convertible, the value at which a security would trade if there were no ***option premium***, i.e. the share price less the option price

introducing broker STOCKHOLDING & INVESTMENTS broker not paid directly by customers a person or organization acting as a broker but not able to accept payment from customers

introduction **1.** MARKETING making product available for first time an act of bringing something into existence or operation for the first time, for example, bringing a new product onto the market for sale for the first time **2.** MARKETS initially listing established company on stock exchange the act of bringing an established company to the Stock Exchange. It is done by getting permission for the shares to be traded on the Stock Exchange, and is used when a company is formed by splitting from an existing larger company and no new shares are being offered for sale.

inventory **1.** BUSINESS all commercial assets owned in the United States, the sum total of the commercial assets of an organization **2.** OPERATIONS & PRODUCTION firm's supply of finished and unfinished products the supply of finished goods, raw materials, and work in progress held by a company.

inventory control OPERATIONS & PRODUCTION keeping optimal level of merchandise on hand the process of making sure that the correct level of inventory is maintained, to be able to meet demand while keeping the costs of holding inventory to a minimum

inventory depreciation ACCOUNTING reduction in value of stored stock a reduction in value of inventory that is held in a warehouse for some time

inventory financing FINANCE obtaining loans against product inventory a method by which manufacturers of consumer products obtain a loan by using their inventory as collateral

inventory record OPERATIONS & PRODUCTION firm's record of inventory a record of the ***inventory*** held by an organization. An inventory record forms an important part of material requirements planning systems. Such records usually make use of some form of part numbering or classification system, and include a description of the part, the quantity held, and the location of all the holdings. A *transaction file* keeps track of inventory use and replenishment.

inventory turnover 1. ACCOUNTING replacement rate of commercial assets an accounting ratio of the number of times ***inventory*** is replaced during a given period. The ratio is calculated by dividing net sales by average inventory over a given period. Values are expressed as times per period, most often a year, and a higher figure indicates a more efficient manufacturing operation.

It is calculated as follows:

Cost of goods sold / Inventory

If COGS is $2 million, and inventory at the end of the period is $500,000, then

2,000,000 / 500,000 = 4

Also called ***stock turns***. **2.** *US* STOCKHOLDING & INVESTMENTS measure of how quickly inventory needs replacing the total value of inventory sold in a year divided by the average value of goods held in stock. This checks that cash is not tied up in inventory for too long, losing its value over time. *UK term* ***stock turnover***

inventory valuation *US* ACCOUNTING estimation of stock value an estimation of the value of inventory at the end of an accounting period. *UK term* ***stock valuation***

inverse floating rate note STOCKHOLDING & INVESTMENTS security with interest varying inversely with base rate a security whose interest rate varies inversely with a ***base interest rate***, rising as it falls and vice versa

inverted market MARKETS when near-term futures are dearest a situation in which near-term ***futures contracts*** cost more than long-term futures for the same commodity. *See also* ***backwardation***

inverted yield curve STOCKHOLDING & INVESTMENTS showing lower interest rates for long-term bonds a visual representation of relative interest rates that shows lower interest rates for long-term bonds than for short-term bonds. *See also* ***yield curve***

invested capital FINANCE firm's stock, retained earnings plus debt the total amount of a company's stock, retained earnings, and long-term debt

investment 1. FINANCE expenditure on assets and securities the spending of money on stocks and other securities, or on assets such as plant and machinery **2.** FINANCE something invested in something such as stocks, real estate, or a project in which money is invested in the expectation of making a profit **3.** STOCKHOLDING & INVESTMENTS money invested an amount of money invested in something in the expectation of making a profit

investment analyst STOCKHOLDING & INVESTMENTS researcher into investment possibilities an employee of a stock exchange company who researches other companies and identifies investment opportunities for clients. *Also called* ***financial analyst***

investment appraisal STOCKHOLDING & INVESTMENTS assessment of future value of new assets analysis of the future profitability of capital purchases as an aid to good management

investment bank BANKING **1.** bank for corporate borrowers a bank that specializes in providing funds to corporate borrowers for startup or expansion **2.** *US* bank for investors and their backers a bank that does not accept deposits but provides services to those who offer securities to investors, and to those investors. *See also* ***commercial bank***. *UK term* ***merchant bank*** ▶ *Abbr* ***IB***

investment bond INSURANCE UK investment in life insurance policy in the United Kingdom, a product where the investment is paid as a single premium into a life insurance policy with an underlying asset-backed fund. The bondholder receives a regular income until the end of the bond's term when the investment (the current value of the fund) is returned to the bondholder. *Also called* ***life insurance bond***

investment borrowing ECONOMICS borrowing money to promote economic growth the borrowing of funds intended to encourage a country's economic growth or to support the development of particular industries or regions by adding to physical or human capital

investment center STOCKHOLDING & INVESTMENTS section responsible for profitable investment a profit center with additional responsibilities for capital investment, and possibly for financing, whose performance is measured by its return on investment

investment club STOCKHOLDING & INVESTMENTS group combining to invest in securities a group of people who join together to make investments in securities

investment committee BANKING bank employees assessing proposals for investment in the United States, a group of employees of an investment bank who evaluate investment proposals

investment company STOCKHOLDING & INVESTMENTS firm investing money of several investors a company that pools for investment the money of several investors. *See also* ***investment fund***

investment dealer *Canada* STOCKHOLDING & INVESTMENTS securities broker a broker dealing in stock, bonds, debentures, and other securities. *Also called* ***broker***

investment fund STOCKHOLDING & INVESTMENTS savings plan that makes investments a savings plan that invests its clients' funds in, for example, corporate start-up or expansion projects. *See also* ***investment company***

investment grade STOCKHOLDING & INVESTMENTS refers to highly rated bond relating to a bond issued by a company, government, or local authority with a rating of BBB or higher, carrying relatively little risk. Trusts or pension funds may be restricted to investing in investment grade securities.

investment grade rating STOCKHOLDING & INVESTMENTS opinion of quality of bond as safe investment an assessment by a ***rating agency*** that a bond carries little risk for the investor. Bonds with ratings between AAA and BBB are considered investment grade.

investment grant STOCKHOLDING & INVESTMENTS government money given to firms for capital assets a government grant to a company to help it invest in capital assets such as buildings, equipment, or new machinery

investment horizon STOCKHOLDING & INVESTMENTS period of time for holding investment the length of time an investor expects to hold an investment, or the holding period over which an investment is analyzed

investment income STOCKHOLDING & INVESTMENTS money earned on investments revenue paid to investors that is derived from their investments, for example, dividends and interest on securities. *See also* ***earned income***

investment management agreement STOCKHOLDING & INVESTMENTS contract between investor and fund manager a contract between an investor and an investment manager. *Abbr* ***IMA***

Investment Management Association STOCKHOLDING & INVESTMENTS association for UK investment professionals the trade body for the UK investment industry, formed in February 2002 following the merger of the Association of Unit Trusts and Investment Funds and the Fund Managers' Association. *Abbr* ***IMA***. *See also* ***Fund Managers' Association***

Investment Management Regulatory Organisation REGULATION & COMPLIANCE UK group regulating investment fund managers in the United Kingdom, an organization that regulated managers of investment funds such as retirement funds, now part of the Financial Services Authority. *Abbr* ***IMRO***

investment manager STOCKHOLDING & INVESTMENTS = ***fund manager***

investment objective STOCKHOLDING & INVESTMENTS long-term financial goal of investments the financial goal that determines how an individual or institution invests its assets, for example, for long-term growth or income

investment portfolio STOCKHOLDING & INVESTMENTS = ***portfolio***

investment professional STOCKHOLDING & INVESTMENTS somebody legally qualified to give investment advice a person who is licensed to offer advice on, and sell, investment products

investment properties FINANCE buildings bought to rent out either commercial buildings such as stores, factories, or offices, or residential dwellings such as houses or apartments, that are purchased by businesses or individuals for renting to third parties

investment revaluation reserve *UK* FINANCE reserve created by firm investing in property the capital reserve where changes in the value of a business's investment properties are disclosed when they are revalued

Investment Services Directive STOCKHOLDING & INVESTMENTS former EU regulations governing investment and market conduct formerly, an EU directive regulating the conduct and operation of investment companies and markets, replaced by the ***Markets in Financial Instruments Directive***. *Abbr* ***ISD***

investment tax credit TAX former US tax advantage in the United States, a tax advantage for investment that was available until 1986

investment trust STOCKHOLDING & INVESTMENTS investment firm with limited shares an investment company with a fixed number of shares available. Investment trusts are ***closed-end investment companies***.

investment vehicle STOCKHOLDING & INVESTMENTS product or firm to invest in a financial product such as stocks, bonds, funds, or futures, or a company, in which somebody can invest money

investomer BUSINESS combined customer and investor a customer of a business who is also an investor *(slang)*

investor STOCKHOLDING & INVESTMENTS person or organization spending money for financial return a person or organization that invests money in something, especially in the stock of publicly owned corporations

investor relations research STOCKHOLDING & INVESTMENTS research into how financial markets view firm research carried out on behalf of an organization in order to gain an understanding of how financial markets regard the organization, its stock, and its sector

invisible asset FINANCE = ***intangible asset***

invisible earnings INTERNATIONAL TRADE foreign currency from services not commodities foreign currency earned by a country in providing services such as banking and tourism, rather than in selling goods

invisible exports INTERNATIONAL TRADE money generated by selling services overseas the profits, dividends, interest, and royalties received from selling a country's services abroad

invisible hand ECONOMICS power of market forces according to the 18th century British economist Adam Smith, the force of the market which drives the economy

invisible imports INTERNATIONAL TRADE money paid to foreign service firms the profits, dividends, interest, and royalties paid to foreign service companies based in a country

invisibles INTERNATIONAL TRADE services that are traded items such as financial and leisure services that are traded by a country, rather than physical goods

invisible trade INTERNATIONAL TRADE buying and selling services between countries trade in items such as financial and other services that are listed in the current account of the ***balance of payments***

invoice FINANCE document requesting payment a document that a supplier sends to a customer detailing the cost of products or services supplied and asking for payment

invoice date FINANCE official date of sending of invoice the date on which an invoice is issued. The invoice date may be different from the delivery date.

invoice discounting FINANCE sale of invoices for less than stated value the selling of invoices at a discount for collection by the buyer, or the payment of invoices at a discount by an intermediary with the customer's eventual payment routed through the intermediary, who takes a fee

invoice price OPERATIONS & PRODUCTION total price as listed on bill the price as given on an invoice, including any discount and sales tax

invoice register ACCOUNTING record of invoices for things bought a list of purchase invoices recording the date of receipt of the invoice, the supplier, the invoice value, and the person to whom the invoice has been passed to ensure that all invoices are processed by the accounting system

invoicing FINANCE requesting payment the process of sending out invoices to customers

involuntary bankruptcy LEGAL bankruptcy petitioned for by creditors a situation in which a petition is filed with the creditors to have a person or corporation declared bankrupt

involuntary liquidation preference STOCKHOLDING & INVESTMENTS payment to particular stockholders before liquidation a payment that a company must make to holders of its preferred stock if it is forced to sell its assets when facing bankruptcy

inward bill INTERNATIONAL TRADE list of merchandise being brought into country a bill of lading for goods arriving in a country from a foreign country

inward investment STOCKHOLDING & INVESTMENTS investment in local area investment by a government or company in its own country or region, often to stimulate employment or develop a business infrastructure

IoD *abbr* CORPORATE GOVERNANCE ***Institute of Directors***

IOD fraud *abbr* FRAUD ***impersonation of the deceased fraud***

IOSCO *abbr* REGULATION & COMPLIANCE ***International Organization of Securities Commissions***

IOU FINANCE note of money borrowed personally a representation of "I owe you" that can be used as legal evidence of a debt, although it is most commonly used as an informal reminder of a minor transaction

IP-backed STOCKHOLDING & INVESTMENTS, RISK describes securities backed by intellectual property used to describe securities whose underlying assets are intellectual property such as patents, copyrights, and trademarks

IPO *abbr* STOCKHOLDING & INVESTMENTS ***initial public offering***

IPRs *abbr* LEGAL ***intellectual property rights***

IRA PENSIONS personal pension plan allowing tax-free deposits in the United States, a pension plan, designed for individuals without a company pension plan, that allows annual sums, subject to limits dependent upon employment income, to be set aside from earnings tax-free. Individuals with a company pension may invest in an IRA, but only from their net income. IRAs, including the Education IRA, designed as a way of saving for children's education, may invest in almost any financial security except real estate. *Full form* ***individual retirement account***

IRA rollover PENSIONS transfer of assets between retirement plans in the United States, a transfer of assets from a tax-deferred qualified retirement plan to a tax-deferred IRA managed by the plan's owner

IRD *abbr* TAX ***Inland Revenue Department***

IRD number TAX New Zealand income tax code for employees a numeric code assigned to all members of the New Zealand workforce for the purpose of paying income tax

IRR *abbr* FINANCE ***internal rate of return***

irrecoverable debt FINANCE loan that will never be repaid a debt that will never be paid to the person to whom it is owed and must be written off, either as a charge to the profit and loss account or against an existing doubtful debt provision

irredeemable bond STOCKHOLDING & INVESTMENTS indefinite government bond a government bond that has no date of maturity but provides interest

irrevocable letter of credit BANKING permanent credit authorization a ***letter of credit*** that cannot be canceled

irrevocable trust FINANCE unalterable trust a trust that cannot be canceled or revised without the agreement of its beneficiary

IRS TAX US government agency for tax collection in the United States, the branch of the federal government charged with collecting the majority of federal taxes. *Full form* ***Internal Revenue Service***

IS *abbr* FINANCE ***income support***

ISA STOCKHOLDING & INVESTMENTS UK tax-free account for savings and investment in the United Kingdom, a tax-free savings account in which up to £7,200 a year can be invested. £3,600 of which can be in cash and the remainder in stocks, or all the investment can be in stocks. Formerly, there were Maxi ISAs and Mini ISAs, each with two components: cash and stocks. *Full form* ***Individual Savings Account***

ISC *abbr* INSURANCE ***Insurance and Superannuation Commission***

ISD *abbr* STOCKHOLDING & INVESTMENTS ***Investment Services Directive***

ISDA *abbr* STOCKHOLDING & INVESTMENTS ***International Swaps and Derivatives Association***

Islamic law LEGAL Muslim religious law the law as interpreted by trained Islamic legal scholars. In strict Islamic countries, all businesses, financial institutions, and products must meet the requirements of Islamic law. *Also called* ***sharia, shariah***

ISMA *abbr* MARKETS ***International Securities Market Association***

issuance costs FINANCE money spent issuing debt the underwriting, legal, and administrative fees required to issue a debt. These fees are significant when issuing debt in the public markets, such as the bond market. However, other types of debt, such as private placements or bank loans, are cheaper to issue because they require less underwriting, legal, and administrative support.

issue STOCKHOLDING & INVESTMENTS stocks or bonds for sale at one time a set of stocks or bonds that a company offers for sale at one time

issue by tender STOCKHOLDING & INVESTMENTS = ***sale by tender***

issued capital STOCKHOLDING & INVESTMENTS = ***share capital***

Issue Department BANKING part of Bank of England issuing currency the department of the Bank of England that is responsible for issuing currency

issued price STOCKHOLDING & INVESTMENTS price of firm's first stock issue the price of shares of stock in a company when they are offered for sale for the first time

issued share capital STOCKHOLDING & INVESTMENTS amount representing shares the type, class, number, and amount of the shares held by stockholders. *See also* ***stockholders' equity***

issued shares STOCKHOLDING & INVESTMENTS shares held by investors those shares that comprise a company's authorized capital that has been distributed to investors. They may be either fully paid or partly paid shares.

issue price STOCKHOLDING & INVESTMENTS original price of securities the price at which securities are first offered for sale

issuer E-COMMERCE organization providing payment cards a financial institution that issues payment cards such as credit or debit cards, pays out to the merchant's account, and bills the customer or debits the customer's account. The issuer guarantees payment for authorized transactions using the payment card. *Also called* ***card-issuing bank, issuing bank***

issuer bid STOCKHOLDING & INVESTMENTS offer to buy own securities an offer made by an issuer for its own securities when it is disappointed by the offers of others

issuer identification number BANKING international number identifying individual bank an internationally agreed six-digit number that uniquely identifies a bank in electronic transactions. *Abbr* ***IIN***

issues management GENERAL MANAGEMENT process of anticipating trends for commercial gain the anticipation and assessment of key trends and themes of the next decade, and the relation of these to the organization. Issues management is informed by ***futures research*** in order to formulate strategic plans and actions.

issuing bank E-COMMERCE = ***issuer***

issuing house FINANCE UK financial institution that launches private companies in the United Kingdom, a financial institution that specializes in the flotation of private companies. *See also* ***investment bank, merchant bank***

istisna'a *or* **istisnah** OPERATIONS & PRODUCTION product manufacturing contract with agreed delivery and price in Islamic financing, a contract for manufacturing a product in which the manufacturer agrees to produce a specified product to be delivered at a specified time for a specified price

IT *abbr* TAX ***income tax***

item ACCOUNTING unit of accounting information a single piece of information included in a company's accounts

itemized deductions TAX expenses allowed to reduce US income tax in the United States, amounts paid by individual taxpayers for expenses that can be deducted to reduce taxable income, for example, medical and dental expenses, charitable contributions, mortgage interest, and losses due to theft

J

jawboning BUSINESS using status to affect decisions using influence, especially the influence of a public position or office, to try to affect the decisions of leaders in the business world

J curve CURRENCY & EXCHANGE line representing falling exchange rate's effect on trade a line on a graph shaped like a letter "J," with an initial short fall, followed by a longer rise, used to describe the effect of a falling exchange rate on a country's balance of trade

Jensen's measure FINANCE = ***risk-adjusted return on capital***

JEPI *abbr* E-COMMERCE ***joint electronic payment initiative***

jikan MARKETS Japanese rule for choosing between identical instructions in Japan, the priority rule relating to transactions on the Tokyo Stock Exchange whereby the earlier of two buy or sell orders received at the same price prevails

JIT *abbr* OPERATIONS & PRODUCTION ***just-in-time***

job BUSINESS assignment a customer order or other piece of work

job action *US* GENERAL MANAGEMENT action to force resolution of dispute a temporary action such as a strike or lockout taken by one side in a labor dispute in an attempt to bring pressure on the other side to settle. *UK term* ***industrial action***

jobber's turn MARKETS UK dealer's profit on transaction formerly, a term used on the London Stock Exchange for a ***spread***, the difference between the buying and selling price that a dealer arranges and takes as profit

jobbing backward *UK* STOCKHOLDING & INVESTMENTS review of actions the analysis of an investment transaction with the benefit of hindsight

job cost ACCOUNTING describes accounting allowing determination of profit per job used to describe a method of accounting whereby a project-oriented business allocates costs to a specific project, thereby having the ability to determine the profitability of individual projects

job lot FINANCE varied items bought or sold together a miscellaneous assortment of items, including securities, that are offered as a single deal

Johannesburg Stock Exchange MARKETS former name of JSE Limited until November of the year 2000, the official name of the JSE Limited, the South African stock exchange

joint account BANKING account shared by two or more people an account, such as one held at a bank or by a broker, that two or more people own in common and can access

joint and several liability LEGAL obligation to meet payment together or individually a legal liability that applies to a group of individuals as a whole and each member individually, so that if one member does not meet his or her liability, the shortfall is the shared responsibility of the others. Most guarantees given by two or more individuals to secure borrowing are joint and several. It is a typical feature of most partnership agreements.

joint bond STOCKHOLDING & INVESTMENTS bond guaranteed by third party a bond that is guaranteed by a party other than the company or government that issued it

joint electronic payment initiative E-COMMERCE proposed protocol for electronic payment a proposed industry standard protocol for electronic payment in e-commerce transactions. *Abbr* ***JEPI***

joint float CURRENCY & EXCHANGE shared exchange relationship within set of currencies a group of currencies that maintains a fixed internal relationship and moves jointly in relation to another currency

joint life annuity INSURANCE annuity lasting until death of both parties an annuity that continues until both parties have died. They are attractive to married couples as they ensure that the survivor has an income for the rest of his or her life.

joint management GENERAL MANAGEMENT running of firm by more than one person the overseeing and control of the affairs of an organization shared by two or more people

joint ownership BUSINESS ownership by several people or organizations ownership by more than one party, each with equal rights in the item owned. Joint ownership is often applied to property or other assets.

joint return TAX single tax return covering spouses in the United States, a tax return filed jointly by a husband and wife

joint stock bank BANKING formerly, commercial bank a term that was formerly used for a commercial bank that is a partnership, as opposed to one that is a ***publicly held corporation***

joint-stock company BUSINESS formerly, public limited company in UK formerly in the United Kingdom, a public company whose stock was owned by many people. Now such a company is called a public limited company or Plc. *See also* ***company limited by shares***

joint venture BUSINESS enterprise undertaken by two or more firms a business project in which two or more independent companies collaborate and share the risks and rewards. *Abbr* ***JV***

journal ACCOUNTING consolidated record of transactions a record of original entry, into which transactions are usually transferred from source documents. The journal may be subdivided into: sales journal/day book for credit sales; purchases journal/day book for credit purchases; cash book for cash receipts and payments; and the journal proper for transactions which could not appropriately be recorded in any of the other journals.

JSE MARKETS *see* ***JSE Limited***

JSE Limited MARKETS South African Stock Exchange the largest stock exchange in Africa, located in Johannesburg, South Africa. *Abbr* ***JSE***

JSE Securities Exchange South Africa MARKETS name of JSE Limited between 2000 and 2005 from 2000 to 2005, the official name of the JSE Limited, the South African stock exchange

ju'alal FINANCE contract for payment for services performed in Islamic financing, a contract for performing a specified act for a specified fee

judgment creditor LEGAL plaintiff in court case for debt in a legal action, the individual or business who has brought the action and to whom the court orders the judgment debtor to pay the money owed. In the event of the judgment debtor not conforming to the court order, the judgment creditor must return to the court to request that the judgment be enforced.

judgment debtor LEGAL defendant in court case for debt in a legal action, the individual or business ordered to pay the judgment creditor the money owed

jumbo mortgage MORTGAGES US mortgage too large for favorable terms in the United States, a mortgage that is too large to qualify for favorable treatment by a government agency

junior capital STOCKHOLDING & INVESTMENTS capital representing stockholders' equity capital in the form of stockholders' equity which is repaid only after the secured loans forming the senior capital have been paid if the firm goes into liquidation

junior debt FINANCE debt with low priority for repayment a debt that has no claim on a debtor's assets, or less claim than another debt. *See also* ***senior debt***. *Also called* ***subordinated debt***

junior mortgage MORTGAGES mortgage with low priority for repayment a mortgage whose holder has less claim on a debtor's assets than the holder of another mortgage. *See also* ***senior mortgage***

junior partner BUSINESS member of business partnership with limited involvement a person whose participation in management and share in the profits of a partnership are very limited

junior security STOCKHOLDING & INVESTMENTS security that is subordinate to another a security whose interest or dividend payment has a lower priority than that of another security issued by the same company

junk bond STOCKHOLDING & INVESTMENTS, RISK high-interest but high-risk bond a high-yielding bond issued on a low-grade security. The issue of junk bonds has most commonly been linked with takeover activity.

junk-rated STOCKHOLDING & INVESTMENTS, RISK describes bond that is risky investment used to describe a bond that is considered by a ***rating agency*** to not be ***investment grade*** and therefore has a higher than average risk. Junk-rated bonds have a rating of BB or less.

just-in-time OPERATIONS & PRODUCTION production method reducing inventory stockpiling a production method that requires necessary materials to be at the place of manufacture or assembly at the appropriate time to minimize holding excess inventory, reducing wastage and expense. *Abbr* ***JIT***

JV *abbr* BUSINESS ***joint venture***

K

K FINANCE 1,000 one thousand: used especially after numbers expressing a sum of money. It derives from kilo-.

kafalah FINANCE agreement to pay debt of another who defaults in Islamic financing, an agreement in which one party assumes responsibility for the debt of another if the debtor should fail to pay

kakaku yusen MARKETS Japanese rule for choosing between differing instructions in Japan, the price priority system operated on the Tokyo Stock Exchange whereby a lower price takes precedence over a higher price for a sell order, and vice versa for a buy order. *See also* ***jikan***

kangaroo MARKETS Australian stock an Australian stock traded on the London Stock Exchange (*slang*)

Kansas City Board of Trade MARKETS specialized US commodities exchange a commodities exchange, established in 1856, that specializes in futures and options contracts for red winter wheat, the Value Line® Index, natural gas, and the ISDEX® Internet Stock Index

kappa STOCKHOLDING & INVESTMENTS relationship between option price change and asset's volatility a ratio between the expected change in the price of an option and a one percent change in the expected volatility of the underlying asset. *Also called* ***lambda, vega***

Keidanren BUSINESS Japan Federation of Economic Organizations the Japanese abbreviation for the Japan Federation of Economic Organizations. Established in 1946, it works toward a resolution of the major problems facing the Japanese and international business communities and the sound development of their economies. Its members include over 1,000 of Japan's leading corporations, including over 50 foreign companies, and over 100 industry-wide groups representing such major sectors as manufacturing, trade, distribution, finance, and energy.

Keough Plan PENSIONS US pension benefiting specific groups in the United States, a pension subject to tax advantage for somebody who is self-employed or has an interest in a small company. *See also* ***stakeholder pension***

kerb market *UK* MARKETS unofficial stock market a stock market that exists outside the stock exchange. The term originates from markets held in the street.

ker-ching FINANCE expression suggesting financial success an expression suggesting that something will be very successful financially (*slang*)

key account management MARKETING management of most important customer relationships the management of the customer relationships that are most important to a company. Key accounts are those held by customers who produce most ***profit*** for a company or have the potential to do so, or those who are of strategic importance. Development of these ***customer relations*** and ***customer retention*** is important to business success. Particular emphasis is placed on analyzing which accounts are key to a company at any one time, determining the needs of these particular customers, and implementing procedures to ensure that they receive premium ***customer service*** and to increase ***customer satisfaction***.

Keynesian economics ECONOMICS economic philosophy of John Maynard Keynes the economic teachings and doctrines associated with ***John Maynard Keynes***

Keynes, John Maynard ECONOMICS British economist with influential theories on macroeconomics a British economist who lived from 1883-1946. He is best known for his theories regarding ***macroeconomics***. He believed that in a ***recession***, the only way to reduce unemployment and improve the economy was for the government to increase spending, even if it meant running a deficit, and to reduce interest rates to encourage borrowing.

key rate FINANCE interest rate on which other rates are based an interest rate that gives the basic rate on which other rates are calculated, for example, the Bank of England's bank rate or the Federal Reserve's discount rate in the United States

kickback FRAUD illicit payment to facilitator in transaction a sum of money paid illegally to somebody in order to gain concessions or favors (*slang*)

kicker STOCKHOLDING & INVESTMENTS attractive extra to standard security an addition to a standard security that makes it more attractive, for example, options and warrants (*slang*). *See also* ***bells and whistles, sweetener***

kiddie tax TAX US tax on youth income in the United States, a tax on the investment income of children and young people up to the age of 24. The amount of the tax is calculated based on their student status and/or earned income.

kill FINANCE stop instruction to stop an instruction or order from being carried out (*slang*)

killer bee BUSINESS facilitator in averting takeover somebody, especially a banker, who helps a company avoid being taken over

killing ◇ make a killing FINANCE to make a lot of money very quickly

kimono ◇ open the kimono GENERAL MANAGEMENT to inspect something that has not been open for examination before, especially a company's accounts

kitchen sink bond STOCKHOLDING & INVESTMENTS, RISK bond created from collection of collateralized mortgage obligations a high-risk bond created by combining ***tranches*** of existing collateralized mortgage obligations

kite 1. FRAUD fraudulent check, bill, or receipt a fraudulent financial transaction, for example, a bad check that is dated to take advantage of the time interval required for clearing **2.** FINANCE sign fraudulent checks to write bad checks in order to take advantage of the time interval required for clearing ◇ fly a kite **1.** FRAUD to use a fraudulent financial document such as a bad check **2.** GENERAL MANAGEMENT to make a suggestion in order to test people's opinion of it

kiwibond CURRENCY & EXCHANGE Eurobond in NZ dollars a ***Eurobond*** denominated in New Zealand dollars

knight MERGERS & ACQUISITIONS firm involved in takeover a term borrowed from chess strategy to describe a company involved in the politics of a ***takeover*** bid. There are three main types of knights. A *white knight* is a company that is friendly to the board of the company to be acquired. If the white knight gains control, it may retain the existing ***board of directors***. A *black knight* is a former white knight that has disagreed with the board of the company to be acquired and has established its own hostile bid. A gray *knight* is a white knight that does not have the confidence of the company to be acquired.

knock-for-knock *UK* INSURANCE with each insurer paying own customer's repair bill used to describe a practice between insurance companies whereby each will pay for the repairs to the vehicle it insures in the event of an accident

knockout option STOCKHOLDING & INVESTMENTS option with condition attached an option to which a condition relating to the underlying security's or commodity's present price is attached so that it effectively expires when it goes ***out of the money***

knowledge capital FINANCE knowledge applicable for profit knowledge that a company possesses and can put to profitable use

knowledge management GENERAL MANAGEMENT use of organization's knowledge for competitive advantage the coordination and exploitation of an organization's knowledge resources, in order to create benefit and competitive advantage

Korea Composite Stock Price Index MARKETS index of traded Korean stocks the index of all the common stocks traded on the Korean stock exchanges. *Abbr* ***KOSPI***

KOSPI *abbr* MARKETS ***Korea Composite Stock Price Index***

krona CURRENCY & EXCHANGE Swedish and Icelandic currency unit a unit of currency used in Sweden and Iceland

Krugerrand CURRENCY & EXCHANGE South African gold coin a South African coin consisting of one ounce of gold, first minted in 1967, bearing the portrait of 19th-century South African president Paul Kruger on the obverse

kurtosis STATISTICS distribution around mean a statistical measure of the distribution of data around a mean, as used in charts that assess the volatility of an investment

L

L ECONOMICS measurement of money supply a measure of the money supply, calculated as the broad money supply plus short-term Treasury securities, savings bonds, and commercial paper

labor HR & PERSONNEL all workers considered as group all the people employed in work, especially those doing manual labor, in a country, company, or industry considered as a group

labor dispute *US* GENERAL MANAGEMENT conflict between workers and management a disagreement or conflict between an ***employer*** and ***employees*** or between the ***employers' association*** and ***labor union***. *UK term* ***industrial dispute***

labor force survey STATISTICS quarterly survey of UK workforce a survey carried out every quarter in the United Kingdom, covering such topics as unemployment and hours of work

labor-intensive OPERATIONS & PRODUCTION requiring many people involving large numbers of workers or high labor costs. *See also* ***capital-intensive***

labor-intensive industry OPERATIONS & PRODUCTION business requiring many workers an industry that needs large numbers of employees and in which labor costs are high in relation to other costs

labor union *US* GENERAL MANAGEMENT organization representing employees' interests an organization of ***employees*** within a trade or profession that has the objective of representing its members' interests, primarily through improving pay and conditions, and provides a variety of services. *UK term* ***trade union***

laddering 1. STOCKHOLDING & INVESTMENTS selling after raising stock price by continued buying the investment strategy of repeatedly buying shares in a newly launched corporation so as to force up the price, then selling the whole investment at a profit **2.** STOCKHOLDING & INVESTMENTS, RISK timed purchase, sale, and reinvestment strategy reducing risk the action of making a series of investments that mature at different times, cashing each one at maturity, then reinvesting the proceeds, thereby reducing the risk of losing large amounts all at once

ladder option STOCKHOLDING & INVESTMENTS, RISK option whose profit is locked in set level an option whose ***strike price*** is reset when the underlying asset breaks through a specified level, locking in the profit between the old and new strike price

Lady Macbeth strategy BUSINESS change in which white knight becomes black knight a change of approach on the part of a presumed white knight, in which it becomes a black knight. A Lady Macbeth strategy is usually associated with ***takeover*** battles and has connotations of treachery.

Laffer curve ECONOMICS, TAX graph showing effects of tax rate changes a graph showing that cuts in tax rates increase output in the economy and thus increase overall tax revenues

laggard MARKETING firm that does not innovate an organization that follows a ***first mover*** to market, or a company that is not the recognized leader in a sector. *See also* ***first mover***

lagging indicator ECONOMICS economic factor confirming change in economic trend a measurable economic factor, for example, corporate profits or unemployment, that changes after the economy has already moved to a new trend, which it can confirm but not predict

laissez-faire economy ECONOMICS economic system in which government does not intervene an economy in which the government does not interfere because it believes that market forces should determine the course of the economy

lambda STOCKHOLDING & INVESTMENTS relationship of option price to underlying asset's volatility a ratio between the expected change in the price of an option and a one percent change in the expected volatility of the underlying asset. *Also called* ***kappa, vega***

lame duck BUSINESS firm with financial problems a company that is in financial difficulties

land bank FINANCE undeveloped land owned by builder or developer the land that a builder or developer has that is available for development

land banking FINANCE acquiring land for future development the practice of buying land that is not needed immediately, but with the expectation of using it in the future

landed costs INTERNATIONAL TRADE costs of shipping and customs clearance costs of goods that have been delivered to a port, unloaded, and passed through customs

landing order INTERNATIONAL TRADE permit to hold goods in bonded warehouse a permit that allows goods to be unloaded into a bonded warehouse without paying customs duty

landlord BUSINESS owner of rented property a person or company that owns a property that is rented

land register REAL ESTATE record of UK property and its owners in the United Kingdom, a list of pieces of land, showing who owns each and what buildings are on it

land tax TAX Australian tax on residential land a form of ***wealth tax*** imposed in Australia on the value of residential land. The level and conditions of the tax vary from state to state.

lapping *US* ACCOUNTING way of concealing missing funds an attempt to hide missing funds by delaying the recording of cash receipts in a business's books. *UK term* ***teeming and lading***

lapse STOCKHOLDING & INVESTMENTS expiry of option without trading the termination of an option without trade in the underlying security or commodity

lapsed option STOCKHOLDING & INVESTMENTS expired right to buy or sell investment an option to buy or sell a security or commodity that is no longer valid because it has expired

lapse rights STOCKHOLDING & INVESTMENTS rights of somebody allowing offer to lapse rights, such as those to a prearranged premium, owned by the person who allows an offer to lapse

large-sized business BUSINESS organization with 250 or more employees an organization that has grown beyond the limits of a ***medium-sized business*** and has 250 or more employees. This definition of a large-sized enterprise is the one adopted by the United Kingdom's Department for Business Enterprise and Regulatory Reform for statistical purposes. It is usually from the ranks of large-sized businesses that ***multinational businesses*** arise.

last quarter ACCOUNTING final period of fiscal year a period of three months from October to the end of the year, or the period of three months at the end of the fiscal year

last survivor policy INSURANCE life insurance policy for two or more an insurance policy covering the lives of two or more people. The sum insured is not paid out until all the policyholders are deceased. *See also* ***joint life annuity***

last trading day MARKETS final trading day in futures or options contract the last day in which trading takes place in a futures or options contract relating to a certain delivery month, after which the contract must be settled

latency MARKETS delay in transmission the delay between the sending of information electronically and its receipt; low latency refers to the rapid execution of a transaction

latent market MARKETING group of potential consumers of proposed product a group of people who have been identified as potential consumers of a product that does not yet exist

launch MARKETING making new product available the process of introducing a new product to the market

laundering FRAUD concealing illegal origins of money the process of passing the profits of illegal activities such as tax evasion into the normal banking system via apparently legitimate businesses

LAUTRO REGULATION & COMPLIANCE former UK regulator a former UK financial authority regulating life insurance and mutual funds. It was brought to an end in 1995. *Full form* ***Life Assurance and Unit Trust Regulatory Organization***

law of diminishing marginal utility ECONOMICS increased consumption of product decreases consumer's satisfaction a general theory in economics stating that each unit of a product consumed adds less satisfaction to the consumer than the previous one, i.e., the ***marginal utility*** of any good or service diminishes as each new unit of it is consumed

law of diminishing returns ECONOMICS increase in one area has limited effect a rule stating that as one factor of production is increased, while others remain constant, the extra output generated by the additional input will eventually fall. The law of diminishing returns therefore means that extra workers, extra capital, extra machinery, or extra land may not necessarily raise output as much as expected. For example, increasing the supply of raw materials to a production line may allow additional output to be produced by using any spare capacity workers have. Once this capacity is fully used, however, continually increasing the amount of raw material without a corresponding increase in the number of workers will not result in an increase of output.

law of supply and demand ECONOMICS *see* ***supply and demand***

lay-away *US* FINANCE paying for product in installments before taking ownership the reservation of an article for purchase by the payment of an initial deposit followed by regular interest-free installments, on completion of which the article is claimed by the buyer

lay off HR & PERSONNEL **1.** terminate somebody's employment because of too little work to dismiss an employee or employees permanently because there is insufficient work to occupy them **2.** temporarily stop somebody's employment to suspend an employee or employees temporarily because there is insufficient work to occupy them

layoff *US* HR & PERSONNEL termination of employment because of too little work dismissal, often temporarily, from work because a job ceases to exist or because of lack of work. Employees who are laid off may qualify for severance pay. If the layoff process is handled incorrectly, the employer may be faced with claims for unfair dismissal. *UK term* ***redundancy***

LBO *abbr* MERGERS & ACQUISITIONS ***leveraged buyout***

LC *or* **L/C** *abbr* BANKING ***letter of credit***

LCH *abbr* BANKING ***London Clearing House***

LCM *abbr* ACCOUNTING ***lower of cost or market***

LDC *abbr* ECONOMICS **1.** ***less developed country*** **2.** ***least developed country***

LDT *abbr* FINANCE ***licensed deposit-taker***

lead INSURANCE first underwriter of Lloyd's policy in an insurance policy from Lloyd's, the first named underwriting syndicate

lead bank BANKING main bank in loan syndicate the primary bank in a loan syndicate, which organizes the transaction in question

leader **1.** GENERAL MANAGEMENT, HR & PERSONNEL firm's executive who motivates others well a business executive who possesses exceptional leadership qualities as well as management skills **2.** MARKETING top performing thing the most successful product or company in a marketplace

leadership GENERAL MANAGEMENT, HR & PERSONNEL ability to guide and motivate others well the capacity to establish direction and to influence and align others toward a common goal, motivating and committing them to action and making them responsible for their performance. Leadership theory is one of the most discussed areas of management, and many different approaches are taken to the topic. Some notions of leadership are related to types of ***authority*** delineated by Max Weber. It is often suggested that leaders possess innate personal qualities that distinguish them from others. Other theories, such as Behaviorist theories of leadership, suggest that leadership is defined by action and behavior, rather than by personality. A related idea is that leadership style is not fixed but should be adapted to different situations, and this is explored in ***contingency theory***. Perhaps the most simple model of leadership is action-centered leadership, which focuses on what an effective leader actually does. These many approaches and differences of opinion illustrate the complexity of the leadership role and the intangibility of the essence of good leadership.

leading economic indicator *or* **leading indicator** ECONOMICS early indication of change in economic trends an economic variable, such as private-sector wages, that tends to show the direction of future economic activity earlier than other indicators. *See also* ***lagging indicator***

leading edge BUSINESS most modern and innovative situated at the forefront of ***innovation***. A leading edge company is ahead of others in such areas as inventing or implementing new technologies, and in entering new markets.

lead manager *UK* STOCKHOLDING & INVESTMENTS = ***lead underwriter***

lead partner BUSINESS dominant partner the organization that takes the lead role in an alliance

leads and lags CURRENCY & EXCHANGE adjusting speed of transactions with exchange rates in businesses that deal in foreign currencies, the practice of speeding up the receipt of payments (leads) if a currency is going to weaken, and slowing down the payment of costs (lags) if a currency is thought to be about to strengthen, in order to maximize gains and reduce losses

lead time **1.** FINANCE, OPERATIONS & PRODUCTION time between starting and finishing the time interval between the start of an activity or process and its completion, for example, the time between ordering goods and their receipt, or between starting manufacturing of a product and its completion **2.** OPERATIONS & PRODUCTION period between order placement and delivery in inventory control, the time between placing an order and its arrival on site. Lead time differs from delivery time in that it also includes the time required to place an order and the time it takes to inspect the goods and receive them into the appropriate store. Inventory levels can afford to be lower and orders smaller when purchasing lead times are short. **3.** OPERATIONS & PRODUCTION, MARKETING period from new product idea to sales readiness in ***new product development*** and manufacturing, the time required to develop a product from concept to market delivery. Lead time increases as a result of the poor sequencing of dependent activities, the lack of availability of resources, poor quality in the component parts, and poor plant layout. The technique of ***concurrent engineering*** focuses on the entire concept-to-customer process with the goal of reducing lead time. Companies can gain a ***competitive advantage*** by achieving a lead time reduction and so getting products to market faster. *Also called* ***cycle time*** *(sense 2)*

lead underwriter *US* STOCKHOLDING & INVESTMENTS institution in charge of new issue the financial institution with overall responsibility for a new issue of shares of stock including its coordination, distribution, and related administration. *UK term* ***lead manager***

lean enterprise OPERATIONS & PRODUCTION efficient business structure with little waste an organizational model that strategically applies the key ideas behind ***lean production***. A lean enterprise is viewed as a group of separate individuals, functions, or organizations that operate as one entity. The goal is to apply lean techniques that create individual breakthroughs in companies and to link these up and down the supply chain to form a continuous value stream to raise the whole chain to a higher level.

lean manufacturing OPERATIONS & PRODUCTION, = ***lean production***

lean operation OPERATIONS & PRODUCTION business with little waste a company following the methodology of ***lean production***, with low ***inventories***. *See also* ***lean production***

lean production OPERATIONS & PRODUCTION efficient manufacturing method with little waste a methodology aimed at reducing waste in the form of overproduction, excessive ***lead time***, or product defects in order to make a business more effective and more competitive. Lean production originates in the production systems established by Toyota in Japan in the 1950s. In the early 1980s there was a significant increase in the application of lean production in Western companies. Lean production is characterized by *lean operations* with low ***inventories***; ***quality management*** through prevention of errors; small batch runs; ***just-in-time*** production; high commitment human resource policies; team-based working; and close relations with suppliers. Concepts that can help an organization move toward lean production include ***continuous improvement*** and ***world class manufacturing***. *Also called* ***lean manufacturing***

LEAPS STOCKHOLDING & INVESTMENTS options with one- to three-year expiry date options that expire between one and three years in the future. *Full form* ***long-term equity anticipation securities***

learning by doing GENERAL MANAGEMENT finding out about job by performing it the acquisition of knowledge or skills through direct experience of carrying out a task. Learning by doing often happens under supervision, as part of a training or ***orientation*** process, and is closely associated with the practical experience picked up by *"sitting with Nellie."* It is an outcome of the research into learning of David Kolb and Reg Revans. A more formalized approach to learning by doing is ***experiential learning***.

learning curve 1. GENERAL MANAGEMENT rate at which new information must be acquired a graphic representation of the acquisition of knowledge or experience over time. A steep learning curve reflects a substantial amount of learning in a short time, and a shallow curve reflects a slower learning process. The curve eventually levels out to a plateau, during which time the knowledge gained is being consolidated. **2.** OPERATIONS & PRODUCTION proportional reduction in effort when production doubles the proportional decrease in effort when production is doubled. The learning curve has its origin in productivity research in the airplane industry of the 1930s, when T. P. Wright discovered that in assembling an aircraft, the time and effort decreased by 20% each time the cumulative number of planes produced doubled. ▶ *Also called* ***experience curve***

learning opportunity GENERAL MANAGEMENT mistake to learn from a positive way of referring to a mistake that somebody has made at work, presenting it as a chance to gain new knowledge

learning organization GENERAL MANAGEMENT customer-focused firm with little hierarchy an organizational model characterized by a flat structure and ***customer-focused*** teams, that engenders the collective ability to develop shared visions by capturing and exploiting employees' willingness, commitment, and curiosity. The concept of the learning organization was proposed by Chris Argyris and Donald Schön as part of their work on organizational learning, but was brought back to public attention in the 1990s by Peter Senge. For Senge, a learning organization is one with the capacity to shift away from views inherent in a traditional hierarchical organization, toward the ability of all employees to challenge prevailing thinking and gain a balanced perspective. Senge believes the five major characteristics of a learning organization are mental models, personal mastery, systems thinking, shared vision, and team learning. Because of the requirement for an open, risk-tolerant culture, which is the opposite of the corporate culture of most organizations today, the learning organization remains, for many, an unattainable ideal.

learning style GENERAL MANAGEMENT way that somebody best acquires knowledge and skills the way in which somebody approaches the acquisition of knowledge and skills. Learning styles have been divided into four main types by Peter Honey and Alan Mumford, in their *Manual of Learning Styles* (1982). The types of learners are the activist, who likes to get involved in new experiences and enjoys the challenges of change; the theorist, who likes to question assumptions and methodologies and learns best when there is time to explore links between ideas and situations; the pragmatist, who prefers practicality and learns best when there is a link between the subject matter and the job in hand and when he or she can try out what he or she has learned; and the reflector, who likes to take his or her time and think things through, and who learns best from activities where he or she can observe and conduct research. One person can demonstrate more than one learning style, and the category or categories that best describe somebody can be determined through use of a learning styles questionnaire.

lease LEGAL **1.** written contract for renting something a written contract for renting a building, a piece of land, or a piece of equipment for a fixed period of time in return for payment of a fee **2.** rent offices, land, or equipment to somebody to rent offices, land, or equipment to a person or business for a fixed period of time specified in a written contract **3.** rent offices, land, or equipment from somebody to use offices, land, or equipment for a fixed period of time specified in a written contract and pay a fee

leaseback LEGAL, FINANCE *see* ***sale and leaseback***

leasehold LEGAL, REAL ESTATE **1.** right to rent property for fixed period the right to possess a property on a lease, for a fixed period of time **2.** piece of property that is rented a property held on a lease granted by the legal owner of the property

leaseholder LEGAL, REAL ESTATE somebody renting piece of property under lease a person who is in possession of a property by way of a lease

least developed country ECONOMICS very poor country with little economic development a country that is not economically advanced, especially a country that borrowed heavily from commercial banks in the 1970s and 1980s to finance its industrial development, and so helped to create an international debt crisis. *Abbr* ***LDC***

leave HR & PERSONNEL paid time away from work work time when an employee is paid, but is not required to be at work. Leave takes several forms and includes time off for vacation. The number of days of vacation is set out in the contract of employment and may be dependent on the employee's length of service. It may also take the form of sick leave, educational leave, or maternity or paternity leave.

ledger ACCOUNTING **1.** book for accounts a book in which account transactions are recorded **2.** book with record of account transactions a collection of accounts, or book of accounts. Credit sales information is recorded, for example, by debtor, in the sales ledger. **3.** book of consolidated accounts a collection of accounts, maintained by transfers from the books of original entry. The ledger may be subdivided as follows: the sales ledger/debtors' ledger contains all the personal accounts of customers; the purchases ledger/creditors' ledger contains all the personal accounts of supplieors; the private ledger contains accounts relating to the proprietor's interest in the business such as capital and drawings; the general ledger/nominal ledger contains all other accounts relating to assets, expenses, revenue, and liabilities.

leg STOCKHOLDING & INVESTMENTS price for security either the highest price offered for a security or the lowest price a seller will accept for a security

legacy system BUSINESS computer system with long-term function an existing computer system that provides a strategic function for a specific part of a business. Inventory management systems, for example, are legacy systems.

legal charge LEGAL legal document showing ownership of UK property in the United Kingdom, a legal document held by the Land Registry showing who has a claim on a property

legal charges LEGAL = ***legal costs***

legal claim LEGAL lawful right or statement of ownership a legally recognized right to the ownership of something, or a statement of such a right

legal costs LEGAL money spent on lawyers' fees the amount of money spent on legal matters, particularly lawyers' fees. *Also called* ***legal charges, legal expenses***

legal currency LEGAL, CURRENCY & EXCHANGE legally accepted money money that is recognized by a government to be legally acceptable for payment of a debt

legal expenses LEGAL = ***legal costs***

legal list LEGAL, STOCKHOLDING & INVESTMENTS securities that financial institutions can legally invest in a list of blue-chip securities in which banks and financial institutions are allowed to invest by the state in which they are based

legal loophole LEGAL legal flaw allowing people to get around law an area in the law that is insufficiently explicit or comprehensive and allows the law to be circumvented

legal tender LEGAL, CURRENCY & EXCHANGE legally accepted paper money and coins paper money and coins that have to be accepted within a given jurisdiction when offered as payment of a debt. *See also* ***limited legal tender***

lemon BUSINESS unsatisfactory product a product that is defective in some way, for example, an investment that is performing poorly (*slang*)

lender FINANCE somebody who lends money a person or financial institution that lends money

lender of last resort BANKING bank lending to troubled commercial banks a central bank that lends money to banks that cannot borrow elsewhere

lending facility BANKING = ***credit facility***

lending limit BANKING maximum amount of money bank can lend a restriction placed on the amount of money a bank can legally lend

lending margin BANKING spread above base rate borrowers agree to pay an agreed spread for lending paid by borrowers, based on a reference rate such as the London Interbank Offered Rate

length of service HR & PERSONNEL how long employee has worked for firm the period in which somebody has been continually employed in an ***organization,*** without breaks in the ***contract of employment***. Length of service may determine entitlement to employment rights or ***fringe benefits***, for example, the amount of annual leave allocated.

less developed country ECONOMICS poorer country with limited economic development a country whose economic development is held back because it lacks the technology and capital to make use of its natural resources to produce goods demanded on world markets. *Abbr* ***LDC***

lessee LEGAL user of something leased the person who has the use of a leased asset

lessor LEGAL provider of something on lease the person who provides an asset being leased

let *UK* REAL ESTATE = ***rent***

letter of acknowledgment GENERAL MANAGEMENT letter saying something has been received a letter written to somebody to say that something that he or she sent has been received

letter of agreement LEGAL simple contract a document that constitutes a simple form of contract

letter of comfort *UK* BANKING = ***letter of moral intent***

letter of credit BANKING letter of authorization from one bank to another a letter issued by a bank that can be presented to another bank to authorize the issue of credit or money. *Abbr* ***L/C***

letter of indemnity LEGAL statement accepting loss from replaced stock certificate a statement that a stock certificate has been lost, destroyed, or stolen and that the stockholder will indemnify the company for any loss that might result from its reappearance after the company has issued a replacement to the stockholder

letter of intent BUSINESS written commitment to do something a document that indicates an intention to do something such as buy a business, grant somebody a loan, or participate in a project. The intention may or may not depend on specific conditions being met and the document is not legally binding. *See also* ***letter of moral intent***

letter of license LEGAL, FINANCE letter giving debtor more time for repayment a letter from a creditor to a debtor who is having problems repaying money owed, giving the debtor a specific period of time to raise the money and an undertaking not to bring legal proceedings to recover the debt during that period

letter of moral intent *US* BANKING parent company's support for subsidiary's loan a letter from a holding company addressed to a bank where one of its subsidiaries wishes to borrow money. The purpose of the letter is to support the subsidiary's application to borrow funds and offer reassurance – although not a guarantee – to the bank that the subsidiary will remain in business for the foreseeable future, often with an undertaking to advise the bank if the subsidiary is likely to be sold. *UK term* ***letter of comfort***

letter of renunciation STOCKHOLDING & INVESTMENTS document transferring new stock a form used to transfer an allotment of shares in a ***rights issue*** to another person

letter security STOCKHOLDING & INVESTMENTS unregistered security salable under certain conditions in the United States, a security that has not been registered with the ***SEC*** but can be sold privately if the buyer signs a letter of intent stating that the security is for investment, not resale, or can be traded publicly if the owner files a Form 144 with the SEC showing that the sale meets conditions that exempts it from registration with the SEC

letters patent LEGAL official document conferring commercial rights on inventor an official document giving somebody the exclusive right to make and sell something that he or she has invented

level load STOCKHOLDING & INVESTMENTS decreasing annual fee an annual fee that is deducted from the assets in a mutual fund to cover management costs and that decreases gradually over time

level term insurance INSURANCE life insurance policy for fixed period a life insurance policy in which an agreed lump sum is paid if the policyholder dies before a specific date. A joint form of this life cover is popular with couples who have children.

leverage FINANCE corporate funding mainly through borrowing a method of corporate funding in which a higher proportion of funds is raised through borrowing than through stock issue. *Also called* ***gearing***. *See also* ***financial leverage***

leveraged bid MERGERS & ACQUISITIONS takeover bid with borrowed finance a takeover bid financed by borrowed money, rather than by a stock issue

leveraged buyout MERGERS & ACQUISITIONS takeover with borrowed finance a takeover using borrowed money, with the purchased company's assets as collateral. *Abbr* ***LBO***

leveraged investment company *US* STOCKHOLDING & INVESTMENTS investment company using borrowed money to expand an investment company that borrows money in order to increase its portfolio. When the market is rising, stocks in a leveraged investment trust rise faster than those in an unleveraged trust, but they fall faster when the market is falling. *UK term* ***geared investment trust***

leveraged required return STOCKHOLDING & INVESTMENTS income from investment exceeding cost of loan the rate of return from an investment of borrowed money needed to make the investment worthwhile

leverage ratios FINANCE, RISK means of quantifying risk from capital ratios that indicate the level of risk taken by a company as a result of its capital structure. A number of different ratios may be calculated, for example, debt ratio (total debt divided by total assets), debt-to-equity or leverage ratio (total debt divided by total equity), or interest cover (earnings before interest and tax divided by interest paid). *Also called* ***gearing ratios***

levy TAX tax that raises money for specific purpose a type of tax on a specific product or service by which a government raises money for a specific purpose

liabilities FINANCE firm's debts the debts of a business, including dividends owed to stockholders

liability FINANCE money lent without guarantee of repayment a debt that has no claim on a debtor's assets, or less claim than another debt

liability insurance INSURANCE insurance against incurring costs insurance against legal liability that the insured might incur, for example, from causing an accident

liability management FINANCE investigation of impact of liabilities on profitability any exercise carried out by a business with the objective of controlling the effect of liabilities on its profitability. This will typically involve controlling the amount of risk undertaken, and ensuring that there is sufficient liquidity and that the best terms are obtained for any funding needs.

LIBID *abbr* MARKETS ***London Interbank Bid Rate***

LIBOR *abbr* MARKETS ***London Interbank Offered Rate***

license *US* LEGAL contract to do or use something for payment a contractual arrangement, or a document representing this, in which one organization gives another the rights to produce, sell, or use something in return for payment

licensed deposit-taker FINANCE UK institution that took deposits and paid interest formerly in the United Kingdom, a type of ***deposit-taking institution*** that was licensed to receive money on deposit from private individuals and to pay interest on it, for example, a bank or savings and loan. *Abbr* ***LDT***

licensed institution FINANCE = ***licensed deposit-taker***

licensing LEGAL making contract to do or use something the transfer of rights to manufacture or market a particular product to another individual or organization through a legal arrangement or contract. Licensing usually requires that a fee, commission, or royalty is paid to the licensor.

licensing agreement LEGAL permission for firm to do or use something an agreement permitting a company to market or produce a product or service owned by another company. A licensing agreement grants a license in return for a fee or royalty payment. Items licensed for use can include patents, trademarks, techniques, designs, and expertise. This kind of agreement is one way for a company to penetrate overseas markets in that it provides a middle path between direct export and investment overseas.

lien LEGAL legal right to hold property against debt a legal right to hold somebody's goods or property until a debt that is secured by the goods or property has been repaid

life annuity INSURANCE annuity with fixed monthly payment until death an annuity that pays a fixed amount per month until the holder's death

life assurance *UK* INSURANCE = ***life insurance***

Life Assurance and Unit Trust Regulatory Organization REGULATION & COMPLIANCE *see* ***LAUTRO***

life assured INSURANCE = ***life insured***

lifeboat 1. FINANCE = ***lifeboat scheme***
2. *S. Africa* BANKING loan to rescue commercial bank a low-interest emergency loan made by a central bank to rescue a commercial bank in danger of becoming insolvent

lifeboat scheme FINANCE rescue measure for business or fund a measure designed to protect or rescue a failing business or fund. *Also called* ***lifeboat*** *(sense 1)*

life cover INSURANCE = ***life insurance***

life cycle MARKETING course of product's development and sales over time the sales pattern of a product or service over a period of time. Typically, a life cycle falls into four stages: introduction, growth, maturity, and decline.

life-cycle costing ACCOUNTING way of assessing asset's cost over time a method of calculating the total cost of a physical asset throughout its life. Life-cycle costing is concerned with all costs of ownership and takes account of the costs incurred by an asset from its acquisition to its disposal, including design, installation, operating, and maintenance costs.

life-cycle fund STOCKHOLDING & INVESTMENTS mutual fund linked to investor's age a mutual fund whose investments vary according to the age of the investor

life-cycle savings motive ECONOMICS reason for saving money over lifetime a reason that a household or individual has for saving at specific times in life so as to have sufficient funds available to spend on anticipated expenses, for example, when starting a family or nearing retirement

life expectancy INSURANCE, PENSIONS how long average person lives the number of years that somebody of a given age is expected to live

life insurance *US* INSURANCE insurance paying others on insured's death insurance that pays a specified sum to the insured person's beneficiaries after the person's death. *Also called* ***life cover***. *UK term* ***life assurance***

life insurance bond INSURANCE = ***investment bond***

life insured *US* INSURANCE person with life insurance policy the person or persons covered by a life insurance policy. The insurance company pays out on the death of the policyholder. *UK term* ***life assured***

life interest REAL ESTATE lifetime right to benefit from property a situation where somebody benefits from a property for the entirety of his or her lifetime

life office INSURANCE, PENSIONS firm offering life insurance in the United Kingdom, a company that provides life insurance and sometimes pension plans

life policy INSURANCE, PENSIONS life insurance contract a contract for insurance that pays a specific sum to the insured person's beneficiaries after the person's death

lifestyle audit TAX comparison of taxpayer's living standards to reported income a study of a taxpayer's living standards and spending to determine if it is consistent with that person's reported income

lifestyle business BUSINESS business run by enthusiasts a typically small business run by individuals who have a strong interest in the product or service offered, for example, handmade greeting cards or jewelry, antique dealing or restoring. Such businesses tend to operate during hours that suit the owners, and generally provide them with a comfortable living.

life table STATISTICS table listing expected life spans by age a table that shows the probabilities of death, survival, and remaining years of life for people of given ages

lifetime customer value BUSINESS = ***lifetime value***

lifetime transfer TAX = ***chargeable transfer***

lifetime value BUSINESS person's accumulated expenditure on brand a measure of the total value to a supplier of a customer's business over the duration of their transactions.

In a consumer business, customer lifetime value is calculated by analyzing the behavior of a group of customers who have the same recruitment date. The revenue and cost for this group of customers is recorded, by campaign or season, and the overall contribution for that period can then be worked out. Industry experience has shown that the benefits to a business of increasing lifetime value can be enormous. A 5% increase in customer retention can create a 125% increase in profits; a 10% increase in retailer retention can translate to a 20% increase in sales; and extending customer life cycles by three years can treble profits per customer. *Also called* ***lifetime customer value***

LIFFE *abbr* MARKETS ***London International Financial Futures and Options Exchange***

lightning strike HR & PERSONNEL strike that happens with little warning in the United Kingdom, a stoppage of work as protest that occurs at very short notice. It may be of short duration and may not be sanctioned by a labor union.

LIMEAN *abbr* BANKING ***London Interbank Mean Rate***

limit STOCKHOLDING & INVESTMENTS specified minimum or maximum price for transaction an amount above or below which a broker is not to conclude the purchase or sale of a security for the client who specifies it

limit down MARKETS maximum daily price fall in option the most that the price of an option may fall in one day on a particular market

Limited BUSINESS part of name of UK limited company when placed at the end of the company's name, used to indicate that a UK company is a limited company

limited company BUSINESS UK firm with individual liability related to investment a British-registered company in which each stockholder is responsible for the company's debts only to the amount that he or she has invested in the company. Limited companies must be formed by at least two directors. *See also* ***private company, publicly held corporation***. *Abbr* ***Ltd***

limited legal tender LEGAL CURRENCY & EXCHANGE bills and coins only usable in small transactions in some jurisdictions, low denomination bills and all coins that may only be submitted up to a specific sum as legal tender in any one transaction

limited liability BUSINESS obligation to pay limited to size of investment the restriction of an owner's loss in a business to the amount of capital he or she has invested in it

limited liability company *UK* BUSINESS = ***corporation***

limited market MARKETS market with few of each security a market in which dealings for a specific security are difficult to transact, for example, because it has only limited appeal to investors or, in the case of stock, because institutions or family members are unlikely to sell it

limited partnership BUSINESS firm with partners responsible for proportion of debts a registered business in which the liability of the partners is limited to the amount of capital they have each provided for the business, and in the running of which the partners may not take part

limit order STOCKHOLDING & INVESTMENTS order to buy or sell security an order to a broker to sell a security at or above an agreed price, or to buy a security at or below an agreed price

limit up MARKETS maximum daily price rise in option the most that the price of an option may rise in one day on a particular market

linear programming GENERAL MANAGEMENT method for optimizing production a mathematical technique used to identify an optimal solution for the deployment of resources to meet organizational objectives. Linear programming uses graphic and algebraic means to calculate which combination of resources, subject to predicted constraints, is most likely to fulfill a given objective.

line management GENERAL MANAGEMENT hierarchy where each employee reports to single manager a hierarchical ***chain of command*** from executive to front-line level. Line management is the oldest and least complex management structure, in which top management have total and direct authority and employees report to only one supervisor. Managers in this type of organizational structure have direct responsibility for giving orders to their subordinates. Line management structures are usually organized along functional lines, although they increasingly undertake a variety of cross-functional duties such as employee development or strategic direction. The lowest managerial level in an organization following a line management structure is supervisory management.

line manager GENERAL MANAGEMENT employee's direct boss an employee's immediate superior, who oversees and has responsibility for the employee's work. A line manager at the lowest level of a large organization is a supervisor, but a manager at any level with direct responsibility for employees' work can be described as a line manager.

line of credit FINANCE means of borrowing money an agreed finance facility that allows a company or individual to borrow money. *Also called* ***bank line, credit line***

line organization GENERAL MANAGEMENT hierarchy with line managers an organizational structure that is based on ***line management***

lipstick entrepreneur BUSINESS independent businesswoman a woman who starts or owns a business. *Also called* ***fempreneur***

liquid FINANCE easy to convert to cash describes an asset that is easily converted to cash

liquid asset ratio FINANCE ratio of liquid to total assets the ratio of liquid assets to total assets. This is an indicator of a company's solvency.

liquid assets FINANCE possible sources of cash cash, and other assets readily convertible into cash without significant loss of capital

liquidate 1. BUSINESS end existence of firm to close a company by selling its assets, paying off any outstanding debts, distributing any remaining profits to the stockholders, and then ceasing trading **2.** STOCKHOLDING & INVESTMENTS convert into cash to sell assets in order to be able to have cash

liquidated damages LEGAL penalty for breaking contract an amount of money somebody pays for breaching a ***contract***

liquidated damages clause LEGAL clause stating penalty for breaking contract a clause in a ***contract*** that sets out the compensation to be paid in the event of a breach or a default of the terms of the contract. The compensation set out in a liquidated damages clause should be a genuine preestimate of the loss suffered as a result of the noncompletion of the contract. An example would be an amount payable per day in the event of the noncompletion of a building project. If the amount specified is not considered a genuine estimate of the losses incurred, and the clause is perceived to be solely an incentive for the completion of the contract, the clause is deemed a penalty clause and is not legally enforceable. However, liquidated damages clauses are often inaccurately referred to as penalty clauses. *See also* ***breach of contract***

liquidation BUSINESS process of ending existence of firm the winding-up of a company, a process during which assets are sold, liabilities settled as far as possible, and any remaining cash returned to the members. Liquidation may be voluntary or compulsory.

liquidation value BUSINESS yield from quick sale of firm's assets the amount of money that a quick sale of all of a company's assets would yield

liquidator BUSINESS seller of insolvent firm's assets the person appointed by a company, its creditors, or its stockholders to sell the assets of an insolvent company. The proceeds of the sale are used to discharge debts to creditors, with any surplus distributed to stockholders.

liquidity FINANCE ability to obtain cash from assets an assessment of the ease with which assets can be converted to cash

liquidity agreement FINANCE agreement to cash in asset an agreement to allow a company to convert an asset into cash

liquidity event FINANCE exit strategy of startup business the means by which founders and initial investors in a new company are able to obtain the money the business has earned by changing their ***equity*** into cash. The company may be sold or there may be a public offering of stock.

liquidity preference FINANCE desire for cash over other investments a choice made by people to hold their wealth in the form of cash rather than bonds or stocks. A general increase in liquidity preference is symptomatic of a financial crisis whereas a general decrease is associated with increased appetite for risk.

liquidity ratio FINANCE = ***cash ratio***

liquidity risk RISK danger of inability to cash in assets the risk that an entity will encounter difficulty in realizing assets or otherwise raising funds to meet commitments associated with financial instruments. *See also* ***funding risk***

liquidity squeeze FINANCE time when money is hard to borrow a situation or period in which money for borrowing is unavailable from finance companies, banks, and other lenders of money. *Also called* ***credit squeeze***

liquidity trap BANKING inability to push interest rates lower a central bank's inability to lower interest rates once investors believe rates can go no lower

liquid market MARKETS market with brisk trading a market in which a large number of trades are being made

liquid savings FINANCE money saved money held in deposit and savings accounts that is easily available if needed and not usually subject to large fluctuations in value

list broker BUSINESS intermediary arranging shared mailing lists a person or organization that makes the arrangements for one company to use another company's direct mail list

listed company BUSINESS firm with stock trading on exchange a company whose stock is quoted on a recognized stock exchange. *Also called* ***quoted company***

listed security STOCKHOLDING & INVESTMENTS, MARKETS security traded on exchange a security that is quoted on a recognized stock exchange

Listing Agreement MARKETS agreement when firm's stock are listed a document that a company signs when being listed on the Stock Exchange, in which the company promises to abide by stock exchange regulations

listing details MARKETS **1.** information published before firm's UK stock exchange listing in the United Kingdom, detailed information about a company, which is published when the company applies for a listing on a stock exchange. The US equivalent is the ***registration statement***. **2.** information about institutions backing issue detailed information published about the institutions that are backing a stock issue

listing requirements MARKETS conditions for security to be traded on exchange the conditions that have to be met before a security can be traded on a recognized stock exchange. Although exact requirements vary from one exchange to another, the two main ones are that the issuing company's assets should exceed a minimum amount and that the required information about its finances and business should have been published.

list price BUSINESS product price given by supplier the price of goods or services published by a supplier. The list price of an item may be discounted to regular customers or for bulk purchases.

list renting BUSINESS making firm's direct mail list available for fee an arrangement in which a company that owns a direct mail list lets another company use it for a fee

litigation LEGAL process of dealing with lawsuit the process of bringing a lawsuit against a person or organization

Little Board MARKETS American Stock Exchange for small firms the New York exchange for lesser companies' stocks and bonds. *Also called* ***American Stock Exchange***. *See also* ***Big Board***

lively market MARKETS stock market with brisk trading an active stock market in which many stocks are being bought or sold

livery MARKETING symbol on corporate property a mark of corporate identity used on something belonging to a company

living wage FINANCE amount of pay needed for normal life a level of pay that provides enough income for normal day-to-day basic requirements

living will LEGAL instructions for allowing death a legal document that specifies the measures you want or do not want taken to prolong your life in the event of a terminal illness or injury. It may also designate a person to make healthcare decisions on your behalf.

Lloyd's INSURANCE = ***Lloyd's of London***

Lloyd's broker INSURANCE agent arranging insurance through Lloyd's an agent who represents a client who wants insurance, and who arranges this insurance for him through a ***Lloyd's underwriting syndicate***

Lloyd's of London INSURANCE London-based insurance market an insurance market based in London made up of a group of member underwriting syndicates that underwrite most types of insurance policy. *Also called* ***Lloyd's***. *See also* ***Lloyd's underwriting syndicate***

Lloyd's underwriting syndicate INSURANCE London-based syndicate underwriting insurance an underwriting syndicate in membership with ***Lloyd's of London***

LME *abbr* MARKETS ***London Metal Exchange***

load STOCKHOLDING & INVESTMENTS administration charge for investment a charge in some investment funds to cover administration, profit, and incidentals. When the primary cost is paid at the beginning this is ***front-end loading***; at the end it is ***back-end loading***. *See also* ***load fund***

load fund STOCKHOLDING & INVESTMENTS mutual fund requiring payment for transactions a mutual fund that charges a fee for the purchase or sale of shares. *See also* ***no-load fund***

loading 1. OPERATIONS & PRODUCTION giving particular jobs to workstation the assignment of tasks or jobs to a workstation. The loading of jobs is worked out through the use of ***master production scheduling***. **2.** *ANZ* FINANCE extra pay for exceptional skills or work environment a payment made to employees over and above the basic wage in recognition of special skills or unfavorable conditions, for example, for overtime or shiftwork

loan FINANCE borrowing arrangement with fixed schedule a borrowing either by a business or a consumer where the amount borrowed is repaid according to an agreed schedule at an agreed interest rate, typically by regular installments over a set period of years. However, the principal may be repayable in one installment. *See also* ***balloon loan, fixed-rate loan, interest-only mortgage, variable interest rate***

loanable funds theory ECONOMICS interest rates are determined by supply and demand the theory that interest rates are determined solely by supply and demand. It assumes that consumers must be offered interest on their savings to induce them not just to spend their income and to make funds available for investment.

loanback 1. FINANCE in US, return of money to lender in the United States, the return to somebody of money that has been given as a loan, often as a way of illegally masking the money's true owner **2.** PENSIONS in UK, arrangement to borrow from pension fund in the United Kingdom, the ability of a holder of a pension fund to borrow money from it

loan capital FINANCE money firm borrows for operations a part of a company's capital that is a loan to be repaid at a later date

loan committee FINANCE group considering nonstandard loan applications a committee that examines applications for special loans, such as higher loans than usually allowed by a bank

loan constant ratio FINANCE ratio of annual payments to original balance the total of annual payments due on a loan as a fraction of the amount of the principal

Loan Council FINANCE Australian federal committee overseeing borrowing by states an Australian federal body, made up of treasurers from the states and the Commonwealth of Australia, that monitors borrowing by state governments

loan loss reserves BANKING sum held by bank to cover bad debts the money a bank holds to cover losses through defaults on loans that it makes

loan note FINANCE written details of loan a written agreement between parties describing the terms of repayment, interest if applicable, and due date of a loan

loan participation BANKING collaboration by banks to make single large loan the grouping together by several banks to share a very large loan to one single customer

loan production cycle FINANCE time between loan application and lending of money the period that begins with an application for a loan and ends with the lending of money

loan schedule FINANCE details of loan payments a list of the payments due on a loan and the balance outstanding after each has been made

loan shark FINANCE lender charging excessively high interest rates somebody who lends money at excessively, often illegally, high rates of interest (*informal*)

loan stock STOCKHOLDING & INVESTMENTS bonds and debentures a fixed-income security given in exchange for a loan

loan to value ratio FINANCE ratio of worth of loan to collateral the ratio of the amount of a loan to the value of the collateral for it. *Abbr* ***LTV ratio***

loan value FINANCE sum available to borrower the amount that a lender is willing to lend a borrower

lobby GENERAL MANAGEMENT group trying to influence decisions of politicians a group that seeks to influence government or legislators on behalf of a specific cause or interest

local MARKETS independent trader in futures or options a trader in futures or options, who occasionally makes trades on behalf of clients, but usually trades on his or her own account

local authority bond STOCKHOLDING & INVESTMENTS UK local government's fixed-interest bond in the United Kingdom, a loan raised by a local authority in the form of a fixed-interest bond, repayable at a specific date. Local authority bonds are similar to US ***Treasury bonds***.

local authority deposits FINANCE money lent to UK local government in the United Kingdom, money deposited with a local authority to earn interest for the depositor

localization MARKETING customizing to geographic audience adapting products, websites, and marketing to the needs of target users in different parts of the world. Studies have shown that if a vendor is serious about selling to foreign marketplaces, localizing is essential. Without localization, sales will be minimal, and returns very high.

lockbox BANKING banking service for checks sent by mail a banking system in which checks sent to a Post Office box rather than to a company are picked up by a bank and deposited in a bank account

lock limit MARKETS market limit on price change per session an occasion in which the trading price of a contract in a ***futures market*** reaches an exchange's specified upward or downward limit during a trading session, causing trading to halt. Lock limits are set to protect investors from large losses in a volatile market.

lockup period MARKETS time when investors cannot sell a specified period of time during which investors, especially insiders and employees of an initial public offering, are unable to sell their shares of stock

logistics OPERATIONS & PRODUCTION controlling flow of materials through firm's processes the management of the movement, storage, and processing of materials and information in the ***supply chain***. Logistics encompasses the acquisition of raw materials and components, manufacturing or processing, and the distribution of finished products to the end user. Each organization focuses on a different aspect of logistics, depending on its area of interest. For example, one might apply logistics to find a way of linking ***physical distribution management*** with earlier events in the supply chain, another to plan its acquisition and storage, while a third might use logistics as a support operation.

logistics management OPERATIONS & PRODUCTION handling of delivery the management of the distribution of products to the market

logo GENERAL MANAGEMENT firm's recognizable symbol a graphic device or symbol used by an organization as part of its corporate identity. A logo is used to facilitate instant recognition of an organization and to reinforce ***brand*** expectations and public image.

Lombard loan RISK loan with securities pledged as collateral a loan granted by a financial institution against pledged collateral in the form of securities

London Bullion Market MARKETS market for gold and silver the world's largest market for gold, where silver is also traded. It is a wholesale market, where the minimum trades are generally 1,000 ounces for gold and 50,000 ounces for silver. Members typically trade with each other and their clients on a principal-to-principal basis so that all risks, including those of credit, are between the two parties to the transaction.

London Chamber of Commerce and Industry BUSINESS UK's largest chamber of commerce in the United Kingdom, the largest chamber of commerce, that strives "to help London businesses succeed by promoting their interests and expanding their opportunities as members of a worldwide business network." *See also* ***ICC***

London Clearing House MARKETS organization trading in contracts for members an organization that acts on behalf of its members as a central counterparty for contracts traded on the London International Financial Futures and Options Exchange, the International Petroleum Exchange, and the London Metal Exchange. When the LCH has registered a trade, it becomes the buyer to every member who sells and the seller to every member who buys, ensuring good financial performance. To protect it against the risks assumed as central counterparty, the LCH establishes margin requirements. *Abbr* ***LCH***. *See also* ***margining***

London Commodity Exchange MARKETS *see* ***London International Financial Futures and Options Exchange***

London Interbank Bid Rate MARKETS UK rate for banks' bidding for deposits on the UK money markets, the rate at which banks will bid to take deposits in Eurocurrency from each other. The deposits are for terms from overnight up to five years. *Abbr* ***LIBID***

London Interbank Mean Rate MARKETS average of two inter-bank interest rates the average of the London Inter Bank Offered Rate and the London Inter Bank Bid Rate, occasionally used as a reference rate. *Abbr* ***LIMEAN***

London Interbank Offered Rate MARKETS UK rate for bank's offering to take deposits on the UK money markets, the rate at which banks will offer to make deposits in Eurocurrency from each other, often used as a reference rate. The deposits are for terms from overnight up to five years. *Abbr* ***LIBOR***

London International Financial Futures and Options Exchange MARKETS exchange for financial futures and options an exchange for trading financial futures and options. Established in 1982, it offered contracts on interest rates denominated in most of the world's major currencies until 1992, when it merged with the London Traded Options Market, adding equity options to its product range. In 1996 it merged with the London Commodity Exchange, adding a variety of soft commodity and agricultural commodity contracts to its financial portfolio. From November 1998, trading gradually migrated from the floor of the exchange to screen-based trading. *Abbr* ***LIFFE***

London Metal Exchange MARKETS market for aluminum, tin, and nickel one of the world's largest nonferrous metal exchanges, that deals in aluminum, tin, and nickel. The primary roles of the exchange are hedging, providing official international reference prices, and appropriate storage facilities. Its origins can be traced back to 1571, though in its present form it dates from 1877. *Abbr* ***LME***

London Traded Options Market MARKETS *see* ***London International Financial Futures and Options Exchange***

long STOCKHOLDING & INVESTMENTS having more shares than wanted having a positive holding as a trader in a security

long bond *or* **long coupon bond** STOCKHOLDING & INVESTMENTS bond that matures after 10 years or more a bond which will mature in more than ten years' time, usually a 30-year bond issued by the US Department of the Treasury

long credit FINANCE loan that borrower can repay over long time credit terms which allow the borrower a long time to pay back the money he or she has borrowed

long-dated STOCKHOLDING & INVESTMENTS maturing after 15 years or more used to describe securities such as bonds that mature after fifteen years or more. *See also* ***short-dated***

long-dated bill STOCKHOLDING & INVESTMENTS bill payable after three or more months a bill that is payable at a date that is not less than three months away

long-dated gilt STOCKHOLDING & INVESTMENTS UK government security maturing in 15 years or more a security issued by the UK government that pays a fixed rate of interest on a regular basis until the redemption date, in 15 years or more, when the principal is returned. *See also* ***gilt-edged security***

long-dated stocks STOCKHOLDING & INVESTMENTS = ***longs***

long firm fraud FRAUD crime of business buying on credit, then disappearing in the United Kingdom, a criminal activity in which somebody sets up an apparently legitimate wholesaling business, obtains fake credit references, trades on credit with wholesale suppliers with no intention of paying for the goods, and then disappears

longitudinal study STATISTICS statistical investigation over period of time a statistical study that produces data gathered over a period of time

long lease REAL ESTATE over 21-year lease in UK in the United Kingdom, a rental agreement that runs at least 21 years

long position MARKETS when dealers avoid selling a situation in which dealers hold securities, commodities, or contracts, expecting prices to rise. *See also* ***short position***

longs STOCKHOLDING & INVESTMENTS long-term government stocks government stocks that will mature more than 15 years after the date of purchase

long-term balance of payments INTERNATIONAL TRADE record of money used in overseas investments a record of movements of capital relating to overseas investments and the purchase of companies overseas

long-term bond STOCKHOLDING & INVESTMENTS bond maturing in 7 years or more a bond that has at least seven years before its redemption date, or, in some markets, a bond with more than seven years until its redemption date

long-term borrowings FINANCE borrowings repayable in several years' time money that is borrowed that does not have to be repaid for a number of years

long-term care insurance INSURANCE insurance against need for costly care insurance that provides coverage for a person who needs ongoing care in a nursing home or their own home

long-term debt FINANCE loans for more than one year loans and debentures that are not due until after at least one year

long-term equity anticipation securities STOCKHOLDING & INVESTMENTS *see* ***LEAPS***

long-term financing FINANCE provision of funding with extended credit forms of funding, such as loans or stock issue, that do not have to be repaid immediately

long-term lease REAL ESTATE lease of 10 years plus a lease that does not expire for at least ten years

long-term liabilities FINANCE debts with extended credit forms of debt such as loans that do not have to be repaid immediately

lookback option MARKETS option with price selected from past prices an option whose price the buyer chooses from all of the prices that have existed during the option's life

loose change CURRENCY & EXCHANGE coins of little value money in the form of coins, especially when the value is small

loose credit ECONOMICS easily available credit to encourage growth a central banking policy to make borrowing easier by lowering interest rates in order to stimulate economic activity

loss ACCOUNTING when costs of activity exceed income from it a financial position in which the ***costs*** of an activity exceed the ***income*** derived from it

loss adjuster *UK* INSURANCE = ***adjuster***

loss assessor INSURANCE in UK, person who assists with insurance claims in the United Kingdom, somebody appointed by an insurance policyholder to assist with his or her claim. *See also* ***claims adjuster***

loss carryback ACCOUNTING application of current-year loss to prior year the process of applying a net operating loss to a previous accounting year in order to reduce tax liability in that year

loss carryforward ACCOUNTING application of current-year loss to future year the process of applying a net operating loss to a following accounting year in order to reduce tax liability in that year

loss control FINANCE, RISK methods of limiting impact of loss of asset the implementation of safety procedures to prevent or limit the impact of a complete or partial loss of an organization's physical assets. Loss control is based on safety audit and prevention techniques. It is concerned with reduction or elimination of losses caused by accidents and occupational ill health. The extent to which it is implemented is usually decided by calculating the total organizational asset cost and weighing this against the likelihood of failure and its worst possible effects on the organization. Loss control was developed in the 1960s as an approach to ***risk management***.

loss leader MARKETING product sold cheaply to attract customers for others a product or service that is sold below the cost of producing it in order to attract more customers to other associated products for purchase

lossmaker BUSINESS product or firm that loses money a product or company that fails to make a profit or break even

loss-making BUSINESS losing money used to describe a business or business activity that is losing money

loss relief TAX in UK, tax relief on previous year's loss in the United Kingdom, an amount of tax not to be paid on one year's profit to offset a loss in the previous year

lot 1. MARKETS smallest quantity traded on exchange the minimum quantity of a commodity that may be purchased on an exchange, for example, 1,000 ounces of gold on the London Bullion Market **2.** BUSINESS unit for sale at auction an item or a collection of related items being offered for sale at an auction **3.** MARKETS group of shares treated together in the United States, a group of shares held or traded together, usually in units of 100 **4.** *US, Canada* REAL ESTATE land for sale a piece of land assigned to be sold. *UK term* ***plot***

lottery GENERAL MANAGEMENT random selection of successful applicants the random method of selecting successful applicants for something, occasionally used when a new stock issue is oversubscribed

lower level domain E-COMMERCE sublevel name at beginning of Internet address the main part of a domain name. For most e-business sites this is usually the company or brand name.

lower of cost or market ACCOUNTING accounting method treating stocks at lower value a method used by manufacturing and supply firms when accounting for their homogenous stocks which involves valuing them either at their original cost or the current market price, whichever is lower. *Abbr* ***LCM***

low gearing *UK* FINANCE low ratio of firm's debt to assets a situation in which a company has only a small amount of debt in proportion to its assets

low latency MARKETS minimal delay relating to an electronic financial network or trading system that offers near-zero delay between transmission and receipt of an electronic signal

low start mortgage MORTGAGES loan with only interest repayment at first a long-term loan, usually for the purchase of real estate, in which the borrower only pays the interest on the loan for the first few years, usually three. After that, the payments increase to cover the interest and part of the original loan, as in an ***amortized mortgage***. Low start mortgages are popular with first-time buyers, as the lower initial costs may free up funds for furnishings or home improvements. *See also* ***mortgage***

loyalty bonus STOCKHOLDING & INVESTMENTS extra shares given after UK privatizations in the United Kingdom in the 1980s, a number of extra shares, calculated as a proportion of the shares originally subscribed, given to original subscribers of privatization issues providing the shares were held continuously for a given period of time

Ltd *abbr UK* BUSINESS ***limited company***

LTV ratio *abbr* FINANCE ***loan to value ratio***

lump sum FINANCE **1.** repaid in one installment used to describe a loan that is repayable with one installment at the end of its term. *See also* ***balloon loan, interest-only mortgage*** **2.** money received in single payment an amount of money received in one payment, for example, the sum payable to the beneficiary of a life insurance policy on the death of the policyholder

luxury tax TAX tax on inessential items a tax on goods or services that are considered nonessential

M

M0 ECONOMICS money available to public for spending an estimate of the amount of money in public circulation, available for use as a means of exchange. *Also called* ***narrow money*** *(sense 2)*

M1 ECONOMICS cash plus bank accounts an estimate of the amount of money held by the public in coins, banknotes, and checking accounts. *Also called* ***narrow money*** *(sense 1)*

M2 ECONOMICS cash plus easily available deposits an estimate of the amount of money held by the public in coins, currency, checking and savings accounts, and deposits

M3 ECONOMICS M1, M2 plus international money an estimate of the amount of money in M1, M2 and large denomination repurchase agreements, institutional money market accounts, and some Eurodollar time deposits

ma and pa shop *UK* BUSINESS = ***mom-and-pop operation***

Macaulay duration MARKETS, RISK measure of interest-rate risk in owning bonds a measure of a bond's sensitivity to changes in interest rates. It is calculated by dividing the present value of the cash flows received by the current market value of the bond. *See also* ***modified duration***

machine hour rate FINANCE proportion of overhead costs an ***overhead absorption rate*** based on the number of hours a machine is used in production

macroeconomics ECONOMICS study of national economic systems the study of national income and the economic systems of nations. *See also* ***microeconomics***

macroeconomy ECONOMICS national economy as whole the broad sectors of a country's economic activity, for example, the financial or industrial sectors, that are aggregated to form its economic system as a whole. *See also* ***microeconomy***

macrohedge RISK reduction of risk on whole portfolio a ***hedge*** that aims to cover the overall risk to an entire investment ***portfolio***. *Also called* ***global hedge***. *See also* ***microhedge***

mail ballot *US* FINANCE election accepting votes returned by mail an election of officers of a company in which the voters send in their ballot papers by mail. *UK term* ***postal vote***

mail form E-COMMERCE webpage for inputting data sent as e-mail a webpage that requires the user to input data such as name, address, or order or shipping information, that is transmitted to an e-merchant via e-mail

mailing *US* MARKETING appeal to specific group through mail a speculative targeting of a specific group of people by mail. A mailing normally contains information, advertising, fundraising requests, or press releases. *Also called* ***mail-out, mailshot***

mailing house MARKETING firm dealing in direct mail projects an organization that specializes in planning, creating, and implementing direct mail campaigns for clients

mailing list MARKETING names and addresses for marketing purposes the names and addresses of a specific group of people compiled for marketing purposes. A mailing list may be compiled internally or bought or rented from an outside agency, and can be used for advertising, fundraising, news releases, or for direct mail or a mailshot. A mailing list is usually compiled for a selected group using one or more criteria, such as men between the ages of 25 and 30, or retired people.

mail order MARKETING method of requesting products from catalog for delivery a form of retailing in which consumers order products from a catalog for delivery to their home

mail-out MARKETING = ***mailing***

mailshot MARKETING = ***mailing***

mailsort MARKETING UK sorting service for direct mail in the United Kingdom, a sorting service offered to organizations by the Post Office, intended to reduce the cost and time spent on direct mail

mainstream corporation tax TAX main UK tax on corporations the principal UK tax on resident companies, paid on profits after deduction of allowable expenses. This was formerly reduced by the amount of ***advance corporation tax*** already paid.

maintenance bond STOCKHOLDING & INVESTMENTS guarantee for period after complete transaction a bond that provides a guarantee against defects for some time after a contract has been fulfilled

majority decision *or* **majority vote** GENERAL MANAGEMENT decision of most people made by voting a decision that represents the wishes of the largest group as shown by a vote, for example, in a board meeting or a shareholders' meeting

majority shareholder STOCKHOLDING & INVESTMENTS stockholder with controlling interest a shareholder with a controlling interest in a company. *See also* ***minority interest***

majority shareholding STOCKHOLDING & INVESTMENTS stockholding in excess of 50% a group of shares of stock that are more than half the total and enough to give control to the person or entity holding them

make or buy GENERAL MANAGEMENT *see* ***purchasing versus production***

maladministration GENERAL MANAGEMENT incompetent management of public affairs failure on the part of an administration to act in a competent manner, especially in public affairs

managed account STOCKHOLDING & INVESTMENTS = ***discretionary account***

managed currency fund CURRENCY & EXCHANGE managed fund investing in currencies a managed mutual fund that makes considered investments in foreign exchange

managed derivatives fund STOCKHOLDING & INVESTMENTS fund investing in derivatives a fund that uses mainly ***futures*** and ***options*** instead of investing in the underlying securities

managed economy ECONOMICS economy controlled by government an economy directed by a government rather than the free market

managed float ECONOMICS exchange rate affected by government action the position when the exchange rate of a country's currency is influenced by government action in the foreign exchange market

managed fund STOCKHOLDING & INVESTMENTS mutual fund investing after research a mutual fund with professional managers who make considered investments, as opposed to an ***index fund***. *Also called* ***managed mutual fund***

managed mutual fund *US* STOCKHOLDING & INVESTMENTS = ***managed fund***

managed rate BANKING financial institution's independently established interest rate a rate of interest charged by a financial institution for borrowing that it sets itself from time to time, rather than following a prescribed margin over base rate

managed unit trust STOCKHOLDING & INVESTMENTS = ***managed fund***

management GENERAL MANAGEMENT, HR & PERSONNEL using firm's resources effectively to achieve goals the use of professional skills for identifying and achieving organizational objectives through the deployment of appropriate resources. Management involves identifying what needs to be done, and organizing and supporting others to perform the necessary tasks. A manager has complex and ever-changing responsibilities, the focus of which shifts to reflect the issues, trends, and preoccupations of the time. At the beginning of the 20th century, the emphasis was both on supporting the organization's administration and managing ***productivity*** through increased efficiency. At the beginning of the 21st century, those original drivers are still much in evidence, although the emphasis has moved to key areas of competence such as people management. Although management is a profession in its own right, its skill set often applies to professionals of other disciplines.

management accountant TREASURY MANAGEMENT financial adviser on management decisions a person who contributes to management's decision-making processes by, for example, collecting and processing data relating to a business's costs, sales, and the profitability of individual activities

management accounting TREASURY MANAGEMENT use of accounting principles to benefit organization the application of the principles of accounting and financial management to create, protect, preserve, and increase value so as to deliver that value to the stakeholders of profit and nonprofit enterprises, both public and private. Management accounting is an integral part of management, requiring the identification, generation, presentation, interpretation, and use of information relevant to formulating business strategy; planning and controlling activities; decision making; efficient resource usage; performance improvement and value enhancement; safeguarding tangible and intangible assets; and corporate governance and internal control.

management accounts TREASURY MANAGEMENT financial report prepared for manager financial information prepared for a manager so that decisions can be made, including monthly or quarterly financial statements, often in great detail, with analysis of actual performance against the budget

management audit GENERAL MANAGEMENT = ***operational audit***

management buyin MERGERS & ACQUISITIONS purchase of business by external managers the purchase of an existing business by an individual manager or management group outside that business. *Abbr* ***MBI***

management buyout MERGERS & ACQUISITIONS takeover of business by its management the purchase of an existing business by an individual manager or management group from within that business. *Abbr* ***MBO***

management by objectives *or* **management by results** GENERAL MANAGEMENT method for achieving goals through series of objectives a method of managing an organization by setting a series of ***objectives*** that contribute toward the achievement of its goals. *Abbr* ***MBO***

management charge *UK* STOCKHOLDING & INVESTMENTS = ***annual management charge***

management company BUSINESS firm that manages aspects of another firm's business a company that takes over responsibility from internal staff for managing facilities such as computer systems, telecommunications, or maintenance. The process is known as ***outsourcing***.

management consultancy *UK* GENERAL MANAGEMENT = ***management consulting***

management consultant GENERAL MANAGEMENT person who gives advice about management methods a person professionally engaged in advising on, and providing, a detached, external view of a company's management techniques and practices. A management consultant may be self-employed, a partner, or employed in a specialist firm. Consultants can be called in for many reasons, but are employed particularly for projects involving business improvement, ***change management***, information technology, and long-term planning.

management consulting *US* GENERAL MANAGEMENT giving advice about management methods the activity of advising on management techniques and practices. Management consulting usually involves the identification of a problem, or the analysis of a specific area of one organization, and the reporting of any resulting findings. The consulting process can sometimes be extended to help put into effect the recommendations made. *UK term* ***management consultancy***

management consulting firm GENERAL MANAGEMENT firm giving management advice a firm of ***management consultants***, offering professional advice on ways to improve efficiency

management fee STOCKHOLDING & INVESTMENTS fee for managing mutual fund a fee paid to a mutual fund manager by a client to cover their services and a variety of administrative costs

management information system OPERATIONS & PRODUCTION *see* ***MIS***

management process GENERAL MANAGEMENT management of human, financial, and material resources the process of planning, implementing, and controlling activities that involve human, financial, and material resources

management team GENERAL MANAGEMENT, HR & PERSONNEL = ***senior management***

management trainee HR & PERSONNEL low-ranking manager learning management methods an employee who holds a low-level management position while undergoing formal training in management techniques

management training HR & PERSONNEL courses teaching management methods planned activities for developing management skills. Management training methods include public or in-company training courses and on-the-job training designed to improve managerial ***competences***. Management training tends to be practical and to focus on specific management techniques. It does not result in a formal degree.

manager GENERAL MANAGEMENT, HR & PERSONNEL employee responsible for part of firm's activities a person who identifies and achieves organizational objectives through the deployment of appropriate resources. A manager can have responsibilities in one or more of five key areas: managing activities; managing resources; managing information; managing people; and managing him- or herself while working within the context of the organizational, political, and economic business environments. There are managers in all disciplines and activities, although some may not bear the title of manager. Some specialize in areas such as personnel, marketing, production, finance, or project management, while others are ***general managers***, applying management skills across all business areas. Very few jobs are entirely managerial, and very few exist without any management responsibilities. It is the capability to harness resources that largely distinguishes a manager from a non-manager.

managerialism GENERAL MANAGEMENT firm's focus on effective management emphasis on efficient management, and the use of systems, planning, and management practice. Managerialism is often used in a critical sense, especially from the perspective of the public sector, to imply overenthusiasm for efficiency, or private sector management techniques and systems, possibly at the expense of service or quality considerations. The term is also used to describe confrontational attitudes, or actions displayed by management toward labor unions.

managing agent INSURANCE administrator of Lloyd's syndicate a person who runs the day-to-day activities of a Lloyd's syndicate

managing director CORPORATE GOVERNANCE limited company's director in charge of daily business the ***chief executive officer*** of a ***limited company*** in the United Kingdom and other countries, who has overall responsibility for its day-to-day operations. *Abbr* ***MD***

managing for value GENERAL MANAGEMENT focusing on long-term value of business an approach to building the long-term value of a business. The term is most frequently used by businesses that are implementing the ***balanced scorecard approach*** and emphasizes the need to make financial and commercial decisions that build the value of the business for its stockholders.

M&A *abbr* MERGERS & ACQUISITIONS ***mergers and acquisitions***

mandarin GENERAL MANAGEMENT important government adviser a high-ranking and influential adviser, especially in government circles

mandatory bid STOCKHOLDING & INVESTMENTS compulsory bid for remaining stock an offer to purchase the remaining shares of a company that a stockholder has to make if he or she acquires at least 30% of that company's stock

mandatory quote period MARKETS time when security prices must be displayed on the London Stock Exchange, the period of time during which prices of securities must be displayed

manpower forecasting GENERAL MANAGEMENT = ***human resource forecasting***

manpower planning GENERAL MANAGEMENT = ***human resource planning***

manufacture OPERATIONS & PRODUCTION making products in factory the large-scale production of goods from raw materials or parts

manufacturer OPERATIONS & PRODUCTION maker of factory products a person or organization involved in the large-scale production of goods from raw materials or parts

manufacturer's agent OPERATIONS & PRODUCTION representative of product-maker for getting contracts a person or organization with authority to act for a ***manufacturer*** in obtaining a ***contract*** with a third party

manufacturing OPERATIONS & PRODUCTION process by which product is made the processes and techniques used in making a product from raw materials or parts

manufacturing account ACCOUNTING accounts showing only production costs a financial statement that shows production costs only, as opposed to a ***profit and loss account***, which shows sales and costs of sales. A manufacturing account will include direct materials and labor costs and the production overhead.

manufacturing cost OPERATIONS & PRODUCTION money needed to make products the expenditure incurred in carrying out the production processes of an organization. The manufacturing cost includes ***direct costs***, for example, labor, materials, and expenses, and indirect costs, for example, subcontracting and overhead.

manufacturing information system OPERATIONS & PRODUCTION computer system for production process a management information system designed specifically for use in a production environment

manufacturing resource planning OPERATIONS & PRODUCTION *see* ***MRP II***

manufacturing system OPERATIONS & PRODUCTION organization of firm's production process a method of organizing production. Manufacturing systems include assembly and ***batch production***, ***flexible manufacturing systems***, ***lean production***, and ***mass production***.

manufacturing to order OPERATIONS & PRODUCTION producing goods to fill requests not for stockpile a production management technique in which goods are produced to meet firm orders, rather than being produced for inventory

Marché des Options Négotiables de Paris MARKETS French traded options market in France, the market that deals in options that can be traded at any time. *Abbr* ***MONEP***

Marché International de France MARKETS French international exchange in France, the international futures and options exchange

margin FINANCE **1.** gap between cost and selling price the difference between the cost and the selling price of a product or service **2.** *ANZ* extra pay for employees' special skills a payment made to workers over and above the basic wage in recognition of special skills

margin account FINANCE account with investment broker who lends money an account with a broker who lends money for investments, held in the name of an investor who pays only a percentage of the price of purchases

marginal 1. FINANCE not worth money spent producing very little benefit in relation to the amount of money spent (*informal*) **2.** OPERATIONS & PRODUCTION barely covering production cost nearly unable to cover the cost of production when selling goods or when goods are being sold

marginal analysis ECONOMICS investigation into economic effects of small changes the study of how small changes in an economic variable will affect an economy

marginal cost OPERATIONS & PRODUCTION extra cost of producing additional item the part of the cost of one unit of product or service that would be avoided if that unit were not produced, or that would increase if one extra unit were produced

marginal costing ACCOUNTING accounting system treating variable and fixed costs differently the accounting system in which variable costs are charged to cost units and fixed costs of the period are written off in full against the aggregate contribution. Its special value is in recognizing cost behavior, and hence assisting in decision making. *Also called* ***variable costing***

marginal costs and benefits ECONOMICS losses and gains resulting from incremental changes the losses or gains to a person or household arising from a small change in a variable, such as food consumption or income received

marginalization ECONOMICS process of becoming less important in world economy the process by which countries lose importance and status because they are unable to participate in mainstream activities such as industrialization or the Internet economy

marginal lender FINANCE lender with lower limit on interest rate a lender who will make a loan only at or above a particular rate of interest

marginal pricing OPERATIONS & PRODUCTION setting prices between variable cost and full cost the practice of basing the selling price of a product on its variable costs of production plus a margin, but excluding fixed costs

marginal revenue OPERATIONS & PRODUCTION money from producing more the revenue generated by additional units of production

marginal tax rate TAX tax rate on income after business expenses the rate of tax payable on a person's income after business expenses have been deducted

marginal utility ECONOMICS satisfaction in using one additional unit satisfaction gained from using one more unit of a product or service

margin call STOCKHOLDING & INVESTMENTS request for additional deposit to margin account a request for a purchaser of a futures contract or an option to deposit more money in his or her ***margin account***, since the fall in the price of the securities or commodity has brought the value of the original deposit below the minimum required

margining STOCKHOLDING & INVESTMENTS, RISK way London Clearing House controls risk the system by which the London Clearing House controls the risk associated with the position of a member of the London International Financial Futures and Options Exchange on a daily basis. To achieve this, members deposit cash or collateral with the London Clearing House in the form of initial and variation margins. The initial margin is the deposit required on all open positions, long or short, to cover short-term price movements and is returned to members by the London Clearing House when the position is closed. The variation margin is the members' profits or losses, calculated daily from the marked-to-market-close value of their position, whereby contracts are revalued daily for the calculation of variation margin and credited to or debited from their accounts.

margin of error GENERAL MANAGEMENT amount allowed for miscalculation an allowance made for the possibility that something has been miscalculated or that conditions change

margin of safety TREASURY MANAGEMENT level of firm's performance above break-even point the difference between the level of activity at which an organization breaks even and the level of activity greater than this point. For example, a margin of safety of $300,000 is achieved when the break-even point is $900,000 and sales reach $1,200,000. This measure can be expressed as a proportion of sales value, as a number of units sold, or as a percentage of ***capacity***.

Margrabe option STOCKHOLDING & INVESTMENTS, RISK = ***exchange option***

marital deductions TAX spouse's nontaxable part of inheritance the part of an estate which, after a death, is not subject to estate tax because it goes to the spouse of the deceased

marital property FINANCE = ***community property***

mark down OPERATIONS & PRODUCTION reduce price of something to make the price of something lower

mark-down OPERATIONS & PRODUCTION **1.** reduction in price an act of reducing the price of something to less than its usual price **2.** percentage reduction in price the percentage amount by which a price has been reduced

marked cheque *UK* BANKING = ***certified check*** *(slang)*

marked price OPERATIONS & PRODUCTION price displayed on product for sale the original displayed price of a product in a store. In a sale, customers may be offered a savings on the marked price.

market 1. FINANCE rate of financial sales the rate at which financial commodities or securities are being sold **2.** ECONOMICS group of consumers with shared need a group of people or organizations unified by common requirements **3.** ECONOMICS group of buyers and sellers trading goods a gathering of sellers and purchasers to exchange commodities ◇ make a market MARKETS to be prepared as a dealer to buy or sell a particular security at the quoted bid or ask price

marketable MARKETING able to be sold successfully possessing the potential to be commercially viable. To determine whether a new product or service is marketable, an assessment needs to be conducted to see if it is likely to make a profit. The assessment is often based on detailed ***market research*** analyzing the potential market, and the projected financial returns and any other benefits for the company.

marketable security STOCKHOLDING & INVESTMENTS security easily sold or exchanged a security that can easily be sold and converted into cash, or exchanged for a different type of security

market analysis MARKETING study of particular market the study of a market to identify and quantify business opportunities

market area MARKETING where market is the geographic location of a particular group of consumers with shared needs

market-based pricing OPERATIONS & PRODUCTION charging what customer will pay setting a price based on the value of the product in the perception of the customer. *Also called* ***perceived value pricing***

market bubble MARKETS short period of inflated prices a stock market phenomenon in which values in a particular sector become inflated for a short period. If the bubble bursts, stock prices in that sector collapse.

market capitalization MARKETS full market value of firm the total market value of a company, calculated by multiplying the price of its shares on the Stock Exchange by the number of shares outstanding. *Abbr* ***market cap***. *Also called* ***market valuation*** *(sense 1)*

market coverage MARKETS how well product satisfies customers' needs the degree to which a product or service meets the needs of a market

market cycle MARKETS sequence of market expansion, contraction, and expansion a period during which a market expands, then slows down, and then expands again

market development MARKETING activities to expand demand for particular product type marketing activities designed to increase the overall size of a market through education and awareness

market driven *or* **market-driven** MARKETING strongly influenced by needs of potential customers using market knowledge to determine the corporate strategy of an organization. A market-driven organization has a customer focus, together with awareness of competitors, and an understanding of the market.

market economist MARKETS specialist in investment a person who specializes in the study of financial structures and the return on investments in the stock market

market economy ECONOMICS economic system not controlled by government an economy in which a ***free market*** in goods and services operates

marketeer MARKETING small firm competing with larger firms a small company that competes in the same market as larger companies. Examples of marketeers are restaurants, travel agents, computer software providers, garages, and insurance brokers.

marketer MARKETING promoter of sales a person who is responsible for developing and implementing marketing policy

marketface MARKETS where suppliers and customers meet the interface between suppliers of goods or services and their customers

market-facing enterprise BUSINESS firm focusing on marketplace and customers an organization that aligns itself with its markets and customers and makes them its priority concern

market-focused organization BUSINESS organization responsive to market needs an organization whose strategies are determined by market requirements rather than organizational demands

market forces MARKETS factors affecting prices influences on sales which bring about a change in prices

market fragmentation MARKETS market consisting of small-scale buyers and sellers a situation in which the buyers or sellers in a market consist of a large number of small organizations

market gap MARKETS situation where no producer is meeting market need an opportunity in a market where no supplier provides a product or service that buyers need

market if touched STOCKHOLDING & INVESTMENTS instruction to trade at specific price an order to trade a security if it reaches a specific price. *Abbr* ***MIT***

marketing MARKETING efforts to promote products the process of building long-term relationships with customers and with other interested parties and to provide value to them. This begins with market research, which analyzes needs and wants in society, and continues with attracting customers and the cultivation of mutually beneficial exchange processes with them. Tools used in this process are diverse and include market segmentation, brand management, PR, logistics, direct response marketing, sales promotion, and advertising. ◊ 4 Ps of marketing MARKETING the variety of integrated decisions made by a marketing manager to ensure successful marketing, in four key areas–product, price, place, and promotion–covering issues such as the type of product to be marketed, brand name, pricing, advertising, publicity, geographic coverage, retailing, and distribution

marketing agreement MARKETING agreement to market another firm's product a contract by which one company agrees to market another company's products

marketing audit MARKETING evaluation of firm's marketing approach an analysis of either the external marketing environment or a company's internal marketing goals, objectives, operations, and efficiency. An external marketing audit covers issues such as economic, political, infrastructure, technological, and consumer perspectives; market size and market structure; and competitors, suppliers, and distributors. An internal marketing audit covers aspects such as the company's mission statement, goals, and objectives; its structure, corporate culture, systems, operations, and processes; product development and pricing; profitability and efficiency; advertising; and deployment of the sales force.

marketing consultancy MARKETING firm creating marketing plan for other firms an organization that plans and develops marketing strategies and programs on behalf of clients

marketing information system MARKETING computer system for managing firm's marketing program an information system concerned with the collection, storage, and analysis of information and data for marketing decision-making purposes. Information for use in marketing information systems is gathered from customers, competitors, and their products, and from the market itself.

marketing management MARKETING responsibility for firm's efforts to promote products one of the main management disciplines, encompassing all the strategic planning, operations, activities, and processes involved in achieving organizational objectives by delivering value to customers. Marketing management focuses on satisfying customer requirements by identifying needs and wants, and developing products and services to meet them.

marketing manager MARKETING person responsible for promoting firm's products somebody who is responsible for planning and controlling marketing activities and budgets for a company

marketing mix MARKETING mixture of techniques for promoting products the variety of integrated decisions made by a marketing manager to ensure successful marketing. These decisions are made in four key areas known as the ***4 Ps of marketing***–product, price, place, and promotion–and cover issues such as the type of product to be marketed, brand name, pricing, advertising, publicity, geographic coverage, retailing, and distribution.

marketing myopia MARKETING mistake of forgetting customers' needs the theory that some organizations ignore the fact that to be successful, the wants of customers must be their central consideration

marketing planning MARKETING process of deciding plan for promoting firm's products the process of producing a ***marketing plan*** incorporating overall marketing objectives and the strategies and programs of action designed to achieve those objectives. Marketing planning requires a careful examination of all strategic issues, including the business environment, the markets themselves, competitors, the corporate ***mission statement***, and organizational capabilities. The resulting marketing plan should be communicated to appropriate staff through an oral briefing to ensure it is fully understood.

market intelligence MARKETING information about particular area of commercial activity a collection of internal and external data on a given market. Market intelligence focuses particularly on competitors, customers, consumer spending, market trends, and suppliers.

market leader MARKETING one with highest market share the product, service, or company that has a dominant ***market share***

market logic MARKETS circumstances governing firm's stock market performance the prevailing forces or attitudes that determine a company's success or failure on the stock market

market maker MARKETS **1.** provider of market for unlisted security a broker or bank that maintains a market for a security that does not trade on any exchange **2.** securities dealer who both buys and sells a securities dealer who offers either to buy or sell stock on the stock market at a guaranteed price **3.** *UK* promoter of trading in one particular firm somebody who works in a stock exchange to facilitate trades in one particular company

market neutral funds STOCKHOLDING & INVESTMENTS hedge funds exploiting temporary fluctuations ***hedge funds*** that are not related to general market movements but that are used to find opportunities to take advantage of temporary slight changes in the relative values of particular financial assets

market order MARKETS instruction to trade security at best available price an order to trade a security at the best price the broker can obtain

market penetration MARKETING percentage of potential sales that firm has made a measure of the percentage or potential percentage of the market that a product or company is able to capture, expressed in terms of total sales or turnover. Market penetration is often used to measure the level of success a new product or service has achieved.

market penetration pricing MARKETING practice of setting prices low to increase sales the policy of pricing a product or service very competitively, and sometimes at a loss to the producer, in order to increase its ***market share***

market position MARKETS product's portion of total sales in market the place held by a product or service in a ***market***, usually determined by its percentage of total sales. An ideal market position is often predefined for a product or service. Analysis of potential customers and competing products can be used with product differentiation techniques to formulate a product to fill the desired market position.

market potential MARKETS predictions about product's sales and earning possibilities a forecast of the size of a market in terms of revenue, numbers of buyers, or other factors

market power MARKETS buyers' or sellers' ability to control market the dominance of a market either by customers, who create a buyer's market, or by a particular company, which creates a seller's market. Individuals or companies retain control of the market by fixing the pricing and number of products available.

market price **1.** MARKETS price consumers are paying the price that buyers are currently paying for a good, service, commodity, etc. **2.** ECONOMICS price at which supply equals demand the theoretical price at which supply equals demand

market quote MARKETS current best stock market price the most up-to-date highest price being offered for a security on a stock exchange

market research MARKETING investigation of commercial activity research conducted to assess the size and nature of a market

market risk MARKETS, RISK risk inherent in securities market or economy investment risk that is attributable to the performance of the stock market or of the economy and cannot be removed by diversification

market risk premium STOCKHOLDING & INVESTMENTS return needed to compensate for risk the extra return required from a high-risk investment to compensate for its higher-than-average risk

market sector *or* **market segment** MARKETS distinctive subsection of consumers a subdivision of a ***market*** with distinctive characteristics. Market sectors are usually determined by market segmentation, which divides a market into different categories. Car buyers, for example, could be put into sectors such as car fleet buyers, private buyers, buyers under 20 years old, and so on. The smaller the sector, the more its members will have in common. Sellers may decide to compete in the whole market or only in segments that are attractive to them or where they have an advantage.

market segmentation MARKETS categorization of buyers by buying habits the division of the market or consumers into categories according to their buying habits

market sentiment MARKETS general feeling among brokers and traders the mood of those participating in exchange dealings that can range from absolute euphoria to downright gloom and despondency and tends to reflect recent company results, economic indicators, and comments by politicians, analysts, or opinion formers. Optimism increases demand and therefore prices, while pessimism has the opposite effect.

market share MARKETING firm's or product's proportion of total sales the proportion of the total market value of a product or group of products or services that a company, service, or product holds. Market share is shown as a percentage of the total value or output of a market, usually expressed in US dollars, pounds sterling, or euros, by weight (tons or tonnes), or as individual units, depending on the commodity. The product, service, or company with a dominant market share is referred to as the ***market leader***.

Markets in Financial Instruments Directive MARKETS, REGULATION & COMPLIANCE EU directive governing conduct of investment companies an EU directive that sets out detailed requirements governing the organization and conduct of business of investment companies, and how regulated markets and multilateral trading facilities should operate. It came into force on November 1, 2007, replacing the Investment Services Directive (ISD), and made significant changes to the regulatory framework to reflect developments in financial services and markets since the ISD was implemented. *Abbr* ***MiFID***

market site E-COMMERCE website shared by several Internet firms a website shared by multiple e-commerce vendors, each having a different specialty, to conduct business over the Internet

market size MARKETS **1.** maximum number of shares traded together the largest number of shares that a market will handle in one trade of a specific security **2.** number of consumers in specific group the size of a group of consumers with shared needs and their buying power

market structure MARKETS organization of particular area of commercial activity the makeup of a particular ***market***. Market structure can be described with reference to different characteristics of a market, including its size and value, the number of providers and their ***market share***, consumer and business purchasing behavior, and growth forecasts. The description may also include a demographic and regional breakdown of providers and customers and an analysis of pricing structures, likely technological impacts, and domestic and overseas sales.

market targeting MARKETING promoting products to specific group of consumers the selection of a particular market sector toward which all marketing effort is directed. Market targeting enables the characteristics of the chosen sector to be taken into account when formulating a product or service and its advertising.

market timing STOCKHOLDING & INVESTMENTS trading determined by market trends an investing strategy of buying and selling securities based on indicators of market trends over relatively short periods of time

market trend MARKETS rising or falling price movements a period during which stock market prices are moving in a particular direction

market valuation MARKETS **1.** = ***market capitalization*** **2.** worth of portfolio on selling the value of a portfolio if all its investments were to be sold at current market prices **3.** professional assessment of current value of real estate the opinion of an expert professional as to the current worth of a piece of real estate

market value FINANCE worth of asset if sold the value of an asset based on what price would be received for it if it were sold

market value added MARKETS difference between market and book value the difference between a company's market value (derived from the stock price), and its economic book value (the amount of capital that stockholders have committed to the firm throughout its existence, including any retained earnings). *Abbr* ***MVA***

marking down MARKETS lowering of price required the reduction by market makers in the price at which they are prepared to deal in a security, for example, because of an adverse report by an analyst, or the announcement or anticipated announcement of a profit warning by a company

mark to market MARKETS securities valuation that reflects current prices daily valuation of the price of securities held in an account at the closing price, or the ***market quote*** if the last sale falls outside the market quote, so that the equity fully reflects current prices

mark up OPERATIONS & PRODUCTION increase price of something to make the price of something higher, especially in order to provide the seller with a profit

markup OPERATIONS & PRODUCTION amount added to make selling price the addition to the cost of goods or services which results in a selling price. The markup may be expressed as a percentage or as an absolute monetary amount.

massaging ACCOUNTING presentation to suggest better performance the adjustment of financial figures to create the impression of better performance (*slang*)

mass market MARKETING area of commercial activity involving much of population a market that covers substantial numbers of the population. A mass market may consist of a whole population or just a segment of that population. Mass customization of products has allowed a greater number of single products to satisfy a mass market.

mass production OPERATIONS & PRODUCTION manufacturing large numbers of same product at once large-scale manufacturing, often designed to meet the demand for a particular product. Mass production methods were developed by Henry Ford, founder of the Ford Motor Company. Mass production involves using a moving production or assembly line on which the product moves while operators remain at their stations carrying out their work on each passing product. Mass production is now challenged by methods including ***just-in-time*** and ***lean production***.

master franchise MARKETING arrangement allowing franchisee to permit further franchises a license issued by the owner of a product or service to another party or master franchisee allowing them to issue further ***franchise*** licenses. A master franchise can benefit the original franchisor, as the master franchisee effectively develops the ***franchise chain*** on their behalf. A master franchise usually grants further licenses within a defined geographic area, and several master franchises may cover a country.

master limited partnership BUSINESS partnership with benefits in tax and liquidity a partnership of a type that combines tax advantages and advantages of liquidity

Master of Business Administration GENERAL MANAGEMENT *see* ***MBA***

master production scheduling OPERATIONS & PRODUCTION method of developing detailed manufacturing plan a technique used in material requirements planning systems to develop a detailed plan for product manufacturing. The *master production schedule*, compiled by a master scheduler, takes account of the requirements of various departments, including sales (delivery dates), finance (inventory minimization), and manufacturing (minimization of setup times), and it schedules production and the purchasing of materials within the capacity of and resources available to the production system.

matador bond STOCKHOLDING & INVESTMENTS foreign bond in Spain a foreign bond issued into the Spanish domestic market by a non-Spanish company (*slang*)

matched bargain *UK* STOCKHOLDING & INVESTMENTS connected sale and rebuying the linked sale and repurchase of the same quantity of the same security. *See also* ***bed and breakfast deal***

matching convention ACCOUNTING accounts basis with matching of sales with costs the basis for preparing accounts that says that profits can only be recognized if sales are fully matched with costs accrued during the same period

material cost OPERATIONS & PRODUCTION price paid for product's raw materials the cost of the raw materials that go into a product. The material cost of a product excludes any ***indirect costs***, for example, overhead or wages, associated with producing the item.

material facts MARKETS **1.** compulsory information for prospectus information about a company that has to be disclosed in a ***prospectus***. *See also* ***listing requirements*** **2.** information insurer must be told in an insurance contract, information that the insured has to reveal at the time that the policy is taken out, for example, that a house is located on the edge of a crumbling cliff. Failure to reveal material facts can result in the contract being declared void.

material information *US* MARKETS information firm must tell exchange price-sensitive developments in a company, for example, proposed acquisitions, mergers, profit warnings, and the resignation of directors, that most stock exchanges require a company to announce immediately to the exchange. *UK term* ***material news***

material news *UK* MARKETS = ***material information***

materials returned note OPERATIONS & PRODUCTION record of unused material a record of the return to stores of unused material

matrix management GENERAL MANAGEMENT managing through both horizontal and vertical reporting structures management based on two or more reporting systems that are linked to the vertical organization hierarchy, and to horizontal relationships based on geographic, product, or project requirements

matrix organization GENERAL MANAGEMENT way of structuring firm both horizontally and vertically organization by both vertical administrative functions and horizontal tasks, areas, processes, or projects. Matrix organization originated in the 1960s and 1970s, particularly within the US aerospace industry, when ***organization charts*** showing how the management of a given project would relate to ***senior management*** were often required to win government contracts. A two-dimensional matrix chart best illustrates the dual horizontal, and vertical, reporting relationships. Matrix organization is closely linked to ***matrix management***.

matrix structure GENERAL MANAGEMENT firm's organization with both horizontal and vertical relationships a form of organizational structure based on horizontal and vertical relationships. The matrix structure is linked closely to ***matrix management***, and is related to ***project management***. It emerged on an improvised rather than a planned basis as a way of showing how people work with or report to others in their organization, project, geographic region, process, or team.

matrix trading STOCKHOLDING & INVESTMENTS trading taking advantage of differences in yields a ***bond swap*** strategy that takes advantages of discrepancies in yields of bonds of different classes

mature FINANCE due for payment having reached maturity

mature economy ECONOMICS economy that has slowed down an economy that is no longer developing or growing rapidly. Such economies tend to have increased consumer spending rather than industrial and manufacturing investment.

maturity STOCKHOLDING & INVESTMENTS period before repayment date of financial instrument the period that will elapse before a financial instrument such as a bond becomes due for repayment or an option expires

maturity date STOCKHOLDING & INVESTMENTS expiration date of option the date on which a financial instrument such as a bond becomes due for repayment or an option expires

maturity value STOCKHOLDING & INVESTMENTS amount payable on mature financial instrument the amount payable when a bond or other financial instrument matures

maturity yield STOCKHOLDING & INVESTMENTS = ***yield***

Maxi ISA STOCKHOLDING & INVESTMENTS former UK tax-free investment formerly, in the United Kingdom, an ***ISA*** in which savers invested tax-free mainly in stocks with a limited cash component. Savers could own only one Maxi ISA. *See also* ***Mini ISA, ISA***

maximize FINANCE increase financial gain as much as possible to take measures to increase something such as your gain on an investment or profit in a business as much as possible

maximum 1. greatest possible amount the largest number, price, quantity, or degree possible or allowed **2.** greatest possible of the largest possible or allowed amount or value

maximum inventory level *US* OPERATIONS & PRODUCTION size above which inventory must not increase an inventory level, set for control purposes, which actual holdings should never exceed. It is calculated as follows:

Reorder level + Economic order quantity – Minimum rate of usage × Minimum lead time

UK term ***maximum stock level***

maximum stock level *UK* OPERATIONS & PRODUCTION = ***maximum inventory level***

maysir FINANCE gambling or speculation prohibited by Islamic law in Islamic financing, gambling with the intention of making an easy profit. It is one of three prohibitions in Islamic law, which is extended to such financial practices as speculation, insurance, futures, and options; the others are ***gharar*** and ***riba***.

MBA GENERAL MANAGEMENT master's degree in business administration a postgraduate degree awarded after a period of study of topics relating to the strategic management of businesses. A Master of Business Administration course can be taken at a business school or university, and covers areas such as finance, personnel, and resource management, as well as the wider business environment and skills such as information technology use. The course is mostly taken by people with experience of managerial work, and is offered by universities worldwide. Part-time or distance learning MBAs are available, so that students can study while still working. There is an increasing number of MBA graduates, as an MBA is seen as a passport to a better job and higher salary. For many positions at a higher level within organizations, an MBA is now a prerequisite. *Full form* ***Master of Business Administration***

MBI *abbr* MERGERS & ACQUISITIONS ***management buyin***

MBIA INSURANCE US firms insuring high-rated municipal bonds a large US-based insurance company whose core business is in high-rated municipal bonds. *Full form* ***Municipal Bond Insurance Association***

MBO *abbr* **1.** MERGERS & ACQUISITIONS ***management buyout*** **2.** GENERAL MANAGEMENT ***management by objectives***

MBS *abbr* MORTGAGES, STOCKHOLDING & INVESTMENTS ***mortgage-backed security***

m-commerce E-COMMERCE sales transactions conducted with portable electronic devices electronic transactions between buyers and sellers using mobile communications devices such as cellphones, personal digital assistants (PDAs), or laptop computers

MD *abbr* CORPORATE GOVERNANCE ***managing director***

mean STATISTICS average statistical value a central value or location for a continuous variable in a statistical study

mean reversion STATISTICS pattern of returning to average value the tendency of a variable such as price to return toward its average value after approaching an extreme position

means 1. resources required to accomplish something the amount of money or resources that are needed to achieve something **2.** way of accomplishing something a method, action, or thing that makes it possible for somebody to do something

means test FINANCE **1.** examination of somebody's eligibility for government aid an inquiry into how much money somebody earns or has in savings to see if they are eligible for government benefits **2.** bankruptcy test in US courts a test used by US courts to see whether somebody wishing to file for bankruptcy has enough income to repay some of the debt, determining which type of bankruptcy that person is eligible for

means-test FINANCE determine if somebody is eligible for government aid to find out how much money somebody earns or has in savings and assets to see if they are eligible for government benefits

measurement error STATISTICS numerical mistake in statistical analysis an error in the recording, calculating, or reading of a numerical value in a statistical study

media independent MARKETING firm that buys advertising for clients an organization that specializes in planning and buying advertising for clients or advertising agencies

median STATISTICS midpoint in set of statistical values the value that divides a set of ranked observations into two parts of equal size

media plan MARKETING evaluation of communication channels for advertising an assessment and outline of the various advertising media to be used for a campaign

media planner MARKETING employee who organizes advertising an employee of an advertising agency or media independent who chooses the media, timing, and frequency of advertising

media schedule MARKETING document detailing advertising plan a document that sets out the choice of media, timing, and frequency of advertising

mediation GENERAL MANAGEMENT effort by outsider to solve disagreement intervention by a third party in a dispute in order to try to reach agreement between the disputing parties. Where a commitment or award is imposed on either party the process is known as ***arbitration***. *Also called* ***conciliation***

medical insurance INSURANCE insurance covering medical expenses arrangement by which a firm promises to pay all or part of the cost of medical treatment

Medicare INSURANCE **1.** US government health insurance for seniors a health insurance program in which the US government pays part of the cost of medical care and hospital treatment for people over 65 **2.** Australia's public health insurance system the Australian public health insurance system. It was created in 1983 and is funded by a levy on income.

medium-dated STOCKHOLDING & INVESTMENTS maturing in 5–10 years used to describe securities such as bonds that mature in five to ten years. *See also* ***long-dated, short-dated***

medium-dated gilt STOCKHOLDING & INVESTMENTS UK government security with 5–10 years' maturity a security issued by the UK government that pays a fixed rate of interest on a regular basis for at least five but no more than ten years until the redemption date, when the principal is returned. *See also* ***gilt-edged security***

medium of exchange FINANCE means of paying for goods anything that is used to pay for goods. Nowadays, this usually takes the form of money (banknotes and coins), but in ancient societies it included anything from cattle to shells.

medium-sized business BUSINESS *see* ***small and medium-sized enterprise***

medium-term bond STOCKHOLDING & INVESTMENTS bond redeemed in 5–10 years a bond that has at least five but no more than ten years before its redemption date. *See also* ***long-term bond***

medium-term note FINANCE borrowing repaid within 5 years borrowing arranged over a period of up to five years. *Abbr* ***MTN***

medium-term noteholder FINANCE investor repaying borrowings within 5 years an investor who borrows money over a period of up to five years

megacorporation *or* **megacorp** *US* BUSINESS extremely large, powerful firm an extremely large and powerful business organization (*informal*)

meltdown MARKETS stock market crash an incidence of substantial losses on the stock market. Black Monday, October 19, 1987, was described as Meltdown Monday in the press the following day.

member 1. STOCKHOLDING & INVESTMENTS shareholder in firm somebody who owns stock in a limited liability company **2.** BUSINESS organization belonging to larger group a business organization that is part of a larger group

member bank BANKING bank in US Federal Reserve System a bank that is a member of the US Federal Reserve System

member firm MARKETS member of London Stock Exchange a firm of brokers or market makers that is a member of the London Stock Exchange

member of a company STOCKHOLDING & INVESTMENTS in UK, registered stockholder in the United Kingdom, a stockholder whose name is recorded in the register of members

members' voluntary liquidation BUSINESS in UK, decision to close down solvent firm in the United Kingdom, a special resolution passed by the members of a solvent company for the closing-down of the organization. Prior to the resolution the directors of the company must make a declaration of solvency. Should the appointed liquidator have grounds for believing that the company is not solvent, the winding-up will be treated as compulsory liquidation. *See also* ***voluntary liquidation***

memorandum of association LEGAL document officially registering UK firm in the United Kingdom, an official company document, registered with the ***Registrar of Companies***. A memorandum of association sets out company name, status, address of the registered office, objectives of the company, statement of ***limited liability***, amount of guarantee, and the amount of authorized share capital.

mentee GENERAL MANAGEMENT somebody being helped to develop professionally a person who, with the help of a ***mentor***, develops their skills and improves their performance so that they can achieve their goals

mentor GENERAL MANAGEMENT experienced person helping another to develop professionally a person experienced in a particular area who helps and encourages a less experienced person to learn and develop

mentoring GENERAL MANAGEMENT more-experienced employees' training of less-experienced employee a form of employee development whereby a trusted and respected person, the ***mentor***, uses his or her experience to offer guidance, encouragement, career advice, and support to another person, the ***mentee***. The aim of mentoring is to facilitate the mentee's learning and development and to enable him or her to discover more about his or her potential. Mentoring can occur informally or it can be arranged by means of an organizational program.

Mentor/mentee relationships can take any form that suits the individuals involved, but in practice there are a few rules that apply to most such arrangements, the most important of which is that anything discussed remains confidential. The relationship also needs to be based on trust and candid communication. A mentor does not have to belong to the same organization as the mentee, but can come from any sphere of the mentee's life (professional association, a community center, your alumni organization, for example) just as long as he or she is not the mentee's direct supervisor or working in the same department. Mentoring does not have to be paid for; in fact it is usually seen as an honor by the mentor. Many accomplished individuals consider it good professional citizenship to participate in the process of helping those coming up after them. It can also frequently be beneficial to volunteer to be a mentor, as many organizations consider mentoring a valuable hallmark of leadership material.

mercantile ECONOMICS relating to trading relating to trade or commercial activity

mercantile agency BUSINESS firm assessing credit status a company that evaluates the creditworthiness of potential corporate borrowers on behalf of other companies. *See also* ***credit bureau***

mercantile paper STOCKHOLDING & INVESTMENTS = ***commercial paper***

mercantilism ECONOMICS economic theory based on importance of international trade the body of economic thought developed between the 1650s and 1750s, based on the belief that a country's wealth depended on the strength of its foreign trade

merchandising MARKETING **1.** activities promoting quick sale of products the process of increasing the market share of a product in retail outlets using display, stocking, and sales promotion techniques **2.** promoting products in connection with movie, celebrity, etc. the promotion and display of goods associated with a specific ***brand***, movie, or celebrity. Merchandising based on a specific movie, for example, may significantly add to its total revenues through appropriate ***licensing*** opportunities. Merchandising may include clothing, toys, food products, or music and often extends well beyond the ***core business*** of the producer of the original product.

merchantable quality OPERATIONS & PRODUCTION UK standard of acceptable product quality in UK law, a minimum standard to which goods being sold must conform. It requires that the goods be reasonably priced given their description, be fit for the purpose for which they were purchased, and be free of defects.

merchant account E-COMMERCE seller's bank account for credit card transactions an account established by a trader to receive the proceeds of credit card transactions

merchant bank 1. E-COMMERCE bank accepting proceeds from seller's credit card transactions a financial institution at which a trader has opened a ***merchant account*** into which the proceeds of credit card transactions are credited after the institution has subtracted its fee **2.** *UK* BANKING = ***investment bank***

merchant number E-COMMERCE identification number for credit card merchant a number that identifies a merchant, printed at the top of the report slip when depositing credit card payments

merger MERGERS & ACQUISITIONS when one organization buys and combines with another the amalgamation of two or more organizations under single ownership, through the direct acquisition by one organization of the net assets or liabilities of the other. A merger can be the result of a friendly ***takeover***, which results in the combining of companies on an equal footing. After a merger, the legal existence of the acquired organization is terminated. There is no standard definition of a merger, as each is different, depending on what is expected from the merger, and on the negotiations, strategy, stock and assets, human resources, and stockholders of the players. Four broad types of mergers are recognized. A *horizontal merger* involves firms from the same industry, while a *vertical merger* involves firms from the same supply chain. A *circular merger* involves firms with different products but similar distribution channels. A ***conglomerate company*** is produced by the union of firms with few or no similarities in production or marketing but that come together to create a larger economic base and greater profit potential. *See also* ***acquisition, consolidation, joint venture, partnership***

merger accounting ACCOUNTING accounting treating combined firm as result of merger a method of accounting that regards a business combination as the acquisition of one company by another. The identifiable assets and liabilities of the company acquired are included in the consolidated balance sheet at their fair value at the date of acquisition, and its results included in the profit and loss account from the date of acquisition. The difference between the fair value of the consideration given and the fair values of the net assets of the entity acquired is accounted for as ***goodwill***.

merger arbitrage MERGERS AND ACQUISITIONS trading securities of merging companies simultaneously in a merger, a hedge fund trader sells short the high-priced securities of the target company and buys the underpriced ones of the acquiring company, and then at a time when prices have reverted to true value, the trade can be liquidated at a profit

merger arbitrageur MERGERS AND ACQUISITIONS trader in securities of merging firms a trader or fund dealing in ***merger arbitrage***

mergers and acquisitions MERGERS & ACQUISITIONS ways in which organizations change ownership a blanket term covering the main ways in which organizations change hands. *Abbr* ***M&A***

merit rating *or* **merit pay** HR & PERSONNEL system for increasing pay based on employees' performance a payment system in which the personal qualities of an employee are rated according to organizational requirements, and a pay increase or bonus is made against the results of this rating. Merit rating has been in use since the 1950s, and examines an employee's input to the organization (for example, their attendance, adaptability, or aptitude) as well as the quality or quantity of work produced. In merit rating programs, these factors may be weighted to reflect their relative importance and the resultant points score determines whether the employee earns a bonus or pay increase.

method study GENERAL MANAGEMENT evaluation of existing techniques to find best one the systematic recording, examination, and analysis of existing and proposed ways of conducting work tasks in order to discover the most efficient and economical methods of performing them. The basic procedure followed in method study is as follows: select the area to be studied; record the data; examine the data; develop alternative approaches; install the new method; maintain the new method. The technique was initially developed to evaluate manufacturing processes but has been used more widely to evaluate alternative courses of action.

metrics GENERAL MANAGEMENT measures of organization's effectiveness the standards used to measure or quantify the activities and success of an organization

mezzanine finance *UK* FINANCE = ***mezzanine financing***

mezzanine financing FINANCE firm's financing following initial investments financing provided to a company after it has received start-up financing. *UK term* ***mezzanine finance***

MFN *abbr* INTERNATIONAL TRADE ***most favored nation***

microbusiness BUSINESS firm with 1–9 employees a very ***small business*** that directly employs fewer than ten people. This definition of small and medium-sized enterprises is the one adopted by the United Kingdom's Department for Business Enterprise and Regulatory Reform for statistical purposes.

microcash E-COMMERCE type of electronic money allowing sub-denomination payments a form of electronic money with no denominations, permitting sub-denomination transactions of a fraction of, for example, a cent

microcredit BANKING financing those not eligible for standard bank loans the extension of credit to entrepreneurs and ***microbusinesses*** that are too poor to qualify for conventional bank loans. *Also called* ***microlending***

microeconomic incentive ECONOMICS financial encouragement to improve market performance a tax benefit or subsidy given to a business to achieve a specific objective such as increased sales overseas

microeconomics ECONOMICS study of consumers' and firms' roles in economy the branch of economics that studies the contribution of groups of consumers or firms, or of individual consumers, to a country's economy. *See also* ***macroeconomics***

microeconomy ECONOMICS individual areas of economy that influence whole economy the narrow sectors of a country's economic activity that influence the behavior of the economy as a whole, for example, consumer choices. *See also* ***macroeconomy***

microfinance *UK* FINANCE = ***microfinancing***

microfinancing *US* FINANCE providing variety of financial services to poor the provision of a range of financial resources such as small loans, insurance, and savings to low-income families in order to help them build businesses and increase their income. *UK term* ***microfinance***. *See also* ***microcredit***

microhedge STOCKHOLDING & INVESTMENTS hedge for one asset or liability a ***hedge*** that relates to a single asset or liability in an investment ***portfolio***. *See also* ***macrohedge***

microlending BANKING = ***microcredit***

microloan FINANCE small loan to low-income borrower a very small loan made to somebody who has a low or no income and nothing to offer as collateral, or to the owner of a small unprofitable business

micromanagement GENERAL MANAGEMENT too close control of subordinate employees' work a style of management where a manager becomes over-involved in the details of the work of subordinates, resulting in the manager making every decision in an organization, no matter how trivial. Micromanagement is a euphemism for meddling, and has the opposite effect to empowerment. Micromanagement can retard the progress of organizational development, as it robs employees of their self-respect.

micromarketing MARKETING promoting products to very small groups marketing to individuals or very small groups. It targets the specific interests and needs of individuals by offering customized products or services. Rather than targeting one large niche market, a micromarketing company targets a large number of very small niches. *See also* ***mass market, niche market***

micromerchant E-COMMERCE online seller accepting microcash a provider of goods or services on the Internet in exchange for electronic money, including ***microcash***

micromort RISK measure of risk of death a one-in-a-million risk of dying

micropayment E-COMMERCE means of paying small sums electronically a payment protocol for small amounts of electronic money, ranging from a fraction of a cent to no more than ten US dollars or euros

micro-profits FINANCE profits after microfinancing the profits made by businesses that have been financed by ***microfinancing***

middleman GENERAL MANAGEMENT go-between in interactions between others an intermediary in a transaction. With direct sales models, manufacturers cut out the middleman by dealing directly with end customers.

middle management HR & PERSONNEL level of managers neither at top nor bottom the position held by managers who are considered neither senior nor junior in an organization. Middle managers were subject to ***delayering*** and ***downsizing*** in the 1980s as organizations sought to reduce costs by removing the layer of managers between those who had direct interface with customers and senior decision-makers.

middle office GENERAL MANAGEMENT staff that works with front and back offices staff who do not interact directly with customers but are involved in making business decisions. Risk management is an example of a middle office function. *See also* ***back office, front office***

middle price *or* **mid-price** *UK* STOCKHOLDING & INVESTMENTS price between bid price and offer price a price, halfway between the bid price and the offer price, that is generally quoted in the press and on information screens

mid-range STATISTICS average of maximum and minimum values the mean of the largest and smallest values in a statistical sample

MiFID *abbr* MARKETS, REGULATION & COMPLIANCE Markets in Financial Instruments Directive

MIGA *abbr* BANKING ***Multilateral Investment Guarantee Agency***

million FINANCE thousand thousands a sum equal to one thousand thousands

millionaire FINANCE person with income over one million a person whose net worth or income is more than one million dollars, pounds, or other unit of currency

mindshare MARKETING public goodwill the attitude toward a product or organization that has been generated among the general public

Mini-Case BUSINESS technique for training business and finance students a set of circumstances used as the basis for solving a business or financial problem, used as a technique for training college students in business and finance

Mini ISA STOCKHOLDING & INVESTMENTS former UK tax-free cash savings account formerly, in the United Kingdom, an ***ISA*** in which savers held cash tax-free. Savers could also have a second Mini ISA in which they held stocks. *See also* ***Maxi ISA, ISA***

minimax regret criterion GENERAL MANAGEMENT choosing course with minimum regret or loss an approach to decision making under uncertainty in which the opportunity cost (regret) associated with each possible course of action is measured, and the decision-maker selects the activity that minimizes the maximum regret, or loss. Regret is measured as the difference between the best and worst possible payoff for each option.

minimum 1. least possible amount the smallest number, price, quantity, or degree possible or allowed **2.** least possible of the smallest possible or allowed amount or value

minimum balance BANKING least amount of money required in account the smallest amount of money which must be kept in an account to qualify for the services provided

minimum inventory level *US* OPERATIONS & PRODUCTION size below which inventory must not decrease an inventory level, set for control purposes, below which holdings should not fall without being highlighted. It is calculated as follows:

Re-order level – Average rate of usage × Average lead time

UK term ***minimum stock level***

minimum lending rate BANKING lowest UK central bank interest rate formerly, the rate at which the Bank of England lent to other banks, now replaced by ***base rate***. *Abbr* ***MLR***

minimum quote size MARKETS minimum number of shares for one transaction the smallest number of shares that a market must handle in one trade of a particular security

minimum reserves BANKING least amount that bank must have in reserve the smallest amount of reserves which a commercial bank must hold with a central bank

minimum stock level *UK* OPERATIONS & PRODUCTION = ***minimum inventory level***

minimum subscription STOCKHOLDING & INVESTMENTS minimum bid for new issue the smallest number of shares or securities that may be applied for in a new issue

minimum wage FINANCE least hourly pay rate legally allowed the lowest hourly rate of pay, usually set by government, to which all ***employees*** are legally entitled

minority interest *or* **minority ownership** CORPORATE GOVERNANCE holding less than half of firm's common stock ownership of less than 50% of a company's common stock, which is not enough to control the company

minority shareholder STOCKHOLDING & INVESTMENTS stockholder with less than 50% of firm's stock a person who owns a group of shares of stock but less than half of the stock in a company. *Also called* ***minority stockholder***

minority shareholding STOCKHOLDING & INVESTMENTS less than 50% of firm's stock a group of shares of stock that somebody has which account for less than half the total shares in a firm

minority stockholder STOCKHOLDING & INVESTMENTS = ***minority shareholder***

minus factor GENERAL MANAGEMENT negative aspect of situation a factor that is unfavorable in some way, for example, because it reduces profitability

minutes CORPORATE GOVERNANCE official notes from meeting an official written record of the proceedings of a meeting. Minutes usually record points for action, and indicate who is responsible for implementing decisions. Good practice requires that the minutes of a meeting be circulated well in advance of the next meeting, and that those attending that meeting read the minutes in advance. Registered companies are required to keep minutes of meetings and make them available at their registered offices for inspection by company members and shareholders.

mirror fund STOCKHOLDING & INVESTMENTS investment trust and mutual fund under same control an investment trust where the manager also runs a mutual fund with the same objectives

MIS OPERATIONS & PRODUCTION computer system with information for management decisions a computer-based system for collecting, storing, processing, and providing access to information used in the management of an organization. Management information systems evolved from early electronic data processing systems. They support managerial decision making by providing regular structured reports on organizational operations. Management information systems may support the functional areas of an organization such as finance, marketing, or production. ***Decision support systems*** and ***EISs*** are types of MIS developed for more specific purposes. *Full form* ***management information system***

misappropriation FRAUD fraudulent use of somebody else's money the illegal use of money by somebody who is not the owner but who has been trusted to look after it

mismanagement GENERAL MANAGEMENT incompetent or illegal handling of firm's resources functional or ethical dereliction of duty due to ignorance, negligence, incompetence, avoidance, or criminality

missing value STATISTICS expected statistical observation that is missing an observation that is absent from a set of statistical data, for example, because a member of a population to be sampled was not at home when the researcher called

mission statement GENERAL MANAGEMENT formal statement of firm's goals a short memorable statement of the reasons for the existence of an organization. *See also* ***vision statement***

MIT *abbr* STOCKHOLDING & INVESTMENTS ***market if touched***

Mittelstand BUSINESS mid-sized German companies a German term that incorporates the meaning of "medium-sized enterprise"

mixed economy ECONOMICS combination of government and private business ownership an economy in which both public and private enterprises participate in the production and supply of goods and services

MLR *abbr* BANKING = ***minimum lending rate***

MMC *abbr* REGULATION & COMPLIANCE ***Monopolies and Mergers Commission***

MMDA *abbr* BANKING ***money market deposit account***

MNC *abbr* BUSINESS ***multinational corporation***

mobile money FINANCE use of cell phones for financial transactions a facility that allows people to use their cell phones and other hand-held devices to handle financial transactions

mobile office GENERAL MANAGEMENT setup of portable office equipment a set of conditions allowing working on the move. Mobile office equipment would typically include a cell phone, laptop computer, and a modem to link the computer to the Internet or a company's main office.

mode STATISTICS most frequent statistical observation in a statistical study, the most frequently occurring value in a set of ranked observations

model building STATISTICS creating structure for statistical observations the process of providing an adequate fit to the data in a set of observations in a statistical study

model risk MARKETS danger of inadequacy of computer modeling the possibility that a computer model on which investment decisions are based may be unreliable in extreme market conditions

modernization GENERAL MANAGEMENT replacing outdated equipment with new investing in new equipment or upgrading existing equipment to bring resources up to date or improve efficiency

modern portfolio theory STOCKHOLDING & INVESTMENTS = ***portfolio theory***

modified accounts ACCOUNTING = ***abbreviated accounts***

modified ACRS TAX US method of assessing asset depreciation in the United States, a system used for computing the depreciation of some assets acquired after 1985 in a way that reduces taxes. The ACRS applies to older assets. *See also* ***accelerated cost recovery system***

modified book value ACCOUNTING = ***adjusted book value***

modified cash basis ACCOUNTING different accounting for short- and long-term assets the bookkeeping practice of accounting for short-term assets on a cash basis and for long-term assets on an accrual basis

modified duration MARKETS, RISK measure of interest-rate risk in owning bonds a measure of a bond's sensitivity to changes in interest rates, based on the assumption that interest rates and bond prices move in opposite directions

mom and pop investors *US* STOCKHOLDING & INVESTMENTS inexperienced investors people who hold or wish to purchase stock but have little experience with or knowledge of the stock market (*slang*)

mom-and-pop operation *US, Canada* BUSINESS small family business a small family-run business, especially in the retail sector. *UK term* ***ma and pa shop***

momentum investor STOCKHOLDING & INVESTMENTS buyer of stock rising in price an investor who buys stock that seems to be moving upward in price

MONEP *abbr* MARKETS ***Marché des Options Négotiables de Paris***

monetarism ECONOMICS belief that increased money causes inflation an economic theory that states that inflation is caused by increases in a country's money supply

monetarist ECONOMICS **1.** believer in monetarism a person who believes that inflation is caused by increases in a country's money supply and that the money supply should remain fairly steady **2.** according to monetarism according to the economic theory of ***monetarism***

monetary FINANCE of money, cash, or liquid assets relating to or involving cash, currency, or assets that are readily convertible into cash

monetary assets ACCOUNTING assets corresponding to amounts in accounts assets such as accounts receivable, cash, and bank balances that are realizable at the amounts stated in the accounts. Other assets such as facilities and machinery, inventories, and marketable securities will not necessarily realize the sum stated in a business's balance sheet.

monetary base ECONOMICS nation's total cash supply the stock of a country's coins, notes, and bank deposits held by the central bank

monetary base control ECONOMICS government restrictions on cash availability the restricting of the amount of ***liquid assets*** in an economy through government controls

monetary items ACCOUNTING items worth the same regardless of inflation monetary assets, such as cash and debtors, and monetary liabilities, such as overdrafts and creditors, whose values stay the same in spite of inflation

monetary policy ECONOMICS government policy regarding money and currency government economic policy concerning a country's rate of interest, its exchange rate, and the amount of money in the economy

Monetary Policy Committee ECONOMICS Bank of England committee that sets interest rates a committee of the Bank of England, chaired by the Governor of the Bank, that has responsibility for setting UK interest rates independently of the British government. Its goal is to set rates with a view to keeping inflation at a defined level and avoiding deflation. *Abbr* ***MPC***

monetary reserve BANKING currency and bullion in central bank the foreign currency and precious metals that a country holds, that provide a cushion for central banking functions

monetary standard CURRENCY & EXCHANGE value on which currency system is based the value underlying the currency in a specific country's monetary system, for example, the ***gold standard***, which in the past many countries used to set the value of their currencies

monetary system ECONOMICS set of government rules controlling nation's money the set of government regulations concerning a country's monetary reserves and its holdings of notes and coins

monetary targets FINANCE government financial targets figures that are given as targets by the government when setting out its budget for the forthcoming year

monetary unit CURRENCY & EXCHANGE standard unit of nation's currency the standard unit of a country's currency, such as the dollar in the United States, the pound sterling in the United Kingdom, or the euro in many other countries of the European Union

monetary working capital adjustment ACCOUNTING adjustment in accounts for inflation an adjustment in ***current cost accounting*** to the historical cost balance sheet to take account of the effect of inflation on the value of debtors, creditors, and stocks of finished goods. *Abbr* ***MWCA***

monetize CURRENCY & EXCHANGE designate as official currency to establish a currency as a country's legal tender

money CURRENCY & EXCHANGE current medium of exchange a medium of exchange that is accepted throughout a country as payment for services and goods and as a means of settling debts ◇ at the money STOCKHOLDING & INVESTMENTS, RISK a situation in which the price an option holder must pay to exercise an option is the same as the current ***market price*** of the underlying security or commodity ◇ at the money forward STOCKHOLDING & INVESTMENTS, RISK a situation in which the price an option holder must pay to exercise an option is the same as the ***forward price*** of the underlying security or commodity

money at call and short notice BANKING **1.** in UK, advances repayable on demand or soon in the United Kingdom, advances made by banks to other financial institutions, or corporate and personal customers, that are repayable either upon demand (call) or within 14 days (short notice) **2.** in UK, balances available on demand or soon in the United Kingdom, balances in an account that are either available upon demand (call) or within 14 days (short notice)

money broker MARKETS in UK, arranger of loans in the United Kingdom, an intermediary who works on the money market, arranging loans between banks, discount houses, and dealers in government securities

moneyer CURRENCY & EXCHANGE coiner of money an archaic term for somebody who is authorized to mint money

money laundering LEGAL concealing illegal origins of money the process of making money obtained illegally appear legitimate by passing it through banks or businesses

moneylender FINANCE lender of money at interest a person whose business is lending money to others for interest

money lying idle FINANCE uninvested money producing no interest money that is not being used to produce interest and that is not invested in business

money management FINANCE, STOCKHOLDING & INVESTMENTS business of investing clients' money the activity of making decisions about income and expenditure, including budgeting, banking arrangements, making investments, and tax payments, either for yourself or on behalf of clients

money manager STOCKHOLDING & INVESTMENTS specialist in investment management a person or company that manages an investment ***portfolio***, usually of ***money market instruments***, on behalf of investors. *See also* ***portfolio manager***

money market MARKETS market for buying and selling financial instruments a market in which short-term financial instruments such as certificates of deposit, Treasury bills, commercial papers, and bank deposits are traded. New York is the major money market, followed by London and Tokyo. *Also called* ***finance market***

money market account BANKING account with high interest rate an account with a financial institution that requires a minimum deposit, and pays a rate of interest, related to the wholesale money market rates, generally higher than retail rates. Most institutions offer a variety of term accounts, with either a fixed rate or variable rate, and notice accounts, with a variety of notice periods at variable rates.

money market deposit account BANKING US savings account in the United States, a type of savings account with deposits invested in the money market and having a high yield. There is often a high minimum deposit and withdrawals require notice. *Abbr* ***MMDA***

money market fund STOCKHOLDING & INVESTMENTS mutual fund investing in short-term securities a mutual fund that invests in short-term debt securities. In the United States these are strictly regulated by the ***Securities and Exchange Commission***.

money market instruments STOCKHOLDING & INVESTMENTS financial products traded on money markets short-term assets and securities, usually maturing within 12 months, that are traded on money markets, for example, certificates of deposit, commercial papers, and Treasury bills

money men FINANCE people working in finance industry the people who provide finance for a venture, campaign, etc.

money national income ECONOMICS unadjusted value of nation's annual output ***GDP*** measured using money value, not adjusted for the effect of inflation

money of account ACCOUNTING unit for accounting purposes a monetary unit that is used in keeping accounts but is not necessarily an actual currency unit

money order BANKING instruction to make payment to someone a written order to pay somebody a sum of money, issued by a bank or post office

money purchase pension *or* **money purchase scheme** PENSIONS UK pension plan to buy annuity in the United Kingdom, a pension plan where the fund that is built up is used to purchase an annuity. The retirement income that the beneficiary receives therefore depends on his or her contributions, any employer contributions, the performance of the investments those contributions are used to buy, the annuity rates, and the type of annuity purchased at retirement.

money purchase plan PENSIONS US pension plan with employer and employee contributing in the United States, a pension plan (a defined benefit plan) in which the participant contributes part and the firm contributes at the same or a different rate

money substitute CURRENCY & EXCHANGE trading goods used to replace currency any goods used as a medium of exchange because of the degree of devaluation of a country's currency

money supply ECONOMICS nation's cash available for purchases the stock of ***liquid assets*** in a country's economy that can be given in exchange for services or goods

monies *or* **moneys** CURRENCY & EXCHANGE sums of money amounts of money, especially those that come from a specific place or have a specific purpose

Monopolies and Mergers Commission REGULATION & COMPLIANCE former UK commission for competition in the United Kingdom, a commission that was replaced by the Competition Commission in April 1999. *Abbr* ***MMC***

monopolistic competition MARKETS situation blocking new competition in market a situation that exists in a market in which there are strong barriers to the entry of new competitors. *Also called* ***imperfect competition***

monopoly ECONOMICS economic situation in which one firm controls market a ***market*** in which there is only one producer or one seller. A company establishes a monopoly by entering a new market or eliminating all competitors from an existing market. A company that holds a monopoly has control of a market and is able to fix prices. For this reason, governments usually try to avoid monopoly situations. However, some monopolies such as government-owned utilities are seen as beneficial to ***consumers***.

monopsony MARKETS situation where only one customer needs product a situation in which there is only one buyer for a specific product or service

Monte Carlo method *or* **Monte Carlo simulation** STATISTICS statistical method of deciding based on uncertainties a statistical method of reducing the uncertainty in estimating future outcomes by running repeated calculations using current and historical data, used in business decision-making that involves a number of uncertain variables such as capital investment and resource allocation. The name of the Monte Carlo method derives from the use of random numbers as generated by a roulette wheel. The numbers are used in repeated simulations, often performed by spreadsheet programs on computers, to calculate a range of possible outcomes, using current and historical data. The technique was developed by mathematicians in the early 1960s for use in nuclear physics and ***operational research*** but has since been used more widely.

month-end ACCOUNTING of end of month relating to the end of each month when financial transactions for the current month are finalized

Moody's Investors Service STOCKHOLDING & INVESTMENTS US firm that rates credit risk of investments a US organization that rates the reliability of a debtor organization on a scale from AAA to C. It also issues ratings on municipal bonds, running from MIG1, the highest rating, to MIG4. *See also* ***Standard & Poor's***

moonlighting HR & PERSONNEL doing second job in addition to main job undertaking a second job, often for cash and in the evenings, in addition to a full-time permanent job

moral hazard RISK danger through protection from consequences of actions a risk that somebody will behave immorally because insurance, the law, or some other agency protects them against loss that the immoral behavior might otherwise cause

moratorium FINANCE postponement a period of delay, for example, additional time agreed on by a creditor and a debtor for recovery of a debt

more bang for your buck *US* FINANCE greater financial benefit greater leverage provided by an investment (*slang*)

Morgan Stanley Capital International Indexes MARKETS worldwide stock market indexes a group of indexes that track stocks traded on stock markets worldwide and are considered benchmarks for international investment portfolios

mortality and expense risk charge INSURANCE charge for annuity guaranteeing benefit and compensating insurer an extra charge paid on some annuities to guarantee that if the policyholder dies, his or her heirs will receive a benefit, and also that the insurance company will be compensated for an annuitant who lives longer than he or she should according to the mortality tables

mortgage MORTGAGES **1.** agreement to lend money for property a financial lending arrangement enabling somebody to borrow money from a bank or other lending institution in order to buy property or land. The original amount borrowed, the ***principal***, is then repaid with interest to the lender over a fixed number of years. *See also* ***amortized mortgage, current account mortgage, endowment mortgage, interest-only mortgage, low start mortgage*** **2.** grant of right to asset of defaulting borrower a borrowing arrangement whereby the lender is granted a legal right to an asset, usually a piece of real estate, should the borrower default on the payments. *See also* ***second mortgage***

mortgage-backed security STOCKHOLDING & INVESTMENTS, MORTGAGES security backed by mortgages a security for which the collateral is the principal and interest on a set of mortgages

mortgage bank BANKING bank dealing in mortgages a financial institution that trades in mortgages

mortgage bond STOCKHOLDING & INVESTMENTS, MORTGAGES debt backed by real estate especially in the United States, a debt secured by real estate

mortgage broker MORTGAGES intermediary between seekers and offerers of mortgages a person or company that acts as an agent between people seeking mortgages and organizations that offer them

mortgage debenture MORTGAGES long-term loan secured against firm's fixed assets a debenture in which the loan is secured against a company's ***fixed assets***

mortgagee MORTGAGES lender in mortgage agreement a person or organization that lends money to a borrower under a mortgage agreement. *See also* ***mortgagor***

mortgage equity analysis MORTGAGES calculation of value of property minus mortgages owed a computation of the difference between the value of a property and the amount owed on it in the form of mortgages

mortgage famine MORTGAGES when house buyers unable to get mortgages a situation where there is not enough money available to offer mortgages to house buyers

mortgage insurance INSURANCE mortgagee's insurance against borrower's default insurance that provides somebody holding a mortgage with protection against default

mortgage lien MORTGAGES claim against mortgaged property a claim against a property that is mortgaged. Mortgagees often own the mortgage lien to secure the loan.

mortgage note MORTGAGES record of mortgage a note that documents the existence and terms of a mortgage

mortgage pool MORTGAGES mortgages on sale together a group of mortgages with similar characteristics packaged together for sale

mortgage portfolio MORTGAGES in US, bank's holdings in mortgages in the United States, the group of mortgages held by a ***mortgage bank***

mortgage rate MORTGAGES interest rate on mortgage the interest rate charged on a mortgage by a lender

mortgage securitizer STOCKHOLDING & INVESTMENTS firm creating and selling groups of mortgage loans as securities a company that collects residential mortgage loans into a package for sale to investors

mortgage tax TAX US tax on mortgage in the United States, a one-time tax paid when a mortgage is taken out

mortgagor MORTGAGES borrower in mortgage agreement somebody who has taken out a mortgage to borrow money. *See also* ***mortgagee***

most distant futures contract MARKETS futures option with longest term a futures option with the latest delivery date of those being considered. *See also* ***nearby futures contract***

most favored nation INTERNATIONAL TRADE foreign country given very good trade terms a foreign country allowed very favorable trade terms by another country. *Abbr* ***MFN***

motion study GENERAL MANAGEMENT evaluation of efficiency of physical work patterns the observation of physical movements involved in the performance of work, and investigation of how these can be made more effective and cost efficient

motivation GENERAL MANAGEMENT giving employees reason to perform their best the creation of stimuli, incentives, and working environments which enable people to perform to the best of their ability in pursuit of organizational success. Motivation is commonly viewed as the magic driver that enables managers to get others to achieve their targets. In the 20th century, there was a shift, at least in theory, away from motivation by dictation and discipline toward motivation by creating an appropriate corporate climate and addressing the needs of individual employees. Although it is widely agreed to be one of the key management tasks, it has frequently been argued that one person cannot motivate others but can only create conditions for others to self-motivate.

mousetrap ◇ build a better mousetrap MARKETING to create a new or better product

mover and shaker GENERAL MANAGEMENT powerful person who initiates things an influential and dynamic person within an organization or group of people

moving average MARKETS average of stock prices that is continually recalculated an average of stock prices on a stock market, in which the calculation is made over a period which moves forward regularly

MPC *abbr* ECONOMICS ***Monetary Policy Committee***

MRP II OPERATIONS & PRODUCTION computer-based system used in manufacturing a computer-based manufacturing, inventory planning, and control system that broadens the scope of production planning by involving other functional areas that influence production decisions. Manufacturing resource planning evolved from material requirements planning to integrate other functions in the planning process. These functions may include engineering, marketing, purchasing, production scheduling, business planning, and finance. *Full form* ***manufacturing resource planning***

MSB *abbr* BANKING ***mutual savings bank***

MTF *abbr* MARKETS ***multilateral trading facility***

MTN *abbr* FINANCE ***medium-term note***

mudaraba *or* **mudarabah** BUSINESS Islamic partnership between investor and entrepreneur in Islamic financing, a type of partnership in which one partner provides the capital while the other provides expertise and management. Each gets a prearranged percentage of the profits, but the partner providing the capital bears any losses.

mudarib BUSINESS entrepreneur in mudaraba partnership in Islamic financing, the entrepreneurial partner in a ***mudaraba*** partnership who provides the expertise and management

multichannel E-COMMERCE using Internet and traditional methods using a combination of online and offline communication methods to conduct business

multicurrency FINANCE offering number of currencies used to describe a loan that gives the borrower a choice of currencies

multifunctional card BANKING plastic card with more than one use a plastic card that may be used for two or more purposes, for example, as an ATM card, a check card, and a debit card

Multilateral Investment Guarantee Agency BANKING part of World Bank Group one of the five institutions that constitute the World Bank Group. MIGA was created in 1988 to promote foreign direct investment into emerging economies by insuring against political risk, with the objective of improving people's lives and reducing poverty. Apart from offering political risk insurance to investors and lenders, MIGA assists emerging countries to attract and retain private investment. *Abbr* ***MIGA***

multilateral netting CURRENCY & EXCHANGE consolidating sums from various sources into one currency a method of putting together sums from various international sources to reduce currency transaction costs, used by groups of companies or banks trading in several currencies at the same time

multilateral trading facility MARKETS system combining third-party commercial interests under the provisions of the ***Markets in Financial Instruments Directive***, a system of bringing together multiple third-party buying and selling interests in financial instruments. *Abbr* ***MTF***

multilevel marketing MARKETING = ***network marketing***

multinational BUSINESS

multinational business *or* **multinational** *or* **multinational company** *or* **multinational corporation** BUSINESS firm operating in more than one country a company that operates internationally, usually with subsidiaries, offices, or production facilities in more than one country

multiparty auction E-COMMERCE Internet selling with buyers making online bids a method of buying and selling on the Internet in which prospective buyers make electronic bids

multiple application STOCKHOLDING & INVESTMENTS more than one application for new share issue the submission of more than one share application for a new issue that is expected to be oversubscribed. In most jurisdictions, this practice is illegal.

multiple exchange rate CURRENCY & EXCHANGE exchange rate varying with transaction's purpose a two-tier rate of exchange used in some countries where the more advantageous rate may be for tourists or for businesses proposing to build a factory

multiple ownership BUSINESS when group owns something together a situation in which something is owned by several parties jointly

multiple regression analysis STATISTICS *see* ***regression analysis***

multiple sourcing OPERATIONS & PRODUCTION using more than one supplier a ***purchasing*** policy of using two or more suppliers for products or services. Multiple sourcing prevents reliance on any one supplier. It encourages competition between suppliers, and ensures access to a wide variety of goods or services. Dealing with more than one supplier can improve access to market information but can also entail more administration.

multiple time series STATISTICS sets of data observed together over time two or more sets of data that are observed simultaneously

multiplier FINANCE factor that multiplies another number or value a number that multiplies another, or a factor that tends to multiply something, for example, the effect of new expenditure on total income and reserves

multiplier effect ECONOMICS effect of increased investment or spending on income a situation in which a small initial change in investment or spending produces a proportionately larger change in national income

multiskilling HR & PERSONNEL training in a variety of skills a process of training employees to do a variety of tasks rather than focusing on single tasks. Employees are therefore available to undertake a number of different jobs and have better general employability.

multitasking E-COMMERCE conducting several tasks together the practice of doing more than one activity or task at a time

multivariate analysis STATISTICS investigation of characteristics of multiple variables any of a number of statistical techniques used in ***operational research*** to examine the characteristics and relationships between multiple variables. Multivariate analysis techniques include ***cluster analysis***, ***discriminant analysis***, and multiple ***regression analysis***.

multivariate data STATISTICS statistical observations involving multiple variables data for which each observation involves values for more than one random variable

mum and dad investors *ANZ* STOCKHOLDING & INVESTMENTS = ***mom and pop investors*** (*slang*)

mumpreneur BUSINESS mother who is independent businesswoman a mother who starts or owns a business

municipal bond *or* **muni** *or* **muni-bond** STOCKHOLDING & INVESTMENTS US government security in the United States, a security issued by states, local governments, and municipalities

municipal bond fund STOCKHOLDING & INVESTMENTS fund investing in municipal bonds a fund that is invested in municipal bonds

Municipal Bond Insurance Association INSURANCE *see* ***MBIA***

murabaha *or* **murabahah** FINANCE when Islamic bank purchases item for customer in Islamic financing, an arrangement in which a bank purchases an item for a customer provided the customer agrees to purchase it from the bank at a prearranged higher price. *See also* ***tawarruq***

Murphy's Law GENERAL MANAGEMENT anything that can go wrong will the principle that if something can go wrong, it will

musharaka *or* **musharakah** BUSINESS Islamic partnership in which all partners invest money in Islamic financing, a type of partnership in which all partners contribute capital to an enterprise, share profits in a prearranged way, and share losses equally

mutual BUSINESS relating to financial organization with members not stockholders used to describe an organization that is run in the interests of its members and that does not have to pay dividends to its stockholders, so surplus profits can be plowed back into the business. In the United Kingdom, building societies and friendly societies were formed as mutual organizations, although in recent years many have demutualized, either by becoming public limited companies or by being bought by other financial organizations, resulting in members receiving cash or share windfall payments. In the United States, *mutual associations*, a type of savings and loan association, and state-chartered mutual savings banks are organized in this way.

mutual company BUSINESS firm owned by its customers a company that is owned by its customers who share in the profits

mutual fund *US* STOCKHOLDING & INVESTMENTS firm trading in investments for clients an investment company that holds a range of stocks in which investors can buy units. *UK term* ***unit trust***

mutual insurance INSURANCE insurance firm owned by policyholders an insurance company that is owned by its policyholders who share the profits and cover claims with their pooled premiums

mutual recognition directive REGULATION & COMPLIANCE EU directive about recognizing other members' practices a directive of the European Union that each country's accounting firms and cross-border services should be recognized by other member states

mutual savings bank BANKING US savings bank run by trustees in the United States, a state-chartered savings bank run in the interests of its members. It is governed by a local board of trustees, not necessarily the legal owners. Most of these banks offer accounts and services that are typical of full-service banks. *Abbr* ***MSB***

muzara'a *or* **muzara'ah** FINANCE payment for land rent by crop share in Islamic financing, an agreement in which a landowner lets somebody farm an area of land in return for part of the crop

MVA *abbr* MARKETS ***market value added***

MWCA *abbr* ACCOUNTING ***monetary working capital adjustment***

N

NAIC *abbr* **1.** INSURANCE, REGULATION & COMPLIANCE ***National Association of Insurance Commissioners*** **2.** STOCKHOLDING & INVESTMENTS ***National Association of Investors Corporation***

naked debenture BUSINESS unsecured debt obligation a debt acknowledged by a company that is without security for the interest or the amount of principal. *See also* ***debenture***

naked option STOCKHOLDING & INVESTMENTS = ***uncovered option***

naked position STOCKHOLDING & INVESTMENTS holding with unhedged securities a situation in which an investor holds securities some of which are not ***hedged***

naked writer STOCKHOLDING & INVESTMENTS offerer of option on another's shares a person selling an option who does not own the underlying shares

name INSURANCE member of Lloyd's insurance group an individual who is a member of the ***Lloyd's underwriting syndicate***, an insurance group based in London

named perils insurance INSURANCE insurance for specific types of risk a type of insurance that provides coverage for only those losses that occur as a result of specifically named risks

NAO *abbr* REGULATION & COMPLIANCE ***National Audit Office***

narrowcasting E-COMMERCE targeting information to restricted group targeting information to a niche audience. Owing to its ability to personalize information to the requirements of individual users, the Internet is generally viewed as a narrowcast rather than a broadcast medium.

narrow market MARKETS market with little trading a market where the trading volume is low. A characteristic of such a market is a wide spread of bid and offer prices.

narrow money ECONOMICS **1.** *US* = ***M1*** **2.** *UK* = ***Mo***

NASD *abbr* STOCKHOLDING & INVESTMENTS ***National Association of Securities Dealers***

NASDAQ[1] *abbr* MARKETS ***NASDAQ Composite Index***

NASDAQ[2] *or* **Nasdaq** MARKETS computerized trading system a computerized quotation system that supports market making in over-the-counter and listed securities. It was established by the ***National Association of Securities Dealers*** in 1971. NASDAQ International has operated from London since 1992.

NASDAQ Composite Index MARKETS US index of high-tech stock prices a specialist US stock price index covering stock of high-technology companies

National Association of Insurance Commissioners INSURANCE, REGULATION & COMPLIANCE US group of insurance regulators in the United States, an organization that brings together the state regulators of insurance. *Abbr* ***NAIC***

National Association of Investors Corporation STOCKHOLDING & INVESTMENTS US organization promoting investment clubs in the United States, an organization that fosters the creation and development of ***investment clubs***. *Abbr* ***NAIC***

National Association of Securities Dealers STOCKHOLDING & INVESTMENTS, REGULATION & COMPLIANCE US organization for traders in securities in the United States, the self-regulatory organization for securities dealers that develops rules and regulations, conducts regulatory reviews of members' business activities, and designs and operates marketplace services facilities. It is responsible for the regulation of the NASDAQ securities market. Established in 1938, it operates subject to the Securities Exchange Commission oversight and has a membership that includes virtually every US broker or dealer doing securities business with the public. *Abbr* ***NASD***

National Audit Office REGULATION & COMPLIANCE UK organization monitoring public spending an independent nongovernmental body in the United Kingdom that examines public spending. The NAO audits the accounts of government agencies and departments, reporting back to Parliament with the results. An officer of the House of Commons, the Comptroller and Auditor General, runs the NAO. It has offices in London, Newcastle, Cardiff, and Blackpool. *Abbr* ***NAO***

national bank BANKING **1.** central bank of state a bank owned or controlled by the state that acts as a bank for a government and implements its monetary policies **2.** US bank in Federal Reserve in the United States, a bank that operates under federal charter and is legally required to be a member of the ***Federal Reserve***

National Credit Union Administration REGULATION & COMPLIANCE US government organization overseeing credit unions in the United States, a federal agency that charters and supervises federal ***credit unions*** and insures savings in federal and most state-chartered credit unions through a fund backed by the US government

national debt ECONOMICS amount of government borrowing the total amount of money that a country's central government has borrowed and is still unpaid

national demand ECONOMICS overall need for products in country's economy the total demand for goods and services made by consumers in an economy

National Guarantee Fund MARKETS insurance fund of Australian Stock Exchange a supply of money held by the Australian Stock Exchange which is used to compensate investors for losses incurred when an exchange member fails to meet its obligations

national income ECONOMICS country's total earnings from goods and services the total earnings from a country's production of goods and services in a specific year

national income accounts FINANCE statistical information on country's economy economic statistics that show the state of a nation's economy over a given period of time, usually a year. *See also* ***GDP, GNP***

National Insurance PENSIONS UK social insurance plan for all adults in the United Kingdom, a compulsory state social insurance plan to which employees and employers contribute. *Abbr* ***NI***. *See also* ***Social Security***

National Insurance contributions PENSIONS money paid into UK social insurance plan in the United Kingdom, payments made by both employers and employees to the government. The contributions, together with other government receipts, are used to finance pensions given by the government and other benefits such as welfare. *Abbr* ***NIC***

National Insurance number PENSIONS person's identifying number for UK social insurance plan a unique number allocated to each UK citizen at the age of 16. It allows HM Revenue & Customs and the Department for Work and Pensions to record contributions and credit them to each person's account. *See also* ***Social Security number***

nationalization GENERAL MANAGEMENT transferring of private firms to state ownership the taking over of privately owned companies by government. Nationalization has strong political connotations. Recent global political trends had moved away from nationalization by introducing more competition and liberalization into markets before the banking crisis of 2008 caused governments to take considerable holdings in financial institutions to save them from collapse. *See also* ***privatization***

National Market System MARKETS system encouraging competition between US stock exchanges in the United States, an inter-exchange network system designed to foster greater competition between domestic stock exchanges. Legislated for in 1975, it was implemented in 1978 with the *Intermarket Trading System* that electronically links eight markets: American, Boston, Cincinnati, Chicago, New York, Pacific, Philadelphia, and the NASD over-the-counter market. It allows traders at any exchange to seek the best available price on all other exchanges that a specific security is eligible to trade on. *Abbr* ***NMS***

National Savings & Investments STOCKHOLDING & INVESTMENTS UK government agency for savings and investment in the United Kingdom, a government agency accountable to the Treasury that offers a variety of savings and investment products directly to the public or through post offices. The funds raised finance government borrowing (the ***national debt***).

National Savings Bank BANKING UK savings plan in the United Kingdom, a savings plan established in 1861 as the Post Office Savings Bank and now operated by National Savings & Investments. *Abbr* ***NSB***

National Savings Certificate STOCKHOLDING & INVESTMENTS UK investment providing tax-free income in the United Kingdom, either a fixed-interest or an index-linked certificate issued for two- or five-year terms by National Savings & Investments with returns that are free of income tax. *Abbr* ***NSC***

National Society of Accountants ACCOUNTING US association of financial professionals in the United States, a non-profit organization of some 17,000 professionals who provide accounting, tax preparation, financial and estate planning, and management advisory services to an estimated 19 million individuals and business clients. Most of the NSA's members are individual practitioners or partners in small to mid-size accounting and tax firms. *Abbr* ***NSA***

natural capitalism ECONOMICS capitalism incorporating environmentalism an approach to capitalism in which protection of the Earth's resources is a strategic priority

natural disaster INSURANCE disaster caused by forces of nature a catastrophe that occurs as a result of forces of nature. Natural disasters include hurricanes, tornados, severe storms, floods, tsunamis, earthquakes, and volcanic eruptions.

NAV *abbr* STOCKHOLDING & INVESTMENTS ***net asset value***

NBV *abbr* ACCOUNTING ***net book value***

NDA *abbr* HR & PERSONNEL **1.** ***nondisclosure agreement*** **2.** ***nondisparagement agreement***

NDP *abbr* ECONOMICS ***net domestic product***

nearby futures contract STOCKHOLDING & INVESTMENTS option with closest delivery date a futures option with the earliest delivery date of those being considered. *See also* ***most distant futures contract***

nearby month STOCKHOLDING & INVESTMENTS next month with futures contract available the earliest month for which there is a ***futures contract*** for a specific commodity. *Also called* ***spot month***. *See also* ***far month***

near-cash STOCKHOLDING & INVESTMENTS easy to convert to cash used to describe an investment that can be quickly converted to cash

near money STOCKHOLDING & INVESTMENTS assets easily cashed in assets such as some types of bank deposit, short-dated bonds, and certificates of deposit that can quickly be turned into cash. *See also* ***quick asset***

negative amortization FINANCE addition to principal following incomplete interest payments an increase in the ***principal*** of a loan due to the inadequacy of payments to cover the interest

negative carry FINANCE when interest payments exceed income on loan interest that is so high that the borrowed money does not return enough profit to cover the cost of borrowing

negative cash flow FINANCE higher expenditures than income a cash flow in which expenditures are higher than income

negative equity FINANCE when property is worth less than it cost a situation in which a fall in prices leads to a property being worth less than was paid for it

negative gearing FINANCE, TAX borrowing money that earns less than interest payments the practice of borrowing money to invest in property or stocks and claiming a tax deduction on the difference between the income and the interest payments

negative goodwill MERGERS & ACQUISITIONS value of company's assets above price paid the gain that a company has when a company it acquires has assets with a market value greater than the price the acquiring company paid for them

negative income tax TAX US tax credits to raise income levels in the United States, payments such as tax credits made to households or individuals to increase their income to a guaranteed minimum level

negative pledge clause STOCKHOLDING & INVESTMENTS condition preventing bond issuer from disadvantaging holders a provision in a bond agreement that prohibits the issuer from doing something that would give an advantage to holders of other bonds

negative yield curve STOCKHOLDING & INVESTMENTS graph plotting interest rates against different maturities a visual representation of relative interest rates showing that they are higher for short-term bonds than they are for long-term bonds

negligence GENERAL MANAGEMENT failure to act responsibly a breach of a duty to act with expected care in conducting activities, resulting in harm to one or more people. Negligence occurs when an organization causes harm or injury through carelessness or inattention to the needs of the groups to which it owes a duty of care. These can include its customers, consumers of its product or service, shareholders, or the local community. Victims of negligence are entitled to claim compensation. Negligence is considered to be ***gross negligence*** if it is the result of excessively careless behavior.

negotiable FINANCE transferable or cashable able to be transfered from one person to another or exchanged for cash

negotiable certificate of deposit FINANCE certificate of deposit that can change hands freely a certificate of deposit with a very high value that can be freely traded

negotiable instrument *or* **negotiable paper** FINANCE document promising to pay cash to holder a document that can be exchanged for cash, for example, a bill of exchange or a check

negotiable order of withdrawal BANKING in US, check drawn on savings account in the United States, a check drawn on a type of savings account that bears interest but allows withdrawals

negotiable order of withdrawal account BANKING = ***NOW account***

negotiable security STOCKHOLDING & INVESTMENTS security that can change ownership a security that can be freely traded to bring its owner some benefit

negotiate FINANCE **1.** sell financial instruments to transfer ownership of financial instruments such as bearer securities, bills of exchange, checks, and promissory notes to somebody else in exchange for money **2.** discuss to agree price of item to reach an agreed price with a buyer or seller by the gradual raising of offers and lowering of the price asked until a mutually agreeable price is reached

negotiated commission FINANCE brokers' commission discussed and agreed with customers a commission that results from bargaining between brokers and their customers, typically large institutions

negotiated issue STOCKHOLDING & INVESTMENTS = ***negotiated offering***

negotiated market MARKETS market where buyers and sellers bargain over prices a market in which each transaction results from negotiation between a buyer and a seller

negotiated offering STOCKHOLDING & INVESTMENTS offer at price negotiated with underwriting syndicate a ***public offering*** of stock, the price of which is determined by negotiations between the issuer and an ***underwriting syndicate***. *Also called* ***negotiated issue***

negotiated sale FINANCE offer at price negotiated with one underwriter a ***public offering*** of stock, the price of which is determined by negotiations between the issuer and a single underwriter

negotiation GENERAL MANAGEMENT attempt to reach agreement a discussion with the goal of resolving a difference of opinion or dispute, or to settle the terms of an agreement or transaction

neoclassical economics ECONOMICS economic theory emphasizing free markets an economic theory that emphasizes the need for the free operation of market forces through supply and demand

nest egg FINANCE savings for retirement savings, usually other than a pension plan or retirement account, that have been set aside for use in somebody's retirement (*informal*)

nester MARKETING person not easily affected by advertising in advertising or marketing, a consumer who is not influenced by advertising hype but prefers value for money and traditional products (*slang*)

net 1. FINANCE remaining after deductions have been made used to describe the amount of something such as a price or salary remaining after all deductions have been made **2.** ACCOUNTING earn amount as profit to make a profit after all expenses have been taken into account

net advantage of refunding ACCOUNTING money raised by replacing debt the amount gained by renewing the funding of debt after interest rates have fallen

net advantage to leasing ACCOUNTING cost difference between leasing and borrowing to buy the amount by which leasing something is financially better than borrowing money and purchasing it

net advantage to merging MERGERS & ACQUISITIONS value gained after merging firms the amount by which the value of a merged enterprise exceeds the value of the preexisting companies, minus the cost of the merger

net assets ACCOUNTING value of assets minus liabilities the amount by which the value of a company's assets exceeds its liabilities, representing its capital

net asset value STOCKHOLDING & INVESTMENTS firm's net market value the value of a company's stock assessed by subtracting any liabilities from the market value. *Abbr* ***NAV***

net asset value per share ACCOUNTING, STOCKHOLDING & INVESTMENTS firm's net market value divided by share number the value of a company's stock assessed by subtracting any liabilities from the market value and dividing the remainder by the number of shares of stock issued

NetBill® E-COMMERCE means of buying digital goods over Internet a micropayment system developed at Carnegie Mellon University for purchasing digital goods over the Internet. After the goods are delivered in encrypted form to the purchaser's computer, the money is debited from the purchaser's prefunded account and the goods are decrypted for the purchaser's use.

net book value ACCOUNTING original cost of asset minus depreciation the historical cost of an asset less any accumulated depreciation or other provision for diminution in value, for example, reduction to net realizable value, or asset value which has been revalued downward to reflect market conditions. *Abbr* ***NBV***. *Also called* ***written-down value***

net borrowings ACCOUNTING borrowings minus cash available the total of all borrowings less the cash in bank accounts and on deposit

net capital ACCOUNTING net assets minus noncash assets the amount by which net assets exceed the value of assets not easily converted to cash

net cash balance ACCOUNTING value of ready cash on a balance sheet, the amount of cash recorded as on hand

net cash flow ACCOUNTING difference between cash inflows and outflows the difference between the amount of money coming in and going out of an organization

net change MARKETS difference between prices on successive days the difference between the price of a security at the close of business from one day to the next

net change on the day MARKETS difference between opening and closing prices the difference between the opening price of a stock at the beginning of a day's trading and the closing price at the end

NetCheque™ E-COMMERCE means of exchanging electronic checks a trademark for an electronic payment system developed at the University of Southern California to allow users to write electronic checks to one another

net current assets ACCOUNTING assets minus liabilities the amount by which the value of a company's current assets exceeds its current liabilities. *Also called* ***net working capital***

net dividend STOCKHOLDING & INVESTMENTS worth of dividend after tax the value of a dividend after the recipient has paid tax on it

net domestic product ECONOMICS total national economic output with factors deducted the figure produced after factors such as depreciation have been deducted from ***GDP***. *Abbr* ***NDP***

net errors and omissions ACCOUNTING size of discrepancies in accounting the net amount of the discrepancies that arise in the calculation of a balance of payments

net exports FINANCE total exports minus total imports a figure showing the total value of exports less the total value of imports

net fixed assets ACCOUNTING worth of fixed assets after depreciation the value of fixed assets after depreciation as shown on a balance sheet

net foreign factor income FINANCE gross national minus gross domestic product income from outside a country, constituting the amount by which a country's gross national product exceeds its gross domestic product

net income ACCOUNTING **1.** income minus expenditures an organization's income less the costs incurred to generate it **2.** income after tax gross income less tax that has been deducted **3.** earnings after tax and other deductions a salary or wage less tax and other statutory deductions. *See also* ***disposable income***

net interest FINANCE interest after tax gross interest less tax that has been deducted

net investment STOCKHOLDING & INVESTMENTS capital invested minus estimated capital consumption an increase in the total capital invested. It is calculated as gross capital invested less an estimated figure for capital consumption or depreciation.

net lease REAL ESTATE lease where lessee pays operating costs a lease that requires the lessee to pay for things that the owner usually pays for. *See also* ***gross lease***

net liquid funds ACCOUNTING money plus salable investments minus short-term borrowings an organization's cash plus its marketable investments less its short-term borrowings such as overdrafts and loans

net loss ACCOUNTING loss taking all expenses into consideration a loss calculated after the deduction of overhead and other expenses

net margin ACCOUNTING percentage of income that is profit the percentage of revenues that is profit, often used an an indicator of cost control

net national product FINANCE national income a country's ***GNP*** adjusted to deduct capital depreciation during the period in question. *Abbr* ***NNP***

net operating income ACCOUNTING income minus expenses the amount by which income exceeds expenditure, before considering taxes, interest, and other expenses

net operating margin ACCOUNTING income minus expenses as percentage of revenues ***net operating income*** as a percentage of revenues. It is an indicator of profitability.

net pay FINANCE total pay minus deductions the amount of pay an employee receives after all deductions such as income tax, social security, or pension contributions. *Also called* ***take-home pay***. *See also* ***disposable income***

net position STOCKHOLDING & INVESTMENTS balance of long and short positions the difference between an investor's long and short ***positions*** in the same security

net present value ACCOUNTING cash inflows minus cash outflows the value of an investment calculated as the sum of its initial cost and the ***present value*** of expected future cash flows.

A positive NPV indicates that the project should be profitable, assuming that the estimated cash flows are reasonably accurate. A negative NPV indicates that the project will probably be unprofitable and therefore should be adjusted, if not abandoned altogether.

NPV enables management to consider the time-value of money it will invest. This concept holds that the value of money increases with time because it can always earn interest in a savings account. When the time-value-of-money concept is incorporated in the calculation of NPV, the value of a project's future net cash receipts in "today's money" can be determined. This enables proper comparisons between different projects.

For example, if Global Manufacturing Inc. is considering the acquisition of a new machine, its management will consider all the factors: initial purchase and installation costs; additional revenues generated by sales of the new machine's products, plus the taxes on these new revenues. Having accounted for these factors in its calculations, the cash flows that Global Manufacturing projects will generate from the new machine are:

Year 1	–100,000 (initial cost of investment)
Year 2	30,000
Year 3	40,000
Year 4	40,000
Year 5	35,000
Net Total	145,000

At first glance, it appears that cash flows total 45% more than the $100,000 initial cost, a sound investment indeed. But the time-value of money shrinks the return on the project considerably, since future dollars are worth less than present dollars in hand. NPV accounts for these differences with the help of present-value tables, which list the ratios that express the present value of expected cash flow dollars, based on the applicable interest rate and the number of years in question.

In the example, Global Manufacturing's cost of capital is 9%. Using this figure to find the corresponding ratios on the present value table, the $100,000 investment cost and expected annual revenues during the five years in question, the NPV calculation looks like this:

Year	Cash flow	Table factor (at 9%)	Present value
1	($100,000) ×	1.000000 =	($100,000)
2	$30,000 ×	0.917431 =	$27,522.93
3	$40,000 ×	0.841680 =	$33,667.20
4	$40,000 ×	0.772183 =	$30,887.32
5	$35,000 ×	0.708425 =	$24,794.88
		NPV =	$16,873.33

NPV is still positive. So, on this basis at least, the investment should proceed. *Abbr* ***NPV***

net price OPERATIONS & PRODUCTION price actually paid the price paid for goods or services after all relevant discounts have been deducted

net proceeds ACCOUNTING gains from transaction minus its cost the amount received from a transaction minus the cost of making it

net profit ACCOUNTING income after expenses an organization's income as shown in a ***profit and loss account*** after all relevant expenses have been deducted. *Also called* ***profit after tax***

net profit margin ACCOUNTING, OPERATIONS & PRODUCTION *see* ***profit margin***

net profit ratio ACCOUNTING ratio of net profit to net sales the ratio of an organization's net profit to its total net sales. Comparing the net profit ratios of companies in the same sector shows which are the most efficient.

net realizable value ACCOUNTING selling price minus costs the value of an asset if sold, allowing for costs

net receipts ACCOUNTING income after all deductions have been made receipts calculated after the deduction of commission, tax, discounts, and other associated expenses. *See also* ***gross receipts***

net relevant earnings TAX income for pension-contribution purposes earnings which qualify for calculating pension contributions and against which relief against tax can be claimed. Such earnings can be income from employment which is not pensionable, for example, the profits of a self-employed sole trader.

net residual value ACCOUNTING value of asset being disposed of the anticipated proceeds of an asset at the end of its useful life, less the costs such as transportation and the commission associated with selling it. It is used when calculating the annual charge for ***straight line depreciation***. *Abbr* ***NRV***

net return ACCOUNTING profit from investment after expenditures the amount received from an investment, taking taxes and transaction costs into account

net salary FINANCE earnings after all deductions have been made the salary remaining after deductions for taxes, social security, medicare, and any employee share of insurance premiums. *See also* ***disposable income***

net sales ACCOUNTING actual value of sales a company's total sales less any relevant discounts such as those given to retailers

net salvage value ACCOUNTING value of project being abandoned, after tax the amount of money remaining after a project has been terminated, taking tax consequences into consideration

net tangible assets ACCOUNTING firm's total assets minus intangible assets the total assets of a company less its intangible assets such as goodwill or intellectual property. *Abbr* ***NTA***

netting MARKETS carrying only net result forward a method of settling financial transactions in which only the net result in a transaction is carried forward

network culture GENERAL MANAGEMENT attitudes and behavior of global networks cultural patterns that are heavily influenced by communication using global networks

net working capital ACCOUNTING = ***net current assets***

network management GENERAL MANAGEMENT supervision of functioning of computer network the coordinated control of computer systems and programs to allow access to and delivery of information to a number of users

network marketing MARKETING trading through independent agents the selling of goods or services through a network of self-employed agents or representatives. Network marketing usually involves several levels of agents, each level on a different commission rate. Each agent is encouraged to recruit other agents. In genuine network marketing, in contrast to ***pyramid selling***, there is an end product or service sold to customers. Another version of network marketing is the loose cooperative relationship between a company, its competitors, collaborators, suppliers, and other organizations affecting the overall marketing function. *Also called* ***multilevel marketing***

network organization GENERAL MANAGEMENT loose association of teams a company or group of companies that has a minimum of formal structures and relies instead on the formation and dissolution of teams to meet specific objectives. A network organization utilizes information and communications technologies extensively, and makes use of knowledge across and within companies along the ***value chain***. *See also* ***virtual organization***

network revolution GENERAL MANAGEMENT dramatic change arising from global networks the fundamental change in business practices triggered by the growth of global networks

network society GENERAL MANAGEMENT society dependent on global networks a society in which patterns of work, communication, and government are characterized by the use of global networks

net worth ACCOUNTING assets minus liabilities the difference between the assets and liabilities of a person or company

net yield ACCOUNTING rate of return after costs and tax the amount produced by an investment after deducting all costs and taxes

new economy ECONOMICS economic system based on e-commerce a term used in the late 1990s and 2000s to describe the e-commerce sector and the ***digital economy***, in which firms mostly trade online rather than in the bricks and mortar of physical premises

new entrant MARKETING new arrival in market or sector an organization or product that has recently come into a market or sector

new issue STOCKHOLDING & INVESTMENTS **1.** new security on sale for first time a new security, such as a bond or stock, being offered to the public for the first time. *See also* ***float, initial public offering*** **2.** issue of new security an additional issue of an existing security, for example, a ***rights issue***

new issue market *or* **new issues market** MARKETS market into which new stock is launched a market where companies can raise finance by issuing additional shares or by a flotation. *See also* ***float, initial public offering, primary market***

newly acquired business BUSINESS business recently bought by another a business in the early stages of the changes caused by having been bought by another company

newly industrialized economy ECONOMICS nation benefiting from industrialization a country whose industrialization has recently started to develop. Mexico and Malaysia are examples of newly industrialized economies.

new metrics GENERAL MANAGEMENT nontraditional standards for measuring business performance standards for measuring or quantifying the activities and success of an organization that incorporate nontraditional approaches

new money FINANCE financing from a new source financing provided by an issue of new shares of stock or by the transfer of money from one account to another

new product development MARKETING stages of bringing something new to market the processes involved in getting a new product or service to market. The traditional ***product development cycle***, the ***stage-gate model***, embraces the conception, generation, analysis, development, testing, marketing, and commercialization of new products or services. Alternative models of new product development fall into two broad categories: ***accelerating time to market models*** and ***integrated implementation models***. These strive to achieve both flexibility and acceleration of development. All activities such as design, production planning, and test marketing are performed in parallel rather than going through a sequential linear progression. *Abbr* ***NPD***

new time MARKETS when stock exchange sales are carried over the period on a stock exchange when sales in the last few days of the previous account are credited to the following account

New York Mercantile Exchange MARKETS US exchange for energy and precious metals the world's largest physical commodity exchange and North America's most important trading exchange for energy and precious metals. It deals in crude oil, gasoline, heating oil, natural gas, propane, gold, silver, platinum, palladium, and copper. *Abbr* ***NYMEX***

New York Stock Exchange MARKETS stock exchange in New York the leading stock exchange in New York, which is self-regulatory but has to comply with the regulations of the US Securities and Exchange Commission. *Abbr* ***NYSE***

New York Stock Exchange Composite Index MARKETS New York stock price index an index designed to track the change in the market value of all common stocks listed on the New York Stock Exchange

New Zealand Stock Exchange MARKETS New Zealand's main market for securities the principal market in New Zealand for trading in securities. It was established in 1981, replacing the Stock Exchange Association of New Zealand and a number of regional trading floors. *Abbr* ***NZSE***

New Zealand Trade Development Board FINANCE New Zealand agency promoting exports and inward investment a government body responsible for promoting New Zealand exports and facilitating foreign investment in New Zealand. *Also called* ***TRADENZ***

next futures contract STOCKHOLDING & INVESTMENTS option for following month an ***option*** to buy or sell for the month after the current month

NI *abbr* PENSIONS ***National Insurance***

NIC *abbr* PENSIONS ***National Insurance contributions***

niche bank *or* **niche banker** BANKING specialist banker a bank or banker specializing in a specific field such as management buyouts

niche company BUSINESS specialist firm a company that produces a product or service that fills a specialized gap in the overall provision of a market

niche market MARKETING specialized market segment a very specialized market segment within a broader segment. A niche market involves specialist goods or services with relatively few or no competitors. Customers may look for exclusiveness or some other differentiating factor such as high status. Alternatively, they may have a specific requirement not satisfied by standard products. *See also* ***micromarketing***

niche player (*informal*) **1.** BANKING = ***niche bank*** **2.** STOCKHOLDING & INVESTMENTS = ***boutique investment house***

nickel *US* FINANCE small margin five hundredths of one percent, expressing a fine margin (*slang*)

NIF *abbr* FINANCE ***note issuance facility***

Nifty Fifty *US* MARKETS institutional investors' favorite stocks the 50 most popular stocks among institutional investors on the New York Stock Exchange from the 1960s until the early 1970s (*informal*)

Nikkei 225 *or* **Nikkei Index** MARKETS Japanese stock price index an index of stock prices on the Tokyo Stock Exchange, the largest stock exchange in Japan

nil paid STOCKHOLDING & INVESTMENTS nothing paid yet with no money yet paid. In the United Kingdom, the term is used in reference to the purchase of newly issued stocks, or to the stocks themselves, when the stockholder entitled to buy new stocks has not yet made a commitment to do so and may sell the rights instead.

nil return *UK* TAX report of no taxable income a report filed with a tax authority showing no transactions or income on which tax is owed

ninja loan FINANCE loan made to somebody with poor credit rating a loan made to somebody who has No INcome, No Job, and no Assets (*slang*). *See also* ***subprime loan***

NMS *abbr* MARKETS ***National Market System***

NNP *abbr* FINANCE ***net national product***

no-claims bonus *or* **no-claims discount** INSURANCE reduced insurance price because no claims are made a reduction of premiums on an insurance policy because no claims have been made

noise GENERAL MANAGEMENT distracting unimportant data irrelevant or insignificant data which overload a feedback process. The presence of noise can confuse or divert attention from relevant information; efficiency in a system is enhanced as the ratio of information to noise increases.

noise trader MARKETS uninformed market participant a participant in the stock market who does not have much knowledge about the securities being traded (*slang*)

no-load fund STOCKHOLDING & INVESTMENTS mutual fund with no fee for trading a mutual fund that does not charge a fee for the purchase or sale of shares. *See also* ***load fund***

nominal 1. FINANCE very much lower than usual level very small when compared with what would be considered usual, especially with reference to a sum of money **2.** ACCOUNTING relating to current prices considered in terms of the stated or original value only, without adjustment for inflation and other changes **3.** GENERAL MANAGEMENT assigned by name assigned to a specific name or category

nominal account ACCOUNTING account recording items according to category a record of revenues and expenditures, liabilities and assets classified by their nature, for example, sales, rent, rates, electricity, wages, or share capital

nominal annual rate FINANCE = ***annual percentage rate***

nominal capital STOCKHOLDING & INVESTMENTS = ***nominal share capital***

nominal cash flow ACCOUNTING cash flow disregarding inflation cash flow in terms of currency, without adjustment for inflation

nominal exchange rate CURRENCY & EXCHANGE stated exchange rate the exchange rate as specified, without adjustment for transaction costs or differences in purchasing power

nominal interest rate FINANCE stated interest rate the interest rate as specified, without adjustment for compounding or inflation

nominal ledger *UK* ACCOUNTING ledger recording money values a record of revenue, operating expenses, assets, and capital

nominal price OPERATIONS & PRODUCTION price disregarding value the price of an item being sold when the price is lower than the full value

nominal share capital STOCKHOLDING & INVESTMENTS maximum amount of firm's share capital the total value of all of a corporation's stock at ***nominal value***. *Also called* **nominal capital**. *See also* ***authorized share capital***

nominal value STOCKHOLDING & INVESTMENTS original value of new stock the original value officially given to a newly issued stock. *Also called* **par value**. *See also* ***capitalization, reserves***

nominal yield STOCKHOLDING & INVESTMENTS dividend as percentage of face value the dividend paid on a share of stock expressed as a percentage of its face value

nominee 1. FINANCE in US, somebody acting for another in the United States, a person who is appointed to deal with financial matters on your behalf **2.** *US* STOCKHOLDING & INVESTMENTS holder of security on another's behalf a financial institution, or an individual employed by such an institution, that holds a security on behalf of the actual owner. While this may be to hide the owner's identity, for example, in the case of a celebrity, it is also to allow an institution managing any individual's portfolio to conduct transactions without the need for the owner to sign the required paperwork. *UK term* ***nominee name***

nominee account BANKING account not in owner's name an account held not in the name of the real owner of the account, but instead in the name of another person, organization, or financial institution. Stocks can be bought and held in nominee accounts so that the owner's identity is not disclosed.

nominee name *UK* STOCKHOLDING & INVESTMENTS = ***nominee***

nonacceptance BANKING rejection of bill of exchange on presentation a refusal to accept a bill of exchange when it is presented, by the person on whom it is drawn

nonbranded goods MARKETING items from unidentified source generic goods such as food produce, pharmaceuticals, or computer keyboards that are not linked to a specific ***brand*** name, manufacturer, or producer. Nonbranded goods are often widely available in street markets or by mail order and are often perceived to be of low quality.

nonbusiness days BANKING days when banks are closed those days when banks are not open for business, for example, public holidays, or Saturdays and Sundays in Western countries

noncallable STOCKHOLDING & INVESTMENTS not able to be repurchased before maturity used to describe a security that the issuer cannot buy back before its maturity date. *See also* ***callable***

noncash item 1. ACCOUNTING entry in income statement not representing cash an item, such as a gain or loss from an investment or depreciation expenses, that occurs on an income statement and is not a receipt of actual money **2.** BANKING financial instruments representing money checks, drafts, and similar items that have money value but are not money themselves

noncompetitive bid MARKETS purchasing US Treasury security at average competitive bid price a method of purchasing US Treasury securities through member banks of the ***Federal Reserve*** in which a buyer agrees to pay a price equal to the average of all competitive bids for that particular week's issue of securities

nonconformance costs OPERATIONS & PRODUCTION = ***quality costs***

nonconforming loan TAX loan not meeting usual conditions a loan that does not conform to the lender's standards, especially those of a US government agency

noncontributory pension plan *US* PENSIONS pension plan financed by employer a pension plan to which the employee makes no payments. *UK term* ***non-contributory pension scheme***

non-contributory pension scheme *UK* PENSIONS = ***noncontributory pension plan***

noncurrent assets FINANCE long-term investments resources that are expected to be held for more than one year. They are reported at the lower of cost and current market value, which means that their values will vary.

nondeductible ACCOUNTING not admissible as deduction not allowed to be deducted from a payment, especially not acceptable as an allowance against income tax

nondisclosure agreement HR & PERSONNEL agreement not to give away company secrets a legally enforceable agreement preventing present or past employees from disclosing commercially sensitive information belonging to the employer to any other party. A nondisclosure agreement can remain in force for several years after an employee leaves a company. In the event of a dispute, a company may be required to prove that the information in question belongs to the company itself, is not in the public domain, or cannot be obtained elsewhere. *Abbr* ***NDA***

nondisparagement agreement HR & PERSONNEL agreement not to criticize employer an agreement that prevents present or past employees from criticizing an employing organization in public. Nondisparagement agreements are a relatively new type of agreement and have arisen primarily to prevent employees putting comments about their employing organization onto the Internet. Case law has yet to determine whether such agreements are legally binding. *Abbr* ***NDA***

nondom *or* **non-domicile** TAX person not paying tax on earnings abroad a person who is exempt from paying tax on foreign earnings because his or her permanent home is in another country

nonexecutive director CORPORATE GOVERNANCE board member without day-to-day involvement a part-time, nonsalaried member of the ***board of directors***, involved in the planning, strategy, and policy making of an organization but not in its day-to-day operations. The appointment of a nonexecutive director to a board is usually made in order to provide independence and balance to that board, and to ensure that good ***corporate governance*** is practiced. A nonexecutive director may be selected for the prestige they bring or for their experience, contacts, or specialist knowledge. *Also called* ***part-time director***. *See also* ***outside director***

nonfinancial asset ACCOUNTING not money or financial contract an asset such as real estate or personal property that is neither money nor a financial instrument

non-financial incentive scheme FINANCE UK program rewarding performance other than with money in the United Kingdom, a program offering benefits such as additional paid vacations, set up to reward employees for improved commitment and performance and as a means of motivation. *See also* ***financial incentive scheme***

noninterest-bearing bond STOCKHOLDING & INVESTMENTS bond with discount rather than interest a bond that is sold at a discount instead of with a promise to pay interest

nonjudicial foreclosure LEGAL in US, reclamation of property without using court in the United States, a foreclosure on real estate without recourse to a court. The mortgage lender issues a notice of mortgage default to the owner, along with a notice of intent to sell the property.

nonline E-COMMERCE not online not provided with an Internet connection, or not done via the Internet

nonlinear programming STATISTICS using some nonlinear equations a process in which the equations expressing the interactions of variables are not all linear but may, for example, be in proportion to the square of a variable

nonline community E-COMMERCE people not using e-mail or Internet the people who do not use e-mail or the Internet for communications, information, or purchasing

nonnegotiable instrument FINANCE financial contract that cannot change hands a financial instrument that cannot be signed over to anyone else. These include ***bills of exchange*** and ***crossed checks***.

nonoperational balances BANKING Bank of England deposits that cannot be withdrawn accounts that banks maintain at the Bank of England without the power of withdrawal

nonparticipating preferred stock STOCKHOLDING & INVESTMENTS preferred stock paying fixed dividend the most common type of preferred stock that pays a fixed dividend regardless of the profitability of the company. *See also* ***participating preferred stock***

nonperforming asset STOCKHOLDING & INVESTMENTS asset providing no income an asset that is not producing income, for example, one that is no longer accruing interest

nonperforming loan FINANCE loan made to borrower likely to default a loan made to a borrower who is not likely to pay any interest nor to repay the principal

nonprofit organization *or* **nonprofit** BUSINESS organization not operated solely for profit an ***organization*** that does not have financial profit as a main strategic objective. Nonprofit organizations include charities, professional associations, labor unions, and religious, arts, community, research, and campaigning bodies. These organizations are not situated in either the ***public*** or ***private sectors***, but in what has been called the *third sector*. Many have paid staff and working capital but their main purpose is not to provide a product or service, but to effect change. They are led by values rather than financial commitments to shareholders. *Abbr* ***NPO***. *See also* ***third sector***

nonqualified annuity PENSIONS US annuity bought with taxed income in the United States, a type of annuity that can be purchased with after-tax income to provide retirement income. Taxes on earnings from the annuity are deferred until money is withdrawn.

nonrandom sampling OPERATIONS & PRODUCTION sampling with unequal chances of selection a ***sampling*** technique that is used when it cannot be ensured that each item has an equal chance of being selected, or when selection is based on expert knowledge of the population. *See also* ***random sampling***

nonrecourse debt FINANCE debt with no liability a debt for which the borrower has no personal responsibility, typically a debt of a limited partnership

nonrecoverable FINANCE that will never be paid back used to describe a debt that will never be paid, for example, because of the borrower's bankruptcy

nonrecurring charge ACCOUNTING unique charge a charge that is made only once

nonrecurring item ACCOUNTING unique item in account in a set of accounts an item that is included on only one occasion

nonresident TAX working abroad used to describe somebody who has left his or her native country to work overseas for a period. Nonresidency has tax advantages, such as exemption from tax on overseas earning. While a US citizen is working overseas for a period of 11 out of 12 months, a limited amount of his or her earned income generated overseas is exempt from US income tax. During a period of nonresidency, many expatriates choose to bank offshore.

Non-Resident Withholding Tax TAX New Zealand levy on nonresidents' investment income a duty imposed by the New Zealand government on interest and dividends earned by a nonresident from investments. *Abbr* ***NRWT***

nonstore retailing *or* E-COMMERCE selling over Internet without building to visit the selling of goods and services electronically without actually establishing a physical store

nonstrategic BUSINESS not related to achievement of long-term goals not related to the long-term objectives of an organization or the resources used to achieve those objectives

non-sufficient funds *UK* BANKING = ***insufficient funds***

nonsystematic risk RISK risk related to particular firm investment risk that is attributable to the performance of a specific company, not to the performance of the stock market or economy, and can be reduced by diversification

nontariff barrier INTERNATIONAL TRADE regulations that make imports more difficult a country's economic regulation on something such as safety standards that impedes imports, often from emerging markets. *Abbr* ***NTB***

nontaxable TAX not liable to tax not subject to tax. In the United Kingdom, interest from ***ISAs***, prize winnings, and statutory redundancy pay are among non-taxable sources of income.

nonvoting share STOCKHOLDING & INVESTMENTS common stock receiving dividend but not voting rights common stock that is paid a dividend from the company's profits, but that does not entitle the stockholder to vote at any meeting of stockholders. Such stock is unpopular with institutional investors. *Also called* ***A share***

norm STATISTICS expected range of values for set in a statistical study, a range of values that is normal for a population or other set

normal distribution STATISTICS expected distribution of random variable in a statistical study, the probability distribution of a random variable

normal profit ECONOMICS minimum profit required for business the minimum level of profit that will attract an entrepreneur to begin a business or remain trading

normal yield curve STOCKHOLDING & INVESTMENTS showing lower yields for short-term bonds a visual representation of interest rates showing higher yields for long-term bonds than for short-term bonds. *See also* ***yield curve***

no-strike agreement HR & PERSONNEL arrangement with union not to call strike a formal understanding between an employer and a labor union that the union will not call its members out on strike. A no-strike agreement is usually won by the employer in exchange for improved terms and conditions of employment, including pay, and sometimes guaranteed employment.

nostro account BANKING account with bank abroad an account that a bank has with a ***correspondent bank*** in another country

notary public LEGAL somebody with authority to officially witness documents a person who has been authorized by a state to witness documents, making them legally accepted, and to administer oaths

notch *S. Africa* HR & PERSONNEL point on scale a position on a scale such as an incremental salary scale

note 1. CURRENCY & EXCHANGE item of paper money a piece of paper money printed by a bank and approved as legal tender. *Also called* ***banknote (sense 1), bill (sense 2)*** **2.** FINANCE document promising to repay borrowed money a written promise to repay money that has been borrowed

note issuance facility FINANCE facility for buying and reselling Eurocurrency notes a credit facility where a company obtains a loan underwritten by banks and can issue a series of short-term ***Eurocurrency*** notes to replace others that have expired. *Abbr* ***NIF***

note of hand FINANCE = ***promissory note***

notes to the accounts *or* **notes to the financial statements** ACCOUNTING information supporting account entries an explanation of specific items in a set of accounts

not-for-profit FINANCE not operated to generate income organized typically for a charitable, humanitarian, or educational purpose and not generating profits for shareholders. In the United States, not-for-profit corporations can apply for tax-exempt status at both the federal and state levels of government. *See also* ***nonprofit organization***

notice of coding TAX information about another's tax code a notice that informs a third party of the code number given to indicate the amount of tax allowances to which somebody is entitled

notice of default *US* LEGAL official notification to defaulter a formal document issued by a lender to a borrower who is in default. *UK term* ***default notice***

notice period HR & PERSONNEL time between resignation or dismissal and leaving the amount of time specified in the terms and ***conditions of employment*** that an ***employee*** must work between resigning from an organization and leaving the employment of that organization

notifying bank BANKING, INTERNATIONAL TRADE = ***advising bank***

notional income ACCOUNTING income not physically received invisible benefit that is not actual money, goods, or services

notional principal amount FINANCE value of loan the value used to represent a loan in calculating ***interest rate swaps***

notional rent ACCOUNTING theoretical rent for firm's own premises an amount of money noted in accounts as rent where the company owns the building it is occupying and so does not pay an actual rent

not negotiable FINANCE not able to change hands absolutely used to describe a check or bill of exchange that cannot be transferred to somebody else. If such a document is given by one person to another, the recipient obtains no better title to it than the signatory. *See also* ***negotiable instrument***

not sufficient funds *UK* BANKING = ***insufficient funds***

novation LEGAL agreed replacement of one party to contract an agreement to change a contract by substituting a third party for one of the two original parties

NOW account BANKING interest-paying US account with checks in the United States, an interest-bearing account with a bank or savings and loan association, on which checks (called ***negotiable orders of withdrawal***) can be drawn. *Full form* ***negotiable order of withdrawal account***

NPD *abbr* MARKETING ***new product development***

NPO *abbr* BUSINESS ***nonprofit organization***

NPV *abbr* ACCOUNTING ***net present value***

NRV *abbr* ACCOUNTING ***net residual value***

NRWT *abbr* TAX ***Non-Resident Withholding Tax***

NSA *abbr* ACCOUNTING ***National Society of Accountants***

NS&I *abbr* STOCKHOLDING & INVESTMENTS ***National Savings & Investments***

NSB *abbr* BANKING ***National Savings Bank***

NSC *abbr* STOCKHOLDING & INVESTMENTS ***National Savings Certificate***

NSF *abbr* BANKING ***non-sufficient funds*** or ***not sufficient funds***

NTA *abbr* ACCOUNTING ***net tangible assets***

NTB *abbr* INTERNATIONAL TRADE ***nontariff barrier***

nuisance parameter STATISTICS unimportant but necessary variable in a statistical model, a parameter that is insignificant in itself but whose unknown value is needed to make inferences about significant variables in a study

null hypothesis STATISTICS lack of significant effect the assumption that there is no relationship between variables that has produced a significant difference

numbered account BANKING bank account without holder's name a bank account identified by a number to allow the holder to remain anonymous

numerical control OPERATIONS & PRODUCTION automation using numerical data the use of numerical data to influence the operation of equipment. It allows the operation of machinery to be automated and usually involves the use of computer systems. Data is generated, stored, manipulated, and retrieved while a process is in operation.

nuncupative will LEGAL oral will a will that is made orally in the presence of a witness, rather than in writing

NYMEX *abbr* MARKETS ***New York Mercantile Exchange***

NYSE *abbr* MARKETS ***New York Stock Exchange***

NZSE *abbr* MARKETS ***New Zealand Stock Exchange***

NZSE10 Index MARKETS index of 10 largest New Zealand firms a measure of changes in stock prices on the New Zealand Stock Exchange, based on the change in value of the stocks of the ten largest companies. *Abbr* ***NZSE10***

NZSE30 Selection Index MARKETS index of 30 largest New Zealand firms a measure of changes in stock prices on the New Zealand Stock Exchange, based on the change in value of the stocks of the 30 largest companies. *Abbr* ***NZSE30***

NZSE40 Index MARKETS index of 40 largest New Zealand firms the principal measure of changes in stock prices on the New Zealand Stock Exchange, based on the change in value of the stocks of the 40 largest companies. The composition of the index is reviewed every three months. *Abbr* ***NZSE40***

O

OBI *abbr* E-COMMERCE ***open buying on the Internet***

object and task technique GENERAL MANAGEMENT budgeting by costing each task in the United States, a method of budgeting that involves assessing a project's objectives, determining the tasks required for their accomplishment, and then estimating the cost of each task

objective GENERAL MANAGEMENT goal of effort an end toward which effort is directed and on which resources are focused, usually to achieve an organization's strategy. There is considerable discussion on whether objective, goal, target, and aim are the same. In general usage, the terms are often interchangeable, so it is important that, if an organization has a particular meaning for one of these terms, it must define it in its documentation. Sometimes an objective is seen as the desired final end result, while a goal is a smaller step on the road to it.

obligation LEGAL legal agreement, especially to pay debt a binding legal agreement, by which somebody is bound to do something, especially to pay an amount of money

obligor FINANCE = ***debtor***

OBSF *abbr* FINANCE ***off-balance-sheet financing***

obsolescence 1. FINANCE loss through becoming out of date the loss of value of a fixed asset due to advances in technology or changes in market conditions **2.** MARKETING becoming out of date the decline of products in a market due to the introduction of better competitor products or rapid technology developments. Obsolescence of products can be a planned process, controlled by introducing deliberate minor cosmetic changes to a product every few years to encourage new purchases. It can also be unplanned, however, and in some sectors the pace of technological change is so rapid that the rate of obsolescence is high Obsolescence is part of the product life cycle, and if a product cannot be turned around, it may lead to product abandonment.

occupational pension PENSIONS in UK, pension plan maintained by employer in the United Kingdom, a pension plan run by an organization for its employees. Occupational pensions are regarded as deferred pay and form part of the total compensation package. Until recently, most plans were based on final salary but there has been a shift toward ***money purchase pensions***, particularly among smaller companies. Alternatively, employers may choose to contribute to an employee's ***personal pension***. *Also called* ***company pension***

OCF *abbr* ACCOUNTING ***operating cash flow***

OCR *abbr* BANKING ***official cash rate***

O/D *abbr* BANKING ***overdraft***

odd lot MARKETS fewer than 100 shares traded together a group of fewer than 100 shares of stock bought or sold together. *Also called* ***broken lot, uneven lot***

OECD INTERNATIONAL TRADE association of nations promoting democracy and free market a group of 30 member countries, with a shared commitment to democratic government and the market economy, that has active relationships with some 70 other countries via nongovernmental organizations. Formed in 1961, its work covers economic and social issues from macroeconomics to trade, education, development, and scientific innovation. Its goals are to promote economic growth and employment in member countries in a climate of stability; to assist the sustainable economic expansion of both member and nonmember countries; and to support a balanced and even-handed expansion of world trade. *Full form* ***Organisation for Economic Co-operation and Development***

OEIC *abbr* STOCKHOLDING & INVESTMENTS ***open-ended investment company***

OEM *abbr* OPERATIONS & PRODUCTION ***original equipment manufacturer***

off-balance-sheet financing FINANCE raising money through items not on balance sheet financing obtained by means other than debt and equity instruments, for example, by partnerships, joint ventures, and leases. *Abbr* ***OBSF***

off-board MARKETS of trading between dealers used to describe the trade of listed securities that does not take place on the stock exchange, or that takes place in the ***over-the-counter market***

offer STOCKHOLDING & INVESTMENTS **1.** *see* ***offering price*** **2.** net value of mutual fund the ***net asset value*** of a mutual fund plus any sales charges. It is the price investors pay when they buy a security.

offer by prospectus STOCKHOLDING & INVESTMENTS UK means of selling securities to public in the United Kingdom, one of the ways available to a ***lead underwriter*** of offering securities to the public. *See also* ***float, initial public offering, new issue, offer for sale***

offer document STOCKHOLDING & INVESTMENTS = ***prospectus***

offered market *UK* MARKETS market with more sellers than buyers a market in which sellers outnumber buyers, giving an advantage to buyers

offer for sale STOCKHOLDING & INVESTMENTS invitation to buy stock an invitation to apply for stock in a company, based on information contained in a prospectus

offering MARKETS security offered for sale an issue of a security that is offered for sale

offering circular STOCKHOLDING & INVESTMENTS = ***prospectus***

offering date MARKETS first day of stock sale the date on which a company offers its stock for sale to the public for the first time

offering price *US* STOCKHOLDING & INVESTMENTS selling price of share of stock the price at which somebody offers a share of a stock, especially a new issue, for sale. *Also called* ***offer price***

offeror STOCKHOLDING & INVESTMENTS maker of bid somebody who makes a bid to buy a ***financial obligation*** such as a debt

offer period MERGERS & ACQUISITIONS time span when takeover bid is open the time after a ***takeover bid*** for a company is first announced until the deal is closed or the offer lapses

offer price *UK* STOCKHOLDING & INVESTMENTS = ***offering price***

Office of Fair Trading REGULATION & COMPLIANCE UK government department protecting consumers a department of the UK government that protects consumers against unfair or illegal business practices. *Abbr* ***OFT***

Office of Management and Budget REGULATION & COMPLIANCE US government office that helps prepare federal budget the US government office, part of the executive branch of the government, that helps the President to prepare the federal budget. *Abbr* ***OMB***

Office of Thrift Supervision REGULATION & COMPLIANCE US agency regulating savings and loan associations an agency within the United States Department of the Treasury that regulates the savings and loan associations to ensure that they operate in a way that protects people's savings. *Abbr* ***OTS***

officer GENERAL MANAGEMENT = ***executive***

official books of account ACCOUNTING institution's financial records the official financial records of an organization set up for educational, professional, religious, or social purposes

official cash rate BANKING government interest rate the current interest rate as set by a central bank. *Abbr* ***OCR***

official development assistance FINANCE money made available to emerging country money that the ***OECD***'s Development Assistance Committee gives or lends to an emerging country

official intervention CURRENCY & EXCHANGE government action to affect exchange rate an attempt by a government to influence the exchange rate by buying or selling foreign currency

official list MARKETS list of securities traded on London Stock Exchange in the United Kingdom, the list maintained by the ***Financial Services Authority*** of all the securities traded on the London Stock Exchange

official receiver LEGAL UK court agent managing bankruptcy in the United Kingdom, an officer of the court who is appointed to wind up the affairs of an organization that goes bankrupt. An official receiver is appointed by the Department for Business, Enterprise & Regulatory Reform and often acts as a ***liquidator***. The job involves realizing any assets that remain to repay debts, for example, by selling property. *Abbr* ***OR***

official return ACCOUNTING legally required financial report a financial report or statement required by law and made by a person or company, for example, a tax return

off-line transaction processing E-COMMERCE recording of credit or debit card transactions the receipt and storage of order and credit or debit card information through a computer network or point-of-sale terminal for subsequent authorization and processing

offset STOCKHOLDING & INVESTMENTS counterbalancing transaction in security a transaction that balances all or part of an earlier transaction in the same security

offset clause INSURANCE insurance condition allowing counterbalancing of credits and debits a provision in an insurance policy that permits the balancing of credits against debits so that, for example, a company can reduce or omit payments to another company that owes it money and is bankrupt

offshore INTERNATIONAL TRADE **1.** send jobs overseas to get cheaper labor to hire workers in foreign countries in order to take advantage of a supply of skilled but relatively cheap labor **2.** located in another country based outside a specific country, especially in a place where taxes are low

offshore account TAX account located in low-tax country an account maintained in a place where taxes are low, to reduce a person's or company's liability to tax where their income originates

offshore banking BANKING banking in foreign banks banking in a foreign country, especially one that has favorable taxation regulations and is considered as a ***tax haven***

offshore company BUSINESS firm registered abroad for financial benefits a company that is registered in a country other than the one in which it conducts most of its business, usually for tax purposes. For example, many ***captive insurance companies*** are registered in the Cayman Islands.

offshore finance subsidiary *UK* BUSINESS = ***offshore financial subsidiary***

offshore financial center FINANCE finance hub in foreign country a country or other political unit that has banking laws intended to attract business from industrialized nations

offshore financial subsidiary *US* BUSINESS firm abroad handling parent company's finances a company created in another country to handle financial transactions, giving the owning company tax and legal advantages in its home country. *UK term* ***offshore finance subsidiary***

offshore fund STOCKHOLDING & INVESTMENTS fund based abroad a fund that is based in a foreign country, usually a country that has favorable taxation regulations

offshore holding company BUSINESS firm abroad owning firms at home a company created in another country to own other companies, giving the owning company legal advantages in its home country

offshore production INTERNATIONAL TRADE making goods abroad for import the manufacture of goods abroad for import to the home market

offshore trading company BUSINESS firm abroad handling parent company's commercial transactions a company created in another country to handle commercial transactions, giving the owning company legal advantages in its home country

offshoring INTERNATIONAL TRADE moving service operations abroad the transfer of service operations to foreign countries in order to take advantage of a supply of skilled but relatively cheap labor

off-the-shelf company BUSINESS UK firm available for purchase in the United Kingdom, a company for which all the legal formalities, except the appointment of directors, have been completed so that a purchaser can transform it into a customized new company with relative ease and low cost

OFT *abbr* REGULATION & COMPLIANCE ***Office of Fair Trading***

OI ACCOUNTING *see* ***EBIT***

oil economy ECONOMICS **1.** economy based on oil revenues an economy that is funded by the revenues from oil resources **2.** economy based on oil an economy that depends on oil supplies for its transportation, agricultural, and energy needs

Old Lady of Threadneedle Street *UK* BANKING Bank of England the Bank of England, which is located in Threadneedle Street in the City of London (*informal*)

oligarch FINANCE rich powerful businessman one of a small group having financial and political power, especially nowadays somebody with extreme personal wealth (*slang*)

oligarchy GENERAL MANAGEMENT control by small group an organization in which a small group of managers exercises control. Within an oligarchy, the controlling group often directs the organization for its own purposes, or for purposes other than the best interests of the organization.

oligopoly MARKETS market with few major sellers a market that is controlled by a few, very large, suppliers

oligopsony MARKETS market with few customers a market in which there are only a few buyers for a specific product or service

OMB *abbr* REGULATION & COMPLIANCE ***Office of Management and Budget***

ombudsman REGULATION & COMPLIANCE independent investigator of complaints a public official who investigates complaints against public departments, large organizations, or business sectors

omitted dividend STOCKHOLDING & INVESTMENTS unpaid regular dividend a regularly scheduled dividend that a company does not pay

omnibus account STOCKHOLDING & INVESTMENTS combined account for broker's convenience an account of one broker with another that combines the transactions of multiple investors for the convenience of the brokers

omnibus survey MARKETING wide-ranging survey a survey covering a number of topics, usually undertaken on behalf of several clients who share the cost of conducting the survey

on account FINANCE by advance payment used to describe an amount of money paid that represents part of a sum of money due to be paid in the future

oncost ACCOUNTING general cost of running business a business cost that cannot be charged directly to a particular good or service and must be apportioned across the business

on demand 1. BANKING allowing immediate withdrawals used to describe an account from which withdrawals may be made without giving a period of notice **2.** FINANCE allowing demand for immediate repayment used to describe a loan, usually an overdraft, that the lender can request the borrower to repay immediately **3.** FINANCE payable immediately to holder used to describe a bill of exchange that is paid upon presentation

one-stop shopping FINANCE provision of complete variety of financial services the ability of a single financial institution to offer a full variety of financial services

one-to-one marketing MARKETING emphasis on individual customers a marketing technique using detailed data, personalized communications, and customized products or services to match the requirements of individual customers

one-way trade INTERNATIONAL TRADE when seller does not buy in return an economic situation in which one country sells to another, but does not buy anything in return

one-year money STOCKHOLDING & INVESTMENTS investment for fixed period of one year money placed on a money market for a fixed period of one year, with either a fixed or variable rate of interest. It can be removed during the fixed term only upon payment of a penalty.

on-hold advertising MARKETING advertising to telephone callers waiting for service telephone advertising aimed at consumers who are being kept on hold while waiting to speak to somebody

online banking E-COMMERCE, BANKING banking service accessible by computer over Internet a system by which customers have bank accounts that they can access directly from their home computers, using the Internet, and can carry out operations such as checking on their account balances, paying invoices, and receiving their salaries electronically

online capture E-COMMERCE means of initiating payment after shipment a payment transaction generated after goods have been shipped, in which funds are transferred from the issuing bank to the acquiring bank and into the merchant account

online catalog E-COMMERCE consolidated catalog on Internet a business-to-business marketplace that collects the catalog data of every supplier in a specific industry and places it on one central Web resource. *Also called* ***procurement portal***

online community E-COMMERCE user network for Internet communication a means of allowing Web users to engage with one another and with an organization through use of interactive tools such as e-mail, discussion boards, and chat systems. They are a means by which a website owner can take the pulse of consumers to find out what they are thinking, and to generate unique content. As stand-alone businesses, online communities have been found to be weak; they work best when they are supporting the need for an organization to collect ongoing feedback.

online shopping E-COMMERCE = ***electronic shopping***

online trading MARKETS trading securities via Internet the process of buying and selling securities over the Internet

onshore FINANCE located in home country based in the home country, especially referring to a company that is registered in the country in which it conducts most of its business, or to funds or activities that are held or located in the home country. *See also* ***offshore***

on-target earnings FINANCE commission equaling amount aimed at the amount earned by somebody working on ***commission*** who has achieved the targets set. *Abbr* ***OTE***

OPEC INTERNATIONAL TRADE association of oil-producing countries an international organization of 11 countries, each one largely reliant on oil revenues as its main source of income, that tries to ensure there is a balance between supply and demand by adjusting the members' oil output. OPEC's headquarters are in Vienna. The current members, Algeria, Indonesia, Iran, Iraq, Kuwait, Libya, Nigeria, Qatar, Saudi Arabia, the United Arab Emirates, and Venezuela, meet at least twice a year to decide on output levels and discuss recent and anticipated oil market developments. *Full form* ***Organization of the Petroleum Exporting Countries***

open account FINANCE **1.** credit offered to buyer without requiring security a credit account offered by a supplier to a purchaser for which the supplier does not require security **2.** unpaid credit an account offered by a business to a customer that is as yet unpaid

open buying on the Internet E-COMMERCE protocol for Internet trading a standard built around a common set of business requirements for electronic communication between buyers and sellers that, when implemented, allows different e-commerce systems to talk to one another. *Abbr* ***OBI***. *See also* ***open trading protocol***

open check *US* BANKING blank signed check a signed check where the amount payable has not been indicated

open cheque *UK* BANKING uncrossed check a check that is not crossed and so may be cashed by the payee at the branch of the bank where it is drawn. *See also* ***crossed cheque***

open credit FINANCE credit offered without requiring security credit given by a supplier to a good customer without requiring security

open economy INTERNATIONAL TRADE economic system with unrestricted international trade an economy that places few restrictions on the movement of capital, labor, foreign trade, and payments into and out of the country

open-end credit *US* FINANCE arrangement allowing borrowing and repaying at will a credit facility that allows the borrower, within an overall credit limit and for a set period, to borrow or repay debt as required. *Also called* ***revolving credit***. *UK term* ***open-ended credit***

open-ended credit *UK* FINANCE = ***open-end credit***

open-ended fund *UK* STOCKHOLDING & INVESTMENTS = ***open-end fund***

open-ended investment company *UK* STOCKHOLDING & INVESTMENTS **1.** = ***open-end fund*** **2.** = ***open-end investment company***

open-ended management company *UK* STOCKHOLDING & INVESTMENTS = ***open-end management company***

open-ended mortgage *UK* MORTGAGES = ***open-end mortgage***

open-end fund *US* STOCKHOLDING & INVESTMENTS mutual fund with varying share numbers a mutual fund that has a variable number of shares. *UK term* ***open-ended fund***. *See also* ***closed-end fund***

open-end investment company *US* STOCKHOLDING & INVESTMENTS firm pooling funds for mutual funds a company with a variable number of shares that it sells to investors and pools for investment in mutual funds. *UK term* ***open-ended investment company***. *See also* ***open-end fund***

open-end management company *US* STOCKHOLDING & INVESTMENTS firm selling mutual funds a company that sells mutual funds. *UK term* ***open-ended management company***

open-end mortgage *US* MORTGAGES mortgage permitting prepayment a mortgage that can be paid off before the closing date originally agreed on. *UK term* ***open-ended mortgage***

opening balance ACCOUNTING amount at beginning of record the value of a financial quantity at the beginning of an accounting period

opening balance sheet ACCOUNTING record of opening balances a record giving details of an organization's financial balances at the beginning of an accounting period

opening bell MARKETS start of day's trading the beginning of a day of trading on a market

opening entry ACCOUNTING first record in account the first entry recorded in an account, for example, the first entry when starting a new business

opening price MARKETS price at start of day's trading the price for a security at the beginning of a day of trading on a market

opening purchase STOCKHOLDING & INVESTMENTS first in series of option purchases the first of a series of purchases to be made in options of a specific type for a specific commodity or security

opening stock *UK* ACCOUNTING = ***beginning inventory***

open interest STOCKHOLDING & INVESTMENTS total of options not yet closed the number of ***options*** contracts that have not yet been exercised, offset, or allowed to expire

open loop system GENERAL MANAGEMENT system with no facility for intervention a management control system that includes no provision for corrective action to be applied to the sequence of activities

open market MARKETS market with unlimited competition a market in which anyone is allowed to buy or sell and compete without restrictions

open market operation MARKETS government transaction in public market a transaction conducted by a central bank in a public market

open market value MARKETS potential price if available to all the price that an asset or security would realize if it was offered on a market open to all

open order MARKETS order remaining open until executed or canceled an order to buy or sell a security that is effective until it is executed or an investor cancels it. *See also* ***good 'til cancel***

open outcry MARKETS verbal exchanges to complete sale the method of making verbal bids and offers used by buyers and sellers on the ***trading floor*** of some exchanges such as the London Metal Exchange

open trading protocol E-COMMERCE e-commerce standard a standard designed to support Internet-based retail transactions, that allows different systems to communicate with each other for a variety of payment-related activities. The ***open buying on the Internet*** protocol is a competing standard. *Abbr* ***OTP***. *See also* ***open buying on the Internet***

operating budget ACCOUNTING plan for firm's income and expenses a forecast of income and expenses that result from the day-to-day activities of a company over a period of time

operating cash flow ACCOUNTING money used and generated in firm's operations the amount used to represent the money moving through a company as a result of its operations, as distinct from its purely financial transactions. *Abbr* ***OCF***

operating costing OPERATIONS & PRODUCTION way of costing output of continuous operation a costing system that is applied to continuous operations in mass production or in the service industries. In the simplest form of operating costing, the costing period is set at a specific length of time, usually a calendar month or four weeks. The costs incurred over the period are related to the number of units produced, and the division of the first by the second gives the average unit cost for the period.

operating costs *or* **operating expenses** ACCOUNTING expenses for firm's ordinary business activities the costs arising from the day-to-day activities of running a company. *Also called* ***running costs***

operating cycle OPERATIONS & PRODUCTION process between investment and income from product the cycle of business activity in which cash is used to buy resources that are converted into products or services and then sold for cash

operating environment OPERATIONS & PRODUCTION combination of external factors affecting business the combination of economic, social, and political factors that affect an organization's activities

operating expenses ACCOUNTING

operating income ACCOUNTING = ***EBIT***

operating lease GENERAL MANAGEMENT lease treated as rent in accounts a lease that is regarded by accountants as rental rather than as a ***capital lease***. The monthly lease payments are simply treated as rental expenses and recognized on the income statement as they are incurred. There is no recognition of a leased asset or liability.

operating leverage ACCOUNTING ratio of fixed to total costs the ratio of a business's fixed costs to its total costs. Fixed costs have to be paid regardless of output, the higher the ratio, the higher the risk of losses in an economic downturn.

operating loss ACCOUNTING firm's loss during ordinary business activities a loss incurred by a company during the course of its usual business

operating margin ACCOUNTING = ***profit margin***

operating profit ACCOUNTING standard income minus standard costs the difference between a company's revenues and any related costs and expenses, not including income or expenses from any sources other than its normal methods of providing a good or service

operating risk ACCOUNTING poor ratio of fixed to total costs the risk of a high ***operating leverage***, when each sale makes a significant contribution to fixed costs

operational audit GENERAL MANAGEMENT assessment of systems and procedures of organization a structured review of the systems and procedures of an organization in order to evaluate whether they are being conducted efficiently and effectively. An operational audit involves establishing performance ***objectives***, agreeing the standards and criteria for assessment, and evaluating actual performance against targeted performance. *Also called* ***management audit, operations audit***

operational costs ACCOUNTING costs of running business the costs incurred by a company during the course of its usual business

operational disciplines OPERATIONS & PRODUCTION activities supporting ongoing operation of business the activities and systems within an organization that ensure that the daily operations required to produce goods and services are running smoothly

operational gearing ACCOUNTING ratio of fixed to total costs the relationship between a company's fixed costs and its total costs. Fixed costs have to be paid before profit can be made, so high operational gearing increases a company's risk.

operational manager OPERATIONS & PRODUCTION manager of goods and services production the person in an organization who is in charge of the activities required to produce goods and services

operational research GENERAL MANAGEMENT analysis of managerial and administrative procedures the application of scientific methods to the solution of managerial and administrative problems, involving complex systems or processes. Operational research strives to find the optimum plan for the control and operation of a system or process. It was originally used during World War II as a means of solving logistical problems. It has since developed into a planning, scheduling, and ***problem solving*** technique applied across the industrial, commercial, and public sectors.

operational risk OPERATIONS & PRODUCTION, RISK risk of loss from internal or external failures the risk of economic loss that an organization faces, resulting from failed or inadequate controls, processes, or systems, or from human or external events

operations OPERATIONS & PRODUCTION production processes activities that are required to produce goods or services for consumers. *See also* ***operations management***

operations audit GENERAL MANAGEMENT = ***operational audit***

operations management OPERATIONS & PRODUCTION overseeing of production processes the maintenance, control, and improvement of organizational activities that are required to produce goods or services for consumers. Operations management has traditionally been associated with manufacturing activities but can also be applied to the service sector.

opinion leader MARKETING influencer of public opinion a high-profile person or organization that can significantly influence public opinion. An opinion leader can be a politician, a religious, business or community leader, a journalist, or an educator. Show business and sports personalities can exert a great deal of influence on young people's leisure lifestyles and buying habits and are consequently frequently used in advertising campaigns.

opinion leader research MARKETING inquiry into top people's views the investigation of the perceptions of ***corporate image*** and reputation among the people at the top of a company, industry, or profession

opinion survey GENERAL MANAGEMENT set of questions to discover people's attitudes a survey conducted to determine what members of a population think about a specific topic

opportunity cost STOCKHOLDING & INVESTMENTS loss through choice of investment an amount of money lost as a result of choosing one investment rather than another

opportunity score MARKETING measure of salability of product before production a measure of the potential marketability of a product or service while it is still in the development stage

optimal portfolio STOCKHOLDING & INVESTMENTS best possible investments a theoretical set of investments that would be the most profitable for an investor

optimize GENERAL MANAGEMENT use resources in best way to allocate such things as resources or capital as efficiently as possible

optimum best best or most desirable out of a number of possible options or outcomes

optimum capacity OPERATIONS & PRODUCTION cheapest quantity to produce the level of output at which the minimum cost per unit is incurred

option 1. STOCKHOLDING & INVESTMENTS contract for trading rights a contract for the right to buy or sell an asset, typically a commodity, under agreed terms. *Also called* ***option contract, stock option*** **2.** BUSINESS opportunity to buy or sell on agreed terms an agreement that somebody may buy or sell a specific asset on predetermined terms on or before a future date

option account STOCKHOLDING & INVESTMENTS account for buying and selling options an account that an investor holds with a broker and uses for trading in ***options***

optionaire STOCKHOLDING & INVESTMENTS millionaire in terms of stock options a millionaire whose wealth consists of or is derived from stock ***options*** (*slang*)

optional redemption provision STOCKHOLDING & INVESTMENTS bond early redemption clause the terms in a bond agreement that allow the issuer (usually) or the lender (less frequently) to redeem it before the final redemption date

option buyer STOCKHOLDING & INVESTMENTS buyer of option an investor who acquires an ***option*** to buy or sell a security, currency, or commodity

option class STOCKHOLDING & INVESTMENTS group of options of same type a set of ***options*** that are identical with respect to type and underlying asset

option contract STOCKHOLDING & INVESTMENTS = ***option***

option dealing MARKETS trading in stock options the activity of buying and selling stock ***options***

option elasticity STOCKHOLDING & INVESTMENTS relative changing values of option and underlying asset the relative change in the value of an ***option*** as a function of a change in the value of the underlying asset

option income fund STOCKHOLDING & INVESTMENTS mutual fund with options a mutual fund that derives income from investing in ***options***

option premium STOCKHOLDING & INVESTMENTS cost of each share in option the amount per share that a buyer pays for an ***option*** to buy or sell a security, currency, or commodity above the exercise price

option price STOCKHOLDING & INVESTMENTS price of option the price of an ***option*** to buy or sell a security, currency, or commodity

option pricing model STOCKHOLDING & INVESTMENTS means of establishing value of options a model that is used to determine the fair value of ***options***. *See also* ***Black-Scholes model***

options clearing corporation REGULATION & COMPLIANCE US organization overseeing trades in options in the United States, an organization responsible for the listing of *options* and clearing trades in them

option seller STOCKHOLDING & INVESTMENTS = ***option writer***

option series STOCKHOLDING & INVESTMENTS group of options representing same thing a collection of options that are identical in terms of class, ***exercise price***, and date of maturity

options market MARKETS **1.** trading options the trading in *options* to buy or sell securities, currencies, or commodities **2.** place for trading options a venue where traders engage in buying and selling ***options***

options on physicals STOCKHOLDING & INVESTMENTS options on physical assets a type of ***option*** that is on real assets rather than financial assets

option trading MARKETS trading in stock options the business of buying and selling stock ***options***

option writer STOCKHOLDING & INVESTMENTS seller of option a person, institution, or other organization that sells an ***option*** to buy or sell a security, currency, or commodity. *Also called* ***option seller***

OR *abbr* LEGAL ***official receiver***

order 1. OPERATIONS & PRODUCTION arrangement between customer and supplier a ***contract*** made between a customer and a supplier for the supply of a variety of goods or services in a determined quantity and quality, at an agreed price, and for delivery at or by a specific time **2.** STOCKHOLDING & INVESTMENTS instruction to trade for investor's own account an occasion when a broker is told to buy or sell a financial product for an investor's own account

order book OPERATIONS & PRODUCTION record of orders waiting to be fulfilled a record of the outstanding orders that an organization has received. An order book may be physical, with the specifications and delivery times of orders recorded in it, or the term may be used generally to describe the health of a company. A full order book implies a successful company, while an empty order book can indicate an organization at risk of business failure.

order confirmation E-COMMERCE e-mail acknowledgment of order an e-mail message informing a purchaser that an order has been received

order-driven system *or* **order-driven market** MARKETS system where stock prices change according to orders on a stock exchange, a price system where prices vary according to the level of orders. *See also* ***quote-driven system***

order imbalance MARKETS backlog in trading of security a situation in which there are more orders to buy or sell a security than can be executed, sometimes resulting in a halt to trading until the situation is resolved

order picking OPERATIONS & PRODUCTION extraction of items requested selecting and withdrawing goods or components from a store or warehouse to meet production requirements or to satisfy customer orders

order point OPERATIONS & PRODUCTION amount triggering reordering the quantity of an item that is on hand when more units of the item are to be ordered

order processing OPERATIONS & PRODUCTION keeping track of orders the tracking of orders made with suppliers and received from customers

orders pending STOCKHOLDING & INVESTMENTS, OPERATIONS & PRODUCTION unfulfilled orders orders that have not yet resulted in transactions

ordinary interest FINANCE interest based on 360-day year interest calculated on the basis of a year having only 360 days

ordinary resolution CORPORATE GOVERNANCE general issue put to vote at annual meeting a resolution put before an annual meeting, usually referring to some general procedural matter, that requires a simple majority of votes to be accepted

ordinary share *UK* STOCKHOLDING & INVESTMENTS = ***common stock***

ordinary share capital *UK* MARKETS capital from sale of ordinary shares the capital of a company raised by selling common stock

organic growth BUSINESS = ***internal growth***

organigram GENERAL MANAGEMENT = ***organization chart***

Organisation for Economic Co-operation and Development INTERNATIONAL TRADE *see* ***OECD***

organization GENERAL MANAGEMENT collection of people and resources with specific purpose an arrangement of people and resources working in a planned manner toward specific strategic goals. An organization can be any structured body such as a business, company, or firm in the private or public sector, or in a nonprofit association.

organization chart GENERAL MANAGEMENT diagram of organization's structure a graphic illustration of an organization's structure, showing hierarchical authority and relationships between departments and jobs. The horizontal dimension of an organization chart shows the nature of job function and responsibility and the vertical dimension shows how jobs are coordinated in reporting or authority relationships. *Also called* ***organigram, org chart***

Organization of the Petroleum Exporting Countries INTERNATIONAL TRADE *see* ***OPEC***

org chart GENERAL MANAGEMENT = ***organization chart***

orientation *US* HR & PERSONNEL formal introduction to new job a process through which a new employee is integrated into an organization, learning about its ***corporate culture***, policies and procedures, and the specific practicalities of his or her job. An orientation program should not consist of a one-day introduction, but should be planned and paced over a few days or weeks. There is a growing use of boot camps, which work to assimilate a new employee rapidly into the culture of the employing organization. *UK term* ***induction***

original cost ACCOUNTING total cost of asset the total cost of acquiring an asset

original equipment manufacturer OPERATIONS & PRODUCTION firm making product from bought-in parts a company that assembles components from other suppliers to produce a complete product. *Abbr* ***OEM***

original face value MORTGAGES amount originally borrowed the amount of the principal of a mortgage on the day it is created

original issue discount STOCKHOLDING & INVESTMENTS discount at bond's first sale the discount offered on the day of sale of a debt instrument

original maturity STOCKHOLDING & INVESTMENTS date for payment of bond a date on which a ***debt instrument*** is due to mature

origination fee MORTGAGES charge for providing mortgage a fee charged by a lender for providing a mortgage, usually expressed as a percentage of the principal

orthogonal STATISTICS statistically unrelated statistically independent

OTC *abbr* FINANCE ***over-the-counter***

OTC bulletin board MARKETS electronic system for quoting unlisted securities an electronic real-time quoting system for unlisted securities that are traded in the over-the-counter market but not traded on the NASDAQ. *Full form* ***over-the-counter bulletin board***

OTC market *abbr* MARKETS ***over-the-counter market***

OTE *abbr* FINANCE ***on-target earnings***

other capital ACCOUNTING uncategorized capital capital that is not listed in specific categories

other current assets ACCOUNTING non-cash assets maturing within year assets that are not cash and are due to mature within a year

other long-term capital ACCOUNTING uncategorized long-term assets long-term capital that is not listed in specific categories in accounts

other long-term liabilities FINANCE obligations with no interest charge in next year obligations such as deferred taxes and employee benefits with terms greater than one year and on which there is no charge for interest in the next year

other prices FINANCE unlisted prices prices that are not listed in a catalog

other short-term capital ACCOUNTING uncategorized short-term assets a residual category in the balance of payments that includes financial assets of less than one year such as currency, deposits, and bills

OTP *abbr* E-COMMERCE ***open trading protocol***

OTS *abbr* REGULATION & COMPLIANCE ***Office of Thrift Supervision***

outgoings *UK* ACCOUNTING = ***costs***

outlay ACCOUNTING money spent for specific purpose money spent on something such as capital assets or operating costs

outlier STATISTICS statistic that is very different from others a statistical observation that deviates significantly from other members of a sample

out-of-pocket expenses ACCOUNTING amount of employee's own money spent on business an amount of an employee's personal money that he or she has spent on company business, especially when considered for reimbursement

out of the money STOCKHOLDING & INVESTMENTS having no intrinsic value used to describe an ***option*** that, if it expired at the current market price, would have no intrinsic value. *See also* ***in the money***

outperform MARKETS do better than other companies to achieve better results in the stock market than other similar companies

output OPERATIONS & PRODUCTION goods produced anything that a company produces, usually referring to physical products but also to services

output gap ECONOMICS difference between economy's production capacity and actual production the difference between the amount of activity that is sustainable in an economy and the amount of activity actually taking place

output method ACCOUNTING accounting technique categorizing costs by output purpose an accounting system that classifies costs according to the outputs for which they are incurred, not the inputs they have bought

output per hour OPERATIONS & PRODUCTION how much is produced each hour the amount of something produced in one hour, especially the amount of a company's product or service

output tax TAX tax due from trader in Australia and New Zealand, the amount of Goods and Services Tax paid to the tax office after the deduction of ***input tax credits***

outside director CORPORATE GOVERNANCE director not employed by firm a member of a company's ***board of directors*** neither currently nor formerly in the company's employment. An outside director is sometimes described as being synonymous with a ***nonexecutive director***, and as usually being employed by a holding or associated company. In the United States, an outside director is somebody who has no relationships at all to a company. In US public companies, compensation and audit committees are generally made up of outside directors, and use of outside directors to select board directors is becoming more common.

outsourcing GENERAL MANAGEMENT **1.** switching from in-house personnel to outside supplier the transfer of the provision of services previously performed by in-house personnel to an external organization, usually under a ***contract*** with agreed standards, costs, and conditions. Areas traditionally outsourced include legal services, transport, catering, and security. An increasing variety of activities, including IT services, training, and public relations are now being outsourced. Outsourcing, or *contracting out*, is often introduced with the goal of increasing efficiency and reducing costs, or to enable the organization to develop greater flexibility or to concentrate on core business activities. The term ***subcontracting*** is sometimes used to refer to outsourcing. **2.** obtaining goods or services from outside suppliers the use of external suppliers as a source of finished products, components, or services

outstanding check ACCOUNTING check issued but not cashed a check which has been written and therefore has been entered in the company's ledgers, but which has not been presented for payment and so has not been debited from the company's bank account

outstanding share STOCKHOLDING & INVESTMENTS share allotted to applicant a share that a company has issued and somebody has bought

outstanding share capital STOCKHOLDING & INVESTMENTS value of stock available to trade the value of all of the stock of a company minus the value of retained shares

outwork GENERAL MANAGEMENT in UK, work done away from premises in the United Kingdom, work performed for a company away from its premises

outworker HR & PERSONNEL in UK, person working away from premises in the United Kingdom, a subcontractor or employee carrying out work for a company away from its premises

overall capitalization rate FINANCE income minus most costs divided by value ***net operating income*** other than debt service divided by value

overall market capacity ECONOMICS amount of product that market can absorb the amount of a service or good that can be absorbed in a market without affecting the price

overall rate of return *or* **overall return** STOCKHOLDING & INVESTMENTS return relative to investment the aggregate of all the dividends received over an investment's life together with its capital gain or loss at the date of its realization, calculated either before or after tax. It is one of the ways an investor can look at the performance of an investment.

overbid FINANCE **1.** bid too much to bid more than necessary to make a successful purchase **2.** too high a bid an amount that is offered that is unnecessarily high for a successful purchase to be made

overborrowed FINANCE having too much debt in comparison to assets used to describe a company that has very high borrowings compared to its assets, and has difficulty in meeting its interest payments

overbought MARKETS inflated by too many buyers used to describe a market or security considered to have risen too rapidly as a result of excessive buying

overbought market MARKETS market with overinflated prices a market where prices have risen beyond levels that can be supported by fundamental analysis. The market for Internet companies in 2001 was overbought and subsequently collapsed when it became clear that their trading performance could not support such price levels.

overcapacity OPERATIONS & PRODUCTION more capacity than needed an excess of capability to produce goods or provide a service over the level of demand

overcapitalized FINANCE having surplus capital used to describe a business that has more capital than can profitably be employed. An overcapitalized company could buy back some of its own stock in the market; if it has significant debt capital it could repurchase its bonds in the market; or it could make a large one-time dividend to stockholders.

overdraft BANKING **1.** deficit in bank account the amount by which the money withdrawn from a bank account exceeds the balance in the account. *Abbr* ***O/D*** **2.** = ***overdraft facility***

overdraft facility BANKING agreement for deficit in bank account a credit arrangement with a bank, allowing a person or company with an account to use borrowed money up to an agreed limit when nothing is left in the account

overdraft line BANKING agreed amount of overdraft an amount in excess of the balance in an account that a bank agrees to pay in honoring checks on the account

overdraft protection BANKING guarantee of payment from overdrawn account a bank service, amounting to a ***line of credit***, that assures that the bank will honor overdrafts, up to a limit and for a fee

overdraw BANKING create deficit in bank account to withdraw more money from a bank account than it contains or than was agreed could be withdrawn

overdrawn BANKING having deficit in bank account in debt to a bank because the amount withdrawn from an account exceeds its balance

overdue FINANCE still owing still to be paid after the date due

overfunding ECONOMICS when UK government sells more stock than necessary in the United Kingdom, a situation in which the government borrows more money than it needs for expenditure, as a result of selling too much government stock

overgeared FINANCE with greater financial commitments than common stock capital describing a company with debt capital and preferred stock that outweigh its ***common stock capital***

overhang MARKETS **1.** large remaining block of one investment, depressing price a large quantity of shares of unsold stock or of a commodity available for sale, which has the effect of depressing the market price **2.** to depress market prices to put downward pressure on stock or commodity prices

overhanging MARKETS

overhead *US* ACCOUNTING = ***overhead costs***

overhead absorption rate ACCOUNTING proportion of overhead attributed to product or service a means of attributing overhead to a product or service, based for example on direct labor hours, direct labor cost, or machine hours (the number of hours for which a machine is in production). The choice of overhead absorption base may be made with the objective of obtaining "accurate" product costs, or of influencing managerial behavior; for example, overhead applied to labor hours or part numbers appears to make the use of these resources more costly, thus discouraging their use.

overhead capacity variance ACCOUNTING gap between budgeted and required overhead the difference between the overhead absorbed, based on budgeted hours, and actual hours worked

overhead costs ACCOUNTING costs incurred in upkeep or running the indirect costs of the day-to-day running of a business, i.e. not money spent on producing goods, but money spent on such things as renting or maintaining buildings and machinery. *Also called* ***overhead, overheads***

overhead expenditure variance ACCOUNTING misjudgment of indirect costs the difference between the budgeted ***overhead costs*** and the actual expenditure

overheads *UK* ACCOUNTING = ***overhead costs***

overinsuring INSURANCE obtaining excessive insurance cover insuring an asset for a sum in excess of its market or replacement value. It is unlikely that an insurance company will pay out more in a claim for loss than the asset is worth or than the cost of replacing it.

overinvested **1.** STOCKHOLDING & INVESTMENTS with too much invested having a higher than desired amount invested in a security, or having a higher amount committed to tracking an index or matching a model portfolio than the index or model suggests **2.** BUSINESS with investment predicated on higher demand used to describe a business that invests heavily during an economic boom only to find that when it starts to produce an income, the demand for the product or service has fallen

overlap profit ACCOUNTING profit assignable to two accounting periods profit that arises in two overlapping accounting periods and on which tax relief can be claimed

overnight position MARKETS trader's commitments at end of trading day a trader's holdings in a security or option at the end of a trading day

overnight rate MARKETS, RISK interest rate on interbank overnight loans the interest rate charged by financial institutions on overnight loans to each other

overnight repo BANKING arrangement for temporary sale for cash a repurchase agreement where banks sell securities for cash and repurchase them the next day at a higher price. This type of agreement is used by central banks as a means of regulating the ***money markets***.

overpayment 1. FINANCE paying too much an act of paying more than is required or reasonable, or the sum paid in such a situation **2.** *UK* ACCOUNTING = ***additional principal payment***

overprice MARKETING charge too high price for something to set the price of a product or service too high, with the result that it is unacceptable to the market

overrated FINANCE with value set too high used to describe something that is valued more highly than it should be

overriding commission *or* **override** *or* **overrider** FINANCE further additional commission a special extra commission which is above all other commissions

overseas company BUSINESS part of firm incorporated abroad a branch or subsidiary of a business that is incorporated in another country

overseas funds FINANCE investment products in foreign countries investment funds that are based in other countries and are not subject to regulation in the home country

Overseas Investment Commission REGULATION & COMPLIANCE New Zealand organization overseeing investment from abroad in New Zealand, an independent body reporting to the government that regulates foreign investment. It was established in 1973 and is funded by the Reserve Bank of New Zealand.

oversold MARKETS depressed by too many sellers used to describe a market or security that is considered to have fallen too rapidly as a result of excessive selling. *See also* ***bear market***

overspend ACCOUNTING **1.** spend more than planned to spend more money than was budgeted or planned or than can be afforded **2.** excess amount spent an amount that is more than was budgeted for spending

overstocked OPERATIONS & PRODUCTION having surplus inventory used to describe a business that has more inventory than it needs

oversubscription MARKETS when investors want more stock than are available a situation in which investors are interested in buying more shares of stock in a new issue than are being made available

over-the-counter FINANCE of trading between dealers used to describe the trade of securities directly between licensed dealers, rather than through an auction system. *Abbr* ***OTC***

over-the-counter market MARKETS market conducted directly between dealers a market in which trading takes place directly between licensed dealers, rather than through an auction system as used in most organized exchanges. *Abbr* ***OTC market***

over-the-counter security STOCKHOLDING & INVESTMENTS security traded directly between dealers a security that is traded directly between licensed dealers on the ***over-the-counter market***

overtrading OPERATIONS & PRODUCTION when firm increases sales and production too rapidly a situation in which a company increases sales and production too much and too quickly, so that it runs short of cash

overvalue FINANCE, GENERAL MANAGEMENT give something too high a value to give a higher value to something or somebody than is justified

own brand *UK* MARKETING = ***private label***

owner 1. LEGAL possessor of legal title to something a person or organization that has legal title to products or services **2.** BUSINESS person having own firm the person who has legal control of a private company

owner-occupier REAL ESTATE somebody who owns home a person who owns the property in which he or she lives

owner-operator BUSINESS = ***sole proprietor***

owner's equity ACCOUNTING total assets minus total liabilities a business's total assets less its total liabilities, being the funds provided by the owners.
See also ***capital, common stock***

ownership of companies BUSINESS holding of stock in firms the possession of stock in companies. Company ownership structures can differ widely. Owners of public companies may be institutions, or individuals, or a mixture of both. Directors are often offered company stock as incentives and more participative companies may offer stock to employees through ***employee ownership*** plans. Private companies are usually owned by individuals, families, or groups of individual stockholders. Nationalized industries are publicly owned. Cooperatives are wholly owned by employees. A separation between the ownership and control of companies became a widely discussed issue during the 20th century, especially in the United States and the United Kingdom where stockholders have tended to be more passive. Managers were viewed as having come to occupy controlling positions as the scale of industry grew. From the 1980s, this position changed to some extent as ***privatization***, ***management buyouts***, restructuring, and ***stock incentive plans*** led to greater stock ownership among managers and produced less passive stockholders.

own label *UK* MARKETING = ***private label***

P

paced line OPERATIONS & PRODUCTION production line moving at steady speed a production line that moves at a constant speed

package and sell STOCKHOLDING & INVESTMENTS sell combined loans to combine a number of loans and sell them to investors as ***mortgage-backed securities***

package deal GENERAL MANAGEMENT agreement including several aspects simultaneously an agreement that covers several different things at the same time

packaging MARKETS combining securities for trade the practice of combining different securities in a single trade

Pac Man defense MERGERS & ACQUISITIONS offer to purchase buyer to avoid firm's takeover a strategy by a company seeking to avoid a hostile takeover, in which the target company makes an offer to purchase the prospective buyer

paid-in capital STOCKHOLDING & INVESTMENTS firm's capital received from investors for stock capital in a business that has been provided by its stockholders

paid up FINANCE fully paid having paid all the money owed

paid-up capital *or* **paid-up share capital** STOCKHOLDING & INVESTMENTS stock issued and paid for an amount of money paid for the issued capital shares of stock, which does not include ***called-up share capital***. *See also* ***fully paid share capital, partly paid capital***

paid-up policy INSURANCE **1.** policy providing life insurance after policyholder stops paying in the United Kingdom, an ***endowment insurance*** policy that continues to provide life insurance while the cost of the premiums is covered by the underlying fund after the policyholder has decided not to continue paying premiums. If the fund is sufficient to pay the premiums for the remainder of the term, the remaining funds will be paid to the policyholder at maturity. **2.** insurance policy with premiums paid in the United States, an insurance policy on which all the premiums have been paid

paid-up share STOCKHOLDING & INVESTMENTS stock paid for in full a stock for which stockholders have paid the full contractual amount. *See also* ***call, called-up share capital, paid-up capital, share capital***

painting the tape MARKETS illegal splitting of orders into smaller units an illegal practice in which traders break large orders into smaller units in order to give the illusion of heavy buying activity. This encourages investors to buy, and the traders then sell as the price of the stock goes up (*slang*).

panda CURRENCY & EXCHANGE Chinese gold or silver collector coin one of a series of Chinese gold and silver bullion collector coins, each featuring a panda, that were first issued in 1982. Struck with a highly polished surface, the smallest gold coin weighs 0.05 ounces, the largest 12 ounces.

P&L *abbr* ACCOUNTING ***profit and loss***

Panel on Takeovers and Mergers MERGERS & ACQUISITIONS UK group overseeing fairness in takeovers in the United Kingdom, the group that issues the ***City Code on Takeovers and Mergers***, a code designed principally to ensure fair and equal treatment of all stockholders in relation to takeovers. *See also* ***City Code on Takeovers and Mergers***

panel study MARKETING study of small group's opinions over time a study that surveys a selected group of people over a period of time

panic buying FINANCE exceptional buying because of fear of shortages an unusual level of buying caused by fear or rumors of product shortages or by severe price rises

panic dumping CURRENCY & EXCHANGE selling currency because of devaluation fears a rush to sell a currency at any price because of fears of a possible devaluation

paper 1. FINANCE record of holdings a certificate of deposits and other securities **2.** STOCKHOLDING & INVESTMENTS issue of stock or bonds to raise capital a rights issue or an issue of bonds launched by a company to raise additional capital **3.** FINANCE all debt issued by firm all funding instruments issued by a company, other than ***equity***

paper company BUSINESS firm without physical presence a company that only exists on paper and has no ***physical assets***

paper gain STOCKHOLDING & INVESTMENTS = ***paper profit***

paper loss STOCKHOLDING & INVESTMENTS drop in value of unsold investment a loss made when an asset has fallen in value but has not been sold. *Also called* ***unrealized loss***

paper millionaire STOCKHOLDING & INVESTMENTS person owning stock valued currently at one million an individual who owns stock that is worth in excess of a million in currency at a specific date, but which may fall in value. In 2001 many of the founders of dot-com companies were paper millionaires. *See also* ***paper profit***

paper money 1. CURRENCY & EXCHANGE bills currency that is not coins **2.** BANKING checks payments in paper form such as checks

paper offer MERGERS & ACQUISITIONS takeover bid with stock rather than cash a takeover bid in which the purchasing company offers its stock in exchange for stock in the company being taken over, as opposed to a cash offer

paper profit ACCOUNTING increase in value on investment not yet sold an increase in the value of an investment that the investor has no immediate intention of realizing

PAR *abbr* BANKING ***prime assets ratio***

paradigm shift GENERAL MANAGEMENT fundamental change a basic change in an accepted pattern of thought or behavior

paradox of saving *or* **paradox of thrift** ECONOMICS cutbacks in expenditure lead to increased expenditure elsewhere the observation that savings made by individuals in their consumption lead to a drop in overall demand which in turn leads to increased spending by a business or government

parafiscal tax TAX tax levied for specific purpose a tax on a specific product or service by which a government raises money for a specific purpose. The money raised is usually paid to a body other than the national tax authority.

parallel economy ECONOMICS = ***black economy***

parallel engineering OPERATIONS & PRODUCTION = ***concurrent engineering***

parallel loan FINANCE = ***back-to-back loan***

parallel pricing OPERATIONS & PRODUCTION competitors' changing of prices together the practice of varying prices in a similar way and at the same time as competitors

paralysis by analysis GENERAL MANAGEMENT substitution of background work for decision making the inability of managers to make decisions as a result of a preoccupation with attending meetings, writing reports, and collecting statistics and analyses. Paralysis of effective ***decision making*** in organizations can occur in situations where there is horizontal conflict, disagreement between different hierarchical levels, or unclear objectives.

parameter STATISTICS quantity relating to entire statistical set a quantity that is numerically characteristic of a whole model or population

parameter design STATISTICS method of limiting variability a process aimed at reducing variation in processes or products

parcel STOCKHOLDING & INVESTMENTS set of securities sold together a group of related securities that are sold at one time

parcel of shares *UK* STOCKHOLDING & INVESTMENTS = ***basket of shares***

parent company BUSINESS firm with subsidiaries a main company in a group that also has one or more subsidiary undertakings

Pareto's Law ECONOMICS idea that income will be distributed similarly everywhere a theory of income distribution that states that regardless of political or taxation conditions, income will be distributed in the same way across all countries

pari passu GENERAL MANAGEMENT ranking equally a Latin phrase that means being of equal rank

Paris Club FINANCE = ***G10***

Paris Interbank Offered Rate BANKING bank releasing money against check the French equivalent of the ***London Interbank Offered Rate***. *Abbr* ***PIBOR***

parity MARKETS price equivalence in different markets a situation when the price of a commodity, foreign currency, or security is the same in different markets. *See also* ***arbitrage***

parity bit E-COMMERCE digit used as check an odd or even digit used to check binary computer data for errors

parity value STOCKHOLDING & INVESTMENTS = ***conversion value***

park STOCKHOLDING & INVESTMENTS (*slang*) **1.** illegally disguise ownership of stock to place owned stock with third parties to disguise their ownership, usually illegally **2.** invest money safely for short time to put money into safe investments while deciding where to invest it in the longer term

parking STOCKHOLDING & INVESTMENTS (*slang*) **1.** illegal transfer of stock to nominee the transfer of stock in a company to a third party such as a nominee or the name of an associate, often illegally **2.** temporarily keeping money in safe investments the practice of putting money into safe investments while deciding where to invest it in the longer term

Parkinson's Law HR & PERSONNEL work expands to fill time available the facetious assertion that work will expand to fill the time available

Parquet MARKETS Paris stock exchange the Bourse, or stock exchange, in Paris, France (*slang*)

part exchange *UK* FINANCE = ***trade-in***

participating bond STOCKHOLDING & INVESTMENTS bond yielding dividends and interest a bond that pays the holder dividends as well as interest

participating insurance INSURANCE insurance offering dividends a form of insurance in which policyholders receive a dividend from the insurer's profits

participating preference share *UK* STOCKHOLDING & INVESTMENTS = ***participating preferred stock***

participating preferred stock *US* STOCKHOLDING & INVESTMENTS stock yielding dividend and share of surplus profit a type of ***preferred stock*** that entitles the holder to a fixed dividend and, in addition, to the right to participate in any surplus profits after payment of agreed levels of dividends to holders of ***common stock*** has been made. *See also* ***nonparticipating preferred stock***. *UK term* ***participating preference share***

participative budgeting TREASURY MANAGEMENT system allowing budget holders to draft own budgets a budgeting system in which all budget holders are given the opportunity to participate in setting their own budgets. *Also called* ***bottom-up budgeting***

partly paid capital *or* **partly paid share capital** STOCKHOLDING & INVESTMENTS capital not paid in full capital composed of shares for which the stockholders have not paid the full value at once, but have paid in installments. *See also* ***fully paid share capital, paid-up capital***

partly paid share STOCKHOLDING & INVESTMENTS stock not paid in full a stock for which stockholders have not paid the full value at once, but have paid in installments. *See also* ***call, partly paid capital***

partner BUSINESS member of business partnership a person who works in a business partnership and shares with one or more other people in the profits or losses of the business

partnership BUSINESS legal relationship between business partners the relationship which exists between persons carrying on business in common with a view to profit. In the United Kingdom, this is regulated by the Partnership Act of 1890, and the liability of the individual partners is unlimited unless provided for by the partnership agreement. The Limited Partnership Act of 1907 allows a partnership to contain one or more partners with limited liability so long as there is at least one partner with unlimited liability. A partnership consists of not more than 20 persons.

partnership accounts **1.** BANKING accounts of business partners the capital and checking accounts of each partner in a partnership **2.** ACCOUNTING record of financial activities accounts that record the business activities of each partner in a partnership

partnership agreement LEGAL legal basis for partnership the document that establishes a partnership, detailing the capital contributed by each partner; whether an individual partner's liability is limited; the apportionment of the profit; salaries; and possibly procedures to be followed, for example, in the event of a partner retiring or a new partner joining. *Also called* ***articles of partnership***

part-owner BUSINESS somebody owning something jointly with others a person who owns something jointly with one or more other people

part-ownership BUSINESS shared ownership of business or property a situation in which two or more people share in the ownership of a business or property

part payment FINANCE amount paid to cover part of debt a partial payment that leaves a balance to pay at some future time

part time HR & PERSONNEL some of standard working hours a proportion of the standard working hours expected in an organization. *See also* ***full time***

part-time director CORPORATE GOVERNANCE = ***nonexecutive director***

party LEGAL somebody involved in legal dispute or agreement a person or organization involved in a legal dispute or legal agreement

par value STOCKHOLDING & INVESTMENTS = ***nominal value***

passbook BANKING = ***bank book***

passing off FRAUD intentionally making one product appear to be another a form of fraud in which a company tries to sell its own product by deceiving buyers into thinking it is another product

passive investment management STOCKHOLDING & INVESTMENTS managing investment portfolio by automatic adjustments the managing of a ***mutual fund*** or other investment portfolio by relying on automatic adjustments such as tracking an index instead of making personal judgments. *See also* ***active fund management***

passive portfolio strategy STOCKHOLDING & INVESTMENTS relying on automatic adjustments to manage investments a plan for managing an investment portfolio that relies on automatic adjustments such as tracking an index

passportable BUSINESS describing financial activities permitted in another European state used to describe activities set out in the relevant EU directives for banking, insurance, insurance mediation, management, and investment services that permit a company registered in the European Economic Area to carry on business in another EEA state

passporting BUSINESS doing business in another European state the exercise by a company registered in the European Economic Area of a right to carry on business in another EEA state

passport in/out BUSINESS do business in another European state to exercise the right to carry on business in another state of the European Economic Area

pass-through security STOCKHOLDING & INVESTMENTS security made up of pool of securities a security that represents an interest in a pool of securities, most commonly ***mortgage-backed securities***, in which the earnings are passed through to investors

patent LEGAL government licence giving sole right to something a type of ***copyright*** granted as a fixed-term monopoly to an inventor by a government to prevent others copying an invention or improvement to a product or process.

The granting of a patent requires the publication of full details of the invention or improvement. The use of the patented information is restricted to the patent holder or any organizations licensed by them.

A patent's value is usually the sum of its development costs, or its purchase price if acquired from someone else. It is generally to a company's advantage to spread the patent's value over several years. If this is the case, the critical time period to consider is not the full life of the patent (17 years in the United States), but its estimated useful life.

For example, in January 2000 a company acquired a patent issued in January 1995 at a cost of $100,000. It concludes that the patent's useful commercial life is ten years, not the 12 remaining before the patent expires. In turn, patent value would be $100,000, and it would be spread (or amortized in accounting terms) over 10 years, or $10,000 each year.

patent attorney LEGAL specialist in law of patents a lawyer who specializes in patents

path analysis STATISTICS method of showing relationships between statistical variables in a statistical study, a method for showing the correlation between variables

pathfinder prospectus *UK* STOCKHOLDING & INVESTMENTS preliminary prospectus to test market a preliminary prospectus used in initial public offerings to gauge the reaction of investors. *US term* ***red eye***

pawnbroker FINANCE person lending money against personal items a person who lends money against the security of a wide variety of chattels, from jewelry to cars. The borrower may recover the goods by repaying the loan and interest by a specific date. Otherwise, the items pawned are sold and any surplus after the deduction of expenses, the loan, and interest is returned to the borrower.

pay FINANCE money paid for work done a sum of money given in return for work done or services provided. Pay, in the form of salary or wages, is generally provided in weekly or monthly fixed amounts, and is usually expressed in terms of the total sum earned per year. It may also be allocated using a ***piece rate*** system, where employees are paid for each unit of work they perform.

payables ledger *US* ACCOUNTING record of accounts to be paid a ledger in which a company records its ***accounts payable***. *UK term* ***purchase ledger***

payable to order FINANCE indicating that payee may be changed the statement on a bill of exchange or check, used to indicate that the payee is able to endorse it to a third party

Pay As You Earn TAX in UK, payment of employees' taxes through employer in the United Kingdom, a system for collecting direct taxes that requires employers to deduct taxes from employees' pay before payment is made. *Abbr* ***PAYE***

pay-as-you-go PENSIONS financing of current pensions by current employees in Canada, a means of financing a pension system whereby benefits of current retirees are financed by current workers

Pay-As-You-Go TAX Australian payment system for business and investment taxes in Australia, a system used for paying income tax installments on business and investment income. PAYG is part of the new tax system introduced by the Australian government on July 1, 2000. *Abbr* ***PAYG***

payback FINANCE **1.** repayment of borrowed money the act of paying back money that has been borrowed **2.** time taken for investment project to break even the time required for the cash revenues from a capital investment project to equal the cost

payback clause LEGAL rules in contract about loan repayment a clause in a contract that states the terms which govern the repayment of a loan

payback period ACCOUNTING time needed to recover project investment costs the length of time it will take to earn back the money invested in a project.

The straight payback period method is the simplest way of determining the investment potential of a major project. Expressed in time, it tells a management how many months or years it will take to recover the original cash cost of the project. It is calculated using the formula:

Cost of project / Annual cash revenues = Payback period

Thus, if a project cost $100,000 and was expected to generate $28,000 annually, the payback period would be:

100,000 / 28,000 = 3.57 years

If the revenues generated by the project are expected to vary from year to year, add the revenues expected for each succeeding year until you arrive at the total cost of the project.

For example, say the revenues expected to be generated by the $100,000 project are:

Revenue	*Total*	*Cum. total*
Year 1	$19,000	$19,000
Year 2	$25,000	$44,000
Year 3	$30,000	$74,000
Year 4	$30,000	$104,000
Year 5	$30,000	$134,000

Thus, the project would be fully paid for in Year 4, since it is in that year the total revenue reaches the initial cost of $100,000. The precise payback period would be calculated as:

((100,000 – 74,000) / (1000,000 – 74,000)) × 365 = 316 days + 3 years

The picture becomes complex when the time-value-of-money principle is introduced into the calculations. Some experts insist this is essential to determine the most accurate payback period. Accordingly, the annual revenues have to be discounted by the applicable interest rate, 10% in this example. Doing so produces significantly different results:

Revenue	*Present value*	*Total*	*Cum. total*
Year 1	$19,000	$17,271	$17,271
Year 2	$25,000	$20,650	$37,921
Year 3	$30,000	$22,530	$60,451
Year 4	$30,000	$20,490	$80,941
Year 5	$30,000	$18,630	$99,571

This method shows that payback would not occur even after five years.

Generally, a payback period of three years or less is desirable; if a project's payback period is less than a year, some contend it should be judged essential.

pay down FINANCE reduce loan amount through payments to reduce the amount of the ***principal*** on a loan by making payments

paydown FINANCE partial repayment of loan a repayment of part of a sum which has been borrowed

PAYE *abbr* TAX ***Pay As You Earn***

payee 1. FINANCE person being paid the person or organization to whom a payment has to be made **2.** BANKING person to whom check is payable the person or organization to whom a check is specified as payable. *Also called* ***drawee***

payer BANKING person paying the person or organization making a payment

PAYG *abbr* TAX ***Pay-As-You-Go***

paying agent FINANCE institution paying interest or repaying capital the institution responsible for making interest payments on a security and repaying capital at redemption. *Also called* ***disbursing agent***

paying banker *UK* BANKING bank releasing money against check the bank on which a bill of exchange or check is drawn

paying-in book *UK* BANKING book of slips for listing bank deposits a book of detachable slips that accompany money or checks being paid into a bank account

paying-in slip *UK* BANKING = ***deposit slip***

payload OPERATIONS & PRODUCTION cargo capacity the amount of cargo that a form of transport can carry

paymaster FINANCE person issuing pay the person responsible for paying an organization's employees or the members of a country's armed services

payment FINANCE **1.** giving of money for goods or services the act of giving an amount of money in exchange for goods or services **2.** money paid for goods or services an amount of money paid in exchange for goods or services

payment by results FINANCE making pay dependent on work output a system of pay that directly links an employee's salary to his or her work output

payment gateway E-COMMERCE intermediary in card payment system a company or organization that provides an interface between a merchant's point-of-sale system, ***acquirer*** payment systems, and ***issuer*** payment systems. *Abbr* ***GW***

payment in advance FINANCE payment made before goods are delivered a payment made for goods when they are ordered and before they are delivered. *See also* ***prepayment***

payment in due course FINANCE payment on fixed future date the payment of a bill of exchange on a fixed date in the future

payment in kind FINANCE something of equivalent value instead of money an alternative form of pay given to employees in place of monetary reward but considered to be of equivalent value. A payment in kind may take the form of use of a car, purchase of goods at cost price, or other nonfinancial exchange that benefits the employee. It forms part of the total pay package rather than being an extra benefit. *See also* ***PIK note***

payment-in-lieu FINANCE money as substitute payment that is given in place of an entitlement

payment terms OPERATIONS & PRODUCTION firm's conditions for reimbursement for goods and services the stipulation by a business as to when it should be paid for goods or services supplied, for example, cash with order, payment on delivery, or within a particular number of days of the invoice date

payoff FINANCE **1.** final repayment a final payment for something that is owed, for example, the outstanding balance of principal and interest on a mortgage or loan **2.** profit or reward of some sort a profit or reward, for example, from a plan or project that is financially successful

payout FINANCE **1.** money given to somebody in difficulties money that is given to help a company or person experiencing difficulties **2.** amount paid a particular sum of money offered, for example, in compensation, or from an insurance policy

payout ratio STOCKHOLDING & INVESTMENTS amount of firm's earnings paid as dividends an expression of the total dividends paid to stockholders as a percentage of a company's net profit in a specific period of time. This measures the likelihood of dividend payments being sustained, and is a useful indication of sustained profitability. The lower the ratio, the more secure the dividend, and the company's future.

The payout ratio is calculated by dividing annual dividends paid on common stock by earnings per share:

Annual dividend / Earnings per share = Payout ratio

Take the company whose earnings per share are $8 and its dividend payout is 2.1. Its payout ratio would be:

2.1 / 8 = 0.263 or 26.3%

A high payout ratio clearly appeals to conservative investors seeking income. When coupled with weak or falling earnings, however, it could suggest an imminent dividend cut, or that the company is short-changing reinvestment to maintain its payout. A payout ratio above 75% is a warning. It suggests the company is failing to reinvest sufficient profits in its business, that the company's earnings are faltering, or that it is trying to attract investors who otherwise would not be interested. *Also called* ***dividend payout ratio***. *See also* ***dividend cover***

PayPal™ E-COMMERCE means of paying over Internet a Web-based service that enables Internet users to send and receive payments electronically. To open a PayPal™ account, users register and provide their credit card or checking account details. When they decide to make a transaction via PayPal™, their card or account is charged for the transfer.

payroll ACCOUNTING record of pay and deductions for each employee a record showing for each employee his or her gross pay, deductions, and net pay. The payroll may also include details of the employer's associated employment costs.

payroll giving plan *US* TAX system for deducting money from salary for charity a plan by which an employee pays money to a charity directly out of his or her salary. The money is deducted by the employer and paid to the charity, and the employee gets tax relief on such donations. *UK term* ***payroll giving scheme***

payroll giving scheme *UK* TAX = ***payroll giving plan***

payroll tax TAX tax on money paid to employees a tax on salary and wages of the people employed by a company

payslip HR & PERSONNEL statement of employee's pay a document given to employees when they are paid, providing a statement of pay for that period. A payslip includes details of deductions such as income tax, social security contributions, pension contributions, and labor union dues.

PBR *abbr* FINANCE ***pre-Budget report***

PBT *abbr* ACCOUNTING ***profit before tax***

P/C *abbr* ACCOUNTING ***petty cash***

PDR *abbr* STOCKHOLDING & INVESTMENTS ***price/dividend ratio***

P/E STOCKHOLDING & INVESTMENTS *see* ***price/earnings multiple, price/earnings ratio***

peak MARKETS highest point or rate the highest price, value, or point reached in a cycle

pecuniary FINANCE of money relating to or involving money

peg 1. CURRENCY & EXCHANGE fix exchange rate of currency against others to fix the exchange rate of one currency against that of another or of a basket of other currencies **2.** FINANCE fix wages and salaries to control inflation to fix wages and salaries during a period of inflation to help prevent an inflationary spiral

P/E multiple *abbr* STOCKHOLDING & INVESTMENTS ***price/earnings multiple***

penalty FINANCE money paid for breaking contract an arbitrary prearranged sum that becomes payable if one party breaks a term of a contract or an undertaking. A common penalty is a high rate of interest on an unauthorized ***overdraft***. *See also* ***overdraft***

penalty clause LEGAL clause stating exaggerated penalty for breaking contract a clause in a ***contract*** that sets out the compensation to be paid in the event of a breach or a default of the terms of the contract when the amount specified is not considered a genuine estimate of the losses incurred, and the clause is perceived to be solely an incentive for the completion of the contract. However, genuine ***liquidated damages clauses*** are often inaccurately referred to as penalty clauses. *See also* ***liquidated damages clause***

penalty rate *ANZ* FINANCE high rate of overtime pay a higher than normal rate of pay awarded for work performed outside normal working hours

penetrated market MARKETING existing customers the customers who already exist within a well-established market

penetration pricing OPERATIONS & PRODUCTION setting low prices to break into market setting prices low, especially for new products, in order to maximize ***market penetration***

pennant MARKETS chart pattern showing converging high and low prices a triangular chart pattern that is formed when a stock's high and low points begin to converge

penny share *UK* STOCKHOLDING & INVESTMENTS = ***penny stock***

penny stock *US* STOCKHOLDING & INVESTMENTS very low-priced stock very low-priced stock, typically under one dollar, that is a speculative investment. *UK term* ***penny share***

pension PENSIONS money received regularly after retirement from paid work money received regularly after retirement, from a government or through a ***personal pension*** or ***occupational pension***. *Also called* ***retirement pension***

pensionable earnings *UK* PENSIONS = ***final average monthly salary***

pension benefit guaranty corporation PENSIONS, INSURANCE US corporation insuring pension benefits for retirees in the United States, a corporation set up by the federal government to insure the retirement benefits of employees of private-sector companies that have established pension plans

pension entitlement PENSIONS amount of retirement income due the amount of income that someone has the right to receive when he or she retires

pension fund PENSIONS **1.** organization investing money to provide future pensions an organization that receives money from employers and employees in order to provide pensions at a later date. The pension funds of large companies and organizations are significant investors in the financial markets. **2.** *UK* = ***retirement fund***

Pension Protection Fund PENSIONS UK fund compensating people when pension providers fail in the United Kingdom, a fund set up by government to compensate people whose pension providers fail. It is funded by a levy on all pension funds. *Abbr* ***PPF***

pension provider PENSIONS firm selling pension products a company ***pension fund***, or company that sells different investment plans that will build up savings for retirement

PEP *abbr* STOCKHOLDING & INVESTMENTS ***Personal Equity Plan***

PER *abbr* STOCKHOLDING & INVESTMENTS ***price/earnings ratio***

per annum FINANCE in a year in one year

P/E ratio *abbr* STOCKHOLDING & INVESTMENTS ***price/earnings ratio***

per capita FINANCE per person average for each person

per capita income ECONOMICS average income of group of people the average income of each of a specific group of people, for example, the citizens of a country

perceived value pricing OPERATIONS & PRODUCTION = ***market-based pricing***

percentage increase STATISTICS increase expressed as percentage an increase calculated on the basis of a rate for one hundred

percentile STATISTICS one of 99 equal divisions of total one of a series of ninety-nine figures below which a percentage of the total falls

perception of risk RISK = ***risk perception***

per diem FINANCE, HR & PERSONNEL rate allowed for each day an amount of money paid per day, for example, for expenses when an employee is working away from the office

perfect capital market ECONOMICS when buying and selling do not affect prices a situation in which the decisions of buyers and sellers have no effect on market price in a ***capital market***

perfect competition ECONOMICS when no single buyer or seller affects price a situation in which no individual buyer or seller can influence prices. In practice, perfect markets are characterized by few or no barriers to entry and by many buyers and sellers.

perfect hedge STOCKHOLDING & INVESTMENTS investment with balanced risks an investment that exactly balances the risk of another investment

performance bond BANKING guarantee against third party failure to perform a guarantee given by a bank or insurance company to a third party stating that it will pay a sum of money if its customer, the account holder, fails to complete a specific contract

performance criteria GENERAL MANAGEMENT standards for judgment the standards used to evaluate a product, service, or employee

performance fund STOCKHOLDING & INVESTMENTS higher-risk investment fund expecting high returns an investment fund designed to produce a high return, reflected in the higher risk involved

performance indicator GENERAL MANAGEMENT criterion for assessing firm's performance a key measure designed to assess an aspect of the qualitative or quantitative performance of a company. Performance indicators can relate to operational, strategic, confidence, behavioral, and ethical aspects of a company's operation and can help to pinpoint its strengths and weaknesses. They are periodically monitored to ensure the company's long-term success.

performance management GENERAL MANAGEMENT helping employees to be successful the facilitation of high achievement by employees. Performance management involves enabling people to perform their work to the best of their ability, meeting and perhaps exceeding targets and standards. For successful performance management, a culture of collective and individual responsibility for the continuing improvement of business processes needs to be established, and individual skills and contributions need to be encouraged and nurtured Where organizations are concerned, performance management is usually known as company performance and is monitored through business appraisal.

performance rating MARKETS, GENERAL MANAGEMENT assessment of stock or firm's performance a judgment of how well a stock or a company has performed

performance-related pay FINANCE payment related to the quality of work a payment system in which the level of pay is dependent on the employee's performance. Performance-related pay can be entirely dependent or only partly dependent on performance. There are usually three stages to a performance-related pay system: determining the criteria by which the employee is assessed, establishing whether the employee has met the criteria, and linking the employee's achievements to the pay structure. Performance measures can incorporate skills, knowledge, and behavioral indicators. The system can be compared to ***payment by results***, which is based solely on quantitative productivity measures.

performance share *UK* STOCKHOLDING & INVESTMENTS = ***performance stock***

performance stock *US* STOCKHOLDING & INVESTMENTS higher-risk stock showing capital growth a stock which is likely to show capital growth rather than income, which is a characteristic of stocks with a higher risk. *UK term* ***performance share***

period bill *UK* FINANCE bill of exchange with specific payment date a bill of exchange payable on a specific date rather than on demand. *Also called* ***term bill***

period-end ACCOUNTING of end of accounting period relating to the end of an accounting period when financial transactions for that period are finalized

periodic inventory review system OPERATIONS & PRODUCTION means of regularly re-ordering inventory a system for placing orders of varying sizes at regular intervals to replenish inventory up to a specified or target level. A periodic inventory review system sets a specific re-order period, but the re-order quantity can vary according to need. The quantity re-ordered is calculated by subtracting existing inventory and on-order inventory from the target level. *Also called* ***fixed interval re-order system***

period of account ACCOUNTING time span covered by UK firm's accounts the period covered by a UK firm's accounts, sometimes coinciding with the firm's ***accounting period***

period of qualification time required to become qualified the time that has to pass before somebody becomes eligible or suitable for something

perk HR & PERSONNEL small supplement to pay a minor benefit that an employee receives in addition to pay, such as the opportunity to buy products cheaply or an interest-free loan for a season ticket (*informal*). *See also* ***fringe benefits***

permanent interest-bearing shares STOCKHOLDING & INVESTMENTS UK stock issued by credit union in the United Kingdom, stock issued by the UK equivalent of a credit union to raise capital because the law prohibits it from raising capital in more conventional ways. *Abbr* ***PIBS***

perpetual bond STOCKHOLDING & INVESTMENTS bond without maturity date a ***bond*** that has no date of maturity and pays interest in perpetuity

perpetual debenture FINANCE debenture without maturity date a ***debenture*** that has no date of maturity and pays interest in perpetuity

perpetual inventory OPERATIONS & PRODUCTION daily inventory check the daily tracking of inventory in order to keep its recorded amount and value up to date

perpetuity PENSIONS annuity that continues indefinitely a form of annuity that entitles the person holding it to receive payments without setting an end date

perquisites HR & PERSONNEL = ***fringe benefits***

per se GENERAL MANAGEMENT as such a Latin phrase meaning by itself or in itself

personal account 1. ACCOUNTING record of amounts for or from individual a record of amounts receivable from or payable to a person or an entity. In the United Kingdom, a collection of these accounts is known either as a sales/debtor ledger or a purchases/creditors ledger, or, more simply, as a ***revenue ledger*** or a ***purchase ledger***. In the United States, the terms ***receivables ledger*** and ***payables ledger*** are used. **2.** BANKING bank account for individual a bank account designed for a private individual rather than a business entity

personal allowance *UK* TAX = ***personal exemption***

personal brand GENERAL MANAGEMENT distinctive way somebody wishes to be seen the public expression and projection of a person's identity, personality, values, skills, and abilities. It aims to influence the perceptions of others, emphasizing personal strengths and differentiating the individual from others.

personal contract HR & PERSONNEL individualized contract of employment a ***contract of employment*** that is negotiated on an employee by employee basis, rather than using a traditional structured system that gives identical contracts to groups of workers

Personal Equity Plan STOCKHOLDING & INVESTMENTS former UK stock-based investment in the United Kingdom, a share-based tax-effective investment replaced by the ISA in 1999. *Abbr* ***PEP***

personal exemption *US* TAX amount somebody can earn without paying income tax the amount of money that an individual can earn without having to pay income tax. *UK term* ***personal allowance***

personal financial planning FINANCE person's short- and long-term financial arrangements short- and long-term financial planning by somebody, either independently or with the assistance of a professional adviser. It will include the use of tax-efficient plans such as Individual Retirement Accounts, ensuring adequate provisions are being made for retirement, and examining short- and long-term borrowing requirements such as overdrafts and mortgages.

Personal Identification Number BANKING *see* ***PIN***

personal income FINANCE money person receives from earnings and other payments the income received by somebody from various sources such as earnings, retirement funds, disability benefits, and dividends from investments

Personal Investment Authority REGULATION & COMPLIANCE UK organization regulating financial service providers in the United Kingdom, a self-regulatory organization that regulates the activities of financial advisers, insurance brokers, and others who give financial advice or arrange financial services for small clients. *Abbr* ***PIA***

personalization E-COMMERCE individualized selection of information by website the process by which a website presents customers with selected information on their specific needs. To do this, personal information is collected on the individual user and employed to customize the website for that person.

personal loan FINANCE loan used for personal purpose a loan from a financial institution to somebody for a personal use such as making home improvements or purchasing an automobile

personal pension PENSIONS pension independent of employer a pension taken out by somebody with a private sector insurance company or bank. A personal pension usually takes the form of a program in which money is paid regularly to a pension provider, who invests it in a pension fund. On retirement, a lump sum is available for the purchase of an annuity that provides weekly or monthly payments

personal pension plan PENSIONS pension provision covering one person not group a pension plan that is set up for one specific person rather than covering a group of employees

personal property FINANCE things belonging to somebody property other than real estate that a person owns

personnel management HR & PERSONNEL appointment, training, and welfare of employees the part of management that is concerned with people and their relationships at work. Personnel management is the responsibility of all those who manage people, as well as a description of the work of specialists. Personnel managers advise on, formulate, and implement personnel policies such as recruitment, conditions of employment, performance appraisal, training, industrial relations, and health and safety. There are various models of personnel management, of which ***human resource management*** is the most recent.

person-to-person lending FINANCE = ***social lending***

per stirpes LEGAL distribution of estate between remaining heirs a method of distributing the assets of an estate, in which the share of assets that would have gone to an heir who predeceases the maker of the will are divided equally among that heir's descendants

PERT *abbr* OPERATIONS & PRODUCTION ***program evaluation and review technique***

petites et moyennes entreprises GENERAL MANAGEMENT small and medium-sized businesses the French for small and medium-sized businesses. *Abbr* ***PME***

petroleum revenue tax TAX UK tax on North Sea oil firms in the United Kingdom, a tax on revenues from companies extracting oil from the North Sea. *Abbr* ***PRT***

petty cash ACCOUNTING amount kept for small payments a small accessible store of cash used for minor business expenses. *Abbr* ***P/C***

petty cash account ACCOUNTING record of small cash receipts and payments a record of relatively small cash receipts and payments, the balance representing the cash in the control of an individual, usually dealt with under an ***imprest system***

petty cash voucher ACCOUNTING document recording petty cash payments a document supporting payments of small amounts of cash to employees under a petty cash system

petty expenses ACCOUNTING small amounts spent on small items small sums of money spent on such items as postage, taxi fares, or copying charges

phantom bid MERGERS & ACQUISITIONS rumored company purchase a reported but nonexistent attempt to buy a company

phantom income TAX income subject to tax though never received income that is subject to tax even though the recipient never actually gets control of it, for example, income from a limited partnership

pharming E-COMMERCE, FRAUD fraudulent poaching of online bank customers the hijacking of online bank customers by infecting web browsers and redirecting them to fake websites, where they are asked to disclose their account details

Phillips curve STATISTICS relationship between unemployment and inflation rate a visual representation of the relationship between unemployment and the rate of inflation

phishing E-COMMERCE, FRAUD fraud to obtain financial information the fraudulent use of e-mail and fake websites to obtain financial information such as credit card numbers, passwords, and bank account information

phoenix activity *or* **phoenix practices** BUSINESS recreating liquidated firm under new name evasion of official responsibilities by the directors of a company that has had to cease doing business, by leaving liabilities in the liquidated business so that the underlying business activity can be immediately resumed under another name free of such liabilities

phoenix company BUSINESS firm formed from identical failed firm a company formed by the directors of a company that has gone into ***receivership***, trading in the same way as the first company and, except in name, appearing to be exactly the same

physical asset ACCOUNTING asset that is not cash or securities an asset such as a building or equipment that has a physical presence, as opposed to cash or securities

physical distribution management OPERATIONS & PRODUCTION overseeing of distribution of manufactured goods the planning, monitoring, and control of the distribution and delivery of manufactured goods

physical market MARKETS futures market involving delivery of commodities a market dealing in ***futures contracts*** that involves physical delivery of the commodities traded, rather than purchases that will be set off against sales in cash transactions and never actually delivered

physical price MARKETS price of commodity for immediate delivery the price of a commodity that is available for immediate delivery, rather than just representing a purchase that will be set off against a sale in a cash transaction and never actually delivered

physicals MARKETS commodities that can be bought and used commodities that are bought and delivered, rather than commodities traded on a ***futures contract***

PIA *abbr* REGULATION & COMPLIANCE ***Personal Investment Authority***

PIBOR *abbr* BANKING ***Paris Interbank Offered Rate***

PIBS *abbr* STOCKHOLDING & INVESTMENTS ***permanent interest-bearing shares***

picture MARKETS details of particular Wall Street stock the price and trading quantity of a specific stock on Wall Street used, for example, in the question to a specialist dealer "What's the picture on ABC?" The response would give the bid and offer price and number of shares for which there would be a buyer and seller (*slang*)

piece rate FINANCE payment according to units completed payment of a predetermined amount for each unit of output by an employee. The rate of pay is usually fixed subjectively, rather than by more objective techniques. Rates are said to be tight when it is difficult for an employee to earn a bonus and loose when bonuses are easily earned. Piece-rate systems are a form of ***payment by results*** or ***performance-related pay***.

piecework FINANCE work paid according to items produced work for which employees are paid in accordance with the number of products produced or pieces of work done and not at an hourly rate

pie chart STATISTICS circle graph divided into sections a chart drawn as a circle divided into proportional sections like portions of a pie

piggyback advertising MARKETING free secondary advertising with another campaign an offer or promotion that runs in parallel with another campaign and incurs no costs

piggyback loan FINANCE loan against same security as existing loan a loan that is raised against the same security as an existing loan

piggyback rights STOCKHOLDING & INVESTMENTS permission to sell existing shares with new shares permission to sell existing shares in conjunction with the sale of similar shares in a new offering

PIK note FINANCE debt finance paying interest on note redemption a form of ***debt financing*** that pays interest only when the note is redeemed, although the interest rate is usually much higher than on ordinary debt. The issue of PIK notes constitutes the payment of interest for tax purposes, so if the notes are issued in the accounting period in which the interest accrues, the interest is tax deductible on an ***accrual basis*** and does not affect cash flow. *Full form* ***payment-in-kind note***

pilot *or* **pilot survey** MARKETING trial to test methodology a preliminary piece of work conducted before full implementation of an activity or process to test its effectiveness

PIN BANKING number verifying card transaction a set of numbers that is used to access an account at an ATM, a computer, or a telephone system, or to verify a credit or debit card at an electronic point of sale. *Full form* ***Personal Identification Number***

pink dollar *US* FINANCE money spent by gays and lesbians money spent by gays and lesbians on goods and services that appeal to them. *UK term* ***pink pound***

pink form STOCKHOLDING & INVESTMENTS in the UK, stock application form for employees in the United Kingdom, a preferential application form for an ***initial public offering*** that is reserved for the employees of the company being floated. *Also called* ***preferential form***

pink paper *UK* FINANCE = ***Financial Times*** (*informal*)

pink pound *UK* FINANCE = ***pink dollar***

pink sheets MARKETS publication giving unlisted securities prices a daily publication of the prices of unlisted securities traded in the ***over-the-counter market*** but that are not traded on the NASDAQ exchange

pink slip ◇ get your pink slip HR & PERSONNEL to be dismissed from employment. (*informal*). *UK terms* ***get your cards, get the sack***

Pink 'Un *UK* FINANCE *Financial Times* an informal name for the London-based newspaper the *Financial Times*. It is printed on pink paper (*informal*).

pip CURRENCY & EXCHANGE smallest unit in currency price the smallest unit of change in the bid or ask price of a currency

pipeline MARKETS SEC procedure for new security issue the procedure required by the US Securities and Exchange Commission before a new security can be issued for sale to the public

piracy FRAUD illegal copying illegal copying of a product such as software or music

pit MARKETS trading area of financial exchange the area of an exchange where trading takes place. It was traditionally an octagonal stepped area with terracing so as to give everyone a good view of the proceedings during the verbal trading called ***open outcry***. *See also* ***ring*** *(sense 1)*

pit broker MARKETS trader in pit of financial exchange a broker who transacts business in the ***pit*** of a futures or options exchange. *Also called* ***floor broker***

pitch MARKETING attempt to persuade somebody to buy an attempt to win business from a customer, especially a presentation by a sales person

PITI MORTGAGES four items in monthly mortgage payment the four items included in a monthly mortgage payment. Lenders use PITI to determine the amount they will lend based on the relationship between monthly income and PITI. *Full form* ***principal, interest, taxes, and insurance***

placement *US* STOCKHOLDING & INVESTMENTS = ***private placement***

placement fee *UK* STOCKHOLDING & INVESTMENTS = ***commission***

placing *UK* MARKETS = ***private offering***

plain vanilla FINANCE standard form of financial product a basic or standard form of a ***financial instrument*** such as an ***option***, ***bond***, or ***swap*** (*slang*)

plank ◇ make somebody walk the plank HR & PERSONNEL to dismiss somebody from employment

planned economy ECONOMICS economic system completely controlled by government an economic system in which the government plans all business activity, regulates supply, sets production targets, and itemizes work to be done. *Also called* ***command economy***. *See also* ***central planning***

planned obsolescence OPERATIONS & PRODUCTION deliberate designing of products to require replacing a policy of designing products to have a limited life span so that customers will have to buy replacements regularly

plan participant HR & PERSONNEL employee in benefit plan an employee enrolled in a employer-sponsored benefit plan

plant ACCOUNTING fixed assets producing goods the capital assets used to produce goods, typically factories, production lines, and large equipment

plastic *or* **plastic money** BANKING debit or credit card a payment system using a debit or credit card, not cash or checks (*informal*). *See also* ***credit card, debit card, multifunctional card***

platform GENERAL MANAGEMENT product supporting others a product used as a basis for building more complex products or delivering services, for example, a communications network is a platform for delivering knowledge or data

platinum MARKETS precious metal traded as commodity a rare precious metal traded on bullion markets

plc *or* **PLC** *abbr* BUSINESS ***public limited company***

plenitude ECONOMICS hypothetical situation with abundant supply of products a hypothetical condition of an economy in which manufacturing technology has been perfected and scarcity is replaced by an abundance of products

plot *UK* REAL ESTATE = ***lot*** *(sense 4)*

plough back *UK* FINANCE = ***plow back***

ploughed back profits *UK* FINANCE = ***plowed back profits***

plow back *US* FINANCE reinvest earnings instead of paying dividends to reinvest a company's earnings in the business instead of paying them out as dividends. *UK term* ***plough back***

plowed back profits *US* FINANCE = ***ploughed back profits***

plug MARKETING advertise something to publicize or advertise a product or service

plum *UK* STOCKHOLDING & INVESTMENTS successful investment an investment that yields a good return (*slang*)

plus tick MARKETS = ***uptick***

PME *abbr* GENERAL MANAGEMENT ***petites et moyennes entreprises***

PN *abbr* FINANCE ***promissory note***

PO *abbr* OPERATIONS & PRODUCTION ***purchase order***

point FINANCE **1.** unit used in calculating a value a unit used for calculation of a value, such as a hundredth of a percentage point for interest rates **2.** unit on scale a single unit on any scale of measurement, such as a salary scale or range of prices

point and click agreement E-COMMERCE = ***click wrap agreement***

poison pill MERGERS & ACQUISITIONS deterrent measure taken to avoid hostile takeover a measure taken by a company to avoid a hostile takeover, for example, the purchase of a business interest that will make the company unattractive to the potential buyer (*slang*). *Also called* ***show stopper***

policyholder INSURANCE person or organization with insurance policy a person or business that has taken out a specific insurance policy

political economy ECONOMICS study of government and economics the study of the ways in which the politics and economic organization of a country interact

political price ECONOMICS bad effect on government of decision the negative impact on a government of a policy decision such as raising interest rates

political risk ECONOMICS possible bad effect on government of decision the potential negative impact on a government of a policy decision such as raising interest rates

Ponzi scheme FRAUD banking fraud a fraudulent pyramid selling activity that offers investors high returns which are paid directly from the money deposited by new investors. When new deposits cannot match payments, the organization fails. The fraud is named after Charles Ponzi, who first set up such a scheme in the United States in 1920.

pool FINANCE collateral underpinning loan a group of mortgages and other collateral that is used to back a loan

poop *US* FINANCE somebody with privileged information a person who has ***inside information*** on a financial deal (*slang*)

pooping and scooping *US* MARKETS illegally spreading rumor to lower stock price an illegal financial practice in which a person or group of individuals attempts to drive down the price of a stock by spreading false unfavorable information. The advent of the Internet has allowed pooping and scooping to become more widespread (*slang*).

population STATISTICS set of people, things, or events in a statistical study, the entire collection of units such as events or people from which a sample may be observed

population pyramid STATISTICS representation of group by sex and age a graphical presentation of data in the form of two histograms with a common base, showing a comparison of a human population in terms of sex and age

pork bellies FINANCE meat of pigs traded as commodity meat from the underside of pig carcasses used to make bacon, traded as ***futures*** on some US commodities exchanges

portable pension *UK* PENSIONS pension savings transferring with employee to new job a ***personal pension*** that moves with an employee when he or she changes employer, as opposed to an ***occupational pension*** that usually does not. *See also* ***stakeholder pension***

portfolio STOCKHOLDING & INVESTMENTS investments held by one owner a set of investments, such as stocks and bonds, owned by one person or organization. *Also called* ***investment portfolio***

portfolio career HR & PERSONNEL work pattern of several employments followed simultaneously an employment pattern that involves working part-time on several different jobs at any one time, rather than on a succession of single full-time jobs. *See also* ***portfolio working***

portfolio immunization STOCKHOLDING & INVESTMENTS measures to maintain investment value measures taken by traders to protect their holdings against loss or undue risk

portfolio insurance STOCKHOLDING & INVESTMENTS options protecting portfolio the use of ***options*** that provide ***hedges*** against the set of investments held

portfolio investment STOCKHOLDING & INVESTMENTS investment seeking spread of assets a form of investment that attempts to achieve a mixture of securities in order to minimize risk and maximize return

portfolio management STOCKHOLDING & INVESTMENTS trading to maximize investor's profit the professional management of investment portfolios with the goal of minimizing risk and maximizing return

portfolio manager STOCKHOLDING & INVESTMENTS specialist in investment management a person or company that specializes in managing an investment portfolio on behalf of investors. *See also* ***money manager***

portfolio theory STOCKHOLDING & INVESTMENTS idea that variety of investments bring best results a strategy for managing a portfolio of investments in order to minimize risk and maximize return by having a variety of types of investments. *Also called* ***modern portfolio theory***. *See also* ***CAPM***

portfolio working HR & PERSONNEL having several employments simultaneously a way of working in which a person follows several simultaneous career pursuits at any one time rather than working full-time for one employer. *See also* ***downshifting, portfolio career***

position STOCKHOLDING & INVESTMENTS size of holding of one owner the number of shares of a security that are owned by a person or organization

position limit STOCKHOLDING & INVESTMENTS maximum holding for individual or group the largest amount of a security that any group or individual may own

positive carry STOCKHOLDING & INVESTMENTS when investment return is greater than cost a situation in which the cost of financing an investment is less than the return obtained from it

positive cash flow FINANCE when firm's income is greater than outflow a situation in which more money is coming into a company than is going out

positive discrimination HR & PERSONNEL favoring appointments from disadvantaged groups preferential treatment, usually through a quota system, to prevent or correct discriminatory employment practices, particularly relating to recruitment and promotion

positive economics ECONOMICS study of verifiable economic theories the study of economic propositions that can be verified by observing the real economy

positive yield curve STOCKHOLDING & INVESTMENTS when long-term investment return exceeds short-term a visual representation of a situation in which the yield on a short-term investment is less than that on a long-term investment. In a long-term investment, an investor expects a higher return because his or her money is tied up and at risk for a longer period of time.

possessor in bad faith REAL ESTATE holder of land not asserting legal right somebody who occupies land even though they do not believe they have a legal right to do so

possessor in good faith REAL ESTATE holder of land asserting legal right somebody who occupies land believing they have a legal right to do so

possessory action REAL ESTATE legal action about land rights a lawsuit over the right to own a piece of land

postal account BANKING account operated only by mail an account for which all dealings are done by post, thereby reducing ***overhead costs*** and allowing a higher level of ***interest*** to be paid

postal vote *UK* FINANCE = ***mail ballot***

post-balance sheet event ACCOUNTING incident affecting accounts after balance sheet completed something that happens after the date when a balance sheet is completed but before it is officially approved by the directors, that affects a company's financial position

Post Big Bang MARKETS describing current London Stock Exchange trading system used to describe the trading mechanism on the London Stock Exchange after the market liberalization changes effected in October 1986. *See also* ***Big Bang***

post-completion audit GENERAL MANAGEMENT independent appraisal of success of project an objective and independent appraisal of the measure of success of a capital expenditure project in progressing the business as planned. The appraisal should cover the implementation of the project from authorization to commissioning and its technical and commercial performance after commissioning. The information provided is also used by management as feedback, which helps the implementation and control of future projects.

postdate GENERAL MANAGEMENT date document or check later than date signed to put a later date on a document or check than the date when it is signed, with the effect that it is not valid until the later date

postindustrial society ECONOMICS economy not reliant on heavy industry a society in which the resources of labor and capital are replaced by those of knowledge and information as the main sources of wealth creation. The postindustrial society involves a shift in focus from manufacturing industries to service industries and is enabled by technological advances.

pot 1. STOCKHOLDING & INVESTMENTS unreleased portion of stock issue the part of a new stock issue that is not released to the public and is only available for purchase by institutional investors **2.** *US* FINANCE amount collected for specific use an amount of money collected from the members of a group for a specific purpose ◇ pot of gold FINANCE a large amount of money, especially one that is achieved by accident or good luck ◇ pot of money FINANCE an amount of money assigned to a specific purpose ◇ pots of money FINANCE an extremely large amount of money

potential GDP ECONOMICS full value of country's production capacity a measure of the real value of the services and goods that can be produced when a country's factors of production are fully employed. *See also* ***GDP***

potentially exempt transfer TAX gift conditionally exempt from UK inheritance tax in the United Kingdom, an outright gift made during a lifetime to a person or to some types of trusts that does not affect the standard of living of the donor. There is no ***inheritance tax*** to be paid on such a gift, but a liability arises if the donor dies within seven years, with that liability decreasing the longer the donor survives. *See also* ***chargeable transfer***

pot trust FINANCE trust for group of people a trust, typically created in a will, for a group of beneficiaries

pound CURRENCY & EXCHANGE main currency unit in UK and other countries a unit of currency used in the United Kingdom and many other countries including Cyprus, Egypt, Lebanon, Malta, Sudan, and Syria

pound cost averaging *UK* STOCKHOLDING & INVESTMENTS = ***dollar cost averaging***

pound sterling CURRENCY & EXCHANGE official UK currency the official term for the currency used in the United Kingdom

poverty trap TAX disadvantage occurring when pay rise reduces total income a situation whereby low-income families are penalized by a progressive tax system: an increase in income is either counteracted by a loss of social benefit payments or by an increase in taxation

power center GENERAL MANAGEMENT most influential section of organization the part of an organization that has the strongest influence on policy

power of appointment LEGAL power of trustee to dispose of real estate the power of a trustee to dispose of interests in real estate to another person

power of attorney LEGAL legal agreement for acting for another a legal document granting one person the right to act on behalf of another in legal and financial matters and, in the United Kingdom since 2007, in decisions on healthcare and welfare

power structure GENERAL MANAGEMENT relative location of influence the way in which power is distributed among different groups or individuals in an organization

pp GENERAL MANAGEMENT on behalf of derived from the Latin "per pro," used beside a signature at the end of a letter, meaning "on behalf of"

PPF *abbr* PENSIONS ***Pension Protection Fund***

PPP *abbr* **1.** CURRENCY & EXCHANGE ***purchasing power parity*** **2.** BUSINESS ***public private partnership***

preauthorized electronic debit *US* BANKING agreed transfer between bank accounts a system in which a payer agrees to let a bank make payments from an account to somebody else's account. *UK term* ***direct debit***

prebilling OPERATIONS & PRODUCTION submitting bill before delivery the practice of submitting a bill for a product or service before it has actually been delivered

pre-Budget report FINANCE fall forecast of UK government's economic plans in the United Kingdom, an economic forecast the government has to present in the fall of each year, reporting on progress since the Budget in the spring and outlining government spending plans prior to the next Budget. *Abbr* ***PBR***

preceding year ACCOUNTING previous fiscal year the year before the ***fiscal year*** in question

preceding year basis ACCOUNTING using previous year's accounts the principle of assessing income or profits based on the figures for the year before the ***fiscal year*** in question. *Abbr* ***PYB***

precious metals FINANCE high value metals rare metals with a high economic value, especially gold, silver, and platinum

predate *US* GENERAL MANAGEMENT **1.** put earlier date on document to put an earlier date than the current date on a document **2.** make something apply from earlier date to make something effective from an earlier date than the current date ▶ *UK term* ***antedate***

predatory lending FINANCE unfair lending practices the practice of encouraging people to borrow in an unfair or unprincipled way, especially if the loan is greater than a borrower can reasonably be expected to repay, or is based on personal property such as a house or car which will be lost if the borrower defaults

predatory pricing OPERATIONS & PRODUCTION setting prices lower than competitors the practice of setting prices for products that are designed to win business from competitors or to damage competitors

pre-emption right *UK* STOCKHOLDING & INVESTMENTS = ***pre-emptive right***

pre-emptive right *US* STOCKHOLDING & INVESTMENTS right of stockholder to first purchase of new stock the right of a stockholder who already owns stock in a company to maintain proportional ownership by being first to purchase stock in a new issue. *UK term* ***pre-emption right***

preference share *UK* STOCKHOLDING & INVESTMENTS = ***preferred stock***

preferential creditor FINANCE creditor who must be paid before others a creditor who is entitled to payment, especially from a bankrupt, before other creditors

preferential form STOCKHOLDING & INVESTMENTS = ***pink form***

preferential issue STOCKHOLDING & INVESTMENTS stock for specific buyers an issue of stock available only to designated buyers

preferential payment FINANCE payment to priority creditor a payment to a ***preferential creditor***, whose debt has first claim on a bankrupt or company that is winding up

preferred risk INSURANCE somebody not regarded as a poor insurance risk somebody considered by an insurance company to be less likely to collect on a policy than the average person, for example, a nonsmoker

preferred stock *US* STOCKHOLDING & INVESTMENTS stock receiving dividend or repayment before others stock that entitles the owner to preference in the distribution of dividends and the proceeds of liquidation in the event of bankruptcy. *UK term* ***preference share***

pre-financing FINANCE securing funding before project begins the practice of arranging funding in advance of the start date of a project

prelaunch MARKETING preparation for product launch the activities that precede the introduction of a new product to the market

preliminary announcement ACCOUNTING initial announcement of firm's financial results an announcement of a company's full-year financial results, which are given out to the press before the detailed annual report is released

preliminary prospectus STOCKHOLDING & INVESTMENTS details about firm given before initial public offering a document issued prior to an ***initial public offering*** that provides details about the company and its financial situation. *Also called* ***red herring***

premarket MARKETS describing transactions before official opening of market used to describe transactions between market members conducted prior to the official opening of the market. *Also called* ***pretrading***

Premiers' Conference FINANCE annual meeting of Australian federal and state heads an annual meeting at which the premiers of the states and territories of Australia meet with the federal government to discuss their funding allocations

premium **1.** FINANCE extra cost for scarcity a higher price paid for a scarce product or service **2.** FINANCE extra charge for high quality a pricing method that uses high price to indicate high quality **3.** STOCKHOLDING & INVESTMENTS price paid for option the price a purchaser of a traded ***option*** pays to its seller **4.** STOCKHOLDING & INVESTMENTS difference between futures price and cash price the difference between the futures price and the cash price of an underlying asset **5.** INSURANCE price of insurance contract the amount paid for an insurance contract, which is needed before the contract is valid ◇ at a premium **1.** FINANCE of a fixed interest security, at an issue price above its nominal value **2.** FINANCE at a price that is considered expensive in relation to others **3.** STOCKHOLDING & INVESTMENTS of a new issue, at a trading price above the one offered to investors

Premium Bond STOCKHOLDING & INVESTMENTS non-interest-bearing UK security eligible for prize draw in the United Kingdom, a nonmarketable security issued by National Savings & Investments at £1 each that pays no interest but is entered into a draw every month to win prizes from £50 to £1 million. There are many lower value prizes, but only one £1 million prize. The bonds are repayable upon demand.

premium income INSURANCE insurance firm's income from premiums the income earned by an insurance company from the money paid for its contracts

premium offer MARKETING offer of free gift with sale a sales promotion technique in which customers are offered a free gift

premium pay plan FINANCE higher pay scale for top employees an enhanced pay scale for high performing employees. A premium pay plan can be offered as an incentive to motivate employees, rewarding such achievements as high productivity, long service, or completion of training with an increased pay package.

premium pricing MARKETING charging high price for high quality the deliberate setting of high prices for a product or service to emphasize its quality or exclusiveness. *Also called* ***prestige pricing***

premoney valuation *or* **premoney value** FINANCE firm's value before capital investors contribute the assessed value of a business before ***venture capital*** or other capital investors make their investment

prepack *or* **prepackaged administration** *or* **prepack administration** BUSINESS UK firm recreated via administration process in the United Kingdom, a business that goes into administration and, having shed its debts, legally emerging as an almost identical company

prepaid interest FINANCE interest paid early interest paid in advance of the date on which it is due

prepayment FINANCE payment of debt before due date the payment of a debt before it is due to be paid

prepayment penalty FINANCE charge made for early payment a charge that may be levied if a payment, such as one on a mortgage or loan, is made before it is due to be paid. The penalty compensates the lender or seller for potential lost interest.

prepayment privilege FINANCE payment before due date without penalty the right to make a payment, such as one on a loan or mortgage, before it is due to be paid, without penalty

prepayment risk FINANCE, RISK risk that prepayment will reduce interest income the risk that a debtor will avoid interest charges by making partial or total payment in advance on a mortgage or loan, especially when interest rates fall

prequalification **1.** FINANCE, MORTGAGES evaluation of likely borrower the process of establishing the financial circumstances of a borrower or mortgage customer before a loan is formally applied for **2.** MARKETING evaluation of likely customer a sales technique in which the potential value of a prospect is carefully evaluated through research

prerefunding STOCKHOLDING & INVESTMENTS using funds from new bond to repay another the process of issuing a longer-term bond in order to take advantage of a drop in interest rates and use the funds to pay off another bond issued earlier

prescribed payments system TAX deduction of tax from Australian casual workers' payments in Australia, a system under which employers are obliged to deduct a specific amount of tax from cash payments made to casual workers

present value FINANCE **1.** future value of asset, discounted for inflation the amount that a future interest in a financial asset is currently worth, discounted for inflation. *Also called* ***discounted value*** **2.** current value of future income, minus accruing interest the value now of an amount of money that somebody expects to receive at a future date, calculated by subtracting any interest that will accrue in the interim

preservation of capital STOCKHOLDING & INVESTMENTS cautious investment strategy an approach to financial management that protects a person's or company's capital by arranging additional forms of finance

pressure group GENERAL MANAGEMENT group formed to lobby for something a body of people who have banded together to campaign on one or more issues of importance to them. A pressure group usually has a formal constitution and coordinates its activities to influence the attitudes or activities of business or government.

prestige pricing MARKETING = ***premium pricing***

pre-syndicate bid STOCKHOLDING & INVESTMENTS advance bid on NASDAQ exchange in the ***NASDAQ*** system, a bid made before a public offering in order to stabilize the price of the stock on offer

pretax TAX before tax before taxes are deducted

pretax profit TAX profit before tax the amount of profit a company makes before taxes are deducted

pretax profit margin TAX profit as a percentage of sales, before tax the profit made by a company, calculated as a percentage of sales and before taxes are considered

pretrading MARKETS = ***premarket***

prevalence STATISTICS how many individuals show same feature in a statistical study, a measure of the number of individuals involved who have a specific characteristic

previous balance ACCOUNTING closing balance of previous accounting period a balance in an account at the end of the ***accounting period*** before the current one

price OPERATIONS & PRODUCTION amount charged to customer an amount of money that a seller charges a customer for a good or service

price-book ratio STOCKHOLDING & INVESTMENTS = ***price-to-book ratio***

price cartel OPERATIONS & PRODUCTION set of firms illegally coordinating prices a group of businesses who make an agreement, often illegally, to maintain prices for a product at a specific level

price ceiling OPERATIONS & PRODUCTION highest price on offer the highest price that a buyer is willing to pay

price change MARKETS price movement of specific stock during day an amount by which the price of a specific share of stock moves during a day's trading

price competition OPERATIONS & PRODUCTION competition on price only a form of competition that is based only on price rather than factors such as quality or design

price controls ECONOMICS government limits on prices to control inflation measures used by a government to set prices in order to protect consumers from rapidly rising prices. Many economists believe that price controls actually hurt the economy by creating shortages and should only be used in an emergency.

price cutting OPERATIONS & PRODUCTION reducing prices to encourage sales a sudden lowering of prices below normal levels in order to boost sales and outsell competitors

price-cutting war OPERATIONS & PRODUCTION = ***price war***

price differential OPERATIONS & PRODUCTION difference in price between similar products a difference in price between products in a range. A basic digital camera, for example, will have a relatively low price compared to the same camera with additional features.

price differentiation OPERATIONS & PRODUCTION pricing same product differently in different markets a pricing strategy in which a company sells the same product at different prices in different markets

price discovery ECONOMICS establishment of price in free market the process by which price is determined by negotiation in a free market

price discrimination OPERATIONS & PRODUCTION selling to different buyers at different prices the practice of selling the same product to different buyers at different prices

price/dividend ratio STOCKHOLDING & INVESTMENTS price of stock divided by annual dividend paid a ratio derived from the price of a stock divided by the annual dividend paid on a share, which gives an indication of how much has to be paid to receive $1 of dividends. *Abbr* ***PDR***

price/earnings multiple STOCKHOLDING & INVESTMENTS stock price divided by its earnings the number of times by which the price of stock is greater than the earnings per share, or ***EPS***. *Abbr* ***P/E multiple***. *See also* ***price/earnings ration***

price/earnings ratio STOCKHOLDING & INVESTMENTS price of stock divided by earnings per share a company's stock price divided by earnings per share.

While earnings per share (EPS) is an actual amount of money, usually expressed in cents per share, the P/E ratio has no units, it is just a number. Thus if a quoted company has a stock price of $100 and EPS of $12 for the last published year, then it has a historical P/E ratio of 8.3. If analysts are forecasting for the next year EPS of, say, $14, then the forecast P/E ratio is 7.1. The P/E ratio is predominantly useful in comparisons with other stocks rather than in isolation. For example, if the average P/E ratio in the market is 20, there will be many stocks with P/E ratios well above and well below this, for a variety of reasons. Similarly, in a particular sector, the P/E ratios will frequently vary from the sector average, even though the constituent companies may all be engaged in similar businesses. The reason is that even two businesses doing the same thing will not always be doing it as profitably as each other. One may be far more efficient, as demonstrated by a history of rising EPS compared with the flat EPS picture of the other over a series of years, and the market might recognize this by awarding the more profitable stock a higher P/E ratio. *Abbr* ***PER***

price effect ECONOMICS how price changes affect economy the impact of price changes on a market or economy

price elasticity of demand ECONOMICS how demand responds to price changes the percentage change in demand divided by the percentage change in price of a good

price elasticity of supply ECONOMICS how supply responds to price changes the percentage change in supply divided by the percentage change in price of a good

price escalation clause LEGAL provision permitting seller to cover increased costs a contract provision that permits the seller to raise prices in response to increased costs

price fixing OPERATIONS & PRODUCTION illegal agreement by producers to coordinate prices an often illegal agreement between producers of a good or service in order to maintain prices at a particular level

price floor OPERATIONS & PRODUCTION lowest price acceptable the lowest price at which a seller is prepared to do business

price index ECONOMICS index measuring inflation an index such as the consumer price index that measures inflation

price indicator ECONOMICS measure of general price trends a measurable variable that can be used as an indicator of the price of something, for example the number of home loans arranged can be an indicator for rising or falling house prices

price-insensitive ECONOMICS describing essential goods or services with unvarying sales used to describe a good or service for which sales remain constant no matter what its price because it is essential to buyers

price instability ECONOMICS situation in which prices change frequently a situation in which the prices of goods alter daily or even hourly

price leadership OPERATIONS & PRODUCTION setting of prevailing market price the establishment of price levels in a market by a dominant company or brand

price ring OPERATIONS & PRODUCTION set of traders illegally coordinating prices a group of individual traders who make an agreement, often illegally, to maintain the price of a product at a specific level

prices and incomes policy ECONOMICS government regulations on prices and wages a policy that limits price or wage increases through government regulations

price-sensitive ECONOMICS describing goods or services with price-dependent sales used to describe a good or service for which sales fluctuate depending on its price, often because it is a nonessential item

price-sensitive information MARKETS information affecting firm's stock price if published as yet unpublished information that will affect a company's stock price. For example, the implementation of a new manufacturing process that will substantially cut production costs would have a positive impact, whereas the discovery of harmful side effects from a recently launched drug would have a negative impact.

price slashing OPERATIONS & PRODUCTION making very large price reduction sudden extreme lowering of a price in order to boost sales

price stability ECONOMICS insignificant changes in prices a situation in which there is little fluctuation in the price of goods or services overall

price support ECONOMICS government spending to keep prices from falling government assistance designed to keep market prices from falling below a minimum level

price-to-book ratio STOCKHOLDING & INVESTMENTS ratio of firm's market value to theoretical value the ratio of the value of all of a company's stock to its ***book value***. *Also called* ***price-book ratio***

price-to-cash-flow ratio STOCKHOLDING & INVESTMENTS ratio of firm's market value to cash flow the ratio of the value of all of a company's stock to its cash flow for the most recent complete fiscal year

price-to-sales ratio STOCKHOLDING & INVESTMENTS ratio of firm's market value to sales the ratio of the value of all of a company's stock to its sales for the previous twelve months, a way of measuring the relative value of a stock when compared with others.

The P/S ratio is obtained by dividing the ***market capitalization*** by the latest published annual sales figure. So a company with a capitalization of $1 billion and sales of $3 billion would have a P/S ratio of 0.33.

P/S will vary with the type of industry. You would expect, for example, that many retailers and other large-scale distributors of goods would have very high sales in relation to their market capitalizations—in other words, a very low P/S. Equally, manufacturers of high-value items would generally have much lower sales figures and thus higher P/S ratios.

A company with a lower P/S is cheaper than one with a higher ratio, particularly if they are in the same sector so that a direct comparison is more appropriate. It means that each share of the lower P/S company is buying more of its sales than those of the higher P/S company.

It is important to note that a stock which is cheaper only on P/S grounds is not necessarily the more attractive stock. There will frequently be reasons why it has a lower ratio than another similar company, most commonly because it is less profitable.

price war OPERATIONS & PRODUCTION cycle of cost cutting to undercut competitors a situation in which two or more companies each try to increase their own share of the market by lowering prices. A price war involves companies undercutting each other in an attempt to encourage more customers to buy their goods or services. In the long term, this can devalue a market and lead to loss of profits, but it can sometimes have short-term success.

price-weighted index ECONOMICS index adjusted for price changes an index of production or market value that is adjusted for changes that occur in prices

pricing model OPERATIONS & PRODUCTION computerized multifactorial system for calculating prices a computerized system for calculating prices, based on a variety of factors including costs and anticipated margins

pricing policy *or* **pricing strategy** OPERATIONS & PRODUCTION way in which businesses determine prices the method of ***decision making*** used for setting the prices for a company's products or services. A pricing policy is usually based on the costs of production or provision with a margin for profit, for example, ***cost-plus pricing***.

primary account number BANKING credit card identifier an identifier for a credit card used in secure electronic transactions

primary commodities MARKETS agricultural bulk produce farm produce that is grown in large quantities, for example corn, rice, or cotton

primary data *or* **primary information** MARKETING information from original research original data derived from a new research study and collected at source, as opposed to previously published material

primary earnings per (common) share STOCKHOLDING & INVESTMENTS profit from each current share of common stock a measure of earnings per share calculated on the basis of the number of shares of ***common stock*** actually held by investors, not including exercisable warrants and options. *See also* ***fully diluted earnings per (common) share, earnings per share***

primary industry BUSINESS type of business involved in obtaining natural resources an industry that deals with obtaining basic raw materials such as coal, wood, or farm products

primary liability FINANCE, INSURANCE responsibility as first payer of financial claims a responsibility to pay before anyone else who also has financial responsibility for financial claims such as damages covered by insurance

primary market MARKETS market for securities offered to investors by issuer the part of the market on which securities are first offered to investors by the issuer. The money from this sale goes to the issuer, rather than to traders or investors as it does in the secondary market. *See also* ***secondary market***

primary product MARKETS natural resource, often used in other products a product which is a basic raw material, for example, wood, milk, or fish

primary sector ECONOMICS part of economy involved in production businesses operating in the sector of a country's economy that is involved in producing goods

prime BANKING = ***prime rate***

prime assets ratio BANKING Australian banks' obligatory holding in secure assets in Australia, the proportion of total liabilities that banks are obliged by the Reserve Bank to hold in highly secure assets such as cash and government securities. *Abbr* ***PAR***

prime bill FINANCE risk-free bill of exchange an agreement that involves no risk of default, setting out an instruction to pay a particular person a fixed sum of money on a particular date or when the person requests payment

prime broker STOCKHOLDING & INVESTMENTS investment bank servicing hedge fund an investment bank that provides borrowing, lending, and settlement services to a ***hedge fund***. Such financial services are often considered the most profitable activity for a major bank but great losses can be incurred if the hedge fund fails.

prime cost OPERATIONS & PRODUCTION cost of producing product, not including overhead the cost involved in producing a product, excluding the general recurring costs of running a business

prime lending BANKING safe lending to creditworthy borrower lending to borrowers who have no delinquencies or defaults and no historical or current financial problems. *Also called* ***vanilla lending***

prime loan BANKING safe loan to creditworthy borrower a loan to a borrower who is regarded as being highly creditworthy, has no obvious financial difficulties and a good payment record, and is therefore very likely to repay the loan. *Also called* ***vanilla loan***

prime rate *or* **prime interest rate** BANKING in US, best interest rate on offer in the United States, the lowest interest rate that commercial banks offer on loans to well-regarded customers. It is analogous to the ***base rate*** in the United Kingdom. *Also called* ***prime***

priming FINANCE = ***pump priming***

principal FINANCE original amount lent the original amount of a loan or investment, not including any ***interest***. *See also* ***mortgage***

principal shareholders *UK* STOCKHOLDING & INVESTMENTS = ***principal stockholders***

principal stockholders *US* STOCKHOLDING & INVESTMENTS owners of majority of stock the people who own the largest percentage of stock in a business or organization. *UK term* ***principal shareholders***

principles-based regulation REGULATION & COMPLIANCE financial industry regulation relying on good practice regulation of the financial industry that relies more on desired regulatory outcomes and principles and less on detailed rules

prior charge percentage STOCKHOLDING & INVESTMENTS = ***priority percentage***

priority percentage STOCKHOLDING & INVESTMENTS share of profit paid to priority stockholders the proportion of a business's net profit that is paid in interest to holders of ***debt capital*** and ***preferred stock***. *Also called* ***prior charge percentage***

prior lien bond STOCKHOLDING & INVESTMENTS bond giving priority claim on debtor's assets a bond whose holder has more claim on a debtor's assets than holders of other types of bonds

prior year adjustment ACCOUNTING alteration to accounts of previous years an adjustment made to accounts for previous years, because of changes in accounting policies or because of errors

private bank BANKING **1.** bank owned by individual or small group a bank that is owned by a single person or a limited number of private stockholders **2.** bank for wealthy clients a bank that provides banking facilities to high net worth individuals. *See also* ***private banking*** **3.** independent bank in country with state-owned institutions a bank that is not state-owned in a country where most banks are owned by the government

private banking BANKING banking services offered to wealthy clients a service offered by some financial institutions to high net worth individuals. In addition to standard banking services, it will typically include portfolio management and advisory services on taxation, including estate planning.

private company BUSINESS company whose stock is not publicly traded a company that is privately owned and whose stock is not offered for sale to the public

private cost ECONOMICS cost to individual consumer or firm of consumption the cost incurred by individuals or companies when they consume resources

private debt FINANCE nongovernmental borrowings money owed by individuals and organizations other than governments

private enterprise ECONOMICS businesses not controlled by government business or industry that is controlled by companies or individuals rather than the government

private equity company BUSINESS private firm funding profitable projects a company not quoted on a public stock market that provides long-term equity finance to unquoted companies by investing money in the form of shares of stock or shares and shareholder loans. Private equity companies provide money for both ***venture capital funds*** and ***buyout*** or ***growth funds***.

private equity financing FINANCE = ***venture capital***

private income FINANCE income separate from salary income from dividends, interest, or rent which is not part of a salary

private investor STOCKHOLDING & INVESTMENTS ordinary person investing money an ordinary person who makes investments and who is not in the business of investing other people's money

private label *US* MARKETING generic product sold under retailer's name a product or range of products offered by a retailer under its own name in competition with branded goods. Private label products, like ***nonbranded goods***, are normally cheaper than branded items but are often perceived to be of lower quality. *Also called* ***own label***. *UK term* ***own brand***

private label MBS BUSINESS US finance company creating and selling bonds in the United States, a finance company other than Fannie Mae, Ginnie Mae, and Freddie Mac that creates and sells mortgage-backed securities or other bonds and is often collateralized by loans which are not eligible for purchase by Freddie Mac

private limited company BUSINESS private UK firm with small number of stockholders in the United Kingdom and some other countries, a company that has a small number of stockholders and whose stock is not traded on the stock exchange

private mortgage insurance INSURANCE insurance to cover default on mortgage an insurance policy that will cover the risk of a mortgagee defaulting on payments, in the case of loss of job, long-term illness, or other financial difficulty

private offering *US* MARKETS finding buyer for many shares in new firm the act of finding a single buyer or a group of institutional buyers for a large number of shares in a new company or a company that is going public. *UK term* ***placing***

private ownership BUSINESS ownership by citizens not by government a situation in which a company is owned by private stockholders, as opposed to being owned by a government

private placement *US* STOCKHOLDING & INVESTMENTS sale of securities directly to investors the sale of securities directly to institutions for investment rather than resale. *UK term* ***private placing***

private placing *UK* STOCKHOLDING & INVESTMENTS = ***private placement***

private property FINANCE property not for general public use property or assets that are owned by a person or group and not for use by the general public

private sector ECONOMICS part of economy not controlled by government the section of the economy that is financed and controlled by individuals or private institutions such as companies, stockholders, or investment groups. *See also* ***public sector***

private sector investment ECONOMICS non-government investment investment by the private enterprise sector of an economy

private treaty FINANCE land sale without auction the sale of land arranged by seller and buyer without a public auction

privatization GENERAL MANAGEMENT transfer from state to private ownership the transfer of a company from ownership by either a government or a few individuals to the public via the issuance of stock

probability STATISTICS how likely it is something will happen the quantitative measure of the likelihood that a given event will occur

probability distribution STATISTICS formula representing probability of values of variables in a statistical study, a mathematical formula showing the probability for each value of a variable

probability measure RISK, STATISTICS evaluation of chance of event occurring in a statistical study, a calculation of the likelihood that a given event will occur

probability plot STATISTICS graph comparing two probability distributions in a statistical study, a graphic plot of data that compares two probability distributions

probability sampling STATISTICS creating statistical sample that could include any individual in a statistical study, a way of sampling in which every individual in a finite population has a known, but not necessarily equal, chance of being included in the sample, which is known as a ***probability sample***

probate LEGAL legal acceptance of validity of will the legal process by which a will is accepted as valid

problem child **1.** *US* BUSINESS troublesome subsidiary company a subsidiary company that is not performing well or is damaging the ***parent company*** in some way (*slang*) **2.** MARKETING underperforming product with high potential a product with a low market share but high growth potential. Problem children often have good long-term prospects, but high levels of investment may be needed to realize the potential, thereby draining funds that may be needed elsewhere. *See also* ***Boston Box***

problem solving GENERAL MANAGEMENT methodology for dealing with management problems a systematic approach to overcoming obstacles or problems in the management process. Problems occur when something is not behaving as it should, when something deviates from the norm, or when something goes wrong. A number of problem-solving methodologies exist, but the most widely used includes these steps: recognizing a problem exists and defining it; generating a variety of solutions; evaluating the possible solutions and choosing the best one; implementing the solution and evaluating its effectiveness in solving the problem.

proceeds FINANCE income from sale the money derived from a sale or other commercial transaction

process box GENERAL MANAGEMENT symbol representing action a primary symbol used in a ***flow chart*** that indicates a process or action taking place. *See also* ***flow chart***

process costing OPERATIONS & PRODUCTION costing method dividing manufacturing cost by units produced a method of costing something that is manufactured from a series of continuous processes, where the total costs of those processes are divided by the number of units produced

processor E-COMMERCE = ***acquirer***

procurement OPERATIONS & PRODUCTION = ***purchasing***

procurement exchange OPERATIONS & PRODUCTION group of companies with combined buying power a group of companies that act together to buy products or services they need at lower prices

procurement manager OPERATIONS & PRODUCTION = ***purchasing manager***

procurement portal E-COMMERCE = ***online catalog***

procyclical ECONOMICS **1.** increasing in line with other factor tending to increase and decrease in tandem with another factor. *See also* ***countercyclical*** **2.** promoting instability likely to increase instability or fluctuation

procyclicality ECONOMICS positive feedback in linked factors a pattern of positive reinforcement in the behavior of linked factors that can intensify fluctuations in a system. For example, credit expands as the financial climate improves, but in a subsequent period of economic contraction credit shrinks and financial constraint increases

producer price index ECONOMICS statistical measure of wholesale prices the ***weighted average*** of the prices of commodities that firms buy from other firms

product OPERATIONS & PRODUCTION, MARKETING marketable good or service anything that is offered to a market that customers can acquire, use, interact with, experience, or consume, to satisfy a want or need. Early ***marketing*** tended to focus on tangible physical goods and these were distinguished from ***services***. More recently, however, the distinction between products and services has blurred, and the concept of the product has been expanded so that in its widest sense it can now be said to cover any tangible or intangible thing that satisfies the consumer. Products that are marketed can include services, people, places, and ideas.

product abandonment OPERATIONS & PRODUCTION, MARKETING discontinuation of particular good or service the ending of the manufacture and sale of a product. Products are abandoned for many reasons. The market may be saturated or declining, the product may be superseded by another, costs of production may become too high, or a product may simply become unprofitable. Product abandonment usually occurs during the decline phase of the ***product life cycle***.

product assortment OPERATIONS & PRODUCTION, MARKETING = ***product mix***

product churning OPERATIONS & PRODUCTION, MARKETING launch of multiple products hoping one will succeed the flooding of a market with new products in the hope that one of them will become successful. Product churning is especially prevalent in Japan, where prelaunch test marketing is often replaced by multiple product launches. Most of these products will decline and disappear, but one or more of the new products churned out may become profitable.

product development OPERATIONS & PRODUCTION, MARKETING modification of product for renewed consumer appeal the revitalization of a product through the introduction of a new concept or consumer benefit. Product development is part of the ***product life cycle***. The concepts or benefits that can be implemented range from modification of the product to simply introducing new packaging.

product development cycle OPERATIONS & PRODUCTION, MARKETING *see* ***new product development***

product differentiation MARKETING promotion of product as different from competition a marketing technique that promotes and emphasizes a product's difference from other products of a similar nature. *Also called* ***differentiation***

product family MARKETING group of similar goods or services a group of products or services that meet a similar need in the market

production versus purchasing OPERATIONS & PRODUCTION = ***purchasing versus production***

productive capacity OPERATIONS & PRODUCTION maximum output achievable at any one time the maximum amount of output that an organization or company can generate at any one time

productive capital FINANCE assets producing income the part of a company's assets that generate an income

productivity OPERATIONS & PRODUCTION measure of production efficiency a measurement of the efficiency of production, taking the form of a ratio of the output of goods and services to the input of factors of production. Labor productivity takes account of inputs of employee hours worked; capital productivity takes account of inputs of machines or land; and marginal productivity measures the additional output gained from an additional unit of input. Techniques to improve productivity include greater use of new technology, altered working practices, and improved training of the workforce.

productivity measurement OPERATIONS & PRODUCTION *see* ***productivity***

product launch MARKETING introduction of new product to market the introduction of a new product to a market. A product launch progresses through a number of important stages: internal communication, which encourages high levels of awareness and commitment to the new product; prelaunch activity, which secures distribution and makes sure that retailers have the resources and knowledge to market the product; launch events at national, regional, or local level; post-event activity, which helps sales forces and retailers make the most of the event; and launch advertising and other forms of customer communication.

product leader MARKETING = ***brand leader***

product liability OPERATIONS & PRODUCTION obligation to accept responsibility for defects in products a manufacturer's, producer's, or service provider's obligation to accept responsibility for defects in their products or services. Faulty products may result in personal injury or damage to property, in which case product liability may result in the payment of compensation to the purchaser.

product life cycle OPERATIONS & PRODUCTION, MARKETING time from development through decline of product the life span of a product from development, through testing, promotion, growth, and maturity, to decline and perhaps regeneration. A new product is first developed and then introduced to the market. Once the introduction is successful, a growth period follows with wider awareness of the product and increasing sales. The product enters maturity when sales stop growing and demand stabilizes. Eventually, sales may decline until the product is finally withdrawn from the market or redeveloped.

product line OPERATIONS & PRODUCTION family of related products a family of related products. Products within a line may be the same type of product, they may be sold to the same type of customer or through similar outlets, or they may all be within a specific price range.

product management OPERATIONS & PRODUCTION control of manufacturing process the process of producing a specification or chart of the manufacturing operations to be carried out by different functions and workstations over a specific time period. Production scheduling takes account of factors such as the availability of plant and materials, customer delivery requirements, and maintenance schedules.

product manager OPERATIONS & PRODUCTION, MARKETING person with oversight of product at all stages a person in charge of ***product management***, who focuses on the marketing of the product but may also be responsible for pricing, packaging, branding, research and development, production, distribution, sales targets, and product performance appraisal

product market OPERATIONS & PRODUCTION, MARKETING selling to business rather than consumer the market in which products are sold to companies rather than directly to consumers. The product market is concerned with purchasing by organizations for their own use, and includes such items as raw materials, machinery, and equipment, which may in turn be used to manufacture items for the consumer market.

product mix OPERATIONS & PRODUCTION, MARKETING variety of products sold by business the variety of product lines that a company produces, or that a retailer stocks. Product mix usually refers to the length (the number of products in the product line), breadth (the number of product lines that a company offers), depth (the different varieties of product in the product line), and consistency (the relationship between products in their final destination) of product lines. *Also called* ***product assortment***

product portfolio OPERATIONS & PRODUCTION, MARKETING products that company handles the range of products manufactured or supplied by an organization

product positioning MARKETING = ***brand positioning***

product range *UK* OPERATIONS & PRODUCTION, MARKETING complete list of products all of the types of products made by one company

product recall OPERATIONS & PRODUCTION removal of defective product from market the removal from sale of products that may constitute a risk to consumers because of contamination, sabotage, or faults in the production process. A product recall usually originates from the product manufacturer but retailers may act autonomously, especially if they believe their outlets are at risk. *See also* ***brand positioning***

profile BUSINESS description of firm a description of the activities of a company, including information on its products or business activities and its finances

profit FINANCE **1.** difference between higher selling price and lower purchase price the difference between the selling price and the purchase price of a product when the selling price is higher. In the case of a security or financial instrument the profit will include any accrued interest. **2.** income exceeding expenditure in business transactions, the amount by which income is greater than expenditure **3.** money made by activity the amount of money that is made from a business undertaking or transaction ◇ turn a profit FINANCE to make a profit from a business activity

profitability FINANCE **1.** extent of profit the degree to which an individual, company, or single transaction achieves financial gain **2.** generation of profit the ability to achieve financial gain from a sale or other commercial transaction

profitability index FINANCE current value of investment divided by original investment the present value of the amount of money an investment will earn divided by the amount of the original investment

profitability threshold FINANCE start point of making profit the point at which a business begins to make profits from its activities or from a specific product

profitable FINANCE producing a profit used to refer to a product, service, or business that achieves financial gain

profit after tax ACCOUNTING = ***net profit***

profit and loss ACCOUNTING difference between income and costs the difference between a company's income and its costs as shown in its accounts. *Abbr* ***P&L***

profit and loss account *or* **profit and loss statement** ACCOUNTING record of firm's external financial transactions the summary record of a company's sales revenues and expenses over a period, providing a calculation of profits or losses during that time. *Also called* ***trading account***

profit before tax ACCOUNTING amount of profit before tax the amount that a company or investor has made, before tax is deducted. *Abbr* ***PBT***

profit center ACCOUNTING business unit responsible for own costs and profits a person, unit, or department within an organization that is considered separately when calculating profit. Profit centers are used as part of management control systems. They operate with a degree of autonomy with regard to marketing and pricing, and have responsibility for their own costs, revenues, and profits.

profit distribution STOCKHOLDING & INVESTMENTS, FINANCE allocation of profits the allocation of profits to different categories of recipients such as stockholders and owners, or for different purposes such as research or investment

profiteering BUSINESS making high profit unethically the practice of making an excessive profit, often in a way that is thought to be unethical or dishonest, or has a detrimental effect on others

profit from ordinary activities ACCOUNTING profits gained from usual business profits earned in the normal course of business, as opposed to profits from extraordinary sources such as windfall payments

profit margin ACCOUNTING, OPERATIONS & PRODUCTION amount by which revenues exceed expenses the amount by which income is greater than expenditure. The profit margin of an individual product is the sale price minus the cost of production and associated costs such as distribution and advertising. The *net profit margin or return on sales* is net income after taxes divided by total sales. On a larger scale, the profit margin is an accounting ratio of company income compared with sales. The profit margin ratio can be used to compare the efficiency and profitability of a company over a number of years, or to compare different companies. The *gross profit margin or operating margin* of a company is its operating, or gross, profit divided by total sales. The level of profit reported is also influenced by the extent of the application of accounting conventions, and by the method of product costing used, for example, ***marginal costing*** or ***absorption costing***.

profit motive BUSINESS desire to make a profit the desire of a business or service provider to make a profit

profit sharing FINANCE allocation of some profit to employees the allocation of a proportion of a company's profit to employees by an issue of stock or other means

profit-sharing debenture STOCKHOLDING & INVESTMENTS employee debenture linking payouts to company performance a ***debenture*** held by an employee, the payments from which depend on the employing company's financial success

profit squeeze BUSINESS reduced profitability compared with the past the inability to maintain a person's or business's profit in a venture, in comparison to previous ventures

profits tax *UK* TAX tax on firm's profit any tax on a company's profits, for example, UK corporation tax (*informal*)

profits warning STOCKHOLDING & INVESTMENTS firm's prediction of low profits an announcement by a company of lower than expected profits for a specific period. *Also called* ***profit warning***

profit-taking STOCKHOLDING & INVESTMENTS sale of investments the act of selling investments in order to receive money for the profit they have made

profit warning STOCKHOLDING & INVESTMENTS = ***profits warning***

pro-forma GENERAL MANAGEMENT preliminary document issued before final version a document issued before all relevant details are known, usually followed by a final version

pro forma balance sheet ACCOUNTING statement of projected financial position after planned transaction in the United States, a projection showing a business's financial statements after the completion of a planned transaction

pro-forma financial statement *UK* ACCOUNTING statement of projected financial position after planned transaction a projection showing a business's likely financial statements after the completion of a planned transaction

pro-forma invoice ACCOUNTING initial basic invoice an invoice that does not include all the details of a transaction, often sent before goods are supplied and followed by a final detailed invoice

program evaluation and review technique *US* OPERATIONS & PRODUCTION way of managing major project a way of planning and controlling a large project, concentrating on scheduling individual activities and completing the project on time. *Abbr* ***PERT***. *UK term* ***programme evaluation and review technique***

programme evaluation and review technique *UK* OPERATIONS & PRODUCTION = ***program evaluation and review technique***

program trading STOCKHOLDING & INVESTMENTS electronic trading of securities the trading of securities electronically, by sending messages from the investor's computer to a market

progressive tax TAX tax with rate rising with income a tax with a rate that increases proportionately with taxable income. *See also* ***proportional tax, regressive tax, flat tax***

progress payment FINANCE payment of project work in stages a payment of a portion of the total contracted price of a project that is made at a agreed stage of completion

project creep GENERAL MANAGEMENT gradual extension of deadlines and targets the gradual alteration of deadlines and expansion of targets as a project progresses

project finance FINANCE funds raised for specific venture money raised for a specific self-contained venture such as a construction or development project

projection FINANCE financial forecast a forecast of conditions that will occur in the future, especially the ways in which they are likely to affect business operations

project management GENERAL MANAGEMENT management of operation and outcome of project the integration of all aspects of a project in order to ensure that the proper knowledge and resources are available when and where needed, and above all to ensure that the expected outcome is produced in a timely, cost-effective manner. The primary function of a *project manager* is to manage the trade-offs between performance, timeliness, and cost.

project risk analysis *or* **project risk assessment** GENERAL MANAGEMENT, RISK assessment of risks to activities the identification of ***risks*** to which a project is exposed, and the assessment of the potential impact of those risks on the project. Project risk analysis forms part of the process of ***project management*** and is a specialized type of ***risk analysis***.

promissory note FINANCE agreement to pay for something received a written contract to pay money to a person or organization for a good or service received. *Abbr* ***PN***

promotion MARKETING = ***sales promotion***

property FINANCE asset owned by somebody ***assets***, such as real estate or goods, that a person or organization owns

property bond STOCKHOLDING & INVESTMENTS bond with property as collateral a bond for which real estate is collateral

property damage insurance INSURANCE insurance for real property insurance against the risk of damage to or on one's real estate

property developer *UK* REAL ESTATE = ***real estate developer***

property tax TAX local tax on real estate a tax that is based on the value of a piece of real estate and paid to a local government

proportional tax TAX tax proportional to value of taxed item a tax that is strictly proportional in amount to the value of the item being taxed, especially income. *See also* ***progressive tax, regressive tax***

proprietary company *ANZ, S. Africa* BUSINESS private limited liability company in Australia and South Africa, a private limited liability company. *Abbr* ***Pty***

proprietary drug OPERATIONS & PRODUCTION patented drug marketed exclusively under brand name a patented drug that is made by a specific company and marketed only by that company under a brand name

proprietary trading MARKETS trading on financial institution's own account trading by a trader in an organization such as an investment bank whose job is to trade on behalf of the bank in order to make large profits for the bank itself, rather than on behalf of the bank's clients

proprietors' interest FINANCE owners' investment in business an amount of money which the owners of a business have invested in the business

pro rata FINANCE at a proportional rate at a rate that is in proportion to something. For example, several investors in a company may share the profits of that company in proportion to their ownership interest.

ProShare MARKETS group representing private investors on London Stock Exchange a group that acts in the interests of private investors in securities on the London Stock Exchange

prospect MARKETING potential client or customer a person or organization considered likely to buy a product or service

prospecting MARKETING identification of potential clients or customers the process of identifying people or organizations that are likely to buy a product or service

prospective dividend STOCKHOLDING & INVESTMENTS = ***forecast dividend***

prospective P/E ratio STOCKHOLDING & INVESTMENTS P/E ratio forecast on expected dividends an assessment of the ***price/earnings ratio*** that can be expected for the future on the basis of forecast dividends

prospect theory GENERAL MANAGEMENT analysis of why individuals make nonrational decisions a branch of decision theory that attempts to explain why individuals make decisions that deviate from rational decision making by examining how the expected outcomes of alternative choices are perceived. The theory is based on the premise that people treat risks associated with perceived losses differently from risks associated with perceived gains. Prospect theory has applications in a wide range of fields, including marketing management, where it is relevant to the way in which choices are presented to the consumer.

prospectus STOCKHOLDING & INVESTMENTS document accompanying sale of securities a description of a company's operations, financial background, prospects, and the detailed terms and conditions relating to an offer for sale or placing of its stock by notice, circular, advertisement, or any form of invitation which offers securities to the public

protectionism INTERNATIONAL TRADE government protection of domestic firms by limiting imports a government economic policy of restricting the level of imports by using measures such as ***tariffs*** and ***nontariff barriers*** in order to protect a country's domestic industries

protective put buying STOCKHOLDING & INVESTMENTS purchase of options to sell something already owned the purchase of ***options*** to sell ***financial instruments*** that are the same as some the purchaser already owns

protective tariff INTERNATIONAL TRADE tax on imports to protect domestic firms a tariff imposed to restrict imports into a country

protest FINANCE proof that bill of exchange is unpaid an official document that proves that a bill of exchange has not been paid

protocol GENERAL MANAGEMENT rules regulating a process a set of rules that govern and regulate a process

prototype GENERAL MANAGEMENT working model of new product or invention an initial version or working model of a new product or invention. A prototype is constructed and tested in order to evaluate the feasibility of a design and to identify problems that need to be corrected. Building a prototype is a key stage in ***new product development***.

provident INSURANCE paying benefits for illness or other need providing benefits in case of illness, old age, or other cases of need

provision ACCOUNTING money earmarked for potential future expense a sum set aside in the accounts of an organization in anticipation of a future expense, often for doubtful debts. *See also* ***bad debt***

provisional tax TAX tax payment based on previous year's income tax paid in advance on the following year's income, the amount being based on the actual income from the preceding year

proxy CORPORATE GOVERNANCE surrogate voter at company meeting somebody who votes on behalf of another person at a company meeting

proxy fight CORPORATE GOVERNANCE consideration of proxy votes in settling disagreement the use of ***proxy votes*** to settle a contentious issue at a company meeting

proxy form *or* **proxy card** CORPORATE GOVERNANCE form that stockholders use to appoint proxy a form that stockholders receive with their invitations to attend an annual meeting, and that they fill in if they want to appoint somebody to vote for them on a resolution

proxy statement CORPORATE GOVERNANCE firm's notification to stockholders of voting rights a notice that a company sends to stockholders, allowing them to vote and giving them all the information they need to vote in an informed way

proxy vote CORPORATE GOVERNANCE vote made by somebody authorized by absent person a vote given by somebody who is present at a company meeting and has been authorized by a person who is not present to vote on his or her behalf

PRT *abbr* TAX ***petroleum revenue tax***

prudence TREASURY MANAGEMENT *see* ***prudence concept***

prudence concept TREASURY MANAGEMENT principle of not anticipating profits in accounts the principle that revenue and profits are not anticipated but are included in the ***profit and loss account*** only when realized in the form either of cash or of other assets, the ultimate cash realization of which can be assessed with reasonable certainty. Provision is made for all known liabilities (expenses and losses) whether the amount of these is known with certainty or is a best estimate in the light of the information available.

prudent FINANCE careful and sensible about money careful and exercising good judgment, especially in financial matters

prudential ratio BANKING, REGULATION & COMPLIANCE in EU, ratio of capital to assets in the European Union, the regulations covering the ratio of capital to assets that a bank should have

prudent man rule FINANCE rule requiring trustees to act carefully the assumption that trustees who make financial decisions on behalf of other people will act carefully, as any prudent person usually would

PSBR *abbr* FINANCE ***public sector borrowing requirement*** *see* ***public sector cash requirement***

psychic income HR & PERSONNEL job satisfaction independent of salary the level of satisfaction derived from a job rather than the salary earned doing it (*slang*)

psychological contract HR & PERSONNEL tacit understanding between employee and employer the set of unwritten expectations concerning the relationship between an employee and an employer. The psychological contract addresses factors that are not defined in a written contract of employment such as levels of commitment, productivity, quality of working life, job satisfaction, attitudes to working flexibly, and the provision and take-up of suitable training. Expectations of both employer and employee can change, so the psychological contract must be reevaluated at intervals to minimize misunderstandings.

Pty *abbr ANZ, S. Africa* BUSINESS private limited liability company

Public Accounts Committee FINANCE UK House of Commons committee monitoring government spending in the United Kingdom, a committee of the House of Commons that examines the spending of each department and ministry

public company BUSINESS = ***publicly held corporation***

public corporation BUSINESS government-owned organization especially in the United Kingdom, a state-owned organization established to provide a specific service, for example, the British Broadcasting Corporation

public debt FINANCE money owed by government the money that a government or a group of governments owes

public deposits FINANCE money of UK government departments in the United Kingdom, the balances to the credit of the government held at the Bank of England

public expenditure FINANCE government spending on citizens' needs spending by the government of a country on items such as pension provision and infrastructure enhancement

public finance law REGULATION & COMPLIANCE financial legislation regulating public-sector organizations legislation relating to the financial activities of government or public-sector organizations

public financing FINANCE money that governments raise and spend the money raised by means of taxation and borrowing, and spent by governments, or the process of raising and spending this money

public funds FINANCE money that government spends money that a government has available for expenditure

public issue STOCKHOLDING & INVESTMENTS offer of stock to public offering a new issue of stock for sale to the public. An issue of this type is often advertised in the press. *See also* ***offer for sale, offer by prospectus***

public-liability insurance INSURANCE insurance against financial liability for injury insurance against the risk of being held financially liable for injury to somebody

public limited company *UK* BUSINESS = ***publicly held corporation****. Abbr* ***plc*** *or* ***PLC***

publicly held corporation *US* BUSINESS organization listed on exchange an organization with common stock listed on a stock exchange. *UK term* ***public limited company***

public monopoly BUSINESS when government is sole supplier of good a situation of limited competition in the public sector, usually relating to nationalized industries

public offering STOCKHOLDING & INVESTMENTS raising of funds via offer of stock a method of raising money used by a company in which it invites the public to apply for shares

public ownership BUSINESS ownership by national government a situation in which a government owns and operates a business

public placement *US* STOCKHOLDING & INVESTMENTS restricted selling of stock in public company the selling of stock in a ***publicly held corporation*** to a limited number of designated buyers. *UK term* ***public placing****. See also* ***private placement***

public placing *UK* STOCKHOLDING & INVESTMENTS = ***public placement****. See also* ***private placement***

public private partnership BUSINESS private-sector involvement in traditionally public-sector service a partnership between government and the private sector for the purpose of more effectively providing services and infrastructure traditionally provided by the public sector. *Abbr* ***PPP***

public sector BUSINESS organizations financed and controlled by government the organizations in the section of the economy that is financed and controlled by central government, local authorities, and publicly funded corporations. *See also* ***private sector***

public sector borrowing requirement FINANCE *see* ***public sector cash requirement***

public sector cash requirement FINANCE difference between revenue and expenses of public sector the difference between the income and the expenditure of the public sector. It was formerly called the ***public sector borrowing requirement***.

public spending ECONOMICS government expenditure spending by the government of a country on publicly provided goods and services

public utility BUSINESS company providing basic service to community a company that provides a service such as electricity, gas, telecommunications, or water that is used by the whole community

published accounts *UK* ACCOUNTING = ***earnings report***

puff MARKETING exaggerate merits of something to overstate the virtues of a product or a service (*informal*)

puffery MARKETING exaggerated claims regarding product or service exaggerated claims made for a product or service. In general, puffery does not constitute false advertising under law (*slang*).

puff piece MARKETING press item for promotional purposes an article in a newspaper or magazine promoting a product or service (*slang*)

pullback MARKETS price drop after rise a fall in the price of a security after it has reached a high

pull strategy MARKETING *see* ***push and pull strategies***

pull system OPERATIONS & PRODUCTION production of goods only as needed by customer a production planning and control system in which the specification and pace of output of a delivery, or supplier, workstation is set by the receiving, or customer, workstation. In pull systems, the customer acts as the only trigger for movement. The supplier workstation can only produce output on the instructions of the customer for delivery when the customer is ready to receive it. Demand is therefore transferred down through the stages of production from the order placed by an end customer. Pull systems are far less likely to result in work-in-progress inventory, and are favored by just-in-time or ***lean production*** systems. *See also* ***push system***

pump-and-dump STOCKHOLDING & INVESTMENTS illegal exaggeration of value of stock for profit an illegal practice in which the owner of a stock makes false claims about the stock, exaggerating its value, then sells it at a profit (*slang*)

pump priming FINANCE injection of funds to boost business the injection of further investment in order to revitalize a company or economy in stagnation, or to help a ***startup*** business over a critical period. Pump priming has a similar effect to the provision of ***seed capital***.

punter STOCKHOLDING & INVESTMENTS speculator in stock market a person who hopes to make a quick profit in a stock market (*slang*)

purchase FINANCE **1.** something bought a product or service that somebody is going to buy or has bought **2.** to buy something to buy a product or service

purchase acquisition MERGERS & ACQUISITIONS, ACCOUNTING accounting procedures for mergers the standard accounting procedures that must be followed when one company merges with another. *Also called* ***acquisition accounting***

purchase contract OPERATIONS & PRODUCTION agreement to buy at stated price a form of agreement to buy specific products at an agreed price

purchase ledger *UK* ACCOUNTING = ***payables ledger***

purchase money mortgage MORTGAGES mortgage used to buy property that is collateral in the United States, a mortgage whose proceeds the borrower uses to buy the property that is collateral for a loan

purchase order OPERATIONS & PRODUCTION document specifying terms of purchase of goods or services a written order for goods or services specifying quantities, prices, delivery dates, and contract terms. *Abbr* ***PO***

purchase price OPERATIONS & PRODUCTION price paid the price that somebody pays to buy a good or service

purchase requisition OPERATIONS & PRODUCTION internal request to purchase goods or services an internal instruction to a buying office to purchase goods or services, stating their quantity and description and generating a ***purchase order***

purchase tax TAX in UK, forerunner of VAT in the United Kingdom, a former tax paid when purchasing nonessential items that was replaced by VAT

purchasing OPERATIONS & PRODUCTION acquisition of goods and services by organization the acquisition of goods and services needed to support the various activities of an organization, at the optimum cost and from reliable suppliers. Purchasing involves defining the need for goods and services; identifying and comparing available supplies and suppliers; negotiating terms for price, quantity, and delivery; agreeing contracts and placing orders; receiving and accepting delivery; and authorizing the payment for goods and services. *Also called* ***procurement***

purchasing by contract OPERATIONS & PRODUCTION = ***contract purchasing***

purchasing department OPERATIONS & PRODUCTION department of firm responsible for purchasing the department in a company that buys raw materials or goods for use in the company. *Also called* ***buying department***

purchasing manager OPERATIONS & PRODUCTION employee responsible for purchasing an individual with responsibility for all activities concerned with purchasing. The responsibilities of a purchasing manager can include ordering, commercial negotiations, and delivery chasing. *Also called* ***buying manager***

purchasing power FINANCE measure of ability to buy goods and services a measure of the ability of a person, organization, or sector to buy goods and services

purchasing power parity CURRENCY & EXCHANGE theory linking exchange rate to purchasing power a theory that the exchange rate between two currencies is in equilibrium when the purchasing power of currency is the same in each country. If a basket of goods costs £100 in the United Kingdom and $150 for an equivalent in the United States, for equilibrium to exist, the exchange rate would be expected to be £1 = $1.50. If this were not the case, *arbitrage* would be expected to take place until equilibrium was restored. *Abbr* ***PPP***

purchasing routine OPERATIONS & PRODUCTION stages in purchase of product or service the various stages involved in organizing the purchase of a product or service

purchasing versus production OPERATIONS & PRODUCTION choice between making or buying needed item a decision on whether to produce goods internally or to buy them in from outside the organization. The goal of purchasing versus production is to secure needed items at the best possible cost, while making optimum use of the resources of the organization. Factors influencing the decision may include: cost, spare ***capacity*** within the organization, the need for tight quality and scheduling control, flexibility, the enhancement of skills that can then be used in other ways, volume and economies of scale, utilization of existing personnel, the need for secrecy, capital and financing requirements, and the potential reliability of supply. *Also called* ***buy or make, make or buy, internal versus external sourcing***

pure competition MARKETS situation in which many sellers compete in market a situation in which there are many sellers in a market and there is free flow of information

pure endowment FINANCE gift with conditions attached a gift that can only be used in the way laid down by its donor

purpose credit STOCKHOLDING & INVESTMENTS credit for purchasing securities credit obtained with the intention of buying and selling securities

push and pull strategies MARKETING contrasting marketing strategies targeting either distributor or customer approaches used as part of a marketing strategy to encourage customers to purchase a product or service. Push and pull strategies are contrasting approaches and tend to target different types of consumers. A ***pull strategy*** targets the end consumer, using advertising, sales promotions, and direct response marketing to pull the customer in. This approach is common in consumer markets. A ***push strategy*** targets members of the distribution channel, such as wholesalers and retailers, to push the promotion up through the channel to the consumers. This approach is more common in industrial markets.

push system OPERATIONS & PRODUCTION production of goods to be sold from inventory a production control and planning system in which demand is predicted centrally and each workstation pushes work out without considering if the next station is ready for it. While the central control aspect of a push system can achieve a balance across workstations, in practice a specific station can experience any one of a number of problems that delay work flow, so affecting the whole system. Push systems are characterized by work-in-progress inventory, lines, and idle time. *See also* ***pull system***

push the envelope GENERAL MANAGEMENT take risk of overstepping normal limits to exceed normal limits, implying a sense of risk at transcending the normal safe limits of operation

put *or* **put option** STOCKHOLDING & INVESTMENTS option to sell stock an option to sell stock within an agreed time at a specific price

put bond STOCKHOLDING & INVESTMENTS bond redeemable at specific date before maturity a bond that can be redeemed at face value at a specified time before its maturity date

put-call ratio MARKETS volume of puts divided by calls a ratio of the volume of *puts* to *calls*, often used as an indicator of the best time to buy or sell stocks

PV *abbr* FINANCE ***present value***

PYB *abbr* ACCOUNTING ***preceding year basis***

pyramiding 1. FINANCE illegal payment of interest from new deposits the illegal practice of using new investors' deposits to pay the interest on the deposits made by existing investors **2.** MERGERS & ACQUISITIONS process of acquiring increasingly large companies the process of building up a major group by acquiring controlling interests in many different companies, each larger than the original company

pyramid selling MARKETING chain selling of goods from distributor to distributor the sale of the right to sell products or services to distributors who in turn recruit other distributors. Sometimes ending with no final buyer, pyramid selling is a form of multilevel marketing, and often involves a system of franchises. It is similar to ***network marketing***, but in many cases no end products are actually sold. Unscrupulous sellers of a pyramid marketing plan profit from the initial fees paid to them by distributors in advance of promised sales income. Pyramid selling is illegal in the United Kingdom.

Q

Q1 *abbr* ACCOUNTING ***first quarter***

Q2 *abbr* ACCOUNTING ***second quarter***

Q3 *abbr* ACCOUNTING ***third quarter***

Q4 *abbr* ACCOUNTING ***fourth quarter***

qard *or* **qard hassan** FINANCE interest-free loan in Islamic financing, a loan, which under Islamic law is always free of profit. A qard may also be a bank deposit, which is considered a loan to a bank for its use but which must be returned to the depositor upon request.

qualification of accounts ACCOUNTING = ***auditors' qualification***

qualification payment FINANCE financial reward for academic qualification an additional payment sometimes made to employees of New Zealand companies who have gained an academic qualification relevant to their job

qualified auditor's report ACCOUNTING = ***adverse opinion***

qualified domestic trust FINANCE trust giving benefits to non-US spouse in the United States, a trust established by a US citizen for a noncitizen spouse that affords tax advantages to the spouse at the time of the citizen's death

qualified lead MARKETING good potential customer a prospective customer whose potential value has been carefully researched

qualified listed security STOCKHOLDING & INVESTMENTS security that can be purchased by regulated entity a security that is eligible for purchase by a regulated entity such as a trust

qualified plan PENSIONS IRS-approved retirement or benefit plan in the United States, a retirement plan or employee benefit plan that meets the requirements of the IRS for special tax consideration

qualified valuer FINANCE professional person conducting valuation a person conducting a valuation who holds a recognized and relevant professional qualification. The person must also have recent post-qualification experience and sufficient knowledge of the state of the market with reference to the location and category of the tangible fixed asset being valued.

qualifying distribution STOCKHOLDING & INVESTMENTS former UK dividend payment formerly in the United Kingdom, the payment to a stockholder of a dividend on which ***advance corporation tax*** was paid

qualifying period FINANCE period needed for eligibility a period of time that has to pass before somebody is eligible for something, for example, a grant or subsidy

qualifying ratio MORTGAGES calculation of mortgage affordability a calculation of how much mortgage a borrower can afford, by comparing his or her monthly income against monthly outgoings

qualifying shares STOCKHOLDING & INVESTMENTS stockholding required before rights are granted the number of shares of stock somebody needs to hold to be eligible for something such as a bonus issue

qualitative analysis GENERAL MANAGEMENT appraisal of project with no quantifiable data the subjective appraisal of a project or investment for which there is no quantifiable data. *See also* ***chartist, quantitative analysis, technical analysis***

qualitative research GENERAL MANAGEMENT research using data that is not measurable research that focuses on "soft" data, for example, attitude research or focus groups. *See also* ***quantitative research***

quality bond STOCKHOLDING & INVESTMENTS bond issued by safe firm a bond issued by an organization that has an excellent credit rating

quality costs OPERATIONS & PRODUCTION costs associated with failure to meet standards costs associated with the failure to achieve conformance to requirements. Quality costs accrue when organizations waste large sums of money because of carrying out the wrong tasks, or failing to perform the right tasks correctly the first time. *Also called* ***nonconformance costs***

quality equity STOCKHOLDING & INVESTMENTS equity with good performance history an equity with a good track record of earnings and dividends. *See also* ***blue chip***

quango *UK* GENERAL MANAGEMENT semi-governmental organization an acronym derived from quasi-autonomous nongovernmental organization, a body outside the civil service but established by the government, answerable to a government minister, and with responsibility in a specific area

quant FINANCE **1.** = ***quantitative analyst*** **2.** = ***quantitative analysis***

quantitative analysis FINANCE numerical assessment of financial variables the use of mathematical and statistical models in the evaluation of financial data of all kinds. *See also* ***chartist, qualitative analysis, technical analysis***

quantitative analyst FINANCE somebody assessing financial variables numerically a person who uses econometric, mathematical, or statistical models to evaluate a project or investment

quantitative easing FINANCE central bank's issue of money to other banks the release by a central bank of sufficient funds to stimulate activity in a banking system that has become sluggish and generate an improvement in the economy. This sometimes means printing money in order to give banks more capital.

quantitative research GENERAL MANAGEMENT analysis of numerical data the gathering and analysis of data that can be expressed in numerical form. Quantitative research involves data that is measurable and can include statistical results, financial data, or demographic data. *See also* ***qualitative research***

quantity discount OPERATIONS & PRODUCTION price reduction for bulk buying a reduction in price given to people who buy large quantities of a product

quantum meruit FINANCE as much as has been earned a Latin phrase meaning "as much as has been earned." A claim for quantum meruit can be for reasonable payment for work that has been done without a full estimate.

quarter 1. ACCOUNTING three-month period a three-month calendar period, often used as a period for reporting earnings, paying taxes, or calculating dividends **2.** CURRENCY & EXCHANGE US coin worth 25 cents a US coin worth one-fourth of a dollar or 25 cents

quarter day *UK* OPERATIONS & PRODUCTION day when some payments become due a day at the end of a quarter, when rents, fees, and other payments become due

quarter-end ACCOUNTING of end of three-month period relating to the end of a three-month ***accounting period*** when financial transactions for that period are finalized

quarterly 1. GENERAL MANAGEMENT happening every three months taking place once in every period of three months **2.** ACCOUNTING company's financial results the results of a corporation, produced each quarter

quarterly report ACCOUNTING financial statement for quarter of tax year a financial statement that covers a quarter of a full fiscal year. In the United States the general practice is to issue quarterly reports. *See also* ***interim financial statement***

quartile STATISTICS one of four equal ranges of values any of the values in a frequency or probability distribution that divide it into four equal parts

quasi-contract LEGAL in UK, court order stipulating legal obligation a decree by a UK court stipulating that one party has a legal obligation to another, even though there is no legally binding contract between the two parties

quasi-loan FINANCE arrangement to pay somebody else's debt an arrangement whereby one party pays the debts of another, on the condition that the sum of the debts will be reimbursed by the indebted party at some later date

quasi-money *UK* STOCKHOLDING & INVESTMENTS = ***near money***

quasi-public corporation BUSINESS firm partly owned by government in the United States, an organization that is owned partly by private or public stockholders and partly by the government

quasi-rent FINANCE difference between production cost and selling cost excess earnings made by a company representing the difference between production cost (the cost of labor and materials) and selling cost

qubes STOCKHOLDING & INVESTMENTS fund tracking NASDAQ-100 an exchange-traded fund that tracks the stocks in the NASDAQ-100 index, which consists mainly of the largest nonfinancial companies traded on the NASDAQ

question mark company STOCKHOLDING & INVESTMENTS uncertain investment prospect a company that offers a doubtful return on investment

quick asset FINANCE asset easily cashed in cash or any asset that can quickly be turned into cash, for example, a bank deposit of some types, a short-dated bond, or a certificate of deposit. *See also* ***near money***

quick ratio FINANCE **1.** measure of somebody's short-term borrowing potential a measure of the amount of cash a potential borrower can acquire in a short time, used in evaluating creditworthiness **2.** ratio of liquid assets to current debts the ratio of a company's liquid assets to its current liabilities, used as an indicator of ***liquidity***

quid pro quo FINANCE something in exchange a Latin phrase meaning "something for something," something given or done in exchange for something else. To be valid, a contract must involve a quid pro quo.

quorum CORPORATE GOVERNANCE minimum number of attendees required for decision-making the minimum number of people required in a meeting for it to be able to make decisions that are binding on the organization. For a company, this number is stated in its ***bylaws***; for a partnership, in its partnership agreement.

quota 1. FINANCE limit of investment by party in joint venture the maximum sum to be contributed by each party in a joint venture or joint business undertaking **2.** STOCKHOLDING & INVESTMENTS ceiling on investment in given situation or market the maximum number of investments that may be purchased and sold in a specific situation or market, as in a US Treasury auction, where bidders may not apply for more than a specific percentage of the securities being offered **3.** INTERNATIONAL TRADE limit of imports or exports the maximum amount of a specific commodity, product, or service that can be imported into or exported out of a country

quota system 1. OPERATIONS & PRODUCTION, INTERNATIONAL TRADE system that limits imports or supplies a system in which imports or supplies of a commodity, for example, are limited to fixed maximum amounts **2.** OPERATIONS & PRODUCTION distribution system allocating items evenly among distributors an arrangement for distribution which allows each distributor only a specific number of items

quote *or* **quotation** FINANCE estimate of price a statement of what a person or company is willing to accept when selling a product or service. *Also called* **bid**

quoted company BUSINESS, MARKETS = ***listed company***

quote-driven system MARKETS system fixing initial stock price by quotes a price system on a stock exchange in which prices are generated by dealers' and market makers' quotes before market forces come into play and prices are determined by the interaction of supply and demand. The London Stock Exchange's dealing system, as well as those of many ***over-the-counter markets***, have quote-driven systems. *See also* ***order-driven system***

quoted securities MARKETS securities listed on exchange securities or stocks that are listed on a recognized stock exchange

R

racket FRAUD illegal money-making deal an illegal business deal that makes a lot of money, involving such activities as bribery or intimidation

raid MARKETS illegal selling of stock the illegal practice of taking a ***short position*** in a large number of shares of stock of a particular company in order to drive the price down. *Also called* ***bear raid***

raider MERGERS & ACQUISITIONS maker of hostile takeover bids a person or company that makes hostile takeover bids, wanted neither by directors nor stockholders

rake it in BUSINESS make large amount of money to make a great deal of money relatively easily (*slang*)

rake-off BUSINESS commission a payment made to an intermediary, often calculated as a percentage of the value of goods or services provided (*slang*)

rally MARKETS price rise after fall a rise in stock prices after a significant fall

ramp MARKETS buy stock to raise price to buy stock with the objective of raising its price rather than as an investment. *See also* ***rigged market***

ramp up GENERAL MANAGEMENT greatly increase efforts or interest to increase significantly your interest or efforts in a particular area

rand CURRENCY & EXCHANGE S. African currency unit the standard unit of currency of the Republic of South Africa, equal to 100 cents

Randlord BUSINESS wealthy businessman in Johannesburg originally a Johannesburg-based mining magnate or tycoon of the late 19th or early 20th centuries, now used informally for any wealthy or powerful Johannesburg businessman

random STATISTICS equally likely to occur relating to a set in which all the members have the same probability of occurrence

random sampling STATISTICS statistical technique for sampling individuals at random an unbiased ***sampling*** technique in which every member of a population has an equal chance of being included in the sample. Based on probability theory, random sampling is the process of selecting and canvassing a representative group of individuals from a specific population in order to identify the attributes or attitudes of the population as a whole. Related sampling techniques include: *stratified sampling,* in which the population is divided into classes, and random samples are taken from each class; *cluster sampling,* in which a unit of the sample is a group such as a household; and *systematic sampling,* which refers to samples chosen by any system other than random selection. *See also* **nonrandom sampling**

random walk 1. MARKETS unpredictable movement in stock prices a movement that cannot be predicted, used to describe movements in stock prices that cannot be forecast **2.** STATISTICS sampling method producing random selection a sampling technique that allows for random selection within specific limits set up by a non-random technique

range STATISTICS spread from smallest to largest value the difference between the smallest and the largest observations in a data set

range pricing BUSINESS logical pricing of products in range the pricing of individual products so that their prices fit logically within a variety of connected products offered by one supplier, differentiated by a factor such as weight of pack or number of product attributes offered

ranking STATISTICS order in which values are arranged the ordered arrangement of a set of variable values

ratchet effect ECONOMICS adjusting more easily to income increases than decreases the result when households adjust more easily to rising incomes than to falling incomes, as, for example, when their consumption drops by less than their income in a recession

rate FINANCE assess value to calculate or assess the value of something, for example, real estate for tax purposes

rateable value FINANCE value calculated according to rule the value of something calculated with reference to a rule. An example is the value of a commercial property taken as a basis for calculating local taxes.

rate cap FINANCE = ***cap***

rate of exchange CURRENCY & EXCHANGE = ***exchange rate***

rate of inflation ECONOMICS percentage increase in prices over year the percentage increase in the price of goods and services calculated over a twelve-month period

rate of interest FINANCE percentage charged on loan or paid on investment a percentage charged on a loan or paid on an investment for the use of the money

rate of return ACCOUNTING, STOCKHOLDING & INVESTMENTS ratio of investment profit to investment cost an accounting ratio of the income from an investment to the amount of the investment, used to measure financial performance.

There is a basic formula that will serve most needs, at least initially:

[(Current value of amount invested – Original value of amount invested) / Original value of amount invested] × 100% = Rate of return

If $1,000 in capital is invested in stock, and one year later the investment yields $1,100, the rate of return of the investment is calculated like this:

[(1,100 – 1,000) / 1,000] × 100% = 100 / 1,000 × 100% = 10%

Now, assume $1,000 is invested again. One year later, the investment grows to $2,000 in value, but after another year the value of the investment falls to $1,200. The rate of return after the first year is:

[(2,000 – 1,000) / 1,000] × 100% = 100%

The rate of return after the second year is:

[(1,200 – 2,000) / 2,000] × 100% = –40%

The average annual return for the two years (also known as average annual arithmetic return) can be calculated using this formula:

(Rate of return for year 1 + Rate of return for year 2) / 2 = Average annual return

Accordingly:

(100% + –40%) / 2 = 30%

The average annual rate of return is a percentage, but one that is accurate over only a short period, so this method should be used accordingly.

The geometric or compound rate of return is a better yardstick for measuring investments over the long term, and takes into account the effects of compounding. This formula is more complex and technical.

The real rate of return is the annual return realized on an investment, adjusted for changes in the price due to inflation. If 10% is earned on an investment but inflation is 2%, then the real rate of return is actually 8%. *Also called* ***return***

rates TAX in UK, forerunner of council tax in the United Kingdom, local UK taxes formerly levied on property and now replaced by ***council tax***

rate tart FINANCE somebody often changing to accounts with better rates somebody who changes loan providers or savings accounts regularly to benefit from better interest rates (*slang*)

rating FINANCE relative assigned value the value or quality that something is assessed as having, for example, the status of a person or company in terms of creditworthiness, or a company or product in terms of suitability for investment. *See also* ***credit rating***

rating agency STOCKHOLDING & INVESTMENTS organization rating firms issuing bonds an organization that gives a rating to companies or other organizations issuing bonds

ratio analysis FINANCE using ratios in financial analysis the use of ratios to measure a company's financial performance, for example, the ***current ratio*** or the ***leverage ratios***

rationalization GENERAL MANAGEMENT measures taken to increase organization's efficiency the application of efficiency or effectiveness measures to an organization. Rationalization can occur at the onset of a downturn in an organization's performance or results. It usually takes the form of cutbacks intended to bring the organization back to profitability and may involve layoffs, plant closures, and cutbacks in supplies and resources. It often involves changes in organization structure, particularly in the form of ***downsizing***. The term is also used in a cynical way as a euphemism for mass layoffs.

raw materials OPERATIONS & PRODUCTION materials from which products are manufactured items bought for use in the manufacturing or development processes of an organization. While most often referring to bulk materials, raw materials can also include components, subassemblies, and complete products.

RBA *abbr* BANKING ***Reserve Bank of Australia***

RBNZ *abbr* BANKING ***Reserve Bank of New Zealand***

RD *or* **R/D** *abbr UK* BANKING ***refer to drawer***

RDG *abbr* ECONOMICS ***regional development grant***

RDP FINANCE government policies addressing economic aftermath of apartheid a policy framework by means of which the South African government intends to correct the socioeconomic imbalances caused by apartheid. *Full form* ***Reconstruction and Development Program***

RDPR *abbr* BANKING ***refer to drawer please re-present***

ready money FINANCE money immediately available cash or money that is immediately available for use

Reaganomics ECONOMICS 1980s economic policies of Ronald Reagan the economic policy of former US President Reagan in the 1980s, who reduced taxes and social security support and increased the national budget deficit to an unprecedented level

real FINANCE after considering inflation after the effects of inflation are taken into consideration

real asset FINANCE physical asset an asset with a physical presence such as land or a building. *See also* ***tangible asset***

real balance effect ECONOMICS results of falling prices and increased consumption the effect on income and employment when prices fall and consumption increases

real capital FINANCE assets with monetary value assets such as buildings or equipment that are used in creating products and can be assigned a monetary value. *See also* ***financial capital***

real earnings FINANCE available income after deductions income that is available for spending after tax and other contributions have been deducted, adjusted for inflation. *Also called* ***real income, real wages***

real economy ECONOMICS goods, services, and jobs the production of goods and services on which jobs, incomes, and consumer spending depend

real estate REAL ESTATE land and improvements in the United States, property that consists of land and anything attached to it, for example, trees and buildings. *Also called* ***realty***

real estate developer *US* REAL ESTATE somebody who develops land or buildings a person or company that develops land or buildings to increase their value. *UK term* ***property developer***

real estate investment trust REAL ESTATE, STOCKHOLDING & INVESTMENTS trust investing in properties and mortgages a publicly traded ***investment trust*** that uses investors' money to invest in properties and mortgages. *Abbr* ***REIT***

real exchange rate CURRENCY & EXCHANGE exchange rate adjusted for inflation a current exchange rate that has been adjusted for inflation

real GDP ECONOMICS GDP adjusted for prices a measure of ***GDP*** adjusted for changes in prices

real growth ECONOMICS economic growth adjusted for prices the increase in productivity, sales, or earnings of a country or a household adjusted for changes in prices

real income FINANCE = ***real earnings***

real interest rate FINANCE interest rate adjusted for inflation an interest rate after a deduction for inflation has been made

real investment FINANCE purchase of real estate or plant, not securities the purchase of assets such as land, real estate, and plant and machinery, as opposed to the acquisition of securities

realize FINANCE sell asset for cash to change an ***asset*** into an amount of money by selling it

realized profit FINANCE profit from sale of something profit made when something has been sold, as opposed to ***paper profit***

real money FINANCE **1.** capital from investors who have not borrowed investment capital provided by investors such as pension funds, some insurance companies, retail mutual funds, and high net worth individuals who are not borrowing it from other sources **2.** bills and coins money available as bills and coins to spend, rather than existing only as items on financial accounts **3.** lots of money a very large amount of money (*informal*)

real option STOCKHOLDING & INVESTMENTS, RISK choice available to investor in tangible investment the opportunity to choose a course of action that an investor has when investing in something tangible such as a business project

real property REAL ESTATE land and permanent improvements in the United States, land and the permanent structures on it

real purchasing power ECONOMICS how much consumer is able to buy the purchasing power of a country or a household adjusted for changes in prices

real rate of return FINANCE rate of return allowing for inflation the rate of return received after a deduction for inflation

real return after tax FINANCE, TAX net income or profit the income or profit made after deductions for taxes and inflation

real time company BUSINESS firm providing immediate response to customers over Internet a company that uses the Internet and other technologies to respond immediately to customer demands

real time credit card processing E-COMMERCE immediate authorization of credit card during online transaction the online authorization of a credit card indicating that the credit card has been approved or rejected during the transaction

real time EDI E-COMMERCE online transactions between businesses and customers online ***electronic data interchange***: the online transfer and processing of business data, for example, purchase orders, customer invoices, and payment receipts, between suppliers and their customers

real time manager E-COMMERCE service manager for Internet customers a manager who is responsible for delivering the immediate service that customers expect, using the Internet and other technologies

real time transaction E-COMMERCE online payment immediately approved or rejected an Internet payment transaction that is approved or rejected immediately when the customer completes the online order form

Realtor REAL ESTATE real estate agent belonging to professional body in the United States, a licensed real estate agent who is a member of the National Association of Realtors

realty REAL ESTATE land and buildings property that consists of land and anything attached to it, for example, trees and buildings. *Also called* ***real estate***

real value FINANCE value of investment in real terms a value of an investment that is maintained at the same level, for example, by making it ***index-linked***

real wages FINANCE = ***real earnings***

rebadge MARKETING sell another company's product under your name to buy a product or service from another company and sell it as part of your own product range

rebate 1. FINANCE money returned when payment is excessive money returned because a payment exceeded the amount required, for example, a tax rebate **2.** FINANCE discount a reduction in the price of goods or services in relation to the standard price **3.** STOCKHOLDING & INVESTMENTS reduce client's commission charge of a broker, to reduce part of the commission charged to the client as a promotional offer

recapitalization FINANCE reorganization of firm's capital the process of changing the way a company's capital is structured, in terms of the balance between debt and equity, usually in response to a major financial problem such as ***bankruptcy***

recapture 1. FINANCE sale with right to buy back a situation in which a seller of an asset retains the right to buy back part or all of the asset **2.** TAX, ACCOUNTING treatment of past deduction as income a situation in which a deduction taken in a previous tax year must be reported as income, for example, when a depreciated asset is sold at a gain

recd *or* **rec'd** *abbr* FINANCE ***received***

receipt BUSINESS acknowledgment of transfer a document acknowledging that something has been received, for example, a payment

receipts FINANCE money from sales the total amount a retailer takes from sales. *Also called* ***takings***. *See also* ***gross receipts, net receipts***

receivables ACCOUNTING money owing but not paid money that has been billed to customers or clients but has not yet been received

receivables ledger *US* ACCOUNTING record of accounts receivable a ledger in which a company records its ***accounts receivable***. *See also* ***payables ledger***. *UK term* ***purchase ledger***

received FINANCE referring to money taken in used in recording payments or sums of money. *Abbr* ***recd, rec'd***

receiver LEGAL person selling firm's assets in insolvency a person appointed to sell the assets of a company that is insolvent. The proceeds of the sale are used to discharge debts to creditors, with any surplus distributed to ***shareholders***.

Receiver of Revenue TAX **1.** S. African tax office a local office of the South African Revenue Service (***SARS***) **2.** S. African Revenue Service the South African Revenue Service (***SARS***) as a whole (*informal*)

receivership LEGAL management of insolvent company by court-appointed official a state of ***insolvency*** prior to ***liquidation***. During receivership, receivers may attempt to undertake ***turnaround management*** or decide that the company must go into liquidation.

recession ECONOMICS slowdown of economic activity a stage of the ***business cycle*** in which economic activity is in slow decline. Recession usually follows a boom, and precedes a ***depression***. It is characterized by rising unemployment and falling levels of output and investment.

recessionary gap ECONOMICS shortfall of demand needed to ensure full employment a shortfall in the amount of ***aggregate demand*** in an economy needed to create full employment

recharacterization PENSIONS movement of US retirement contributions in the United States, the process of transferring a contribution made to one type of Individual Retirement Account (***IRA***) to another type, or reversing a prior conversion such as from a ***traditional IRA*** to a ***Roth IRA***

reciprocal holdings STOCKHOLDING & INVESTMENTS mutual stockholdings that prevent takeover bids a situation in which two companies own stock in each other to prevent takeover bids

reciprocal trade INTERNATIONAL TRADE trade between countries trade between two countries, usually based on an agreement that benefits both countries

recognized investment exchange MARKETS in UK, financial exchange recognized by FSA in the United Kingdom, a stock exchange, futures exchange, or commodity exchange recognized by the ***Financial Services Authority***. *Abbr* ***RIE***

recognized professional body BUSINESS in UK, organization recognized by FSA in the United Kingdom, a professional organization that regulates its members and is recognized by the ***Financial Services Authority***. *Abbr* ***RPB***

recommended retail price *UK* BUSINESS = ***suggested retail price***

reconciliation ACCOUNTING accounting adjustment in line with authoritative information adjustment of a record, such as somebody's own record of bank account transactions, to match more authoritative information

reconciliation statement ACCOUNTING document verifying date of independently recorded transaction a document used to verify that two independent records of the same financial transactions agree as of a particular date

Reconstruction and Development Program FINANCE *see* ***RDP***

record date GENERAL MANAGEMENT date of computer data entry the date when a computer data entry or record is made

recourse FINANCE right of lender to demand repayment of loan a right of a lender to compel a borrower to repay money borrowed, or, in some cases, to take assets belonging to the borrower if the money is not repaid

recourse agreement FINANCE installment plan agreement allowing retailer to repossess an agreement in an installment plan whereby the retailer repossesses the goods being purchased in the event that the purchaser fails to make regular payments

recoverable ACT TAX former part of UK corporation tax formerly in the United Kingdom, ***advance corporation tax*** that could be set against the ***corporation tax*** payable for the period

recoverable amount ACCOUNTING value of asset if sold or when used the value of an asset, either the price it would bring if sold, or its value to the company when used, whichever is the larger figure

recovery ECONOMICS return to normal economic activity after downturn the return of a country to economic health after a crash or a depression

recovery fund STOCKHOLDING & INVESTMENTS fund investing in recovery stock a fund that invests in ***recovery stock*** that it considers likely to return to a previous higher price

recovery stock STOCKHOLDING & INVESTMENTS underperforming stock now recovering a stock that has fallen in price because of poor business performance, but is now expected to climb as a result of an improvement in the company's prospects

rectification note OPERATIONS & PRODUCTION authorization to improve poor product the authorization for more work to be done to improve a product that did not originally meet the required standard

recurring billing transaction E-COMMERCE automatic rebilling of customer's credit card a means of electronic payment based on the automatic charging of a customer's credit card in each payment period

recurring payments E-COMMERCE series of automatic payments preauthorized by customer a means of electronic payment that permits a merchant to process multiple authorizations by the same customer either as multiple payments for a fixed amount or recurring billings for varying amounts

red BANKING color for debits the color of debit or overdrawn balances in some bank statements ◇ in the red FINANCE, BANKING, ACCOUNTING in debt, or losing money

Red Book FINANCE copy of UK finance minister's Budget speech a copy of the Chancellor of the Exchequer's speech published on the day of the Budget. It can be regarded as the United Kingdom's financial statement and report.

Red chips STOCKHOLDING & INVESTMENTS good Chinese companies Chinese companies that are considered risk-free and worth investing in

red day *US* FINANCE unprofitable day a day on which no profit has been made (*slang*)

redeem **1.** FINANCE pay off loan or debt to carry out the repayment of a loan or a debt **2.** BUSINESS exchange voucher for something to exchange a voucher, coupon, or stamp for a gift or a reduction in price **3.** STOCKHOLDING & INVESTMENTS exchange security for cash to exchange a security for cash

redeemable bond STOCKHOLDING & INVESTMENTS bond that will be repaid a bond that is redeemable

redeemable gilt STOCKHOLDING & INVESTMENTS gilt that will be repaid a gilt that is redeemable

redeemable government stock STOCKHOLDING & INVESTMENTS stock redeemable for cash government stock that can be redeemed for cash at some time in the future

redeemable preference share *UK* STOCKHOLDING & INVESTMENTS = ***redeemable preferred stock***

redeemable preferred stock *US* STOCKHOLDING & INVESTMENTS preference share that firm may buy back a type of preferred stock that a company has the right to buy back at a specific date and for a specific price. *Also called* ***callable preferred stock***. *UK term* ***redeemable preference share***

redeemable security STOCKHOLDING & INVESTMENTS security redeemable at face value a security that can be redeemed at its face value at a specific date in the future

redeemable shares STOCKHOLDING & INVESTMENTS shares of stock that may be repurchased stock that is issued on terms that may require it to be bought back by the issuer at some future date, at the discretion either of the issuer or of the holder

redemption STOCKHOLDING & INVESTMENTS ending of financial obligation repayment of a financial obligation, frequently used in connection with preferred stock, debentures, and bonds

redemption date STOCKHOLDING & INVESTMENTS date for repayment of redeemable security the date on which a redeemable security is due to be repaid

redemption value STOCKHOLDING & INVESTMENTS value of security at redemption the value of a security at the time it is redeemed

redemption yield STOCKHOLDING & INVESTMENTS yield on security up to redemption a yield on a security including interest and its value up to the time it is redeemed. *See also* ***yield to maturity***

red eye *US* STOCKHOLDING & INVESTMENTS preliminary prospectus to test market information in the form of a ***preliminary prospectus*** used in ***initial public offerings*** to gauge the reaction of investors (*slang*). *UK term* ***pathfinder prospectus***

red herring STOCKHOLDING & INVESTMENTS = ***preliminary prospectus***

rediscount FINANCE discount bill of exchange for second time to discount a bill of exchange that has already been discounted by a commercial bank

redistribution of wealth ECONOMICS sharing of wealth across population the process of sharing wealth among the entire population, often through taxation

redistributive effect ECONOMICS, TAX wealth equalization resulting from taxes and benefits the tendency toward equalization of people's wealth that results from a ***progressive tax*** or selective benefit

redlining FINANCE, LEGAL discrimination against borrowers because of neighborhood of residence the illegal practice by financial institutions of discriminating against prospective borrowers because of the area of the town or city in which they live

red screen market MARKETS in UK, market with low prices in the United Kingdom, a market where the prices are down and are being shown as red on the dealing screens

red tape GENERAL MANAGEMENT excessive bureaucracy excessive bureaucracy or unwillingness to depart from rules and regulations

reducing balance depreciation CURRENCY & EXCHANGE *see* ***depreciation***

reducing balance method ACCOUNTING = ***accelerated depreciation***

redundancy *UK* HR & PERSONNEL = ***severance***

redundancy package *UK* HR & PERSONNEL = ***severance package***

redundancy payment *UK* FINANCE, HR & PERSONNEL = ***severance pay***

redundant capacity OPERATIONS & PRODUCTION = ***surplus capacity***

reengineering GENERAL MANAGEMENT *see* ***business process reengineering***

reference BANKING = ***banker's reference***

reference population STATISTICS standard set for statistical comparison a standard against which a statistical population under study can be compared

reference rate FINANCE rate used as benchmark a benchmark interest rate, for example, a bank's own set rate or the ***London Interbank Offered Rate***. Lending rates are often expressed as a margin over a reference rate.

reference site E-COMMERCE customer website showcasing new technology a customer website where a new technology is being used successfully

referred share STOCKHOLDING & INVESTMENTS ex dividend stock a stock that is ***ex dividend***, the right to dividends remaining with the vendor

refer to drawer *UK* BANKING refuse to pay check from underfunded account to refuse to pay a check because the account from which it is drawn has too little money in it. *Abbr* ***RD, R/D***

refer to drawer please re-present BANKING shown on refused UK check in the United Kingdom, marked on a check by the paying banker to indicate that there are currently insufficient funds to meet the payment, but that the bank believes sufficient funds will be available shortly. *See also* ***refer to drawer***. *Abbr* ***RDPR***

refinance FINANCE replace loan to replace one loan with another, especially at a lower rate of interest or at a longer maturity

refinancing FINANCE **1.** replacing one loan with another the process of taking out a loan to pay off other loans **2.** new loan that repays old loan a loan taken out for the purpose of repaying another loan or loans

reflation ECONOMICS increasing employment by increasing demand a method of reducing unemployment by increasing an economy's ***aggregate demand***. *See also* ***recession***

refugee capital FINANCE resources entering country through necessity people and other financial resources that come into a country because they have been forced to leave their own country for economic or political reasons

refund BUSINESS return of purchase price to buyer the reimbursement of the purchase price of a good or service, for reasons such as manufacturing flaws or dissatisfaction with the service provided

refundable BUSINESS able to be repaid able or liable to be paid back

refunding FINANCE issuance of new bonds to replace old the process of a government's renewing of the funding of a debt by issuing new bonds to replace those that are about to mature

regeneration ECONOMICS revitalization of rundown industrial or business areas the redevelopment of industrial or business areas that have suffered decline, in order to increase employment and business activity

regional development grant ECONOMICS grant encouraging business in UK regions in the United Kingdom, a grant given to encourage a business to establish itself in a specific part of the country. *Abbr* ***RDG***

regional fund STOCKHOLDING & INVESTMENTS mutual fund investing in geographic region a mutual fund that invests in the markets of a particular geographic region

regional stock exchange MARKETS stock exchange outside country's main financial center a stock exchange that is not in the main financial center of a country

registered bond STOCKHOLDING & INVESTMENTS bond with ownership recorded by issuer a bond the ownership of which is recorded on the books of the issuer

registered broker MARKETS broker registered on exchange a broker who is registered as a member of a particular stock exchange

registered capital FINANCE = ***authorized capital***

registered check BANKING check written on temporary bank account a check written on a bank's account on behalf of a customer who does not have a bank account but who gives the bank funds to hold to cover the check

registered company REGULATION & COMPLIANCE UK firm registered with Companies House in the United Kingdom, a company that has filed official documents with the ***Registrar of Companies*** at Companies House. A registered company is obliged to conduct itself in accordance with company law. All organizations must register in order to become companies.

registered investment advisor STOCKHOLDING & INVESTMENTS professionally recognized US financial manager a person or company that is registered with the US Securities and Exchange Commission and usually manages the portfolios of others

registered name REGULATION & COMPLIANCE name of UK firm registered with Companies House in the United Kingdom, the name of a company as it is registered at Companies House. It must appear, along with the company's registered number and office, on all its letterheads and orders. *See also* ***company, corporation***

registered number REGULATION & COMPLIANCE number assigned to registered UK firm in the United Kingdom, a unique number assigned to a company registered at Companies House. It must appear, along with the company's registered name and office, on all its letterheads and orders. *See also* ***company, corporation***

registered office REGULATION & COMPLIANCE in UK, company's official mailing address in the United Kingdom, the official address of a company, which is reproduced on its letterheads and registered with Companies House, to which all legal correspondence and documents must be delivered

registered representative STOCKHOLDING & INVESTMENTS qualified US seller of securities a person who is licensed by the US Securities and Exchange Commission to sell securities, after having passed the required examinations

registered security *or* **registered share** STOCKHOLDING & INVESTMENTS security with holder's name recorded by issuer a security for which the holder's name is recorded in the books of the issuer. *See also* ***nominee***

registered share capital STOCKHOLDING & INVESTMENTS = ***authorized share capital***

registered trademark LEGAL unique mark identifying product with producer a unique legally registered mark on a product, that may be a symbol, words, or both, connecting the product to the trader or producer of that product

register of companies REGULATION & COMPLIANCE in UK, list of registered firms in the United Kingdom, the list of companies maintained at Companies House. *See also* ***company, corporation***

register of directors and secretaries REGULATION & COMPLIANCE firm's record of directors and secretaries a record that every ***registered company*** in the United Kingdom must maintain of the names and residential addresses of directors and the company secretary together with their nationality, occupation, and details of other directorships held. Public companies must also record the date of birth of their directors. The record must be kept at the company's registered office and be available for inspection by stockholders without charge and by members of the public for a nominal fee.

register of directors' interests REGULATION & COMPLIANCE, STOCKHOLDING & INVESTMENTS firm's record of directors' holdings a record that every ***registered company*** in the United Kingdom must maintain of the stocks and other securities that have been issued by the company and are held by its directors. It has to be made available for inspection during the company's ***annual meeting***.

registrar CORPORATE GOVERNANCE keeper of official records a person or organization responsible for keeping official records, for example, the person who keeps a record of stockholders in a company

Registrar of Companies LEGAL, CORPORATE GOVERNANCE official holding record of registered UK companies the person charged with the duty of holding and registering the official startup and constitutional documents of all ***registered companies*** in the United Kingdom

registration REGULATION & COMPLIANCE **1.** official listing or recording of information the process of recording something such as names, data, or other required information on an official list **2.** provision of required documentation before selling company stock in the United States, the process by which a company files documents with the ***SEC*** prior to offering stock for sale to the public. The document must contain detailed financial information that has been certified by an outside accountant, information about the company's management, and details of the public offering.

registration fee 1. REGULATION & COMPLIANCE money paid to have something registered money paid to cover the cost of having something, such as a company, registered **2.** GENERAL MANAGEMENT fee for attending event money paid to take part in an event or activity, for example, a conference or training session

registration statement REGULATION & COMPLIANCE document produced by US corporation issuing securities in the United States, a document that corporations planning to issue securities to the public have to submit to the ***SEC***. It features details of the issuer's management, financial status, and activities, and the purpose of the issue. *See also* ***shelf registration***

regression analysis STATISTICS method of determining relationships between variables a ***forecasting*** technique used to establish the relationship between quantifiable variables.
In regression analysis, data on dependent and independent variables is plotted on a scatter graph or diagram, and trends are indicated through a line of best fit. The use of a single independent variable is known as *simple regression analysis,* while the use of two or more independent variables is called *multiple regression analysis*.

regressive tax TAX tax where rate falls as income increases a tax with a rate that decreases proportionally as the value of the item being taxed, especially income, rises. Social security taxes are regressive. *See also* ***progressive tax, proportional tax***

regulated superannuation fund TAX Australian superannuation fund regulated by legislation an Australian superannuation fund that is regulated by legislation and therefore qualifies for tax concessions. To attain this status, a fund must either show that its main function is the provision of pensions, or adopt a corporate trustee structure.

regulation REGULATION & COMPLIANCE control of activities using laws and rules the use of laws or rules stipulated by a government or regulatory body, such as the ***Securities and Exchange Commission*** in the United States or the ***Financial Services Authority*** in the United Kingdom, to provide orderly procedures and to protect consumers and investors

regulation D REGULATION & COMPLIANCE rule allowing sale of securities without SEC registration in the United States, a regulation that allows some smaller companies to offer their securities for sale without having to register them with the ***Securities and Exchange Commission***

regulation S-X REGULATION & COMPLIANCE US rules on financial reports in the United States, a regulation that controls the form and content of financial reports filed with the ***Securities and Exchange Commission***

regulation T REGULATION & COMPLIANCE rule on extensions of credit in the United States, a federal law that regulates extensions of credit by brokers and dealers and specifies initial margin requirements and payment rules on some securities transactions

regulation Z REGULATION & COMPLIANCE rule requiring transparency in loans in the United States, a federal law requiring that all lenders and credit card issuers disclose in writing all the costs and terms associated with obtaining the loan or credit

regulator REGULATION & COMPLIANCE government official who monitors businesses and markets a government official or body that monitors the behavior of companies and the level of competition in particular markets, for example, telecommunications or energy

regulatory body *or* **regulatory agency** REGULATION & COMPLIANCE organization regulating firms' activities an independent organization, usually established by government, that regulates the activities of companies in an industry

regulatory framework REGULATION & COMPLIANCE system of regulations and enforcement a system of regulations and the means to enforce them, usually established by a government to regulate a specific activity. *Also called* ***regulatory regime***

regulatory pricing risk INSURANCE, RISK risk that government will regulate insurance company's prices the risk an insurance company faces that a government will regulate the prices it can charge

regulatory regime REGULATION & COMPLIANCE = ***regulatory framework***

rehypothecation FINANCE pledge of client's securities as loan collateral an arrangement in which a broker pledges securities in a client's margin account as collateral for a loan from a bank

reimbursement FINANCE repayment of expense incurred repayment of money spent for an agreed or official purpose or taken as a loan, or money paid as compensation for a loss

reinsurance INSURANCE reduction of insurance risk by transferring policy a method of reducing risk by transferring all or part of an insurance policy to another insurer

reinsurer INSURANCE provider of insurance to insurers an insurer to whom another insurer transfers all or part of an insurance policy to reduce risk

reintermediation E-COMMERCE reintroduction of intermediaries in traditional retail channels the reintroduction of intermediaries found in traditional retail channels. *See also* ***disintermediation***

reinvestment STOCKHOLDING & INVESTMENTS **1.** investing of money again the act of investing money again in the same securities **2.** firm's investing of earnings in own business the act of investing a company's earnings in its own business by using them to create new products for sale

reinvestment rate FINANCE interest rate available for reinvested income the interest rate at which an investor is able to reinvest income received from an investment

reinvestment risk FINANCE, RISK risk that reinvestment will be at lower rate the risk that an investor will be unable to earn the same rate of return on the proceeds of an investment as he or she earns on the investment as a result of declining interest rates

reinvestment unit trust STOCKHOLDING & INVESTMENTS mutual fund using dividends to buy more stock in the United Kingdom, a mutual fund that uses dividends to buy more shares in the company issuing them. *See also* ***accumulation unit***

REIT *abbr* REAL ESTATE, STOCKHOLDING & INVESTMENTS ***real estate investment trust***

rejects OPERATIONS & PRODUCTION inferior products or merchandise units of output that fail a set quality standard and are subsequently rectified, sold as substandard, or disposed of as scrap

related company BUSINESS firm that other firm invests in a company in which another company makes a long-term capital investment in order to gain control of it or influence its decisions

relationship management MARKETING effort to maintain good customer relations the process of fostering good relations with customers to build loyalty and increase sales

relative income hypothesis ECONOMICS belief that people care about others' incomes the theory that consumers are concerned less with their absolute living standards than with consumption relative to other consumers

relevant interest *ANZ* STOCKHOLDING & INVESTMENTS legal position enabling investor to buy and sell the legal status held by stock investors who can legally dispose of, or influence the disposal of, stocks

relocation GENERAL MANAGEMENT transfer of business to new location the transfer of a business from one location to another. Relocation occurs for a variety of reasons, including the need for more space, the desire to centralize operations, or to be nearer to suppliers, customers, or raw materials.

reminder BUSINESS, FINANCE letter reminding of obligation to pay invoice a letter to remind a customer that he or she has not paid an invoice

remittance BUSINESS, FINANCE money sent as payment money that is sent to pay a debt or to pay an invoice

remittance advice *or* **remittance slip** BUSINESS, FINANCE detailed document accompanying payment a document sent with payment, giving details of what invoices are being paid and credits, if any, being taken

remitting bank BANKING = ***collecting bank***

remuneration FINANCE, HR & PERSONNEL = ***earnings***

remuneration package HR & PERSONNEL employee's total pay, including bonuses and benefits the salary, pension contributions, bonuses, and other forms of payment or benefits that an employer gives an employee

renewal notice INSURANCE document advising of need to renew insurance a document, usually in the form of an invoice, sent by an insurance company asking the insured person to renew the insurance for a particular period of time

renewal premium INSURANCE payment to renew insurance a payment to an insurance company to renew insurance for a particular period of time

renounceable document LEGAL evidence of temporary ownership in the United Kingdom, written proof of ownership for a limited period, for example, a letter of allotment of shares of stock in a ***rights issue***. *See also* ***letter of renunciation***

rent **1.** FINANCE arrangement to use equipment for money an arrangement whereby customers pay money to be able to use a car, boat, or piece of equipment owned by another person or firm for a period of time **2.** REAL ESTATE arrangement to use buildings or land for money money paid to use an office, building, or piece of farmland, for example, owned by another person for a period of time **3.** FINANCE allow somebody use of something for money to use or allow somebody to use, an office, building, or piece of farmland, for example, in return for a regular payment. *Also called* ***let***

rental value REAL ESTATE level of rent at current market rate a full value of the rent for a property if it were charged at the current market rate, usually calculated between rent reviews

rent control LEGAL, REAL ESTATE limit on amount chargeable as residential rent regulation by a government restricting the amount somebody can charge to rent a residential property

renting back FINANCE = ***sale and leaseback***

rent review LEGAL, REAL ESTATE increase in rent during term of lease an increase in rents that is carried out during the term of a lease. Most leases allow for rents to be reviewed every three or five years.

renunciation STOCKHOLDING & INVESTMENTS = ***letter of renunciation***

reorder level OPERATIONS & PRODUCTION fixed limit triggering new order of inventory a level of inventory at which a replenishment order should be placed. Traditional "optimizing" systems use a variation on the computation of maximum usage multiplied by maximum lead, which builds in a measure of safety.

reorganization bond STOCKHOLDING & INVESTMENTS US bond for creditors of firm being reorganized in the United States, a bond issued to creditors of a business that is undergoing a form of ***Chapter 11*** reorganization. Interest is normally only paid when the company can make the payments from its earnings.

repatriation FINANCE return of foreign investment earnings to home country the act of sending money earned on foreign investments to the home country of their firm or owner

repayable FINANCE to be repaid used to describe money that is to be paid back, usually in a particular way, for example, in monthly installments

repayment FINANCE **1.** repaying of money the act of paying money back, usually in a particular way, for example, in monthly installments **2.** money repaid money that is paid back, usually in a particular way, for example, in monthly installments

repayment mortgage *UK* MORTGAGES = ***amortized mortgage***

repeat business BUSINESS, MARKETING continuing orders from same supplier the placing of order after order with the same supplier. Repeat business can be implemented by an agreement between the customer and supplier for purchase on a regular basis. It is often used where there are small numbers of customers, or high volumes per product and low product variety. There is market competition for the first order only, and customization is usually available for the initial purchase only. Sales and marketing have a diminished role once the business has been gained.

replacement cost *or* **replacement price** ACCOUNTING today's cost of replacing something the cost of replacing an asset or service with its current equivalent

replacement cost accounting ACCOUNTING means of evaluating firm's assets a method of valuing company assets based on their replacement cost

replacement cost depreciation ACCOUNTING depreciation based on current replacement cost depreciation based on the actual cost of replacing the asset in the current year

replacement ratio ECONOMICS difference between wages and unemployment benefits the ratio of the total resources received when unemployed to those received when in employment

replacement value INSURANCE today's cost of replacing something the cost of replacing an insured asset with its current equivalent

repo 1. FINANCE = ***repurchase agreement*** **2.** MARKETS open-market buying and selling by US Federal Reserve in the United States, an open-market operation undertaken by the ***Federal Reserve*** to purchase securities and agree to sell them back at a stated price on a future date **3.** BANKING Bank of England's repurchase agreement in the United Kingdom, a Bank of England repurchase agreement with ***market makers*** in ***gilt-edged securities***. It is used to provide securities for ***short positions***.

reporting entity CORPORATE GOVERNANCE organization providing financial information to stockholders any organization such as a limited company that reports its accounts to its stockholders

repositioning MARKETING marketing old product in new ways a marketing strategy that changes aspects of a product or brand in order to change ***market position*** and alter consumer perceptions

repossession FINANCE return of merchandise after default on time payments the return of goods purchased through an installment plan when the purchaser fails to make the required regular payments. *See also* ***recourse agreement***

repudiation FINANCE refusing to honor debt a refusal to pay or acknowledge a debt or similar contract

repurchase FINANCE buy back shares in mutual fund to buy back shares, for example, when a fund manager buys back the shares in a mutual fund after an investor sells, or when companies repurchase shares instead of or in addition to paying a dividend to shareholders

repurchase agreement MARKETS agreement to both sell and buy back security in the bond and money markets, a spot sale of a security combined with its repurchase at a later date and pre-agreed price. In effect, the buyer is lending money to the seller for the duration of the transaction and using the security as collateral. Dealers finance their positions by using repurchase agreements. *Also called* ***repo (sense 1)***

request form E-COMMERCE Web page with blanks for user data an interactive Web page that accepts user-provided data—for example, name, address, or shipping information—that can be saved for recurring use or sent by e-mail to the page owner

required beginning date PENSIONS, TAX date to start pension payments in the United States, the date on which the ***IRS*** requires that distributions to a participant in a ***qualified retirement plan*** begin

required rate of return FINANCE lowest acceptable return the minimum return for a proposed project investment to be acceptable. *See also* ***discounted cash flow***

required reserve ratio *or* **required reserves** BANKING ratio of bank's reserves to deposits the proportion of a bank's deposits that must be kept in reserve.

In the United Kingdom and in certain European countries, there is no compulsory ratio, although banks will have their own internal measures and targets to be able to repay customer deposits as they forecast they will be required. In the United States, specified percentages of deposits—established by the Federal Reserve Board—must be kept by banks in a non-interest-bearing account at one of the twelve Federal Reserve Banks located throughout the country.

In Europe, the reserve requirement of an institution is calculated by multiplying the reserve ratio for each category of items in the reserve base, set by the European Central Bank, with the amount of those items in the institution's balance sheets. These figures vary according to the institution.

The required reserve ratio in the United States is set by federal law, and depends on the amount of checkable deposits a bank holds. Up to $9.3M the required reserve ratio is 0%, from $9.3M to $43.9M it is 3% and above $43.9M it is 10%. These breakpoints are reviewed annually in accordance with money supply growth. No reserves are required against certificates of deposit or savings accounts.

The reserve ratio requirement limits a bank's lending to a certain fraction of its demand deposits. The current rule allows a bank to issue loans in an amount equal to 90% of such deposits, holding 10% in reserve. The reserves can be held in any combination of till money and deposit at a Federal Reserve Bank. *Also called* ***bank reserve ratio, reserve ratio, reserve requirement***

requisition OPERATIONS & PRODUCTION firm's purchase order an official order form used by companies when purchasing a product or service

resale price maintenance MARKETING UK agreement with supplier restricting retail price formerly in the United Kingdom, an agreement between suppliers or manufacturers and retailers, restricting the price that retailers can ask for a product or service. Resale price maintenance was designed to enable all retailers to make a profit. The Resale Prices Act now prevents this practice on the grounds that it is uncompetitive. Now, unless they can prove that resale price maintenance is in the public interest, manufacturers can only recommend a retail price. *Abbr* ***RPM***

reschedule FINANCE arrange new payment schedule for debt to arrange a new payment schedule and new conditions for the repayment of a debt

rescission LEGAL cancellation of contract an act of rescinding or annulling a contract

research STOCKHOLDING & INVESTMENTS evaluation of information to aid investing the examination of statistics and other information regarding past, present, and future trends or performance that enables analysts to recommend to investors which stocks to buy or sell in order to maximize their return and minimize their risk. It may be used either in the top-down approach (where the investor evaluates a market, then an industry, and finally a specific company) or the bottom-up approach (where the investor selects a company and confirms his or her findings by evaluating the company's sector and then its market). Careful research is likely to help investors find the best deals, in particular ***value shares*** or ***growth equities***. *See also* ***technical analysis***

reserve FINANCE business profits withheld to cover unexpected costs profits in a business that have not been paid out as dividends but have been set aside in the business to cover any unexpected costs. *Also called* ***reserve fund***

reserve account E-COMMERCE = ***holdback***

reserve bank BANKING bank that holds money for other banks in the United States, a bank such as a Federal Reserve bank that holds the reserves of other banks

Reserve Bank of Australia BANKING central bank of Australia Australia's central bank, which is responsible for managing the Commonwealth's monetary policy, ensuring financial stability, and printing and distributing currency. *Abbr* ***RBA***

Reserve Bank of New Zealand BANKING central bank of New Zealand New Zealand's central bank, which is responsible for managing the government's monetary policy, ensuring financial stability, and printing and distributing currency. *Abbr* ***RBNZ***

reserve currency CURRENCY & EXCHANGE foreign currency kept for international trading foreign currency that a central bank holds for use in international trade

reserve for fluctuations CURRENCY & EXCHANGE money to absorb exchange rate differences money set aside to allow for changes in the values of currencies

reserve fund FINANCE = ***reserve***

reserve price FINANCE minimum price in auction a price for a particular lot, set by the vendor, below which an auctioneer may not sell

reserve ratio BANKING = ***required reserve ratio***

reserve requirement BANKING = ***required reserve ratio***

reserves 1. FINANCE money held for contingencies and opportunities a sum of money held by a person or organization to finance unexpected business opportunities. *See also* ***war chest*** **2.** BANKING money that bank holds for withdrawals the money that a bank holds to ensure that it can satisfy its depositors' demands for withdrawals **3.** ACCOUNTING, STOCKHOLDING & INVESTMENTS profit not distributed plus stock subscriptions in a company balance sheet, the total of profits not yet distributed to shareholders and the amount subscribed for stock in excess of the ***nominal value***

residential property REAL ESTATE dwellings houses, apartments, or other dwellings in which people and their families live

residual value ACCOUNTING value of asset after depreciation a value of an asset after it has been depreciated in the company's accounts

residuary legatee LEGAL person inheriting after specific bequests the person to whom a testator's estate is left after specific bequests have been made

residue FINANCE money left over money that has not been spent or paid out

resizing HR & PERSONNEL = ***upsizing***

resolution CORPORATE GOVERNANCE proposal to be voted on at meeting a proposal put to a meeting, for example, an ***annual meeting*** of shareholders, on which those present and eligible can vote. *See also* ***extraordinary resolution, special resolution***

resource driver ACCOUNTING **1.** *see* ***cost driver*** **2.** unit for measuring usage and assignment of resources a measurement unit that is used to assign resource costs to ***activity cost pools*** based on some measures of usage. For example, it may be used to assign office occupancy costs to purchasing or accounting services within a company.

resources OPERATIONS & PRODUCTION total means by which organization achieves its purpose anything that is available to an organization to help it achieve its purpose. Resources are often categorized into finance, property, premises, equipment, people, and raw materials.

response bias STATISTICS difference between answer given and actual fact the disparity between information that a survey respondent provides and data analysis, for example, a person claiming to watch little television but giving answers showing 30 hours' weekly viewing

response rate STATISTICS how many people respond to survey the proportion of subjects in a statistical study who respond to a researcher's questionnaire

responsibility accounting ACCOUNTING record-keeping that shows individual responsibilities the keeping of financial records with an emphasis on who is responsible for each item

responsibility center GENERAL MANAGEMENT organizational center for which manager is completely accountable a department or organizational function whose performance is the direct responsibility of a specific manager

restated balance sheet ACCOUNTING accounts reorganized to emphasize selected feature a balance sheet reframed to serve a specific purpose such as highlighting depreciation on assets

restatement ACCOUNTING revised financial statement a revision of a company's earlier financial statement

restraint of trade GENERAL MANAGEMENT, HR & PERSONNEL restriction of right to compete against former employer a term in a contract of employment that restricts a person from carrying on their trade or profession if they leave an organization. Generally illegal, it is usually intended to prevent key employees from leaving an organization to establish a competing organization.

restricted security STOCKHOLDING & INVESTMENTS security bought in unregistered sale a security acquired in an unregistered private resale from the issuer or an affiliate of the issuer, and whose sale must meet certain conditions laid down by the ***Securities and Exchange Commission***

restricted surplus *US* FINANCE funds unavailable for dividend payments reserves that are not legally available for distribution to stockholders as dividends. *UK term* ***undistributable reserves***

restricted tender STOCKHOLDING & INVESTMENTS conditional offer for stock an offer to buy stock only under specific conditions

restrictive covenant FINANCE agreement to retain loan collateral an agreement by a borrower not to sell an asset that he or she has used as collateral for a loan

restructure BUSINESS reorganize firm's financial basis to reorganize the financial basis of a company

result ACCOUNTING account produced at end of trading period a profit or loss account for a company at the end of a trading period

result-driven GENERAL MANAGEMENT focused on outcome rather than process used to describe a type of corporate strategy focused on outcomes and achievements. A result-driven organization concentrates on meeting objectives, delivering to the required time, cost, and quality, and holds performance to be more important than procedures.

résumé *US* HR & PERSONNEL document summarizing job history and skills a document that provides a summary of personal career history, skills, and experience. A résumé is usually prepared to aid in a job application. A job advertisement may ask either for a résumé or instead may require a candidate to complete an application form.

Every résumé should include the following: the jobseeker's name and contact details; a clear and concise description of his or her career objective; some kind of outline of work experience; and a list of education and degrees. It is important to customize a résumé to the type of job or career being applied for, and to make sure it has impact: a hiring manager receives an average of over 120 résumés for every job opening.

There are four basic types of résumé: the chronological, the functional, the targeted, and the capabilities résumé. A chronological résumé is useful for people who stay in the same field and do not make major career changes. They should start with and focus on the most recent positions held. A functional résumé is the preferred choice for those seeking their first professional job, or those making a major career change. It is based around 3–5 paragraphs, each emphasizing and illustrating a particular skill or accomplishment. A targeted résumé is useful for jobseekers who are very clear about their job direction and need to make an impressive case for a specific job. Like a functional résumé, it should be based around several capabilities and accomplishments that are relevant to the target job, focusing on action and results. A capabilities résumé is used for people applying for a specific job within their current organization. It should focus on 5–8 skills and accomplishments achieved with the company.

The format of a résumé should also be considered—whether it is to be printed out, incorporated into an e-mail, posted on a website, or burned onto a CD-ROM. Different layout and design elements, such as the choice of fonts or inclusion of multimedia, are suitable for each medium, and should be thought through carefully. *UK term* ***CV***

retail BUSINESS **1.** sale of goods to general public the sale of small quantities of goods to the general public **2.** sell goods to general public to sell goods in small quantities to the general public

retail banking BANKING financial services for individuals services provided by commercial banks to individuals as opposed to business customers that include current accounts, deposit and savings accounts, as well as credit cards, mortgages, and investments. In the United Kingdom, although this service was traditionally provided by high street banks, separate organizations, albeit offshoots of established financial institutions, more recently began to provide Internet and telephone banking services, though the credit crunch of 2008 has set back their operations. *See also* ***wholesale banking***

retail cooperative BUSINESS retailers who cut costs by purchasing collectively an organization for the collective purchase and sale of goods by a group who share profits or benefits. Retail cooperatives were the first offshoot of the ***cooperative movement*** and profits were originally shared among members through dividend payments proportionate to a member's purchases.

retail deposit BANKING money held in bank on somebody's behalf a sum of money held in a bank on behalf of an individual

retail depositor BANKING individual bank customer an individual who deposits money in a bank, as opposed to a business customer

retailer BUSINESS store selling directly to customer an outlet through which products or services are sold to customers. Retailers can be put into three broad groups: independent traders, multiple stores, or retail cooperatives.

retailer number BANKING retailer's identification number for depositing credit card payments the identification number of the retailer, printed at the top of the report slip when depositing credit card payments

retail investor STOCKHOLDING & INVESTMENTS small investor a private investor who buys and sells stock

retail price BUSINESS price for small quantity a price charged to customers who buy in limited quantities *Also called* ***shop price***

retail price index ECONOMICS list of average prices charged to consumers a listing of the average levels of prices charged by retailers for goods or services. The retail price index is calculated on a set variety of items, and usually excludes luxury goods. It is updated monthly, and provides a running indicator of changing costs. *Abbr* ***RPI***

retained earnings *US* ACCOUNTING = ***retained profits***

retained profits ACCOUNTING firm's profits kept as reserves, expansion, or investment the amount of profit remaining after tax and distribution to stockholders that is retained in a business and used as a reserve or as a means of financing expansion or investment. *Also called* ***retained earnings, retentions***

retainer FINANCE money advanced to retain somebody's services money paid in advance to somebody so that they will work for you and not for someone else

retention 1. FINANCE withholding of payment the holding back of money due until a condition has been fulfilled **2.** HR & PERSONNEL keeping existing employees the process of keeping the loyalty of existing employees and persuading them not to work for another company

retentions ACCOUNTING = ***retained profits***

retire 1. FINANCE pay off loan to pay the balance owed on a loan **2.** HR & PERSONNEL stop working at end of career to leave a job or career voluntarily at the usual age or time for doing so

retirement 1. FINANCE payment of loan balance the act of paying the balance owed on a loan **2.** HR & PERSONNEL act of retiring the act of leaving a job or career voluntarily at the usual age or time for doing so **3.** HR & PERSONNEL time after retiring the time that follows the end of a person's working life

retirement annuity PENSIONS pension paid as annuity to retired person an annuity paid to a person when they reach a specific age, derived from a fund built up over time

retirement benefits PENSIONS pension payments to retired person benefits that are payable by a pension plan to somebody who retires

retirement fund *US* PENSIONS money set aside to pay pensions of retirees a large sum of money made up of contributions from employees and their employer which provides pensions for retired employees. *UK term* ***pension fund***

retirement pension PENSIONS = ***pension***

retrenchment FINANCE cost reductions to improve profitability the reduction of costs or spending in order to maintain or improve profitability, especially in response to changed economic circumstances

return 1. ACCOUNTING, STOCKHOLDING & INVESTMENTS = ***rate of return*** **2.** TAX = ***tax return***

return date ACCOUNTING in UK, date for required annual return in the United Kingdom, a date by which a company's annual return has to be made to the ***Registrar of Companies***

return on assets ACCOUNTING net income as percentage of total assets a measure of profitability calculated by expressing a company's net income as a percentage of total assets. *Abbr* ***ROA***

return on capital *or* **return on capital employed** ACCOUNTING ratio used for measuring profitability by UK firms in the United Kingdom, a ratio of the net profit made in a fiscal year in relation to the ***capital employed***. It is used as a measure of business profitability. *Abbr* ***ROC, ROCE***

return on equity FINANCE relationship between net income and stockholders' funds the ratio of a company's net income as a percentage of shareholders' funds.

Return on equity is easy to calculate and is applicable to the majority of industries. It is probably the most widely used measure of how well a company is performing for its shareholders.

It is calculated by dividing the net income shown on the income statement (usually of the past year) by shareholders' equity, which appears on the balance sheet:

Net income / Owners' equity = Return on equity

For example, if net income is $450 and equity is $2,500, then:

450 / 2,500 = 0.18 × 100% = 18% return on equity

Return on equity for most companies should be in double figures; investors often look for 15% or higher, while a return of 20% or more is considered excellent. Seasoned investors also review five-year average ROE, to gauge consistency. *Abbr* ***ROE***

return on invested capital *or* **return on investment** FINANCE profit as percentage of investment a ratio of the profit made in a financial year as a percentage of an investment

The most basic expression of ROI can be found by dividing a company's net profit (also called net earnings) by the total investment (total debt plus total equity), then multiplying by 100 to arrive at a percentage:

Net profit / Total investment = ROI

If, say, net profit is $30 and total investment is $250, the ROI is:

30 / 250 = 0.12 × 100% = 12%

A more complex variation of ROI is an equation known as the Du Pont formula:

(Net profit after taxes / Total assets) = (Net profit after taxes / Sales) × Sales / Total assets

If, for example, net profit after taxes is $30, total assets are $250, and sales are $500, then:

30 / 250 = 30 / 500 × 500 / 250 =12% = 6% × 2 = 12%

Champions of this formula, which was developed by the Du Pont Company in the 1920s, say that it helps reveal how a company has both deployed its assets and controlled its costs, and how it can achieve the same percentage return in different ways.

For shareholders, the variation of the basic ROI formula used by investors is:

Net income + (Current value – Original value) / Original value = ROI

If, for example, somebody invests $5,000 in a company and a year later has earned $100 in dividends, while the value of the shares is $5,200, the return on investment would be:

100 + (5,200 – 5,000) / 5,000 = (100 + 200) / 5,000 = 300 / 5,000 = 0.06 × 100% = 6% ROI

It is vital to understand exactly what a return on investment measures, for example, assets, equity, or sales. Without this understanding, comparisons may be misleading. It is also important to establish whether the net profit figure used is before or after provision for taxes. *Abbr* ***ROI, ROIC***

return on net assets FINANCE profit as percentage of firm's assets a ratio of the profit made in a fiscal year as a percentage of the assets of a company. *Abbr* ***RONA***

return on sales ACCOUNTING profit or loss as percentage of sales a company's operating profit or loss as a percentage of total sales for a given period, typically a year. *Abbr* ***ROS***. *See also* ***profit margin***

returns to scale ECONOMICS increase in output related to increases in inputs the proportionate increase in a country's or company's output as a result of increases in all its inputs

revaluation CURRENCY & EXCHANGE increase in value of nation's currency a rise in the value of a country's currency in relation to other currencies

revaluation method ACCOUNTING asset depreciation using change in value over year a method of calculating the depreciation of assets by which the asset is depreciated by the difference in its value at the end of the year over its value at the beginning of the year

revaluation of assets ACCOUNTING asset depreciation using change in value since acquisition the revaluation of a company's ***assets*** to take account of inflation or changes in value since the assets were acquired. The change in value is credited to the ***revaluation reserve account***.

revaluation of currency CURRENCY & EXCHANGE altering currency value to affect balance of payments an increase in the value of a currency in relation to others. In situations where there is a ***floating exchange rate***, a currency will usually find its own level automatically but this will not happen if there is a ***fixed exchange rate***. Should a government have persistent ***balance of payment*** surpluses, it may exceptionally decide to revalue its currency, making imports cheaper but its exports more expensive.

revaluation reserve CURRENCY & EXCHANGE money held to cover fluctuations in foreign currencies money set aside to account for the fact that the value of assets may vary as a result of accounting in different currencies

revaluation reserve account ACCOUNTING account for asset depreciation an account to which the change in value of a company's assets is credited during a ***revaluation of assets***

revalue ACCOUNTING reassess value of something to value something again, usually setting a higher value on it than before

revenue FINANCE income from product or service the income generated by a product or service over a period of time

revenue account ACCOUNTING business account for recording income an account in a business used for recording receipts from sales, services, commissions, and other income associated with the business's activities

revenue anticipation note STOCKHOLDING & INVESTMENTS, TAX government means of raising money a government-issued ***debt instrument*** for which expected income from taxation is collateral

revenue bond STOCKHOLDING & INVESTMENTS US government bond a bond that a US state or a local government issues, to be repaid from the money made from the project financed with it

revenue center FINANCE center for generating income without costs a part of a business that raises revenue but has no responsibility for costs, for example, a sales center

revenue expenditure ACCOUNTING money spent on inventory purchases for current-year sale expenditure on purchasing stock, but not on capital items, which is then sold during the current accounting period

revenue ledger ACCOUNTING record of total income a record of all the income received by an organization. *Also called* ***sales ledger***

revenue officer TAX employee in tax office a person working in the government tax offices

revenue recognition ACCOUNTING determination of when income becomes revenue an accounting principle that determines when income is recognized as revenue. In ***cash accounting***, revenue is recognized not when services were performed or products delivered but when payment is actually received. Following the ***accrual concept***, revenue is recognized when payment is earned no matter when it is actually received.

revenue reserves FINANCE, ACCOUNTING undistributed earnings held as stockholders' funds ***retained profits*** that are shown in the company's balance sheet as part of the stockholders' funds

revenue sharing **1.** TAX distribution of US federal taxes to states distribution to states by the federal government of money that it collects in taxes **2.** BUSINESS income sharing within limited partnerships the distribution of income within ***limited partnerships***, where there are both general and limited partners

revenue stamp TAX stamp certifying receipt of tax payment a stamp that a government issues to certify that somebody has paid a tax

revenue tariff TAX national tax on imports or exports a tax levied on imports or exports to raise revenue for a national government

reversal FINANCE change in status a change to the opposite, for example, from being profitable to unprofitable, or, in the case of a stock price from rising to falling

reversal stop MARKETS price that triggers change between buying and selling a price at which a trader stops buying and starts selling a security, or vice versa

reverse leverage FINANCE **1.** higher expenditures than income a cash flow in which expenditures are higher than income **2.** borrowing at higher interest rate than investments pay the borrowing of money at a rate of interest higher than the expected rate of return on investing the money borrowed

reverse mortgage MORTGAGES arrangement using mortgage as collateral for annuity payment a financial arrangement in which a lender such as a bank takes over a mortgage and then pays an annuity to the homeowner

reverse split STOCKHOLDING & INVESTMENTS exchange of fewer new shares for old shares the issuing to stockholders of a fraction of one share for every share that they own. *See also* ***stock split***

reverse takeover MERGERS & ACQUISITIONS takeover by lesser company the ***takeover*** of a large company by a smaller one, or the takeover of a public company by a private one

reverse yield gap FINANCE, STOCKHOLDING & INVESTMENTS amount by which expenditure exceeds yield or income the amount by which bond yield exceeds equity yield, or interest rates on loans exceed rental values as a percentage of the costs of properties

reversing entry ACCOUNTING final debit or credit entry reversing earlier entry a debit or credit entry in a chart of accounts that is made at the end of an accounting period to reverse an entry

reversionary annuity PENSIONS annuity paid on person's death an annuity paid to somebody on the death of another person

reversionary bonus INSURANCE annual bonus on life assurance policy an annual bonus on a life assurance policy, declared by the insurer

revocable trust FINANCE trust that can be revoked a trust whose provisions can be amended or canceled

revolving charge account FINANCE account with renewable credit for buying goods a charge account with a company for use in buying that company's goods with ***revolving credit***

revolving credit FINANCE = ***open-end credit***

revolving fund FINANCE fund receiving revenue from projects it finances a fund the resources of which are replenished from the revenue of the projects that it finances

revolving loan BANKING loan allowing money repaid to be borrowed again a loan facility whereby the borrower can choose the number and timing of withdrawals against their bank loan and any money repaid may be reborrowed at a future date. Such loans can be made available to both businesses and personal customers.

riba FINANCE interest charge or unfair profit in Islamic financing, interest or any unjust profit made by a lender in a financial transaction. It is one of three prohibitions in Islamic law, the others being ***gharar*** and ***maysir***.

rider INSURANCE additional provision added to contract an additional clause or provision added to an insurance policy, which becomes part of the policy

RIE *abbr* MARKETS ***recognized investment exchange***

rigged market MARKETS illegal trading practice to attract investors a market where two or more parties are buying and selling securities among themselves to give the impression of active trading with the intention of attracting investors to purchase the stocks. This practice is illegal in most jurisdictions.

right of survivorship LEGAL joint owner's right after death of other the right of a surviving joint owner of property to acquire the interest of a deceased joint owner

rights issue STOCKHOLDING & INVESTMENTS raising capital by offering existing stockholders additional stock the raising of new capital by giving existing stockholders the right to subscribe to new shares or ***debentures*** in proportion to their current holdings. These shares of stock are usually issued at a discount to market price. A stockholder not wishing to take up a rights issue may sell the rights. *Also called* ***rights offer***

rightsizing GENERAL MANAGEMENT restructuring of company to most effective size corporate restructuring, or rationalization, with the goal of reducing costs and improving efficiency and effectiveness. Rightsizing is often used as a euphemism for ***downsizing***, or ***delayering***, with the suggestion that it is not as far-reaching. Rightsizing can also be used to describe increasing the size of an organization, perhaps as an attempt to correct a previous downsizing, or delayering, exercise.

rights offer STOCKHOLDING & INVESTMENTS = ***rights issue***

rights offering STOCKHOLDING & INVESTMENTS offering additional stock to existing stockholders an offering for sale of a ***rights issue***, in proportion to the holdings of existing stockholders

ring MARKETS **1.** trading floor a trading area at an exchange, especially a commodity exchange. *See also* ***pit*** **2.** session on London Metal Exchange a trading session on the ***London Metal Exchange***, which deals in copper, lead, zinc, aluminum, tin, and nickel

ring-fence **1.** FINANCE separate profitable elements to safeguard business to separate valuable assets or profitable businesses from others in a group that are unprofitable and may make the whole group collapse **2.** FINANCE use money for specific projects to identify money from specific sources and only use it in agreed areas or for specific projects. *See also* ***hypothecation*** **3.** BUSINESS not let firm's liquidation affect others in group to allow one company within a group to go into liquidation without affecting the viability of the group as a whole or any other company within it

ring member MARKETS member of London Metal Exchange a member of the ***London Metal Exchange***, dealing in copper, lead, zinc, aluminum, tin, and nickel

ring trading MARKETS business conducted on trading floor business conducted in the trading area of a commodity exchange

rising bottoms MARKETS graph showing stock's rising price following low prices a pattern on a graph of the price of a security or commodity against time that shows an upward price movement following a period of low prices (*slang*). *See also* ***chartist***

risk RISK **1.** possibility of suffering harm or loss the possibility of suffering damage or loss in the face of uncertainty about the outcome of actions, future events, or circumstances. Organizations are exposed to various types of risk, including damage to property, injury to personnel, financial loss, and legal liability. These may affect profitability, hinder the achievement of objectives, or lead to business interruption or failure. Risk may be deemed high or low, depending on the probability of an adverse outcome. Risks that can be quantified on the basis of past experience are insurable and those that cannot be calculated are uninsurable. **2.** potential for negative outcome a condition in which there exists a quantifiable dispersion in the possible outcomes from any activity

risk-adjusted return on capital STOCKHOLDING & INVESTMENTS, RISK return on capital evaluated in terms of risks return on capital calculated in a way that takes into account the risks associated with income. *Also called* ***Jensen's measure, Treynor ratio***

risk analysis RISK determination of how risks might affect organization the identification of risks to which an organization is exposed and the assessment of the potential impact of those risks on the organization. The goal of risk analysis is to identify and measure the risks associated with different courses of action in order to inform ***decision making***. In the context of business decision making, risk analysis is especially used in investment decisions and capital investment appraisal. Risk analysis may be used to develop an organizational ***risk profile***, and also may be the first stage in a ***risk management*** program.

risk arbitrage MARKETS, RISK trading without guaranteed profit simultaneous buying and selling without certainty of profit, though at relatively low risk. It is particularly employed by ***hedge fund*** managers.

risk arbitrageur RISK somebody engaged in risk arbitrage a person whose business is ***risk arbitrage***

risk assessment RISK determination of how risky something is the determination of the level of risk in a specific course of action. Risk assessments are an important tool in areas such as health and safety management and environmental management. Results of a risk assessment can be used, for example, to identify areas in which safety can be improved. Risk assessment can also be used to determine more intangible forms of risk, including economic and social risk, and can inform the scenario planning process. The amount of risk involved in a specific course of action is compared to its expected benefits to provide evidence for decision making.

risk asset ratio BANKING, RISK proportion of assets that carry risk the proportion of a bank's total capital assets that carry risk. *See also* ***risk-weighted asset***

risk-averse STOCKHOLDING & INVESTMENTS, RISK having desire to avoid risk in investment wanting to achieve the best return that can be had on an investment while taking the least possible risk

risk aversion STOCKHOLDING & INVESTMENTS, RISK desire to avoid risk in investment a desire to achieve the best return that can be had on an investment while taking the least possible risk

risk-based capital assessment BANKING, RISK bank's value based on risk attached to assets an internationally approved system of calculating a bank's capital value by assessing the risk attached to its assets. Cash deposits and gold, for example, have no risk, while loans to less-developed countries have a high risk.

risk-bearing economy of scale BUSINESS, RISK employing diversification to reduce risk conducting business on such a large scale that the risk of loss is reduced because it is spread over so many independent events, as in the issuance of insurance policies

risk capital FINANCE, RISK = ***venture capital***

risk factor RISK degree of risk in enterprise the degree of risk in a project or other business activity

risk-free return STOCKHOLDING & INVESTMENTS, RISK money from safe investment the profit made from an investment that involves no risk

risk management RISK **1.** actions intended to reduce or eliminate risks the variety of activities undertaken by an organization to control and minimize threats to the continuing efficiency, profitability, and success of its operations. The process of risk management includes the identification and analysis of risks to which the organization is exposed, the assessment of potential impacts on the business, and deciding what action can be taken to eliminate or reduce risk and deal with the impact of unpredictable events causing loss or damage. Risk management strategies include taking out insurance against financial loss or legal liability and introducing safety or security measures. **2.** understanding and dealing with inevitable risks the process of understanding and managing the risks that an organization is inevitably subject to in attempting to achieve its corporate objectives. For management purposes, risks are usually divided into categories such as operational, financial, legal compliance, information, and personnel.

risk manager GENERAL MANAGEMENT, HR & PERSONNEL RISK employee managing business risk the person in an organization who is in charge of assessing and managing business risks

risk perception RISK nonobjective view of risk the way in which people and organizations view risk, based on their concerns and experiences, but not necessarily on objective data. Risk perceptions can influence such things as business policies and investment decisions. *Also called* ***perception of risk***

risk premium FINANCE, RISK extra payment received by somebody taking risks an extra payment, for example, increased dividend or higher than usual profits, for taking risks

Risk Priority Number RISK number used to quantify risk a measure used in ***Failure Mode and Effects Analysis*** to quantify risk. It is a product of the severity, probability of occurrence, and ability to detect failure. *Abbr* ***RPN***

risk profile RISK **1.** description of risks facing organization an outline of the risks to which an organization is exposed. An organizational risk profile may be developed in the course of ***risk analysis*** and used for ***risk management***. It examines the nature of the threats faced by an organization, the likelihood of adverse effects occurring, and the level of disruption and costs associated with each type of risk. **2.** analysis of willingness to take risks an analysis of the willingness of individuals or organizations to take risks. A risk profile describes the level of risk considered acceptable by an individual or by the leaders of an organization, and considers how this will affect decision making and corporate strategy.

risk tolerance STOCKHOLDING & INVESTMENTS, RISK ability to withstand stress of investing the ability of an investor to handle the uncertainty and money losses inherent to investing

risk-weighted asset FINANCE, RISK asset weighted by its riskiness an asset weighted by factors relating to its riskiness, used by financial institutions in managing their capital requirements. *See also* ***risk asset ratio***

ROA *abbr* ACCOUNTING ***return on assets***

road show STOCKHOLDING & INVESTMENTS events to interest potential investors a series of presentations to potential investors and brokers given by the management of a company prior to issuing securities, especially in an ***initial public offering***, intended to create interest in the offering

ROC *abbr* ACCOUNTING ***return on capital***

ROCE *abbr* ACCOUNTING ***return on capital employed***

rocket scientist FINANCE innovative finance worker an employee of a financial institution who creates innovative securities that usually include derivatives (*slang*)

rodo kinko FINANCE Japanese provider of loans to small businesses in Japan, a financial institution that specializes in providing credit for small businesses

ROE *abbr* FINANCE ***return on equity***

rogue trader MARKETS stock dealer acting illegally a dealer in stocks who uses illegal methods to make profits

ROI *abbr* FINANCE ***return on investment***

ROIC *abbr* FINANCE ***return on invested capital***

roll down MARKETS close then open option position at lower price to close a position on one option and open another at a lower ***strike price***

rolled-up coupon *UK* STOCKHOLDING & INVESTMENTS interest coupon added to capital value of security an interest coupon on a security that is not paid out, but added to the capital value of the security

rolling account MARKETS stock exchange system with no fixed settlement days a system in which there are no fixed settlement days, but stock exchange transactions are paid at a fixed period after each transaction has taken place, as opposed to the UK system, in which a settlement day is fixed each month

rolling budget ACCOUNTING budget that moves with time a budget that moves forward on a regular basis, for example, a budget covering a twelve-month period that moves forward each month or quarter

roll-out MARKETING launch of program the full-scale implementation of an advertising campaign or marketing program

rollover FINANCE extension of credit or period of loan an extension of credit or of the period of a loan, though not necessarily on the same terms as previously

rollover IRA PENSIONS US personal retirement plan transferred to individual control in the United States, an ***IRA*** that is created when the assets of a ***qualified retirement plan*** arranged by an employer are transferred out of the employer-sponsored plan into an IRA managed by the owner of the plan. *Also called* ***conduit IRA***. *See also* ***traditional IRA***

roll up FINANCE loan payments including interest the addition of interest amounts to principal in loan payments

Romalpa clause LEGAL clause withholding title to goods pending full payment a clause in a contract whereby the seller provides that title to the goods does not pass to the buyer until the buyer has paid for them

RONA *abbr* FINANCE ***return on net assets***

rort *ANZ* GENERAL MANAGEMENT (*slang*) **1.** dishonest practice an illegal or underhand strategy **2.** work a system to manipulate or break the rules of a system for personal gain

ROS *abbr* ACCOUNTING ***return on sales***

Roth 401(k) PENSIONS employee plan with taxed contributions and untaxed payments in the United States, a qualified employee retirement plan, to which the employee contributes after-tax dollars but whose distributions are tax-exempt

Roth IRA PENSIONS personal plan with taxed contributions and untaxed payments in the United States, an ***IRA*** whose contributions unlike ***traditional IRAs*** are not tax-deductible, but whose distributions are tax-exempt

round figures FINANCE numbers adjusted to nearest 10, 100, 1,000, etc. figures that have been adjusted up or down to the nearest 10, 100, 1,000, and so on

rounding STATISTICS expressing number as simpler estimated value the practice of reducing the number of significant digits in a number, for example, expressing a figure that has four decimal places with only two decimal places

round lot MARKETS 100 shares of stock traded together a group of 100 shares of stock bought or sold together in one transaction

routing number BANKING = ***ABA routing number***

royalties FINANCE share of income paid to creator of product a proportion of the income from the sale of a product paid to its creator, for example, an inventor, author, or composer

RPB *abbr* BUSINESS ***recognized professional body***

RPI *abbr* ECONOMICS ***retail price index***

RPIX ECONOMICS indicator of inflation excluding mortgages in the United Kingdom, an index based on the ***retail price index*** that excludes mortgage interest payments and is regarded as an indication of the *underlying rate of inflation*

RPIY ECONOMICS indicator of inflation excluding indirect tax and mortgages in the United Kingdom, an index based on the ***retail price index*** that excludes mortgage interest payments and indirect taxation

RPM *abbr* MARKETING ***resale price maintenance***

RPN *abbr* RISK ***Risk Priority Number***

RRP *abbr* BUSINESS ***recommended retail price***

R-squared STOCKHOLDING & INVESTMENTS benchmarked measure of investment performance a measure of how much of the performance of an investment can be explained by the performance of a ***benchmark index***

rubber check BANKING check returned because of insufficient funds a check that cannot be cashed because the person writing it does not have enough money in the account to pay it (*slang*)

rule 144 REGULATION & COMPLIANCE rule on selling certain securities an ***SEC*** rule that specifies the conditions under which somebody holding ***restricted*** or ***control securities*** can sell them to the public

rule of 72 STOCKHOLDING & INVESTMENTS method of calculating growth of investment a calculation that an investment will double in value at compound interest after a period shown as 72 divided by the interest percentage, so interest at 10% compounded will double the capital invested in 7.2 years

rule of 78 STOCKHOLDING & INVESTMENTS calculation of interest rebate on loan repaid early a method used to calculate the rebate on a loan with front-loaded interest that has been repaid early. It takes into account the fact that as the loan is repaid, the share of each monthly payment related to interest decreases, while the share related to principal increases.

rumortrage *US* MARKETS securities trading based on rumor of takeover speculation in securities issued by companies that are rumored to be the target of an imminent takeover attempt (*slang*)

run 1. BANKING, CURRENCY & EXCHANGE simultaneous withdrawal of money by bank customers an incidence of bank customers, or owners of holdings in a specific currency, simultaneously withdrawing their entire funds because of a lack of confidence in the institution **2.** STATISTICS unbroken sequence in statistical series an uninterrupted sequence of the same value in a statistical series

running account credit BANKING UK arrangement for borrowing and reborrowing limited sum in the United Kingdom, an overdraft facility, credit card, or similar system that allows customers to borrow up to a specific limit and reborrow sums previously repaid by either writing a check or using their card

running costs ACCOUNTING = ***operating costs***

running total ACCOUNTING total carried over to next column a total carried from one column or set of figures to the next

running yield STOCKHOLDING & INVESTMENTS = ***current yield***

runoff MARKETS display of closing prices the process of displaying the closing prices of every stock on an exchange on the ***ticker***

run-off STOCKHOLDING & INVESTMENTS reduction in value of mortgage-backed securities a decline in the value of ***mortgage-backed securities***, caused by borrowers refinancing at lower interest rates or defaulting on their loans, resulting in losses by investors in the securities

S

SA *abbr* BUSINESS **1.** ***Sociedad Anónima*** **2.** ***Sociedade Anônima*** **3.** ***Société Anonyme***

sack ◇ get the sack HR & PERSONNEL = ***get your pink slip*** (*informal*)

SADC *or* **SADEC** INTERNATIONAL TRADE organization for economic development in southern Africa an organization that aims to harmonize economic development in southern Africa. The member countries are Angola, Botswana, the Democratic Republic of the Congo, Lesotho, Malawi, Mauritius, Mozambique, Namibia, Seychelles, South Africa, Swaziland, Tanzania, Zambia, and Zimbabwe. *Full form* ***Southern African Development Community***

safe custody STOCKHOLDING & INVESTMENTS = ***safe keeping***

safe hands STOCKHOLDING & INVESTMENTS **1.** investors buying securities to hold for longer term investors who buy securities and are unlikely to sell in the short- to medium-term **2.** securities held by friendly investors securities held by investors who are not likely to sell them

safe investment STOCKHOLDING & INVESTMENTS investment unlikely to lose value an investment such as a bond that is not likely to fall in value

safe keeping STOCKHOLDING & INVESTMENTS holding by financial institutions of customers' valuable documents a service provided by a financial institution in which stock certificates, deeds, wills, or a locked deed box are held by it on behalf of customers.

Securities are often held under the customer's name in a locked cabinet in the vault so that if the customer wishes to sell, the bank can forward the relevant certificate to the broker. A will is also usually held in this way so that it may be handed to the executor on the customer's death. Deed boxes are always described as "contents unknown to the bank." Most institutions charge a fee for this service. *Also called* ***safe custody***

safety margin OPERATIONS & PRODUCTION extra time or space allowed for safety an extra amount of time or space allowed to make sure that something can be done safely

SAIF *abbr* INSURANCE ***Savings Association Insurance Fund***

salam FINANCE agreement to pay now for goods delivered later in Islamic financing, a contract for the purchase of goods to be delivered at a specified time in the future. Payment for the goods is made in advance.

salaried partner BUSINESS partner paid regular salary a partner, often a junior one, who receives a regular salary that is detailed in the partnership agreement

salary FINANCE payment for work a form of pay given to employees at regular intervals in exchange for the work they have done. Traditionally, a salary is a form of remuneration given to professional employees on a monthly basis. In modern usage, the word refers to any form of pay that employees receive on a regular basis. A salary is usually paid straight into an employee's account.

salary ceiling HR & PERSONNEL **1.** top of relevant pay range the highest level in a pay range that an employee can achieve under his or her contract **2.** restriction on size of pay an upper limit on pay imposed by government or fixed according to labor union and employer agreements

salary reduction plan HR & PERSONNEL = ***flexible spending account***

salary reduction simplified employee pension PENSIONS voluntary pay deductions for pension in the United States, a ***simplified employee pension plan*** that is funded by voluntary employee salary reductions

salary review HR & PERSONNEL regular reconsideration of employee's pay a reassessment of an individual employee's rate of pay, usually conducted on an annual basis

salary sacrifice scheme HR & PERSONNEL exchange of future pay rise for other benefit in the United Kingdom, an agreement between ***employer*** and ***employees*** by which the employees relinquish a right to future cash in exchange for a noncash benefit of some sort

sale and leaseback FINANCE seller's leasing of previously sold asset the leasing back by the former owner of an asset, usually buildings, that has been sold to a third party. *Also called* **leaseback, renting back**

sale by tender FINANCE sale to party invited to make offer the sale of an asset to interested parties who have been invited to make an offer. The asset is sold to the party that makes the highest offer. *See also* ***tender***

sales MARKETING **1.** selling the activity of selling a company's products or services **2.** income from selling the income generated by selling a company's products or services **3.** department for selling the department within a company that deals with selling its products or services

sales analysis MARKETING examination of reports of poor sales an examination of the reports of sales to discover why items have or have not sold well

sales charge STOCKHOLDING & INVESTMENTS purchase fee on some mutual funds a fee charged to the purchaser of some types of mutual funds

sales figures MARKETING total amount of money spent by consumers the total amount of money spent by consumers, for example, in a particular product category, a particular region of the country, or within a particular time period. Sales figures are often used by analysts to judge how well an economy is doing.

sales force MARKETING team responsible for selling a group of salespeople or sales representatives responsible for the sales of either a single product or the entire range of an organization's products. *Also called* ***sales team***

sales forecast MARKETING estimation of future sales a prediction of future sales, based mainly on past sales performance. Sales forecasting takes into account the economic climate, current sales trends, company capacity for production, company policy, and ***market research***. A sales forecast can be a good indicator of future sales in stable market conditions, but may be less reliable in times of rapid market change.

sales ledger ACCOUNTING = ***revenue ledger***

sales mix profit variance FINANCE varying profitability of products in range the differing profitability of different products within a product range

sales promotion MARKETING concentrated activities to sell product activities, usually short-term, designed to attract attention to a particular product and to increase its sales, using advertising and publicity. Sales promotion usually runs in conjunction with an advertising campaign that offers free samples or money-off coupons. The product may be offered at a reduced price and the campaign may be supported by additional telephone or door-to-door selling or by competitions. *Also called* ***promotion***

sales revenue FINANCE income from sales the income generated by sales of goods or services

sales tax *US* TAX tax on item sold, collected at purchase a tax that is paid on each item sold and is collected when the purchase is made. *UK term* ***VAT***. *Also called* ***turnover tax***

sales team MARKETING = ***sales force***

sales turnover FINANCE amount of sales in specific period the total amount sold within a specific time period, usually a year. Sales turnover is often expressed in monetary terms but can also be expressed in terms of the total amount of stock or products sold.

sales volume FINANCE number of items sold the number of units of a product sold

sales volume profit variance FINANCE difference between actual and forecast profits the difference between the profit on the number of units actually sold and the forecast figure

Sallie Mae FINANCE US company investing in student loans the largest source of student loans and administrator of college savings plans in the United States. Created in 1972 as a government-sponsored entity, it became completely privatized in 2004 and is a stockholder-owned company traded on the New York Stock Exchange. Sallie Mae purchases loans from lenders, pools them, and sells them to investors. *Full form* ***Student Loan Marketing Association***

salvage value ACCOUNTING = ***scrap value***

sample STATISTICS representative subgroup of larger group to be investigated a subset of a population in a statistical study chosen so that selected properties of the overall population can be investigated

sample size STATISTICS number of individuals in subgroup to be investigated the number of individuals included in a statistical survey

sample survey STATISTICS statistical analysis of subgroup of larger population a statistical study of a sample of individuals designed to collect information on specific subjects, such as buying habits or voting behavior

sampling 1. MARKETING providing free samples a sales promotion technique in which customers and prospects are offered a free sample of a product **2.** STATISTICS selecting representative subgroup from population under investigation the selection of a small proportion of a set of items being studied, from which valid inferences about the whole set or population can be made. Sampling makes it possible to obtain valid research results when it is impracticable to survey the whole population. The size of the sample needed for valid results depends on a number of factors, including the uniformity of the population being studied and the level of accuracy required. The technique is based on the laws of probability, and a number of different sampling methods can be used, including ***random sampling*** and ***nonrandom sampling***.

sampling design STATISTICS plan for selecting representative subgroup the procedure by which a particular sample is chosen from a population

sampling error STATISTICS discrepancy between whole population and subgroup investigated the difference between the population characteristic being estimated in a statistical study and the result produced by the sample investigated

sampling units STATISTICS items chosen from whole population for investigation the items chosen for sampling from a larger population by a sampling design

sampling variation STATISTICS differences between various subgroups of same population variation between different samples of the same size taken from the same population

samurai bond STOCKHOLDING & INVESTMENTS bond sold by foreign institution in Japan a bond issue denominated in yen and issued in Japan by a foreign institution. *See also* ***shibosai bond, shogun bond***

sandbag MERGERS & ACQUISITIONS prolong negotiations in hostile takeover in a hostile ***takeover*** situation, to enter into talks with the bidder and attempt to prolong them as long as possible, in the hope that a ***white knight*** will appear and rescue the target company (*slang*)

S&L *abbr* BANKING ***savings and loan association***

S&P *abbr* STOCKHOLDING & INVESTMENTS ***Standard & Poor's***

S&P 500 *abbr* MARKETS ***Standard & Poor's 500 Index***

S&P Index *abbr* MARKETS ***Standard & Poor's 500 Index***

Santa Claus rally MARKETS year-end stock price rise a rise in stock prices in the last week of the year (*slang*). *Also called* ***year-end bounce***

Sarbanes–Oxley Act REGULATION & COMPLIANCE US law covering financial reporting and accountability a corporate governance law that came into effect in the United States in 2005. Created in the aftermath of a series of high-profile financial scandals, including Enron and WorldCom, Sarbanes–Oxley seeks to overhaul corporate financial reporting by improving its accuracy and reliability. Though it is an American law, its reach is global and has affected the way that large companies and audit firms do business. Chief executives are to take full responsibility for the accuracy of all financial results by signing a statement to that effect, thereby putting paid to the so-called "aw shucks" defense strategy adopted by senior executives involved in earlier financial scandals. Under this strategy, the accused maintained that they were simply not aware of the distortion of financial reporting that took place under their governance. *Abbr* ***SOX***

sarf CURRENCY & EXCHANGE currency trading in Islamic financing, the buying and selling of currencies

SARL *abbr* BUSINESS ***société à responsabilité limitée***

SARS *abbr* TAX ***South African Revenue Service***

saucer MARKETS chart shape showing stock price rising from low a dish-shaped chart that indicates that the price of a stock has reached its low and is beginning to rise

Save as You Earn STOCKHOLDING & INVESTMENTS method of saving attracting tax relief in the United Kingdom, a system for employees to save on a regular basis toward buying shares in their company that is encouraged by the government through tax concessions. *Abbr* ***SAYE***

savings FINANCE money reserved for future use money set aside by consumers for various purposes such as meeting contingencies or providing an income during retirement. Savings (money in deposit and savings accounts) differ from investments such as stocks in that they are not usually subject to price fluctuations and are thus considered safer. *Also called* ***liquid savings***

savings account BANKING account paying interest an account with a bank or savings and loan association that pays interest. *See also* ***fixed rate, gross interest, net interest***

savings and loan association BANKING chartered bank offering services for consumers in the United States, a ***chartered bank*** that offers savings accounts, pays dividends, and invests in new mortgages. *Abbr* ***S&L***. *Also called* ***building and loan association***. *See also* ***thrift institution***

Savings Association Insurance Fund INSURANCE insurance for federal and state savings in the United States, an insurer of deposits in federal savings banks and federal and state savings and loan associations operated by the Federal Deposit Insurance Corporation. *Abbr* ***SAIF***

savings bank BANKING bank managing small investments a bank that specializes in managing small deposits from customers with personal savings. *See also* ***thrift institution***

savings bond STOCKHOLDING & INVESTMENTS = US savings bond

savings certificate STOCKHOLDING & INVESTMENTS = ***National Savings Certificate***

savings function ECONOMICS measurement of how much people will save an expression of the extent to which people save money instead of spending it

savings ratio ECONOMICS measurement of proportion of income saved the proportion of the income of a country or household that is saved in a particular period

savings-related share option scheme STOCKHOLDING & INVESTMENTS arrangement allowing UK employees to buy stock in the United Kingdom, an arrangement that allows employees of a company to buy company shares of stock with money which they have contributed to a savings scheme

SAYE *abbr* STOCKHOLDING & INVESTMENTS ***Save as You Earn***

SC *abbr* REGULATION & COMPLIANCE ***Securities Commission***

scale GENERAL MANAGEMENT system of graded levels a system that is graded into various levels

scalp MARKETS make profits on many quick trades to make many quick trades in a single day for many small gains

scarce currency CURRENCY & EXCHANGE money traded in foreign exchange market a currency that is traded in a foreign exchange market and for which demand is persistently high relative to its supply

scarcity ECONOMICS situation in which demand exceeds supply a situation in which the demand for something exceeds the supply. This can apply to anything from consumer goods to raw materials.

scarcity value FINANCE value of rare item in great demand the value something has because it is rare and a large demand exists for it

scatter STATISTICS how much observations differ from average observation the amount by which a set of observations deviates from its mean

scatter chart *or* **scatter diagram** *or* **scatter plot** STATISTICS graph showing relationship between variables a chart or diagram that plots a sample of values for two variables for a set of data, in two dimensions

scenario GENERAL MANAGEMENT postulated state of affairs or sequence of events a possible future state of affairs or sequence of events. Scenarios are imagined or projected on the basis of current circumstances and trends and expectations of change in the future.

scenario planning GENERAL MANAGEMENT imagining future conditions or events for planning strategy a technique that requires the use of a scenario in the process of strategic planning to aid the development of corporate strategy in the face of uncertainty about the future The process of identifying alternative scenarios of the future, based on a variety of differing assumptions, can help managers anticipate changes in the business environment and raise awareness of the frame of reference within which they are operating. The scenarios are then used to assist in both the development of strategies for dealing with unexpected events and the choice between alternative strategic options.

schedule 1. FINANCE long-term plan a plan of how an activity will be carried out over a period of time, drawn up in advance. For example, a repayment schedule sets out how debts will be paid. **2.** FINANCE list of interest rates a list of rates of interest that apply to a range of investments **3.** LEGAL list attached to contract a list, especially a list forming an additional document attached to a contract **4.** TAX form relating to UK income tax in the United Kingdom, a form relating to a particular kind of income liable for income tax **5.** INSURANCE details of insurance cover details of the items covered by insurance, sent with the policy

Schedule A TAX UK tax schedule governing income from property in the United Kingdom, a schedule under which tax is charged on income from land or buildings

Schedule B TAX UK tax schedule governing income from woodlands in the United Kingdom, a schedule under which tax was formerly charged on income from woodlands

Schedule C TAX UK schedule taxing income from public sources in the United Kingdom, a schedule to the Finance Acts under which tax was charged on income from public sources such as government stock

Schedule D TAX UK tax schedule governing income from trades in the United Kingdom, a schedule under which tax is charged on income from trades or professions, interest, and other earnings not derived from being employed

Schedule E TAX UK tax schedule governing income from salaries in the United Kingdom, a schedule under which tax is charged on income from salaries, wages, or retirement funds

Schedule F TAX UK tax schedule governing income from dividends in the United Kingdom, a schedule under which tax is charged on income from dividends

scheme *UK* arrangement or method a plan, arrangement, or way of working

scheme of arrangement FINANCE UK plan for avoiding bankruptcy proceedings in the United Kingdom, a plan offering ways of paying debts, drawn up by a person or company to avoid bankruptcy proceedings

scientific management GENERAL MANAGEMENT, HR & PERSONNEL managing using systematic approaches an analytical approach to managing activities by optimizing efficiency and productivity through measurement and control. Scientific management theories were dominant in the 20th century, and many management techniques such as ***benchmarking***, ***total quality management***, and ***business process reengineering*** result from a scientific management approach.

scrap value ACCOUNTING value of asset if scrapped the value of an asset if it is sold for scrap. *Also called* ***salvage value***

screening study STATISTICS statistical investigation of prevalence of particular disease a medical statistical study of a population, conducted to investigate the prevalence of a disease

scrip MARKETS security or certificate for it a security, for example, a share or bond, or the certificate issued to show that somebody has been allotted such a security

scrip dividend STOCKHOLDING & INVESTMENTS dividend paid with stock a dividend paid by the issue of additional company shares, rather than by cash

scrip issue *UK* STOCKHOLDING & INVESTMENTS = ***stock split***

scripophily STOCKHOLDING & INVESTMENTS collecting of old stocks and bonds the collecting of stock or bond certificates that have been canceled, for their historical, aesthetic, or rarity value

Sdn *abbr* BUSINESS ***Sendirian***

SDR *abbr* CURRENCY & EXCHANGE ***Special Drawing Right***

SEAQ MARKETS London Stock Exchange's system for UK securities transactions the London Stock Exchange's system for UK securities. It is a continuously updated computer database of quotations that also records prices at which transactions have been struck. *Full form* ***Stock Exchange Automated Quotations system***

SEAQ International MARKETS London Stock Exchange's system for overseas securities transactions the London Stock Exchange's system for overseas securities. It is a continuously updated computer database of quotations that also records prices at which transactions have been struck. *Full form* ***Stock Exchange Automated Quotations system International***

seasonal adjustment ACCOUNTING accounts adjustment for seasonal distortion of figures an adjustment made to accounts to allow for any short-term seasonal factors such as Christmas sales that may distort the figures

seasonal business BUSINESS trade influenced by time of year trade that is affected by seasonal factors, for example, trade in goods such as suntan products or Christmas trees

seasonality OPERATIONS & PRODUCTION situation in which business varies between seasons variations in production or sales that occur at different but predictable times of the year

seasonal products MARKETING items sold at particular time of year products that are only marketed at particular times of the year, for example, Christmas trees or fireworks

seasonal unemployment HR & PERSONNEL unemployment that changes with seasons unemployment that rises and falls according to the season

seasonal variation STATISTICS changes in data based on time of year the variation of data according to specific times of the year such as the winter months or a tourist season

seasoned equity STOCKHOLDING & INVESTMENTS stocks traded for 90 days stocks that have traded for more than 90 days on a regulated market, long enough to be purchased by ***retail investors***

seasoned issue STOCKHOLDING & INVESTMENTS offering from established company a stock issue that has traded for more than 90 days on a regulated market, long enough to be purchased by ***retail investors***. *See also* ***unseasoned issue***

seat MARKETS stock exchange membership membership in a stock exchange

SEATS MARKETS Australian Stock Exchange's electronic trading system the electronic screen-trading system operated by the Australian Stock Exchange. It was introduced in 1987. *Full form* ***Stock Exchange Automatic Trading System***

SEC *abbr* REGULATION & COMPLIANCE ***Securities and Exchange Commission***

SEC fee STOCKHOLDING & INVESTMENTS US SEC trading fee in the United States, a small fee that the Securities and Exchange Commission charges for the sale of securities listed on a stock exchange

secondary bank BANKING finance company funding installment-plan deals a finance company that provides money for installment-plan deals

secondary industry OPERATIONS & PRODUCTION industry manufacturing goods from raw materials an industry that uses basic raw materials to produce manufactured goods

secondary issue STOCKHOLDING & INVESTMENTS offer of already traded stock an offer of listed stocks that have previously been publicly traded

secondary market MARKETS market buying and selling other than new issues a market that trades in existing stocks rather than new stock issues, for example, a stock exchange. The money earned from these sales goes to the dealer or investor, not to the issuer. *See also* ***primary market***

secondary offering MARKETS offering of securities already on market an offering of securities of a kind that is already on the market

secondary product OPERATIONS & PRODUCTION product made from raw materials a product that has been processed from raw materials. *See also* ***primary product***

Secondary Tax on Companies TAX *see* ***STC***

second half ACCOUNTING second 6-month period in fiscal year the period of six months that is the second part of any fiscal year

secondment HR & PERSONNEL temporary assignment to work elsewhere in the United Kingdom, the temporary transfer of a member of staff to another organization for a defined length of time, usually for a specific purpose. Secondment has grown in popularity in recent years, primarily for career development purposes. Secondments between the public and private sectors have been used as a mechanism to share management techniques and to disseminate best practice.

second mortgage MORTGAGES loan using already-mortgaged property as collateral a loan that uses the equity on a mortgaged property as security and is taken out with a different lender from the first mortgage. The second mortgagee has to record its interest and cannot be paid off on foreclosure until the first mortgagee is paid off.

second quarter ACCOUNTING second of four divisions of fiscal year the period of three months from April to the end of June, or the period of three months following the first quarter of the fiscal year. *Abbr* ***Q2***

second-tier market MARKETS more informal financial market than main market a market in stocks where the listing requirements are less onerous than for the main market, as in, for example, London's ***Alternative Investment Market***

secretary of the board CORPORATE GOVERNANCE *see* ***company secretary***

Secretary of the Treasury FINANCE US government official overseeing finance a senior member of the US government in charge of financial affairs

secret reserves FINANCE = ***hidden reserves***

Section 21 company BUSINESS S. African nonprofit organization in the Republic of South Africa, a company established as a nonprofit organization

sector 1. ECONOMICS businesses in economy providing similar products or services a part of the economy in which businesses produce the same type of product or provide the same type of service **2.** STOCKHOLDING & INVESTMENTS securities in particular industry or market a group of securities in one type of industry or market, for example, the banking sector or the industrial sector

sector fund STOCKHOLDING & INVESTMENTS fund invested in a particular sector a fund that is invested in only one sector of the stock market

sector index MARKETS list of firms specializing in specific markets an index of companies specializing in specific markets whose stocks are listed on a general or specialist stock exchange

secular STOCKHOLDING & INVESTMENTS developing over many years underlying movement over a long period, usually a number of years

secular trend STATISTICS pattern of change in data collected over time the underlying development of a series of measurements collected over a time period of several years to assess long-term trends and seasonal fluctuations

secured FINANCE *see also* ***collateral, security***

secured bond STOCKHOLDING & INVESTMENTS bond with asset as collateral a bond for which real estate or goods have been pledged as collateral

secured creditor FINANCE creditor with legal claim on defaulting debtor's assets a person or organization that is owed money and has a legal claim to some or all of the borrower's assets if the borrower fails to repay the money owed

secured debt FINANCE debt backed by assets a debt that is guaranteed by assets that have been pledged. *See also* ***unsecured debt***

secured loan FINANCE loan guaranteed by borrower's assets as security a loan that is guaranteed by the borrower giving assets as security

secure server E-COMMERCE computer system protecting card transactions over Internet a combination of hardware and software that secures e-commerce credit card transactions so that there is no risk of unauthorized people gaining access to credit card details online

securities account TREASURY MANAGEMENT account record of financial assets an account that shows the value of financial assets held by a person or organization

securities analyst FINANCE professional studying effectiveness of firms and their securities a professional person who studies the performance of securities and the companies that issue them

Securities and Exchange Commission REGULATION & COMPLIANCE US agency overseeing financial transactions of public companies the US government agency responsible for establishing standards of financial reporting and accounting for public companies. *Abbr* ***SEC***

Securities and Futures Authority REGULATION & COMPLIANCE US organization for supervising financial advisers and facilitators in the United States, a self-regulatory organization responsible for supervising the activities of institutions advising on corporate finance activity, or dealing or facilitating deals in securities or derivatives. *Abbr* ***SFA***

Securities and Investments Board REGULATION & COMPLIANCE former UK organization regulating securities markets in the United Kingdom, the organization that formerly had the responsibility of regulating the securities markets, now superseded by the FSA. *Abbr* ***SIB***

Securities Commission REGULATION & COMPLIANCE New Zealand monitoring organization for securities market a statutory body responsible for monitoring standards in the New Zealand securities markets and for promoting investment in New Zealand. *Abbr* ***SC***

securities deposit account BANKING electronic deposit account for securities a brokerage account in which deposits of securities are registered electronically, without receipt of an actual certificate

Securities Institute of Australia FINANCE organization of Australian financial industry professionals a national professional body that represents people involved in the Australian securities and financial services industry. *Abbr* ***SIA***

Securities Investor Protection Corporation INSURANCE US corporation insuring clients of securities firms in the United States, a corporation created by Congress in 1970 that is a mutual insurance fund established to protect clients of securities firms. In the event of a firm being closed because of bankruptcy or financial difficulties, the corporation will step in to recover clients' cash and securities held by the firm. Its reserves are available to satisfy cash and securities that cannot be recovered up to a maximum of $500,000, including a maximum of $100,000 on cash claims. *Abbr* ***SIPC***

securities lending FINANCE lending of securities between brokers the loan of securities from one broker to another in the process of ***selling short***

securitization MORTGAGES, STOCKHOLDING & INVESTMENTS changing debt into securities the process of changing financial assets such as mortgages and loans into securities. The practice of selling mortgages to investors by repackaging the loans as ***loan notes*** paying a rate of interest that international banks and fund managers found attractive became widespread and eventually contributed to the financial difficulties experienced by banks and other financial institutions worldwide in 2008.

securitized mortgage STOCKHOLDING & INVESTMENTS mortgage exchanged for securities a mortgage that has been converted into securities. *See also* ***securitization***

securitized paper STOCKHOLDING & INVESTMENTS documents representing securitization the ***bond*** or ***promissory note*** resulting from changing financial ***assets*** such as mortgages and loans into ***securities***

security 1. STOCKHOLDING & INVESTMENTS financial asset that can be bought and sold a tradable financial asset, for example, a bond, stock, or a warrant **2.** FINANCE guarantee of payment of debt an asset pledged as collateral for a loan or other borrowing

security deposit FINANCE deposit forfeited in transaction if buyer backs out an amount of money paid before a transaction occurs to compensate the seller in the event that the transaction is not concluded because the buyer defaults

security investment company MARKETS firm engaged in securities trading a financial institution that specializes in the analysis and trading of securities

security printer FINANCE printer of valuable documents a printer who prints paper money, stock prospectuses, and confidential government documents

seed capital *or* **seed money** FINANCE money needed to start new business a usually modest amount of money used to convert an idea into a viable business. Seed capital is a form of ***venture capital***.

segmentation STATISTICS separating statistical data into categories the division of the data in a study into categories

seigniorage CURRENCY & EXCHANGE difference between money's production cost and its value the difference between the cost of producing a currency and the face value of the currency. If the money is worth more than it cost to produce, the government makes a profit.

selection bias STATISTICS distortion of data by unmeasured variables in a statistical study, the distorting effect on variables of the methods that have been used to collect the data

selective pricing FINANCE pricing according to market setting different prices for the same product or service in different markets. This practice can be broken down as follows: category pricing, which involves cosmetically modifying a product such that the variations allow it to sell in a number of price categories; customer group pricing, which involves modifying the price of a product or service so that different groups of consumers pay different prices; peak pricing, setting a price which varies according to the level of demand; and service level pricing, setting a price based on the specific level of service chosen from a range.

self-assessment TAX UK system allowing taxpayers to estimate taxes owed in the United Kingdom, a system that enables taxpayers to assess their own income tax and capital gains tax payments for the fiscal year

self-certification FINANCE borrower's unconfirmed statement of income a statement by a borrower of their income, without confirmation by an employer or accountant, made in order to obtain a loan

self-certified mortgage MORTGAGES mortgage granted based on borrower's statement of income a mortgage granted on the basis of a borrower's statement of their income rather than an employer's or accountant's statement. Self-certified mortgages are usually granted to self-employed people whose income varies during the year but who have good credit ratings.

self-employed HR & PERSONNEL working but not on any firm's payroll working for yourself, or not on the payroll of a company

self-financing FINANCE financing of project from own resources the process by which a company finances a project or business activity from its own resources, rather than by applying for external financing

self-insurance INSURANCE setting money aside for possible loss the practice of saving money to pay for a possible loss rather than taking out an insurance policy against it

Self Invested Personal Pension Plan PENSIONS UK pension plan with great freedom of investment in the United Kingdom, a pension plan that allows the holder a much wider choice of investments than a conventional plan, and allows the investments to be held directly rather than by a third party. The plan holder can control the investment strategy or can appoint a fund manager or stockbroker to manage the fund. *Abbr* ***SIPP***

self-liquidating FINANCE paying for itself providing enough income to pay off the amount borrowed for financing

self-liquidating premium MARKETING self-financing promotional technique a sales promotion technique that pays for itself, in which customers send money and vouchers or proof of purchase to obtain a premium gift

self-liquidating promotion MARKETING self-financing sales activity a sales promotion in which the cost of the campaign is covered by the incremental revenue generated by the promotion

self-regulation REGULATION & COMPLIANCE regulation of industry by own members the regulation of an industry by its own members, usually by means of a committee that issues guidance and sets standards that it then enforces

self-regulatory organization REGULATION & COMPLIANCE **1.** in US, organization that is its own authority in the United States, an organization that polices its own members, for example, a stock exchange **2.** in UK, professional body responsible for financial activities in the United Kingdom, a professional body licensed by the ***FSA*** and responsible for policing the range of investment activities undertaken by its members, ensuring that compensation is available in cases of negligence or fraud, and ensuring that there is sufficient professional indemnity ▶ *Abbr* ***SRO***

self-tender STOCKHOLDING & INVESTMENTS US firm's offer to buy back stock in the United States, the repurchase by a corporation of its stock by way of a tender

sell and build GENERAL MANAGEMENT practice of only producing when order paid for an approach to manufacturing in which the producer creates a product only when a customer has placed an order and paid for it, rather than creating and stocking products that have not been ordered

seller's market MARKETS market in which sellers can get top price a market in which sellers can dictate prices, typically because demand is high or there is a product shortage

selling costs *or* **selling overhead** OPERATIONS & PRODUCTION expenses involved in selling something the amount of money needed for the advertising, sales representatives' commissions, and other expenses involved in selling something

selling price OPERATIONS & PRODUCTION price at which something is sold the price at which somebody is willing to sell something

selling price variance OPERATIONS & PRODUCTION discrepancy between actual and planned selling prices the difference between the actual selling price and the budgeted selling price

selling season MARKETS good time for selling a period in which market conditions are favorable to sellers

sell-off MARKETS wave of selling that lowers security's price rapid or widespread selling that causes a sudden drop in the price of a security or a drop in a market

sell short MARKETS sell borrowed security anticipating price drop to sell commodities, currencies, or securities that have been borrowed from a third party in the expectation that prices will fall before the commodities, currencies, or securities are bought back and the loan redeemed, so ensuring a profit. *Also called* ***short*** *(sense 3)*

semiannual FINANCE paying or payable twice a year paying, or requiring payment, every six months

semi-variable cost *or* **semi-fixed cost** OPERATIONS & PRODUCTION production costs that vary somewhat according to quantity the amount of money paid to produce a product, which increases, though less than proportionally, with the quantity of the product made

Sendirian BUSINESS "Limited," in company name the Malay term for "limited." Companies can use "Sendirian Berhad" or "Sdn Bhd" in their name instead of "plc." *Abbr* ***Sdn***

senior capital FINANCE loan capital with priority for payment capital in the form of ***secured loans*** to a company that, in the event of liquidation, is repaid before ***junior capital*** such as stockholders' equity

senior debt FINANCE debt with higher claim on assets than others a debt whose holder has more claim on the debtor's assets than the holder of another debt. *See also* ***junior debt***

senior management GENERAL MANAGEMENT, HR & PERSONNEL those at top level of organization the managers and executives at the highest level of an organization. Senior management includes the ***board of directors***. Senior management has responsibility for ***corporate governance***, ***corporate strategy***, and the interests of all the organization's ***stakeholders***. *Also called* ***management team***

senior mortgage MORTGAGES mortgage with higher claim on assets than others a mortgage whose holder has more claim on the debtor's assets than the holder of another mortgage with the same mortgagee. *See also* ***junior mortgage***

sensitivity analysis ACCOUNTING analysis of effect of small adjustments to calculation the analysis of the effect of a small change in a calculation on the final result

SEP *abbr* PENSIONS ***simplified employee pension plan***

separable net assets ACCOUNTING assets that can be sold separately assets that can be separated from the rest of the assets of a business and sold off

sequestration LEGAL act of seizing property by court order the act of taking and keeping property on the order of a court, especially of seizing property from somebody who is in contempt of court

sequestrator LEGAL person seizing property by court order a person who takes and keeps property on the order of a court

serial correlation STATISTICS correlation of variable over period of time the correlation of a variable with itself over different points in time, used as an indicator of the future performance of something such as a security or economy. *Also called* ***autocorrelation***

serial entrepreneur BUSINESS person who repeatedly starts new enterprises an ***entrepreneur*** who sets up a string of new ventures, one after the other

seriation STATISTICS arrangement of objects in series the process of arranging a set of objects in a series on the basis of similarities or dissimilarities

series STOCKHOLDING & INVESTMENTS bonds or savings certificates issued over time a group of bonds or savings certificates, issued over a period of time but all bearing the same interest

Serious Fraud Office REGULATION & COMPLIANCE UK government department investigating major commercial fraud in the United Kingdom, a government department in charge of investigating major fraud in companies. *Abbr* ***SFO***

SERPS PENSIONS UK plan for earnings-related pensions in the United Kingdom, a state program that was designed to pay retired employees an additional pension to the standard state pension. It was replaced by the ***State Second Pension***. *Full form* ***State Earnings-Related Pension Scheme***

service MARKETING system or activity meeting need any activity with a mix of tangible and intangible outcomes that is offered to a market with the goal of satisfying a customer's need or desire. Early marketing tended to distinguish a service from a physical good, but more recently these two have been seen as interrelated because service delivery frequently has physical aspects. For example, in a restaurant, service is provided by a waiter but physical goods, such as the food and the dining room, are also involved. In modern marketing, all forms of services and goods can be seen as products.

service charge 1. FINANCE, BANKING sum or additional sum paid for service a fee for any service provided, or an additional fee for any improvements to an existing service. For example, residents in apartment buildings may pay an annual maintenance fee, or banks may charge a fee for operating an account or obtaining foreign currency for customers (also called a ***bank charge***). **2.** MARKETING payment to serving staff a gratuity usually paid in restaurants and hotels. A service charge may be voluntary or may be added as a percentage to the bill.

service contract HR & PERSONNEL employment contract for senior executive a contract of employment for executive directors that lays down the conditions of employment and details of any bonus that may be paid, and outlines the procedure for ending employment

service cost center FINANCE cost center serving other cost centers in organization a cost center providing services to other cost centers. When the output of an organization is a service rather than goods, an alternative name is usually used, for example, support cost center or utility cost center.

service/function costing ACCOUNTING cost accounting for services within organization ***cost accounting*** for services or functions, for example, canteens, maintenance, or personnel

service industry BUSINESS industry specializing in service not products an industry that does not make products, but instead offers a service such as banking, insurance, or transport

service level agreement LEGAL contract giving details of service to be performed a contract between a service provider and a customer that specifies in detail the level of service (quality, frequency, flexibility, charges, etc.) to be provided over the contract period, as well as the procedures to implement in the case of default

servicing borrowing FINANCE paying interest the process of paying the interest that is due on a loan

set-aside ACCOUNTING = ***reserves***

set-off FINANCE offset of debts or loss against gain an agreement between two parties to balance one debt against another or a loss against a gain

settle STOCKHOLDING & INVESTMENTS finalize security sale to transfer property such as securities from a seller to a buyer in return for payment

settlement **1.** FINANCE payment the payment of an outstanding debt, invoice, account, or charge **2.** STOCKHOLDING & INVESTMENTS finalizing security sale the transfer of property such as securities from a seller to a buyer in return for payment **3.** E-COMMERCE transfer of payment to account of e-business the portion of an electronic transaction during which the customer's credit card is charged for the transaction and the proceeds are deposited into the ***merchant account***

settlement date FINANCE due date for paying debt or charge the date on which an outstanding debt or charge is due to be paid, or when cash offered for securities or derivatives of them must be delivered

settlement day MARKETS **1.** in UK, final day for paying for stock in the United Kingdom, the day on which shares of stock bought must be paid for. On the London Stock Exchange the account period is three business days from the day of trade. **2.** in US, day when securities become purchaser's property in the United States, the day on which securities bought actually become the property of the purchaser

setup costs ACCOUNTING amount spent to make equipment usable the costs associated with making a workstation or equipment available for use. Setup costs include the personnel needed to set up the equipment, the cost of downtime during a new setup, and the resources and time needed to test the new setup to achieve the specification of the parts or materials produced.

setup fees E-COMMERCE amount spent arranging to accept Internet payments the costs associated with establishing a ***merchant account***, for example, application and software licensing fees and point-of-sale equipment purchases

setup time OPERATIONS & PRODUCTION time spent to make equipment fully productive the time it takes to prepare, calibrate, and test a piece of equipment to produce a required output

seven-day money MARKETS money-market funds with seven-day term funds that have been placed on the money market for a term of seven days

severally LEGAL not jointly as separate individuals or entities, not jointly

severance *US* HR & PERSONNEL dismissal or discharge from employment dismissal from employment because the job or worker is considered no longer necessary. *UK term* ***redundancy***

severance package *US* HR & PERSONNEL benefits for dismissed or discharged employee a package of benefits that an employer gives to an employee who is dismissed. *UK term* ***redundancy package***

severance pay *US* FINANCE payment to dismissed or discharged employee a payment made by an employer to an employee when the employee who has been dismissed or discharged leaves the organization. *Also called* ***unemployment compensation***. *UK term* ***redundancy payment***

SFA *abbr* REGULATION & COMPLIANCE ***Securities and Futures Authority***

SFAS *abbr* REGULATION & COMPLIANCE ***Statement of Financial Accounting Standards***

SFE *abbr* MARKETS ***Sydney Futures Exchange***

SFO *abbr* REGULATION & COMPLIANCE ***Serious Fraud Office***

SGX *abbr* MARKETS ***Singapore Exchange***

shadow economy ECONOMICS = ***black economy***

shadow market MARKETS = ***black market***

shadow price ECONOMICS estimated cost of new economic activity the amount that engaging in a new economic activity is likely to cost a person or an economy. *See also* ***opportunity cost***

shakeout MARKETS exiting of timid investors during financial crisis the elimination of weak or cautious investors during a crisis in the financial market (*slang*)

share STOCKHOLDING & INVESTMENTS = ***stock***

share account **1.** STOCKHOLDING & INVESTMENTS account with credit union paying dividends in the United States, an account with a credit union that pays dividends rather than interest **2.** BANKING member's account in UK building society in the United Kingdom, an account at a building society where the account holder is a member of the society. Account holders who are not members are offered a deposit account. *See also* ***deposit account***

share at par STOCKHOLDING & INVESTMENTS stock valued at face value a share whose value on the stock market is the same as its face value

share buyback STOCKHOLDING & INVESTMENTS = ***buyback***

share capital STOCKHOLDING & INVESTMENTS capital from sale of stock the amount of ***nominal share capital*** that a company raises by issuing shares of stock. Share capital does not reflect any subsequent increase or decrease in the value of stock sold; it is capital raised, irrespective of changes in stock value in the secondary markets. *Also called* ***issued capital***. *See also* ***stockholders' equity, reserves***

share certificate *UK* STOCKHOLDING & INVESTMENTS = ***stock certificate***

shared drop MARKETING delivery of simultaneous promotional offers a sales promotion technique in which a number of promotional offers are delivered by hand to ***prospects*** at the same time

shared values GENERAL MANAGEMENT = ***core values***

share exchange STOCKHOLDING & INVESTMENTS exchange of individual stockholdings for shares in fund a service provided by some collective investment plans whereby they exchange investors' existing individual stockholdings for shares in their funds. This saves the investor the expense of selling holdings, which can be uneconomical when dealing with small stockholdings.

share-for-share offer STOCKHOLDING & INVESTMENTS bidder's offer of shares as payment for company a type of ***takeover bid*** where the bidder offers its own shares, or a combination of cash and shares, for the target company

shareholder STOCKHOLDING & INVESTMENTS **1.** somebody owning stock in corporation a person or organization that owns shares in a limited company or partnership. A shareholder has a stake in the company and becomes a member of it, with rights to attend the ***annual meeting***. Since shareholders have invested money in a company, they have a vested interest in its performance and can be a powerful influence on company policy; they should consequently be considered ***stakeholders*** as well as shareholders. Some pressure groups have sought to exploit this by becoming shareholders in order to get a particular viewpoint or message across. At the same time, in order to maintain or increase the company's market value, managers must consider their responsibility to shareholders when formulating strategy. It has been argued that on some occasions the desire to make profits to raise returns for shareholders has damaged companies, because it has limited the amount of money spent in other areas (such as the development of facilities, or health and safety). *Also called* **stockholder** **2.** participant in pooled investment a person who owns shares of a fund or ***investment trust***

shareholders' equity *or* **shareholders' funds** STOCKHOLDING & INVESTMENTS = ***stockholders' equity***

shareholders' perks STOCKHOLDING & INVESTMENTS benefits for stockholders besides dividends benefits offered to stockholders in addition to dividends, often in the form of discounts on the company's products and services. *Also called* ***stockholder perks***

shareholder value STOCKHOLDING & INVESTMENTS total return to stockholders including dividends and appreciation the total return to the stockholders in terms of both dividends and share price growth, calculated as the present value of future free cash flows of the business discounted at the weighted average cost of the capital of the business less the market value of its debt. *Also called* ***stockholder value***

shareholder value analysis STOCKHOLDING & INVESTMENTS firm's value based on return to stockholders a calculation of the value of a company made by looking at the returns it gives to its stockholders. *Abbr* ***SVA***. *Also called* ***stockholder value analysis***

shareholding *UK* STOCKHOLDING & INVESTMENTS = ***stockholding***

share incentive scheme *UK* HR & PERSONNEL = ***stock incentive plan***

share index *UK* MARKETS = ***index***

share issue STOCKHOLDING & INVESTMENTS offer to sell shares in business the offering for sale of shares in a business. The capital derived from share issues can be used for investment in the core business or for expansion into new commercial ventures.

share of voice MARKETING comparative amount spent on advertising an individual company's proportion of the total advertising expenditure in a sector

share option *UK* STOCKHOLDING & INVESTMENTS = ***stock option***

share option scheme *UK* STOCKHOLDING & INVESTMENTS = ***stock option plan***

shareowner STOCKHOLDING & INVESTMENTS = ***shareholder***

share premium STOCKHOLDING & INVESTMENTS amount paid for share above declared value the amount payable for a share above its ***nominal value***. Most shares are issued at a ***premium*** to their nominal value. Share premiums are credited to the company's ***share premium account***.

share premium account ACCOUNTING account where firms credit share premiums the special reserve in a company's balance sheet to which ***share premiums*** are credited. Expenses associated with the issue of shares may be written off to this account.

share register STOCKHOLDING & INVESTMENTS list of stockholders a list of the stockholders in a particular company

share shop STOCKHOLDING & INVESTMENTS office where stock is traded the name given by some financial institutions to an office open to the public where stock may be bought and sold

shares of negligible value STOCKHOLDING & INVESTMENTS worthless shares in defunct firm shares that are considered as having no value in income tax terms because the company has ceased to exist. The shares of companies in receivership are not deemed to be of negligible value, although they may eventually end up as such.

share split STOCKHOLDING & INVESTMENTS = ***scrip issue stock split***

share tip *UK* STOCKHOLDING & INVESTMENTS = ***stock tip***

Share Transactions Totally Electronic MARKETS *see* ***STRATE***

shareware E-COMMERCE program available free but chargeable for continued use software distributed free of charge, but usually with a request that users pay a small fee if they like the program

share warrant STOCKHOLDING & INVESTMENTS document stating right to hold stock a document stating that somebody has the right to a number of shares of stock in a company

sharia *or* **shariah** LEGAL = ***Islamic law***

sharia-compliant FINANCE in accordance with Islamic law used to describe financial activities and investments that comply with Islamic law, which prohibits the charging of interest and involvement in any enterprise associated with activities or products forbidden by Islamic law

shark watcher US MARKETS firm that identifies takeover targets a firm that specializes in monitoring the stock market for potential takeover activity (*slang*)

Sharpe ratio STOCKHOLDING & INVESTMENTS formula for calculating relationship between risk and return a method of determining the relationship between investment risk and return, calculated by subtracting the return on a risk-free investment from the rate of return on a portfolio of investments and dividing the result by the standard deviation of the return

sharp practice FRAUD underhand business methods business methods that are not illegal but are not entirely open and honest

shelf registration STOCKHOLDING & INVESTMENTS in US, statement registering future securities sale in the United States, a ***registration statement*** filed with the ***Securities and Exchange Commission*** two years before a corporation issues securities to the public. The statement, which has to be updated periodically, allows the corporation to act quickly when it considers that the market conditions are right without having to start the registration procedure from scratch.

shelfspace MARKETING area available for product in store the amount of space allocated to a product in a retail outlet

shell company BUSINESS registered firm whose shares no longer trade a company that has ceased to trade but is still registered, especially one sold to enable the buyer to begin trading without having to establish a new company

shibosai STOCKHOLDING & INVESTMENTS sale of securities direct to investors the Japanese term for a ***private placement***, which is the sale of securities direct to institutions for investment rather than resale

shibosai bond STOCKHOLDING & INVESTMENTS yen-denominated bond sold direct by issuing company a bond denominated in yen sold direct to investors by the foreign issuing company. *See also* ***samurai bond, shogun bond***

shift differential FINANCE extra pay for working unpopular shift payment made to employees over and above their basic rate to compensate them for the inconvenience of working in shifts. A shift differential usually takes account of the time of day when the shift is worked, the duration of the shift, the extent to which weekend working is involved, and the speed of rotation within the shift.

shingle ◇ hang out your shingle GENERAL MANAGEMENT to start a business or announce the startup of a new business

shinyo kinku BANKING Japanese bank financing small businesses in Japan, a financial institution that provides financing for small businesses

shinyo kumiai BANKING Japanese credit union financing small businesses in Japan, a credit union that provides financing for small businesses

shirkah FINANCE contract between people going into business for profit in Islamic financing, a contract between two or more people who launch a business or financial enterprise in order to make a profit. *Also called* ***musharaka***

shogun bond STOCKHOLDING & INVESTMENTS non-yen bond sold in Japan by non-Japanese institution a bond denominated in a currency other than the yen that is sold on the Japanese market by a non-Japanese financial institution. *Also called* ***geisha bond***. *See also* ***samurai bond, shibosai bond***

shop price OPERATIONS & PRODUCTION = ***retail price***

short 1. FINANCE asset behind security benefiting from asset's fall an asset underlying a security in which a dealer has a ***short position*** and so gains by a fall in the asset's value **2.** MARKETS investor selling short an investor who is holding a ***short position*** **3.** MARKETS = ***sell short***

short bill FINANCE bill payable at short notice a bill of exchange that becomes payable at short notice

short-change FRAUD give customer too little change to give a customer less change than is right, either by mistake or in the hope that it will not be noticed, or to treat somebody less than fairly

short covering MARKETS purchase of security benefiting from asset's fall the buying back of foreign exchange, commodities, or securities by a firm or individual that has been ***selling short***. Such purchases are undertaken when the market has begun to move upward, or when it is thought to be about to do so.

short credit FINANCE credit terms demanding repayment soon terms of borrowing that allow the customer only a little time to pay

short-dated STOCKHOLDING & INVESTMENTS maturing in 5 years or less used to describe securities such as bonds that mature in five years or less. *See also* ***long-dated, medium-dated***

short-dated bill FINANCE bill payable almost immediately a bill that is payable within a few days

short-dated gilts STOCKHOLDING & INVESTMENTS UK government security maturing within 5 years fixed-interest securities issued by the UK government that mature in less than five years from the date of purchase. *Also called* ***shorts***. *See also* ***gilt-edged security***

shortfall FINANCE amount missing from expected total an amount that is missing that would make the total expected sum

shorting MARKETS = ***short selling***

short interest STOCKHOLDING & INVESTMENTS quantity of security sold and not repurchased the total number of shares of a specific security that investors have sold short and have not repurchased in anticipation of a price decline

short investor MARKETS seller of securities expecting to repurchase them somebody who sells shares they have borrowed in order to buy expecting to be able to buy them back later at a lower price

short position STOCKHOLDING & INVESTMENTS selling unbought security hoping price will decline a situation in which somebody sells commodities, currencies, or securities they have borrowed for a fee in the expectation that they will be able to buy them back and return the loan at a lower price, so making a profit. *See also* ***long position***

shorts STOCKHOLDING & INVESTMENTS = ***short-dated gilts***

short sale STOCKHOLDING & INVESTMENTS sale of borrowed security anticipating cheap repurchase a sale of borrowed commodities, currencies, or securities in the expectation that prices will fall before they have to be bought back and then returned to the original owner

short selling MARKETS selling borrowed security anticipating cheap repurchase the practice of selling borrowed commodities, currencies, or securities in the expectation that prices will fall before they have to be bought back and then returned to the original owner. *Also called* ***shorting***

short-term bond STOCKHOLDING & INVESTMENTS bond maturing within 2 years a bond on the corporate bond market that has an initial maturity of less than two years

short-term capital FINANCE money on short-term loan funds raised for a period of less than 12 months, for example, by a bank loan, to cover a short-term shortage. *See also* ***working capital***

short-term debt FINANCE debt due within year debt that has a term of one year or less

short-term economic policy ECONOMICS economic planning for near future an economic policy with objectives that can be met within a period of months or a few years

short-term forecast MARKETS forecast covering few months only a forecast that covers a period of a few months

short-termism GENERAL MANAGEMENT emphasis on quick results not long-term goals an approach to business that concentrates on short-term results rather than long-term objectives

short-term loan FINANCE loan repayable in weeks a loan that has to be repaid within a year, usually within a few weeks

short-term security STOCKHOLDING & INVESTMENTS security maturing within 5 years a security that matures in less than five years

show stopper MERGERS & ACQUISITIONS = ***poison pill*** (*slang*)

shrinkage OPERATIONS & PRODUCTION **1.** reduction in firm's inventories a reduction in the amount of inventory held by a company, often caused by production processes **2.** goods lost to theft or damage a term used to describe goods that leave a retail outlet but are not logged as sales. Shrinkage can include goods that are stolen by shoplifters, or are damaged or broken.

SI *abbr* LEGAL ***statutory instrument***

SIA *abbr* FINANCE ***Securities Institute of Australia***

SIB *abbr* REGULATION & COMPLIANCE ***Securities and Investments Board***

SIC *abbr* BUSINESS ***Standard Industrial Classification***

SICAV *abbr* BUSINESS ***société d'investissement à capital variable***

sickness and accident insurance INSURANCE policy paying creditors during sickness or injury a form of insurance for ill health that may be sold with some form of credit, for example, a credit card or personal loan. In the event of the borrower being unable to work because of accident or illness, the policy covers the regular payments to the credit card company or lender.

sideline cash FINANCE = ***idle capital***

sight bill FINANCE bill of exchange payable immediately a bill of exchange payable when it is presented, rather than at a given length of time after presentation or after a date indicated on the bill

sight deposit BANKING bank deposit withdrawable immediately a bank deposit against which the depositor can immediately make a withdrawal

sight draft FINANCE bill of exchange payable immediately a bill of exchange that is payable on delivery. *See also* ***time draft***

sight letter of credit FINANCE letter of credit presented along with required documents a ***letter of credit*** that is paid when the necessary documents have been presented

signatory LEGAL somebody signing contract or document a person who signs a contract or other legal document

signature guarantee BANKING stamp or seal validating signature a stamp or seal, usually from a bank or a broker, that vouches for the authenticity of a signature

signature loan FINANCE = ***unsecured loan***

silent partner *US* BUSINESS investment partner with no active management role a person or organization that invests money in a company but takes no active part in the management of the business. Although silent partners are inactive in the operation of the business, they have legal obligations and benefits of ownership, and are therefore fully liable for any debts. *UK term* ***sleeping partner***

silly money FINANCE excessively high or low sum an amount of money that is regarded as excessively large or, occasionally, small (*informal*)

silver MARKETS precious metal traded as commodity a precious metal traded on commodity markets such as the London Metal Exchange

simple interest FINANCE interest paid on principal only interest charged simply as a constant percentage of the principal and not compounded. *See also* ***compound interest***

simple moving average STATISTICS method of sampling giving every unit equal chance the selection of units from a population in such a way that every possible combination of selected units is equally likely to be in the sample chosen

simplified employee pension plan PENSIONS IRA funded by employer a type of ***qualified plan*** that provides employers with a way of making contributions toward their employees' and their own retirement. Contributions are paid directly into an ***IRA*** set up for each person. *Abbr* ***SEP***

simulation GENERAL MANAGEMENT representation of possible situation or system the construction of a mathematical model to imitate the behavior of a real-world situation or system in order to test the outcomes of alternative courses of action. Simulation techniques are used in situations where real-life experimentation would be impossible, costly, or dangerous, and for training purposes.

simultaneous engineering OPERATIONS & PRODUCTION = ***concurrent engineering***

Singapore dollar CURRENCY & EXCHANGE Singapore's unit of currency Singapore's unit of currency, whose exchange rate is quoted as S$ per US$

Singapore Exchange MARKETS Singapore stock and monetary exchange the institution resulting from the merger in 1999 of the Stock Exchange of Singapore and the Singapore International Monetary Exchange. It provides securities and derivatives trading, securities clearing and depository, and derivatives clearing services. *Abbr* ***SGX***

single-currency CURRENCY & EXCHANGE denominated in same currency used to describe an international transaction denominated entirely in one currency

single customs document INTERNATIONAL TRADE standardized customs form a standard, universally used form for the passage of goods through customs

single entry ACCOUNTING book-keeping system using only one entry per transaction a type of bookkeeping where only one entry, reflecting both a credit to one account and a debit to another, is made for each transaction

single-figure inflation ECONOMICS inflation below 10% inflation that is rising at less than 10% per annum

single market MARKETS organization of European nations the European Union in its role as an economic organization. *See also* ***EU***

single-payment bond STOCKHOLDING & INVESTMENTS bond redeemed with single payment at maturity a bond redeemed with a single payment combining principal and interest at maturity

single premium assurance *UK* INSURANCE = ***single premium insurance***

single premium deferred annuity TAX deferred annuity funded with single initial payment an annuity that is paid for with a single payment at inception and pays returns regularly after a set date. It gives a tax advantage.

single premium insurance *US* INSURANCE life insurance paid for with single initial premium life coverage where the premium is paid in one lump sum when the policy is taken out, rather than in installments. *UK term* ***single premium assurance***

single tax TAX tax to cover everything one major tax that supplies all revenue, especially on land

sinker STOCKHOLDING & INVESTMENTS bond paid from debt repayment reserve a bond whose principal and interest payments are paid out of the issuer's ***sinking fund***

sinking fund FINANCE money set aside for debt payments money put aside periodically to settle a liability or replace an asset. The money is invested to produce a required sum at an appropriate time.

SIPC *abbr* INSURANCE ***Securities Investor Protection Corporation***

SIPP *abbr* PENSIONS ***Self Invested Personal Pension Plan***

sister company BUSINESS company belonging to same group a company that belongs to the same group of companies as another

SIV *abbr* STOCKHOLDING & INVESTMENTS ***structured investment vehicle***

six-month money MARKETS money invested for 6 months funds invested on the money market for a period of six months

size of firm BUSINESS relative size of company for government records a method of categorizing companies according to size for the purposes of government statistics. Divisions are typically ***microbusiness***, ***small business***, ***medium-sized business***, and ***large-sized business***.

skewness STATISTICS lack of statistical symmetry a lack of symmetry in a ***probability distribution***

skimming FRAUD stealing small amounts from customer accounts the unethical and usually illegal practice of taking small amounts of money from accounts that belong to other individuals or organizations

skin in the game FINANCE amount of entrepreneur's money invested in business the amount of an entrepreneur's own money that they have invested in their business, considered by ***venture capitalists*** as an indication of the entrepreneur's commitment to making the business successful

sleeper **1.** STOCKHOLDING & INVESTMENTS stock with potential to rise in value a stock that has not risen in value for some time, but may suddenly do so in the future **2.** BUSINESS product that sells after period of sluggish sales a product that does not sell well for some time, then suddenly becomes very popular

sleeping partner *UK* BUSINESS = ***silent partner***

slippage STOCKHOLDING & INVESTMENTS discrepancy between estimated and actual costs the difference between the estimated costs of buying or selling a security and the actual costs of the transaction

slowdown ECONOMICS minor decrease in economic activity a fall in demand that causes a lowering of economic activity, less severe than a ***recession*** or ***slump***

slow payer FINANCE somebody slow to pay debts a person or company that does not pay debts on time

slump ECONOMICS major decrease in economic activity a severe downturn phase in the business cycle

slumpflation ECONOMICS decrease in economic activity with increased inflation a collapse in all economic activity accompanied by wage and price inflation. This happened, for example, in the United States and Europe in 1929 (*slang*).

slush fund FINANCE fund used for bribery or corruption a fund used by a company for illegal purposes such as bribing officials to obtain preferential treatment for planned work or expansion

small and medium-sized enterprise BUSINESS firm with under 250 employees an organization that is in the ***startup*** or growth phase of development and has fewer than 250 employees. This definition of a small and medium-sized enterprise is the one adopted by the United Kingdom's Department for Business Enterprise and Regulatory Reform for statistical purposes. *Abbr* ***SME***

small business BUSINESS firm with under 50 employees managed by owner an organization that is small in relation to the potential market size, is managed by its owners, and has fewer than 50 employees. This definition of a small business is the one adopted by the United Kingdom's Department for Business Enterprise and Regulatory Reform for statistical purposes.

small change FINANCE money in coins a small quantity of coins of mixed value that somebody might carry, often used to suggest a sum of no significance

small claim LEGAL in UK, claim for less than £5,000 in the United Kingdom, a claim for less than £5,000 in the County Court

Small Order Execution System MARKETS NASDAQ system for trading small lots automatically on the NASDAQ, an automated execution system for bypassing brokers when processing small order agency executions of NASDAQ securities up to 1,000 shares

small print GENERAL MANAGEMENT details and conditions printed smaller than main text details in an official document such as a contract that are usually printed in a smaller size than the rest of the text and, while often important, may be overlooked. Items often referred to as "small print" may include deliberately hidden charges, unfavorable terms, or loopholes.

smart card E-COMMERCE plastic card with built-in microprocessor a small plastic card containing a microprocessor that can store and process transactions and maintain a bank balance, thus providing a secure, portable medium for electronic money. Financial details and personal data stored on the card can be updated each time the card is used.

smart market E-COMMERCE market only using electronic communications a market in which all transactions are performed electronically using network communications

SME *abbr* BUSINESS ***small and medium-sized enterprise***

smoothing methods STATISTICS ways of removing irregularities in statistical data procedures used in fitting a set of observations in a study into a statistical model, often by creating a graph of the data

smurf FRAUD somebody involved in money-laundering someone who passes money obtained illegally through banks or businesses in order to make it appear legitimate

snake CURRENCY & EXCHANGE currencies formerly in European Exchange Rate Mechanism formerly, the group of currencies within the European Exchange Rate Mechanism whose exchange rates were allowed to fluctuate against each other within specific bands or limits

snowball sampling STATISTICS method of creating samples based on existing samples a form of sampling in which existing sample members suggest potential new sample members, for example, personal acquaintances

snowflake STATISTICS graph of multiple variables a graph that shows ***multivariate data***

social business *or* **social enterprise** BUSINESS business run for positive social change a business whose main objective is to make positive social change in areas such as poverty, education, health, the environment, etc.

social lending FINANCE direct lending between people the practice of one person offering to lend money to another, without the involvement of a bank or other institution, especially through the Internet. *Also called* ***person-to-person lending***. *See also* ***ZOPA***

socially conscious investing STOCKHOLDING & INVESTMENTS = ***ethical investment***

social marginal cost ECONOMICS cost to society of change in economic variable the additional cost to a society of a change in an economic variable, for example, the price of gas or bread

social security INSURANCE, PENSIONS government financial support system a system of financial support in a variety of areas of personal need provided by a government, for example for retired people, those with young children, or those unemployed or unable to work

Social Security INSURANCE, PENSIONS US government assistance program for elderly and disabled in the United States, the federal insurance program that provides income for retirees and their dependents and survivors, disability income, and healthcare for seniors. The program is funded by required contributions from employers and working individuals.

Social Security number INSURANCE, PENSIONS, TAX person's identifying number for US social insurance plan in the United States, a unique nine-digit number assigned to each person within the Social Security system, which is used for taxation and identification purposes and does not change throughout the person's life. *Abbr* ***SSN***

Sociedad Anónima BUSINESS Spanish public corporation a Spanish company with a status comparable to a public corporation. *Abbr* ***SA***

Sociedade Anónima BUSINESS Portuguese public corporation a Portuguese company with a status comparable to a public corporation. *Abbr* ***SA***

Società a responsabilità limitata BUSINESS Italian private corporation an Italian unlisted company with a status comparable to a private corporation. *Abbr* ***Srl***

Società per Azioni BUSINESS Italian public corporation an Italian company with a status comparable to a public corporation. *Abbr* ***SpA***

Société Anonyme BUSINESS French public corporation a French company with a status comparable to a public corporation. *Abbr* ***SA***

société à responsabilité limitée BUSINESS French unlisted corporation a French unlisted company with a status comparable to a private corporation. *Abbr* ***SARL***

société d'investissement à capital variable BUSINESS French investment company a French company managing an investment fund with capital varying according to the number of investors at any one time. *Abbr* ***SICAV***

Society for Worldwide Interbank Financial Telecommunication BANKING *see* ***SWIFT***

socioeconomic ECONOMICS relating to social and economic factors involving both social and economic factors. Structural unemployment, for example, has socioeconomic causes.

socioeconomic segmentation MARKETING separation of market into socioeconomic groups the division of a market according to the different socioeconomic categories within it

Sod's Law *UK* GENERAL MANAGEMENT = ***Murphy's Law***

soft capital rationing ACCOUNTING management's imposition of limit on capital investment a restriction on an organization's ability to invest capital funds caused by an internal budget ceiling being imposed by management. *See also* ***capital rationing***

soft commissions FINANCE brokerage commissions rebated to institutional customer brokerage commissions that are rebated to an institutional customer in the form of, or to pay for, research or other services

soft commodities MARKETS commodities other than solid raw materials commodities such as foodstuffs that are neither metals nor other solid raw materials. *Also called* ***softs***. *See also* ***future, hard commodities***

soft-core radicalism MARKETING exploitation of customers' environmental and ethical concerns a marketing technique that plays on people's concerns about environmental and ethical issues in order to sell them a product (*slang*)

soft currency CURRENCY & EXCHANGE currency that is weak or expected to fall a currency that is weak, usually because there is an excess of supply and a belief that its value will fall in relation to others. *See also* ***hard currency***

soft dollars MARKETS payment by brokers for management firms' business rebates given by brokers to money management firms in return for funds' transaction business

soft landing ECONOMICS slowdown of economic activity without recession the situation when a country's economic activity has slowed down but demand has not fallen far enough or rapidly enough to cause a recession

soft loan FINANCE loan on highly favorable terms a loan on exceptionally favorable terms, for example, for a project that a government considers worthy

soft market MARKETS market with falling prices a market in which prices are falling because there are more sellers than buyers

softs MARKETS = ***soft commodities***

sold short STOCKHOLDING & INVESTMENTS borrowed and sold anticipating price drop used to refer to commodities, currencies, or securities that somebody borrows and sells, then buys back and repays in the expectation that prices will have fallen. *See also* ***sell short***

sole agency *UK* BUSINESS = ***exclusive agency***

sole agent *UK* BUSINESS = ***exclusive agent***

sole distributor BUSINESS retailer with exclusive right to sell something a retailer who is the only one in an area who is allowed by the manufacturer to sell a specific product or service

sole practitioner BUSINESS professional practicing alone the proprietor of a professional practice, who is personally responsible for all its debts

sole proprietor BUSINESS person operating business alone somebody who owns and runs an unincorporated business by himself or herself. Sole proprietors are taxed at the personal income level and are personally liable for all business losses or debts; in the event of bankruptcy personal possessions may be forfeited. *Also called* ***sole trader, owner-operator***

sole proprietorship BUSINESS business of one person a business operated by a sole proprietor, who is personally responsible for all its debts

sole trader BUSINESS = ***sole proprietor***

solicit FINANCE request money to ask another person or company for money

solvency FINANCE situation of being able to pay all debts situation in which a person or organization is able to pay all debts on their due date. *See also* ***insolvency***

solvency margin FINANCE business's assets minus liabilities a business's ***liquid assets*** that exceed the amount required to meet its liabilities

solvency ratio **1.** FINANCE ratio of assets to liabilities a ratio of assets to liabilities, used to measure a company's ability to meet its debts **2.** INSURANCE in UK, measure of insurance company's financial condition in the United Kingdom, the ratio of an insurance company's net assets to its non-life premium income

solvent FINANCE able to pay all one's debts used to refer to a situation in which the assets of an individual or organization are worth more than their liabilities

sort code *UK* BANKING number identifying UK bank branch a combination of numbers that identifies a bank branch on official documentation such as bank statements and checks. *See also* ***ABA routing number***

source and application of funds statement ACCOUNTING = ***cash flow statement***

sources and uses of funds statement ACCOUNTING = ***cash flow statement***

South African Revenue Service TAX S. African tax authority the government body that is responsible for collecting taxes and ensuring compliance with tax law in South Africa. *Abbr* ***SARS***

Southern African Development Community INTERNATIONAL TRADE *see* ***SADC***

sovereign bond STOCKHOLDING & INVESTMENTS government bond in foreign currency a bond issued by a national government denominated in a foreign currency

sovereign loan FINANCE bank loan to foreign government a loan by a financial institution to an overseas government, usually of an emerging country. *See also* ***sovereign risk***

sovereign money STOCKHOLDING & INVESTMENTS money in sovereign wealth funds the money that is invested in ***sovereign wealth funds***

sovereign risk FINANCE risk that foreign government may default on loan the risk that an overseas government may refuse to repay or may default on a ***sovereign loan***

sovereign wealth fund STOCKHOLDING & INVESTMENTS very wealthy state investment fund an investment fund owned by a government with very large amounts of money at its disposal. There is concern that such a fund would be able to buy stakes in another country's strategic industries. *Abbr* ***SWF***

SOX *abbr* REGULATION & COMPLIANCE ***Sarbanes–Oxley Act***

SpA *abbr* BUSINESS ***Società per Azioni***

spam MARKETING unwanted e-mailed advertising e-mailed direct mail regarded as an invasion of personal privacy. *See also* ***direct mail***

special clearing BANKING = ***special presentation***

Special Commissioner TAX UK Treasury official who hears income tax appeals in the United Kingdom, an official appointed by the Treasury to hear cases where a taxpayer is appealing against an income tax assessment

special damages FINANCE damages awarded for calculable loss damages awarded by a court to compensate for a loss that can be calculated, for example, the expense of repairing something

special deposit **1.** MORTGAGES in US, mortgage money for home improvements in the United States, an amount of money set aside for the renovation or improvement of a property as part of a mortgage **2.** BANKING commercial bank's required deposit in Bank of England a large sum of money that a commercial bank has to deposit with the Bank of England

Special Drawing Right CURRENCY & EXCHANGE country's entitlement to receive IMF loans an accounting unit used by the ***International Monetary Fund***, allocated to each member country for use in loans and other international operations. The value is calculated daily on the weighted values of a group of currencies shown in dollars. *Abbr* ***SDR***

Special Economic Zone INTERNATIONAL TRADE Chinese free trade region in China, an area where trade is conducted under special conditions and largely free of state control

specialist **1.** BUSINESS person or company specializing in one thing a person or company that deals with one particular type of product, or with one subject **2.** MARKETS stock exchange member acting as market maker a member of a stock exchange who maintains an inventory of particular stocks, selling to or buying from brokers in order to maintain a stable market for those stocks

special notice STOCKHOLDING & INVESTMENTS late announcement of proposal for stockholder meeting notice of a proposal to be put before a meeting of the stockholders of a company that is issued less than 28 days before the meeting

special presentation BANKING direct delivery of check to paying banker the sending of a check directly to the paying banker rather than through the clearing system. *Also called* ***special clearing***. *See also* ***advice of fate***

special purpose bond STOCKHOLDING & INVESTMENTS bond for one particular project a bond for one particular project, financed by levies on the people who benefit from the project

special resolution CORPORATE GOVERNANCE vote held on exceptional issue in the United Kingdom, an exceptional issue that is put to the vote at a company's general meeting, for example, a change to the company's articles of association, requiring 21 days' notice

special situation STOCKHOLDING & INVESTMENTS expectation of stock price rise the expectation that a stock will increase in value as a result of a change in the company such as a merger

specie CURRENCY & EXCHANGE coins that are legal tender coins, as opposed to pieces of paper money, that are legal tender

specific charge FINANCE = ***fixed charge***

specific order costing ACCOUNTING way to track costs billed by separate contractors the basic cost accounting method used where work consists of separately identifiable contracts, jobs, or batches

speculation FINANCE purchase made on basis of large anticipated gain a purchase made solely to make a profit when the price or value of something increases

speculative bubble MARKETS = ***bubble***

speculator MARKETS somebody taking risks to make quick profit somebody who buys goods, stock, or foreign currency with a higher-than-average risk in the hope that it will rise quickly in value

spending money CURRENCY & EXCHANGE personal money money that is available for small ordinary personal expenses

spinning MARKETS offering stock to preferred customers a practice of questionable legality in which brokerage firms offer stock in ***initial public offerings*** that are in high demand to preferred customers, in order to obtain or keep their business

spin-off GENERAL MANAGEMENT firm formed from larger one a company or subsidiary formed by splitting away from a parent company. A spin-off company can, for example, be created when research and development yields a new product that does not fit into the company's current portfolio, or when a company wants to explore a new venture related to its current activities. It can also be formed from a demerger, in which acquired companies or parts of a business are separated in order to create a more streamlined parent organization. A spin-off is often entrepreneurial in spirit, but the backing of the parent company can provide financial stability.

split STOCKHOLDING & INVESTMENTS = ***stock split***

split annuity INSURANCE combined immediate and deferred annuity product a combination of two products, an immediate annuity and a deferred annuity, each having a single premium. The immediate annuity provides monthly income over a set period and the deferred annuity provides capital growth to replace the original principal, on a fixed interest basis.

split-capital investment trust *or* **split-capital trust** STOCKHOLDING & INVESTMENTS = ***split-level investment trust***

split commission FINANCE transaction fee divided among multiple parties commission that is divided between two or more parties in a transaction

split coupon bond STOCKHOLDING & INVESTMENTS = ***zero coupon bond***

split-level investment trust *or* **split-level trust** STOCKHOLDING & INVESTMENTS investment trust combining income shares and capital shares an investment trust with two categories of shares: ***income shares***, which receive income from the investments, but do not benefit from the rise in their capital value, and ***capital shares***, which increase in value as the value of the investments rises. Income shareholders receive all or most of the income generated by the trust and a predetermined sum at liquidation, while capital shareholders receive no interest but the remainder of the capital at liquidation. *Also called* ***split trust, split-capital investment trust, split-capital trust***

split payment FINANCE payment greatly subdivided a payment that is divided into small units

split trust STOCKHOLDING & INVESTMENTS = ***split-level investment trust***

sponsor **1.** FINANCE person or company giving money for venture a person or company that pays money to help with an activity or to pay for a business venture **2.** FINANCE firm giving money to sport for advertising rights a company that pays to help a sport, in return for advertising rights **3.** STOCKHOLDING & INVESTMENTS backer of an initial public offering an organization such as an investment bank that backs an initial public offering **4.** BUSINESS somebody giving job recommendation somebody who recommends another person for a job **5.** MARKETING company purchasing advertising on TV program a company that pays part of the cost of making a television program by taking advertising time on the program

sponsorship **1.** FINANCE financial support financial backing for an activity or business venture **2.** MARKETING financial support as means of advertising a form of advertising in which an organization provides funds for something such as a television program or sports event in return for exposure to a target audience

spot MARKETING broadcast advertisement a commercial broadcast on television or radio

spot cash CURRENCY & EXCHANGE cash paid on the spot cash paid immediately for something bought

spot currency market CURRENCY & EXCHANGE, MARKETS market for currency deliverable at time of sale a market that deals in foreign exchange for immediate rather than future delivery. *See also* ***spot market***

spot exchange rate CURRENCY & EXCHANGE, MARKETS current exchange rate the exchange rate used for immediate currency transactions

spot goods MARKETS commodity deliverable immediately a commodity traded on the ***spot market***, for immediate delivery

spot interest rate MARKETS current interest rate an interest rate that is determined when a loan is made

spot market MARKETS market for items deliverable at time of sale a market that deals in commodities or foreign exchange for immediate rather than future delivery. *See also* ***spot currency market***

spot month MARKETS = ***nearby month***

spot price MARKETS current price the price for immediate delivery of a commodity or currency

spot rate MARKETS current rate of interest to maturity on security the rate of interest to maturity currently offered on a particular type of security

spot transaction MARKETS transaction for immediate delivery a transaction in commodities or foreign exchange for immediate delivery

spread 1. MARKETS difference between buying and selling price for security the difference between the buying and selling price of a security achieved by a ***market maker*** on a stock exchange **2.** STOCKHOLDING & INVESTMENTS mix of investments the range of the investments in a particular portfolio

spread betting STOCKHOLDING & INVESTMENTS betting on stock movements within specified range betting on the movement of a stock price in relation to a range of high and low values. If the price moves outside the range on a specific day, the bettor wins a multiple of the original stake times the number of points outside the range.

spreadsheet GENERAL MANAGEMENT software organizing data in columns a computer program that provides a series of ruled columns in which data can be entered, manipulated, and analyzed

sprinkling trust STOCKHOLDING & INVESTMENTS trust in which trustees have discretion over distributions a trust with multiple beneficiaries where the trustees have discretion over how the trust's income is distributed

Square Mile FINANCE British financial center an area of London where the British financial center is located. *Also called* ***City of London***

squeeze ECONOMICS government restriction of available credit a government policy of restriction, commonly affecting the availability of credit in an economy

Srl *abbr* BUSINESS ***Società a responsabilità limitata***

SRO *abbr* REGULATION & COMPLIANCE ***self-regulatory organization***

SSAPs *abbr* REGULATION & COMPLIANCE, ACCOUNTING ***Statements of Standard Accounting Practice***

SSN *abbr* INSURANCE, PENSIONS, TAX ***Social Security number***

stabilization fund ECONOMICS government reserve for international financial support a fund created by a government for use in maintaining its official exchange rate when necessary

stag STOCKHOLDING & INVESTMENTS somebody buying new stock for immediate resale somebody who buys ***initial public offerings*** at the offering price and sells them immediately to make a profit

staged payments FINANCE payments made in stages payments that are made in stages over a period of time

stage-gate model MARKETING way of bringing something new to market the traditional model of ***new product development***, comprising the conception, generation, analysis, development, testing, marketing, and commercialization of new products or services. *See also* ***new product development***

stagflation ECONOMICS situation with high unemployment and inflation a situation in which both inflation and unemployment exist at the same time in an economy. There was stagflation in the United Kingdom and the United States in the 1970s, for example.

stagnation ECONOMICS situation with no economic progress a situation in which no progress is being made, especially in economic matters

stakeholder BUSINESS party with vested interest in firm's success a person or organization with a legitimate interest in the successful operation of a company or organization. A stakeholder may be an employee, customer, supplier, partner, or even the local community within which an organization operates.

stakeholder pension PENSIONS in UK, low-cost pension supplementing state plan a pension bought from a private company in which the retirement income depends on the level of contributions made during a person's working life. Stakeholder pensions are designed for people without access to a pension from their employment, and are intended to provide a low-cost supplement to a pension from the government. A stakeholder pension plan can either be trust-based, like an occupational pension plan, or contract-based, similar to a personal pension. Employers must provide access to a stakeholder pension plan for employees, subject to some exceptions, although they are not required to establish a stakeholder pension plan themselves. Membership of a stakeholder pension plan is voluntary. *See also* ***Keough Plan***

stakeholder theory STOCKHOLDING & INVESTMENTS theory that stockholders' interests needn't harm stakeholders the theory that an organization can enhance the interests of its stockholders without damaging the interests of its wider ***stakeholders***. Stakeholder theory grew in response to the ***economic theory of the firm***. One of the difficulties of stakeholder theory is allocating importance to the values of different groups of stakeholders, and a solution to this is proposed by ***stakeholder value analysis***.

stakeholder value analysis STOCKHOLDING & INVESTMENTS assessment of stakeholders' views for corporate planning purposes a method of determining the values of the ***stakeholders*** in an organization for the purposes of making strategic and operational decisions. Stakeholder value analysis is one method of justifying an approach based on ***stakeholder theory*** rather than the ***economic theory of the firm***. It involves identifying groups of stakeholders and eliciting their views on particular issues in order that these views may be taken into account when making decisions.

stale bull STOCKHOLDING & INVESTMENTS investor seeking to sell nonperforming security an investor who bought stocks hoping that they would rise, and now finds that they have not risen and wants to sell them

stamp duty LEGAL in UK, duty verified with postage stamp in the United Kingdom, a duty that is payable on some legal documents and is shown to have been paid by a stamp being affixed to the document

standard OPERATIONS & PRODUCTION benchmark measurement a benchmark measurement of resource usage, set in defined conditions on the basis of expected, potentially attainable, prior or comparable performance standards. Standards may be set at attainable levels, which assume efficient levels of operation but include allowances for normal loss, waste, and machine downtime, or at ideal levels, which make no allowance for the above losses and are only attainable under the most favorable conditions.

standard agreement *or* **standard contract** LEGAL contract containing usual language a printed contract form that contains the usual language applicable to a particular situation

Standard & Poor's STOCKHOLDING & INVESTMENTS major US bond-rating corporation in the United States, a corporation that rates bonds according to the credit-worthiness of the organizations issuing them. Standard & Poor's also issues several stock market indices, for example, the *Standard & Poor's Composite Index*. *Abbr* ***S&P***

Standard & Poor's 500 Index MARKETS US index of 500 stock prices a US index of 500 general stock prices selected by the Standard & Poor agency. *Abbr* ***S&P Index***

Standard & Poor's rating STOCKHOLDING & INVESTMENTS US stock rating service a stock rating service provided by the US agency Standard & Poor's

standard cost FINANCE calculated future cost as basis of estimates a future cost that is calculated in advance and against which estimates are measured

standard costing ACCOUNTING comparison of standard and actual costs a control procedure that compares standard costs and revenues with actual results to obtain variances, which are used to stimulate improved performance

standard deduction TAX untaxed part of person's income in the United States, a proportion of personal income that is not subject to tax for people who do not itemize their deductions. It is calculated based on marital status, number of children or dependents, and whether or not a person is aged 65 or older. *See also* ***itemized deductions***

standard deviation STATISTICS quantity expressing difference from mean a measure of how dispersed a set of numbers are around their mean

standard hour OPERATIONS & PRODUCTION amount of work expected per hour the amount of work achievable, at standard efficiency levels, in an hour

Standard Industrial Classification BUSINESS US system for identifying businesses with their activity in the United States, a system used for categorizing and coding businesses according to the type of activity in which they are engaged. *Abbr* ***SIC***

standard letter GENERAL MANAGEMENT letter sent to several correspondents a letter that is sent without change to a number of correspondents

standard of living ECONOMICS people's ability to buy desired goods and services a measure of economic well-being based on the ability of people to buy the goods and services they desire

standard rate TAX in UK, usual rate of VAT in the United Kingdom, the rate of ***VAT*** usually payable on goods or services

standby credit 1. BANKING = ***backup credit*** **2.** ECONOMICS credit that can be used by emerging countries credit drawing rights given to an emerging country by an international financial institution, to fund industrialization or other growth policies

standby fee FINANCE fee for additional loan a fee paid to obtain ***standby credit***

standby loan ECONOMICS loan to emerging country for specific purposes a loan given to an emerging country by an international financial institution, to fund technology hardware purchase or other growth policies

standing instructions GENERAL MANAGEMENT procedural instructions normally in effect instructions, which may be revoked at any time, for a specific procedure to be undertaken in the event of a specific occurrence; for example, an instruction that money in a savings account for a fixed term should be placed on deposit for a further period when the term expires

standing order *UK* BANKING = ***automatic debit***

standing room only MARKETING illusion of high demand to encourage sales a sales technique whereby customers are given the impression that there are many other people waiting to buy the same product at the same time (*slang*)

staple commodity FINANCE basic item of trade any basic food or a raw material that is important in a country's economy

star 1. STOCKHOLDING & INVESTMENTS outstanding investment an investment that is performing extremely well **2.** BUSINESS fast-growing business with high market share in the ***Boston Box*** model, a business with a high market share and high growth rate. *See also* ***Boston Box***

startup BUSINESS new business, especially in technology sector a relatively new, usually small business, particularly one supported by venture capital and within those sectors closely linked to new technologies

startup costs FINANCE money required to launch new business the initial sum required to establish a business or to get a project under way. The costs will include the capital expenditure and related expenses before the business or project generates revenue.

startup financing *or* **start-up financing** FINANCE first stage in financing new project the first stage in financing a new project, which is followed by several rounds of investment capital as the project gets under way

state bank BANKING bank chartered by US state in the United States, a commercial bank chartered by one of the states rather than having a federal charter

state capitalism ECONOMICS capitalistic system where government controls most production a way of organizing society in which the state controls most of a country's means of production and capital

State Earnings-Related Pension Scheme PENSIONS *see* ***SERPS***

state enterprise BUSINESS nationalized or largely nationalized firm an organization in which the government or state has a controlling interest

statement BANKING list of bank account transactions a summary of all transactions, for example, deposits or withdrawals, that have occurred in an account at a bank or savings and loan association over a given period of time

statement of account ACCOUNTING **1.** list of recent transactions a summary of transactions that have occurred between two parties over a given period of time **2.** list of commercial transactions a list of sums due, usually comprising unpaid invoices, items paid on account but not offset against particular invoices, credit notes, debit notes, and discounts

statement of affairs ACCOUNTING list of assets and liabilities showing financial condition a statement in a prescribed form, usually prepared by a receiver, showing the estimated financial position of a debtor or a company that may be unable to meet its debts. It contains a summary of the debtor's assets and liabilities, with the assets shown at their estimated realizable values. The various classes of creditors, such as preferential, secured, partly secured, and unsecured, are shown separately.

statement of cash flows ACCOUNTING list of cash transactions a statement that documents actual receipts and expenditures of cash

statement-of-cash-flows method ACCOUNTING accounting system based on business's cash flow a method of accounting that is based on flows of cash rather than balances on accounts

statement of changes in financial position ACCOUNTING list of business's income and expenditures a financial report of a company's incomes and outflows during a period, usually a year or a quarter

Statement of Financial Accounting Standards REGULATION & COMPLIANCE in US, declaration of standards governing financial reporting in the United States, a statement detailing the standards to be adopted for the preparation of financial statements. *Abbr* ***SFAS***

statement of source and application of funds ACCOUNTING = ***cash flow statement***

statement of total recognized gains and losses ACCOUNTING list of changes in stockholders' equity a financial statement showing changes in stockholders' equity during an accounting period

Statements of Standard Accounting Practice REGULATION & COMPLIANCE, ACCOUNTING UK rules for preparation of financial statements rules laid down by the UK Accounting Standards Board for the preparation of financial statements. *Abbr* ***SSAPs***

state of indebtedness FINANCE situation of owing money the situation that exists when somebody owes money

state ownership BUSINESS ownership of industry by government a situation in which an industry is taken over from private ownership and run by a government

state pension PENSIONS UK government pension in the United Kingdom, the basic pension entitlement provided by the government for a retired person

State Second Pension PENSIONS additional UK government pension in the United Kingdom, an additional pension entitlement over and above the basic pension provided by the government, available to people who had caring responsibilities or long-term illness or disability as well as to those who were employed

statistic STATISTICS item of numerical data a piece of information in numerical form, obtained from analysis of a large quantity of numerical data

statistical discrepancy STATISTICS discrepancy arising from different calculation methods the amount by which sets of figures differ, usually because of a difference in the methods of calculation

statistical expert system STATISTICS computer program for performing statistical analysis a computer program used to conduct a statistical analysis of a set of data

statistical model STATISTICS techniques for analyzing data in statistical study the particular methods used to investigate the data in a statistical study

statistical quality control STATISTICS methods for checking consistency of statistical samples the process of inspecting samples of a product to check for consistent quality according to given parameters

statistical significance STATISTICS status as statistical pointer in a statistical study, a value assigned to the likelihood that something has occurred by chance

statistics STATISTICS **1.** numerical data information in numerical form, obtained from analysis of a large quantity of numerical data **2.** study of numerical data the collection, analysis, and presentation of large quantities of numerical data

status inquiry FINANCE credit check the act of checking on a customer's credit rating

statute-barred debt FINANCE debt that is uncollectable after time limit a debt that cannot be pursued as the time limit laid down by law has expired

statute of limitations LEGAL time limit for bringing lawsuit a law that allows only a fixed period of time during which somebody can start legal proceedings to claim property or compensation for damage

statutory auditor ACCOUNTING, REGULATION & COMPLIANCE in UK, officially qualified auditor in the United Kingdom, a professional person qualified to conduct an audit required by the Companies Act

statutory body BUSINESS group created by law an organized group with a particular function that has been established by government legislation

statutory instrument LEGAL in UK, legislation not needing full Parliamentary approval in UK law, a form of legislation that allows the provision of an Act of Parliament to be brought into force or altered without full Parliamentary approval. *Abbr* ***SI***

statutory regulations REGULATION & COMPLIANCE UK financial regulations based on Parliamentary acts in the United Kingdom, regulations covering financial dealings that are based on Acts of Parliament, for example, the Financial Services Act, as opposed to the rules of self-regulatory organizations, which are non-statutory

statutory voting CORPORATE GOVERNANCE system granting one vote per share a system of voting in which stockholders in a company have one vote per share of stock owned

STC TAX S. African tax on dividends in South Africa, a tax that is levied on corporate dividends. *Full form* ***Secondary Tax on Companies***

stealth tax TAX initially unnoticed tax a new tax or tax increase, especially an indirect tax, that is introduced without much public attention, or an additional charge that is effectively a tax although not officially classed as one

sterling CURRENCY & EXCHANGE UK currency the standard currency (pounds and pence) used in the United Kingdom

sterling area CURRENCY & EXCHANGE formerly, countries using sterling as trading currency formerly, the area of the world where the pound sterling was the main trading currency

sterling balances CURRENCY & EXCHANGE trade balances expressed in sterling a country's trade balances expressed in pounds sterling

sterling index CURRENCY & EXCHANGE index measuring sterling against other currencies an index that shows the current value of sterling against a group of other currencies

stipend FINANCE regular payment to office-holder a regular remuneration or allowance paid as a salary to an office-holder such as a member of the clergy

stock 1. STOCKHOLDING & INVESTMENTS fixed interest investment a form of security issued in fixed units at a fixed rate of interest. The technical difference between stocks and shares is that a company that fixes its capital in terms of a monetary amount and then sells different proportions of it to investors creates stock, while a company that creates a number of shares of equal nominal value and sells different numbers of them to investors creates shares. For all practical purposes they are the same. In the United States, all equity instruments are called stocks, whereas in the United Kingdom, they are called shares. **2.** *UK* OPERATIONS & PRODUCTION = ***inventory***

stockalypse STOCKHOLDING & INVESTMENTS collapse in stock prices a sudden and dramatic drop in the price of stock *(slang)*

stockbroker STOCKHOLDING & INVESTMENTS professional agent for securities a person or company that arranges the sale and purchase of stocks and other securities, usually for a commission. *Also called* ***broker***

stockbroking STOCKHOLDING & INVESTMENTS dealing in stock the business of dealing in stocks and other securities for clients

stock buyback STOCKHOLDING & INVESTMENTS = ***buyback***

stock certificate *US* STOCKHOLDING & INVESTMENTS document representing ownership in firm a document that certifies ownership of stock in a company. *UK term* ***share certificate***

stock control *UK* OPERATIONS & PRODUCTION = ***inventory control***

stock depreciation *UK* ACCOUNTING = ***inventory depreciation***

stock dividend STOCKHOLDING & INVESTMENTS dividend paid as additional shares of stock a dividend paid to a stockholder in the form of additional stock rather than cash

stock exchange MARKETS market for securities a registered place where securities are bought and sold. *Also called* ***stock market*** *(sense 2)*

Stock Exchange Automated Quotations system MARKETS *see* ***SEAQ***

Stock Exchange Automated Quotations system International MARKETS *see* ***SEAQ International***

Stock Exchange Automatic Trading System MARKETS *see* ***SEATS***

stock exchange listing MARKETS presence on official stock list the fact of being on the official list of stocks that can be bought or sold on a stock exchange

stockholder *US* STOCKHOLDING & INVESTMENTS somebody with shares in company a person or organization that owns one or more shares of stock in a company. *UK term* ***shareholder***

stockholder perks *US* STOCKHOLDING & INVESTMENTS = ***shareholders' perks***

stockholders' equity *US* FINANCE firm's share capital and reserves the part of a company's financial assets consisting of ***share capital*** and ***retained profits***. *Also called* ***shareholders' equity, shareholders' funds***

stockholder value *US* STOCKHOLDING & INVESTMENTS = ***shareholder value***

stockholder value analysis *US* STOCKHOLDING & INVESTMENTS = ***shareholder value analysis***

stockholding *US* STOCKHOLDING & INVESTMENTS ownership of shares in firm the stock in a ***corporation*** owned by a stockholder. *Also called* ***shareholding***

stock incentive plan *US* HR & PERSONNEL offering shares in firm to employees a type of financial ***incentive plan*** in which employees can acquire shares in the company in which they work and so have an interest in its financial performance. A stock incentive plan is a type of ***employee stock ownership plan***, in which employees may be given stock by their employer, or stock may be offered for purchase at an advantageous price, as a reward for personal or group performance. *UK term* ***share incentive scheme***

stockjobber MARKETS former UK dealer in securities the equivalent of a ***market maker*** on the London Stock Exchange before the ***Big Bang*** of October 1986. Stockjobbers could not deal directly with private investors. *See also* ***market maker***

stockjobbing MARKETS former trading activities on stock exchange formerly, the business of buying and selling shares from other traders on a stock exchange

stock level OPERATIONS & PRODUCTION quantity of goods in inventory the quantity of goods kept in inventory. *Also called* ***inventory level***

stock market MARKETS **1.** trading in securities the activity or profession of trading in securities **2.** = ***stock exchange***

stock market crash MARKETS = ***crash***

stock market index MARKETS = ***index***

stock market manipulation MARKETS efforts to influence stock prices an attempt or series of attempts to influence the price of stocks by buying or selling in order to give the impression that the stocks are widely traded

stock market rating MARKETS stock price indicating firm's value the price of a stock on the stock market, which shows how investors and financial advisers generally consider the value of the company

stock market valuation MARKETS firm's value based on stock price the value of a company based on the current market price of its stock

stock option STOCKHOLDING & INVESTMENTS right to buy or sell on agreed terms the right of an option holder to buy or sell a specific stock on predetermined terms on, or before, a future date. *Also called* ***option***. *UK term* ***share option***

stock option plan *US* STOCKHOLDING & INVESTMENTS employees' right to buy company stock a program in which an employee is given the option to buy a specific number of shares of stock at a future date, at an agreed price. Stock options provide a financial benefit to the recipient only if the stock price rises over the period the option is available. If the stock price falls over the period, the employee is under no obligation to buy. There may be a tax advantage to the employees who participate in such a program. Share options may be available to all employees or operated on a discretionary basis. *UK term* ***share option scheme***

stockout OPERATIONS & PRODUCTION unavailability of part from stock the situation where the stock of a particular component or part has been used up and has not yet been replenished. Stockouts result from poor stock control or the failure of a ***just-in-time*** supply system. They can result in delays in the delivery of customer orders and can damage the reputation of the business.

stockpicker STOCKHOLDING & INVESTMENTS buyer choosing stock somebody who is choosing which stock to buy. *See also* ***bottom-up approach***

stock quote MARKETS current price of stock trading on stock exchange the highest ***bid price*** or lowest ***ask price*** of a share of stock at any point in time during a trading day

stocks and shares STOCKHOLDING & INVESTMENTS firms' capital owned by public the units of ownership in public companies. The technical difference between stocks and shares is that a company that fixes its capital in terms of a monetary amount and then sells different proportions of it to investors creates stock, while a company that creates a number of shares of equal nominal value and sells different numbers of them to investors creates shares. For all practical purposes they are the same. In the United States, all equity instruments are called stocks, whereas in the United Kingdom, they are called shares.

stock split *US* STOCKHOLDING & INVESTMENTS numerical increase of shares without affecting total value an act of issuing stockholders with at least one more share for every share owned, without affecting the total value of each holding. A stock split usually occurs because the stock price has become too high for easy trading. *Also called* ***share split, split***. *See also* ***bonus shares, reverse split***. *UK term* ***scrip issue***

stock symbol MARKETS short form of firm's name a shortened version of a company's name, usually made up of two to four letters, used in screen-based trading systems and newspaper listings

stocktaking OPERATIONS & PRODUCTION counting items held in stock the process of measuring the quantities of stock held by an organization. Inventory can be held both in stores and within the processes of the operation.

stock tip *US* STOCKHOLDING & INVESTMENTS expert's recommendation on stock a recommendation about a stock published in the financial press, usually based on research published by a financial institution. *UK term* ***share tip***

stock turnover *UK* STOCKHOLDING & INVESTMENTS = ***inventory turnover***

stock turns ACCOUNTING = ***inventory turnover***

stock valuation *UK* ACCOUNTING = ***inventory valuation***

stokvel BANKING S. African savings association in South Africa, an informal, widely used cooperative savings program that provides small-scale loans

stop-go ECONOMICS alternately tightening and loosening economic policies the alternate tightening and loosening of fiscal and monetary policies, characteristic of the UK economy in the 1960s and 1970s

stop limit order MARKETS order to trade stock above specific price an order to trade only if and when a security reaches a specified price

stop-loss order *or* **stop-loss** *or* **stop order** MARKETS instruction to sell stock if price falls an instruction to a stockbroker to sell a stock if the price falls to a specified level.

stop price MARKETS specified trading price the price at which to sell or buy a security specified in a ***stop-loss order***

store card FINANCE credit card used exclusively in department store a credit card issued by a large department store, which can only be used for purchases in that store

story stock STOCKHOLDING & INVESTMENTS stock reported on in press a stock that is the subject of a press or financial community story that may affect its price

straddle STOCKHOLDING & INVESTMENTS simultaneous security purchase of put and call options the act of buying a ***put option*** and a ***call option*** for the same number of shares of the same security at the same time with the same ***strike price*** and expiration date. This allows the buyer to make a profit if the price rises or falls. *See also* ***strangle***

straight line depreciation ACCOUNTING reducing value of asset evenly over its lifetime a form of ***depreciation*** in which the cost of a fixed asset is spread equally over each year of its anticipated lifetime

Straits Times Industrial Index MARKETS Singapore stock exchange indicator an index of 30 Singapore stocks, the most commonly quoted indicator of stock market activity in Singapore

strangle MARKETS simultaneously trading differently priced put and call options a strategy in which a ***put option*** and a ***call option*** with the same expiration date but different ***strike prices*** on the same asset are either bought or sold. *See also* ***straddle***

STRATE MARKETS S. African electronic exchange system the electronic stock transactions system of the South African stock exchange, JSE Limited. *Full form* ***Share Transactions Totally Electronic***

strategic analysis GENERAL MANAGEMENT assessment of business procedures and environment the process of evaluating the business environment within which an organization operates and the organization itself as part of a process of formulating long-term objectives

strategic business unit GENERAL MANAGEMENT section with own marketing strategy a division within a large organization that shares the organization's market and customer focus but has responsibility for the development of its own marketing strategy. A single overall strategic approach is often inappropriate in large diversified organizations or multinational companies.

strategic financial management FINANCE handling firm's money to achieve firm's goals the identification of the strategies capable of maximizing an organization's net present value, the allocation of scarce capital resources, and the implementation and monitoring of a particular strategy

strategic management GENERAL MANAGEMENT management for longer-term objectives the development of corporate strategy, and the management of an organization according to that strategy. Strategic management focuses on achieving and maintaining a strong competitive advantage. It involves the application of corporate strategy to all aspects of the organization, and especially to decision making. As a discipline, strategic management developed in the 1970s, but it has evolved in response to changes in organization structure and corporate culture. With greater empowerment, strategy has become the concern not just of directors but also of employees at all levels of the organization.

strategic marketing MARKETING direct selling to customers a method of selling products directly to customers, bypassing traditional retailers or distributors

strategy GENERAL MANAGEMENT structured course of action for longer-term objectives a planned course of action undertaken to achieve the goals and objectives of an organization. The overall strategy of an organization is known as corporate strategy, but strategy may also be developed for any aspect of an organization's activities such as environmental management or manufacturing strategy.

stratified random sampling STATISTICS selecting random subgroups from stratified statistical population sampling carried out at random from each stratum of a stratified population. *See also* ***random sampling***

stratified sampling STATISTICS *see also* ***random sampling***

street *US* MARKETS describing person with market awareness used to describe somebody who is considered to be well informed about the market (*slang*)

Street MARKETS US financial industry the financial industry in the United States, located in and around Wall Street

street name MARKETS brokerage house holding customer's investments in the United States, a way of registering a customer's security in which a broker or brokerage holds the security in the brokerage house's name to facilitate transactions

stress test BANKING review of system's stability a stringent set of checks on the stability and security of a system or of an organization such as a bank

strike price STOCKHOLDING & INVESTMENTS price fixed by seller the price for a security or commodity that underlies an ***option***. *Also called* ***exercise price*** *(sense 2)*

strip STOCKHOLDING & INVESTMENTS separation of coupons from bond for sale individually the separation of the coupons from the principal of a bond in order to sell them separately as a package of interest coupons and a bond that repays principal without interest. *See also* ***strips***

strippable bond STOCKHOLDING & INVESTMENTS bond separable into principal and interest payments a bond that can be divided into separate zero-coupon bonds, representing its principal and interest payments, which can be traded independently

stripped bond STOCKHOLDING & INVESTMENTS bond separated into principal and interest payments a bond that has been divided into separate zero-coupon bonds, representing its principal and interest payments, which can be traded independently

stripped stock STOCKHOLDING & INVESTMENTS stock without dividend rights stock for which the rights to dividends have been split off and sold separately

stripping STOCKHOLDING & INVESTMENTS splitting bond into two parts for separate trading the process of separating the coupons from the principal of a bond in order to sell them separately as a package of interest coupons and a bond that repays principal without interest. *See also* ***strips***

strips STOCKHOLDING & INVESTMENTS bond parts allowing interest or principal payments only the parts of a ***stripped bond*** that entitle the owner to interest payments only, or to the payment of principal only

strong currency CURRENCY & EXCHANGE currency with relatively high value a currency that has a high value against other currencies

structural adjustment ECONOMICS change in basic framework of economy the reallocation of resources in response to alterations in the composition of the output of an economy as it experiences changes between the contribution of different business sectors. *Also called* ***structural change***

structural change ECONOMICS = ***structural adjustment***

structural fund STOCKHOLDING & INVESTMENTS mutual fund invested in EU economic development a type of ***mutual fund*** that invests in projects that contribute to the economic development of poorer nations in the European Union

structural inflation ECONOMICS inflation with no specific cause inflation that naturally occurs in an economy, without any particular triggering event

structural unemployment ECONOMICS unemployment caused by change in basic economic framework unemployment resulting from a change in demand or technological advances, which cause a surplus of labor in a particular location or skills area

structured investment vehicle STOCKHOLDING & INVESTMENTS product with short-term borrowing funding high-yielding securities a product that borrows money in the short-term credit market to invest in high-yielding, longer-dated securities. *Abbr* ***SIV***

structured product STOCKHOLDING & INVESTMENTS customized investment a type of investment designed to meet an investor's specific needs

stub equity STOCKHOLDING & INVESTMENTS **1.** money from high risk bond sales the money raised through the sale of large quantities of high risk bonds, as in a ***leveraged buyout*** **2.** stock with greatly reduced price a stock whose price has seriously fallen due to major financial problems. Stub stock is a risky investment with great potential if the company regains its strength.

Student Loan Marketing Association FINANCE *see* ***Sallie Mae***

subcontracting GENERAL MANAGEMENT, OPERATIONS & PRODUCTION employing another to fulfill part of contract the delegation to a third party of some or all of the work that somebody has contracted to do. Subcontracting usually occurs where the contracted work such as the construction of a building requires a variety of skills. Responsibility for the fulfillment of the original contract remains with the original contracting party. Where the fulfillment of a contract depends on the skills of the person who has entered into the contract, as in the painting of a portrait, then the work cannot be subcontracted to a third party. The term subcontracting is sometimes used to describe ***outsourcing*** arrangements.

subject to collection FINANCE depending on repayment dependent upon the ability to collect the amount owed

subordinated debt FINANCE = ***junior debt***

subordinated loan FINANCE debt whose repayment ranks after all others a loan that ranks below all other borrowings with regard to both the payment of interest and principal. *See also* ***pari passu***

subprime loan FINANCE loan made to borrower unlikely to repay a loan made to somebody who does not meet the usual or standard qualifications for borrowing the amount in question. In 2007–8, a world financial crisis was precipitated by defaults on subprime mortgage loans.

subscribed capital *or* **subscribed share capital** STOCKHOLDING & INVESTMENTS = ***issued share capital***

subscriber 1. STOCKHOLDING & INVESTMENTS somebody who buys stocks in new firm a buyer, especially one who buys stocks in a new company or new issues **2.** BUSINESS original stockholder a person who signs a company's ***memorandum of association***

subscription price STOCKHOLDING & INVESTMENTS price of new stock offered for sale the price at which new shares of stock in an existing company are offered for sale

subscription share STOCKHOLDING & INVESTMENTS share of stock in new firm a stock purchased by a subscriber when a new company is formed

subsidiary BUSINESS = ***subsidiary company***

subsidiary account BANKING individual account for one owner of joint account an account for one of the individual people or organizations that jointly hold another account

subsidiary company BUSINESS firm controlled by another a company that is controlled by another. A subsidiary company operates under the control of a parent or ***holding company***, which may have a majority on the subsidiary's ***board of directors***, or a majority shareholding in the subsidiary—giving it majority voting rights—or it may be named in a contract as having control of the subsidiary. If all of the stock in a company is owned by its parent, it is known as a ***wholly-owned subsidiary***. A subsidiary that is located in a different country from the parent is a *foreign subsidiary company*.

subsidized FINANCE having financial assistance for which a ***subsidy*** has been paid

subsidy FINANCE financial assistance for activity or firm financial assistance to a company or group of people, usually given by a government, to encourage new developments of benefit to the public or to support an industry for a period of time. Subsidies are regarded as restrictive in international trade if by supporting a domestic industry they make imports more expensive.

subsistence allowance FINANCE money for living expenses away from home ***expenses*** paid by an employer, usually within preset limits, to cover the cost of accommodations, meals, and incidental expenses incurred by employees when away on business

subtreasury FINANCE subordinate treasury a place where some of a nation's money is held

sub-underwriter MARKETS firm underwriting stock issue a company that underwrites an issue, taking shares of stock from the main underwriters

subvention FINANCE financial support given officially money given by a government or official body to support an activity

suggested retail price *US* BUSINESS sale price suggested by manufacturer the price at which a manufacturer suggests a product should be sold on the retail market, though this may be reduced by the retailer. *UK term* ***recommended retail price***

suit GENERAL MANAGEMENT employee in formal role a business executive who works for a large corporation, especially in a relatively faceless management role (*slang*)

suitability rules REGULATION & COMPLIANCE rules ensuring that client can afford an investment guidelines that brokers and others selling or recommending investments are required to follow to ensure that investors are financially able to handle the risks involved in investing

sukuk FINANCE asset-backed interest-free bond in Islamic financing, the equivalent of a bond, which represents undivided shares in ownership of tangible assets. Under Islamic law it cannot earn interest.

sum FINANCE **1.** money a particular amount of money **2.** total amount of something the total amount of any given item, such as stocks or securities **3.** total of added numbers the total arising from the addition of two or more numbers

sum at risk FINANCE, RISK how much of something investors might lose an amount of any given item, such as money, stocks, or securities, that an investor might lose

sum insured INSURANCE largest amount insurance firm will pay the maximum amount that an insurance company will pay out in the event of a claim

sum of digits method *or* **sum-of-the-year's-digits depreciation** ACCOUNTING = ***accelerated depreciation***

sums chargeable to the reserve ACCOUNTING sums debited to company's reserves sums that can be debited to a company's reserves

sunk cost ACCOUNTING completed cost unrelated to future decisions a cost that has been irreversibly incurred or committed prior to a decision point, and cannot therefore be considered relevant to subsequent decisions

sunshine law REGULATION & COMPLIANCE US law requiring openness in the United States, a law that requires public disclosure of a government act or government proceedings

superannuation PENSIONS money yielding income, usually in retirement money providing an income for somebody who no longer works, usually because they are older than the normal age for retirement

superannuation plan PENSIONS Australian pension plan in Australia, a pension plan that may be personal or operated by an employer

superannuation scheme PENSIONS New Zealand pension plan in New Zealand, a pension plan that may be personal or operated by an employer

supertax TAX **1.** high tax on high earnings a high rate of tax levied on the income of the highest earners **2.** former UK tax in the United Kingdom, a tax rate levied from 1919 to 1973 on the income of the highest earners. *Also called* ***surtax***

supplementary benefit HR & PERSONNEL formerly in UK, government payments for poor people formerly, in the United Kingdom, payments from the government to people with very low incomes. It was replaced by ***income support***.

supplementary capital BANKING = ***Tier 2 capital***

supplier OPERATIONS & PRODUCTION firm providing what another firm needs a company that provides materials, components, goods, or services for another company

supply and demand ECONOMICS quantity of available goods and desire for them the quantity of goods available for sale at a given price, and the level of consumer need for those goods. The balance of supply and demand fluctuates as external economic factors—for example, the cost of materials and the level of competition in the marketplace—influence the level of demand from consumers and the desire and ability of producers to supply the goods. Supply and demand is recognized as an economic force, and is often referred to as the ***law of supply and demand***.

supply chain GENERAL MANAGEMENT, OPERATIONS & PRODUCTION network of firms involved in production process the network of manufacturers, wholesalers, distributors, and retailers, who turn raw materials into ***finished goods*** and services and deliver them to consumers. Supply chains are increasingly being seen as integrated entities, and closer relationships between the organizations throughout the chain can bring competitive advantage, reduce costs, and help to maintain a loyal customer base.

supply chain management OPERATIONS & PRODUCTION overseeing of relationships between firms in supply chain the management of the movement of goods and flow of information between an organization and its suppliers and customers, to achieve strategic advantage. Supply chain management covers the processes of managing materials, physical distribution, purchasing, information, and logistics.

supply price OPERATIONS & PRODUCTION price at which something is provided the price at which goods or services are supplied

supply shock ECONOMICS event causing reduced supply of necessity an event that causes a sudden reduction, or perceived reduction, in the production or availability of a product or resource necessary to an economy

supply-side economics ECONOMICS economic theory stressing incentives for suppliers a branch of economics that emphasizes the production of goods through incentives as a means of stimulating economic growth

support price ECONOMICS product price subsidized by government the price of a product that is fixed or stabilized by a government so that it cannot fall below a specific level

support ratio ECONOMICS = ***dependency ratio***

surcharge OPERATIONS & PRODUCTION charge added to standard charge a charge added to the standard charge for a specific product or service

surety FINANCE **1.** guarantor somebody who promises to cover another person's obligations **2.** guarantee for loan the ***collateral*** given as security when a person, business, or organization takes out a loan

surplus ACCOUNTING = ***budget surplus***

surplus capacity OPERATIONS & PRODUCTION ability to produce more than customers require the capability of a factory or workstation to produce output over and above the level required by consumers or subsequent processes. Surplus capacity is a product of materials, personnel, and equipment that are superfluous, or not working to maximum ***capacity***. Some surplus capacity is required in any production system to deal with fluctuations in demand, and as a backup in case of failure. Excessive surplus capacity, however, adds to the cost of the production process as work-in-process inventory or finished-goods storage increases, and can result in ***overcapacity***. If a workstation has no surplus capacity its workloads cannot be increased, so it is at risk of becoming a ***bottleneck***. *Also called* ***redundant capacity***

surrender INSURANCE relinquish insurance policy before maturity to cancel an insurance policy before the contracted date for maturity

surrender charge FINANCE penalty for early withdrawal of invested money a charge levied when somebody withdraws money invested before the date allowed

surrender value INSURANCE money paid by insurance firm for canceled policy the sum of money offered by an insurance company to somebody who cancels a policy before it has completed its full term

surtax TAX **1.** tax paid on top of other taxes a tax paid in addition to another tax, typically levied on a corporation with very high income = ***supertax***

survey MARKETING, STATISTICS collection of data from group on particular topic the collection of data from a given population for the purpose of analysis of a particular issue. Data is often collected from only a sample of a population, and this is known as a ***sample survey***. Surveys are used widely in research, especially in ***market research***.

survivalist enterprise *S. Africa* BUSINESS small firm with no paid workers a business that has no paid employees, generates income below the poverty line, and is considered the lowest level of microbusiness

sushi bond STOCKHOLDING & INVESTMENTS Japanese bond a bond that is not denominated in yen and is issued in any market by a Japanese financial institution. This type of bond is often bought by Japanese institutional investors (*slang*).

suspended trading MARKETS halt in trading of stock a period when trading in a specific stock or on an exchange is stopped, usually in response to information about a company, or concern about rapid movement of the stock price. *See also* ***trading halt***

suspense account BANKING temporary holding account an account in which debits or credits are held temporarily until sufficient information is available for them to be posted to the correct accounts

sustainable advantage GENERAL MANAGEMENT lasting competitive advantage a competitive advantage that can be maintained over the long term, as opposed to one resulting from a short-term tactical promotion

sustainable development GENERAL MANAGEMENT development that does not disadvantage future generations development that meets the needs of the present without compromising the ability of future generations to meet their own needs. The concept of sustainable development was introduced by the Brundtland Report, the first report of the World Commission on Environment and Development, established by the United Nations in 1983. It advocates the integration of social, economic, and environmental considerations into policy decisions by business and government. Particular emphasis is given to social, cultural, and ethical implications of development. Sustainable development can be achieved through ***environmental management*** and is a feature of a socially responsible business.

SVA *abbr* STOCKHOLDING & INVESTMENTS ***shareholder value analysis***

swap 1. FINANCE, STOCKHOLDING & INVESTMENTS trade of payment terms between two firms an arrangement whereby two organizations contractually agree to exchange payments on different terms, for example, in different currencies, or one at a fixed rate and the other at a floating rate. *See also* ***asset swap, bond swap, interest rate swap*** **2.** FINANCE exchange an exchange of credits or liabilities

swap book STOCKHOLDING & INVESTMENTS list of exchanges wanted a broker's list of stocks or securities that clients wish to swap

swaption STOCKHOLDING & INVESTMENTS right to exchange an ***option*** giving the right but not the obligation to enter into a ***swap*** contract (*slang*)

sweat equity FINANCE unpaid work by firm's founder work done for little or no pay by the owner or partners of a new company in the early stages of the company's activities

sweep facility BANKING automatic service moving money to different account the automatic transfer of sums from a checking account to a deposit account, or from any low interest account to a higher one. For example, a personal customer may have the balance transferred just before receipt of their monthly salary, or a business may stipulate that when a balance exceeds a specific sum, the excess is to be transferred.

sweetener 1. GENERAL MANAGEMENT incentive an incentive offered to somebody to take a particular course of action **2.** STOCKHOLDING & INVESTMENTS attractive extra feature on investment product a feature added to a security to make it more attractive to investors **3.** STOCKHOLDING & INVESTMENTS high-yield investment added to lower yield collection a security with a high yield that has been added to a portfolio to improve its overall return. *See also* ***kicker***

SWF *abbr* STOCKHOLDING & INVESTMENTS ***sovereign wealth fund***

SWIFT BANKING society supporting common global financial transactions network a nonprofit cooperative organization with the mission of creating a shared worldwide data processing and communications link and a common language for international financial transactions. Established in Brussels in 1973 with the support of 239 banks in 15 countries, it now has over 7,000 live users in 192 countries, exchanging millions of messages valued in trillions of dollars every business day. *Full form* ***Society for Worldwide Interbank Financial Telecommunication***

swing trading MARKETS buying and selling stock after sudden price changes the trading of stock in order to take advantage of sudden price movements that occur especially when large numbers of traders have to cover short sales

switch 1. STOCKHOLDING & INVESTMENTS replace one investment product in set with another to exchange a specific security with another within a portfolio, usually because the investor's objectives have changed **2.** STOCKHOLDING & INVESTMENTS swap involving exchange rates a type of ***swap*** that involves different currencies and interest rates. *See also* ***swap*** **3.** OPERATIONS & PRODUCTION move goods elsewhere to move a commodity from one location to another

Switch BANKING UK debit card a debit card formerly used in the United Kingdom

switching STOCKHOLDING & INVESTMENTS buying and selling different futures contracts simultaneously the simultaneous sale and purchase of contracts in futures with different expiration dates, as, for example, when a business decides that it would like to take delivery of a commodity earlier or later than originally contracted

switching discount STOCKHOLDING & INVESTMENTS lower charge to existing customers for exchanging funds the discount available to holders of collective investments who move from one fund to another offered by the same fund manager. The discount is usually a lower initial charge compared to the one made to new investors, or to existing investors who make a further investment.

SWOT analysis GENERAL MANAGEMENT, MARKETING assessment of strengths, weaknesses, opportunities, and threats an assessment of the "Strengths, Weaknesses, Opportunities, and Threats" in an organization. SWOT analysis is used in the early stages of strategic and ***marketing planning***, in ***problem solving*** and ***decision making***, or for making staff aware of the need for change. It can be used at a personal level when determining possible career development.

SYD *abbr* ACCOUNTING ***sum-of-the-year's-digits depreciation*** = ***accelerated depreciation***

Sydney Futures Exchange MARKETS main Australian commodity exchange the principal market in Australia for trading financial and commodity futures. It was established in 1962 as a wool futures market, the Sydney Greasy Wool Futures Exchange, but adopted its current name in 1972 to reflect its widening role. *Abbr* ***SFE***

symmetrical distribution STATISTICS even distribution of statistical data around central value a distribution of statistical data that is symmetrical about a central value

syndicate **1.** BUSINESS group joining together for business activity a group of people or companies that come together for a specific business activity, especially when they jointly contribute capital to a project **2.** GENERAL MANAGEMENT distribute item to several outlets to agree to distribute an article, a cartoon, a television show, or other work to several different outlets, publications, or broadcasting companies **3.** BANKING get large loan underwritten by international banks to arrange for a large loan to be underwritten by several international banks

syndicated research MARKETING data on commercial trends trend data supplied by research agencies from their regularly operated retail audits or consumer panels

systematic risk RISK risk related to securities market or economy investment risk that is attributable to the performance of the stock market or the economy

systematic sampling STATISTICS *see* ***random sampling***

systematic withdrawal STOCKHOLDING & INVESTMENTS regular payment from mutual fund to shareholder an arrangement in which a mutual fund pays out a specific amount to the shareholder at regular intervals. *See also* ***withdrawal plan***

systems analysis GENERAL MANAGEMENT assessment of efficiency of business operation the examination and evaluation of an operation or task in order to identify and implement more efficient methods, usually through the use of computers. Systems analysis can be broken down into three main areas: the production of a statement of objectives; determination of the best methods of achieving these objectives in a cost-effective and efficient way; and the preparation of a ***feasibility study***. *Also called* ***systems planning***

systems approach GENERAL MANAGEMENT use of computers in business organization a technique employed for organizational ***decision making*** and ***problem solving*** involving the use of computer systems. The systems approach uses ***systems analysis*** to examine the extent to which a system's components are interrelated and interdependent. When working together, these components produce an effect greater than the sum of the parts. System components might comprise departments or functions of an organization or business which work together for an overall objective.

systems audit GENERAL MANAGEMENT auditing approach an approach to ***auditing*** that utilizes a ***systems approach***. By using a systems audit to assess the internal control system of an organization, it is possible to assess the quality of the accounting system and the level of testing required from the financial statements. One shortcoming of systems audit is that it does not consider audit risk.

systems planning GENERAL MANAGEMENT = ***systems analysis***

T

T+ FINANCE number of days for completing business deal an expression of the number of days allowed for settlement of a transaction

tactical plan GENERAL MANAGEMENT short-term plan a short-term plan for achieving the objectives of a person, business, or organization

tail **1.** MARKETS difference between acceptable yields in US Treasury auction the spread between the average yield accepted in an auction of US government securities and the highest yield accepted **2.** STOCKHOLDING & INVESTMENTS numbers after decimal point in bond price the figures that come after the decimal point in the quoted price of a bond

tailgating MARKETS broker trading stock immediately after client does the practice by a broker of buying or selling a security immediately after a client's transaction, in order to take advantage of the impact of the client's deal

takaful INSURANCE insurance comprised of pool of funds Islamic insurance in which all participants are members and contribute to a pool of funds that provide assistance in the event of loss on the part of any of the participants. An Islamic insurance arrangement avoids the prohibitions against gambling and interest in Islamic law.

take a flier FINANCE guess to speculate about what might happen (*slang*)

take a hit FINANCE lose money to make a loss on an investment (*slang*)

take a view MARKETS form expectation of how market will perform to form an opinion on the likely direction a market will take, and take a position that will be of benefit if the opinion proves correct

takeaway MARKETING customer's impressions of product the impressions that a consumer forms about a product or service

take-home pay FINANCE = ***net pay*** (*informal*)

takeout STOCKHOLDING & INVESTMENTS selling stock in firm the act of removing capital that was originally invested in a new company by selling stock

takeout financing FINANCE long-term borrowing long-term loans taken out to replace short-term financing

takeover MERGERS & ACQUISITIONS **1.** when one firm takes control of another the acquisition by a company of a controlling interest in the voting share capital of another company, usually achieved by the purchase of a majority of the voting stocks **2.** = ***takeover bid***

takeover approach *UK* MERGERS & ACQUISITIONS price offered for takeover the price at which a prospective buyer offers to purchase a controlling interest in a business or corporation. *US term* ***tender offer***

takeover battle MERGERS & ACQUISITIONS result of firm's resistance to acquisition the activities surrounding a ***contested takeover bid***. The bidder may raise the offer price and write to the stockholders extolling the benefits of the takeover. The board may contact other companies in the same line of business, hoping that a ***white knight*** may appear. It could also take action to make the company less desirable to the bidder. *See also* ***poison pill***

takeover bid MERGERS & ACQUISITIONS firm's attempt to buy another an attempt by one company to acquire another. A takeover bid can be made either by a person or an organization, and usually takes the form of an approach to shareholders with an offer to purchase. The bidding stage is often difficult and fraught with politics, and various forms of ***knight*** may be involved.

Takeover Panel MERGERS & ACQUISITIONS, REGULATION & COMPLIANCE = ***City Panel on Takeovers and Mergers***

takeover ratio *UK* MERGERS & ACQUISITIONS indicator of likelihood that firm is acquisition target the ***book value*** of a company divided by its market capitalization. If the resulting figure is greater than one, then the company is a candidate for a takeover. *See also* ***appreciation, asset stripping***

takeover target MERGERS & ACQUISITIONS firm another company wants to purchase a company that another company has chosen to acquire by buying enough of its stock to control it

taker 1. STOCKHOLDING & INVESTMENTS buyer of option the buyer of an ***option*** to buy or sell at a particular price and time **2.** FINANCE borrower somebody who takes out a loan

take-up rate STOCKHOLDING & INVESTMENTS percentage of stockholders agreeing to buy more stock the percentage of acceptances of an offer to existing stockholders to buy more stock in a specific company

takings FINANCE = ***receipts***

talon STOCKHOLDING & INVESTMENTS form for ordering bond coupons a form attached to a ***bearer bond*** that the holder of the bond uses to order new coupons when those attached to the bond have been depleted

tangible asset ACCOUNTING firm's material resource an asset that has a physical presence, for example, buildings, cash, and stock. Leases and securities, although not physical in themselves, are classed as tangible assets because the underlying assets are physical. *See also* ***intangible asset***

tangible asset value *or* **tangible net worth** ACCOUNTING asset value expressed per share the value of all the assets of a company less its intangible assets such as goodwill, shown as a value per share

tangible book value ACCOUNTING value of all firm's material resources the book value of a company after intangible assets, patents, trademarks, and the value of research and development have been subtracted

tank STOCKHOLDING & INVESTMENTS drop steeply in price to fall suddenly and steeply, especially with reference to stock prices (*slang*)

tap CD FINANCE certificate of deposit issued on demand an issue of a ***certificate of deposit***, normally in a large denomination, at the request of a specific investor

tape ◇ don't fight the tape STOCKHOLDING & INVESTMENTS don't go against the direction of the market

taper relief TAX UK system for adjusting capital gains tax payable in the United Kingdom, a system of reduction in the capital gains tax payable on the disposal of assets by relating the proportion of the capital gain charged to tax to the length of time the asset has been owned. The reduction differs for business assets and non-business assets.

tap stock STOCKHOLDING & INVESTMENTS UK government stock issued over time in the United Kingdom, a government stock that is made available over a period of time in varying amounts

target 1. GENERAL MANAGEMENT goal of effort an end toward which effort is directed and on which resources are focused, usually to achieve an organization's strategy. **2.** MERGERS & ACQUISITIONS = ***target company***

target audience MARKETING likely consumers of product or service a group of people considered likely to buy a product or service

target cash balance FINANCE amount of money firm wants available the amount of cash that a company would like to have readily available

target company MERGERS & ACQUISITIONS firm subject to acquisition a company that is the object of a ***takeover bid***

targeted repurchase MERGERS & ACQUISITIONS buying back stock from firm's potential buyer a company's purchase of its own stock from somebody attempting to buy the company

target population STATISTICS group to be investigated in statistical study in a statistical study, a sample set of units such as events or people that is to be observed

target savings motive ECONOMICS desire to save money for particular goal the wish to have a specific item or to achieve a specific goal that gives people a reason to save

target stock level OPERATIONS & PRODUCTION supply of stored goods that meets likely customer demand the level of inventory that is needed to satisfy all demand for a product or component over a specific period

tariff 1. INTERNATIONAL TRADE government tax on imports or exports a government duty imposed on imports or exports to stimulate or dampen economic activity **2.** OPERATIONS & PRODUCTION list of prices a list of prices at which goods or services are supplied

Tariff Concession Scheme TAX Australian program for reduced duties on some imports a system operated by the Australian government in which imported goods that have no locally produced equivalent attract reduced duties. *Abbr* ***TCS***

tariff office INSURANCE UK insurance firm charging regulated premiums in the United Kingdom, an insurance company whose premiums are based on a scale set collectively by several companies

TARP *abbr* FINANCE ***Troubled Asset Relief Program***

tawarruq FINANCE sale for cash of item purchased by installments in Islamic financing, an arrangement in which somebody purchases an item from a bank on a deferred payment plan, then sells it immediately to obtain money. *See also* ***murabaha***

tax TAX government charge on people and firms a charge levied by a government on individuals and companies to pay for public services. Tax may be taken directly from income or indirectly through a sales tax or other indirect tax.

tax abatement TAX temporary reduction in tax owed a reduction in the amount of tax owed, usually for a short period of time

taxability TAX liability to tax the extent to which a good or individual is subject to a tax

taxable base TAX amount that can be taxed the amount of income that is subject to taxation, after allowances and deductions have been made

taxable gain *US* TAX profit liable to capital gains tax a profit from the sale of an asset that is subject to ***capital gains tax***. *UK term* ***chargeable gain***

taxable income TAX income that can be taxed the proportion of the income of a person, business, or organization that is subject to taxes

taxable matters TAX products that can be taxed goods or services that fall into a category of things that is subject to a tax

taxable supply TAX goods subject to VAT a supply of goods that are subject to tax in countries that have ***VAT***

tax adjustment TAX change to amount of tax owed a change made to the amount of tax owed

tax adviser TAX = ***tax consultant***

tax allowance TAX portion of UK income not taxed in the United Kingdom, a part of somebody's income that is not taxed. There are different reasons for receiving a tax allowance and they vary according to age and personal circumstances.

tax and price index ECONOMICS, TAX UK measure of household buying power in the United Kingdom, an index number showing the percentage change in gross income that taxpayers need if they are to maintain their real ***disposable income***

tax assessment TAX calculation of property value for tax an official calculation of the value of property for the purposes of taxation

taxation TAX **1.** system of raising public revenue the system of raising revenue for public funding by taxing individuals and organizations **2.** amount raised by tax the amount of money raised by imposing a tax

tax auditor *US* TAX official checking tax returns a government employee who investigates taxpayers' returns. *UK term* ***tax inspector***

tax avoidance TAX way of managing finances to pay less tax the organization of a taxpayer's affairs so that the minimum tax liability is incurred. Tax avoidance involves making the maximum use of all legal means of minimizing liability to taxation. *See also* ***tax evasion, tax break***

tax base TAX value of things taxed the taxable value of all property, goods, and activities taxed by a government

tax bracket TAX group of incomes with same tax rate a range of income levels subject to marginal tax at the same rate

tax break TAX special reduction in taxes an investment that is tax-efficient or a legal arrangement that reduces the liability to tax. *See also* ***tax avoidance, tax shelter***

tax code TAX **1.** number indicating UK tax allowance in the United Kingdom, a number given to indicate the amount somebody can earn before tax has to be paid **2.** US laws on tax in the United States, the system of laws and regulations regarding taxation

tax concession *UK* TAX tax reduction encouraging investment a tax reduction allowed, for example, to encourage investment in a particular type of industry

tax consultant TAX professional adviser on taxes a professional who advises on all aspects of taxation from tax avoidance to estate planning. *Also called* ***tax adviser***

tax court TAX US court deciding cases involving federal taxes in the United States, a court that deals with disputes between taxpayers and the Internal Revenue Service

tax credit TAX **1.** sum offset against tax a sum of money that can be offset against tax **2.** portion of UK dividend already taxed in the United Kingdom, the part of a dividend on which the company has already paid tax, so that the stockholder is not taxed on it **3.** deduction from individual's income tax liability an amount that can be subtracted directly to reduce somebody's income tax liability

tax-deductible TAX subtracted before tax calculation allowed to be removed from the total of income that will be subject to tax

tax-deferred TAX taxed later not to be taxed until a later time

tax deposit certificate TAX UK certificate showing advance payment of tax in the United Kingdom, a certificate showing that a taxpayer has deposited money in advance of an expected tax payment. The money earns interest while on deposit.

tax dodge TAX illegal way of avoiding taxes any illegal method of paying less tax than a person or company is obliged to pay (*informal*)

tax dollars TAX US taxes funding government the income taxes paid in the United States to fund the government

tax domicile TAX somebody's legal home for tax purposes a place that a government levying a tax considers to be somebody's home

tax-efficient TAX reducing tax due financially advantageous by leading to a reduction of the taxes that have to be paid

tax evasion TAX illegally not paying taxes the illegal practice of paying less money in taxes than is due. *See also* ***tax avoidance***

tax evasion amnesty TAX official forgiveness by government for not paying taxes a government measure that gives freedom from punishment to people who have evaded a tax

tax-exempt TAX **1.** not subject to expected tax not subject to tax though falling into a category of things that are usually subject to tax **2.** tax-free falling into a category of things that is legally exempted from a tax

tax exemption TAX **1.** freedom from specific tax liability freedom from having to pay specific taxes that would ordinarily be collected **2.** portion of income not taxed a part of somebody's income on which tax does not have to be paid

Tax-Exempt Special Savings Account STOCKHOLDING & INVESTMENTS *see* ***TESSA***

tax exile TAX **1.** living abroad to avoid tax residence in another country in order to avoid paying taxes in the home country **2.** person or firm moving abroad to avoid taxes a person or business that leaves a country to avoid paying taxes

tax-favored asset TAX resource taxed at lower rate an asset that receives more favorable tax treatment than some other asset

tax file number TAX Australian taxpayer's number in Australia, a unique identification number assigned to each taxpayer. *Abbr* ***TFN***

Tax File Number Withholding Tax TAX *see* ***TFN Withholding Tax***

tax-free TAX not subject to tax not subject to an expected tax

tax harmonization TAX making tax laws in different areas similar the enactment of taxation laws in different jurisdictions, such as neighboring countries, provinces, or states of the United States, that are consistent with one another

tax haven TAX place with attractively low tax rates a country that has generous tax laws, especially one that encourages noncitizens to base operations in the country to avoid higher taxes in their home countries

tax holiday *UK* TAX period when tax is waived an exemption from tax granted for a specific period of time, for example, when just starting out in business (*informal*)

tax incentive TAX lowering of taxes on specific activities a tax reduction given to encourage or support specific courses of action

tax inspector *UK* TAX = ***tax auditor***

tax invoice TAX in Australia and New Zealand, invoice specifying tax in Australia and New Zealand, a document issued by a supplier which stipulates the amount charged for goods or services as well as the amount of ***Goods and Services Tax*** payable

tax law TAX legislation regulating taxation the body of laws on taxation, or a specific law on an aspect of taxation

tax liability TAX tax payable by person or organization the amount of tax that a person or organization has to pay

tax lien TAX legal notice to recover tax a legal order to hold somebody's goods or property until a debt that is secured by the goods or property has been repaid

tax loophole TAX flaw in law allowing tax avoidance an ambiguity in a tax law that enables some individuals or companies to avoid or reduce taxes

tax loss TAX financial loss claimable against tax a transaction that results in a reduced tax liability, even though it may not be associated with an actual cash loss, for example, a loss associated with depreciation

tax loss carry back TAX using current losses to lower past year's taxes the reduction of taxes in a previous year, by subtraction from income for that year of losses suffered in the current year

tax loss carry forward TAX using current losses to lower future taxes the reduction of taxes in a future year, by subtraction from income for that year of losses suffered in the current year

tax obligation TAX how much tax is owed the amount of tax that a person, business, or organization owes

tax on capital income TAX tax on selling assets a tax on a business's income from sales of capital assets

tax payable TAX how much tax is due the amount of tax a person or company has to pay

taxpayer TAX somebody paying tax a person, business, or organization that pays a tax

tax planning TAX planning of tax avoidance the process of planning how to avoid paying too much tax, for example by investing in tax-exempt bonds

tax rate TAX percentage of income due in tax the rate at which a tax is payable, usually expressed as a percentage

tax refund TAX overpaid tax money returned to taxpayer an amount that a government gives back to a taxpayer who has paid more taxes than were due

tax relief TAX reduction in taxes deductions and exemptions allowed taxpayers for specific expenses or losses they may have incurred, or because of their age or status as a caregiver, etc

tax return TAX form for calculating and reporting taxes owed an official form on which a company or individual enters details of income and expenses, used to assess tax liability. *Also called* ***return***

tax revenue FINANCE, TAX money from taxes the money that a government receives in taxes from any source

tax sale TAX government's sale of property for unpaid tax in the United States, the sale of an item by a government to recover overdue taxes on a taxable item

tax shelter TAX arrangement to avoid tax a financial arrangement designed to avoid or reduce tax liability. *See also* ***abusive tax shelter, tax break***

tax subsidy TAX special lowering of taxes for business a tax reduction that a government gives a business for a particular purpose, usually to create jobs.

tax system TAX processes for taxation an organized and integrated method for imposing and collecting taxes

tax threshold *UK* TAX point at which tax rate changes a point at which another percentage of tax is payable

tax treaty TAX agreement between nations concerning taxes an international agreement that deals with taxes, especially taxes by several countries on the same individuals

tax year TAX period for which taxes are calculated a 12-month period covered by a statement for taxation purposes about income, spending, and allowable deductions

T-bill *abbr* STOCKHOLDING & INVESTMENTS ***Treasury bill***

T-bond *abbr* STOCKHOLDING & INVESTMENTS ***Treasury bond***

TCO *abbr* GENERAL MANAGEMENT ***total cost of ownership***

T-commerce E-COMMERCE business via TV business that is conducted by means of interactive television

TCS *abbr* TAX ***Tariff Concession Scheme***

TDB *abbr* FINANCE ***Trade Development Board***

teaser MARKETING advertising that interests customers in learning more an advertisement that gives a little information about a product in order to attract customers by making them curious to know more

teaser rate MORTGAGES special temporary interest rate to attract customers a temporary concessionary interest rate offered on mortgages or credit cards in order to attract new customers (*informal*)

technical analysis STOCKHOLDING & INVESTMENTS examination of changes in investment prices the analysis of past movements in the prices of financial instruments, currencies, commodities, etc., with a view to predicting future price movements by applying analytical techniques. *See also* ***fundamental analysis, qualitative analysis, quantitative analysis***

technical correction MARKETS when stock price changes to match true value a situation where a stock price or a currency moves up or down because it was previously too low or too high, due to technical factors

technical rally MARKETS short-term price increase against prevailing market decrease a temporary rise in security or commodity prices while the market is in a general decline. This may be because investors are seeking bargains, or because analysts have noted a support level.

technical reserves *UK* INSURANCE = ***insurance reserves***

Technology and Human Resources for Industry Programme FINANCE *see* ***THRIP***

technology stock STOCKHOLDING & INVESTMENTS shares in technology firms stock issued by a company that is involved in new technology

TED spread MARKETS yield difference between LIBOR and US Treasury bills the difference in yield between commercial ***LIBOR*** rates and US ***Treasury bills***. *Full form* ***Treasury Eurodollar spread***

teeming and lading *UK* ACCOUNTING = ***lapping***

telebanking BANKING = ***telephone banking***

telecommuter GENERAL MANAGEMENT, HR & PERSONNEL = ***teleworker***

teleconferencing GENERAL MANAGEMENT meetings conducted via telephones or TV channels the use of telephone or television channels to connect people in different locations in order to conduct group discussions, meetings, conferences, or courses

telegraphic transfer BANKING means of moving money abroad a method of transferring funds from a bank to a financial institution overseas, using telephone or cable. *Abbr* ***TT***

teleimmersion GENERAL MANAGEMENT advanced teleconferencing creating impression of physical immediacy an enhanced teleconferencing technology that uses banks of video cameras linked to computers, enabling users in remote locations to collaborate as if they were in the same room

telephone banking BANKING accessing bank account by telephone a system in which customers can access their accounts and a variety of banking services 24 hours a day by telephone. *Also called* ***telebanking***

telephone number salary FINANCE very high salary a six- or seven-figure salary, especially one aspired to or considered undeserved (*informal*)

teleworker GENERAL MANAGEMENT, HR & PERSONNEL employee who works largely remotely an employee who spends a substantial amount of working time away from the employer's main premises and communicates with the organization through the use of computing and telecommunications equipment. *Also called* ***telecommuter***

teller *US* BANKING bank employee dealing with customers face to face an employee in a bank or savings and loan association who deals in person with customers' deposits and withdrawals. *UK term* ***cashier***

tenancy in common LEGAL joint ownership without right to inherit other's share a type of ownership in property in which two or more people each have the right to enjoy the entire property but have no right to automatically inherit other owners' shares

tenant REAL ESTATE somebody renting place to live or work a person or company that rents a house, apartment, or office to live or work in

tenbagger STOCKHOLDING & INVESTMENTS investment with big increase in value an investment that increases in value ten times over its purchase price (*slang*)

tender 1. STOCKHOLDING & INVESTMENTS make offer for investment product at auction to bid for securities at auction. The securities are allocated according to the method adopted by the issuer. In the standard auction style, the investor receives the security at the price they tendered. In a Dutch style auction, the issuer announces a strike price after all the tenders have been examined. This is set at a level where all the issue is sold. Investors who submitted a tender above the strike price just pay the strike price. The Dutch style of auction is increasingly being adopted in the United Kingdom. US Treasury bills are also sold using the Dutch system. *See also* ***offer for sale, sale by tender*** **2.** GENERAL MANAGEMENT submit price to do work to offer to undertake work or supply goods at a specific price, usually in response to an invitation to bid for a work contract in competition with other suppliers **3.** OPERATIONS & PRODUCTION statement outlining acceptable price for job a statement of what a person or company is willing to accept when offering to undertake a major piece of work or supply goods, given in response to request to bid competitively for the work. *See also* ***quote***

tenderer *UK* OPERATIONS & PRODUCTION = ***bidder***

tender offer *US* MERGERS & ACQUISITIONS price offered for takeover the price at which a prospective buyer offers to purchase a controlling interest in a business or corporation. *UK term* ***takeover approach***

10-K ACCOUNTING US firm's official yearly financial statement the filing of a US company's annual accounts with the New York Stock Exchange

tenor FINANCE period before bill of exchange can be paid the period of time that has to elapse before a bill of exchange becomes payable

10-Q ACCOUNTING US firm's official quarterly financial statement the filing of a US company's quarterly accounts with the New York Stock Exchange

term STOCKHOLDING & INVESTMENTS period before investment product is fully payable the period of time that has to elapse from the date of the initial investment before a security or other investment such as a term deposit or endowment insurance becomes redeemable or reaches its maturity date

term assurance *UK* INSURANCE = ***term insurance***

term bill FINANCE = ***period bill***

term deposit BANKING savings held for a specified period in the United Kingdom, a deposit account held for a fixed period. Withdrawals are either not allowed during this period, or they involve a fee payable by the depositor.

terminal bonus INSURANCE bonus received at policy maturity date in the United Kingdom, a bonus received when insurance comes to an end

terminal date *UK* STOCKHOLDING & INVESTMENTS end date for futures contract the day on which a ***futures contract*** expires and the buyer must take delivery. *Also called* ***delivery date***

terminal market MARKETS place for trading futures contracts an exchange on which futures contracts or spot deals for commodities are traded

termination clause LEGAL clause detailing termination of contract a clause that explains how and when a contract can be terminated

term insurance INSURANCE insurance that is valid for specified period insurance, especially life insurance, that is in effect for a specified period of time. *UK term* ***term assurance***

term loan FINANCE debt arrangement for specified period a loan for a fixed period, usually called a ***personal loan*** when it is for non-business purposes. While a personal loan is usually at a fixed rate of interest, a term loan to a business may be at either a fixed or variable rate. Term loans may be either secured or unsecured. An early payment fee is usually payable when such a loan is repaid before the end of the term. *See also* ***balloon loan, bullet loan***

terms STOCKHOLDING & INVESTMENTS conditions attached to new issue the conditions that apply to an issue of shares of stock

term share BANKING building society account for specified period in the United Kingdom, a share account in a building society that is for a fixed period of time. Withdrawals are usually not allowed during this period. However, if they are, then a fee is usually payable by the account holder.

terms of sale OPERATIONS & PRODUCTION agreed conditions attached to sale the conditions attached to a sale and agreed to by buyer and seller, for example, payment due dates, method of payment, and delivery date

term structure of interest rates STOCKHOLDING & INVESTMENTS discount pattern for each year to maturity a set of interest rates for each year to maturity of fixed-rate securities such as bonds of differing ***term***. *See also* ***yield to maturity***

terotechnology OPERATIONS & PRODUCTION techniques designed to optimize life of assets a multidisciplinary technique that combines the areas of management, finance, and engineering with the goal of optimizing life-cycle costs for physical assets and technologies. Terotechnology is concerned with acquiring and caring for physical assets. It covers the specification and design for the reliability and maintainability of plant, machinery, equipment, buildings, and structures, including the installation, commissioning, maintenance, and replacement of this plant, and also incorporates the feedback of information on design, performance, and costs.

tertiary industry BUSINESS business providing a service an industry that does not produce raw materials or manufacture products but offers a service such as banking, retailing, or accountancy

tertiary sector ECONOMICS part of economy involving nonprofit organizations the part of the economy made up of nonprofit organizations such as consumer associations

TESSA STOCKHOLDING & INVESTMENTS former untaxed UK bank account a former UK savings account in which investors could save up to £9,000 over a period of five years and not pay any tax, provided they made no withdrawals over that time. *Full form* ***Tax Exempt Special Savings Account***

test STOCKHOLDING & INVESTMENTS assessment of likely stock price movements in technical analysis, a way of determining whether to buy or sell a stock by observing if it is likely to rise above or drop below specific price levels that it has had difficulty breaking through in the past

testacy LEGAL possession of valid will at death the legal position of somebody who has died leaving a valid will

testate LEGAL having valid will at death used to refer to somebody who has died leaving a valid will

testator LEGAL somebody with valid will a person who has made a valid will or left a legacy

testatrix LEGAL woman with valid will a woman who has made a valid will or left a legacy

test level STOCKHOLDING & INVESTMENTS barrier price level a specific price level that a stock has had difficulty breaking through in the past. In technical analysis, it is used in determining whether to buy or sell a stock.

TFN *abbr* TAX ***tax file number***

TFN Withholding Tax TAX Australian tax when information missing in Australia, a levy imposed on financial transactions involving somebody who has not disclosed his or her tax file number. *Full form* ***Tax File Number Withholding Tax***

theta STOCKHOLDING & INVESTMENTS ratio of option's decreasing value to decreasing time a ratio between the rate of decrease in the value of an option and the decrease in time as it approaches expiration. *Also called* ***time decay***

thin market MARKETS exchange where little trading is happening a market where the trading volume is low. A characteristic of such a market is a wide spread of bid and offer prices.

third market MARKETS secondary stock exchange a market other than the main stock exchange in which stocks are traded

third party LEGAL person other than two main parties to contract a person other than the two main parties involved in a contract, for example, in an insurance contract, anyone who is not the insurance company nor the person who is insured

third-party network *or* **third-party service provider** E-COMMERCE = ***value-added network***

third quarter ACCOUNTING third of four divisions of fiscal year the period of three months from July to the end of September, or the period of three months following the second quarter of the fiscal year. *Abbr* ***Q3***

third sector ECONOMICS part of economy involving nonprofit organizations the part of the economy made up of ***nonprofit organizations*** such as charities, professional associations, labor unions, and religious, arts, community, research, and campaigning bodies. *See also* ***nonprofit organization***

three-dimensional management *or* **3-D management** GENERAL MANAGEMENT theory of management styles a theory outlining eight styles of management that differ in effectiveness, four that are effective and four that are less effective. Different styles may be used in different types of work settings and managers modify their style to suit different circumstances.

360 degree branding LEGAL, STOCKHOLDING & INVESTMENTS supporting brand identity by all marketing activity taking an inclusive approach in branding a product by bringing the brand to all points of consumer contact

3i BANKING bank-owned group providing company finance a finance group owned by the big British commercial banks which provides finance to other companies, especially small ones

three steps and a stumble MARKETS if interest rates increase three times, stocks fall a rule of thumb used on the US stock market that if the Federal Reserve increases interest rates three times consecutively, stock market prices will go down

threshold GENERAL MANAGEMENT starting point the point at which something begins or changes

threshold agreement FINANCE UK contract promising pay raise in specific situation in the United Kingdom, a contract that says that if the cost of living goes up by more than an agreed amount, pay will go up to match it

threshold company BUSINESS emerging company a company that is on the verge of becoming well established in the business world

threshold price OPERATIONS & PRODUCTION lowest sale price for imports into EU in the European Union, the lowest price at which farm produce imported into the EU can be sold

thrift 1. FINANCE care in managing money a cautious attitude toward the management of money, shown by saving, or spending it carefully and looking for good value **2.** BANKING private local US bank for small investors in the United States, a private local bank, savings and loan association, or credit union, that accepts and pays interest on deposits from small investors

thrift institution BANKING US institution acting like savings bank in the United States, an institution that is not a bank but accepts savings deposits and makes loans to savers. *See also* ***savings and loan association, savings bank***

THRIP FINANCE S. African program supporting industry research and development in South Africa, a collaborative program involving industry, government, and educational and research institutions, which supports research and development in technology, science, and engineering. *Full form* ***Technology and Human Resources for Industry Programme***

TIBOR *abbr* MARKETS ***Tokyo Interbank Offered Rate***

tick STOCKHOLDING & INVESTMENTS smallest amount price or rate can change the least amount by which a value such as the price of a stock or a rate of interest can rise or fall, for example, a hundredth of a percentage point or an eighth of a dollar ◇ have ticks in all the right boxes GENERAL MANAGEMENT to be on course to meet a series of objectives

ticker *or* **ticker tape** MARKETS continuous display of stock prices the electronic display of stock prices that stream across a computer or television screen. The information was formerly produced on continuous paper tape.

ticker symbol MARKETS letters representing stocks traded on stock exchange letter or letters used to identify the stocks or funds listed for trade on a stock exchange

tied loan FINANCE loan to foreign country to buy lender's products a loan made by one national government to another on the condition that the funds are used to purchase goods from the lending nation

Tier 1 capital BANKING bank's core capital funds the core capital of a bank, mainly consisting of stockholders' funds, which is used by regulators as a measure of a bank's stability

Tier 1 capital ratio BANKING ratio of bank's core to supplementary funds the relationship between the amount of Tier 1 capital and other capital held by a bank. *See also* ***capital adequacy ratio***

Tier 2 capital BANKING bank's supplementary funds funds such as undisclosed reserves, held by a bank in addition to its core capital of stockholders' funds. *Also called* ***supplementary capital***

tiger MARKETS Hong Kong, S. Korea, Singapore, or Taiwan any of the key markets in the Pacific Basin region except Japan, i.e. Hong Kong, South Korea, Singapore, and Taiwan

tight money ECONOMICS situation where borrowing money is difficult a situation where it is expensive to borrow because of restrictive government policy or high demand

tight money policy ECONOMICS government policy restricting money supply a government policy to restrict money supply, usually by raising interest rates, making it more difficult to borrow and spend money

TILA *abbr* LEGAL ***Truth in Lending Act***

time and material pricing FINANCE determining price based on work and materials a form of ***cost-plus pricing*** in which price is determined by reference to the cost of the labor and material inputs to the product or service

time bargain MARKETS stock exchange trade for future date a stock market transaction in which the securities are deliverable at a future date beyond the exchange's normal settlement day

time decay STOCKHOLDING & INVESTMENTS = ***theta***

time deposit BANKING US savings arrangement for specified period a US savings account or a certificate of deposit, issued by a financial institution. While the savings account is for a fixed term, deposits are accepted with the understanding that withdrawals may be made subject to a period of notice. Banks are authorized to require at least 30 days' notice. While a certificate of deposit is equivalent to a term account, passbook accounts are generally regarded as funds readily available to the account holder.

time draft BANKING type of US bill of exchange a bill of exchange drawn on and accepted by a US bank. It is either an ***after date*** bill or ***after sight*** bill.

times covered STOCKHOLDING & INVESTMENTS ability of net profit to pay firm's dividend the number of times a company's dividends to ordinary stockholders could be paid out of its net after-tax profits. This measures the likelihood of dividend payments being sustained, and is a useful indication of sustained profitability. *Also called* ***dividend cover***

time series STATISTICS collection of data at intervals a series of measurements collected at uniformly spaced intervals of time, sometimes over a period of several years, used to assess long-term trends and seasonal fluctuations

time spread MARKETS simultaneously buying and selling options with different maturities the purchase and sale of options in the same commodity or security with the same price and different ***maturities***

time value MARKETS market value minus face value the premium at which an option is trading relative to its ***intrinsic value***

time value of money FINANCE potential growth in value over time the principle that a specific amount of money is worth more now than it will be at a date in the future, because the sum available now can be invested and will have grown in value by the date in the future

tip STOCKHOLDING & INVESTMENTS recommendation given by expert a piece of useful expert information, for example, a recommendation about a product or a ***stock tip***

tip-off STOCKHOLDING & INVESTMENTS confidential information a piece of confidential information about something that is going to happen, or a warning based on confidential financial or commercial information. *See also* ***insider dealing, money laundering***

title LEGAL right of ownership a legal right to the ownership of property. If somebody has good title to a property, proof of ownership is beyond doubt.

title deed LEGAL document showing real estate ownership a document showing who is the owner of real estate

title insurance INSURANCE protection from problems in legal title an insurance policy that protects a purchaser or lender from loss of real property due to defects in the ***title***

toasted FINANCE having suffered financial losses used to refer to someone or something that has lost money (*slang*)

Tobin tax TAX **1.** levy on foreign currency dealings a tax imposed on foreign transactions with the aim of securing greater economic stability and protecting currencies from speculators. It was proposed by US economist James Tobin (1918-2002). **2.** levy on financial transactions a tax imposed on a financial transaction of any kind

toehold purchase *or* **toehold** MERGERS & ACQUISITIONS small stake in corporation in the United States, the acquisition of less than 5% of the outstanding stock in a company that is targeted for a takeover. At the 5% level, the acquiring company must notify the Securities and Exchange Commission and the targeted company of its plans.

token charge OPERATIONS & PRODUCTION small charge levied as token gesture a small charge that does not cover the real costs of providing the goods or services

token payment FINANCE small payment made as token gesture a small payment made only so that a payment of some sort is seen to be made

Tokyo Interbank Offered Rate MARKETS in Japan, rate for banks' offers of deposits on the Japanese money markets, the rate at which banks will offer to make deposits in yen with each other, often used as a reference rate. The deposits are for terms from overnight up to five years. *Abbr* ***TIBOR***

tombstone FINANCE newspaper notice detailing large loan for business a notice in the financial press giving details of a large lending facility, or large equity or debt securities offerings, to a business. It may relate to a management buyout or to a package that may include an ***interest rate cap*** and ***collars*** to finance a specific package. More than one bank may be involved. Although it may appear to be an advertisement, technically in most jurisdictions it is regarded as a statement of fact and therefore falls outside the advertisement regulations. The borrower generally pays for the advertisement, though it is the financial institutions that derive the most benefit.

top-down approach GENERAL MANAGEMENT leadership style with managers driving changes an autocratic style of leadership in which strategies and solutions are identified by senior management and then cascaded down through an organization. The top-down approach can be considered a feature of large bureaucracies. A number of management gurus have criticized it as an out-of-date style that leads to stagnation and business failure. *See also* ***bottom-up approach***

top management HR & PERSONNEL senior members of firm the upper-level managers of an organization or company, especially the ***senior management*** or a ***board of directors*** (*informal*)

top slicing 1. STOCKHOLDING & INVESTMENTS sale of holding yielding original cost of investment selling part of a stockholding that will realize a sum that is equal to the original cost of the investment. What remains therefore represents potential pure profit. **2.** TAX in UK, assessment of tax on mature investments in the United Kingdom, a complex method used by HM Revenue & Customs for assessing what tax, if any, is paid when some investment bonds or endowment policies mature or are cashed in early

total absorption costing ACCOUNTING accountant's method of pricing goods and services a method used by a cost accountant to price goods and services, allocating both direct and indirect costs. Although this method is designed so that all of an organization's costs are covered, it may result in opportunities being missed because of high prices. Consequently sales may be lost that could contribute to overheads. *See also* ***marginal costing***

total assets FINANCE sum of assets owned by person or organization the total value of all current and long-term assets owned by a person or organization

total cost OPERATIONS & PRODUCTION sum of costs of producing amount of something all the costs of producing a specific amount of something, including fixed costs and variable costs

total cost of ownership GENERAL MANAGEMENT cost including all aspects of ownership a structured approach to calculating the ***costs*** associated with buying and using a product or service. Total cost of ownership takes the purchase cost of an item into account but also considers related costs such as ordering, delivery, subsequent usage and maintenance, supplier costs, and after-delivery costs. Originally designed as a process for measuring IT expense after implementation, total cost of ownership considers only financial expenses and excludes any ***cost-benefit analysis***. *Abbr* ***TCO***

total overhead cost variance ACCOUNTING difference between actual and absorbed overhead costs the difference between the overhead costs absorbed and the actual overhead costs incurred, both fixed and variable

total quality management GENERAL MANAGEMENT integrated system of business planning an integrated and comprehensive system of planning and controlling all business functions so that products or services are produced which meet or exceed customer expectations. TQM is a philosophy of business behavior, embracing principles such as employee involvement, continuous improvement at all levels, and customer focus, as well as being a collection of related techniques, such as full documentation of activities, clear goal-setting, and performance measurement from the customer perspective, that are aimed at improving quality. *Abbr* ***TQM***

total responsibility management GENERAL MANAGEMENT procedures ensuring responsible business practices systems and procedures to ensure responsible business practices and management. It is used to describe the codes of practice and systems that organizations are developing to manage their social, environmental, and ethical responsibilities in response to pressures from stakeholders, emerging global standards, general social trends, and institutional expectations. Some issues, linked to labor, ecology, and community, are included because they are subject to increasing assessment or regulation, while others are raised intermittently as a result of public controversies.

total return STOCKHOLDING & INVESTMENTS percentage change in overall value of investment the total percentage change in the value of an investment over a specified time period, including capital gains, dividends, and the investment's appreciation or depreciation.

The total return formula reflects all the ways in which an investment can earn or lose money, resulting in an increase or decrease in the investment's ***net asset value*** (NAV):

(Dividends + Capital gains distributions +/– Change in NAV) / Beginning NAV = Total return

If, for instance, you buy a stock with an initial NAV of $40, and after one year it pays an income dividend of $2 per share and a capital gains distribution of $1, and its NAV has increased to $42, then the stock's total return would be:

$(2 + 1 + 2) / 40 = 5 / 40 = 0.125 \times 100\% = 12.5\%$

The total return time frame is usually one year, and it assumes that dividends have been reinvested. It does not take into account any sales charges that an investor paid to invest in a fund, or taxes they might owe on the income dividends and capital gains distributions received.

total revenue FINANCE total income from all sources all income from all sources

total utility ECONOMICS consumer's total satisfaction from good or service the overall satisfaction that a consumer receives from consuming a particular quantity of a specific good or service

touch MARKETS difference between best bid and offer prices the difference between the best bid and the best offer price quoted by all market makers for a specific security

touch price MARKETS best gap between bid and offer prices the largest available difference between the bid and offer prices of a security

toxic FINANCE, STOCKHOLDING & INVESTMENTS adversely affecting financial status damaging to financial health. The term as applied to loans, debt, assets, and financial instruments such as mortgages, bonds and other securities refers to finance that is risky and potentially seriously damaging not only to the owner but to the financial system as a whole (*informal*).

toxic waste STOCKHOLDING & INVESTMENTS high-risk securities new securities with unusually high risk, often notes that have as collateral the riskiest portions of numerous issues of otherwise relatively low-risk debt (*slang*)

TQM *abbr* GENERAL MANAGEMENT ***total quality management***

tracker fund STOCKHOLDING & INVESTMENTS = ***index fund***

tracking 1. STOCKHOLDING & INVESTMENTS investing to match a market index the practice of buying investments in order to achieve the same or a similar return to a market index **2.** MARKETING research into changing perception of product or organization research designed to monitor changes in the public perception of a product or organization over a period of time

tracking error STOCKHOLDING & INVESTMENTS degree to which fund fails to track index the deviation by which an ***index fund*** fails to replicate the index it is aiming to mirror

tracking stock STOCKHOLDING & INVESTMENTS stock with dividends linked to performance of subsidiary a stock whose dividends are tied to the performance of a subsidiary of the corporation that owns it

trade OPERATIONS & PRODUCTION **1.** carry on a business to buy and sell products, or carry on a business **2.** buying and selling the business of buying and selling goods or, in some situations, bartering goods **3.** particular type of business a particular type of business, or the people or companies dealing in the same type of product **4.** one transaction a single activity of buying or selling that is carried out

trade agreement INTERNATIONAL TRADE trading agreement between countries an international agreement between countries over general terms of trade

trade association OPERATIONS & PRODUCTION organization promoting interests of particular trade a membership organization of businesses in the same trade that promotes the interests of the businesses

trade balance INTERNATIONAL TRADE = ***balance of trade***

trade barrier INTERNATIONAL TRADE government-imposed impediment to international trade a condition imposed by a government to limit the free exchange of goods internationally. Nontariff barriers, safety standards, and tariffs are typical trade barriers.

trade bill FINANCE bill of exchange between trading partners a bill of exchange between two businesses that trade with each other. *See also* ***acceptance credit***

trade credit FINANCE credit offered to trading partner credit offered by one business when trading with another. Typically this is for one month from the date of the invoice, but it could be for a shorter or longer period.

trade cycle INTERNATIONAL TRADE period of cyclical fluctuations in trade a period during which trade expands, then slows down, then expands again

trade date STOCKHOLDING & INVESTMENTS date of a purchase or sale the date on which a buyer and seller reach an agreement for the purchase and sale of an asset

trade debt FINANCE debt from normal trading a debt that originates during the normal course of trade

trade debtor FINANCE debtor with debt incurred through normal trading a person or company that owes money to a company as a result of the normal activities of trading

trade deficit INTERNATIONAL TRADE extent to which imports exceed exports the difference in value between a country's imports and exports when its imports exceed its exports. *Also called* ***balance of payments deficit***. *See also* ***trade gap***

trade description REGULATION & COMPLIANCE legal description of product a description of a product provided by the manufacturer and controlled for accuracy by the ***Trade Descriptions Act***

Trade Descriptions Act REGULATION & COMPLIANCE UK legislation governing product description in the United Kingdom, an act that limits the way in which products can be described so as to protect customers from wrong descriptions made by manufacturers

Trade Development Board INTERNATIONAL TRADE agency promoting trade with Singapore companies a Singapore government agency that was established in 1983 to promote trade and explore new markets for Singapore products, and offers various programs of assistance to companies. *Abbr* ***TDB***

trade discount OPERATIONS & PRODUCTION price reduction for person in same trade a reduction in price given to a customer in the same trade

traded option STOCKHOLDING & INVESTMENTS option bought and sold on exchange an option that can be continuously traded on an exchange

trade gap INTERNATIONAL TRADE gap between imports and exports the difference between the value of a country's imports and that of its exports. *See also* ***trade deficit***

trade-in *US* FINANCE using old product as partial payment for new the act of giving an old product as part of the payment for a new one. *UK term* ***part exchange***

trade investment STOCKHOLDING & INVESTMENTS investment of one business in another the action or process of one business making a loan to another, or buying stock in another. The latter may be the first stages of a friendly ***takeover bid***.

trademark GENERAL MANAGEMENT unique mark identifying product with producer an identifiable mark on a product that may be a symbol, words, or both, that connects the product to the trader or producer of that product and gives the producer or trader protection from fraudulent use. Any use of the trademark without permission gives the owner the right to sue for damages. In the United States, trademarks are controlled by the United States Patent and Trademark Office. In the United Kingdom, a trademark can be registered at the Register of Trademarks maintained by the Intellectual Property Office.

trade mission INTERNATIONAL TRADE foreign visit for purpose of discussing trade a visit by businesspeople from one country to another for the purpose of discussing trade between their respective nations

trade name MARKETING proprietary name of product or service the proprietary name given by the producer or manufacturer to a product or service. A trade name occasionally becomes the generic name for products of a similar nature, for example, "Thermos" is often applied to all insulated flasks, and "Kleenex" to all tissues.

TRADENZ *abbr* BUSINESS ***New Zealand Trade Development Board***

tradeoff OPERATIONS & PRODUCTION exchange of items or concessions in business deal an act of exchanging one thing for another as part of a business deal

trade point MARKETS informal, minor stock exchange a stock exchange that is less formal than the major exchanges

trader MARKETS **1.** = ***floor trader*** **2.** = ***market maker***

trader's index MARKETS *see* ***TRIN***

trade surplus INTERNATIONAL TRADE extent to which exports exceed imports the difference in value between a country's imports and exports when its exports exceed its imports. *Also called* ***balance of payments surplus***

trade union *UK* GENERAL MANAGEMENT, HR & PERSONNEL = ***labor union***

trade war INTERNATIONAL TRADE competition between countries for market share a competition between two or more countries for a share of international or domestic trade

trade-weighted index CURRENCY & EXCHANGE measure of country's currency against trading partners' currencies an index that measures the value of a country's currency in relation to the currencies of its trading partners

trading MARKETS buying and selling goods the business of buying and selling goods or assets

trading account ACCOUNTING = ***profit and loss account***

trading area BUSINESS area where business is concentrated the area in which a company does most of its business, or the area around a city that is the main center of a region

trading company BUSINESS firm that buys and sells goods a company that specializes in buying and selling goods

trading floor MARKETS where dealers trade face to face an area in a stock exchange or similar market where dealers meet to trade with each other personally

trading halt MARKETS cessation of trade in firm's stock a stoppage of trading in a stock on an exchange, usually in response to information about a company, or concern about rapid movement of the stock price. *See also* ***suspended trading***

trading limit MARKETS maximum amount allowed to single trader the maximum amount of a product that can be traded by a single trader

trading loss FINANCE sales income lower than expenditure a situation in which the amount of money an organization receives in sales is less than its expenditure

trading partner 1. BUSINESS, INTERNATIONAL TRADE firm or country doing business with another one of two or more businesses or countries that engage in trade with each other **2.** E-COMMERCE partner in electronic data interchange transaction the merchant, customer, or financial institution with whom an EDI (***electronic data interchange***) transaction takes place. Transactions can be either between senders and receivers of EDI messages or within distribution channels in an industry, for example, financial institutions or wholesalers.

trading pit MARKETS *see* ***pit***

trading profit ACCOUNTING = ***gross profit***

trading range MARKETS difference between highest and lowest prices the difference between the highest and lowest price for a stock or bond over a period of time. *Also called* ***historical trading range***

trading session MARKETS one trading day in stock or commodities market a period of one day of buying and selling at a stock or commodities exchange from the opening bell to the closing bell

trading stamp OPERATIONS & PRODUCTION stamp exchanged for goods in store a special stamp given away by a store, which the customer can collect and exchange later for free goods

traditional IRA PENSIONS retirement savings facility in the United States, the original ***IRA***, that allows individuals to set up retirement accounts, contributions to which are tax-deductible up to a specific amount depending on income. *See also* ***rollover IRA, Roth IRA***

training levy TAX UK tax funding government's training programs in the United Kingdom, a tax to be paid by companies to fund the government's training programs

tranche STOCKHOLDING & INVESTMENTS one installment in series one of a series of installments, used, for example, when referring to loans to companies, government securities that are issued over a period of time, or money withdrawn by a country from the IMF

tranche CD BANKING certificate of deposit sold in series over time a ***certificate of deposit*** that is part of a set that is sold by the issuing bank over a period of time. Each of the CDs in a tranche has the same maturity date.

transaction 1. BUSINESS business negotiation an act of negotiating something or carrying out a business deal **2.** MARKETS instance of trading an instance of buying or selling a security, currency, or commodity **3.** E-COMMERCE item of business transmitted electronically any item or collection of sequential items of business that are enclosed in encrypted form in an electronic envelope and transmitted between trading partners

transaction costs STOCKHOLDING & INVESTMENTS direct costs of buying or selling asset incremental costs that are directly attributable to the buying or selling of an asset. Transaction costs include commissions, fees, and direct taxes.

transaction e-commerce E-COMMERCE electronic selling the electronic sale of goods and services, either business-to-business or business-to-customer

transaction exposure CURRENCY & EXCHANGE, RISK risk in international trade from changing exchange rates the risk that an organization may incur major losses from the effects of foreign exchange rate changes during the time it takes to arrange the export or import of goods or services. Transaction exposure is present from the time a price is set.

transaction file OPERATIONS & PRODUCTION means of tracking inventory a file for keeping track of inventory use and replenishment. *See also* ***inventory record***

transaction history STOCKHOLDING & INVESTMENTS record of trades with broker a record of all of an investor's transactions with a broker

transaction message *or* **transaction set** E-COMMERCE electronic document exchanged in e-commerce transaction the EDI (***electronic data interchange***) equivalent of a paper document, exchanged as part of an e-commerce transaction, comprising at least one data segment representing the document sandwiched between a header and a trailer. It is called a transaction message in the UN/EDIFACT protocol and a transaction set in the ANSI X.12 protocol.

transactions motive ECONOMICS desire to keep cash for upcoming purchases the motive that consumers have to hold money for their likely purchases in the immediate future

transfer 1. BANKING movement of money between banks the movement of money through the domestic or international banking system, between banks in a ***clearing system***, or between particular bank accounts. *See also* ***BACS, Fedwire, SWIFT*. 2.** STOCKHOLDING & INVESTMENTS change of ownership the change of ownership of an asset or security

transferable LEGAL **1.** legally able to be passed on able to be legally passed into somebody else's ownership **2.** document eligible to be passed on a document such as a bearer bond that can be passed legally into somebody else's ownership

transfer agent STOCKHOLDING & INVESTMENTS agent handling transfers of ownership an agent employed by a corporation to keep a record of the owners of securities and handle transfers of ownership

transferee LEGAL somebody to whom an asset is transferred a person who receives ownership of an asset that is being transferred

transferor LEGAL somebody transferring asset to another a person who transfers the ownership of an asset or security to another person

transfer out fee STOCKHOLDING & INVESTMENTS fee for closing broker's account a fee payable when an investor closes an account with a broker

transfer price OPERATIONS & PRODUCTION price for goods or services within firm the price at which goods or services are transferred between different units of the same company. If those units are located in different countries, the term ***international transfer pricing*** is used.

The extent to which the transfer price covers costs and contributes to (internal) profit is a matter of policy. A transfer price may, for example, be based upon marginal cost, full cost, market price, or negotiation. Where the transferred products cross national boundaries, the transfer prices used may have to be agreed with the governments of the countries concerned.

transfer pricing OPERATIONS & PRODUCTION pricing method used between departments of organization a pricing method used when supplying products or services from one part of an organization to another. The transfer pricing method can be used to supply goods either at cost or at profit if profit targets are to be achieved. This can cause difficulties if an internal customer can buy more cheaply outside the organization. Multinational businesses have been known to take advantage of this pricing policy by transferring products from one country to another in order for profits to be higher in the country where corporation tax is lower.

transfer stamp REAL ESTATE, TAX mark on UK deeds showing payment of stamp duty in the United Kingdom, the mark embossed onto ***title deeds*** when property is transferred to signify that ***stamp duty*** has been paid

transfer value PENSIONS in UK, value of somebody's pension rights in the United Kingdom, the value of a person's rights in a pension when they are given up on acquiring rights in a new pension, for example, when somebody changes the company providing the pension. *See also* ***vested rights***

transit time OPERATIONS & PRODUCTION delay after completing operation the period between the completion of an operation and the availability of the material at the next workstation

translation exposure CURRENCY & EXCHANGE, RISK risk on business from changing exchange rates the risk that the balance sheet and income statement may be adversely affected by foreign exchange rate changes

transmission E-COMMERCE electronic data sent between trading partners digital data sent electronically from one trading partner to another, or from a trading partner to a ***value-added network***

transmission control standards E-COMMERCE format for exchanging electronic business data the defined format by which to address the ***electronic envelopes*** used by trading partners to exchange business data

transnational business *or* **transnational company** *or* **transnational corporation** *or* **transnational** BUSINESS = ***multinational business***

transparency MARKETS when information is freely available the condition in which nothing is hidden. This is an essential condition for a free market in securities. Prices, the volume of trading, and factual information must be available to all.

trash and cash MARKETS driving stock price down to repurchase more cheaply a trade of a security in which a trader sells a stock, then spreads negative information about the company whose stock they just sold, causing the stock's price to decline and enabling the trader to buy it back at a low price and make a profit

travel accident insurance INSURANCE travel insurance provided by credit card company a form of insurance coverage offered by some credit card companies when the whole or part of a travel arrangement is paid for with the card. In the event of death resulting from an accident in the course of travel, or the loss of eyesight or a limb, the credit card company will pay the cardholder, or his or her estate, a pre-stipulated sum. *See also* ***travel insurance***

traveler's checks BANKING checks for cashing in foreign country checks bought by a traveler that are valid for use at home or abroad, but are generally cashed in a foreign country. Only a countersignature is required from the holder for verification. *UK term* ***traveller's cheques***

travel insurance INSURANCE insurance for various risks associated with travel a form of insurance coverage that provides medical cover while abroad as well as covering the policyholder's possessions and money while traveling. Many travel insurance policies also reimburse the policyholder if a holiday has to be canceled and pay compensation for delayed journeys. *See also* ***travel accident insurance***

traveller's cheques BANKING = ***traveler's checks***

treasurer TREASURY MANAGEMENT officer responsible for money a person who is responsible for the funds and other assets of an organization

Treasurer FINANCE Australian government minister responsible for financial and economic matters in Australia, the minister responsible for financial and economic matters in a national, state, or territory government

treasuries STOCKHOLDING & INVESTMENTS US government securities negotiable debt instruments issued by the US government. *See also* ***Treasury bill, Treasury bond, Treasury note***

treasury TREASURY MANAGEMENT section of firm responsible for financial matters the department of a company or corporation that deals with all financial matters

Treasury FINANCE government department responsible for finance and economy in some countries, the government department responsible for the nation's financial policies as well as the management of the economy

Treasury bill STOCKHOLDING & INVESTMENTS discounted short-term security a short-term security issued by the US or UK government that is sold at a discount from face value and pays no interest but can be redeemed for full face value at maturity. *Abbr* ***T-bill***

Treasury bill rate STOCKHOLDING & INVESTMENTS effective interest earned from holding Treasury bill the rate of interest obtainable by holding a ***Treasury bill***. Although Treasury bills are non-interest bearing, by purchasing them at a discount and holding them to redemption, the discount is effectively the interest earned by holding these instruments. The Treasury bill rate is the discount expressed as a percentage of the issue price. It is annualized to give a rate per annum.

Treasury bond STOCKHOLDING & INVESTMENTS US government bond a bond issued by the US government that bears fixed interest. *Abbr* ***T-bond***

treasury direct STOCKHOLDING & INVESTMENTS trading system for US Treasury bills in the United States, a system offered through Federal Reserve banks that allows investors to buy and sell ***Treasury bills*** directly from the Federal Reserve

Treasury Eurodollar spread MARKETS *see* ***TED spread***

treasury inflation protected security STOCKHOLDING & INVESTMENTS US government security protected from inflation a security issued by the US government with principal and coupon payments that are increased automatically to protect against inflation

treasury management TREASURY MANAGEMENT firm's handling of all financial matters the corporate handling of all financial matters, the generation of external and internal funds for business, the management of currencies and cash flows, and the complex strategies, policies, and procedures of corporate finance

Treasury note STOCKHOLDING & INVESTMENTS **1.** US 2–10-year government security a fixed-interest security issued by the US government that can mature within two to ten years **2.** short-term debt instrument issued by Australian government a short-term debt instrument issued by the Australian federal government. Treasury notes are issued on a tender basis for periods of 13 and 26 weeks.

treasury stock STOCKHOLDING & INVESTMENTS shares of firm's stock bought back by firm shares of a company's stock that have been bought back by the company and not canceled. In the United States, these shares are shown as deductions from equity; in the United Kingdom, they are shown as assets in the balance sheet.

treaty 1. LEGAL written agreement between nations a written agreement between nations, such as the Treaty of Rome (1957), that was the foundation of the European Union **2.** INSURANCE contract in which reinsurer accepts insurer's risks a contract between an insurer and the reinsurer whereby the latter is to accept risks from the insurer **3.** REAL ESTATE = ***private treaty***

trend STATISTICS regular movement of variable values over time the movement in a specific direction of the values of a variable over a period of time

trendline STATISTICS pattern of change in variable values over time a visual representation of the direction of change shown by variables over a period of time

Treynor ratio ECONOMICS = ***risk-adjusted return on capital***

trial balance ACCOUNTING draft balance in bookkeeping in a double-entry bookkeeping system, a draft calculation of debits and credits to see if they balance

trickle-down theory ECONOMICS belief that benefits spread downward in economy the theory that financial and other benefits received by big businesses and wealthy people eventually spread down through an economy to the rest of society

trillion one million millions a sum equal to one million millions (1 plus 12 zeros). An older use in the United Kingdom was a larger number, 1 plus 18 zeros.

TRIN MARKETS measure of rising to falling stocks a market indicator calculated by dividing the advancing stocks by declining stocks and comparing it to the volume of advances to declines. A result less than one is considered bullish, and a result greater than one is considered bearish. *Full form* ***trader's index***

tripartite authority REGULATION & COMPLIANCE UK system of financial regulators in the United Kingdom, the financial regulatory system composed of the Treasury, Financial Services Authority, and the Bank of England

triple A STOCKHOLDING & INVESTMENTS = ***AAA***

triple bottom line GENERAL MANAGEMENT firm's environmental and social behavior, together with profitability environmental sustainability and social responsibility used as criteria when judging the overall performance of a company, in addition to purely financial considerations

triple I organization GENERAL MANAGEMENT corporate culture focusing on information, intelligence, and ideas a type of ***corporate culture*** in which the focus is on three areas: information, intelligence, and ideas. The triple I organization recognizes the value of information and learning. It minimizes the distinction between managers and workers, concentrating instead on people and the need to pursue learning, including personal, lifelong, and organizational learning, in order to keep up with the pace of change.

triple tax exempt TAX exempt from US tax at all levels in the United States, used to describe bonds, interest payments, and other sources of income that are exempt from federal, state, and local taxes

triple witching hour MARKETS joint maturity date for futures and options a time when stock options, stock index futures, and options on such futures all mature at once. Triple witching hours occur quarterly and are usually marked by highly volatile trading.

Troubled Asset Relief Program FINANCE federal government support for lenders in the United States, a federal government program established in response to the credit crunch of 2007-2008 by which the Treasury was authorized to buy mortgage-backed securities from financial institutions in an attempt to provide them with funds that would enable them to return to lending. *Abbr* ***TARP***

troubleshooter FINANCE consultant employed by firm in difficulty an independent person, often a consultant, who is called in by a company in difficulties to help formulate a strategy for recovery

trough ECONOMICS low point in economic cycle the lowest point or period in an economic cycle before the situation begins to improve

troy ounce FINANCE unit of weight for precious metals the traditional unit used when weighing precious metals such as gold or silver. It is equal to approximately 1.097 ounces avoirdupois or 31.22 grams.

true and fair view *UK* ACCOUNTING auditor-confirmed statement of firm's financial position a correct statement of a company's financial position as shown in its accounts and confirmed by the auditors

true copy LEGAL copy of legal document attested by notary an exact copy of a legal document, as declared before a ***notary public***

true interest cost FINANCE real interest rate paid on debt security the effective rate of interest paid by the issuer on a debt security that is sold at a discount

trump MARKETING make competitor's product appear useless by comparison to make something such as a competitor's product appear useless because what you have is so much better *(slang)*

trust 1. FINANCE assets held for somebody else money or property held by one person or a group of people (the trustees) with a legal obligation to administer them for another person's benefit. *See also* ***blind trust*** **2.** *US* BUSINESS cartel a group of companies that act together with the effect of reducing competition and controlling prices

trust account BANKING account held for somebody else money held by one person (the trustee), often a professional, on behalf of the owner of the funds in it, for example, a minor

trust bank BANKING Japanese bank offering banking and trustee services a Japanese bank that acts commercially in the sense of accepting deposits and making loans and also in the capacity of a trustee

trust company BUSINESS firm administering trusts a company whose business is administering trusts on behalf of trustees

trust corporation BANKING US institution sometimes performing banking activities a US state-chartered institution that may undertake banking activities

trust deed LEGAL document outlining trust a document that sets out the regulations governing a trust

trustee FINANCE somebody holding assets in trust a person who, either individually or as a member of a board, has a legal obligation to administer assets for another person's benefit

trustee in bankruptcy FINANCE somebody managing bankrupt's finances somebody appointed by a court to manage the finances of a bankrupt person or company

trustee investment STOCKHOLDING & INVESTMENTS investment made by trustee an investment that is made by a trustee and is subject to legal restrictions

trusteeship FINANCE **1.** status of trustee the position of a ***trustee*** with a legal obligation to administer assets for another person's benefit **2.** time as trustee the term during which somebody acts as a ***trustee***

trust fund FINANCE set of assets held in trust assets held in trust by a ***trustee*** or board of trustees for the trust's beneficiaries

trust officer FINANCE manager of assets of trust somebody who manages the assets of a trust, especially for a bank that is acting as a ***trustee***

Truth in Lending Act LEGAL US law requiring transparent disclosure of credit terms in the United States, a law requiring lenders to disclose the terms of their credit offers accurately so that consumers are not misled and are able to compare the various credit terms available. The Truth in Lending Act requires lenders to disclose the terms and costs of all loan plans, including the following: annual percentage rate, points, and fees; the total of the principal amount being financed; payment due date and terms, including any balloon payment where applicable and late payment fees; features of variable-rate loans, including the highest rate the lender would charge, how it is calculated and the resulting monthly payment; total finance charges; whether the loan is assumable; the existence of any application fees or any annual or one-time service fees; and whether there are any pre-payment penalties. Where applicable, it also requires the lender to confirm the address of the property securing the loan. *Abbr* ***TILA***

TT *abbr* BANKING ***telegraphic transfer***

turbulence GENERAL MANAGEMENT sudden changes affecting performance unpredictable and swift changes in an organization's external or internal environments, or in an economy, that affect its performance. The late 20th century was considered a turbulent environment for business because of the rapid growth in technology and globalization, and the frequency of restructuring and merger activity. 2008 was an especially turbulent period for financial markets, when banks worldwide could not meet their loans and had to receive government support.

turkey FINANCE poor performer an investment or business that is performing badly (*informal*)

turn MARKETS market maker's profit the difference between the bid and offer prices of a ***market maker***

turnaround *US* **1.** FINANCE return of profitability a term for the act of making a company profitable again **2.** OPERATIONS & PRODUCTION value of sales divided by value of inventory a term for the value of goods sold during a year divided by the average value of goods held in stock **3.** OPERATIONS & PRODUCTION preparation of vehicle for another commercial trip a term for the process of emptying a ship, plane, etc., and getting it ready for another commercial trip **4.** OPERATIONS & PRODUCTION processing and dispatching of orders a term for the time it takes to process orders and send out the goods ▶ *UK term* ***turnround***

turnaround management GENERAL MANAGEMENT implementation of rescue measures for failing organization the implementation of a set of actions required to save an organization from business failure and return it to operational normality and financial solvency. Turnaround management usually requires strong leadership and can include restructuring and job losses, an investigation of the root causes of failure, and long-term programs to revitalize the organization.

Turnbull REGULATION & COMPLIANCE UK internal control guidance in the United Kingdom, a best-practice framework for internal control in UK listed companies, originally established in 1999 and subsequently updated

turnkey contract GENERAL MANAGEMENT agreement to control project until handover to client an agreement in which a contractor designs, constructs, and manages a project until it is ready to be handed over to the client and operation can begin immediately

turnover 1. ACCOUNTING firm's total sales revenue the total sales ***revenue*** of an organization for an accounting period. This is shown net of ***VAT***, trade discounts, and any other taxes based on the revenue in a ***profit and loss account***. **2.** MARKETS total value of stocks traded during year the total value of stocks bought and sold on an exchange during the year. This covers both sales and purchases, so each transaction is counted twice. **3.** HR & PERSONNEL rate of change of staff the rate at which staff leave and are replaced in an organization

turnover ratio OPERATIONS & PRODUCTION frequency of firm's changes in inventory during year a measure of the number of times in a year that a business's inventory changes completely. It is calculated as the cost of sales divided by the average book value of inventory.

turnover tax TAX **1.** *US* = ***sales tax*** **2.** *UK* = ***VAT***

turnround *UK* FINANCE = ***turnaround***

20-F BUSINESS document giving detailed information about non-US companies a document compiled by non-US companies listed on the New York Stock Exchange for the Securities and Exchange Commission that gives detailed corporate information

twenty-four hour trading MARKETS constant financial trading the possibility of trading in currencies or securities at any time of day or night, because there are always trading floors open at different locations in different time zones. A financial institution with offices in the Far East, Europe, and the United States can offer its clients 24-hour trading-either by the client contacting their offices in each area, or by the customer's local office passing the orders on to another center.

two-tier tender offer MERGERS & ACQUISITIONS offering premium for initial stock in acquisition attempt in the United States, a ***takeover bid*** in which the acquirer offers to pay more for shares bought early than for those acquired at a later date, in order to encourage stockholders to accept the offer, thus gaining control quickly. This form of bidding is outlawed in some jurisdictions, including the United Kingdom.

U

UBR *abbr* TAX ***uniform business rate***

UCC *abbr* REGULATION & COMPLIANCE ***uniform commercial code***

UCITS STOCKHOLDING & INVESTMENTS EU rules for mutual funds a set of directives that regulate mutual funds throughout all the countries of the European Union. *Full form* ***Undertakings for Collective Investment in Transferable Securities***

UGMA *abbr* REGULATION & COMPLIANCE ***Uniform Gifts to Minors Act***

UHNWI *abbr* FINANCE ***ultra high net worth individual***

UIF *abbr* INSURANCE ***Unemployment Insurance Fund***

UIT *abbr* STOCKHOLDING & INVESTMENTS ***unit investment trust***

UKFI *abbr* FINANCE ***UK Financial Investments Ltd***

UK Financial Investments Ltd FINANCE firm managing UK government's banking investments a company that manages the UK government's investments in the Royal Bank of Scotland plc, Lloyds Banking Group, Bradford & Bingley, Northern Rock plc and Northern Rock Asset Management plc. It was set up in 2008 after the government had to step in to overcome serious difficulties in independent banks. *Abbr* ***UKFI***

ultra high net worth individual FINANCE person with $30 million plus a person whose net assets, excluding the value of a home, are worth more than

$30 million. About 100,000 people worldwide fall into this category. *Abbr* ***UHNWI***

ultra vires LEGAL beyond scope of organization's authority a Latin phrase meaning "beyond the powers," used to refer to an activity that normally falls beyond the scope of the instrument from which an organization's authority is derived, and thus may be challenged by the courts. A corporation's powers are limited by the objectives in its charter. Most objectives tend to be wide-ranging, but, should a corporation's directors act outside of these objectives, any resulting agreement may be unenforceable.

ultra vires activity FINANCE something disallowed by rules an act that is not permitted by applicable rules such as those of a corporate charter. Such acts may lead to contracts being void.

umbrella fund STOCKHOLDING & INVESTMENTS offshore investment in other offshore concerns a collective investment based offshore that invests in other offshore collective investments

umbrella organization BUSINESS organization embracing several member organizations a large organization that includes a number of member organizations and works to protect their shared interests

unbalanced growth ECONOMICS different parts of economy growing at different rates the situation that occurs when some sectors of an economy grow at different rates from others

unbundling 1. MERGERS & ACQUISITIONS dividing of firm before selling it off the dividing of a company into separate constituent companies, often to sell all or some of them after a takeover **2.** STOCKHOLDING & INVESTMENTS splitting returns on security for separate sale the separation of the components of a security in order to sell them separately

uncalled share capital STOCKHOLDING & INVESTMENTS unpaid proportion of stock value the amount of the ***nominal value*** of shares for which the company has not requested payment. It may not be intended that this payment should be requested unless the company goes into ***liquidation***.

uncollectable FINANCE describing debt that is written off used to describe a debt that must be written off, either as a charge to the ***profit and loss account*** or against an existing doubtful debt provision

uncollected funds BANKING value residing in deposit that bank cannot negotiate money deriving from the deposit of an instrument that a bank has not been able to negotiate

unconditional bid MERGERS & ACQUISITIONS takeover bid offering payment irrespective of stock volume in a takeover battle, a situation in which a bidder will pay the offered price irrespective of how many shares are acquired, typically after the acquisition of a majority of the shares

unconsolidated STOCKHOLDING & INVESTMENTS not grouped together used to describe shares, holdings, loans, or subsidiaries that are not combined into a single unit

uncontested bid GENERAL MANAGEMENT offer of contract to single bidder the offering of a contract by a government or other organization to one bidder only, without competition

uncovered bear STOCKHOLDING & INVESTMENTS person selling stock not yet acquired a person who sells stock which he or she does not hold, hoping to be able to buy stock back at a lower price when it is time to settle

uncovered option STOCKHOLDING & INVESTMENTS option whose seller does not own associated asset a type of ***option*** in which the underlying asset is not owned by the seller, who risks considerable loss if the price of the asset falls. *Also called* ***naked option***

UNCTAD INTERNATIONAL TRADE UN department dealing with development and finance a part of the United Nations system dealing with the integrated treatment of development and interrelated issues in trade, finance, technology, and investment. *Full form* ***United Nations Conference on Trade and Development***

undated bond STOCKHOLDING & INVESTMENTS bond without maturity date a bond to which no maturity date has been assigned

underbanked STOCKHOLDING & INVESTMENTS describing new issue with few sellers used to describe a new issue without enough brokers to sell it

undercapitalized FINANCE with insufficient capital used to describe a business that has insufficient capital for its requirements

underemployed capital FINANCE capital not producing enough income capital that is not being used effectively to produce income

underlying asset STOCKHOLDING & INVESTMENTS asset with option an asset that is associated with an ***option*** or other derivative or structured note

underlying inflation *or* **underlying rate of inflation** MORTGAGES inflation rate not considering mortgage costs a measure of inflation that does not take mortgage costs into account

underlying security STOCKHOLDING & INVESTMENTS security with option a security that is associated with an ***option***

undermargined account BANKING account with funds insufficient for margin requirements an account that does not have enough funds to cover its margin requirements, resulting in a ***margin call***

underspend FINANCE **1.** spend less than intended or allowed to spend less than the amount that was budgeted for spending **2.** smaller amount spent than expected an amount that is less than the amount that was budgeted for spending

undersubscribed STOCKHOLDING & INVESTMENTS describing stock issue with some stock unsold used to describe a new issue in which not all shares are sold, and part of the issue remains with the underwriters

undertaking 1. BUSINESS business a commercial business or company 2. LEGAL formal promise a promise, especially a legally binding one

Undertakings for Collective Investment in Transferable Securities STOCKHOLDING & INVESTMENTS *see* ***UCITS***

underused liquidity FINANCE cash not being optimally used available capital that is not being put to effective use in developing a business

undervaluation FINANCE valuation at less than true worth the assessment of an asset as having a value that is less than its expected value or worth

undervalued FINANCE describing asset available for less than value used to describe an asset that is offered for sale at a price lower than its expected value or worth

undervalued currency CURRENCY & EXCHANGE currency available cheaply a currency that costs less to buy with another currency than it is worth in goods

underwrite STOCKHOLDING & INVESTMENTS, INSURANCE, RISK be liable for potential losses to assume risk, especially for a new issue or an insurance policy. *Also called* ***write***

underwriter 1. STOCKHOLDING & INVESTMENTS guarantor of public offering an institution or group of institutions who, for a fee, guarantee a public offering from a corporation and, if it fails to find enough buyers, will purchase the remaining shares 2. INSURANCE insurance risk assessor a person who establishes insurance risk and issues insurance policies for an ***insurance company*** or syndicate, paying the insured party if a specified loss occurs. *Also called* ***writer*** *(sense 1). See also* ***Lloyd's underwriting syndicate***

underwriters' syndicate STOCKHOLDING & INVESTMENTS group guaranteeing public offering a group of institutions who, for a fee, guarantee a public offering from a corporation and, if it fails to find enough buyers, will purchase the remaining shares

underwriting STOCKHOLDING & INVESTMENTS guaranteeing of public offering the activity of guaranteeing a public offering from a corporation for a fee, agreeing to buy any shares that remain unsold

underwriting commission *or* **underwriting fee** STOCKHOLDING & INVESTMENTS fee guaranteeing purchase of new stock a fee paid by a company to the ***underwriters*** for guaranteeing the purchase of new shares in that company.

underwriting income INSURANCE profit from insurance premiums the money that an insurance company makes because the premiums it collects exceed the claims it pays out

underwriting spread STOCKHOLDING & INVESTMENTS difference between stock costs and income from sale an amount that is the difference between what an organization pays for an issue and what it receives when it sells the issue to investors

underwriting syndicate STOCKHOLDING & INVESTMENTS group of institutions selling new securities to investors a group of financial institutions who join to sell new securities to investors, and agree to buy any that are unsold themselves

undischarged bankrupt LEGAL somebody still officially classed as bankrupt a person who has been declared bankrupt and has not yet been released from that status by a court

undistributable reserves *UK* FINANCE = ***restricted surplus***

undistributed profit STOCKHOLDING & INVESTMENTS profit not paid out as dividend profit that has not been distributed as dividends to stockholders

UNDP ECONOMICS UN agency providing human development grants a part of the United Nations system with goals that include the elimination of poverty, environmental regeneration, job creation, and advancement of women. It is the world's largest source of grants for sustainable human development. *Full form* ***United Nations Development Program***

unearned income FINANCE money not received from employment income received from sources such as investments or interest on savings rather than from employment. *See also* ***earned income***

unearned increment REAL ESTATE increase in property value not created by owner an increase in the value of a property that arises from causes other than the owner's improvements or expenditure

unearned premium INSURANCE money repaid from terminated insurance policy the amount of money repaid by an insurance company when a policy is terminated

uneconomic FINANCE not producing profits not profitable for a country, firm, or investor in the short or long term

unemployment ECONOMICS people wanting to work but not finding jobs the situation in which some members of a country's labor force are willing to work but cannot find employment

unemployment compensation *US* HR & PERSONNEL = ***severance pay***

Unemployment Insurance Fund INSURANCE employee insurance against potential unemployment in South Africa, a system administered through payroll deductions that insures employees against loss of earnings through being made unemployed by such causes as retrenchment, illness, or maternity. *Abbr* ***UIF***

unencumbered REAL ESTATE property with no mortgage used to describe a property that is not subject to a mortgage

uneven lot MARKETS = ***odd lot***

unfair competition BUSINESS dubious way of gaining competitive advantage the practice of trying to do better than another company by using underhand techniques such as importing foreign goods at very low prices or wrongly criticizing a competitor's products

unfunded debt FINANCE debt to be repaid within a year short-term debt requiring repayment within a year of being issued

ungeared *UK* FINANCE = ***unleveraged***

ungluing MERGERS & ACQUISITIONS splitting up established networks the process of breaking up traditional supply chains or groups of cooperating organizations after taking control of the element of mutual interest that holds them together

uniform business rate TAX tax on UK local businesses in the United Kingdom, the rate of tax set by central government that is to be collected from businesses by local government. *Abbr* ***UBR***

uniform commercial code REGULATION & COMPLIANCE US laws regulating commercial transactions in the United States, a set of laws governing commercial transactions that has been adopted totally or in part by all 50 states. *Abbr* ***UCC***

uniform costing OPERATIONS & PRODUCTION identical approach to costing the use by several businesses of the same costing methods, principles, and techniques

Uniform Gifts to Minors Act REGULATION & COMPLIANCE US standards protecting assets given to children in the United States, a set of standards for protecting financial assets that have been given to minors. *Abbr* ***UGMA***

Uniform Transfers to Minors Act REGULATION & COMPLIANCE US regulations protecting noncash gifts to children in the United States, a set of standards for protecting noncash assets that have been given to minors. *Abbr* ***UTMA***

unincorporated BUSINESS describing business without status of company used to describe a business that is operating as a partnership or sole trader and has not been made into a company

uninsurable risk INSURANCE risk for which insurance is unavailable an event that is met with so rarely that it is impossible to calculate a probability of occurrence and therefore impossible to calculate a suitable price for insurance. *See also* ***insurable risk, risk***

unique selling point *or* **unique selling proposition** MARKETING *see* ***USP***

unissued share capital *or* **unissued capital** *UK* STOCKHOLDING & INVESTMENTS = ***unissued stock***

unissued stock *US* STOCKHOLDING & INVESTMENTS capital stock not yet issued the proportion of a company's ***capital stock*** that is authorized but has not been issued. *UK term* ***unissued share capital***

unit STOCKHOLDING & INVESTMENTS **1.** securities traded together a collection of securities traded together as a single item **2.** single mutual fund share of stock a share in a mutual fund

unitary taxation TAX taxing of international firm based on worldwide income a method of taxing a corporation based on its worldwide income rather than on its income in the country of the tax authority

unit cost OPERATIONS & PRODUCTION cost of producing single item the cost of one item, calculated on the basis of production and overhead costs for a number of such items produced together

United Nations Conference on Trade and Development INTERNATIONAL TRADE *see* ***UNCTAD***

United Nations Development Program ECONOMICS *see* ***UNDP***

unit investment trust STOCKHOLDING & INVESTMENTS investment company offering units in unmanaged portfolio an investment company that offers an unmanaged portfolio of securities to investors through brokers, typically in units of $1,000 each. *Abbr* ***UIT***

unit-linked insurance INSURANCE insurance policy linked to unit trust in the United Kingdom, an insurance policy that is linked to the security of units in a unit trust or fund

unit of account CURRENCY & EXCHANGE currency unit used for payments a unit of a country's currency that can be used in payment for goods or in a firm's accounting

unit of trade STOCKHOLDING & INVESTMENTS smallest amount that can be traded the smallest quantity that can be bought or sold of a share of stock, or a contract included in an ***option***

unit price OPERATIONS & PRODUCTION price of single item the price of one item, calculated on the basis of the cost of production and overhead costs for a number of such items produced together

unit trust *UK* STOCKHOLDING & INVESTMENTS = ***mutual fund***

universal life insurance INSURANCE life insurance that accrues savings a type of life insurance policy that builds up savings and allows the insurer to change the amount of premiums and the coverage

unleveraged *US* FINANCE describing firm with no borrowings used to describe a company that has no borrowed money. *UK term* ***ungeared***

unlimited liability FINANCE full responsibility for debts full responsibility for the obligations of a ***general partnership***. This may include the use of personal assets to pay debts.

unlimited risk RISK risk with unlimited potential loss a risk whose potential loss is unlimited, for example, in futures trading

unlisted company BUSINESS, MARKETS company with stock not listed on exchange a company whose shares are not listed on an exchange

unlisted securities STOCKHOLDING & INVESTMENTS stocks not listed on exchange stocks that are not listed on an exchange. *Also called* ***unquoted investments, unquoted shares***

unlisted securities market MARKETS market for minor stocks a market for stocks that are not listed on a recognized exchange. *Abbr* ***USM***

unprofitable FINANCE not profitable not producing a profit

unquoted MARKETS having no publicly stated price used to describe a security that has no publicly stated price because it is not listed on an exchange

unquoted investments STOCKHOLDING & INVESTMENTS = ***unlisted securities***

unquoted shares STOCKHOLDING & INVESTMENTS = ***unlisted securities***

unrealized capital gain ACCOUNTING profitable investment not yet sold a profit from the holding of an asset worth more than its purchase price, but not yet sold

unrealized profit/loss ACCOUNTING profit or loss from asset not yet sold a profit or loss that need not be reported as income, for example, deriving from the holding of an asset worth more or less than its purchase price, but not yet sold

unreason GENERAL MANAGEMENT unorthodox approaches that bring business success the process of thinking the unlikely and doing the unreasonable that can be a means by which an organization or individual achieves success

unremittable gain ACCOUNTING in UK, capital gain that cannot be imported in the United Kingdom, a capital gain that cannot be imported into the taxpayer's country, especially because of currency restrictions

unseasoned issue STOCKHOLDING & INVESTMENTS issue of stocks to SEC-approved investors an issue of stocks that a dealer may only sell to specific qualifying investors as agreed by the US Securities and Investment Commission. *See also* ***seasoned issue***

unsecured creditor FINANCE creditor making unsecured loans a creditor who is owed money, but has no security from the debtor for the debt. Unsecured creditors are at risk of losing everything, as official procedures may absorb most of the money remaining after a business failure and small creditors may not be paid.

unsecured debt FINANCE money borrowed without collateral an amount of money borrowed without the borrower providing ***collateral*** to the lender

unsecured loan FINANCE loan provided without collateral a loan made without ***collateral*** provided to the lender by the borrower. *Also called* ***signature loan***

unstable equilibrium ECONOMICS easily disrupted balance of supply and demand a market situation in which, if there is a movement of price or quantity away from the equilibrium, existing forces will push the price even further away

unsubsidized FINANCE without financial assistance for which no ***subsidy*** has been paid. *See also* ***subsidized***

up market MARKETS rising stock market a stock market that is rising or is at its highest level

upside potential STOCKHOLDING & INVESTMENTS potential for value of security to go up the possibility that a security will increase in value. *See also* ***downside risk***

upsizing HR & PERSONNEL increase in activities and staff expansion and restructuring of business activities, including an increase in the number of staff employed. *Also called* ***resizing***. *See also* ***downsizing***

upstairs market MARKETS area of exchange where major institutions trade the place where traders for major brokerages and institutions do business at an exchange

upstream OPERATIONS & PRODUCTION at earlier stage at a point earlier in the production process. *See also* ***downstream***

upstream progress GENERAL MANAGEMENT commercial progress in difficult conditions advancement against opposition or in difficult conditions. A company or project can make upstream progress if it moves toward achieving its objectives despite impediments. *See also* ***downstream progress***

upswing MARKETS rise in stock prices following fall an upward movement in stock prices following a period of steady or falling prices

uptick MARKETS trade at price higher than in previous trade a transaction in which the price of a specific security is higher than the price in the transaction immediately preceding it. *Also called* ***plus tick***

upturn ECONOMICS upward trend an upward trend in sales, profits, a stock market, or an economy

urbun FINANCE forfeitable deposit paid by buyer to seller in Islamic financing, money paid by a buyer to a seller at the time of execution of a contract that will be forfeited if the contract is canceled by the buyer

used credit FINANCE used part of offered credit the portion of a ***line of credit*** that is no longer available for use

use of proceeds FINANCE details of intended investment use detailed information for investors on how money invested in an undertaking will be put to use

U-shaped recovery ECONOMICS slow exit from recession a pattern of recovery after a recession shaped like the letter U, showing a gradual improvement of conditions

USM *abbr* MARKETS ***unlisted securities market***

USP MARKETING feature distinguishing specific product a specific feature that differentiates a product from similar products. *Full form* ***unique selling point***

US savings bond STOCKHOLDING & INVESTMENTS US Federal government savings product in the United States, a bond that can be bought from the Federal government. *Also called* ***savings bond***

usury FINANCE lending money at high rates the practice of lending money at a rate of interest that is either unlawful or considered to be excessively high

utility **1.** BUSINESS company that provides a service to community a public service company, for example, one that supplies water, gas, or electricity or that runs public transportation **2.** ECONOMICS customer satisfaction the usefulness or satisfaction that a consumer gets from a product

UTMA *abbr* REGULATION & COMPLIANCE ***Uniform Transfers to Minors Act***

V

valuation FINANCE estimate of worth an estimate of how much something is worth

value FINANCE **1.** worth measured in money the amount of money that something is worth **2.** estimate worth of something in money to estimate how much money something is worth

value added GENERAL MANAGEMENT **1.** difference between cost of materials and selling price the difference between the cost of bought-in materials and the eventual selling price of the finished product **2.** valuable distinguishing features of product or service the features that differentiate one product or service from another, and thus create value for the customer. Value added is a customer perception of what makes a product or service desirable over others and worth a higher price. Value added is more difficult to measure without a physical end product, but value can be added to services as well as physical goods, through the process of ***value engineering***. *Also called* ***added value*** *(sense 1)*

value-added network E-COMMERCE organization providing messaging and communications services an organization that provides messaging-related functions and EDI (***electronic data interchange***) communications services, for example, protocol matching and line-speed conversion, between trading partners. *Abbr* ***VAN***. *Also called* ***third-party network, third-party service provider***

value-added reseller BUSINESS trader selling repackaged items bought at retail a merchant who buys products at retail and packages them with additional items for sale to customers. *Abbr* ***VAR***

value-added tax TAX *see* ***VAT***

value-adding intermediary GENERAL MANAGEMENT distributor adding value to product before sale a distributor who adds value to a product before selling it to a customer, for example, by installing software or a modem in a computer

value analysis OPERATIONS & PRODUCTION technique of eliminating unnecessary costs a cost reduction and problem-solving technique that analyzes an existing product or service in order to reduce or eliminate any costs that do not contribute to value or performance. Value analysis usually focuses on design issues relating to the function of a product or service, looking at the properties that make it work, or which are ***USPs***.

value-at-risk STOCKHOLDING & INVESTMENTS, RISK *see* ***Var***

value chain BUSINESS business activities adding value to products or services the sequence of business activities by which, in the perspective of the end user, value is added to products or services produced by an organization

value date FINANCE transfer date a date on which a transaction takes place

value driver FINANCE something adding value to product or service an activity or organizational focus that enhances the value of a product or service in the perception of the consumer and which therefore creates value for the producer. Advanced technology, reliability, or reputation for customer relations can all be value drivers.

value engineering OPERATIONS & PRODUCTION activity that aids design of product an activity that helps to design products that meet customer needs at the lowest cost while assuring the required standards of quality and reliability

value for customs purposes only INTERNATIONAL TRADE declared value of item imported into US what somebody importing something into the United States declares that it is worth

value for money audit ACCOUNTING examination of firm's effectiveness in using resources an investigation into whether proper arrangements have been made for securing economy, efficiency, and effectiveness in the use of resources. *Abbr* ***VFM***. *Also called* ***comprehensive auditing***

value innovation GENERAL MANAGEMENT approach to business growth concentrating on new markets a strategic approach to business growth, involving a shift away from a focus on the existing competition to one of trying to create entirely new markets. Value innovation can be achieved by implementing a focus on innovation and creation of new market possibilities.

value investing STOCKHOLDING & INVESTMENTS investing based on company's value an investment strategy based on the value of a company rather than simply on its stock price

value map MARKETING extra value differentiating product or service the level of value that the market recognizes in a product or service and that helps to differentiate it from competitors

value proposition FINANCE proposed profit-making plan a proposed plan for making a profit, presented, for example, to a potential investor

value share *or* **value stock** STOCKHOLDING & INVESTMENTS currently underpriced stock a stock that is considered to be currently underpriced by the market, and therefore an attractive investment prospect

value to the business *or* **value to the owner** FINANCE asset's minimum assessable value the lower of the figures for the ***recoverable amount*** and the ***replacement cost*** of an asset. *Also called* ***deprival value***

VAN *abbr* E-COMMERCE ***value-added network***

vanilla lending FINANCE = ***prime lending***

vanilla loan FINANCE = ***prime loan***

Var *or* **VAR** STOCKHOLDING & INVESTMENTS assessment of likely depreciation of asset or investment a risk assessment measure that is used to establish how much the market value of an asset or a portfolio is likely to decrease over a specific period of time. *Full form* ***value-at-risk***

VAR *abbr* BUSINESS ***value-added reseller***

variable STATISTICS piece of data studied in statistical analysis an element of data whose changes are the object of a statistical study

variable annuity INSURANCE annuity without fixed payments an ***annuity*** that offers no guarantee but has potential for a greater return, usually based on the performance of a stock or mutual fund. *See also* ***annuity***

variable costing ACCOUNTING = ***marginal costing***

variable interest rate FINANCE interest rate that fluctuates during loan period an interest rate that changes, usually in relation to a standard index, during the period of a loan

variable life assurance *UK* INSURANCE = ***variable life insurance***

variable life insurance *US* INSURANCE life insurance where benefits vary with investment performance a type of whole-life insurance policy providing a death benefit that varies according to the performance of an investment portfolio managed by the insurance company. *UK term* ***variable life assurance***

variable rate FINANCE interest rate that fluctuates a rate of interest on a loan that is not fixed, but can change with the current bank interest rates. *Also called* ***floating rate***

variable rate note FINANCE note with interest rate linked to index a note whose interest rate is tied to an index, such as the prime rate in the United States or the London Interbank Offering Rate in the United Kingdom. *Abbr* ***VRN***

variance **1.** GENERAL MANAGEMENT difference between actual and predicted performance a measure of the difference between actual performance and forecast, or standard, performance **2.** ACCOUNTING difference between planned and actual cost the difference between a planned, budgeted, or standard cost and the actual cost incurred. The same comparisons may be made for revenues.

variation margin STOCKHOLDING & INVESTMENTS, RISK daily profits or losses the profits or losses of members of the ***London Clearing House***, calculated daily from the marked-to-market-close value of their position. *See also* ***initial margin***

VAT TAX tax added at each manufacturing stage a tax added at each stage in the manufacture of a product. It acts as a replacement for a ***sales tax*** in almost every industrialized country outside North America. It is levied on selected goods and services, paid by organizations on items they buy, and then charged to customers. *Full form* ***value-added tax***

VAT declaration TAX in UK, statement of VAT income in the United Kingdom, a statement to ***Her Majesty's Revenue & Customs*** declaring that proportion of a business's income that is liable to ***VAT***

VAT inspector TAX UK government official checking payment of VAT a UK government official who examines VAT returns and checks that VAT is being paid

VAT paid TAX in UK, with VAT paid in the United Kingdom, indicating an item on which ***VAT*** has already been paid

VAT receivable TAX with VAT not yet collected with the VAT for an item not yet collected by a taxing authority

VAT registration TAX listing as firm eligible for some refunding of VAT the process of listing with a European government as a company eligible for the return of VAT in some cases

vault cash BANKING cash used for bank's everyday needs cash held by a bank in its vaults, used for day-to-day needs

VC *abbr* FINANCE ***venture capitalist***

VCM *abbr* MARKETS ***Venture Capital Market***

VCT *abbr* BUSINESS ***venture capital trust***

vega STOCKHOLDING & INVESTMENTS relationship of option price to underlying asset's volatility a ratio between the expected change in the price of an option and a 1% change in the expected volatility of the underlying asset. *Also called* ***kappa, lambda***

velocity of circulation of money ECONOMICS how quickly money moves around economy the rate at which money circulates in an economy

vendor FINANCE seller a person or organization that sells goods, services, shares, or property

vendor placing STOCKHOLDING & INVESTMENTS business vendor's exchanging of acquired stock for cash the practice of issuing stock to acquire a business, where an agreement has been made to allow the vendor of the business to place the stock with investors for cash

venture capital FINANCE finance for new businesses or projects money used to finance new companies or projects, especially those with high earning potential and high risk. *Also called* ***risk capital***

venture capital fund FINANCE fund providing venture capital a fund that invests in finance houses providing ***venture capital***

venture capitalist FINANCE firm or individual providing venture capital a finance company or private individual specializing in providing venture capital. *Abbr* ***VC***

Venture Capital Market MARKETS closed sector of Johannesburg exchange for developing companies a sector on the South African stock exchange for listing smaller developing companies that was closed to new listings in 2004 due to low liquidity. *Abbr* ***VCM***. *See also* ***Development Capital Market***

venture capital trust BUSINESS in UK, trust investing in smaller firms in the United Kingdom, a trust that invests in smaller firms that need capital to grow. *Abbr* ***VCT***

venture funding FINANCE second round of funding for new firm the round of funding for a new company that follows the provision of seed capital by venture capitalists

venture management GENERAL MANAGEMENT collaboration encouraging entrepreneurism and innovation the collaboration of various sections within an organization to encourage an ***entrepreneurial*** spirit, increase innovation, and produce successful new products more quickly. Venture management is used within large organizations to create a small-firm, entrepreneurial atmosphere, releasing innovation and talent from promising employees. It cuts out bureaucracy and bypasses traditional management systems. The collaboration is generally between research and development, corporate planning, marketing, finance, and purchasing functions.

venturer FINANCE partner in joint venture one of two or more parties involved in a ***joint venture***

verbal contract GENERAL MANAGEMENT oral, not written, agreement an agreement that is oral and not written down. It remains legally enforceable by the parties who have agreed to it.

verification ACCOUNTING in-depth examination of firm's assets and liabilities in an audit, a substantive test of the existence, ownership, and valuation of a company's assets and liabilities

vertical diversification GENERAL MANAGEMENT, MERGERS & ACQUISITIONS developing new areas in supply chain ***diversification*** in which a company moves into a different level of the ***supply chain***, for example, a manufacturing company becoming a retailer. *See also* ***diversification***

vertical equity TAX principle that tax rates vary with income the principle that people with different incomes should pay different rates of tax

vertical form ACCOUNTING presentation of debits and credits in single column the presentation of a financial statement in which the debits and credits are shown in one column of figures

vertical integration GENERAL MANAGEMENT combining of operations in supply chain the practice of combining some or all of the sequential operations of the ***supply chain*** between the sourcing of ***raw materials*** and sale of the final product. Vertical integration can be pursued as a strategy through the acquisition of ***suppliers***, ***wholesalers***, and ***retailers*** to increase control and reliability. It can also be achieved when a company gains strong control over suppliers or distributors, usually by exercising purchasing power.

vertical market MARKETS market geared toward one product type a market that is oriented to one particular specialty, for example, plastics manufacturing or transportation engineering

vertical merger MERGERS & ACQUISITIONS combining of firms in same supply chain the amalgamation of two or more organizations from the same ***supply chain*** under single ownership, through the direct *acquisition* by one organization of the net assets or liabilities of the other. *See also* ***merger***

vested employee benefits HR & PERSONNEL benefits not linked to job employee benefits that are not conditional on future employment by the company in question, for example, a pension plan

vested interest FINANCE personal interest in maintaining status quo a special interest in keeping an existing state of affairs for personal gain

vested rights PENSIONS in US, value of pension on leaving job the value of somebody's rights in a pension if he or she leaves a job

vesting HR & PERSONNEL in US, continuing right to receive employer contributions the right of an employee participating in a benefit plan to employer contributions to the plan, whether or not the employee continues working for the company

VFM *abbr* ACCOUNTING ***value for money audit***

v-form FINANCE graph line showing value falling then rising a graphic representation of something that had been falling in value and is now rising

viatical settlement INSURANCE proceeds from sale of terminal patient's insurance policy the proceeds received from the sale of a life insurance policy to a third party by somebody who is terminally ill

virement *UK* ACCOUNTING transfer of money between accounts or budgets a transfer of money from one account to another or from one section of a budget to another

virtual bank BANKING, E-COMMERCE bank only accessible electronically a financial institution that offers banking services via the Internet, ATMs, and telephone but does not have a physical location for customers to visit

virtual hosting E-COMMERCE hosting option with user responsible for software a type of hosting suitable for small and medium-sized businesses, in which the customer uses space on a network vendor's server that is also used by other organizations. The hosting company agrees to deliver minimum access speeds and data transfer rates, and to conduct basic hardware maintenance, but the customer is responsible for managing the content and software.

virtualization E-COMMERCE creation of product or service with electronic existence the creation of a product, service, or organization that has an electronic rather than a physical existence

virtual organization E-COMMERCE temporary partnerships between firms via communications technologies a temporary network of companies, suppliers, customers, or employees, linked by information and communications technologies, with the purpose of delivering a service or product. A virtual organization can bring together companies in partnering or outsourcing arrangements, enabling them to share expertise, resources, and cost savings until objectives are met and the network is dissolved. Such organizations are virtual not only in the sense that they exist largely in cyberspace, but also in that they are unconstrained by the traditional barriers of time and place. A greater level of trust is required between employer and employee or coworkers, or partner organizations, because they will be working out of one another's sight for most of the time. *See also* ***network organization, virtual team***

virtual team GENERAL MANAGEMENT remote employees collaborating via communications technologies a group of employees using information and communications technologies to collaborate from different work bases. Members of a virtual team may work in different parts of the same building or may be scattered across a country or around the world.

visible INTERNATIONAL TRADE describing tangible goods imported or exported used to describe real products or goods that are imported or exported

visible trade INTERNATIONAL TRADE buying and selling physical goods trade in physical goods and merchandise

vision statement GENERAL MANAGEMENT statement of organization's aims a statement giving a broad, aspirational image of the future that an organization is aiming to achieve

voetstoots FINANCE in S. Africa, at buyer's risk in South Africa, used to describe a sale or purchase for which there is no warranty or guarantee

Volcker rule BANKING US restriction on banks' investment activities in the United States, a federal government proposal, in response to the global banking crisis of 2007-2008, that no bank or financial institution that contains a bank can own, invest in, or sponsor, for its own profit, hedge funds, private equity funds, or proprietary trading operations that are unrelated to serving customers. The effect of this is to separate banking operations from trading activities.

volume discount OPERATIONS & PRODUCTION discount to customer for quantity purchase the discount given to a customer who buys a large quantity of goods

volume of retail sales BUSINESS how much consumers buy the amount of trade in goods conducted in the retail sector of an economy in a particular period

volume of trade MARKETS number of stocks sold during trading day the number of shares sold on a stock exchange during a day's trading

volume variances ACCOUNTING monetary differences when actual and budgeted activity diverges differences in costs or revenues compared with budgeted amounts, caused by differences between the actual and budgeted levels of activity

voluntary arrangement FINANCE agreement with terms not legally binding an agreement the terms of which are not legally binding on the parties

voluntary bankruptcy LEGAL bankruptcy declared by debtor ***bankruptcy*** in which the debtor files a petition claiming inability to meet his or her debts, as opposed to involuntary bankruptcy, where one or more creditors bring a petition against the debtor. *See also* ***bankruptcy***

voluntary liquidation BUSINESS unforced liquidation supported by stockholders liquidation of a solvent company that is supported by the stockholders

voluntary registration TAX in UK, optional VAT registration by small company in the United Kingdom, registration for ***VAT*** by a trader whose turnover is below the registration threshold. This is usually done in order to reclaim tax on inputs.

vostro account BANKING local bank account held for foreign bank an account held by a local bank on behalf of a foreign bank

votes on account FINANCE extra money for UK government department in the United Kingdom, money granted by Parliament to allow government departments to continue spending in a fiscal year before final authorization of the totals for the year

voting shares *UK* STOCKHOLDING & INVESTMENTS = ***voting stock***

voting stock *US* STOCKHOLDING & INVESTMENTS stock giving voting rights stock whose owners have the right to vote at the company's annual meeting and any extraordinary meetings. *UK term* ***voting shares***

voting trust STOCKHOLDING & INVESTMENTS group with voting rights from stockholders a group of individuals who have collectively received voting rights from stockholders

voucher ACCOUNTING evidence for accounting entry a document supporting an entry in a company's accounts

vouching ACCOUNTING auditor's matching of vouchers with accounting entries an auditing process in which documentary evidence is matched with the details recorded in an accounting record in order to check for validity and accuracy

Vredeling Directive GENERAL MANAGEMENT proposal requesting multinational firms to consult employees a proposal, presented to the European Council of Ministers in 1980, for obligatory information, consultation, and participation of employees at headquarters level in multinational enterprises

VRN *abbr* FINANCE ***variable rate note***

V-shaped recovery ECONOMICS rapid exit from recession a pattern of recovery after a recession shaped like the letter V, showing rapid smooth improvement in conditions

vulture capitalist FINANCE venture capitalist benefiting investors, not entrepreneur client a ***venture capitalist*** who exploits entrepreneurs by structuring deals on their behalf in such a way that the investors benefit rather than the entrepreneurs (*slang*)

vulture fund STOCKHOLDING & INVESTMENTS investment fund specializing in discounted items a mutual fund that specializes in acquiring investments such as bonds that have been downgraded or ***distressed property***

W

wage FINANCE money regularly paid for work done the money paid to an employee in return for work done, especially when it is based on an hourly rate and is paid weekly

wage drift FINANCE = ***earnings drift***

wage freeze ECONOMICS government restraints on wage increases a government policy of preventing pay raises in order to combat inflation

wage incentive FINANCE monetary reward for employee's performance a monetary benefit offered as a reward to those employees who perform well in an agreed way

wage indexation ECONOMICS linking of pay raises to cost of living the linking of increases in wages to the percentage rise in the cost of living

wage policy *US* ECONOMICS government policy on wage levels a government policy setting wages and wage increases for workers, for example, setting minimum wage requirements. *UK term* ***wages policy***

wage-price spiral ECONOMICS = ***inflationary spiral***

wage restraint FINANCE curbs on pay raises the act of keeping increases in wages under control and in proportion to increases in workers' productivity

wages FINANCE money in return for work a form of pay given to employees in exchange for the work they have done. Traditionally, the term wages applied to the weekly pay of manual, or nonprofessional workers. In modern usage, the term is often used interchangeably with salary.

wages costs ACCOUNTING costs of paying employees the costs of paying employees for their work. Along with other costs such as pension contributions, these costs typically form the largest single cost item for a business.

wages payable account ACCOUNTING in UK, account showing expenditure on employees in the United Kingdom, an account showing the gross wages and employer's ***National Insurance*** contributions paid during a specific period

wages policy *UK* ECONOMICS = ***wage policy***

waiting time OPERATIONS & PRODUCTION period of inactivity enforced by machine breakdown the period for which an operator is available for production but is prevented from working by shortage of material or tooling, or by machine breakdown

waiver LEGAL avoidance of legal condition an act of giving up a right or removing the conditions of a rule

waiver of premium INSURANCE policy provision to suspend premium payments a provision of an insurance policy that suspends payment of premiums, for example, if the insured receives a disabling injury

wakalah FINANCE contract appointing agent in Islamic financing, a contract in which one person appoints another person to act as an agent on their behalf in a transaction

wallet technology E-COMMERCE software facilitating payment by digital cash a software package providing ***digital wallets*** or purses on the computers of merchants and customers to facilitate payment by digital cash

wallflower STOCKHOLDING & INVESTMENTS unappealing investment an investment that does not attract a lot of interest from potential investors (*slang*)

wall of worry MARKETS stock market moving up with fallbacks a stock market that moves generally upward but that also has many losing sessions is said to be "climbing the wall of worry"

wallpaper STOCKHOLDING & INVESTMENTS major stock issue financing takeovers a disparaging term used to describe a situation where a company issues and sells many new shares in order to finance a series of takeovers (*slang*)

Wall Street MARKETS **1.** US financial markets a collective name for the financial industry in the United States **2.** financial district of New York City a street in Manhattan in and around which the ***New York Stock Exchange*** and other important financial institutions are located

Wall Street bonus FINANCE large financial reward for US employee a very large sum of money, in addition to annual salary, paid to an employee in New York's financial industry for effective performance in increasing his or her company's profits. *See also* ***City bonus***

Wall Street Journal FINANCE US financial newspaper a respected daily newspaper published by Dow Jones & Company in New York City, with Asian and European editions, that covers US and international business and financial news and topics

war babies STOCKHOLDING & INVESTMENTS defense industry securities securities in companies that work as contractors in the defense industry (*slang*)

war chest MERGERS & ACQUISITIONS reserves for financing takeovers a large amount of money held by a person or a company in ***reserves*** that can be used to finance the ***takeover*** of other companies (*slang*)

warehouse capacity OPERATIONS & PRODUCTION available storage space in warehouse the space available in a warehouse for storing goods

war loan STOCKHOLDING & INVESTMENTS UK government bond paying fixed interest a UK government bond that pays a fixed rate of ***interest*** and has no final ***redemption date***. War loans were originally issued to finance military expenditure.

warrant STOCKHOLDING & INVESTMENTS contract to buy stocks in future a contract that gives the right to buy a predetermined number of shares of stock in the future

warrantee LEGAL somebody given warranty a person who is given a warranty by a ***warrantor***

warrantor LEGAL somebody giving warranty a person who gives a warranty to a ***warrantee***

warrant premium STOCKHOLDING & INVESTMENTS extra paid for buying and exercising warrant a premium paid to buy and exercise a warrant, above the price of buying the shares of stock directly without the warrant

warrants risk warning notice STOCKHOLDING & INVESTMENTS broker's statement of risks of options trading a statement that a broker in the United Kingdom gives to clients to alert them to the risks inherent in trading in options

warranty 1. INSURANCE insured person's statement that information provided is correct a statement made by somebody who is being insured that the facts stated by that person are true **2.** LEGAL legal document promising quality of goods a legal document that promises that a machine will work properly or that an item is of good quality **3.** LEGAL promise in contract a promise explicitly stated in a contract

wash sale STOCKHOLDING & INVESTMENTS sale and repurchase of same stock the sale and then immediate repurchase of a block of stock. In the United States it may be used as a means of creating fictitious trading volume. *See also* **bed and breakfast deal**

wasting asset ACCOUNTING asset that is consumed to earn income a ***fixed asset*** that is consumed or exhausted in the process of earning income, for example, a mine or a quarry

watchdog REGULATION & COMPLIANCE organization regulating particular industry an independent organization set up to police a particular industry, ensuring that member companies do not act illegally

watch list MARKETS list of securities to be monitored a list of securities that a brokerage firm, exchange, or regulatory agency is watching closely. These may be securities of firms targeted for takeovers, those planning to issue new securities, or those suspected of rules violations.

watered stock STOCKHOLDING & INVESTMENTS stock with value lower than capital invested stock in a company that is worth less than the total ***capital*** invested

watermark LEGAL symbol in document proving authenticity a design inserted into documents to prove their authenticity. For example, banknotes all carry watermarks to prevent forgery.

WC *abbr* FINANCE ***working capital***

WDA *abbr* ACCOUNTING, TAX ***writing-down allowance***

WDV *abbr* ACCOUNTING ***written-down value*** = ***net book value***

weak market MARKETS stock market with falling prices a stock market in which prices tend to fall because there are no buyers

wealth ECONOMICS real estate or investments physical assets such as a house or financial assets such as stocks and bonds that can yield an income for their holder

wealth tax TAX tax on accumulated wealth a tax on somebody's accumulated wealth, as opposed to their income

wear and tear ACCOUNTING degeneration of asset owing to normal use the deterioration of a tangible ***fixed asset*** as a result of normal use. This is recognized for accounting purposes by ***depreciation***.

web commerce E-COMMERCE = ***e-commerce***

web marketplace E-COMMERCE online community for commercial trade a business-to-business web community that brings business buyers and sellers together. Although their exact nature can vary considerably, there are essentially three types of web-based B2B marketplace: online catalogs, auctions, and exchanges.

wedge MARKETS representation of converging highs and lows in market analysis, a chart pattern in which the lines that connect the highs and lows are gradually converging while moving in the same direction

WEF *abbr* ECONOMICS ***World Economic Forum***

weighted average STATISTICS average reflecting relative importance of individual values an average of quantities that have been adjusted by the addition of a statistical value to allow for their relative importance in a set of items

weighted average cost of capital FINANCE average cost of firm's capital the average cost of a company's financing (equity, debentures, bank loans) weighted according to the proportion each element bears to the total pool of capital. Weighting is usually based on market valuations, current yields, and costs after tax. The weighted average cost of capital is often used as the ***hurdle rate*** for investment decisions, and as the measure to be minimized in order to find the optimal capital structure for the company.

weighted average cost price FINANCE cost of each item in inventory a value for the cost of each item of a specific type in an inventory, taking into account what quantities were bought at what prices

weighted average number of ordinary shares *UK* STOCKHOLDING & INVESTMENTS = ***weighted average number of shares outstanding***

weighted average number of shares outstanding *US* STOCKHOLDING & INVESTMENTS figure used for calculating earnings per share the number of shares of common stock at the beginning of a period, adjusted for shares canceled, bought back, or issued during the period, multiplied by a time-weighting factor. This number is used in the calculation of ***earnings per share***. *UK term* ***weighted average number of ordinary shares***

weighted index ECONOMICS index with importance affecting value an index in which some important items are given more value than less important ones

weighting STATISTICS giving more importance to some values the assigning of greater importance to particular items in a data set

weightlessness GENERAL MANAGEMENT quality ascribed to knowledge economy a quality considered to characterize an economy that is based on knowledge or other intangibles rather than on physical assets

Wheat Report ACCOUNTING report examining principles and methods of US accounting a report produced by a committee in 1972 that set out to examine the principles and methods of accounting in the United States. Its publication led to the establishment of the ***FASB***.

whisper number *or* **whisper estimate** FINANCE rumored earnings an estimate of a company's earnings that is based on rumors.

whisper stock STOCKHOLDING & INVESTMENTS stock predicted to rise in value a stock about which there is talk of a likely change in value, usually upward and often related to a takeover

whistle ◇ blow the whistle on somebody or something GENERAL MANAGEMENT to engage in ***whistleblowing*** with regard to some malpractice, misconduct, corruption, or mismanagement

whistleblowing GENERAL MANAGEMENT exposure of misconduct within organization speaking out to the media or the public on malpractice, misconduct, corruption, or mismanagement witnessed in an organization. Whistleblowing is usually undertaken on the grounds of morality or conscience, or because of a failure of business ethics on the part of the organization being reported.

white-collar crime FRAUD crime by white-collar worker a crime committed by somebody in the course of doing a ***white-collar job***, for example, embezzlement

white-collar job HR & PERSONNEL job involving no physical labor a position of employment that does not involve physical labor, for example, a job in an office. The term refers to the white shirt and tie supposedly worn by office workers. *See also* ***blue-collar job***

white-collar worker HR & PERSONNEL office worker a person whose job involves working in an office

white elephant BUSINESS product or service underperforming against development costs a product or service that has not sold well, despite large amounts of money being pumped into its development

white goods MARKETING large household appliances large household electrical appliances such as ranges, refrigerators, and freezers.

white knight MERGERS & ACQUISITIONS preferred buyer whose action thwarts takeover a person or company liked by a company's management, who buys the company when a hostile company is trying to buy it. *See also* ***knight***

whitemail MERGERS & ACQUISITIONS issue of cheap shares of stock to prevent takeover a method used by a company that is the target of a takeover bid to prevent the takeover, in which the target company issues a large number of shares of stock below the market price to friendly investors. The company wanting to acquire the target must buy the shares in order to be successful.

White Paper BUSINESS report stating UK government's policy a report issued by the UK government as a statement of government policy on a particular problem. *See also* ***Green Paper***

white squire MERGERS & ACQUISITIONS shareholder whose stock purchases prevent takeover bid somebody who purchases a significant, but not controlling, number of shares of stock in order to prevent a ***takeover bid*** from succeeding. A white squire is often invited to purchase the shares by the company to be acquired, and may be required to sign an agreement to prevent him or her from later becoming a ***black knight***.

whiz kid BUSINESS young person enjoying huge business success a young, exceptionally successful person, especially one who makes a lot of money in large financial transactions, including takeovers (*informal*)

whole-life assurance *UK* INSURANCE = ***whole-life insurance***

whole-life insurance *or* **whole-life policy** *US* INSURANCE insurance policy paying out on death an insurance policy in which the insured person pays a fixed premium each year and the insurance company pays a sum when he or she dies. *UK term* ***whole-life insurance***

whole loan MORTGAGES mortgage sold in entirety a mortgage loan that is sold to an investor along with all of its rights and responsibilities

wholesale BUSINESS describing business of selling goods to retailers relating to the business of buying goods from manufacturers and selling them in large quantities to retailers who then sell in smaller quantities to the general public

wholesale banking BANKING banking services provided by merchant banks banking services between investment banks and other financial institutions. *See also* ***retail banking, commercial bank***

wholesale funded BANKING funded by short-term borrowing used to describe a bank whose funds come from other banks and financial institutions in the form of short-term loans rather than from long-term deposits

wholesale funding BANKING funding of banks through short-term borrowing a method of funding banks by short-term borrowing from other banks and financial institutions

wholesale market MARKETS, BANKING = ***interbank market***

wholesale price BUSINESS price for bulk purchases of items for resale a price charged to customers who buy large quantities of an item for resale in smaller quantities to others

wholesale price index ECONOMICS government indicator of inflation level a government-calculated index of wholesale prices, indicative of inflation in an economy

wholesaler OPERATIONS & PRODUCTION intermediary between producer and retailer a business that purchases goods from a manufacturer or producer and sells them to a retailer or distributor

wholly-owned subsidiary BUSINESS firm completely owned by another a company that is completely owned by another company. A wholly-owned subsidiary is a ***registered company*** with board members who all represent one ***holding company*** or corporation. Board members may be directly from the holding company or acting as its nominees, or they may be from other wholly-owned subsidiaries of the holding company.

whoops *US* FINANCE disparaging name for Washington state power company a disparaging way of referring to the Washington Public Power Supply System, a municipal corporation in the US state of Washington that built and operated power plants. Delays, cost overruns, and mismanagement in the construction of nuclear power plants caused the company to default on the $2.25 billion in bonds, the largest bond default in US history before the events of 2008.

widow-and-orphan stock *US* STOCKHOLDING & INVESTMENTS dependable stock a stock considered extremely safe as an investment

will LEGAL document stating distribution of property after death a legal document in which a person says what should happen to his or her property after he or she dies

wimbledonization *UK* BUSINESS migration of ownership of British industry the process of the ownership of British industry gradually moving out of the country. The term derives from the major tennis tournament of Wimbledon, where the contest is still played in the UK but the high-profile players are from other countries *(slang)*.

windfall gains and losses FINANCE unforeseen gains and losses large financial gains and losses that occur unexpectedly

windfall profit FINANCE large unexpected profit a large profit that is made unexpectedly and may be subject to extra tax

windfall tax *UK* TAX = ***excess profits tax***

winding-up LEGAL dissolving firm the legal process of closing down a company

winding-up petition LEGAL petition to court to liquidate company a formal request to a court for the compulsory liquidation of a company

window dressing GENERAL MANAGEMENT artificial inflation of firm's success the practice of making a business seem more profitable or more efficient than it really is

wind up LEGAL close business down to close down a business or organization and sell its assets

WIP *abbr* OPERATIONS & PRODUCTION ***work in process***

wire house MARKETS brokerage with electronically connected branch offices a brokerage firm whose branch offices are linked by a communications system that allows them to rapidly share data relating to financial markets and individual securities

wire room **1.** BANKING bank department dealing with payment orders the department in a financial institution that originates, receives, and transmits payment orders **2.** MARKETS brokerage department dealing with securities orders the department in a brokerage firm that receives and transmits securities orders to the floor of the exchange or the trading department

wire transfer E-COMMERCE electronic transfer of funds a transfer of money from one account to another electronically

witching hour *US* MARKETS time when financial instrument becomes due the time when a type of derivative financial instrument such as a ***put***, a ***call***, or a contract for advance sale becomes due *(slang)*

withdraw **1.** BANKING take money from account to remove money from an account **2.** FINANCE rescind offer to retract an offer that has been made

withdrawal STOCKHOLDING & INVESTMENTS income disbursement from open-end mutual fund the regular disbursement of dividend or capital gain income from an open-end mutual fund

withdrawal plan STOCKHOLDING & INVESTMENTS regular payment to shareholder from mutual fund an arrangement in which a mutual fund pays out a specific amount to a shareholder at regular intervals. *See also* ***systematic withdrawal***

withholding *or* **withholding tax** TAX **1.** US employee's income tax deducted at source in the United States, the money that an employer pays directly to the government as a payment of the income tax of the employee **2.** tax on dividend or interest paid directly to government the money deducted from a dividend or interest payment that a financial institution pays directly to the government as a payment of the income tax on the recipient **3.** tax in place of dividends the tax that a company must pay because it chose not to pay ***dividends*** that would subject its owners to higher taxes

with profits INSURANCE describing insurance policy paying share of profits used to describe an insurance policy that guarantees the policyholder a share in the profits of the fund in which the premiums are invested

working capital FINANCE firm's money available for trading the funds that are readily available to operate a business.

Working capital comprises the total net ***current assets*** of a business minus its ***current liabilities.***

Current assets – Current liabilities

Current assets are cash and assets that can be converted to cash within one year or a normal operating cycle; current liabilities are monies owed that are due within one year.

If a company's current assets total $300,000 and its current liabilities total $160,000, its working capital is:

$300,000 - $160,000 = $140,000

Abbr ***WC***

working capital productivity FINANCE measure of firm's productivity a way of measuring a company's efficiency by comparing working capital with sales or turnover.

It is calculated by first subtracting ***current liabilities*** from ***current assets,*** which is the formula for working capital, then dividing this figure into sales for the period.

Sales / (Current assets – Current liabilities) = Working capital productivity

If sales are $3,250, current assets are $900, and current liabilities are $650, then:

3250 / (900 – 650) = 3250 / 250 = 13 working capital productivity

In this case, the higher the number the better. Sales growing faster than the resources required to generate them is a clear sign of efficiency and, by definition, productivity.

The working capital to sales ratio uses the same figures, but in reverse:

Working capital / Sales = Working capital to sales ratio

Using the same figures in the example above, this ratio would be calculated:

250 / 3250 = 0.077 × 100% = 7.7%

For this ratio, obviously, the lower the number the better.

Some experts recommend doing quarterly calculations and averaging them for a given year to arrive at the most reliable number.

working capital ratio ACCOUNTING = ***current ratio***

working capital turnover FINANCE sales divided by average working capital a figure equal to sales divided by average working capital

Working Time Directive *or* **Working Hours Directive** HR & PERSONNEL EU directive concerning maximum working hours a European Union directive concerning the maximum number of hours an employee can work. The directive currently limits weekly working hours to a maximum of 48, but employees can choose to opt out and work more hours than this.

work in process *US* OPERATIONS & PRODUCTION products currently being made any product that is in the process of being made. Such items are included in inventories and usually valued according to their production costs. *Abbr* ***WIP***. *UK term* ***work in progress***

work in progress *UK* OPERATIONS & PRODUCTION = ***work in process***

work simplification GENERAL MANAGEMENT elimination of nonessential tasks the streamlining of business practices that attempts to eliminate tasks that do not add value to an idea or process. Tasks in a procedure are analyzed to see if unnecessary steps can be eliminated, thereby reducing complexity as much as possible, enabling workers to complete tasks more quickly. Work simplification is most suited to manufacturing processes and low-skilled jobs. It can lead to cost savings and better use of resources, but it has been criticized for resulting in workers specializing in only one task and for making work repetitive and monotonous.

World Bank BANKING group of institutions funding less developed countries one of the largest sources of funding for the less industrially developed countries in the world. It is made up of five organizations: the International Bank for Reconstruction and Development, the International Development Association, the International Finance Corporation, the Multilateral Investment Guarantee Agency, and the International Centre for Settlement of Investment Disputes. The World Bank was founded at the 1944 Bretton Woods Conference and has over 180 member countries. Its head office is located in Washington, DC, but the Bank has field offices in over 100 countries. Its focus has shifted dramatically since the 1980s, when over one-fifth of its lending was made up of investment in the energy industry. Its current priorities are education, health, and nutrition in the most economically challenged countries of the world.

world class manufacturing GENERAL MANAGEMENT level of manufacturing excellence recognized internationally a position of international manufacturing excellence, achieved by developing a culture based on factors such as continuous improvement, problem prevention, zero defect tolerance, customer-driven ***just-in-time*** production, and ***total quality management***

World Economic Forum ECONOMICS organization seeking to effect global economic improvement an independent economic organization whose goal is to "improve the state of the world." Based in Switzerland, the WEF was formed in the 1970s by Professor Klaus Schwab, who set out to bring together the CEOs of leading European companies in order to discuss strategies that would enable Europe to compete in the global marketplace. Since then, over 1,000 companies around the world have become members of the WEF and its interests have diversified to cover health, corporate citizenship, and peace-building activities. However, it has attracted criticism from some quarters, and antiglobalization protesters gather regularly at its meetings. *Abbr* ***WEF***

world economy ECONOMICS = ***global economy***

World Trade Organization INTERNATIONAL TRADE international organization established to reduce trade restrictions an international organization set up with the goal of reducing restrictions in trade between countries. *Abbr* ***WTO***

wrap account STOCKHOLDING & INVESTMENTS brokerage account charging periodic fee a client account with a broker in which the broker charges a set quarterly or annual fee covering transaction and management costs instead of charging per transaction

wrap fund STOCKHOLDING & INVESTMENTS fund investing in various underlying mutual funds a registered fund that, while not itself a mutual fund, has similar status to that of a stockbroker's portfolio and invests in a variety of underlying mutual funds, each of which is treated as a discrete holding, often in the form of an insurance bond. *Also called* ***wrapper***

wrapper STOCKHOLDING & INVESTMENTS = ***wrap fund***

writ LEGAL document starting legal process an official document issued by a judge requiring a specific action

write STOCKHOLDING & INVESTMENTS, RISK = ***underwrite***

write-down ACCOUNTING assignment of lower value to asset the recording of an asset at a lower value than previously

write-off **1.** ACCOUNTING reduction in recorded value of asset a reduction in the recorded value of an asset, usually to zero **2.** INSURANCE cancellation of debt the total loss or cancellation of a bad debt **3.** INSURANCE something damaged beyond repair for insurance claims, something that is so badly damaged that it cannot be repaired and will have to be replaced

writer **1.** INSURANCE = ***underwriter*** **2.** STOCKHOLDING & INVESTMENTS seller of traded option somebody who is selling a ***traded option***

write-up ACCOUNTING increase in book value of asset an increase made to the book value of an asset to adjust for an increase in market value

writing-down allowance ACCOUNTING, TAX tax relief on acquired assets that lose value in the United Kingdom, a form of capital allowance giving tax relief to companies acquiring ***fixed assets*** that are then depreciated. This allowance forms part of the system of ***capital allowances***. *Abbr* ***WDA***

written-down value ACCOUNTING = ***net book value***

wrongful trading LEGAL continued trading by directors aware of impending insolvency in the United Kingdom, the continuation of trading when a company's directors know that it cannot avoid insolvent liquidation

W-shaped recession ECONOMICS = ***double dip recession***

WTO *abbr* INTERNATIONAL TRADE ***World Trade Organization***

X

X STOCKHOLDING & INVESTMENTS with no dividend right a symbol used in newspapers to designate a stock or bond that is trading ***ex dividend***

X.12 E-COMMERCE = ***ANSI X.12 standard***

xa *abbr* STOCKHOLDING & INVESTMENTS ***ex-all***

XBRL FINANCE computer language for financial reporting a computer language used for financial reporting. It allows companies to publish, extract, and exchange financial information through the Internet and other electronic means. *Full form* ***Extensible Business Reporting Language***

xd *abbr* STOCKHOLDING & INVESTMENTS ***ex dividend***

xr *abbr* STOCKHOLDING & INVESTMENTS ***ex-rights***

xw STOCKHOLDING & INVESTMENTS trading without a warrant to buy shares a symbol used in newspapers to designate a stock that is trading without a warrant to buy shares of stock

Y

Yankee bond STOCKHOLDING & INVESTMENTS foreign bond in US market a bond issued in the US domestic market by a non-US company

yard CURRENCY & EXCHANGE one billion currency units used by traders for one billion units of any currency (*slang*)

year end ACCOUNTING end of fiscal year the end of the financial year, when a company's accounts are prepared

year-end ACCOUNTING of end of fiscal year relating to the end of a fiscal year

year-end bounce MARKETS = ***Santa Claus rally*** (*slang*)

year-end closing ACCOUNTING statements at end of firm's fiscal year the financial statements issued at the end of a company's fiscal year

year to date ACCOUNTING period from start of fiscal year to now the period from the start of a fiscal year to the current time. A variety of financial information, such as a company's profits, losses, or sales, may be displayed on this basis. *Abbr* ***YTD***

yen CURRENCY & EXCHANGE Japanese currency the basic unit of currency used in Japan

yield STOCKHOLDING & INVESTMENTS percentage that is annual income from investment a percentage of the amount invested that is the annual income from an investment.

Yield is calculated by dividing the annual cash return by the current share price and expressing that as a percentage.

Yields can be compared against the market average or against a sector average, which in turn gives an idea of the relative value of the share against its peers. Other things being equal, a higher yield share is preferable to that of an identical company with a lower yield.

An additional feature of the yield (unlike many of the other share analysis ratios) is that it enables comparison with cash. Cash placed in an interest-bearing source like a bank account or a government stock produces a yield—the annual interest payable. This is usually a safe investment. The yield from this cash investment can be compared with the yield on shares, which are far riskier. This produces a valuable basis for share evaluation.

Share yield is less reliable than bank interest or government stock interest yield, because, unlike banks paying interest, companies are under no obligation at all to pay dividends. Frequently, if they go through a bad patch, even the largest companies will cut dividends or abandon paying them altogether.

yield curve STOCKHOLDING & INVESTMENTS graph showing comparable interest on bonds a visual representation of relative interest rates of short- and long-term bonds. It can be normal, flat, or inverted.

yield gap STOCKHOLDING & INVESTMENTS difference in return between equities and bonds an amount representing the difference between the yield on a safe equity investment and the yield on a riskier bond investment. *See also* ***reverse yield gap***

yield management FINANCE price adjustment that secures maximum profits securing maximum profits from available capacity by manipulating pricing to gain business at different times, and from differing market segments. Yield management is used particularly in service industries such as the airline, hotel, and equipment rental industries, where there are heavy fixed overheads and additional revenue has a big impact on bottom line profitability. Increasing computing power has enabled organizations to integrate complex information from different sources (for example, customer travel histories and current information on bookings) and use mathematical models to analyze the possibility of increasing profitability. Hotel businesses, for example, can use price offers to increase "revenue per available room," or "RevPAR," on the basis of yield management analysis.

yield to call STOCKHOLDING & INVESTMENTS yield on bond at potential call date the yield on a bond at a date when the bond can be called

yield to maturity *US* STOCKHOLDING & INVESTMENTS investor's total return if security held to maturity the total return to an investor if a fixed interest security is held to maturity, in other words, the aggregate of gross interest received and the capital gain or loss at redemption, annualized. *Abbr* ***YTM***. *UK term* ***gross redemption yield***

yield to worst MARKETS lowest possible bond yield the lowest possible yield from a bond, calculated using the lower of the yield to maturity or any ***yield to call***

YK *abbr* BUSINESS ***yugen kaisha***

YTD *abbr* ACCOUNTING ***year to date***

YTM *abbr* STOCKHOLDING & INVESTMENTS ***yield to maturity***

yugen kaisha BUSINESS private limited liability corporation in Japan in Japan, a private limited liability corporation. Usually, the number of stockholders must be under 50. The minimum capital of a limited liability corporation is 3 million yen. The nominal value of each share must be 50,000 yen or more. *Abbr* ***YK***

Z

ZBB *abbr* ACCOUNTING ***zero-based budgeting***

Z bond STOCKHOLDING & INVESTMENTS bond paying interest after paying all other holders a bond whose holder receives no interest until all of the holders of other bonds in the same series have received theirs

zero-balance account BANKING bank account for outgoings, holding no residual funds a bank account that does not hold funds continuously, but has money automatically transferred into it from another account when claims arise against it

zero-based budgeting ACCOUNTING budgeting method requiring costs to be justified a method of budgeting that requires each cost element to be specifically justified, as though the activities to which the budget relates were being undertaken for the first time. Without approval, the budget allowance is zero. *Abbr* ***ZBB***

zero coupon bond STOCKHOLDING & INVESTMENTS discounted bond paying no interest a bond that pays no interest and is sold at a large discount. *Also called* ***accrual bond, split coupon bond***

zero-coupon security STOCKHOLDING & INVESTMENTS government security without interest a government security that pays no interest but is sold at a discount from its face value

zero-fund *or* FINANCE provide no money for project to assign no money to a business project without actually canceling it (*slang*)

zero growth ECONOMICS no increase in output a lack of increase in the output of a business or economy between one period, such as one quarter, and the next. *See also* ***recession***

zero-rated TAX on which no sales tax is paid used to describe an item on which a buyer pays no sales tax

zero-rated supplies *or* **zero-rated goods and services** TAX goods or services not liable for VAT in the United Kingdom, taxable items or services on which ***VAT*** (Value Added Tax) is charged at zero rate, for example, food, books, public transport, and children's clothes.

zero-rating TAX sales tax rating of 0% the rating of a product or service at 0% sales tax

zero-sum game FINANCE gain by one results in loss by another a situation in which a gain by one participant results in another participant's equivalent loss

zombie *US* BUSINESS firm still trading although insolvent a business that continues to trade supported by its bank even though it is insolvent and unlikely to recover (*slang*)

ZOPA BANKING website facilitating loans between users a personal loan exchange website that allows web users to lend to and borrow from each other directly. *Full form* ***Zone of Possible Agreement***

Z score STATISTICS, FINANCE measure of bankruptcy risk a statistical measure used to determine the likelihood of bankruptcy from a company's credit strength